THE USE OF FORCE

International Politics and Foreign Policy, Second Edition

Edited by

Robert J. Art and
Kenneth N. Waltz

UNIVERSITY
PRESS OF
AMERICA

LANHAM • NEW YORK • LONDON

University Press of America,™ Inc.

4720 Boston Way
Lanham, MD 20706

3 Henrietta Street
London WC2E 8LU England

Printed in the United States of America

ISBN (Perfect): 0-8191-3425-2
ISBN   (Cloth): 0-8191-3424-4

First Edition © 1971 by
Little, Brown & Co., Inc.

Preface from the First Edition

The subject of this book, the use of military power in twentieth-century international politics, is by no means new. In putting the book together, however, we have adopted a strangely neglected perspective by emphasizing the relation of technology to military strategy and foreign policy. In making the selections, we have kept these questions in mind: (1) What role has the threatened or actual use of military force played in international politics? (2) How has military power changed in the last seventy years? (3) How have changes in the instruments of force affected the use of force by statesmen? (4) What materials will help most to answer the first three questions?

Two types of selections are included: those which treat general problems or principles directly and those which deal with applications of force and, in doing so, illustrate general principles. An introduction by the editors is included to enable the student to follow the intricacies of the subject, to understand the dilemmas faced by statesmen, and to identify recurrent patterns in military strategy and foreign policy.

Robert J. Art
Kenneth N. Waltz

THE USE
OF FORCE

Contents

Technology, Strategy, and
the Uses of Force

ROBERT J. ART
KENNETH N. WALTZ

The dropping of an atomic bomb on Hiroshima in August of 1945 was heralded at the time as inaugurating a new era in the relations of states. The awesome power of the atom made disarmament necessary according to some, world government imperative according to others, and war impossible according to many. Nearly forty years after the event we can no longer be so sure. Wars have been fought; disarmament and world government have been as difficult as ever to achieve. Indeed, the accumulation of nuclear weapons in the arsenals of America and Russia, and the spread of nuclear weapons to today's total of six states, have not produced any widespread agreement that disarmament and world government are desirable as ends in themselves.

No one would deny that nuclear power in the hands of separate states has made the world different. But just what differences can be attributed to nuclear weaponry is not clear enough to permit their identification with certainty and the specification of their causes with precision. Is it, for example, because of the beneficent presence of nuclear weapons that the world has enjoyed a longer period of peace since 1945 than had been known in this century—if peace is defined as the absence of general war among the major states of the world? The second world war followed upon the first one within twenty-one years. As of 1982, thirty-eight years had elapsed since the Allies' victory over the Axis powers. Conflict marks all human affairs. In the past quarter of a century, conflict has generated hostility among states and has at times issued in violence among the weaker and the smaller ones. Even though the more powerful states of the world have occasionally been direct participants (most noticeably the United States and China), war has been confined geographically and limited in the number of states engaged in the fighting. Remarkably, general war has been avoided in a period of rapid and far-reaching changes—decolonization; the rapid economic growth of some states; the formation, the tightening, and the loosening of blocs; the emergence of new technologies and strategies of nuclear and guerrilla warfare. The prevalence of peace, together with the fighting of circumscribed wars, indicates a high

1

ability of the international system to absorb changes and to contain conflict and hostility.

One may be inclined to say simply that the destructive power of nuclear weapons has dissuaded their possessors from using them, that local wars did not become global wars for fear of the world's destruction. But such a dampening effect can never be reliably assumed, nor did it emerge spontaneously. Intricate decisions in foreign and in military policy have constantly been required.

They are decisions made within a wide range of choice. Since the early fifties, American defense spending has run to well less than 10 per cent of gross national product (GNP). To suggest a range of feasible variation, one may notice that in 1944 American military expenditure exceeded 40 per cent of GNP and that in 1947 and again in 1948 it fell below 5 per cent of GNP. In the first two years of President Eisenhower's administration, the amount of federal spending for national defense fell by 27 per cent, and in the first year of President Kennedy's administration, it rose by 10.3 per cent.[1] In the first year of the Reagan administration it rose by 7 per cent in real terms. Clearly, American defense expenditures could be increased or decreased by 25 per cent over a few years without profoundly disturbing the American economy. Countries with capacious economies and fertile technologies have a wide range of choice in military policy. Such choice is heavily affected by the strategic ideas that come to prevail.

One of the most striking effects of the fission and fusion of atoms is found in the burgeoning of strategic studies. "At least until World War I," Bernard Brodie wrote, the study of military strategy "could proceed profitably from the study of campaigns going back to antiquity."[2] Because the instruments of warfare changed little and slowly, the principles of warfare endured. Nelson's flagship at the battle of Trafalgar was forty years old and none the worse for its age. The sailing ships of 1850 were little different from those in use two centuries earlier, and naval guns had, if anything, changed even more slowly.[3] In a book completed in 1960 one can read, however, of a revolution in weapons taking place every five years since the end of World War II.[4]

"War stimulates invention, but the army resists it!"[5] If prior to this century technological change was slow, military adaptation was still slower. The interests of military men vested in their regiments and

[1] Malcolm W. Hoag, "What New Look in Defense?" *World Politics,* XXII (October, 1969), 1, 3.

[2] Bernard Brodie, *Some Strategic Implications of the Nuclear Revolution* (University of Utah: Institute of International Studies, no date), p. 3.

[3] See the selection by Samuel P. Huntington in Part III.

[4] Herman Kahn, *On Thermonuclear War,* 2nd ed. (Princeton: Princeton University Press, 1961), pp. 311–315.

[5] Lewis Mumford, *Technics and Civilization* (London: George Routledge, 1934), p. 95. And see the selection by Edward L. Katzenbach, Jr., in Part II.

fleets, with traditions, customary ways of recruitment, and established systems of weaponry acting as impediments to change. Strategic studies were written largely by peripheral military figures—more men of the pen than men of the sword—who challenged professional orthodoxy but whose influence was weakened by the positions they occupied on the fringes of the military establishment. With the dominance of science and technology, civilians have now come to enjoy almost a monopoly in the field of strategic studies. They are not confined to the fringes of the policy-making establishment; they have instead invaded its heartland. The change that has been worked is striking. The vested interest of civilian strategists has not been in helping to preserve traditional military arrangements by providing suitable rationales for them. They have instead established a vested interest in innovation. Their reputations have been made by working changes in our perspectives, by challenging and reversing old maxims, and by showing that unthinkable weapons can usefully be thought about. Thus, the two great revolutions in the military thought of our time have been produced, in nuclear warfare, largely by intellectuals, and in guerrilla warfare, largely by political revolutionaries.[6]

Even the production of nuclear weapons of a form and quantity that give to men the power to destroy man has not meant that military strategy would be written on a clean slate. Slow annihilation has always been possible. In razing Carthage and sowing the site with salt so that new life could not emerge, Rome showed a capability for extirpation and a capacity for ruthlessness usually, but wrongly, identified with modern totalitarianism. The Thirty Years' War, ending in 1648, inflicted death upon perhaps a third of the people who lived in the area of Germany. In the same area, the extent of death and destruction during World War II approached the havoc that would have been wreaked by model-T atomic bombs. It is not that in the nuclear age near annihilation has suddenly become possible. It always had been. What is new is that *sudden* annihilation has become possible.[7]

THE NEED FOR FORCE

The web of social and political life is spun out of inclinations and incentives, deterrent threats and punishments. Eliminate the latter two, and the ordering of society will depend entirely upon the former—an anarchic ideal that is unworkable this side of the Garden of Eden. Depend entirely upon threat and punishment, and the ordering of society will be based on pure coercion. International politics

---

[6] The considerable literature on guerrilla warfare is not represented in this volume, partly because of the limits of space and partly because good readers on the subject are available. See especially Franklin Mark Osanka, ed., *Modern Guerrilla Warfare* (New York: Free Press, 1962).

[7] See the selection by Thomas C. Schelling in Part I.

tends toward the latter condition. The daily presence of force and recurrent reliance upon it mark the affairs of nations. Since Thucydides in Greece and Kautilya in India, the use of force and the possibility of controlling it have been the preoccupations of international political studies. They still preoccupy the men who are responsible for the military and foreign policies of their nations.

The reason that statesmen are preoccupied with the use of force is because international politics is anarchic.[8] There exists no central authority above states clothed with the power and the authority to resolve disputes that inevitably arise among them. Unlike domestic politics, therefore, international politics takes place in a condition in which no single agency has a legitimate monopoly on the use of force. Simply put, there is no government among states. Politics among nations is the politics of the ungoverned.

From this fact flow five important consequences for state behavior, each of which bears vitally upon the role that military power plays in international politics. *First,* all states must fend for themselves. Although a state is free to set whatever goals it wishes to aim for, each must provide the wherewithall to attain them. No state can confidently rely on the goodwill of other states over the long term. No state can realistically calculate that its friends of today will remain its friends of tomorrow. No state can count on other nations to provide for its welfare unless it is in the others' self-interest to do so. No state can look to an international government to give it the resources necessary to attain its ends. In anarchy states must be entrepreneurs. They must supply the means to attain their proclaimed objectives. Anarchy, in short, demands self-help.

Second, all states must make provisions for their physical security. That which makes given states and particular statesmen secure is no easy matter to determine, in part because states vary in their resources and geographical placement; in part because security is a state of mind experienced by individuals who, by definition, vary widely in their psychological makeups. First and foremost, however, the concept of security refers to the capability of a state to prevent others from physically harming it, either by invading it or by raining destruction upon it. Security is the protection of the homeland from military attack. The provision for physical security does not exhaust all the goals any state seeks, but it is the prerequisite for the attainment of all the rest. If a state fails to provide for its military defense, then it will find its other goals, whether those be the material well-being of its citizenry or the political freedom of its populace, to be highly

[8] Material in this section and at the end ("The Future of Force") has been taken from Robert J. Art, "Military Power," in James Hart and Thomas Prout.

vulnerable to disruption, curtailment, or sabotage by other nations. Most states most of the time enjoy some degree of security. A few states a great deal of the time enjoy more security than most others. But whether all states experience some security or whether a few are more nearly secure than all others, the basic point still stands: all states all of the time must make provisions for their defense. It is precisely because anarchy demands self-help that all states do what they can to protect their homelands from attack.

Third, in an anarchic setting, each state must put concern for its short-term position relative to others above concern for the long-term absolute gain of all. Not the welfare of all but the success of each is the focus of state action. This concern for relative position follows naturally from the first two consequences for states acting in anarchy. If a state must help itself and if a state must provide for its own defense, then each state has no choice but to concern itself with how it is doing relative to the others. And with no government above states to redistribute resources, how well any state does in its international affairs must depend on how many resources it can muster by its own efforts relative to what the others by their own efforts muster. In anarchy, then, state egoism, not state altruism, is the credo of state action.

The necessity to focus on the short term often requires states to sacrifice *their own* long-term well being. In anarchy, trust is hard to come by. And, yet, trust in the good faith of others is essential if each state is to focus on the long term because long-term gain usually requires a statesman to take risks in the short term. Each must have confidence that the others will not take advantage of him during that period. Put another way, all must be prepared to take the same risks. Anarchy, however, breeds skepticism about the motives of others and constrains a statesman to focus on what other states can do, not on what they say they intend to do. This is the familiar problem of distinguishing between capability and intention. A statesman does not always reject the well-meaning intentions of others and plan instead on the basis of their actual capabilities when he formulates his actions, but he almost never can discount the power of others and more often than not will emphasize their capabilities over their intentions. The tragedy that results for international political action is that all can be damned if each opts for short-term gain, but none finds it easy to escape from doing so. Anarchy literally constrains statesmen to be shortsighted.

Fourth, all states in anarchy are in a position of strategic inter-dependence. No state, that is, has complete control over its own fate because what it can achieve in the realm of international politics hangs heavily on the actions of others. No state can therefore plan its actions without first anticipating the likely responses of others. The strategy of each depends upon the strategies of all. In this sense, international politics, with few great powers, all of whom have to fend for themselves, is akin to the oligopolistic competitive model of microeconomic theory. There are no formal rules of behavior and no possibility of predicting exact outcomes from initial conditions. One can speak only of wide ranges of possible outcomes. The emphasis of action is not on the positive but on the negative; unfavorable surprise is deemed to be more injurious than favorable surprise is beneficial. States will concentrate more on the avoidance of defeats than they will on the winning of victories. In international relations, just as in oligopolistic competition, strategies of behavior are interdependent; outcomes in general are indeterminate; and avoidance of defeats is mightily prized. In international relations, just as in oligopolistic competition, the stakes of the game are quite high; the interactions wave widely between cutthroat competition and tacit collusion; and the costs of defeat are framed often in terms of ceasing to survive. In both realms, moreover, one does not have the choice of declining to play simply because one does not like the rules of the game. One has to play merely to survive, much less prosper. Neither realm is one for gentlemen.

Fifth and last, states in anarchy cannot afford to be moral. The possibility for moral behavior rests upon the existence of an effective government that can deter and punish illegal actions. In anarchy, there is no government; hence there are no laws. International law reflects merely the prevailing consensus among states about their common self-interests. Such "laws" are followed only when useful to states. They are violated usually with impunity, whenever states find it inexpedient to observe them. If there is neither government nor laws, then there can be no concept of legal rights. States have a "right" only to what they can achieve by their own efforts. No state has a legal or moral right to exist or to prosper, only the "right" to do all that is in its power to do. In this sense, right does not mean legality, but rather the freedom to choose whatever is deemed most effective to attain a given end. The preconditions for morality are absent in international politics. Every state, as a consequence, has to be prepared to do that which is necessary for its interests as it defines them. Anarchy is the realm where all can, and many do, play "dirty pool."

How do these five factors bear upon the role that military power plays in international relations? Quite directly, for each of these factors dictates that military force must be integral to a state's conduct of its foreign policy. Fending for itself requires a state to muster the necessary resources, including military power. Provision for physical security obviously necessitates military forces. Concern for relative position dictates calculations regarding power ratios. Strategic interdependence and the absence of morality mean that each state, if it wishes to be effective, must be prepared to play according to the rules set by the "dirtiest" player.

All of this is straightforward. But there is a deeper underpinning to the central role that military power plays in international politics. Too many analysts assume that military power has no utility if it is not physically used against an opponent or if no threats to employ it are made. Most of the time, most states are at peace with their neighbors, not warring with them. Even so, international relations is referred to, correctly so, as a "state of war." The reason is clear: The ever-present possibility that any state can always resort to force if it so chooses causes all to prepare for that eventuality. "Aggressor" states prepare for war; therefore, "peaceful" states must do so too. It is the necessity to prepare for war, not its incessant occurrence, that has caused analysts to term international politics a state of war. Because resort to force is the ultimate recourse of all states, the seriousness of a state's intentions is conveyed fundamentally by its having a credible military posture. Without it, a state's diplomacy generally lacks effectiveness. Hence force need not be physically used to be politically useful, and threats need not be overtly made to be communicated. The mere presence of a credible military option is often sufficient to make the point. Indeed, the capability to resort to military force if all else fails serves as the most effective brake against having to do so. Lurking behind the scenes, unstated but explicit, lies the military muscle that gives meaning to the posturings of the diplomats. Diplomacy is the striking of compromises by parties with differing perspectives and clashing interests. The ultimate ability of each to resort to force disciplines the diplomats. Precisely because each knows that all can come to blows if they do not strike compromises do the diplomats engage in the hard work necessary to construct them. There is truth to the old adage: "The best way to keep the peace is first to prepare for war."

Military power thus yields political leverage on the entire range of issues with which a state concerns itself. The correspondence between a state's relative military strength and the successes it achieves in its foreign policies, however, is not direct. States are not successful politically according to the way they rank militarily. International politics is too complex for that. Other factors intervene, such as the relative skills of statesmen, their differing tolerances for risk taking, the conformity of the actions of others to initial calculations, and differences in the amount of political leverage that can be gained from military strength in each of the types of non-military issues with which states deal. But even though the relation between military power and political success is neither readily apparent nor simple to calculate, *there is a relation*. Military power is necessary for survival. If it brings a good deal of security to a state, military strength can be a liberating force because it enables a state to focus more of its energies and resources on nonsecurity matters. A state with a large reservoir of military strength can bluff better, bargain more toughly, threaten to resort to force with more credibility, and prevail more often than states with a small reservoir. "Reputation for power is power" said Hobbes. The stronger a nation is perceived to be militarily, the less likely will it have to use that power physically. Whether he be a statesman or a domestic political figure, the ability of a political actor to prevail over others without overt resort to his powers is the measure of his strength relative to them.

In anarchy, force and politics are connected. By itself, military power guarantees neither survival nor prosperity. But it is almost always the essential ingredient for both. Force is the bedrock of international political action. It is also the dominant tool—the one that can override all the others. As a consequence, all the foreign policy interests that a state pursues are vitally, though unequally, affected by military power. The simplest reason why states need force is that they cannot get along without it.

DEFENSE AND DETERRENCE

Atomic and hydrogen bombs are new things under the sun, but the military and political strategies that have accompanied them are not wholly so. Revolutions in weapons systems have not destroyed the continuity of strategy partly because the range of national objectives has not changed much. States still seek to preserve themselves; some states continue to entertain ends that can be gained only at the expense of others. Partly, also, continuity remains because nuclear power, though revolutionary in the magnitude of its destructive force and in the speed of its deliverability, is nevertheless still only an instrument of force—usable to threaten and deter, to punish and destroy. And these are the ways in which force in the hands of rulers has always been used. The continuity of strategy means that much that is useful in the present can be learned from contemplating the strategies and the practices of the past. We should not slip into thinking that because some things are new nothing has endured.

We should also guard against the opposite error of believing that because some principles remain valid nothing has changed. What then is new in the strategies of the nuclear age? The most general and fundamental answer is this: the immense and sudden destructive power of nuclear-tipped missiles has shifted the emphasis of strategic planners from victory and defense to deterrence.[9] Concern over the use of force to strike for victory or to hold off an attacker is not absent in present-day strategic discourse, nor was concern over deterring an enemy's

---

[9] See the selection by Robert E. Osgood in Part I.

attack so that a defense would not have to be mounted absent in the old days. But the distinction between victory and defense, on the one hand, and deterrence, on the other, has been sharpened; and the emphasis has shifted from the first to the second.

In the 1930s, Stanley Baldwin had stressed that the bomber would always get through, a dictum that helped to demoralize England.[10] Despite such seeming or momentary advantages for the offense, prior to the age of nuclear-tipped missiles, advances in offensive arms had always been countered by improved defenses. The possibility of successful defense made a world of independent states tolerable. By the mid-1950s, however, the approximate equality of offensive forces at an awesomely potent level seemed to produce a world of states comparable to Hobbes's state of nature among men. The misery of that world, as Hobbes imagined it, rested on everyone's ability to do harm to anyone else. The weakest man could kill the strongest man by striking at him while he slumbered.[11] The metaphors that appeared early in the atomic age reflected the vision of Hobbes. Two scorpions in a bottle: each can kill the other but in doing so the killer authors his own death. Two cowboys armed with six-guns on the western frontier with neither being sure of the other's intention: each must try to shoot first, not in anger, but out of fear that if he does not the other fellow will. In the strategic trade, this is known as "preemption."

The equality of offensive forces and the absence of effective defenses, however, have not presented to states the impossible alternatives of unavoidable death or unattainable world government, but have instead permitted the contriving of a third way.[12] The logic of Hobbes does not apply to a state among states as it does to a man among men. States can devise strategies and produce the means for their implementation as men acting alone cannot possibly do. One way to counter an intended offense is to build fortifications and to muster forces that look forbiddingly strong. The other way to inhibit a

[10] Both Britain and Germany believed that no defense against the other country's bomber force could be effectively mounted. Each of them initially accepted the doctrine that only a preemptive blow against the other country's bomber force could save the homeland from devastation. And yet, when World War II came, neither launched a preemptive strike. For the restraints at work between Britain and Germany in the initial phase of World War II, see the selection by George H. Quester in Part II. For an assessment of the effects that beliefs about bomber destruction had on foreign policy in the 1930s, see Herbert S. Dinerstein, "The Impact of Airpower on the International Scene, 1933-1940," *Military Affairs,* XXIX (Summer, 1965), 65-71.

[11] Thomas Hobbes, *Leviathan* (Oxford: Blackwell, no date), p. 80.

[12] As examples of those who, in effect, have accepted the logic of Hobbes and followed it to the world-government conclusion, see Robert Maynard Hutchins, "The Constitutional Foundations for World Order," in *Foundations for World Order* (Denver: University of Denver Press, 1949), pp. 99-105; Bertrand Russell, *New Hopes for a Changing World* (New York: Simon and Schuster, 1951), pp. 93-93; Kahn, *On Thermonuclear War,* pp. 6-7.

country's intended aggressive moves is to scare that country out of making them by threatening to visit unacceptable punishment upon it. "To deter" literally means to stop someone from doing something by frightening him. In contrast to dissuasion by defense, dissuasion by deterrence operates by frightening a state out of attacking, not because of the difficulty of launching an attack and carrying it home, but because the expected reaction of the opponent will result in one's own severe punishment.[13]

In a simple two-party situation, state A's deterrent force accomplishes its purpose by frightening state B out of making the military strike that it would have made had the deterrent threat been ineffective. What B would actually have done had A's force been absent or weaker can only be surmised. Claims for the success of deterrence must rest on assertions about why something did *not* happen. Neither logically nor empirically, however, can one conclusively demonstrate why something did not happen. The abstract and rationalist quality of recent military analysis has often been criticized. But this quality is inescapable because of the emphasis put on deterrence and because nuclear weapons have never been used in a world in which two or more countries possessed them. When there is no opportunity to learn from direct experience, and hopefully will be none, military analysis can only proceed by reasoned abstractions and on the basis of appropriate analogies. The criticism is often turned in another direction. The conclusions of the strategists, it is said, rest on the assumption that in the heat of a crisis the rulers of states will decide with cool rationality whether to press their nuclear buttons. This criticism, too, is wide of the mark. A strategist's assumption that rulers will behave rationally cannot directly affect their behavior. That much is obvious. In a nuclear world, however, the incentives to cautious and reasoned behavior are strong. It is important to make them still stronger by devising strategies and by deploying forces in ways that will reduce the chances of reckless behavior and of desperate decisions by military commanders and statesmen.

VICTORY AND DEFENSE

The distinctions between defense and deterrence, the conditions conducive to preemptive and offensive uses of military power, the effects that military technology can have on strategic planning, and the constraints that foreign policy goals can create for military planners—all these points can best be made clear by examples. Two good ones are French and German strategic planning prior to World War I and American strategic planning after World War II. The com-

---

[13] Definitions of "defense" and "deterrence," of course, vary from one author to another.

parisons and contrasts between these two periods will also bring out the qualitative differences in strategic planning in the nuclear and pre-nuclear ages.

At approximately the same time but for different reasons, France and Germany adopted offensive strategies that committed each of them to strike with full force at the other. A country may adopt an offensive strategy simply because it wants to conquer its opponent in order to gain some tangible advantage. Even without such an ambition, a country may adopt an offensive strategy out of its concern for security and its conviction that a good offense is the best defense, or even that it is the only defense possible. France fits well into the first category; Germany into the second.

Germany was wedged in between two great powers, France and Russia, who were diplomatically united by the alliance they had formed in 1894.[14] Germany had to expect that if she went to war against either France or Russia, the other would come in against her. Under these trying circumstances, Alfred von Schlieffen, Chief of the Great German General Staff from 1891 to 1905, developed and refined a daring strategy.[15] Schlieffen predicated his plan upon a belief that was widespread throughout military and civilian circles in the several decades prior to 1914: modern warfare, were it to be drawn out, would wreck the highly complex and delicately balanced industrial economies of all the participants, Germany included. Confronting the prospect of a protracted two-front war, German officials could see no way to avoid their country's being ground to pieces between her two antagonists other than by concentrating her armies in the west and striking to defeat France before wheeling eastward to meet the slower-moving armies of Russia. To defeat two enemies without fighting a sustained two-front war required that one of them be eliminated before the forces of the other could become fully effective.

The Schlieffen Plan was a bold one and entailed many risks. Execution of the Plan rested on Germany's physical ability to move more rapidly than her adversaries and on her psychological ability to take the risk of leaving the eastern front open in the first weeks of the war. If her army did not move rapidly enough, the French army would gain the time to redeploy forces to counter the advance through northern France. Quick victory in the west would be possible only if the German army could outflank the French fortresses facing the Rhine by skirting them and going through Belgium. The Schlieffen Plan thus

[14] Among other provisions, the Franco-Russian Alliance of 1894 committed Russia to deploy one-third of her army against Germany in the east if France and Germany should go to war.
[15] The Schlieffen Plan was formally adopted in 1906. The following discussion relies heavily on Gerhard Ritter's *The Schlieffen Plan* (London: Oswald Wolff, 1958), especially pp. 17–69.

required Germany to violate Belgian neutrality and run the grave risk of bringing Britain into the war. The prospect of British entry intensified the need for speed: France would have to be beaten before either Russian or British armies could roll into action with full force. If her military and political leaders did not have the nerve to leave the eastern front lightly defended at the outset of the war, then her army would be too weak in the west to overwhelm the French. The success of the strategy thus depended upon surprise, rapid advance through Belgium and northern France, and great nerve on the part of commanders and statesmen.

The geographic situation of Germany, along with diplomatic developments, strongly affected the military policy she adopted. Shortly before World War I, France too adopted an offensive strategy, but not for reasons of geography or diplomacy. For France, national ambitions and military beliefs reinforced each other. Only by taking the offensive in any future European war could France hope to regain Alsace and Lorraine. To adopt a defensive strategy, moreover, would have implied France's acquiescence in her defeat at the hands of Prussia in 1870 and the acceptance of a permanent position of inferiority to Germany. At the same time, French military leaders were imbued with an almost mystical faith in the efficacy of élan—human will, drive, energy, spirit. The most famous and influential exponent of this line of thinking among the French military before World War I was General Ferdinand Foch, director of L' École Superieure de la Guerre, or War College, where the French Army's intellectual elite studied. Long before Mao Tse-tung, Foch preached the doctrine of men over weapons, or what Bernard Brodie has called "the subordination of the material to the moral."[16] The following excerpts from his *Principles of War* capture the essence of his doctrine:

> In order that our army be victorious, it must have a moral superiority to that which the enemy possesses or receives from his commander. To organize battle consists in enhancing our own spirit to the highest degree in order to break that of the enemy.
>
> A battle won, is a battle in which one will not confess oneself beaten. The will to conquer: such is victory's first condition.
>
> Therefore: War = the domain of moral force. Victory = moral superiority in the victors; moral depression in the vanquished. Battle = a struggle between two wills.[17]

Foch, in short, put his faith in the all-conquering human spirit.

---

[16] For a comprehensive discussion of Foch's doctrines, see chapter 2 of Brodie's *Strategy in the Missile Age* (Princeton: Princeton University Press, 1959).

[17] Marshal Foch, *The Principles of War,* translated by Hilaire Belloc (London: Chapman and Hall, 1919), pp. 286–287.

The belief that the spirit could triumph over the material firmly wedded French strategists to the offense. Commitment to the offense led the French in May of 1913 to adopt something called "Plan 17." This provided for a massive thrust by the entire French army eastward into Germany, and left the Belgian frontier to the north unprotected. Thus, while the Germans were planning to move most of their army around the French defenses on the Franco-German border by marching through Belgium, the French were preparing to move their forces out from these defenses headlong into Germany. The French and German commitment to the offense led both to opt literally for carrying the battle to the enemy.

Not only did the commitment to the offense cause the French to neglect their defenses on the Belgian frontier before the war. It also led them during the war to a tragically costly use of their infantry. Perhaps the greatest irony for France in World War I was that the faith in élan both saved her from defeat and bled her white. The emphasis on will led General Joffre, Chief of the General Staff, to refuse to admit defeat in August and September of 1914. Joffre's sheer stubbornness was one of the ingredients in the French army's successful stand at the Battle of the Marne. Success there spelled doom for the Schlieffen Plan. And yet, at the same time, the faith that the French military had in élan caused France to lose more men on the western front than either Britain or Germany. Believing in élan, the French generals hurtled masses of men against the withering fire of opposing forces that were dug in and well armed with machine guns and artillery. This strategy gained little and lost much. After the first few months of the war, battle lines did not change significantly, but millions of lives were sacrificed. Events proved the futility of this tactic, and yet military leaders on both sides continued to believe in its efficacy, repeated it over and over, and achieved the same result—or lack of result. Clearly, military doctrine about how the infantry could best be used did not lead to its best use in World War I. Men may die easily, but beliefs do not.

Two sides, quite evenly balanced and both driving for victory, may well land themselves in a stalemate. That this happened in World War I should not have been very surprising. But notice that this result was not inevitable. Instead the outcome, wanted by no one, was a product of technology, capability, military strategy, and political policy. The message conveyed by the two opposed alliances of European states, and by the military arrangements they had made, was this: if a major state on either side should mobilize, all the great powers would do so, and mobilization would mean war. As the Chief of the Great German General Staff wrote to his Austrian counterpart in January of 1909, "two mobilized armies such as the German and French will not be able to stand face to face without a passage at arms." Writing with remarkable prescience, he nevertheless drew a falsely optimistic conclusion. That mobilization means war is, he reasoned, "familiar enough to the whole European diplomacy, and in that fact lies the guarantee that none of the Great Powers will light the torch of war on account of Serbian ambitions, which would put the fire to the roof of all Europe."[18]

Unfortunately, contemplating a future situation that would pit the armies of the opposed sides against each other deterred neither of them. To understand why will make clear the difference between conditions that emphasize victory and defense and those that lead to the possibility of deterrence. Whether offensive strategies convey threats that deter depends partly on the design of forces and the strategy for their use and partly on physical capabilities and technology. Both France and Germany planned to take the offensive at the outset of a war. Both aimed for victory. Both believed that the key to victory lay in an offensive first strike against the other's forces. Each knew that to be the first to strike required that it be the first to complete full mobilization. German leaders realized that the success of the Schlieffen Plan depended upon Germany's greater speed of mobilization and movement. The mere increased likelihood of French mobilization would therefore strongly pressure Germany to order the actual mobilization of her forces. Under these circumstances, a threat of preparation or action by one state does not deter another from taking action, but instead creates a strong incentive for counteraction. Military technology was such that the steps that reduced a nation's vulnerability to attack also increased its readiness to launch a war.[19] In a climate of fear, the fact that defensive preparations could be viewed as offensive preparations meant that they would in fact be viewed as such. One who believes in the maxim that "a good offense is the best defense" scares the hell out of his opponent each time he makes efforts merely intended to improve his defensive position! If two or more states believe in the maxim, the situation becomes highly unstable.

At first glance, French and German plans look like deterrent strategies whereby neither side plans to defend itself but instead, if struck, plans to strike back at the other. The effectiveness of a deterrent threat rests on the ability of the threatener to punish his would-be attacker with reasonable certainty and speed. If A's striking first to hurt B does not eliminate, or reduce to limits that A finds tolerable, B's ability to hurt A by mounting a retaliatory blow, then B has the

[18] From the correspondence between Helmuth von Moltke and Conrad von Hötzendorf, as quoted in Alfred Vagts, *Defense and Diplomacy* (New York: King's Crown Press, 1956), p. 97.
[19] Cf. Thomas C. Schelling, *Arms and Influence* (New Haven: Yale University Press, 1966), pp. 221–227.

ability to deter A. For mutual deterrence, A's capability must be comparable to B's.

As events showed, both Germany and France had the ability to hurt each other severely, but to do the damage would take considerable time. How that time could be used was a question of immense importance. Armies were the means of attack; they were also the means of defense. Both sides might initially mount an invasion, as in fact they did, but either side (France, it turned out) could be forced to abandon its invasion and go on the strategic defensive by the success of the other's offensive strike. Each side could hope that its offensive first strike would eliminate the other side's offensive power—and thus its ability to retaliate. The initial success of one side would then determine the course of the war. Therefore, worries about preemption dominated, and mutual offensive capabilities and strategies had little deterrent effect.

A defensive strategy, had anyone adopted one, would have changed the situation. It would have, that is, if two conditions could have been met: first, that defensive preparations not also appear to be preparations for an attack, and, second, that a smaller number of troops dug in to defend be able to hold off a larger number attacking. As has just been indicated, the first of these conditions was not satisfied in the years immediately before 1914; and neither was the second one, for reasons that can easily be stated.

It may be true that "a good offense is the best defense." Depending on circumstances, however, it may instead be true that a good defense is the best means of dissuading an enemy from launching an attack. Until the latter part of the nineteenth century, the defense was thought to have an advantage in land warfare of 3 to 2 or even of 3 to 1.[20] A favorable ratio for the defense has a stabilizing effect, for any increase of one country's offensive capability can be negated by a lesser increment of its adversary's defensive strength. If state A adds three army corps, for example, state B can counter this conservatively by adding only two. To play such a game is expensive (and perhaps futile) for A, and that should make an arms race less likely. It should also make a first strike appear less beneficial. If victory is state A's aim, then B's construction of a powerful defense may dissuade state A from actively seeking it. In eras in which strategic emphasis falls upon defense and victory, a state may be dissuaded from attacking because the quality of the opponent's defense makes the achievement of victory unlikely.

French and German military planners, dazzled by Bismarck's

---

[20] B. H. Liddell Hart gives the even higher estimate of 5:1 for the Normandy campaign in World War II. For a historical sketch of the increasingly favorable ratios that the defense has enjoyed since 1800, see his *Deterrent or Defense* (London: Stevens and Sons, 1960), pp. 97–110. See also the selections by Robert Jervis and Glenn H. Snyder in "When Wars Occur" in Part I.

lightning victories over Denmark, Austria, and France, forgot
Clausewitz's demonstrations of the advantages of defense. The conviction that the defense enjoyed little if any advantage increased their
impatience to strike the first blow and made the avoidance of war
more difficult.

DETERRENCE IN THE NUCLEAR AGE

A state unprepared to counter a weapon invites the use of that
weapon against itself. In the nuclear age, the problem has been to
devise a strategy that will discourage the use of weapons against which
no defense yet exists.[21] Economically most capable and technologically
most advanced, the United States has been the fashion leader in
nuclear strategy, with the Soviet Union following along after some
few years have elapsed.[22] To look at recent American strategy and
problems attendant upon it will illustrate some strategic principles and
show how strategy has responded to changes in technology.

The Soviet Union did not explode an atomic device until 1949 and
had no intercontinental atomic capability until the early 1950s. In
these years, American strategy emphasized preparation for victory
should war occur, rather than deterrence of it. With little conventional
force in being, the strategy relied on bombing capability plus the
nation's vast mobilization potential. World War III, if it came, would
look like World War II, but with American atomic bombs added.
Coherence of strategy, however, was not achieved. The military's
emphasis on B-36 bombers and supercarriers clashed with President
Truman's persistent and unavailing advocacy of Universal Military
Training.

The Eisenhower administration's New Look shifted American doctrine abruptly from a war-fighting to a war-deterring strategy. One
stimulant to change was the desire to find a strategy that the country
could afford and could stick to without gearing its responses to the
wayward actions of other states. The Korean war was another stimulant
to change. In his claim that we would never fight another one like that,
Defense Secretary Wilson succinctly conveyed the intention. Never
again would America fight a war in which she denied herself the use of
her best (i.e., atomic) weapons. The threat to drop A-bombs, as various
statements of Secretary Dulles made clear, was intended to deter other
states from starting wars or carrying them through.[23] The threat of
"massive retaliation" would bring a halt to all aggression, whether
undertaken by big or small states, by conventional troops or guerrilla
warriors.

[21] See the selection by Colin S. Gray in Part IV for a discussion of the defensive
value of ABM systems.
[22] See the speeches by John Foster Dulles and Nikita S. Khrushchev in Part I.
[23] See Dulles's statement in Part I.

The New Look was a radical military strategy propounded for the sake of serving conservative ends at home: balancing the budget at a low level of federal expenditure. With unbalanced forces and a simple program of action, radical strategies seek to meet all the important contingencies a nation is likely to face. Strong strategies make bold bets. The Schlieffen Plan, the Maginot Line, Japan's initial plan for war against the United States, and America's New Look policy—all of these fall into the same category, and none of them worked very well.[24]

Deterrent strategies, whether or not they are strong ones, encounter two basic problems. The first is the threatener's credibility. To be effective, a deterrent threat has to be believed. One state must believe that the other can deliver the threatened punishment and that under certain circumstances it may do so. Otherwise the state that is threatened will not be deterred. The second problem is posed by the actions that a threatened state may take. Confronted with a strong defense, a would-be aggressor may attempt to outflank the defense or to overcome it. Confronted with a powerful deterrent, a would-be aggressor may seek to reduce its effect by taking measures to protect its population or by striking to destroy a large part of the adversary's deterrent force.

The deterrent threat is a threat to punish someone if he undertakes certain loosely specified acts. The state to which the threat is addressed must at least believe that the punishment *may* be administered. In the old Indochina war, the threats made in 1954 by President Eisenhower, Secretary Dulles, and others to retaliate massively neither stopped the advance of Ho Chi Minh's forces nor slowed the flow of supplies to them. Would Moscow or Peking be bombed because artillery pieces were shipped to Ho's forces through Russia and China? To make a nuclear threat against such actions plausible, the country issuing the threat would have to make itself look like a monster. The threat of wreaking massive destruction would be credible only against actions of the utmost evil. The problem of making the punishment fit the crime bedeviled the New Look doctrine. Could the credibility of the threat be established despite the wide disparity between action and threatened reaction? This question could not be affirmatively answered.

A further difficulty soon emerged. The New Look doctrine was formulated in the presence of the Soviet Union's growing nuclear arsenal, and this brought into question the credibility of nuclear threats made to deter conventional aggression in a bilateral nuclear world. Why should Russians credit American retaliatory threats once the Soviet Union had developed the ability to respond in kind?

The existence of two nuclear countries raised questions about the

---

[24] On the strategic intention of Japan, see Sir George Sansom's essay in Part II.

design and the vulnerability of the bomber forces and, later, the missile forces by which nuclear warheads would be delivered. Would they be directed at cities or at the other fellow's delivery systems? If bombers and missiles might become targets, how could they be protected? Mutual vulnerability of forces would lead to mutual fear of surprise attack by giving each nuclear power a strong incentive to strike first. If either country could eliminate the other's bombers and missiles in one surprise blow, then both of them would be encouraged to mount a sudden attack if only for fear that if one did not the other one would. Here the temptation to preempt appears in extreme form. It is as though the two cowboys confronting each other were armed with hair-trigger revolvers. Put differently, the situation is like the one just before World War I, but now with the problem compounded by fantastic increases in destructive power and in the speed of its deliverability.[25]

To reduce or eliminate the temptation to preempt, offensive forces must be protected. They must be made invulnerable, or nearly so, for example, by keeping bomber forces dispersed, and alert, and a portion of them airborne, by placing missiles under the sea in order to render them invisible, by putting them in concrete silos, or by placing anti-ballistic missiles around them. If neither of two countries can knock out the other's means of delivery, then cities become the main targets. A strike by one country at the other country's cities leaves its missiles intact, and they can then be expected to destroy the first country's cities in a retaliatory blow. From about 1956 onward, both the United States and the Soviet Union have sought, apparently with considerable success, to maintain second-strike countercity capabilities at a minimum. Insofar as they succeeded, both were deterred from unleashing their strategic nuclear forces. The invulnerability of retaliatory weapons to destruction by a first strike is the surest guarantee against such a strike. Thus both superpowers are pressed to spend huge sums designing and deploying weapons so that neither will ever have to use them. The "assured destruction" of cities that would be wrecked by the retaliatory blow becomes the keystone of deterrence.[26]

With large portions of their delivery systems in a state of near invulnerability, both states can afford to wait to see whether acts that might ambiguously threaten vital interests were in fact designed to do so. In contrast, vulnerability of missile forces would produce mutual fear of preemption, obviously a highly unstable and dangerous condi-

---

[25] Worries about the dangers in the vulnerability of delivery systems and about the consequent temptation to preempt were often expressed in the middle and later 1950s. See especially Albert Wohlstetter, "The Delicate Balance of Terror," *Foreign Affairs*, XXXVII (January, 1958).

[26] See the selections by Glenn H. Snyder and Thomas C. Schelling in Part I.

tion. The incentive to avoid it is strong. This urge, which represents a general requirement of any nuclear deterrent strategy, is one of the two major impulses of America's (and Russia's) military policies. In American policy, it is concretely expressed in the insistence upon maintaining multiple weapons systems with each of them able to deliver the amount of destructive force deemed sufficient to deter the Soviet Union—long-range bombers, land-based missiles (Minutemen), and sea-based missiles. If a Russian technological breakthrough should make one system vulnerable, the other two would still be available. Thus, multiple assured destruction (or MAD, to use Warner Schilling's acronym) is maintained. More generally, of course, the premium placed on the invulnerability of missiles is expressed in the ceaseless efforts made in research and development lest someone else's innovations exceed one's own in ingenuity and destructiveness.[27]

The second major impulse of American military policy is found in the commitments made by the United States to the countries of NATO and in the extension of security commitments of some sort to forty-odd countries. In a condition of mutual deterrence, the United States may not be able to rely on strategic nuclear threats to dissuade the Soviet Union from acting in ways that are damaging, say, to Western European states. As early as April of 1959, Undersecretary of State Herter expressed the thought in extreme form in the following statement:

> I can't conceive of the President involving us in an all-out nuclear war unless the facts showed clearly that we are in danger of devastation ourselves, or that actual moves have been made toward devastating ourselves.[28]

The conditions that make nuclear deterrence credible may also make it incredible that either state will launch a nuclear strike at the other in response to actions it has taken against third countries. What protection, then, do these states gain from America's nuclear arsenal? The Soviet Union would presumably still be deterred by its fear that the United States would retaliate massively, not only in response to blows aimed at America, but also in response to large-scale attacks on America's major allies. America's strategic deterrent would then cover only those actions which Americans might view as endangering their basic security. One can well imagine that some acts of aggression would impress allied states as intolerable and yet not be severe enough threats to the United States to merit her retaliating at the risk of her own destruction. To say that two states deter each other means that

---

[27] See the selections by Samuel P. Huntington and Warner R. Schilling in Part III.

[28] Quoted in Dean Acheson, "The Practice of Partnership," *Foreign Affairs*, XLI (January, 1963), pp. 251-252.

they create a condition of strategic stability. Strategic stability, however, makes it possible to use force on a fairly large scale without much danger of anyone's pressing the nuclear buttons.

One who follows this reasoning carefully will understand why the establishment in the late 1950s of an American-Russian system of mutual second-strike deterrence had the following consequences: the decreased confidence of allies in the protection afforded by American or Russian nuclear weapons, the loosening of alliances, and the increased desire of lesser powers to have their own nuclear weapons. If American and Russian forces are secure against each other's first strike and if their cities are vulnerable to each other's second strike, then both of them will be reluctant to use strategic weapons on behalf of third states. Neither of the superpowers can fire its missiles without the near certainty of being struck in return. Once two states possess invulnerable delivery systems, third countries become uneasy about relying on nuclear guarantees. The smaller states of the world then have good reason to want nuclear weapons of their own. Strategic stability for the superpowers can be purchased only at the expense of increasing the incentives for nuclear proliferation. The more America's allies have questioned her commitments to them, the more they have wanted to find other means of guaranteeing their security.[29]

The nuclear superiority enjoyed by America in the early 1950s created a fear in Europe that the United States would too easily succumb to a temptation to retaliate massively. The arrival of strategic stability produced the opposite worry. In the words of a senior British general: "McNamara is practically telling the Soviets that the worst they need expect from an attack on West Germany is a conventional counterattack."[30] The countries in Europe, separate or united, have an incentive to adopt destabilizing military programs. Thus, in the 1964 *Statement on Defence,* the "unique contribution" of Britain's V-bombers and Polaris submarines was described as being to dissuade a potential enemy from attacking Europe "in the mistaken belief that the United States would not act unless America herself were attacked."[31] The contribution of Britain's nuclear force, it appears, has consisted in placing a British finger firmly on the American trigger. Where Britain led, France soon followed. The French Institute of Strategic Studies has justified nuclear diffusion in part with the argument that the uncertainty produced by a third power's nuclear force "considerably augments the opponent's belief in the possibility of a

    [29] See the selections by Kenneth N. Waltz and Lewis Dunn in Part IV for contrasting views on the consequences for world peace that may derive from the further spread of nuclear weapons.
    [30] Quoted by Eldon Griffiths, "The Revolt of Europe," *Saturday Evening Post,* CCLXIII (March 9, 1963), 19.
    [31] *Statement on Defence: 1964,* Cmnd. 2270 (London: HMSO, 1964), p. 6, par. 7.

first strike" (italics added).[32] It is understandable that lesser powers should, by mounting nuclear weapons, want to be able to decide when the United States should risk destruction, but it is also easy to see that the United States will resist such an outcome. A force well protected will, for example, be less easily triggered, whether by allied or enemy action.

The United States and the Soviet Union have taken the insecurity of third states to be a part of the problem of their own foreign and military policies. If each worried only about what the other could do to its own homeland, then both might be content with the stability promised by mutual possession of second-strike deterrent forces. What is described above as the first impulse of American military policy would exhaust their motivations. But because their interests extend beyond their boundaries (concern for the security of allies; desire to dampen the enthusiasm of smaller states for the acquisition of nuclear weapons), either may develop a desire to do more than deter the other by means of second-strike forces. When either does so, the military policies of both are affected—simply because each must react to the other. Let us again carry through the reasoning for the American case since, as previously indicated, America's strategic revisions have usually come first, to be followed later by Russia's.

From the desire to cater to interests beyond the national domain, either or both of two military requirements may arise: to increase the country's strength in conventional arms and to create a first-strike capability. To protect client states, an alliance leader needs either a war-fighting or a first-strike capability. If both of these should be lacking, then, say, a conventional Russian thrust into Europe would pose the choice of appeasement or annihilation. Weakness on the ground makes fighting a war impossible; mutual invulnerability inhibits making a strategic strike. If appeasement or annihilation are the choices, the former is likely to be preferred.

McNamara's policy of flexible response was designed to remedy both tactical and strategic weakness. American troops in Europe created a tangible identification of America's fate with Europe's. With at least several thousand tactical nuclear warheads and more than one hundred medium range missiles in the area of the European command, the forces available to NATO also represented something of a war-fighting capability. Facing it, Russia would either have to move with considerable force and thus raise the risk of American strategic retaliation, or she would have to forgo the use of force. At the

<hr>

[32] The conclusion is reported by André Beaufre, retired general and director of the Institute, in his essay on "Nuclear Deterrence and World Strategy," in Karl H. Cerny and Henry W. Briefs, eds., *NATO in Quest of Cohesion* (New York: Praeger, 1965), p. 221.

same time, the enlargement and the improvement of American missile forces created a qualified first-strike capability: that is, the ability to destroy enough Russian missiles on first strike to reduce significantly the amount of damage done by her expected retaliatory blow.

If both had second-strike deterrent forces, the Soviet Union would find it difficult to believe that the United States would initiate a nuclear strike in response to a move—even a severely damaging one—by the Soviet Union against a third country. So long as the United States had only a second-strike capability, its European allies would also find it difficult to believe that the United States could generate from its expensive nuclear arsenal and the ability to protect them. A first-strike (i.e., counterforce) capability would spread the deterrent benefits of the American nuclear force from the homeland to countries abroad. Just as a second-strike force may be unleashed in response to an attack on the homeland, so a first-strike force may be unleashed in response to one abroad.

To extend the coverage of America's nuclear weapons beyond the national borders requires the ability to reduce the damage that can be done by the Soviet Union in retaliation. A first-strike capability will do this, and protection of population by ballistic missile defenses and shelters would add to the effect. Expected damage would nevertheless still be extensive. A first strike would obviously be made only in the face of extreme provocation; the war-fighting capability would take care of other cases. The United States with its varied arsenal could then choose to use just the right amount and type of force for the occasion and would presumably have the Russians stopped at all levels.[33]

Nowadays, obviously, a first strike capability is difficult (and probably impossible) to achieve. An American or Russian first strike at the other's weapons could reduce the amount of damage that could be done in retaliation. But the thousands of warheads that would survive could wreak immense if not catastrophic damage. Thus, arguments in the 1970s turned less on doubts about the ability to strike back and more on doubts about whether the will to do so would survive in the country hit first. To describe superiority in weapons as constituting a first-strike capability may help in catering to the interests of allies. It is also a way of heightening competition in armaments.

ARMS RACES IN THE NUCLEAR AGE

A brief look at developments from 1957 to 1982 will make clear how military capabilities, strategic policy, foreign-policy ends, and national apprehensions interacted to bring about an arms race. The

---

[33] The policy of flexible response, still official NATO strategy, has recently come under increasing criticism, especially with regard to the first use of tactical nuclear weapons that the policy calls for. See the selections in Part IV by Bundy *et. al.* and Kaiser *et. al.*

launching of Sputnik in 1957 created great fears in America that
Russia's lead in rocketry would enable her to build a missile force
large enough to give her a first-strike capability within a few years.
This view was widely publicized by the Gaither Committee, a blue-
ribbon panel appointed by President Eisenhower to assess the
significance of Sputnik's launching for the United States. Predicating
their estimates on what the Russians could build (their capability)
rather than on what they were likely to build (their intentions), the
Committee predicted that a missile gap would materialize—one that
the United States would not be able to overcome until 1960 or 1961,
even were it to begin immediately to make strenuous efforts to redress
the balance.[34] The Eisenhower administration, looking at Russia's
intentions instead of her capabilities, differed with the Committee's
conclusions, but it never succeeded in dispelling the doubts cast by its
critics. John F. Kennedy used the predicted missile gap against
Richard Nixon in the campaign for the presidency. Upon coming into
office, Kennedy accelerated the efforts begun by the previous administration to ensure America's retaliatory capability and initiated new
ones.[35]

Near the end of 1961, it became apparent to defense officials that
the predicted missile gap had failed to materialize. In fact, a missile
gap had opened up in America's favor. Beginning with a statement in
October of 1961 by Deputy Secretary of Defense Roswell Gilpatric,
the Kennedy administration began to stress America's overwhelming
superiority. In December of 1961, Paul Nitze, then Assistant Secretary
of Defense for International Security Affairs, put the case for
American superiority very clearly:

> . . . It appears to be the consensus of the intelligence community, both
> in the United States and in the United Kingdom, that the Soviet deploy-
> ment of ICBM's has proceeded less rapidly than it was once feared it might.
> There has never been any doubt that the West possesses by far the greater
> nuclear force, including delivery capability. . . . We believe that this force
> . . . and the NATO forces . . . give the West a definite nuclear superiority.
> We further believe this superiority can be maintained into the future. . . .
> Furthermore, we believe this superiority, particularly when viewed from
> the Soviet side, to be strategically important in the equations of deterrence
> and strategy.[36]

Evidently the Soviet Union agreed with Nitze, for in September of

[34] The same situation occurred nearly fifty years earlier when, in 1909, the British
were seized by fears of a possible "dreadnought gap" vis-à-vis Germany. See the selection by Robert J. Art in Part II.
[35] See William W. Kaufmann, *The McNamara Strategy* (New York: Harper and
Row, 1964), pp. 47–56.
[36] Quoted in *ibid.*, pp. 108–109.

1962 it began to introduce medium range and intermediate range ballistic missiles into Cuba. The various motives that the Russians may have had at that time are not completely clear. But one point seems certain: by introducing missiles into Cuba, they were resorting to a "quick fix" to redress their strategic inferiority.[37] As a result of American statements, the Russians knew that the Americans now knew what the Russians had always known: they had not built as many ICBM's as they could have. Moreover, the showdown and retreat from Cuba in October of 1962 apparently convinced the Russian leaders that such inferiority vis-à-vis the United States was extremely dangerous. The Chinese may have been correct in asserting that the Soviet Union was "adventuristic" when it put missiles into Cuba and "cowardly" when it took them out. Adventurousness and cowardice, however, were both born of strategic inferiority. To avoid these two extremes in the future, the Soviet Union would have to increase its strategic nuclear forces drastically. It did so. By the end of the decade, it was approaching parity with the United States. In late 1969, the United States had 1,054 land-based ICBM's and 656 sea-based missiles; the Soviet Union, 1,050 and 160, respectively.[38]

The American response after 1957 to a predicted missile gap, and the Russian response after 1961 to a real missile gap, clearly demonstrate that each superpower will refuse to accept a situation in which the other might have a first-strike capability. From the standpoint of the balance of terror, such a refusal is conducive to stability because it reduces the likelihood of preemption. From the standpoint of arms control, such a refusal can be disastrous. Both countries have an interest in taking measures to discourage preemption. Both also have an interest in holding down defense expenditures. The difficulty lies in trying to figure out how much is enough to ensure a second-strike capability and how much is so much as to create fear that a first-strike capability is being sought. In their efforts to determine how much to have, the two superpowers have not helped each other. Russian boasts of superiority from 1957 onward did little to restrain America's fears and to discourage her from looking at capabilities rather than intentions in her intelligence estimates. American boasts of superiority from 1961 onward did little to inhibit the Russians from undertaking a massive land-based and sea-based missile buildup. Each boasted, however, because each found itself in a situation where boasts could serve other interests. After 1957, the Soviet Union found it advantageous to use a presumed superiority in order to undertake a general political offensive in its foreign policy. After 1961, the United States

---

[37] See the selection by Albert and Robert Wohlstetter in Part II.
[38] These figures are taken from the Institute of Strategic Studies, *The Military Balance, 1969–70* (London: The Institute of Strategic Studies, 1969), p. 55.

found it advantageous to use a known superiority to try to convince her allies that they did not need national nuclear establishments.

In the nuclear arms race from 1957 to 1970, then, the two superpowers experienced intense and conflicting pressures. For their own protection, they had to maintain retaliatory capabilities at the least. For their alliance commitments and other interests, they were tempted to strive for superiority and to make full diplomatic use of any real or presumed advantage. Complicating matters even further were the difficulties inherent in trying to infer each other's unknown strategic intentions from well-known strategic capabilities. If the two superpowers had been interested solely in preserving their respective second-strike capabilities, the arms race would have been easier to manage. The problem, of course, is that each had interests beyond the dissuasion of an attack by the other on its homeland. Both used their strategic nuclear forces to serve larger political purposes.

These same pressures operated from 1972 to 1982, during the period when both formal and tacit limits on the nuclear arms race were in effect. In 1972, America and Russia signed the Strategic Arms Limitation Treaty (SALT I). By their agreement, for indefinite duration, anti-ballistic missiles (ABM) were severely constrained in both the number that could be deployed and in the qualitative improvements that were permissible.[39] Offensive missile systems (but not strategic bombers) were frozen at then present levels for five years.

Analysts disagree as to why the Russians agreed to the Treaty, but surely fear about the consequences of an effective American ABM system and desire to gain access to Western technology to improve the Soviet economy's performance played their parts. The ABM component of SALT I prevented the United States from deploying systems that could threaten the costly and extensive buildup in offensive weapons that the Soviet Union had engaged in for the previous ten years. The Accord as a whole promised to usher in a new era in American-Russian political relations that would facilitate trade between the two. For their part, the Americans wanted to avoid another expensive round of strategic nuclear competition. They saw SALT I as a way to cap the number of *both* Russian and American offensive systems. The quantitative and qualitative limits imposed on ABM systems would obviate an offense/defense race; the quantitative limits

---

[39] The ABM Treaty prohibited the following: deployment of a nationwide defense; development, testing, and deployment of air-based, sea-based, space-based, and mobile ABM systems and components; testing of non-ABM systems in an ABM-mode. Each nation was limited to two sites for deployment—at the national capital and at an ICBM-field—with 100 ABM launchers and interceptor missiles permitted at each site. Development, testing, and deployment of ABMs was thus restricted to the fixed land-based mode. See Mason Willrich and John B. Rhinelander, editors, *SALT—The Moscow Agreements and Beyond* (New York: The Free Press, 1974), pp. 126–143 and 277–295.

put on Russia's offensive forces would reduce the political pressures on the United States to match Russia weapon for weapon.

The ABM treaty is still in force. No formal treaty on offensive systems is now in effect because President Carter asked the Senate to defer debate on the Salt II treaty following the Soviet Union's invasion of Afghanistan. Both nations, however, have continued to improve their offensive forces. In fact, an intense qualitative race in offensive systems has gone on during the past decade; a moderate one in defensive systems.[40]

Why? Why have they continued to race so intensely when the 1972 Accord might have meliorated it? The reasons, as usual, are complex; but, at the minimum, the same intense and conflicting pressures that operated from 1957 to 1970 were present in the 1972 to 1982 period. As a consequence, the SALT I Accord did not end the superpower nuclear arms race. It merely redirected it.

Because the 1972 Accord only loosely constrained qualitative improvements in offensive systems,[41] both powers continued to improve them, especially their accuracy. The net result for each, however, is that their fixed-site, land-based ballistic missiles have become increasingly vulnerable to attack. Recent Secretaries of Defense have reported that over 90% of America's Minuteman force will shortly be vulnerable to a surprise Russian attack unless the United States takes countermeasures, such as a launch on warning (LOW) policy or an ABM hard-point defense of selected missile fields.[42] By the early 1990s, Russia's fixed land-based missiles will be similarly vulnerable once the United States begins to deploy the Trident II missile.

The meaning of this development for nuclear deterrence, assured destruction, crisis stability, and alliance relations is not clear, though hotly debated.[43] What is clear is that the debate over what is sufficient for deterrence no longer revolves mainly around the concept of assured destruction. Since the advent of superpower strategic parity, many have thought that the ability to fight limited strategic nuclear wars is needed. This is the context in which to view Secretary of Defense Schlesinger's limited nuclear options, Secretary Brown's countervailing strategy, and Secretary Weinberger's call for the ability

---

[40] See the selection by Warner R. Schilling in Part III for a comprehensive discussion of this period.

[41] The qualitative constraint was put only on land-based missiles and indirectly by setting limits on ICBM silo dimensions. The purpose of this provision was to constrain the Russians from converting older silos to house their newer generations of heavy missiles. See Mason and Willrich, pp. 143–146 and 296–300.

[42] See *Department of Defense Annual Report for Fiscal Year 1981*, 29 January 1980, by Harold Brown (Washington: GPO), pp. 5 and 6 and 85–88; *FY 1982 Report* (by Harold Brown), 19 January 1981, pp. 52–59 and 109–111; *FY 1973 Report* (by Caspar Weinberger), 31 January 1982, Chap. I, pp. 41–42 and Chap. III, pp. 57–58.

[43] See the selections by Robert Jervis, Desmond Ball, and Paul Nitze in Part IV.

to wage a protracted nuclear war.[44] Thus, by making an all-out exchange between the superpowers less credible, parity has led, at least in the United States, to the search for lesser and more credible nuclear options. And that, in turn, has pushed analysts to look at what fighting a sustained nuclear war might mean. To many, the ability to conduct a protracted nuclear war has now become a component of how to deter it.

The presumed logic of parity, combined with the minimal constraints on offensive improvements, helped produce the qualitative offensive arms race of the last ten years.[45] But larger political factors have also been at work. Russia achieved formal recognition of coequal strategic nuclear status with the SALT I Accord. She has used the security that this nuclear shield has provided to extend the reach of her influence. While not fully a global power, she is no longer merely a regional one. Surely part of the reason for the continuing modernization of her forces is the determination to maintain a strategic nuclear force "second to none" because of the presumed, if intangible, political benefits thought to derive from it.

For her part, America has reacted ambiguously and fitfully to the loss of nuclear superiority, alternately embracing and rejecting parity. As in earlier times, the United States has been torn between the desire to achieve a stable relation with Russia and the desire to reap the benefits thought to derive from superiority. Unwilling to break the tacit offensive accord unilaterally, the United States has resorted to both doctrinal and hardware fixes to the problem of alliance commitments. Schlesinger's limited nuclear options was a doctrinal change intended to restore the credibility of the American nuclear guarantee to Europe after parity had been enshrined.[46] The deployment of long range theater nuclear forces (LRTNF) to Western Europe, agreed upon by NATO in December 1979, was a hardware response to continuing European concerns about the credibility of the American nuclear guarantee.[47] The large scale deployment of cruise missiles at sea and in the air, the contemplated deployment of the MX, and the Trident II deployment bespeak America's determination, because of the larger political image involved, not to have a strategic force second to Russia's. Once again, the two superpowers have been driven

---

[44] See the selections by James Schlesinger and Harold Brown in Part I.

[45] The qualitative race in ABM research and development has been muted because of the severe constraints imposed by the 1972 Accord. For reasons not clear, the Russians have continued to improve their ABM system around Moscow. Area or population defense is no longer taken seriously in the United States, but ICBM vulnerability has led to serious work on hard-point or ICBM defense.

[46] See Lynn Ethridge Davis, *Limited Nuclear Options*, Adelphi Paper No. 121 (London: International Institute for Strategic Studies, 1976).

[47] See the selection by Robert J. Art and Stephen E. Ockenden in Part II for a full explanation of these points.

by their larger foreign policy interests to design forces beyond what simply protecting themselves would require.

THE FUTURE OF FORCE

If the past be any guide to the future, military power will remain central to the course of international relations. As long as anarchy obtains, force will remain the final arbiter to resolve the disputes that arise among states. As has always been the case, most disputes will be settled short of the physical use of force. But as long as the active use of force is possible, military power will vitally affect the way in which states deal with one another in peacetime as well as in war.

This is a conclusion not universally nor even widely held today. Adherents of three schools of thought challenge it. First are those who argue that nuclear weapons make war, nuclear or conventional, between America and Russia or between the NATO Alliance and the Warsaw Pact, unthinkable. One hopes that is the case. But, as we have argued, one does not measure the utility of force simply by the frequency with which it is actively used. To argue that force is on the wane because war in Europe has not occurred is to confuse effect with cause. The probability of war between America and Russia or between NATO and the Warsaw Pact is practically nil precisely because the military planning and deployments of each, together with the fears of escalation to general nuclear war, keep it that way. The absence of war in the European theater, does not signify the irrelevance of military power to East-West relations but rather the opposite. The estimates of relative strength between these two sets of forces, moreover, intimately affect the political and economic relations between Eastern and Western Europe. A stable balance of forces creates a political climate conducive to trade. An unstable balance of forces heightens political tensions that are disruptive to trade. The odds against general war are high, but the mere possibility shapes the peacetime relations of European powers with one another and with their superpower protectors.

Second are those who argue that the common problems of mankind, such as pollution and the feared scarcity of raw materials, have made both military power and war passé. They argue that the common problems of nations not only make war obsolete but also make it imperative that nations cooperate to solve them. This argument, however, is less a statement of fact about the present than a fervent hope for the future. Cooperation among nations today, such as it is, cannot make us sanguine about their ability to manage their conflicts for the good of all. The circumstances of states differ and so do their interests and perspectives. They have different solutions to the same problems and, indeed, different ideas about what the problems are. Thus China and India are concerned about the deleterious affects of population growth on their standards of living. But Nigeria, whose source of power and influence within Africa rests partly on a population that is huge by African standards, is not. As long as anarchy obtains, no agency is able to create and enforce a consensus among states. Therefore, military power deployed by individual states plays a vital role both in defining what the problems are and in hastening or delaying their solutions.

Third are those who proclaim that the nations of the world have become so economically intertwined that military power is no longer useful. Nations whose economic interests are deeply entangled cannot use force against one another without harming themselves in the process. The intertwining of interests renders force unusable. This view of the world is odd. American military power created and sustained the political conditions under which the American, Canadian, Japanese, and Western Europe economies have flourished and have become even more entangled. It is strange to argue that force has no utility among states whose interests are closely united when force has been responsible for uniting them. The Japanese, Canadians, and Western Europeans know that they remain dependent for their security on American military power, especially the American nuclear umbrella. Almost inevitably the United States uses the military dependence of others to further its own political and economic interests. America's military preeminence conditions her relations with others. It is the cement of economic interdependence.

A simple example will clarify the point. In 1945, convinced that competitive devaluations of currencies deepened and lengthened the depression of the 1930s, America pressed for fixed exchange rates. Her view prevailed, and the Bretton Woods structure of fixed exchange rates, with small permissible variations monitored by the International Monetary Fund, was set up and lasted until 1971. In that year, because of the huge overflow of dollars over a twenty-five year period, the United States found it to its best interests to close the gold window—that is, to suspend the commitment to pay out gold for dollars that a nation turned in. Under Bretton Woods the value of each nation's currency was tied to the American dollar, which in turn was fixed at thirty-five dollars per ounce of gold. By closing the gold window, the United States shattered that standard, caused the price of an ounce of gold in dollars to soar, destroyed the fixed benchmark according to which all currencies were measured, and ushered in the era of floating exchange rates. In sum, America both made and unmade the Bretton Woods system. In 1945 she persuaded her allies. In 1971 she acted unilaterally and against their wishes.

Under both fixed and floating exchange rates, moreover, the United States has confronted her major allies with an unpleasant choice. Either they could accept and hold onto the dollars flowing out of the United States and thereby add to their inflation at home by increasing their money supplies; or they could refuse the dollars, watch the value of their currencies in relation to the dollar rise, make their exports more expensive (exports upon which all these nations heavily rely), and threaten a decline in exports with the concomitant risk of recession. America's economic and military strength has enabled her for over twenty years to confront her major allies with the choice of inflation or recession. America did not have to use military power directly to structure the choice this way nor to make or break the system. Her economic strength gave her considerable bargaining power. But without her military preeminence and the military dependence of others, she could not have acted as she did.

Some also argue that the United States can no longer use its military power against Third World nations to achieve its aims because of its dependence on their raw materials or because of its need to sell them manufactured goods.[48] In order to assess the validity of this argument, four factors must be kept in mind. First, the efficacy of military power should not be confused with the will to use it. In the mid and late 1970s, as a consequence of the war in Vietnam, America's foreign policy elite was reluctant to commit conventional forces, believing that the American public would not tolerate such action. Second, although a superior military position can give one state a bargaining edge over another in their economic relations, bargains must nevertheless be struck. Short of outright conquest, the economic relations between two states are settled on the basis of each state's perception of its economic interests, on differences in the strength, size, and diversity of their economies, on differences in the degree to which each state coordinates the activities of its interest groups and hence centrally manages its economy, and on the differences in their military dependence.

Third, in the 1950s and 1960s, America's economic and military power far surpassed that of any other nation. With the emergence of the Soviet Union as a global military power in the 1970s, America's freedom to intervene around the world, unimpeded by concerns about the responses of another global power, has declined. So too has America's economic freedom worldwide waned. Whether measured by the diminished role of the dollar as the world's reserve currency, by the persistently unfavorable trade balance, by the smaller percentage of the world's trade accounted for by American imports and exports, by the decline in the productivity of its labor force, or by the greater dependence on imported raw materials, the United States economy is less self-sufficient than it once was. It is, therefore, wrongheaded to assert that America's diminished ability to get what it wants economically from allies and neutrals is due mainly to the devaluation

---

[48] See the selections by Huntington, Waltz, and Epstein in Part IV.

of military power. To assert that military power is devalued because it cannot solve economic problems when economic problems have never been readily solved by military measures is wrongheaded.

Fourth, force cannot be used efficiently when ambivalence exists over the ends to be achieved. America's increasing dependence on imported oil illustrates the problem. Many have taken the decision by the United States not to use military power to get OPEC nations to lower the price of their oil as signalling the devaluation of military power. It would be absurd to deny that the efforts of OPEC countries to strengthen themselves militarily have reduced America's ability to use military power against them. It would be equally absurd to ignore that some of the restraints on the use of force arise from America's ambivalence about the price it should pay for imported oil. In the short term, America's interest is to have a stable supply of cheap oil. In the long term, however, a low price for foreign oil would lead, as it had led before, to increased dependence. In the short term, expensive oil worsens the nation's balance of payments deficit, increases inflation, and lessens aggregate demand. In the long term, it promotes conservation, the search for more oil, the development of alternative energy sources, and the likelihood of a decreasing dependence on foreign energy imports. Military power is not useful for solving an economic problem that has no simple or single best solution. Certainly much of America's restraint in dealing with OPEC stems from uncertainty over what is in her own best economic interest, or even from tacit agreement that a rise in the price of imported oil is in America's long term interest.

American action aside, the record of the late 1970s fails to support the assertion that military power is on the wane. Recent Russian successes in Angola, Ethiopia, Southern Yemen, Afghanistan, and Cambodia have all been predicated on the use of Russian military power, sometimes in concert with Cuba. Russia continues to pour huge resources into her military machine. Evidently she does not believe that force has lost its efficacy. Military power remains a vital instrument of foreign policy in the relations of Third World nations. Recall these events from the years of 1978 to 1982: The Tanzanian-Ugandan War, the Northern Yemen-Southern Yemen War, the Ethiopian-Samalian War, the Sino-Vietnam War, the Cambodian-Vietnam War, the Libyan-Egyptian border clashes, the Libyan-backed insurgency in Chad, the Angolan-backed insurgency in Southern Zaire, the Moroccan takeover of the Spanish Sahara, the Algerian-backed Polisaro War against Morocco, and the Israeli war against the PLO in Lebanon. Moreover, nuclear weapons continue to entice and lure such non-nuclear powers as Pakistan and Brazil. China strives to modernize its obsolete military forces. The NATO Alliance committed itself to a three percent real increase in its military spending. Above and beyond that, sentiment in the United States has supported a tremendous increase in military spending.

The attractions of force endure. They must. As long as the nations of the world refuse to yield their sovereignty to a higher power, military power and foreign policy will be inexorably linked. Until the nature of international politics is transformed, mankind will continue to suffer the costs and reap the benefits of the use of force.

Part I
Theories About
The Use of Force

States coexist in a condition of anarchy. If a state is attacked, it has to defend itself with whatever means it can muster. Because no authoritative agency can be called on to resolve disputes among states, statesmen often find it convenient, and sometimes find it necessary, to threaten or to use force. Military force is important, if not central, in international politics. It brings some order out of chaos, and it helps to make and enforce the rules of the game.

Since force is so important internationally, the following questions arise: How can states most effectively employ military force in pursuit of national goals? What effects has the growth in national military power had on the ways in which force has been used? What kinds of military threats are productive, and what kinds counterproductive? Have nuclear weapons changed the nature of international politics or drastically altered the ways in which states can use military power? These are the questions that the authors of the selections in Part I explore. Robert Jervis looks at the different ways defensive and offensive strategies affect the probabilities that cooperation and peace or conflict and war will prevail. The first of the selections by Glenn Snyder asks what conditions make deterrent balances stable. Robert E. Osgood provides a historical analysis of the changes in the military capabilities of states and of the effects that changes have had on the ways in which force has been used. With conventional weapons, deterrence and defense had tended to fuse; Thomas C. Schelling shows how nuclear weapons have separated these two functions. The second of the selections by Snyder distinguishes between the functions of pre-attack deterrence and post-attack defense in his discussion of the dilemmas that nuclear technology has created for strategists. Finally, the selections under "Nuclear Strategies: The Record" deal more specifically with the kinds of choices that statesmen have made in their plans for the use of nuclear weapons.

Cooperation Under The
Security Dilemma

ROBERT JERVIS

I. ANARCHY AND THE SECURITY DILEMMA

The lack of an international sovereign not only permits wars to occur, but also makes it difficult for states that are satisfied with the
status quo to arrive at goals that they recognize as being in their common interest. Because there are no institutions or authorities that can
make and enforce international laws, the policies of cooperation that
will bring mutual rewards if others cooperate may bring disaster if
they do not. Because states are aware of this, anarchy encourages
behavior that leaves all concerned worse off than they could be, even
in the extreme case in which all states would like to freeze the status
quo. This is true of the men in Rousseau's "Stag Hunt." If they
cooperate to trap the stag, they will all eat well. But if one person
defects to chase a rabbit—which he likes less than stag—none of the
others will get anything. Thus, all actors have the same preference
order, and there is a solution that gives each his first choice: (1)
cooperate and trap the stag (the international analogue being cooperation and disarmament); (2) chase a rabbit while others remain at their
posts (maintain a high level of arms while others are disarmed); (3) all
chase rabbits (arms competition and high risk of war); and (4) stay at
the original position while another chases a rabbit (being disarmed
while others are armed).[1] Unless each person thinks that the others
will cooperate, he himself will not. And why might he fear that any
other person would do something that would sacrifice his own first
choice? The other might not understand the situation, or might not be
able to control his impulses if he saw a rabbit, or might fear that some

From "Cooperation Under the Security Dilemma," *World Politics,* Vol. 30, no. 2
(January 78). Copyright © 1978 by Princeton University Press. Excerpts, pp. 167–170,
187–214, reprinted by permission of Princeton University Press.
    * I am grateful to Robert Art, Bernard Brodie, and Glenn Snyder for comments,
and to the Committee on Research of the UCLA Academic Senate for financial support. An earlier version of this essay appeared as Working Paper No. 5, UCLA Program in Arms Control and International Security.
    [1] This kind of rank-ordering is not entirely an analyst's invention, as is shown by the
following section of a British army memo of 1903 dealing with British and Russian
railroad construction near the Persia-Afghanistan border:

other member of the group is unreliable. If the person voices any of these suspicions, others are more likely to fear that he will defect, thus making them more likely to defect, thus making it more rational for him to defect. Of course in this simple case—and in many that are more realistic—there are a number of arrangements that could permit cooperation. But the main point remains: although actors may know that they seek a common goal, they may not be able to reach it.

Even when there is a solution that is everyone's first choice, the international case is characterized by three difficulties not present in the Stag Hunt. First, to the incentives to defect given above must be added the potent fear that even if the other state now supports the status quo, it may become dissatisfied later. No matter how much decision makers are committed to the status quo, they cannot bind themselves and their successors to the same path. Minds can be changed, new leaders can come to power, values can shift, new opportunities and dangers can arise.

The second problem arises from a possible solution. In order to protect their possessions, states often seek to control resources or land outside their own territory. Countries that are not self-sufficient must try to assure that the necessary supplies will continue to flow in wartime. This was part of the explanation for Japan's drive into China and Southeast Asia before World War II. If there were an international authority that could guarantee access, this motive for control would disappear. But since there is not, even a state that would prefer the status quo to increasing its area of control may pursue the latter policy.

When there are believed to be tight linkages between domestic and foreign policy or between the domestic politics of two states, the quest for security may drive states to interfere pre-emptively in the domestic politics of others in order to provide an ideological buffer zone. Thus, Metternich's justification for supervising the politics of the Italian states has been summarized as follows:

The conditions of the problem may . . . be briefly summarized as follows:

a) If we make a railway to Seistan while Russia remains inactive, we gain a considerable defensive advantage at considerable financial cost;

b) If Russia makes a railway to Seistan, while we remain inactive, she gains a considerable offensive advantage at considerable financial cost;

c) If both we and Russia make railways to Seistan, the defensive and offensive advantages may be held to neutralize each other; in other words, we shall have spent a good deal of money and be no better off than we are at present. On the other hand, we shall be no worse off, whereas under alternative (b) we shall be much worse off. Consequently, the theoretical balance of advantage lies with the proposed railway extension from Quetta to Seistan.

W. G. Nicholson, "Memorandum on Seistan and Other Points Raised in the Discussion on the Defence of India," (Committee of Imperial Defence, March 20, 1903). It should be noted that the possibility of neither side building railways was not mentioned, thus strongly biasing the analysis.

Every state is absolutely sovereign in its internal affairs But this implies
that every state must do nothing to interfere in the internal affairs of any
other. However, any false or pernicious step taken by any state in its
internal affairs may disturb the repose of another state, and this consequent disturbance of another state's repose constitutes an interference in
that state's internal affairs. Therefore, every state—or rather, every
sovereign of a great power—has the duty, in the name of the sacred right of
independence of every state, to supervise the governments of smaller states
and to prevent them from taking false and pernicious steps in their internal
affairs.[2]

More frequently, the concern is with direct attack. In order to protect themselves, states seek to control, or at least to neutralize, areas
on their borders. But attempts to establish buffer zones can alarm
others who have stakes there, who fear that undesirable precedents
will be set, or who believe that their own vulnerability will be increased.
When buffers are sought in areas empty of great powers, expansion
tends to feed on itself in order to protect what is acquired, as was
often noted by those who opposed colonial expansion. Balfour's complaint was typical: "Every time I come to a discussion—at intervals
of, say, five years—I find there is a new sphere which we have got to
guard, which is supposed to protect the gateways of India. Those
gateways are getting further and further away from India, and I do
not know how far west they are going to be brought by the General
Staff."[3]
  Though this process is most clearly visible when it involves territorial expansion, it often operates with the increase of less tangible
power and influence. The expansion of power usually brings with it an
expansion of responsibilities and commitments; to meet them, still
greater power is required. The state will take many positions that are
subject to challenge. It will be involved with a wide range of controversial issues unrelated to its core values. And retreats that would be
seen as normal if made by a small power would be taken as an index of
weakness inviting predation if made by a large one.
  The third problem present in international politics but not in the
Stag Hunt is the security dilemma: many of the means by which a state
tries to increase its security decrease the security of others. In domestic
society, there are several ways to increase the safety of one's person
and property without endangering others. One can move to a safer
neighborhood, put bars on the windows, avoid dark streets, and
keep a distance from suspicious-looking characters. Of course these

[2] Paul Schroeder, *Metternich's Diplomacy at Its Zenith, 1820–1823* (Westport,
Conn.: Greenwood Press 1969), 126.
[3] Quoted in Michael Howard, *The Continental Commitment* (Harmondsworth,
England: Penguin 1974), 67.

measures are not convenient, cheap, or certain of success. But no one save criminals need be alarmed if a person takes them. In international politics, however, one state's gain in security often inadvertently threatens others. In explaining British policy on naval disarmament in the interwar period to the Japanese, Ramsey MacDonald said that "Nobody wanted Japan to be insecure."[4] But the problem was not with British desires, but with the consequences of her policy. In earlier periods, too, Britain had needed a navy large enough to keep the shipping lanes open. But such a navy could not avoid being a menace to any other state with a coast that could be raided, trade that could be interdicted, or colonies that could be isolated. When Germany started building a powerful navy before World War I, Britain objected that it could only be an offensive weapon aimed at her. As Sir Edward Grey, the Foreign Secretary, put it to King Edward VII: "If the German Fleet ever becomes superior to ours, the German Army can conquer this country. There is no corresponding risk of this kind to Germany; for however superior our Fleet was, no naval victory could bring us any nearer to Berlin." The English position was half correct: Germany's navy was an anti-British instrument. But the British often overlooked what the Germans knew full well: "in every quarrel with England, German colonies and trade were . . . hostages from England to take." Thus, whether she intended it or not, the British Navy constituted an important instrument of coercion. . . .[5]

II. OFFENSE, DEFENSE, AND THE SECURITY DILEMMA

Another approach starts with the central point of the security dilemma—that an increase in one state's security decreases the security of others—and examines the conditions under which this proposition holds. Two crucial variables are involved: whether defensive weapons and policies can be distinguished from offensive ones, and whether the defense or the offense has the advantage. The definitions are not always clear, and many cases are difficult to judge, but these two variables shed a great deal of light on the question of whether status-quo powers will adopt compatible security policies. All the variables discussed so far leave the heart of the problem untouched. But when defensive weapons differ from offensive ones, it is possible for a state

[4] Quoted in Gerald Wheeler, *Prelude to Pearl Harbor* (Columbia: University of Missouri Press 1963), 167.

[5] Quoted in Leonard Wainstein, "The Dreadnought Gap," in Robert Art and Kenneth Waltz, eds., *The Use of Force* (Boston: Little, Brown 1971), 155; Raymond Sontag, *European Diplomatic History, 1871-1932* (New York: Appleton-Century-Croits 1933), 147. The French had made a similar argument 50 years earlier; see James Phinney Baxter III, *The Introduction of the Ironclad Warship* (Cambridge: Harvard University Press 1933), 149. For a more detailed discussion of the security dilemma, see Jervis, *Perception and Misperception in International Politics* (Princeton: Princeton University Press 1976), 62-76.

to make itself more secure without making others less secure. And when the defense has the advantage over the offense, a large increase in one state's security only slightly decreases the security of the others, and status-quo powers can all enjoy a high level of security and largely escape from the state of nature.

OFFENSE-DEFENSE BALANCE

When we say that the offense has the advantage, we simply mean that it is easier to destroy the other's army and take its territory than it is to defend one's own. When the defense has the advantage, it is easier to protect and to hold than it is to move forward, destroy, and take. If effective defenses can be erected quickly, an attacker may be able to keep territory he has taken in an initial victory. Thus, the dominance of the defense made it very hard for Britain and France to push Germany out of France in World War I. But when superior defenses are difficult for an aggressor to improvise on the battlefield and must be constructed during peacetime, they provide no direct assistance to him.

The security dilemma is at its most vicious when commitments, strategy, or technology dictate that the only route to security lies through expansion. Status-quo powers must then act like aggressors; the fact that they would gladly agree to forego the opportunity for expansion in return for guarantees for their security has no implications for their behavior. Even if expansion is not sought as a goal in itself, there will be quick and drastic changes in the distribution of territory and influence. Conversely, when the defense has the advantage, status-quo states can make themselves more secure without gravely endangering others.[6] Indeed, if the defense has enough of an advantage and if the states are of roughly equal size, not only will the security dilemma cease to inhibit status-quo states from cooperating, but aggression will be next to impossible, thus rendering international anarchy relatively unimportant. If states cannot conquer each other, then the lack of sovereignty, although it presents problems of collective goods in a number of areas, no longer forces states to devote their primary attention to self-preservation. Although, if force were not usable, there would be fewer restraints on the use of nonmilitary instruments, these are rarely powerful enough to threaten the vital interests of a major state.

Two questions of the offense-defense balance can be separated. First, does the state have to spend more or less than one dollar on defensive forces to offset each dollar spent by the other side on forces

---

[6] Thus, when Wolfers (fn. 10) 126, argues that a status-quo state that settles for rough equality of power with its adversary, rather than seeking preponderance, may be able to convince the other to reciprocate by showing that it wants only to protect itself, not menace the other, he assumes that the defense has an advantage.

that could be used to attack? If the state has one dollar to spend on increasing its security, should it put it into offensive or defensive forces? Second, with a given inventory of forces, is it better to attack or to defend? Is there an incentive to strike first or to absorb the other's blow? These two aspects are often linked: if each dollar spent on offense can overcome each dollar spent on defense, and if both sides have the same defense budgets, then both are likely to build offensive forces and find it attractive to attack rather than to wait for the adversary to strike.

These aspects affect the security dilemma in different ways. The first has its greatest impact on arms races. If the defense has the advantage, and if the status-quo powers have reasonable subjective security requirements, they can probably avoid an arms race. Although an increase in one side's arms and security will still decrease the other's security, the former's increase will be larger than the latter's decrease. So if one side increases its arms, the other can bring its security back up to its previous level by adding a smaller amount to its forces. And if the first side reacts to this change, its increase will also be smaller than the stimulus that produced it. Thus a stable equilibrium will be reached. Shifting from dynamics to statics, each side can be quite secure with forces roughly equal to those of the other. Indeed, if the defense is much more potent than the offense, each side can be willing to have forces much smaller than the other's, and can be indifferent to a wide range of the other's defense policies.

The second aspect—whether it is better to attack or to defend—influences short-run stability. When the offense has the advantage, a state's reaction to international tension will increase the chances of war. The incentives for pre-emption and the "reciprocal fear of surprise attack" in this situation have been made clear by analyses of the dangers that exist when two countries have first-strike capabilities.[7] There is no way for the state to increase its security without menacing, or even attacking, the other. Even Bismarck, who once called preventive war "committing suicide from fear of death," said that "no government, if it regards war as inevitable even if it does not want it, would be so foolish as to leave to the enemy the choice of time and occasion and to wait for the moment which is most convenient for the enemy."[8] In another arena, the same dilemma applies to the policeman in a dark alley confronting a suspected criminal who appears to be holding a weapon. Though racism may indeed be present, the security dilemma can account for many of the tragic shootings of innocent people in the ghettos.

[7] Schelling (fn. 20), chap. 9.
[8] Quoted in Fritz Fischer, *War of Illusions* (New York: Norton 1975), 377, 461.

Beliefs about the course of a war in which the offense has the advantage further deepen the security dilemma. When there are incentives to strike first, a successful attack will usually so weaken the other side that victory will be relatively quick, bloodless, and decisive. It is in these periods when conquest is possible and attractive that states consolidate power internally—for instance, by destroying the feudal barons—and expand externally. There are several consequences that decrease the chance of cooperation among status-quo states. First, war will be profitable for the winner. The costs will be low and the benefits high. Of course, losers will suffer; the fear of losing could induce states to try to form stable cooperative arrangements, but the temptation of victory will make this particularly difficult. Second, because wars are expected to be both frequent and short, there will be incentives for high levels of arms, and quick and strong reaction to the other's increases in arms. The state cannot afford to wait until there is unambiguous evidence that the other is building new weapons. Even large states that have faith in their economic strength cannot wait, because the war will be over before their products can reach the army. Third, when wars are quick, states will have to recruit allies in advance.[9] Without the opportunity for bargaining and re-alignments during the opening stages of hostilities, peacetime diplomacy loses a degree of the fluidity that facilitates balance-of-power policies. Because alliances must be secured during peacetime, the international system is more likely to become bipolar. It is hard to say whether war therefore becomes more or less likely, but this bipolarity increases tension between the two camps and makes it harder for status-quo states to gain the benefits of cooperation. Fourth, if wars are frequent, statesmen's perceptual thresholds will be adjusted accordingly and they will be quick to perceive ambiguous evidence as indicating that others are aggressive. Thus, there will be more cases of status-quo powers arming against each other in the incorrect belief that the other is hostile.

When the defense has the advantage, all the foregoing is reversed. The state that fears attack does not pre-empt—since that would be a wasteful use of its military resources—but rather prepares to receive an attack. Doing so does not decrease the security of others, and several states can do it simultaneously; the situation will therefore be stable, and status-quo powers will be able to cooperate. When Herman Kahn argues that ultimatums "are vastly too dangerous to give because . . . they are quite likely to touch off a pre-emptive strike,"[10] he incorrectly assumes that it is always advantageous to strike first.

---

[9] George Quester, *Offense and Defense in the International System* (New York: John Wiley 1977), 105–06; Sontag (fn. 5), 4–5.
[10] Kahn (fn. 23), 211 (also see 144).

More is involved than short-run dynamics. When the defense is dominant, wars are likely to become stalemates and can be won only at enormous cost. Relatively small and weak states can hold off larger and stronger ones, or can deter attack by raising the costs of conquest to an unacceptable level. States then approach equality in what they can do to each other. Like the .45-caliber pistol in the American West, fortifications were the "great equalizer" in some periods. Changes in the status quo are less frequent and cooperation is more common wherever the security dilemma is thereby reduced.

Many of these arguments can be illustrated by the major powers' policies in the periods preceding the two world wars. Bismarck's wars surprised statesmen by showing that the offense had the advantage, and by being quick, relatively cheap, and quite decisive. Falling into a common error, observers projected this pattern into the future.[11] The resulting expectations had several effects. First, states sought semi-permanent allies. In the early stages of the Franco-Prussian War, Napoleon III had thought that there would be plenty of time to recruit Austria to his side. Now, others were not going to repeat this mistake. Second, defense budgets were high and reacted quite sharply to increases on the other side. It is not surprising that Richardson's theory of arms races fits this period well. Third, most decision makers thought that the next European war would not cost much blood and treasure.[12] That is one reason why war was generally seen as inevitable and why mass opinion was so bellicose. Fourth, once war seemed likely, there were strong pressures to pre-empt. Both sides believed that whoever moved first could penetrate the other deep enough to disrupt mobilization and thus gain an insurmountable advantage. (There was no such belief about the use of naval forces. Although Churchill made an ill-advised speech saying that if German ships "do not come out and fight in time of war they will be dug out like rats in a hole,"[13] everyone knew that submarines, mines, and coastal fortifications made this impossible. So at the start of the war each navy prepared to

[11] For a general discussion of such mistaken learning from the past, see Jervis (fn. 5), chap. 6. The important and still not completely understood question of why this belief formed and was maintained throughout the war is examined in Bernard Brodie, *War and Politics* (New York: Macmillan 1973), 262–70; Brodie, "Technological Change, Strategic Doctrine, and Political Outcomes," in Klaus Knorr, ed., *Historical Dimensions of National Security Problems* (Lawrence: University Press of Kansas 1976), 290–92; and Douglas Porch, "The French Army and the Spirit of the Offensive, 1900–14," in Brian Bond and Ian Roy, eds,. *War and Society* (New York: Holmes & Meier 1975), 117–43.

[12] Some were not so optimistic. Gray's remark is well-known: "The lamps are going out all over Europe; we shall not see them lit again in our life-time." The German Prime Minister, Bethmann Hollweg, also feared the consequences of the war. But the controlling view was that it would certainly pay for the winner.

[13] Quoted in Martin Gilbert, *Winston S. Churchill, III, The Challenge of War, 1914–1916* (Boston: Houghton Mifflin 1971), 84.

defend itself rather than attack, and the short-run destabilizing forces that launched the armies toward each other did not operate.)[14] Furthermore, each side knew that the other saw the situation the same way, thus increasing the perceived danger that the other would attack, and giving each added reasons to precipitate a war if conditions seemed favorable. In the long and the short run, there were thus both offensive and defensive incentives to strike. This situation casts light on the common question about German motives in 1914: "Did Germany unleash the war deliberately to become a world power or did she support Austria merely to defend a weakening ally," thereby protecting her own position?[15] To some extent, this question is misleading. Because of the perceived advantage of the offense, war was seen as the best route both to gaining expansion and to avoiding drastic loss of influence. There seemed to be no way for Germany merely to retain and safeguard her existing position.

Of course the war showed these beliefs to have been wrong on all points. Trenches and machine guns gave the defense an overwhelming advantage. The fighting became deadlocked and produced horrendous casualties. It made no sense for the combatants to bleed themselves to death. If they had known the power of the defense beforehand, they would have rushed for their own trenches rather than for the enemy's territory. Each side could have done this without increasing the other's incentives to strike. War might have broken out anyway, just as DD is a possible outcome of Chicken, but at least the pressures of time and the fear of allowing the other to get the first blow would not have contributed to this end. And, had both sides known the costs of the war, they would have negotiated much more seriously. The obvious question is why the states did not seek a negotiated settlement as soon as the shape of the war became clear. Schlieffen had said that if his plan failed, peace should be sought.[16] The answer is complex, uncertain, and largely outside of the scope of our concerns. But part of the reason was the hope and sometimes the expectation that breakthroughs could be made and the dominance of the offensive restored. Without that hope, the political and psychological pressures to fight to a decisive victory might have been overcome.

The politics of the interwar period were shaped by the memories of the previous conflict and the belief that any future war would resemble it. Political and military lessons reinforced each other in ameliorating the security dilemma. Because it was believed that the First World War had been a mistake that could have been avoided by

[14] Quester (fn. 33), 98–99. Robert Art, *The Influence of Foreign Policy on Seapower,* II (Beverly Hills: Sage Professional Papers in International Studies Series, 1973), 14–18, 26–28.
[15] Konrad Jarausch, "The Illusion of Limited War: Chancellor Bethmann Hollweg's Calculated Risk, July 1914," *Central European History, II* (March 1969), 50.
[16] Brodie (fn. 8), 58.

skillful conciliation, both Britain and, to a lesser extent, France were highly sensitive to the possibility that interwar Germany was not a real threat to peace, and alert to the danger that reacting quickly and strongly to her arms could create unnecessary conflict. And because Britain and France expected the defense to continue to dominate, they concluded that it was safe to adopt a more relaxed and nonthreatening military posture.[17] Britain also felt less need to maintain tight alliance bonds. The Allies' military posture then constituted only a slight danger to Germany; had the latter been content with the status quo, it would have been easy for both sides to have felt secure behind their lines of fortifications. Of course the Germans were not content, so it is not surprising that they devoted their money and attention to finding ways out of a defense-dominated stalemate. *Blitzkrieg* tactics were necessary if they were to use force to change the status quo.

The initial stages of the war on the Western Front also contrasted with the First World War. Only with the new air arm were there any incentives to strike first, and these forces were too weak to carry out the grandiose plans that had been both dreamed and feared. The armies, still the main instrument, rushed to defensive positions. Perhaps the allies could have successfully attacked while the Germans were occupied in Poland.[18] But belief in the defense was so great that this was never seriously contemplated. Three months after the start of the war, the French Prime Minister summed up the view held by almost everyone but Hitler: on the Western Front there is "deadlock. Two Forces of equal strength and the one that attacks seeing such enormous casualties that it cannot move without endangering the continuation of the war or of the aftermath."[19] The Allies were caught in a dilemma they never fully recognized, let alone solved. On the one hand, they had very high war aims; although unconditional surrender had not yet been adopted, the British had decided from the start that the removal of Hitler was a necessary condition for peace.[20] On the other hand, there were no realistic plans or instruments for allowing the Allies to

[17] President Roosevelt and the American delegates to the League of Nations Disarmament Conference maintained that the tank and mobile heavy artillery had reestablished the dominance of the offensive, thus making disarmament more urgent (Boggs, fn. 28, pp. 31, 108), but this was a minority position and may not even have been believed by the Americans. The reduced prestige and influence of the military, and the high pressures to cut government spending throughout this period also contributed to the lowering of defense budgets.

[18] Jon Kimche, *The Unfought Battle* (New York: Stein 1968); Nicholas William Bethell, *The War Hitler Won: The Fall of Poland, September 1939* (New York: Holt 1972); Alan Alexandroff and Richard Rosecrance, "Deterrence in 1939," *World Politics*, XXIX (April 1977), 404–24.

[19] Roderick Macleod and Denis Kelly, eds., *Time Unguarded: The Ironside Diaries, 1937–1940* (New York: McKay 1962), 173.

[20] For a short time, as France was falling, the British Cabinet did discuss reaching a negotiated peace with Hitler. The official history ignores this, but it is covered in P. M. H. Bell, *A Certain Eventuality* (Farnborough, England: Saxon House 1974), 40–48.

impose their will on the other side. The British Chief of the Imperial General Staff noted, "The French have no intention of carrying out an offensive for years, if at all"; the British were only slightly bolder.[21] So the Allies looked to a long war that would wear the Germans down, cause civilian suffering through shortages, and eventually undermine Hitler. There was little analysis to support this view—and indeed it probably was not supportable—but as long as the defense was dominant and the numbers on each side relatively equal, what else could the Allies do?

To summarize, the security dilemma was much less powerful after World War I than it had been before. In the later period, the expected power of the defense allowed status-quo states to pursue compatible security policies and avoid arms races. Furthermore, high tension and fear of war did not set off short-run dynamics by which each state, trying to increase its security, inadvertently acted to make war more likely. The expected high costs of war, however, led the Allies to believe that no sane German leader would run the risks entailed in an attempt to dominate the Continent, and discouraged them from risking war themselves.

Technology and Geography. Technology and geography are the two main factors that determine whether the offense or the defense has the advantage. As Brodie notes, "On the tactical level, as a rule, few physical factors favor the attacker but many favor the defender. The defender usually has the advantage of cover. He characteristically fires from behind some form of shelter while his opponent crosses open ground."[22] Anything that increases the amount of ground the attacker has to cross, or impedes his progress across it, or makes him more vulnerable while crossing, increases the advantage accruing to the defense. When states are separated by barriers that produce these effects, the security dilemma is eased, since both can have forces adequate for defense without being able to attack. Impenetrable barriers would actually prevent war; in reality, decision makers have to settle for a good deal less. Buffer zones slow the attacker's progress; they thereby give the defender time to prepare, increase problems of logistics, and reduce the number of soldiers available for the final assault. At the end of the 19th century, Arthur Balfour noted Afghanistan's "non-conducting" qualities. "So long as it possesses

[21] Macleod and Kelly (fn. 43), 174. In flat contradiction to common sense and almost everything they believed about modern warfare, the Allies planned an expedition to Scandinavia to cut the supply of iron ore to Germany and to aid Finland against the Russians. But the dominant mood was the one described above.
[22] Brodie (fn. 8), 179.

few roads, and no railroads, it will be impossible for Russia to make effective use of her great numerical superiority at any point immediately vital to the Empire." The Russians valued buffers for the same reasons; it is not surprising that when Persia was being divided into Russian and British spheres of influence some years later, the Russians sought assurances that the British would refrain from building potentially menacing railroads in their sphere. Indeed, since railroad construction radically altered the abilities of countries to defend themselves and to attack others, many diplomatic notes and much intelligence activity in the late 19th century centered on this subject.[23]

Oceans, large rivers, and mountain ranges serve the same function as buffer zones. Being hard to cross, they allow defense against superior numbers. The defender has merely to stay on his side of the barrier and so can utilize all the men he can bring up to it. The attacker's men, however, can cross only a few at a time, and they are very vulnerable when doing so. If all states were self-sufficient islands, anarchy would be much less of a problem. A small investment in shore defenses and a small army would be sufficient to repel invasion. Only very weak states would be vulnerable, and only very large ones could menace others. As noted above, the United States, and to a lesser extent Great Britain, have partly been able to escape from the state of nature because their geographical positions approximated this ideal.

Although geography cannot be changed to conform to borders, borders can and do change to conform to geography. Borders across which an attack is easy tend to be unstable. States living within them are likely to expand or be absorbed. Frequent wars are almost inevitable since attacking will often seem the best way to protect what one has. This process will stop, or at least slow down, when the state's borders reach—by expansion or contraction—a line of natural obstacles. Security without attack will then be possible. Furthermore, these lines constitute salient solutions to bargaining problems and, to the extent that they are barriers to migration, are likely to divide ethnic groups, thereby raising the costs and lowering the incentives for conquest.

Attachment to one's state and its land reinforce one quasi-geographical aid to the defense. Conquest usually becomes more difficult the deeper the attacker pushes into the other's territory. Nationalism spurs the defenders to fight harder; advancing not only

---

[23] Arthur Balfour, "Memorandum," Committee on Imperial Defence, April 30, 1903, pp. 2–3; see the telegrams by Sir Arthur Nicolson, in G. P. Gooch and Harold Temperley, eds., *British Documents on the Origins of the War,* Vol. 4 (London: H.M.S.O. 1929), 429, 524. These barriers do not prevent the passage of long-range aircraft; but even in the air, distance usually aids the defender.

lengthens the attacker's supply lines, but takes him through unfamiliar and often devastated lands that require troops for garrison duty. These stabilizing dynamics will not operate, however, if the defender's war materiel is situated near its borders, or if the people do not care about their state, but only about being on the winning side. In such cases, positive feedback will be at work and initial defeats will be insurmountable.[24]

Imitating geography, men have tried to create barriers. Treaties may provide for demilitarized zones on both sides of the border, although such zones will rarely be deep enough to provide more than warning. Even this was not possible in Europe, but the Russians adopted a gauge for their railroads that was broader than that of the neighboring states, thereby complicating the logistics problems of any attacker—including Russia.

Perhaps the most ambitious and at least temporarily successful attempts to construct a system that would aid the defenses of both sides were the interwar naval treaties, as they affected Japanese-American relations. As mentioned earlier, the problem was that the United States could not defend the Philippines without denying Japan the ability to protect her home islands.[25] (In 1941 this dilemma became insoluble when Japan sought to extend her control to Malaya and the Dutch East Indies. If the Philippines had been invulnerable, they could have provided a secure base from which the U.S. could interdict Japanese shipping between the homeland and the areas she was trying to conquer.) In the 1920's and early 1930's each side would have been willing to grant the other security for its possessions in return for a reciprocal grant, and the Washington Naval Conference agreements were designed to approach this goal. As a Japanese diplomat later put it, their country's "fundamental principle" was to have "a strength insufficient for attack and adequate for defense."[26] Thus, Japan agreed in 1922 to accept a navy only three-fifths as large as that of the United States, and the U.S. agreed not to fortify its Pacific islands.[27] (Japan had earlier been forced to agree not to fortify the islands she had taken from Germany in World War I.) Japan's navy would not be large enough to defeat America's anywhere other than close to the home islands. Although the Japanese could still take the Philippines,

---

[24] See, for example, the discussion of warfare among Chinese warlords in Hsi-Sheng Chi, "The Chinese Warlord System as an International System," in Morton Kaplan, ed., *New Approaches to International Relations* (New York: St. Martin's 1968), 405–25.

[25] Some American decision makers, including military officers, thought that the best way out of the dilemma was to abandon the Philippines.

[26] Quoted in Elting Morrison, *Turmoil and Tradition: A Study of the Life and Times of Henry L. Stimson* (Boston: Houghton Mifflin 1960), 326.

[27] The U.S. "refused to consider limitations on Hawaiian defenses, since these works posed no threat to Japan." Braisted (fn. 27), 612.

not only would they be unable to move farther, but they might be weakened enough by their efforts to be vulnerable to counterattack. Japan, however, gained security. An American attack was rendered more difficult because the American bases were unprotected and because, until 1930, Japan was allowed unlimited numbers of cruisers, destroyers, and submarines that could weaken the American fleet as it made its way across the ocean.[28]

The other major determinant of the offense-defense balance is technology. When weapons are highly vulnerable, they must be employed before they are attacked. Others can remain quite invulnerable in their bases. The former characteristics are embodied in unprotected missiles and many kinds of bombers. (It should be noted that it is not vulnerability *per se* that is crucial, but the location of the vulnerability. Bombers and missiles that are easy to destroy only after having been launched toward their targets do not create destabilizing dynamics.) Incentives to strike first are usually absent for naval forces that are threatened by a naval attack. Like missiles in hardened silos, they are usually well protected when in their bases. Both sides can then simultaneously be prepared to defend themselves successfully.

In ground warfare under some conditions, forts, trenches, and small groups of men in prepared positions can hold off large numbers of attackers. Less frequently, a few attackers can storm the defenses. By and large, it is a contest between fortifications and supporting light weapons on the one hand, and mobility and heavier weapons that clear the way for the attack on the other. As the erroneous views held before the two world wars show, there is no simple way to determine which is dominant. "[T]hese oscillations are not smooth and predictable like those of a swinging pendulum. They are uneven in both extent and time. Some occur in the course of a single battle or campaign, others in the course of a war, still others during a series of wars." Longer-term oscillations can also be detected:

The early Gothic age, from the twelfth to the late thirteenth century, with its wonderful cathedrals and fortified places, was a period during which the attackers in Europe generally met serious and increasing difficulties, because the improvement in the strength of fortresses outran the advance in the power of destruction. Later, with the spread of firearms at the end of the fifteenth century, old fortresses lost their power to resist. An age ensued during which the offense possessed, apart from short-term setbacks, new advantages. Then, during the seventeenth century, especially after about 1660, and until at least at the outbreak of the War of the Austrian Succession in 1740, the defense regained much of the ground it had lost

---

[28] That is part of the reason why the Japanese admirals strongly objected when the civilian leaders decided to accept a seven-to-ten ratio in lighter craft in 1930. Stephen Pelz, *Race to Pearl Harbor* (Cambridge: Harvard University Press 1974), 3.

since the great medieval fortresses had proved unable to meet the bombardment of the new and more numerous artillery.[29]

Another scholar has continued the agrument: "The offensive gained
an advantage with new forms of heavy mobile artillery in the nineteenth century, but the stalemate of World War I created the impression that the defense again had an advantage; the German invasion in
World War II, however, indicated the offensive superiority of highly
mechanized armies in the field."[30]

The situation today with respect to conventional weapons is
unclear. Until recently it was believed that tanks and tactical air power
gave the attacker an advantage. The initial analyses of the 1973 Arab-
Israeli war indicated that new anti-tank and anti-aircraft weapons
have restored the primacy of the defense. These weapons are cheap,
easy to use, and can destroy a high proportion of the attacking
vehicles and planes that are sighted. It then would make sense for a
status-quo power to buy lots of $20,000 missiles rather than buy a few
half-million dollar tanks and multi-million dollar fighter-bombers.
Defense would be possible even against a large and well-equipped
force; states that care primarily about self-protection would not need
to engage in arms races. But further examinations of the new
technologies and the history of the October War cast doubt on these
optimistic conclusions and leave us unable to render any firm judgment.[31]

Concerning nuclear weapons, it is generally agreed that defense is
impossible—a triumph not of the offense, but of deterrence. Attack
makes no sense, not because it can be beaten off, but because the
attacker will be destroyed in turn. In terms of the questions under consideration here, the result is the equivalent of the primacy of the
defense. First, security is relatively cheap. Less than one percent of the
G.N.P. is devoted to deterring a direct attack on the United States;
most of it is spent on acquiring redundant systems to provide a lot of
insurance against the worst conceivable contingencies. Second, both
sides can simultaneously gain security in the form of second-strike

[29] John Nef, *War and Human Progress* (New York: Norton 1963), 185. Also see
ibid., 237, 242–43, and 323; C. W. Oman, *The Art of War in the Middle Ages* (Ithaca,
N.Y.: Cornell University Press 1953), 70–72; John Beeler, *Warfare in Feudal Europe,
730–1200* (Ithaca, N.Y.: Cornell University Press 1971), 212–14; Michael Howard, *War
in European History* (London: Oxford University Press 1976), 33–37.

[30] Quincy Wright, *A Study of War* (abridged ed.; Chicago: University of Chicago
Press 1964), 142. Also see 63–70, 74–75. There are important exceptions to these
generalizations—the American Civil War, for instance, falls in the middle of the period
Wright says is dominated by the offense.

[31] Geoffrey Kemp, Robert Pfaltzgraff, and Uri Ra'anan, eds., *The Other Arms
Race* (Lexington, Mass.: D. C. Heath 1975); James Foster, "The Future of Conventional Arms Control," *Policy Sciences,* No. 8 (Spring 1977), 1–19.

capability. Third, and related to the foregoing, second-strike capability can be maintained in the face of wide variations in the other side's military posture. There is no purely military reason why each side has to react quickly and strongly to the other's increases in arms. Any spending that the other devotes to trying to achieve first-strike capability can be neutralized by the state's spending much smaller sums on protecting its second-strike capability. Fourth, there are no incentives to strike first in a crisis.

Important problems remain, of course. Both sides have interests that go well beyond defense of the homeland. The protection of these interests creates conflicts even if neither side desires expansion. Furthermore, the shift from defense to deterrence has greatly increased the importance and perceptions of resolve. Security now rests on each side's belief that the other would prefer to run high risks of total destruction rather than sacrifice its vital interests. Aspects of the security dilemma thus appear in a new form. Are weapons procurements used as an index of resolve? Must they be so used? If one side fails to respond to the other's buildup, will it appear weak and thereby invite predation? Can both sides simultaneously have images of high resolve or is there a zero-sum element involved? Although these problems are real, they are not as severe as those in the prenuclear era: there are many indices of resolve, and states do not so much judge images of resolve in the abstract as ask how likely it is that the other will stand firm in a particular dispute. Since states are most likely to stand firm on matters which concern them most, it is quite possible for both to demonstrate their resolve to protect their own security simultaneously.

OFFENSE-DEFENSE DIFFERENTIATION

The other major variable that affects how strongly the security dilemma operates is whether weapons and policies that protect the state also provide the capability for attack. If they do not, the basic postulate of the security dilemma no longer applies. A state can increase its own security without decreasing that of others. The advantage of the defense can only ameliorate the security dilemma. A differentiation between offensive and defensive stances comes close to abolishing it. Such differentiation does not mean, however, that all security problems will be abolished. If the offense has the advantage, conquest and aggression will still be possible. And if the offense's advantage is great enough, status-quo powers may find it too expensive to protect themselves by defensive forces and decide to procure offensive weapons even though this will menace others. Furthermore, states will still have to worry that even if the other's military posture shows that it is peaceful now, it may develop aggressive intentions in the future.

Assuming that the defense is at least as potent as the offense, the differentiation between them allows status-quo states to behave in ways that are clearly different from those of aggressors. Three beneficial consequences follow. First, status-quo powers can identify each other, thus laying the foundations for cooperation. Conflicts growing out of the mistaken belief that the other side is expansionist will be less frequent. Second, status-quo states will obtain advance warning when others plan aggression. Before a state can attack, it has to develop and deploy offensive weapons. If procurement of these weapons cannot be disguised and takes a fair amount of time, as it almost always does, a status-quo state will have the time to take countermeasures. It need not maintain a high level of defensive arms as long as its potential adversaries are adopting a peaceful posture. (Although being so armed should not, with the one important exception noted below, alarm other status-quo powers.) States do, in fact, pay special attention to actions that they believe would not be taken by a status-quo state because they feel that states exhibiting such behavior are aggressive. Thus the seizure or development of transportation facilities will alarm others more if these facilities have no commercial value, and therefore can only be wanted for military reasons. In 1906, the British rejected a Russian protest about their activities in a district of Persia by claiming that this area was "only of [strategic] importance [to the Russians] if they wished to attack the Indian frontier, or to put pressure upon us by making us think that they intend to attack it."[32]

The same inferences are drawn when a state acquires more weapons than observers feel are needed for defense. Thus, the Japanese spokesman at the 1930 London naval conference said that his country was alarmed by the American refusal to give Japan a 70 percent ratio (in place of a 60 percent ratio) in heavy cruisers: "As long as America held that ten percent advantage, it was possible for her to attack. So when America insisted on sixty percent instead of seventy percent, the idea would exist that they were trying to keep that possibility, and the Japanese people could not accept that."[33] Similarly, when Mussolini told Chamberlain in January 1939 that Hitler's arms program was motivated by defensive considerations, the Prime Minister replied that "German military forces were now so strong as to make it impossible for any Power or combination of Powers to attack her successfully.

---

[32] Richard Challener, *Admirals, Generals, and American Foreign Policy, 1898-1914* (Princeton: Princeton University Press 1973), 273; Grey to Nicolson, in Gooch and Temperley (fn. 47), 414.

[33] Quoted in James Crowley, *Japan's Quest for Autonomy* (Princeton: Princeton University Press 1966), 49. American naval officers agreed with the Japanese that a ten-to-six ratio would endanger Japan's supremacy in her home waters.

She could not want any further armaments for defensive purposes; what then did she want them for?"[34]

Of course these inferences can be wrong—as they are especially likely to be because states underestimate the degree to which they menace others.[35] And when they are wrong, the security dilemma is deepened. Because the state thinks it has received notice that the other is aggressive, its own arms building will be less restrained and the chances of cooperation will be decreased. But the dangers of incorrect inferences should not obscure the main point: when offensive and defensive postures are different, much of the uncertainty about the other's intentions that contributes to the security dilemma is removed.

The third beneficial consequence of a difference between offensive and defensive weapons is that if all states support the status quo, an obvious arms control agreement is a ban on weapons that are useful for attacking. As President Roosevelt put it in his message to the Geneva Disarmament Conference in 1933: "If all nations will agree wholly to eliminate from possession and use the weapons which make possible a successful attack, defenses automatically will become impregnable, and the frontiers and independence of every nation will become secure."[36] The fact that such treaties have been rare—the Washington naval agreements discussed above and the anti-ABM treaty can be cited as examples—shows either that states are not always willing to guarantee the security of others, or that it is hard to distinguish offensive from defensive weapons.

Is such a distinction possible? Salvador de Madariaga, the Spanish statesman active in the disarmament negotiations of the interwar years, thought not: "A weapon is either offensive or defensive according to which end of it you are looking at." The French Foreign Minister agreed (although French policy did not always follow this view): "Every arm can be employed offensively or defensively in turn. . . . The only way to discover whether arms are intended for purely defensive purposes or are held in a spirit of aggression is in all cases to enquire into the intentions of the country concerned." Some evidence for the validity of this argument is provided by the fact that much time in these unsuccessful negotiations was devoted to separating offensive from defensive weapons. Indeed, no simple and unambiguous definition is possible and in many cases no judgment can be reached. Before the American entry into World War I, Woodrow Wilson wanted to arm merchantmen only with guns in the back of the

[34] E. L. Woodward and R. Butler, eds., *Documents on British Foreign Policy, 1919-1939,* Third series, III (London: H.M.S.O. 1950), 526.

[35] Jervis (fn. 5), 69-72, 352-55.

[36] Quoted in Merze Tate, *The United States and Armaments* (Cambridge: Harvard University Press 1948), 108.

ship so they could not initiate a fight, but this expedient cannot be applied to more common forms of armaments.[37]

There are several problems. Even when a differentiation is possible, a status-quo power will want offensive arms under any of three conditions. (1) If the offense has a great advantage over the defense, protection through defensive forces will be too expensive. (2) Status-quo states may need offensive weapons to regain territory lost in the opening stages of a war. It might be possible, however, for a state to wait to procure these weapons until war seems likely, and they might be needed only in relatively small numbers, unless the aggressor was able to construct strong defenses quickly in the occupied areas. (3) The state may feel that it must be prepared to take the offensive either because the other side will make peace only if it loses territory or because the state has commitments to attack if the other makes war on a third party. As noted above, status-quo states with extensive commitments are often forced to behave like aggressors. Even when they lack such commitments, status-quo states must worry about the possibility that if they are able to hold off an attack, they will still not be able to end the war unless they move into the other's territory to damage its military forces and inflict pain. Many American naval officers after the Civil War, for example, believed that "only by destroying the commerce of the opponent could the United States bring him to terms.[38]

A further complication is introduced by the fact that aggressors as well as status-quo powers require defensive forces as a prelude to acquiring offensive ones, to protect one frontier while attacking another, or for insurance in case the war goes badly. Criminals as well as policemen can use bulletproof vests. Hitler as well as Maginot built a line of forts. Indeed, Churchill reports that in 1936 the German Foreign Minister said: "As soon as our fortifications are constructed [on our western borders] and the countries in Central Europe realize that France cannot enter German territory, all these countries will begin to feel very differently about their foreign policies, and a new constellation will develop."[39] So a state may not necessarily be reassured if its neighbor constructs strong defenses.

More central difficulties are created by the fact that whether a weapon is offensive or defensive often depends on the particular situation—for instance, the geographical setting and the way in which the weapon is used. "Tanks . . . spearheaded the fateful German thrust through the Ardennes in 1940, but if the French had disposed of

[37] Boggs (fn. 28), 15, 40.
[38] Kenneth Hagan, *American Gunboat Diplomacy and the Old Navy, 1877–1889* (Westport, Conn.: Greenwood Press 1973), 20.
[39] Winston Churchill, *The Gathering Storm* (Boston: Houghton 1948), 206.

a properly concentrated armored reserve, it would have provided the
best means for their cutting off the penetration and turning into a
disaster for the Germans what became instead an overwhelming
victory.''⁴⁰ Anti-aircraft weapons seem obviously defensive—to be
used, they must wait for the other side to come to them. But the
Egyptian attack on Israel in 1973 would have been impossible without
effective air defenses that covered the battlefield. Nevertheless, some
distinctions are possible. Sir John Simon, then the British Foreign
Secretary, in response to the views cited earlier, stated that just
because a fine line could not be drawn, "that was no reason for saying
that there were not stretches of territory on either side which all practical men and women knew to be well on this or that side of the line."
Although there are almost no weapons and strategies that are useful
only for attacking, there are some that are almost exclusively defensive. Aggressors could want them for protection, but a state that relied
mostly on them could not menace others. More frequently, we cannot
"determine the absolute character of a weapon, but [we can] make a
comparison . . . [and] discover whether or not the offensive potentialities predominate, whether a weapon is more useful in attack or in
defense.''⁴¹

The essence of defense is keeping the other side out of your
territory. A purely defensive weapon is one that can do this without
being able to penetrate the enemy's land. Thus a committee of military
experts in an interwar disarmament conference declared that
armaments "incapable of mobility by means of self-contained
power," or movable only after long delay, were "only capable of
being used for the defense of a State's territory.''⁴² The most obvious
examples are fortifications. They can shelter attacking forces, especially when they are built right along the frontier,⁴³ but they cannot
occupy enemy territory. A state with only a strong line of forts, fixed
guns, and a small army to man them would not be much of a menace.
Anything else that can serve only as a barrier against attacking troops
is similarly defensive. In this category are systems that provide warning of an attack, the Russian's adoption of a different railroad gauge,
and nuclear land mines that can seal off invasion routes.

If total immobility clearly defines a system that is defensive only,
limited mobility is unfortunately ambiguous. As noted above, short-

⁴⁰ Brodie, *War and Politics* (fn. 35), 325.
⁴¹ Boggs (fn. 28), 42, 83. For a good argument about the possible differentiation between offensive and defensive weapons in the 1930's, see Basil Liddell Hart, "Aggression and the Problem of Weapons," *English Review,* Vol. 55 (July 1932), 71–78.
⁴² Quoted in Boggs (fn. 28), 39.
⁴³ On these grounds, the Germans claimed in 1932 that the French forts were offensive (*ibid.,* 49). Similarly, fortified forward naval bases can be necessary for launching
an attack; see Braisted (fn. 27), 643.

range fighter aircraft and anti-aircraft missiles can be used to cover an attack. And, unlike forts, they can advance with the troops. Still, their inability to reach deep into enemy territory does make them more useful for the defense than for the offense. Thus, the United States and Israel would have been more alarmed in the early 1970's had the Russians provided the Egyptians with long-range instead of short-range aircraft. Naval forces are particularly difficult to classify in these terms, but those that are very short-legged can be used only for coastal defense.

Any forces that for various reasons fight well only when on their own soil in effect lack mobility and therefore are defensive. The most extreme example would be passive resistance. Noncooperation can thwart an aggressor, but it is very hard for large numbers of people to cross the border and stage a sit-in on another's territory. Morocco's recent march on the Spanish Sahara approached this tactic, but its success depended on special circumstances. Similarly, guerrilla warfare is defensive to the extent to which it requires civilian support that is likely to be forthcoming only in opposition to a foreign invasion. Indeed, if guerrilla warfare were easily exportable and if it took ten defenders to destroy each guerrilla, then this weapon would not only be one which could be used as easily to attack the other's territory as to defend one's own, but one in which the offense had the advantage: so the security dilemma would operate especially strongly.

If guerrillas are unable to fight on foreign soil, other kinds of armies may be unwilling to do so. An army imbued with the idea that only defensive wars were just would fight less effectively, if at all, if the goal were conquest. Citizen militias may lack both the ability and the will for aggression. The weapons employed, the short term of service, the time required for mobilization, and the spirit of repelling attacks on the homeland, all lend themselves much more to defense than to attacks on foreign territory.[44]

Less idealistic motives can produce the same result. A leading student of medieval warfare has described the armies of that period as follows: "Assembled with difficulty, insubordinate, unable to maneuver, ready to melt away from its standard the moment that its short period of service was over, a feudal force presented an assemblage of unsoldierlike qualities such as have seldom been known to coexist. Primarily intended to defend its own borders from the Magyar, the Northman, or the Saracen . . . , the institution was utterly unadapted to take the offensive."[45] Some political groupings can be similarly

---

[44] The French made this argument in the interwar period; see Richard Challener, *The French Theory of the Nation in Arms* (New York: Columbia University Press 1955), 181–82. The Germans disagreed; see Boggs (fn. 28), 44–45.

[45] Oman (fn. 53), 57–58.

described. International coalitions are more readily held together by fear than by hope of gain. Thus Castlereagh was not being entirely self-serving when in 1816 he argued that the Quadruple Alliance "could only have owed its origin to a sense of common danger; in its very nature it must be conservative; it cannot threaten either the security or the liberties of other States."[46] It is no accident that most of the major campaigns of expansion have been waged by one dominant nation (for example, Napoleon's France and Hitler's Germany), and that coalitions among relative equals are usually found defending the status quo. Most gains from conquest are too uncertain and raise too many questions of future squabbles among the victors to hold an alliance together for long. Although defensive coalitions are by no means easy to maintain—conflicting national objectives and the free-rider problem partly explain why three of them dissolved before Napoleon was defeated—the common interest of seeing that no state dominates provides a strong incentive for solidarity.

Weapons that are particularly effective in reducing fortifications and barriers are of great value to the offense. This is not to deny that a defensive power will want some of those weapons if the other side has them: Brodie is certainly correct to argue that while their tanks allowed the Germans to conquer France, properly used French tanks could have halted the attack. But France would not have needed these weapons if Germany had not acquired them, whereas even if France had no tanks, Germany could not have foregone them since they provided the only chance of breaking through the French lines. Mobile heavy artillery is, similarly, especially useful in destroying fortifications. The defender, while needing artillery to fight off attacking troops or to counterattack, can usually use lighter guns since they do not need to penetrate such massive obstacles. So it is not surprising that one of the few things that most nations at the interwar disarmament conferences were able to agree on was that heavy tanks and mobile heavy guns were particularly valuable to a state planning an attack.[47]

Weapons and strategies that depend for their effectiveness on surprise are almost always offensive. That fact was recognized by some of the delegates to the interwar disarmament conferences and is the principle behind the common national ban on concealed weapons. An earlier representative of this widespread view was the mid-19th-century Philadelphia newspaper that argued: "As a measure of defense, knives, dirks, and sword canes are entirely useless. They are fit only for attack, and all such attacks are of murderous character.

[46] Quoted in Charles Webster, *The Foreign Policy of Castlereagh, II, 1815–1822* (London: G. Bell and Sons 1963), 510.
[47] Boggs (fn. 28), 14–15, 47–48, 60.

Whoever carries such a weapon has prepared himself for homicide.''[48]

It is, of course, not always possible to distinguish between forces that are most effective for holding territory and forces optimally designed for taking it. Such a distinction could not have been made for the strategies and weapons in Europe during most of the period between the Franco-Prussian War and World War I. Neither naval forces nor tactical air forces can be readily classified in these terms. But the point here is that when such a distinction is possible, the central characteristic of the security dilemma no longer holds, and one of the most troublesome consequences of anarchy is removed.

Offense-Defense Differentiation and Strategic Nuclear Weapons. In the interwar period, most statesmen held the reasonable position that weapons that threatened civilians were offensive.[49] But when neither side can protect its civilians, a counter-city posture is defensive because the state can credibly threaten to retaliate only in response to an attack on itself or its closest allies. The costs of this strike are so high that the state could not threaten to use it for the less-than-vital interest of compelling the other to abandon an established position.

In the context of deterrence, offensive weapons are those that provide defense. In the now familiar reversal of common sense, the state that could take its population out of hostage, either by active or passive defense or by destroying the other's strategic weapons on the ground, would be able to alter the status quo. The desire to prevent such a situation was one of the rationales for the anti-ABM agreements; it explains why some arms controllers opposed building ABM's to protect cities, but favored sites that covered ICBM fields. Similarly, many analysts want to limit warhead accuracy and favor multiple re-entry vehicles (MRV's), but oppose multiple independently targetable re-entry vehicles (MIRV's). The former are more useful than single warheads for penetrating city defenses, and ensure that the state has a second-strike capability. MIRV's enhance counterforce capabilities. Some arms controllers argue that this is also true of cruise missiles, and therefore do not want them to be deployed either. There is some evidence that the Russians are not satisfied with deterrence and are seeking to regain the capability for defense. Such an effort, even if not inspired by aggressive designs, would create a severe security dilemma.

What is most important for the argument here is that land-based ICBM's are both offensive and defensive, but when both sides rely on Polaris-type systems (SLBM's), offense and defense use different weapons. ICBM's can be used either to destroy the other's cities in

    [48] Quoted in Philip Jordan, *Frontier Law and Order* (London: University of Nebraska Press 1970), 7; also see 16–17.
    [49] Boggs (fn. 28), 20, 28.

retaliation or to initiate hostilities by attacking the other's strategic missiles. Some measures—for instance, hardening of missile sites and warning systems—are purely defensive, since they do not make a first strike easier. Others are predominantly offensive—for instance, passive or active city defenses, and highly accurate warheads. But ICBM's themselves are useful for both purposes. And because states seek a high level of insurance, the desire for protection as well as the contemplation of a counterforce strike can explain the acquisition of extremely large numbers of missiles. So it is very difficult to infer the other's intentions from its military posture. Each side's efforts to increase its own security by procuring more missiles decreases, to an extent determined by the relative efficacy of the offense and the defense, the other side's security. That is not the case when both sides use SLBM's. The point is not that sea-based systems are less vulnerable than land-based ones (this bears on the offense-defense ratio) but that SLBM's are defensive, retaliatory weapons. First, they are probably not accurate enough to destroy many military targets.[50] Second, and more important, SLBM's are not the main instrument of attack against other SLBM's. The hardest problem confronting a state that wants to take its cities out of hostage is to locate the other's SLBM's, a job that requires not SLBM's but anti-submarine weapons. A state might use SLBM's to attack the other's submarines (although other weapons would probably be more efficient), but without anti-submarine warfare (ASW) capability the task cannot be performed. A status-quo state that wanted to forego offensive capability could simply forego ASW research and procurement.

There are two difficulties with this argument, however. First, since the state's SLBM's are potentially threatened by the other's ASW capabilities, the state may want to pursue ASW research in order to know what the other might be able to do and to design defenses. Unless it does this, it cannot be confident that its submarines are safe. Second, because some submarines are designed to attack surface ships, not launch missiles, ASW forces have missions other than taking cities out of hostage. Some U.S. officials plan for a long war in Europe which would require keeping the sea lanes open against Russian submarines. Designing an ASW force and strategy that would meet this threat without endangering Soviet SLBM's would be difficult but not impossible, since the two missions are somewhat different.[51] Furthermore, the Russians do not need ASW forces to combat submarines carrying out conventional missions; it might be in

[50] See, however, Desmond Ball, "The Counterforce Potential of American SLBM Systems," *Journal of Peace Research,* XIV (No. 1, 1977), 23–40.
[51] Richard Garwin, "Anti-Submarine Warfare and National Security," *Scientific American,* Vol. 227 (July 1972), 14–25.

America's interest to sacrifice the ability to meet a threat that is not likely to materialize in order to reassure the Russians that we are not menacing their retaliatory capability.

When both sides rely on ICBM's, one side's missiles can attack the other's, and so the state cannot be indifferent to the other's building program. But because one side's SLBM's do not menace the other's, each side can build as many as it wants and the other need not respond. Each side's decision on the size of its force depends on technical questions, its judgment about how much destruction is enough to deter, and the amount of insurance it is willing to pay for—and these considerations are independent of the size of the other's strategic force. Thus the crucial nexus in the arms race is severed.

Here two objections not only can be raised but have been, by those who feel that even if American second-strike capability is in no danger, the United States must respond to a Soviet buildup. First, the relative numbers of missiles and warheads may be used as an index of each side's power and will. Even if there is no military need to increase American arms as the Russians increase theirs, a failure to respond may lead third parties to think that the U.S. has abandoned the competition with the U.S.S.R. and is no longer willing to pay the price of world leadership. Furthermore, if either side believes that nuclear "superiority" matters, then, through the bargaining logic, it will matter. The side with "superiority" will be more likely to stand firm in a confrontation if it thinks its "stronger" military position helps it, or if it thinks that the other thinks its own "weaker" military position is a handicap. To allow the other side to have more SLBM's—even if one's own second-strike capability is unimpaired—will give the other an advantage that can be translated into political gains.

The second objection is that superiority *does* matter, and not only because of mistaken beliefs. If nuclear weapons are used in an all-or-none fashion, then all that is needed is second-strike capability. But limited, gradual, and controlled strikes are possible. If the other side has superiority, it can reduce the state's forces by a slow-motion war of attrition. For the state to strike at the other's cities would invite retaliation; for it to reply with a limited counterforce attack would further deplete its supply of missiles. Alternatively, the other could employ demonstration attacks—such as taking out an isolated military base or exploding a warhead high over a city—in order to demonstrate its resolve. In either of these scenarios, the state will suffer unless it matches the other's arms posture.[52]

These two objections, if valid, mean that even with SLBM's one

---

[52] The latter scenario, however, does not require that the state closely match the number of missiles the other deploys.

cannot distinguish offensive from defensive strategic nuclear weapons. Compellence may be more difficult than deterrence,[53] but if decision makers believe that numbers of missiles or of warheads influence outcomes, or if these weapons can be used in limited manner, then the posture and policy that would be needed for self-protection is similar to that useful for aggression. If the second objection has merit, security would require the ability to hit selected targets on the other side, enough ammunition to wage a controlled counterforce war, and the willingness to absorb limited countervalue strikes. Secretary Schlesinger was correct in arguing that this capability would not constitute a first-strike capability. But because the "Schlesinger Doctrine" could be used not only to cope with a parallel Russian policy, but also to support an American attempt to change the status quo, the new American stance would decrease Russian security. Even if the U.S.S.R. were reassured that the present U.S. Government lacked the desire or courage to do this, there could be no guarantee that future governments would not use the new instruments for expansion. Once we move away from the simple idea that nuclear weapons can only be used for all-out strikes, half the advantage of having both sides rely on a sea-based force would disappear because of the lack of an offensive-defensive differentiation. To the extent that military policy affects political relations, it would be harder for the United States and the Soviet Union to cooperate even if both supported the status quo.

Although a full exploration of these questions is beyond the scope of this paper, it should be noted that the objections rest on decision makers' beliefs—beliefs, furthermore, that can be strongly influenced by American policy and American statements. The perceptions of third nations of whether the details of the nuclear balance affect political conflicts—and, to a lesser extent, Russian beliefs about whether superiority is meaningful—are largely derived from the American strategic debate. If most American spokesmen were to take the position that a secure second-strike capability was sufficient and that increments over that (short of a first-strike capability) would only be a waste of money, it is doubtful whether America's allies or the neutrals would judge the superpowers' useful military might or political will by the size of their stockpiles. Although the Russians stress war-fighting ability, they have not contended that marginal increases in strategic forces bring political gains; any attempt to do so could be rendered less effective by an American assertion that this is

---

[53] Thomas Schelling, *Arms and Influence* (New Haven: Yale University Press 1966), 69–78. Schelling's arguments are not entirely convincing, however. For further discussion, see Jervis, "Deterrence Theory Re-Visited," Working Paper No. 14, UCLA Program in Arms Control and International Security.

nonsense. The bargaining advantages of possessing nuclear "superiority" work best when both sides acknowledge them. If the "weaker" side convinces the other that it does not believe there is any meaningful difference in strength, then the "stronger" side cannot safely stand firm because there is no increased chance that the other will back down.

This kind of argument applies at least as strongly to the second objection. Neither side can employ limited nuclear options unless it is quite confident that the other accepts the rules of the game. For if the other believes that nuclear war cannot be controlled, it will either refrain from responding—which would be fine—or launch all-out retaliation. Although a state might be ready to engage in limited nuclear war without acknowledging this possibility—and indeed, that would be a reasonable policy for the United States—it is not likely that the other would have sufficient faith in that prospect to initiate limited strikes unless the state had openly avowed its willingness to fight this kind of war. So the United States, by patiently and consistently explaining that it considers such ideas to be mad and that any nuclear wars will inevitably get out of control, could gain a large measure of protection against the danger that the Soviet Union might seek to employ a "Schlesinger Doctrine" against an America that lacked the military ability or political will to respond in kind. Such a position is made more convincing by the inherent implausibility of the arguments for the possibility of a limited nuclear war.

In summary, as long as states believe that all that is needed is second-strike capability, then the differentiation between offensive and defensive forces that is provided by reliance on SLBM's allows each side to increase its security without menacing the other, permits some inferences about intentions to be drawn from military posture, and removes the main incentive for status-quo powers to engage in arms races.

IV. FOUR WORLDS

The two variables we have been discussing—whether the offense or the defense has the advantage, and whether offensive postures can be distinguished from defensive ones—can be combined to yield four possible worlds.

	OFFENSE HAS THE ADVANTAGE	DEFENSE HAS THE ADVANTAGE
OFFENSIVE POSTURE NOT DISTINGUISHABLE FROM DEFENSIVE ONE	1 Doubly dangerous	2 Security dilemma, but security requirements may be compatible.
OFFENSIVE POSTURE DISTINGUISHABLE FROM DEFENSIVE ONE	3 No security dilemma, but aggression possible. Status-quo states can follow different policy than aggressors. Warning given.	4 Doubly stable

The first world is the worst for status-quo states. There is no way to get security without menacing others, and security through defense is terribly difficult to obtain. Because offensive and defensive postures are the same, status-quo states acquire the same kind of arms that are sought by aggressors. And because the offense has the advantage over the defense, attacking is the best route to protecting what you have; status-quo states will therefore behave like aggressors. The situation will be unstable. Arms races are likely. Incentives to strike first will turn crises into wars. Decisive victories and conquests will be common. States will grow and shrink rapidly, and it will be hard for any state to maintain its size and influence without trying to increase them. Cooperation among status-quo powers will be extremely hard to achieve.

There are no cases that totally fit this picture, but it bears more than a passing resemblance to Europe before World War I. Britain and Germany, although in many respects natural allies, ended up as enemies. Of course much of the explanation lies in Germany's ill-chosen policy. And from the perspective of our theory, the powers' ability to avoid war in a series of earlier crises cannot be easily explained. Nevertheless, much of the behavior in this period was the product of technology and beliefs that magnified the security dilemma. Decision makers thought that the offense had a big advantage and saw little difference between offensive and defensive military postures. The era was characterized by arms races. And once war seemed likely, mobilization races created powerful incentives to strike first.

In the nuclear era, the first world would be one in which each side relied on vulnerable weapons that were aimed at similar forces and each side understood the situation. In this case, the incentives to strike first would be very high—so high that status-quo powers as well as aggressors would be sorely tempted to pre-empt. And since the forces could be used to change the status-quo as well as to preserve it, there would be no way for both sides to increase their security simultaneously. Now the familiar logic of deterrence leads both sides to see the dangers in this world. Indeed, the new understanding of this situation was one reason why vulnerable bombers and missiles were replaced. Ironically, the 1950's would have been more hazardous if the decision makers had been aware of the dangers of their posture and had therefore felt greater pressure to strike first. This situation could be recreated if both sides were to rely on MIRVed ICBM's.

In the second world, the security dilemma operates because offensive and defensive postures cannot be distinguished; but it does not operate as strongly as in the first world because the defense has the advantage, and so an increment in one side's strength increases its security more than it decreases the other's. So, if both sides have reasonable subjective security requirements, are of roughly equal power, and the variables discussed earlier are favorable, it is quite likely that status-quo states can adopt compatible security policies. Although a state will not be able to judge the other's intentions from the kinds of weapons it procures, the level of arms spending will give important evidence. Of course a state that seeks a high level of arms might be not an aggressor but merely an insecure state, which if conciliated will reduce its arms, and if confronted will reply in kind. To assume that the apparently excessive level of arms indicates aggressiveness could therefore lead to a response that would deepen the dilemma and create needless conflict. But empathy and skillful statesmanship can reduce this danger. Furthermore, the advantageous position of the defense means that a status-quo state can often maintain a high degree of security with a level of arms lower than that of its expected adversary. Such a state demonstrates that it lacks the ability or desire to alter the status-quo, at least at the present time. The strength of the defense also allows states to react slowly and with restraint when they fear that others are menacing them. So, although status-quo powers will to some extent be threatening to others, that extent will be limited.

This world is the one that comes closest to matching most periods in history. Attacking is usually harder than defending because of the strength of fortifications and obstacles. But purely defensive postures are rarely possible because fortifications are usually supplemented by armies and mobile guns which can support an attack. In the nuclear era, this world would be one in which both sides relied on relatively invulnerable ICBM's and believed that limited nuclear war was impossible. Assuming no MIRV's, it would take more than one attacking missile to destroy one of the adversary's. Pre-emption is therefore unattractive. If both sides have large inventories, they can ignore all but drastic increases on the other side. A world of either ICBM's or SLBM's in which both sides adopted the "Schlesinger Doctrine" would probably fit in this category too. The means of preserving the status quo would also be the means of changing it, as we discussed earlier. And the defense usually would have the advantage, because compellence is more difficult than deterrence. Although a state might succeed in changing the status-quo on issues that matter much more to it than to others, status-quo powers could deter major provocations under most circumstances.

In the third world there may be no security dilemma, but there are security problems. Because states can procure defensive systems that do not threaten others, the dilemma need not operate. But because the offense has the advantage, aggression is possible, and perhaps easy. If the offense has enough of an advantage, even a status-quo state may take the initiative rather than risk being attacked and defeated. If the offense has less of an advantage, stability and cooperation are likely because the status-quo states will procure defensive forces. They need not react to others who are similarly armed, but can wait for the warning they would receive if others started to deploy offensive weapons. But each state will have to watch the others carefully, and there is room for false suspicions. The costliness of the defense and the allure of the offense can lead to unnecessary mistrust, hostility, and war, unless some of the variables discussed earlier are operating to restrain defection.

A hypothetical nuclear world that would fit this description would be one in which both sides relied on SLBM's, but in which ASW techniques were very effective. Offense and defense would be different, but the former would have the advantage. This situation is not likely to occur; but if it did, a status-quo state could show its lack of desire to exploit the other by refraining from threatening its submarines. The desire to have more protecting you than merely the other side's fear of retaliation is a strong one, however, and a state that knows that it would not expand even if its cities were safe is likely to believe that the other would not feel threatened by its ASW program. It is easy to see how such a world could become unstable, and how spirals of tensions and conflict could develop.

The fourth world is doubly safe. The differentiation between offensive and defensive systems permits a way out of the security dilemma; the advantage of the defense disposes of the problems discussed in the previous paragraphs. There is no reason for a status-quo power to be tempted to procure offensive forces, and aggressors give notice of their intentions by the posture they adopt. Indeed, if the advantage of the defense is great enough, there are no security problems. The loss of the ultimate form of the power to alter the status quo would allow greater scope for the exercise of nonmilitary means and probably would tend to freeze the distribution of values.

This world would have existed in the first decade of the 20th century if the decision makers had understood the available technology. In that case, the European powers would have followed different policies both in the long run and in the summer of 1914. Even Germany, facing powerful enemies on both sides, could have made herself secure by developing strong defenses. France could also have made her frontier almost impregnable. Furthermore, when crises arose, no one would have had incentives to strike first. There would have been no competitive mobilization races reducing the time available for negotiations.

In the nuclear era, this world would be one in which the super-powers relied on SLBM's, ASW technology was not up to its task, and limited nuclear options were not taken seriously. We have discussed this situation earlier; here we need only add that, even if our analysis is correct and even if the policies and postures of both sides were to move in this direction, the problem of violence below the nuclear threshold would remain. On issues other than defense of the homeland, there would still be security dilemmas and security problems. But the world would nevertheless be safer than it has usually been.

The Conditions of Stability

GLENN H. SNYDER

We may say that a "balance of terror" exists when each side has somewhat more than the minimum strike-back requirement—i.e., when neither side, in striking first, can destroy enough of the opponent's forces to make the latter's retaliation bearable. But the *existence* of a deterrent balance is something different from the *stability* of the balance. Stability in one sense refers to the degree of change in the military, technological, or political situation which is necessary to give one side a sufficient first-strike capability or sufficient incentive to strike first. For example, the balance would be unstable if either side required only a small additional expenditure of resources to achieve a first-strike capability which could reduce the opponent's retaliation to acceptable proportions. It would also be unstable if some moderately conceivable technological or scientific breakthrough—say, in air defense or in devices for tracking mobile missile launchers—suddenly gave one side a first-strike capability. Or it might be unstable if the commitment of one side's honor and prestige in a policy declaration made it willing to accept significantly greater retaliatory damage, so that a first-strike capability which previously had been insufficient became sufficient to justify a first strike.

A second form of instability would be a force relationship which produced strong fears on one or both sides that the other was about to strike first, thus creating an incentive to strike first to pre-empt the other's attack.

Stability, at any given time, is a function of two factors: the extent to which either side's strike-back capability exceeds the necessary minimum, and the "attacker-to-target ratio." The latter refers to the amount of attacking forces required to eliminate a given amount of the defender's forces; it may also be called the degree of "structural stability." Both factors together determine the degree of effort required of the attacker to achieve a sufficient first-strike capability.

Stability is highest when both sides have much more than the minimum strike-back capability and when the attacker-to-target ratio is high. Then a very large increase in either side's forces would be necessary to obtain a sufficient first-strike capability; only a very major and rather fantastic scientific discovery would overcome the deterrent balance; and no political commitment or threat would be likely to increase either side's values at stake to a degree necessary to offset the costs of all-out war. And with such a configuration of forces, neither side would be likely to fear a first strike by the other, so there could be no incentive for pre-emptive attack.

At the other extreme, the balance would be very unstable if both sides just barely had a minimum strike-back capability and if the attacker-to-target ratio were low, so that only a slight increase in one side's forces, or a minor technological breakthrough, or a small rise in political tension, would create a situation in which one side felt it could rationally strike first. Incentives to pre-empt would be high

From *Deterrence and Defense: Toward a Theory of National Security* by Glenn H. Snyder, pp. 97–109. Copyright © 1961 by Princeton University Press for the Center of International Studies, Princeton University. Reprinted by permission of Princeton University Press. Some footnotes have been omitted.

because of mutual fears that the opponent had, or would soon develop, a sufficient first-strike capability.

Of course, there could be many intermediate degrees of stability between these extremes. For example, if one side could muster a wide margin of forces over its minimum deterrent, while the other side just barely met this criterion, stability would be fairly high if the stronger country were a status-quo power with little incentive to strike first. But stability would depend on the continuance of benevolent intentions on the part of the stronger side.

Even with a high degree of structural and over-all stability in the sense just discussed, there may be countervailing factors which make for instability. For example, even though a very major unilateral scientific breakthrough would be required to give one side a first-strike capability, if such breakthroughs are possible or likely, the situation may be unstable. The sudden perfection of a good anti-missile defense system by one side would drastically shift the balance of terror in its favor, whatever the previous degree of structural and over-all stability. Or if one or both sides entertain a policy of firing missiles on warning alone, there may be serious dangers of accidental war. However, . . . the danger of accidental war is closely related to the degree of stability on other counts; when neither side has anything approaching a sufficient first-strike capability, there is little likelihood of their being "trigger-happy."

It is instructive to consider the degree of structural stability which would seem likely to exist with various types and combinations of weapons.

If both sides were to rely entirely on fixed land-based missiles, reasonably well-hardened and dispersed, the attacker-to-target ratio would depend largely on the accuracy of the attacking missiles and their lethal radius, the latter defined as distance from the point of impact within which the target would be destroyed.[1] For example, if accuracy were such that there was a .50 chance of a single missile landing within the lethal radius, four missiles would have to be fired to achieve upward of a .90 chance of killing the target and the situation would be, structurally, very stable. The attacker would need many more missiles than the defender to be sure of getting off with acceptable retaliatory damage. But if there were a .50 chance of an attacking missile landing within a circle of only half the lethal radius, the attacker would have a .94 chance of destroying the target with a single missile. Then the balance of terror would be structurally unstable; one side might be willing to strike, for example, if its missile stocks only equaled the defender's and if it were willing to accept the retaliatory

---

[1] Lethal radius is a function of the "hardness" of the target—the amount of blast pressure it can withstand—and the yield of the warhead. . . .

destruction which approximately 6 per cent of the defender's missiles could inflict.

The degree of preponderance, if any, which the attacker needs, is sensitive not only to the attacker-to-target ratio, but also to the absolute number of missiles which the defender has. This follows from the fact that the damage which the attacker will accept is constant, while the number of defending missiles which escape the first strike, with given accuracy and lethal radius, varies with the total number of defending missiles. For example, suppose retaliation against cities by 25 missiles is just unacceptable damage for the attacker, the defender has 50 missiles, and the attacker has a .5 chance of killing any particular missile site with any one missile. Then the attacker needs only 50 missiles for a sufficient first-strike capability. If both sides are symmetrical in their accuracies and willingness to accept damage, each has a sufficient first-strike capability and the situation is unstable. But if one side increases to 100, the other must fire 200 (two at each of the defending sites) to be confident of retaliation by only 25 missiles. If the defender increases to 200, the attacker needs 600. If the defender increases to 300, the attacker needs 1,200, and so on.[2] The less accurate the attacker's missiles, the faster his first-strike requirement multiplies as the defender increases his stocks. Thus, when the number of missiles on both sides is reasonably large, the requirement for a sufficient first-strike capability will be some multiple of the requirement for a minimum strike-back capability, and the multiple itself will be greater, the larger the number of the defender's missile sites. It is thus characteristic of the missile arms race, in seeming contrast to traditional arms races with conventional weapons, that it becomes more stable as it proceeds. The incentives to continue the arms race diminish rapidly as the numbers of weapons increase on both sides. The country which wishes to have only a minimum deterrent need have one that amounts to only a fraction of the opponent's striking force when the former's number of dispersed weapons is large relative to the number of weapons which would cause unacceptable

---

[2] The mathematical reason for this "multiplier effect" is that increasing numbers of attacking missiles are wasted in "overkills" as the defender's launching sites increase in number. When both have 50 missiles, the attacker reduces the retaliating force to 25 by firing one missile at each defending site. When the defender has 100, the attacker must reduce the probability of missing each target to .25, to have a statistical likelihood of reducing the number of retaliating missiles to 25. The attacker must fire two missiles per target: the probability that both will hit the target is .25, the probability that one or the other will hit is .50, and the probability of a miss by both is .25. When more than one missile is fired at a target, the probability that the target is missed is the product of the probabilities of a miss with each missile. When the defender has 200, the attacker must fire three per target to reduce the probability of a miss per target to .125 ($.50 \times .50 \times .50$). With 300 defending missiles, the probability of a miss must be reduced to .0625 or $(.50)^4$, requiring four missiles per target.

damage to the opponent's cities.[3] By similar reasoning, the country which contemplates a first strike can provide itself with the necessary capability only be resource expenditures very much larger than the expenditures the opponent must make to counter and re-establish the deterrent balance.

Of course, improvements in accuracy, reliability, and payload of missiles would work against the stabilizing effect of increased numbers. On the other hand, increased hardening and dispersal would be stabilizing.[4] In general, it does not seem that a system of numerous hardened and well-dispersed sites at fixed bases would ever become seriously unstable in a structural sense (barring a substantial breakthrough in active defense against missiles), since it is hard to believe any aggressor would be so sure of the accuracy and reliability of his missiles and target intelligence as to be confident of eliminating each of the defending sites with a single missile. Two missiles per site would seem about the minimum for any aggressor who is not a pathological risk-taker. Even with this ratio, over-all instability could of course occur if the aggressive-minded side were allowed to gain a very large preponderance in weapons.

Statements of comparable precision regarding mobile systems, both land- and sea-based, are more difficult to make. A land-based mobile system may be highly invulnerable, and hence may contribute to overall stability, if methods for continuous aerial surveillance of its movements are not devised. However, if space photography develops to the point where surveillance becomes possible, missile trains may become more vulnerable than fixed-base missiles. Since they are "soft" installations, lethal radius against them will be high; a moving train might not be able to get out of range of the blast between the time an enemy space satellite transmits a "fix" and the enemy fires a missile with a high-yield warhead against that fix. If missile trains carry several missiles (as in current U.S. plans) one successful attacking missile could eliminate more than one defending missile, in which case the mobile system might be considerably less stable than the fixed-base system. Also the generalization made above, about the balance of terror becoming more stable as it proceeds to higher levels of armament, might not hold if both sides relied heavily on rail-mobile

[3] A further conclusion might be that, as missile stocks increase, the "competition" between numbers of missiles and passive defense measures as means of preserving a minimum punitive deterrent comes more and more to favor the former, provided the accuracy and reliability of the enemy's missiles do not increase proportionately.

[4] Hardening and dispersal are complementary measures. The greater the hardening, the lesser the degree of dispersal which is necessary to make sure a single attacking missile does not destroy more than one defending missile site. Thus hardening can produce administrative and logistical economies by allowing the closer clustering of missile sites.

missiles. At some point in his accumulation of missiles, an aggressor would reach the point where he could simply blanket the defender's railroad system with enough blast "overpressure" to destroy all trains.

Missile-firing submarines are in a somewhat different category, since they are not subject to attack by missiles, but rather by other submarines and other ships, as well as by aircraft. Here the crucial first-strike requirement is not for numbers of attacking weapons, but rather for the development of technical means of identification, tracking, and coordinated attacks. Since the enemy may develop such means in secret, sole reliance on Polaris submarines might create an unstable situation. Also, Polaris submarines do not benefit from the stabilizing effect of numbers, since each successful attack on a submarine would mean the loss of 16 missiles.

With aircraft against aircraft, stability depends on the degree to which defending aircraft are protected and dispersed, the efficiency of the defender's warning systems, and the efficiency of the attacker's air defenses. If the defender's warning system is not reliable, and if his aircraft are unsheltered and only moderately dispersed, the situation may be very unstable, since one attacking bomber can destroy several bombers which are caught on the ground. But if the defender does have a very good warning system which cannot be penetrated by sneak attacks or evaded by "end runs," a minimum strike-back capability can be assured by an ability to get enough aircraft into the air, after receipt of warning, to penetrate the attacker's air defenses in sufficient strength to inflict unacceptable damage. The number of attacking bombers is virtually irrelevant. With reliable warning, the balance is likely to be stable unless the attacker is confident that his air defenses can achieve a very high kill rate against the retaliating bombers.[5]

When the prospective attacker has large numbers of missiles and the defender relies entirely on aircraft, similar reasoning applies. If the defender does not have a good warning system against missiles, if his aircraft are unprotected and undispersed, and if the attacker has enough missiles to hit all the defender's airbases, the defender must have enough bombers on continuous airborne alert to inflict unacceptable damage after attrition by the attacker's air defenses. If the defender does have a good warning system against missiles, he needs the same number of aircraft on ground alert, but the degree of alertness must be much higher than when the attacker uses aircraft, because of the very short flight-time of missiles.

When both sides have mixed forces, as we must expect in the foreseeable future, stability depends, of course, on some combination of the factors just discussed.

---

[5] Of course, warning systems are vulnerable to destruction. The situation could be unstable if the attacker were willing to gamble that destruction of the defender's warning system would not cause immediate retaliation.

Both structural stability and over-all stability are ultimately economic functions. Structural stability depends on the amount of economic resources which an incipient attacker must invest to gain a capacity to eliminate a given amount of the defender's forces, compared with the amount of resources which the defender must invest to counter the attacker's increase. For example, if the cost of building a "hardened" missile site, requiring three enemy firings for a sure kill, were substantially less than the cost to the enemy of building three additional missiles, the balance would be fairly stable structurally. It is conceivable that the cost of building the three attacking missiles would be less than the cost of the hardened missile, since missiles designed for attack do not have to be protected. Then the balance would be structurally unstable, since the defender would have to spend more than the attacker to offset the attacker's increase. Or if a 10 per cent increase in the attacker's air defense kill rate would cost him considerably more than a 10 per cent increase in the defender's aircraft on air alert or high ground alert, this would make for stability. But *over-all* stability depends not only on structural stability but also on the *total amount* of expenditure which the attacker must make to gain a sufficient first-strike capability. This, of course, is a function of the margin of insurance which the defender has provided himself in building his strike-back force.

We have left the question of pre-emptive attack for separate consideration because it involves certain factors not pertaining to other forms of instability—principally its incentive, which does not stem from the prospect of gain, but from the desire to forestall losses from a first strike by the opponent which is believed to be imminent. In the usual analysis of pre-emptive war, a spiral of mutual reinforcing fears and counterfears is postulated: A begins to fear that B intends to strike first, from which A derives some incentive to deliver a forestalling strike; B, realizing that A is subject to such fears, begins to fear A's forestalling attack, from which B develops some incentive to strike first even if, originally, it had entertained no such intention; A, recognizing that B fears a pre-emptive strike by A, has its fears of B's first strike reinforced, and feels even greater pressure to strike first; B, guessing that A feels this pressure, develops still greater fears and incentives to strike first, . . . and so on for as many regressive steps as either side might wish to contemplate. If such a spiral of expectations and incentives did occur, either side might be willing to accept much greater retaliatory damage after its own first strike than it would accept if the pre-emptive motivation did not exist.

The following analysis will attempt to show that although pre-emptive attack is at least conceivable when manned bombers are the mainstay of each side's strategic nuclear power, it is unlikely even then, and it becomes increasingly unlikely as both sides come to rely more and more on long-range ballistic missiles.

If there were to be a serious danger of pre-emptive attack, it would have to follow from the existence of two conditions: (1) that there is a substantial if not decisive first-strike advantage—i.e., that if war is expected with certainty, it is much better to strike first than second; and (2) that one side believes the other side is very likely to strike first.

The first condition is often taken as axiomatic. The advantage of getting in the first blow in all-out war is said to follow from the benefits of surprise;[6] from the advantage of being able to choose the most propitious time of attack; and, above all, from the effect of the first blow in establishing an asymmetry of surviving forces favoring the attacker. The defender must strike back with a disorganized and badly decimated force, in the face of air defenses and civil defenses which are alerted. Although the defender can inflict some damage in retaliation, this damage is as nothing compared with the damage which the "defender" could have inflicted if he had been allowed to strike first.

The "advantage of striking first" which we are presently discussing is not the advantage which follows from having a sufficient first-strike capability. When a country bent on aggression has such a capability, it has an incentive to strike, simply because the victim's retaliatory blow would be tolerable—tolerable when measured against the expectation of gains from the attack. The "advantage of striking first," as it relates to the question of pre-emptive attack, means that even though a retaliation blow would be unacceptable when measured against objectives other than pre-emption, it is nevertheless preferred to the costs of taking the opponent's first strike. It implies simply that if war is believed to be imminent, one's own losses are minimized by getting in the first blow.

Whether there is an advantage in getting in the first blow depends on a combination of *strategic* and *intrinsic* considerations. In strategic terms, there is a strike-first advantage when the side striking first can destroy more of the opponent's strategic nuclear capability in doing so than it loses of its own. In intrinsic terms, a strike-first advantage exists when the destruction to one's population and economy which would be suffered in the opponent's first strike is greater than the destruction which the opponent could inflict in a retaliatory blow.

There may be a strategic advantage in striking first when the bulk of each side's striking forces is made up of manned bombers, if one assumes that a considerable number of the defender's aircraft will be caught on the ground. One attacking airplane can eliminate several on the ground, since the defender is likely to have several planes at each base and since each attacking aircraft may be able to hit several bases

---

[6] Although surprise is usually mentioned among the advantages of striking first, surprise would be minimal under conditions conducive to pre-emption—i.e., when both sides have strong fears of impending attack by the opponent.

in succession, carrying, as it may, a multiple bomb load. So the side which strikes first may be able to achieve a considerable preponderance of forces even though it may have struck from a prewar position of inferiority. However, even if such a strike-first advantage did exist in this sense, it would hardly trigger off a spiral of fears and counter-fears leading to pre-emptive attack unless each side had a first-strike capability which could be construed by the other as being sufficient or nearly sufficient to make a first-strike rational for non-pre-emptive reasons. And even if this condition did exist, either side, rather than striking first because of uncertain fears that the other intended to strike, would be more likely to take measures—such as putting more aircraft on a high alert status—which would reduce the other's first-strike capability.

There may not be a first-strike advantage in an all-missile or predominantly missile environment if one makes four quite plausible assumptions: that the targets of a first strike would be the opponent's missile bases; that missile sites are well dispersed and hardened, or mobile; that a given number of missiles aimed at missile bases would cause less damage to the population and economy than a smaller number of retaliating missiles aimed at cities; and that the primary targets of a retaliatory blow would be cities.

Consider first a situation in which both sides rely entirely on fixed-base ICBM's, and missiles on both sides are equally accurate, reliable, and vulnerable. Suppose each side has 100 ICBM's. If accuracies, reliabilities, and vulnerabilities are all very high, we might imagine an extreme case in which each protagonist would feel absolutely confident that a single attacking missile could eliminate one of the opponent's launching sites before its missile was fired. Then of course there would be an advantage in striking first, since, although the attrition of forces on both sides would be equal and complete, all the war damage would be concentrated on the side which received the first (and only) blow.

But this is an extreme case which is hardly likely to be realized. The attacker probably will always have to lose more missiles in attacking than he is able to destroy of the defender's. Let us suppose, to give technology and the attacker's confidence the benefit of every doubt, that the missile-to-target ratio drops as low as 2:1. Then, with equal numbers of missiles on each side, it *may* not be advantageous to strike first. The attacker would lose two missiles for every one of the defender's which is destroyed. Firing off his entire stock of 100 missiles, the attacker would have to expect retaliation by at least 50 missiles against his cities. Rather than accept this result, the "attacker" might prefer to let the other side strike first against his missile sites. For either side, a first-strike advantage would *not* exist if the damage from 50 retaliatory missiles on its cities were expected to be greater than the by-product damage to population which would be expected from the enemy's first strike with 100 missiles directed at missile sites, not cities. Or, following another line of reasoning, each side might well believe that it would be best to let the other use up all its striking power, leaving the attacked side with a residual force which could be used to compel the attacker to capitulate. Thus, even with the low missile-to-target ratio of 2:1, there may be disadvantages in striking first. Obviously, with higher missile-to-target ratios, the supposed "strike-first advantage" becomes even more doubtful.

It is sometimes overlooked, in discussions of pre-emptive attack, that the act of pre-emption tends to convert the other side's target system from primarily counterforce to primarily countercity. If pre-emption cannot virtually eliminate the opponent's striking forces, this conversion may result in the pre-emptor's suffering more damage than he would have absorbed as the result of the opponent's first strike. Although pre-emption then would reduce the number of missiles landing on one's own territory, the ones which did arrive would hit where they would do maximum damage.

The primary object of getting in the first blow is to reduce the damage to oneself, as compared with what it would be if the opponent were allowed to strike first. But if it takes two or more missiles to eliminate one, missiles may be more useful for reducing the enemy's damage-producing capacity when they function as targets than when they are used as instruments of attack. With a missile-to-target ratio of 2:1 for both sides, two missiles destroy one in attacking, but "destroy" four as targets. The strategic advantage in *not* striking first varies as the square of the missile-to-target ratio, when the latter is greater than 1:1, and roughly equal for both sides. The strategic disadvantage may be enough in itself to discourage pre-emption if an important objective is to gain the best possible position in the post-strike balance of forces for bargaining purposes. But there may also be an intrinsic disadvantage in striking first if the gain from reducing the number of missiles impacting on one's own territory is overwhelmed by the extra costs incurred in making cities rather than forces the enemy's primary targets.

Let us suppose, however, that each side prefers to strike first rather than accept a first strike by the other, possibly because neither can be sure that the other would avoid cities on a first strike. Continuing to assume a 2:1 missile-to-target ratio and equal forces on each side, the strength of the incentive for either side to launch a pre-emptive first strike would then depend on its estimate of the likelihood that the other intended to strike, as well as on the amount by which the damage suffered from the other side's first strike was expected to exceed the damage from the other side's retaliatory blow after one's own first strike. In other words, neither side would contemplate pre-emption unless it believed that the probability of a first strike by the other (p), times the population-economic costs which this strike would cause (c), was greater than the retaliatory damage (d) which would follow its own pre-emptive strike. Thus the *minimum* condition for "incentive to pre-empt" can be expressed by the formula: $pc > d$.

It must be emphasized, however, that this is a minimum condition. Even if pc were very much larger than d, the estimated probability of the other side's first strike probably would have to approach unity to create a very strong incentive to pre-empt. It is very hard to believe that any country would deliberately accept the *certainty* of severe retaliatory damage in preference to the *uncertain* prospect of being the recipient of a first strike. As long as there existed any significant chance of avoiding war altogether, inaction would be preferred to striking first.

It is possible, however, that one side—let us say, the Soviet Union—might have other than pre-emptive motivation for striking first, so that the addition of even uncertain fears of a first strike by the United States to the motives already existing might be enough to trigger a Soviet first strike. The greater the Soviets' non-pre-emptive incentives to strike, the less certain they would have to be of a U.S. intent to strike first in order to be willing to strike first themselves.

But a pre-emptive motivation is hardly likely to arise unless *both* sides have a very substantial first-strike counterforce capability. Neither side can develop an incentive to pre-empt unless the other side appears to have enough strength to be willing to strike first for non-pre-emptive reasons. And if one side does begin to fear attack by the other, it cannot consider pre-emption unless it also has a large first-strike counterforce capability. In an all-missile environment, it would be possible for both sides simultaneously to have a sufficient first-strike capability only when the total number of missiles on each side was relatively low—relative, that is, to the number of retaliating missiles which each would tolerate as a price for the non-pre-emptive gains which it could expect from striking first—and when the missile-to-target ratio was also low. This condition would exist in the hypothetical case just presented: when each side has 100 missiles, when the missile-to-target ratio is 2:1, and when each is willing to accept retaliatory damage by 50 missiles. Then either might begin to fear an attack and might decide to pre-empt. But again, for pre-emption to seem rational, the pre-emptor would have to prefer 50 missiles on his cities to 100 missiles aimed at his missile-launching sites. If each side had 500 missiles, neither would have any fear of sur-prise attack (because each would know the other would not willingly accept a retaliatory blow by 250 or more missiles), so there would be no incentive to pre-empt.

We must conclude that when both sides' strategic arsenals are composed primarily of missiles, the danger of pre-emptive war is very small—first, because there may be no advantage in striking first even if one is sure the other intends to strike; and, secondly, because of the unlikelihood that both sides simultaneously will have a capability approaching sufficient first-strike proportions. Pre-emptive war would be more likely if both sides relied chiefly on manned bombers, but even in this case the danger would be rather small because neither side would be likely to trade the certainty of retaliation for the uncertainty of a first strike by the other, even if both sides had a substantial first-strike capability.

We have assumed equal striking forces on each side. When the forces are unequal, there might still be no advantage for either side in striking first in a predominantly missile environment, so long as a first strike by the other side would be less costly than its retaliatory strike. Of course, the greater the preponderance achieved by one side, the less retaliatory damage it would have to expect, and the more likelihood that it would see an advantage in striking first. On the other hand, the greater its preponderance, the less need for the stronger side to fear a first strike by the other; hence if it does strike first, it is not likely to be for pre-emptive reasons. . . .

The Expansion of Force

ROBERT E. OSGOOD

THE TRANSFORMATION OF FORCE

Sources of the expansion of force. Between the full establishment of the modern military state in the eighteenth century and the dawn of

From *Force, Order and Justice* by Robert Osgood and Robert Tucker, pp. 41–70 and 118–120. Copyright 1967 by The Johns Hopkins Press. Reprinted by permission. Portions of the text and some footnotes have been omitted.

the nuclear age, military power underwent a transformation as remarkable as its transformation in the nuclear age. As in the nuclear age, the chief impetus of this transformation came from the tremendous expansion in the destructive power available to the most advanced states; but the sources of expansion were rooted deeply in social and political changes. . . .

One can sum up the sources of the expansion of military power in the following terms, arranged in the approximate chronological sequence of their initial impact upon international politics: the rationalization, centralization, popularization, professionalization, and modernization of military power.

In many ways these developments have fostered disorder and complicated the problem of controlling and restraining military power. But since they seem as irreversible as modern Western civilization, we must wonder whether they condemn us to novel and terrible destruction or whether they may provide the foundation of a new international order of unprecedented stability.

The rationalization of force under the state. The modern state, applying a rational, instrumental approach to power and war in the wake of the relatively disorganized conflict of the Middle Ages, became the primary agent of the expansion of force. Man's approach to war had been highly rationalized in relatively orderly periods before. It did not become entirely divorced from motives of glory, adventure, and mission in the eighteenth century. When transferred to the nation-state after the French Revolution, these motives were more compelling than during the Crusades. Nevertheless, a significant change in man's approach to war took place with the state's establishment of internal order in the eighteenth century. As military power became the instrument of state policy, the religious and messianic, the social or agonistic, and the personal motives of war became subordinate to a utilitarian approach oriented toward using power with studied efficiency. This rationalization of military power has become increasingly comprehensive, calculated, and technical since the last part of the nineteenth century. Although we take this approach for granted as part of our civilization, this was not always the prevailing attitude.

In the Middle Ages, from roughly the eleventh century through much of the fourteenth, war was more a way of life than a calculated instrument of policy. It was virtually a continuous but small-scale activity that men took for granted.[1] The small scale resulted from the smallness of the armies, the short term of service, and the physical

---

[1] In perhaps the greatest battle of the Middle Ages, Bouvines (1214), the French had 11,000 cavalry and about 20,000 militia infantry, fighting a coalition with 11,000 cavalry and 70,000 infantry. . . .

difficulty of keeping forces in the field for more than a few weeks at a time. Moreover, armies lacked the weapons and logistics to overcome the defensive advantage of castles and fortresses or to hold territory. The most successful commanders relied on maneuver, while generally avoiding pitched battles, where all might be lost in a day. Strategic direction was weak or entirely missing, although some commanders displayed great tactical skill.

Battles were, in effect, extensions of personal disputes arising primarily from the network of conflicting jurisdictions and loyalties involved in feudal obligations and dynastic claims. They needed no other justification. Except for the Crusades and the later years of the semi-national Hundred Years' War (1338–1452), wars were fought for the security, status, and enrichment of kings and for the emotional and economic gratification of the nobility. They were permeated by the chivalric values of personal honor, glory, and vengeance. We need not enter the controversy over the extent to which these values— especially the gentler ones of magnanimity and fair play—were actually lived up to. There are many examples in the Middle Ages of the mutual observation of rules of fair contest and of ceremonial restraints in the conduct of warfare. There are also many examples of one or both sides violating such rules and restraints. The important point here is that social and personal motives were so pervasive that war was more like a continuing enterprise or recreation than a recurrent political necessity. Consequently, boldness, vengeance, adventure, plunder, and sometimes even generosity frequently overrode tactical or strategic considerations. In the spirit of knight-errantry, kingdoms went to war in the most reckless and unpremeditated way; armies fought in the most amateurish and capricious fashion.[2]

Chivalry as a code of military conduct was largely destroyed during the fourteenth through sixteenth centuries by infantries with crossbows and longbows, by Swiss pikemen, gunpowder, and the growth of national allegiance. Still, the instrumental approach to war remained subordinate to its social or agonistic aspect. The chaotic Religious Wars of the sixteenth and seventeenth centuries dissolved what was left of the old codes of combat and injected a new intensity into warfare. Yet war did not become an instrument of policy in the modern sense.

War was scarcely under the effective control of rulers. Armies were often little more than undisciplined bands of marauders living off the

---

[2] . . . A lack of planning and calculation continued to characterize warfare after the Hundred Years' War. For example, France's repeated costly military adventures in Italy in the sixteenth century were undertaken without any calculation of possible material gains and losses. Her expeditions against Naples were militarily impossible tasks undertaken with neither naval supremacy nor effectual control of Lombardy and central Italy. . . .

land, since states lacked organizational control of them and were unable to provide logistical support. War was a clash of dynastic and religious sectarian allegiances. Above all, it was, in Sir George Clark's words, a "general melee," a "collision of societies."[3] Even in fifteenth- and sixteenth-century Italy, which saw the origins of modern diplomacy, the formation of military coalitions, and the consolidation of several fairly cohesive political units absorbed in Machiavellian competition, war was governed by feudal and dynastic interests rather than by the interests of nations or modern states.

In the second half of the seventeenth century, as the religious issues waned, monarchs began to construct internal order by establishing effective control over economic and political life. The growing internal power of governments facilitated their control of war and gave war political direction. In the coalitions formed against Louis XIV's drive toward Continental hegemony, diplomacy became absorbed in efforts to shape the configurations of state interest and power. Concomitantly, effective control of the military establishments, marked by improved military discipline, the formulation of military codes restraining plunder and piracy, and the creation of more efficient and larger standing armies, laid the foundation for the war system of the eighteenth century, in which force and the threat of force were to serve as instruments of state policy. Through these developments modern *Realpolitik*, foreshadowed in Renaissance Italy, emerged on a larger scale than ever before, backed by the organized power of the state.

In the eighteenth century kings became identified with modern sectarian states, yet states transcended the monarchy to encompass the people and the land as well. The development of centralized authority and of financial and bureaucratic structures capable of raising revenue enabled the state to create and control professional standing armies in order to enforce civil order and support external policies. In the aftermath of Louis XIV's failure to establish a European order based on French hegemony, the ambitions and rivalries of military states led to a pattern of calculated, circumspect relations based upon alignments of countervailing power. The stakes of politics were predominantly dynastic, turning largely upon marriages and inheritances, territory and commerce, but the common unit of political currency was now more clearly the power of the state to make war. This currency was freely exchanged in limited quantities for limited ends. Yet these limitations were, in a sense, the result of the weakness as well as the strength of the state.

The constraints on force. The rulers of eithteenth-century Europe lacked the mobility and firepower and the base of mass enthusiasm

---

[3] Sir George Clark, *War and Society in the Seventeenth Century* (Cambridge: Cambridge University Press, 1958), pp. 25ff.

that were essential to wage Napoleonic war. Equally important, they lacked the political system and the administrative capacity to mobilize the whole nation and its resources for war. The expensive standing armies and artillery of the period imposed a severe strain on the limited capacity of governments to tax the people and finance protracted campaigns. The stringencies upon seapower were even greater, since no state could afford to train seamen in time of peace, and the quantity and quality of seamen that could be dragged into the service by press gangs were not conducive to large-scale warfare. Throughout the eighteenth century, war on land and at sea had to be attenuated or terminated because it threatened financial ruin, owing to the destruction of commerce at sea and the expense of keeping armies and navies fighting.

These limiting conditions were in accord with the political necessities of the ruling classes. To have waged war for larger purposes with greater violence would have required popular states (whether autocratic or representative) and, therefore, the end of the Old Regime. Besides, the stilted tactics and clumsy logistics of warfare seemed appropriate to the social differences of the time. They reflected on the one hand the aristocratic and mercantilist outlook of the ruling classes, who liked their battlefield amenities and wished to limit the expenditure of life and money, and on the other hand the apathy and unreliability of the soldiery, who, having been drawn from the nonproductive segments of society and feeling little allegiance to the state, had to be disciplined to the stylized, drill-like maneuvers of the time in order to be kept reasonably efficient.

Yet the social and political constraints upon war would not have been so limiting without the material and technological constraints, which, in fact, persisted for decades after the French Revolution. The military inventions of the eighteenth century did not notably increase the scope, tempo, or intensity of warfare. The important changes in weapons since the Middle Ages—notably the development of muskets and artillery, fortresses, and heavily armed sailing ships—were assimilated only very gradually. The relative strength of the defense coutinued to retard the pace of war. Indeed, the greater use of artillery further encumbered logistics; and material shortages, especially in metal, fuel, and saltpeter, hampered exploitation of the new technology. The nearest thing to a modern arms race was the competitive establishment and enlargement of standing armies, but this competition was not accompanied by comparable competition in weapons.

European industry, still mainly dependent on craftsmanship, had not yet developed much standardization or mass production, either in civilian or military technology. Transportation and communication did not become significantly faster and cheaper. There was little or no pressure for innovations in military technology from monarchs, and there was considerable resistance to it on the part of the nobility and soldiery: the nobility, because innovations threatened their supremacy as a fighting class; the soldiery, because they feared the destructiveness of new weapons. Military inventions were not the product of a systematic response to military needs; they were largely a by-product of civilian technology. Science was not oriented toward practical invention, even for civilian uses; and scientists were generally hostile to the thought of applying their learning to military uses.[4]

These basic material, technological, political, economic, and social constraints enable us to speak of the eighteenth century before the French Revolution as a century of limited wars. The generalization is too sweeping, since these wars were not notably different from those of the seventeenth century in their number, frequency, scope, duration, intensity, and deadliness to combatants. Indeed, when the typical wars of maneuver and position were punctuated with pitched battles, the improved discipline of the armies, together with the continuing low level of medical science, produced extremely high casualty rates. In one important respect, however, the limited wars of the eighteenth century were comparatively moderate: they caused significantly less destruction of civilian life, property, and welfare, with the exception of the devastating Seven Years' War in Prussia. This limitation distinguished them from the *grande mêlée* of the Religious Wars and made them a discriminating tool of statecraft.

In this respect kings and statesmen, anxious to avoid the excesses of the Thirty Years' War and determined to employ no more force than necessary to achieve modest and well-defined objectives, kept war limited. Limited war in turn generally served them as a means of policy commensurate with their ends. Thus the limited scope of land warfare was well suited to the limited territorial goals that states usually sought. War at sea was frequently little more than commercial war with an admixture of violence. Diplomatic bargains resolved what force could not decide.

Harbingers of military dynamism. Yet even in this century of limited war there were harbingers of a new military dynamism. The rulers of Prussia, despite the many limitations on military power, demonstrated the capacity of the state to improve its relative position in the hierarchy of states by generating military power. By the end of the seventeenth century Frederick William, the Great Elector of Brandenburg-Prussia, had already shown the capacity of an absolute monarch to utilize the material, human, and administrative resources

---

[4] . . . In the eighteenth century the sailing warship was technologically the most complicated military machine, but it remained substantially unchanged, and its effectiveness continued to depend on relative skill of operation rather than on technological advantage. . . .

of the state to build a superior standing army.[5] In the eighteenth century his successors, Frederick William I and Frederick the Great, added limited military conscription, intensive tactical training, efficient artillery barrages, and skillful generalship to raise Prussia through conquests and diplomacy to the front rank of states, although France, Russia, and Austria had from ten to twenty times the population and corresponding advantages in wealth, resources, trade, and territory.[6]

England provides the other striking example of an eighteenth-century state capitalizing upon military superiority based on efficient use of natural and human resources. By concentrating on naval power and a merchant marine and keeping military adventures on the Continent to a minimum, England compensated for her scarce native material resources by using her strategic geographical position, her substantial population, and her financial and trading prowess to become the dominant commercial and colonial power, with hegemony on the seas.

As Prussia based its military ascendance on the army and the control of land, England based its hegemony on the navy and control of overseas commerce. Through its army Prussia acquired and controlled land and population, which in turn were major ingredients in strengthening the army. Through its navy England acquired colonies and controlled commerce, which in turn provided the money to hire soldiers and subsidize allies on land while supporting a navy that could strangle the commerce of adversaries. Both were pre-eminent examples of states operating as successful military organizations, although the relatively unobtrusive impact upon domestic life of a standing navy, as compared to a standing army, helped England avoid the conspicuous militarism that arose in Prussia. Both provided impressive examples of the internal expansion of military power, which subsequent generations would emulate in the nineteenth century.

Moreover, in the rationalism of the eighteenth century there was also a harbinger of the technological explosion that transformed the scale of military power in the half century before World War I. In this

---

[5] . . . The greatest organizer of an efficient standing army in the seventeenth century was Sweden's King Gustavus Adolphus, although great advancements in rationalizing military organizations were also made by Richelieu in the army and by Colbert in the navy, under Louis XIV. Where Gustavus had about 30,000 men under arms in 1631, Louis XIV is said to have maintained a military establishment of 400,000, with field armies approaching 100,000—a size not to be duplicated until the French Revolution. . . .

[6] . . . In size of population, Prussia, with 2½ million, was twelfth among European states in 1740, but largely through conquest this population had doubled by 1786. The Prussian army under Frederick the Great grew to about 200,000, with a field army of about 53,000, at the beginning of the Seven Years' War (as compared to an average size of 47,000 among first-rank field armies in the eighteenth century). Four-fifths of Prussia's revenue went into the army.

century modern materialism—faith in the inevitable progressive increase of man's mastery of inanimate things for practical ends—became a sacred standard. The standard eroded the remnants of medieval moral and aesthetic constraints upon weaponry and lay the cultural foundation for the uninhibited advancement of military technology. The invention of more powerful weapons was presumed to be a mark of advancing civilization. The perfection of firearms, some hoped, would make wars so destructive that they would be quickly terminated or avoided altogether. Thus Europe was being prepared for a revolution in military technology that would be the counterpart of the industrial revolution—that astonishing explosion of man's ingenuity and productivity ignited in England two hundred years ago.[7]

Yet before the rise of popular nationalism and the onset of the industrial-technological revolution, military power could not approach the volatility, dynamism, mass, and intensity it attained in the nineteenth and twentieth centuries. Consequently, the military managers of the eighteenth century were spared the problems of control which afflicted their successors and were permitted the illusion of mastering the still latent energy of destruction. In the hands of enlightened statemen and generals, military establishments seemed to be calculable and safe instruments of policy.[8]

Confidence in the calculability of war was consonant with the stress on rigid tactical principles of maneuver and position and with elaborate rules of siege and surrender. It reflected the prevalent faith in the ability of men to rationalize all human activity by discovering the precise, mechanical laws of its operation. Some analysts foresaw a universal military science that would be so exact as to render war futile and unnecessary. There was reason for such confidence, for although the outcome of war depended on many imponderables, the principal elements of military power were sufficiently ponderable to facilitate roughly accurate comparisons in advance of war. In war itself they remained fairly stable, and victory turned upon the most skillful use

---

[7] Among the civilian innovations of the eighteenth-century industrial revolution which transformed military technology in the latter part of the nineteenth were the steam engine, iron metallurgy, the shift from wood to coal for fuel, the rise of industrial chemistry, the establishment of a machine tool industry, and the beginnings of the science of electricity. . . .

[8] "By and large a statesman in 1750 or 1815, if he possessed information on the size of armies, on the men who led them, and on the relative wealth of the rulers, probably had a better chance of estimating the power of a foreign state than he would have today. Much of the necessary information was actually common knowledge in the chancelleries of Europe." Edward V. Gulick, *Europe's Classical Balance of Power* (Ithaca: Cornell University Press, 1955), p. 28.

of largely unchanging weapons and tactical rules known to everyone.

In reality, of course, war was not as precisely calculable as its theorists professed. The vicissitudes of physical environment and human skill on the battlefield and especially at sea, where weather and unreliable communications interfered more with command and control, repeatedly led to miscalculations. The chief significance of the limitations on armed forces was that, together with the rough equality of combinations of opposing forces, they rendered the consequences of miscalculations less serious.

Thus Frederick II, who was increasingly impressed by the role of chance in war and diplomacy as he gained experience, reflected upon the results of the War of the Austrian Succession (1740–48) with a certain melancholy satisfaction: "Since the art of war has been so well understood in Europe, and policy has established a certain balance of power between sovereigns, grand enterprises but rarely produce such effects as might be expected. An equality of forces, alternate loss and success, occasion the opponents at the end of the most desperate war, to find themselves much in the same state of reciprocal strength as at the commencement."

The wars of the French Revolution and Napoleon's military adventures would reveal a dynamism and decisiveness in war that Frederick II could not have imagined. But this new dimension of force also created a new dimension of miscalculation—and new efforts to master force.

The wars of the French Revolution showed what unprecedented concentration of military energy the popularization of war could produce even before the technological transformation preceding World War I. Although Carnot, as Minister of War in 1799, directed the first concerted effort to mobilize scientific talent for war, Napoleon was indifferent to technological innovations. Nevertheless, Napoleon magnified the force of war tremendously by exploiting the new sources of organized violence released by popular nationalism and ideological fervor. Following the course of the revolutionary leaders who preceded him, he transformed warfare into a national crusade, involving not just tactical maneuver and attrition of the enemy's supply lines but annihilation of the enemy's forces, occupation of his territory, and even political conversion of his people. With universal military conscription and comprehensive material and economic mobilization, he created a "nation in arms." To the revolutionary tactics of offensive mobility, surprise, the concentration of overwhelming numbers on a single point, massed artillery fire, and destructive pursuit, he added the extravagant ambition of a bold field commander, to give war a terrible new impact and momentum.

Truly, "The wars of Kings were at an end; the wars of peoples were beginning."[9] The sheer scale of the resulting violence made the impact of war as unpredictable and uncontrollable as it was momentous. In Clausewitz's terms, it made war more nearly "a thing in itself."

Yet, although the potential autonomy and dynamism of popular, massive war had been revealed, the European wars of the following century, from 1815 to 1914, were relatively limited. Indeed, there were fewer significant wars in the European state systems than in the period from the defeat of Louis XIV to the French Revolution.[10] There were none of the scope or duration of the Seven Years' War and only one, the Crimean War, that was a general war involving several major powers. In the Crimean and Franco-Prussian Wars the field armies were several times larger than those of the seventeenth and eighteenth centuries—in the hundreds of thousands instead of twenty or thirty thousand—but the percentage of combat casualties was not much different, and civilian destruction was localized. The wars of this period are notable for their short duration and the small number of battles and participating states, as compared to the eighteenth or twentieth centuries. They were fought and settled for limited objectives, they were localized, and they were quickly terminated. . . .

The explanation of limited war in the period between the Napoleonic Wars and World War I, as in the eighteenth century, seems to lie in circumstances that were partly fortuitous, partly technological and economic, and partly the result of deliberate restraints upon the political objectives of war. Although the material and technical limits upon war were not so constraining as before the French Revolution, the destructive potential of armies was still sufficiently restricted to enable states to keep combat within bounds in the absence of a political occasion for fighting a general war of annihilation.

The Austro-Prussian War and the Franco-Prussian War were limited chiefly by Prussia's ability to bring superior force to bear quickly and by Bismark's willingness to negotiate a limited victory consistent with a new equilibrium of power. The Russo-Japanese War

---

[9] This is Marshal Foch's pronouncement occasioned by the famous cannonade at Valmy (1792), which marked the end of the Prussian offensive. Foch, *The Principles of War*, trans. Hilaire Belloc (New York: Henry Holt & Co., 1918), p. 29. Much earlier, Goethe and Clausewitz, among others, had interpreted the battle at Valmy as the end of the old warfare and the beginning of the new. Actually, Valmy was tactically insignificant, but it was strategically and politically significant because a citizen army withstood a model eighteenth-century army and permitted the Revolutionary forces to go on to future victories. . . .

[10] Of course, what one regards as a militarily and politically significant war is somewhat subjective. By our reckoning there were either nine or sixteen such wars in the eighteenth century and either seven or thirteen in the latter period, depending upon what criteria are used. However, the number of belligerents and the duration of wars were markedly greater in the eighteenth century. In the eighteenth century the period from 1763 to the French Revolution was generally peaceful in the sense that there was no more than one large war and only a few small wars. In nineteenth-century Europe the periods 1815–1854 and 1871–1914 were equally peaceful.

of 1904-05 was limited chiefly by Japan's sudden naval victory, by its satisfaction with a local victory, and by the material incapacity of both belligerents to carry the war to the other's homeland. The Crimean War was limited by its location—the same war in Austria might well have become a world war—and by the incompetence and inefficiency of the belligerents. These and other wars in this period remained local largely because the European system of political alignments, as in the eighteenth century, was relatively fragmented and loosely knit before the emergence of the two great alliances that clashed in 1914.

The new management of force. Although war itself remained limited in the period after the Napoleonic Wars and before World War I, military power expanded greatly. The professionalization and modernization of military power in the latter half of this period created an unprecedented peacetime war potential. But the success of states in preserving a relatively peaceful and orderly international system while greatly expanding its military basis concealed the latent dangers of the new military potential.

In the latter half of the nineteenth century, military power in Europe came under the systematic direction of a new class of specialists in military organization and planning. Professionally dedicated to maximum military efficiency, these specialists directed their nation's human, material, technological, and economic resources toward the creation in peacetime of military machines capable of inflicting maximum destruction upon the enemy's forces in war. The systematic training of these military specialists, with their highly developed staffs and administrative procedures, codes of professional conduct, formulation of war plans, conduct of war games, and development of strategic and tactical doctrine marked the application to the management of force of those methods of modern production that were transforming private industry.

The outstanding model of military management was the Prussian General Staff. By capitalizing on two great new military resources, universal compulsory peacetime conscription and the railways-and-telegraph system, the Staff led Prussia to two rapid, stunning victories over Austria in 1866 and France in 1871.[11] The quickness and

[11] The conscription system introduced by the Prussian military reformers enabled Prussia to combine a relatively small, highly professional standing army with a large military potential and thereby to join numbers with skill at a tolerable cost. The system entailed compulsory universal service for several years with the regular army and the regular reserve and then with a civilian militia. The military organization of the railways entailed first constructing a railway network, then mobilizing the army, transporting it with weapons and supplies to the right spot at the right time, and finally deploying the forces properly. Prussia made many mistakes in conscription and railway organization in the war with Austria, but the General Staff studied the experience and profited from it. Michael Howard, *The Franco-Prussian War* (New York: Macmillan, 1961), pp. 18-29. Howard's study shows how substantially Prussia's success depended upon superior organization of mobilization and railway utilization.

completeness of Prussia's destruction of the fighting capacity of the dominant military power in Europe were particularly remarkable. It convincingly demonstrated to the rest of Europe the necessity of systematically developing peacetime military potential under professional, scientific management. Thereafter all the major states on the Continent created general staffs, railway networks, and systems of universal peacetime military service.

As we shall see in examining the political consequences of the expansion of military power, the new military machines provided statesmen with a powerful political instrument; but, unfortunately, the statesmen permitted the machines to follow a logic of their own—the narrow logic of military efficiency held by the professional managers. Thus instead of becoming a flexible instrument of policy short of war, the new peacetime military potential became, in effect, an independent force largely divorced from political control. Because the military machines were geared so strictly to fighting a war, they tended to foreclose new opportunities for using force short of war. . . .

The expanded function of strategy called for a systematic integration of military plans with foreign policy. In the hands of military professionals, however, strategy tended, on the one hand, to exalt the romantic emphasis of Foch on *will* and the all-out offensive and, on the other hand, to emphasize meticulous operational planning for military efficiency measured by the maximum force that could be brought to bear upon the enemy. The result was a kind of strategic monism that simplified planning but did not serve policy.

Thus the war mobilization plans of the general staffs in the years of armed peace after the Franco-Prussian War seriously limited the opportunities for diplomatic accommodation and committed governments in certain contingencies to an almost automatic shift into general war, as though their war machines had only one forward gear and no brakes. The prevailing military assumption that a future war would be swift and decisive like the Franco-Prussian War and that a long war would ruin a nation's economy and incur the danger of revolution put a premium on striking first with superior forces. This requirement in turn led military staffs to commit their governments to plans for total mobilization only and to regard mobilization as an inevitable prelude to all-out war. When mobilization began, diplomacy would stop. For the sake of military efficiency, military plans were directed toward meeting a single contingency with one kind of response. The whole machinery was inflexibly geared to the complicated, exacting logistics of the railway networks, with the objects of concentrating the maximum force at a single military point as quickly as possible. Consequently, when Austria declared war against Serbia in 1914, Austria, Russia, and Germany forfeited the diplomatic opportunities for avoiding war that partial mobilization against each other might have afforded, lest they lose precious time in fully mobilizing for the war that their military staffs considered inevitable.[12]

Actually, despite their commitment to full mobilization, each of these governments, at the behest of statesmen, tried to resist and, except in Germany, temporarily succeeded in resisting the prescribed automatic response by undertaking partial mobilization so as not to provoke the potential adversary into war or draw others into war. In the end, however, the military, pleading military necessity, prevailed and full mobilization was instituted, thereby turning military foresight into a self-fulfilling prophecy. In this way the attempt to manage military power more precisely and calculably made it more autonomous and less subject to control.

Thus mobilization plans seriously limited opportunities for diplomatic accommodation and, once they had been put into effect, virtually assured general war. In the end, the ineffective political control of peacetime military preparations proved to be even more dangerous to international order than the tremendous increase of destructive power that accompanied the outbursts of industrial and technological energy. On the other hand, the modernization and hence increasing complexity of military power created a far more serious problem of peacetime political control than had existed before.

The technological revolution in military power. Competitive arming in a dynamic military technology further enhanced the role of military power as an autonomous political force. The modern arms race originated in an unprecedented surge of military invention in the last quarter of the nineteenth century.

The rifled gun barrel, together with improvements in gunpowder and firing mechanisms, led to tremendous improvements of range and accuracy. The development of breech-loading rifles and artillery, along with improved recoil mechanisms late in the century, greatly increased rapidity of fire. As significant as the accelerated rate of invention was the reduction of time between invention, mass production, and tactical assimilation of weapons, due to the effective co-ordination of economic and technological-scientific resources and to systematic battlefield experimentation and analysis.[13]

---

[12] Thus Dobrorolski, in charge of mobilization in Russia, insisted, "The whole plan of mobilization is worked out ahead to its end in all its details. When the moment has been chosen, one only has to press the button, and the whole state begins to function automatically with the precision of a clock's mechanism. . . . Once the moment has been fixed, everything is settled; there is no going back; it determines mechanically the beginning of war." Quoted in Sidney B. Fay, *The Origins of the World War* (2nd ed. rev.; New York: Macmillan, 1930), p. 481.

[13] . . . Despite the increased rate of assimilation, the French, although they developed the machine gun shortly before the Franco-Prussian War, failed to exploit its potentialities because they used it like artillery instead of like rifles against infantry at close range. Improved models by the Americans Gatling and Browning and the Englishman Maxim were developed in the last half of the century, but the full significance of the machine gun was not demonstrated until World War I.

As land warfare was transformed by the utilization of railways and the telegraph, maritime warfare was transformed by the invention of the iron-hulled, steam-propelled warship. The rapid development of the battleship and the profusion of offensive and defensive naval technology to counter it were unprecedented in the history of military innovation. This weapon system changed more in the latter half of the nineteenth century than it had in the preceding ten centuries.

The development of the battleship altered the distribution of power, stimulated far-reaching rivalries, and shaped new political alignments. More than ever before a single weapon became the pre-eminent test and symbol of national greatness. It was integrally linked to foreign policy in the gospel of seapower according to Mahan. Mahan's great popularity as a strategist (particularly in England, Germany, and France) was based on his view that seapower was the royal road to national wealth and prestige. It would enable states to enlarge and protect overseas imperial holdings and commerce with an integrated system of colonies, bases, and merchant marine, supported by a fleet of line-of-battle ships designed to control the sea lanes, not merely to raid commerce and protect ports.

The rapid improvement of battleships created the first modern technological arms races. The arms race is a somewhat misleading metaphor for a competitive advancement of the type, quantity, and quality of weapons between adversaries seeking an advantageous ratio of military strength. In the latter part of the nineteenth century it became a major form of power politics and greatly enhanced the role of military power in peacetime.

From the 1850s through the 1880s France precipitated an arms race with Britain by attempting to offset numerical inferiority in warships with superiority in ironclad battleships, guns, and commerce-destroying torpedo boats and light cruisers, in accordance with the strategic concepts of the *Jeune École* navalists.[14] The resulting competition was most conspicuous in the contest between offensive guns and defensive armor. France eventually abandoned the competition without approaching naval equality chiefly because of disorder in French politics, growing fear of the German army, and friendlier political relations with Britain.

---

[14] This school of navalists, echoing the old view of naval warfare as an extension of commercial warfare, did not anticipate starving England but only cutting off enough food and raw materials to cause an economic panic by raising insurance rates. The British decided to counter this danger by providing national insurance and devising new tactics to protect merchant vessels. Arthur J. Marder, *The Anatomy of British Sea Power* (New York: Alfred A. Knopf, 1940), chap. vi.

Germany launched another naval race with Britain in 1898, primarily to compete with her as a colonial world power. The British naval program, based on the famous two-power standard, had been designed to offset a Franco-Russian combination. Germany's program, coinciding with an alleviation of the Russian threat by virtue of the Anglo-Japanese Alliance and the Russo-Japanese War, shifted the focus of Britain's naval program to Germany. In October, 1905, Britain laid down the original *Dreadnought* and in February, 1906, launched it. The *Dreadnought* had greater speed and several times greater long-range firepower than previous battleships. Germany soon followed suit, and in 1912 First Lord of the Admiralty Churchill announced a British naval standard of 60 per cent superiority over Germany in dreadnoughts, while threatening to lay two keels for every one German keel unless Germany would reciprocally slow down or freeze construction without any political conditions. By 1914 the German government had abandoned this competition for fear of encouraging further British naval expansion and pressing German taxpayers too heavily, as well as because of more urgent demands imposed by military preparations on land.

The role of dreadnoughts foreshadowed the revolutionary role of submarines and airpower in that they were intended not merely to defeat the enemy's forces but to exert a far-reaching effect upon its livelihood and status. They would do this, moreover, not merely by harassing commerce directly but primarily by securing or denying control of sea lanes vital to a nation's welfare and greatness. What is more, they were admirably suited to sustaining in peacetime a world policy and position through the conspicuous representation of a nation's might in distant places. This had been the more or less conscious strategy of British seapower since the latter part of the eighteenth century, but Mahan made it explicit and popularized it, and the modern battleship dramatized its efficacy.

The development of steamships with screw propellers relieved sea maneuvers from dependence on the vagaries of the wind and currents and completely outmoded sailing vessels. It greatly enhanced the defensive strength of advanced industrial nations, especially such insular powers as Japan and the U.S. It also greatly enhanced the geographical extension of the power of nations that could develop coaling bases and colonies. Therefore it became the mainstay of the great imperial contests and the virtually global struggles for hegemony that agitated international politics in the two decades or so preceding World War I.

In these ways the dreadnought exemplified the momentous impact of technological innovation upon international politics. It demonstrated the growing impact of armed forces, as well as their growing dependence, upon the nation as a whole.

It also posed the question of whether the new technology could be controlled. This question was posed in one form by the new factor of uncertainty in warfare and military planning, injected by the accelerated rate of technological innovation. The dreadnought complicated the calculation of relative military power and made more difficult the control and prediction of the outcome of war. To integrate the new battleships into war plans and production programs, certain assumptions had to be made about their military function. The assumption that a surprise attack with naval forces-in-being would be decisive provided the strategic impetus for naval competition, just as the assumption that the army that struck first with the most firepower would have a decisive advantage impelled the arms race in land weapons. Yet forces-in-being at the moment of a hypothetical war would depend not only on existing weapons but, equally, on future weapons produced by the building programs in the shipyards—programs that were complex and, in the case of challenging states, shrouded in secrecy.

In 1909 official and private British sources indicated that Germany might build 17 or even 21 dreadnoughts by 1912 instead of the officially announced 13. This estimate turned out to be wrong. It was based on information concerning an increase in German shipbuilding capacity; an increase in Krupp's capacity to produce gun mountings; the secret accumulation of nickel for use in guns, armor, and mountings; and an acceleration of contracts for ships. In effect, the alarmists based estimates of production on their view of Germany's capabilities, whereas more moderate advocates of a naval build-up credited Germany's announced intentions. England, unlike Germany, did not keep production details secret. The details of its naval program were publicly debated in Parliament and in the press. On the other hand, the public debate was often a confusing guide to those concerned with estimating the future of England's naval program.

The secrecy, complexity, and dynamism of building programs meant that naval programs had to be based on uncertain estimates not only of an adversary's relative capacity but also of its *intentions* to increase the quantity and quality of its navy. Yet the adversary's intentions could be affected by many imponderable internal and external considerations, including its estimate of one's own capacity and intentions. Therefore one state might try to alter the other's intentions by threatening and bargaining with a construction program and, perhaps, by linking this game with political proposals.

After some controversy, the British built the more powerful dreadnoughts, although they knew that this would lead to expensive and possibly dangerous competition with Germany in a weapon in which British superiority would not be as great as in pre-dreadnought battleships. The decisive argument for doing so was simply that Britain's refraining from building dreadnoughts would not prevent Germany from building them but only give Germany a head start. After competitive building started, however, the British tried to induce the Germans to agree to a reciprocal reduction of the tempo of competition or at least to an exchange of construction information in order to mitigate exaggerated suspicions of rates of construction. But the German government was unwilling thus to concede British superiority without some political *quid pro quo,* such as British neutrality in the event of a Franco-German war. The British government, on the other hand, was unwilling to break the Anglo-French entente. Winston Churchill, First Lord of the Admiralty, tried in vain to get German agreement to proportional reductions or to a joint holiday in construction of dreadnoughts while threatening, otherwise, to outbuild Germany by a precise ratio or number of ships. In the end, Germany defeated its political purpose by driving Britain closer to France. At the same time, it had to concede British superiority in the naval competition.

The difficulties of using the new peacetime power of weapons as a finely calculated instrument of policy were demonstrated in the failure of Admiral Tirpitz's too-clever "risk" strategy, which foundered on miscalculations of British policies and capabilities. Tirpitz developed his "risk theory" as a strategy for advancing Germany's political status and security vis-à-vis Britain by improving its relative naval power without obtaining naval equality. According to this strategy England would prefer to make concessions to Germany in the colonial field or possibly even enter into a military commitment with Germany rather than risk a clash with a smaller German navy, if, in the event of such a clash, that navy were strong enough to leave England inferior in the face of a Franco-Russian naval combination. The underlying assumptions of this strategy, if they ever had any merit, were invalidated by the Anglo-Russian entente, the Anglo-French rapprochement, the Admiralty's decision to concentrate the British fleet in the North Sea, and England's decision to build dreadnoughts. But the German government continued to pursue Tirpitz's strategy and brought about the very political result—consolidation of the Triple Entente—that it was intended to prevent, while inciting Britain to enter a competition Germany could not win.

As the Anglo-German naval competition illustrates, the nature of the new technology gave arms races a kind of self-generating impetus based on the interactions of opposing military capabilities and intentions, real and estimated. This interaction produced a mode of peacetime power politics that resembled maneuvering and bargaining of eighteenth-century wars, except that the stakes of the game were larger, the rules less reliable, and the whole game more volatile and subjective.

Moreover, because the game was expensive, because it impinged upon national pride and affected international tensions and the prospect of war, and because even nondemocratic governments felt the need to elicit popular consent for arms policies, arms races were also deeply involved in the vagaries of public opinion and internal politics —an involvement which the armed services and the armaments manufacturers stimulated and exploited. Thus during both the Anglo-French and Anglo-German naval races there were a number of naval scares in England, causing widespread, although unwarranted, fears of sudden naval attack and invasion. News of French and German naval increases created considerable public apprehension and touched off controversies with political overtones in the government and press. There were lively public disputes over future German naval strength and the proper number of ships to be built in the British program.

In England, as elsewhere, it was widely assumed that the outcome of crises like the two in Morocco depended upon naval superiority. Therefore all governments that could afford a navy, as well as some that could not, pointed to the navy as a symbol of national might and pride. The involvement of the public in military policies through arms races, demonstrations of military prowess, and crises added a further dimension of subjectivity and incalculability to the use of military power short of war.

The difficulties of planning in peacetime for the effective use of military power in war were no less severe. For in addition to all the other complicating factors in arms races, the new high rate of technological innovation and obsolescence deprived the military managers of one of the crucial, though increasingly inadequate, criteria for determining military requirements: wartime experience. Thus the London *Times* of November 19, 1895, noted: "A modern navy is a totally untried weapon of warfare. It is the resultant of a host of more or less conflicting theories of attack and defense. The seaman, the gunner, the torpedoist, the engineer, and the naval constructor each has his share in the creation of the modern man-of-war, each presses the paramount claim of his own department, and the result is a marvel of theory, compromise, and complication."[15]

To some extent, formulation of strategic doctrine, conduct of war games, and mathematical calculations of projected operations compensated for lack of experience,[16] but they also tended to foster a

---

[15] Quoted in Marder, *The Anatomy of British Sea Power, op. cit.,* p. 9.

[16] War games, however, often led to false conclusions. Thus the British Royal Navy's maneuvers of 1892 supported the belief that torpedo boats had little chance of success against fleets at sea. *Ibid.,* p. 166. But the first real example of this new technology in battle, provided by Japan against Russia in the war of 1904-5, contributed much to Japan's astonishing victory when torpedo boats attacked the Russian squadron in Port Arthur and sank a Russian flagship and three other ships in the decisive Battle of Tsushima.

dangerous illusion of precision and predictability. The meticulous planning and rehearsal of complex military operations and the single-minded pursuit of maximum wartime efficiency tended not only to overlook the contingent and unpredictable elements of war; equally important, the inflexibility of military plans had unexpected and often quite adverse political consequences. Germany's Schlieffen Plan, before World War I, is the most notable case in point.

Under Chief of Staff Von Schlieffen's command, this plan followed his predecessor Waldersee's crucial assumption that a full-scale two-front war with France and Russia was inevitable. The elder Moltke had planned a quick war and a settlement with Russia in the East while offering France neutrality or fighting her with a holding action if necessary. But Waldersee, coming into office after the formation of the Franco-Russian Alliance, planned a full-scale war against Russia, preceded by a quick knockout blow against France. This foreclosed the possibility of keeping a Balkan war localized, since even if a war with the Russians were to originate in the Balkans, Germany would have to strike first against France. Moreover, the Schlieffen Plan envisaged an attack through Belgium even if, as proved to be the case, France were to refrain from invading Belgium first and England were to regard the invasion of Belgium as requiring her intervention.

Strategic prognostications in other countries showed the same lack of foresight. On the eve of World War I the general staffs of the major European antagonists were universally convinced that their forces, with the help of allied forces, would be victorious and that victory would come from a quick, decisive contest like the Prussian victory over France in 1871.[17] They believed in Marshall Foch's mystical doctrine of *l'offensive brutale et à outrance*. Foch's stress of offensive action went along with his advocacy of "absolute" or total war, in opposition to the eighteenth-century limited wars of maneuver and position. It was associated with his belief in the decisiveness of the moral factor in war: the will to victory. It was in accord with the widespread belief that a modern war of attrition would be such a severe strain on industrial economies that nations would have to end a war quickly rather then face bankruptcy and revolution.

---

[17] The Elder Moltke and Joffre were exceptions in foreseeing a war of attrition, but neither undertook preparations for such a war. Only Lord Kitchener, who became war minister after war was declared, urged preparation for a long war of attrition. England's War Council, however, regarded his views as extravagant whimsy. . . . The most detailed and well-reasoned prophecy of a war of attrition was made by Ivan S. Bloch in his six-volume work, *The Future of War in Its Technical, Economic, and Political Relations* (1897–99), which predicted that the increased firepower of guns would force entrenchment and stalemate. However, Bloch shared the consensus that modern war would be economically and socially catastrophic, or "impossible," as he put it. . . .

The military staffs were, therefore, completely unprepared for the war of stalemate and attrition that ensued when the devastating firepower unleashed by the new weapons, unaccompanied by comparable innovations in tactical mobility, drove troops into the trenches and exacted unimagined casualties for negligible advances.[18]

World War I. In World War I the principal object of war was conceived to be the annihilation of the enemy's forces. Yet the British blockade and the German submarine campaign put whole nations under siege as never before. In the end Britain was bankrupted, France and Britain had lost a terrible portion of their youth, Italy was on the brink of political chaos, Russia and Germany were racked with revolution, the Austro-Hungarian Empire had vanished, and the Ottoman Empire was dismembered. Only the American Civil War, the first conflict to reveal fully the momentous destructive power generated by modern technology and the popularization of war, could have prepared the world of 1914 for the protracted, profligate expenditure of lives, homes, and money; but the lessons of that war were largely ignored in Europe.

Thus, contrary to the illusion of precision and calculability conveyed by advanced professional management—but contrary also to the conviction that sheer morale and the will to victory would be decisive—total war proved to be far more intractable to intelligent direction than the managers expected. This was partly the result of unwarranted faith in the simple military axioms that led armies into massive assaults in the expectation of quick, decisive victories and partly the result of the enormous dimensions of force and the immense complexity of military establishments, which multiplied the frequency and repercussions of unanticipated developments.

World War I precipitated a torrent of technological innovations, fostered for the first time by a comprehensive mobilization of scientific talent. These innovations included not only the improvement of previous weapons but also the introduction of new weapons: the airplane, the tank, poison gas, and the submarine. Each of these weapons and the interaction of all of them with other weapons, with tactical innovations, and with new factors of logistics and materiel affected the conflict in unexpected ways. The submarine, which had been only an ineffective novelty in previous wars, came close to being a truly decisive weapon.

Of course, all these innovations provided only a faint foretaste of the proliferation of decisive technology in World War II,[19] in which

---

[18] . . . According to the official French history of the war, *Les Armées Françaises dans la grande guerre* (1922–25), French casualties in the month of August alone amounted to about 300,000 out of a field army of 1,600,000.

[19] In World War II the mobilization of scientific and engineering talent for military purposes was especially comprehensive and effective in England. The British program

the participants were as unprepared for mechanized, mobile, blitz-krieg warfare as they had been unprepared for trench warfare in 1914. In the interwar period mechanized mobile warfare had been espoused by a few prophets in England and France—notably, Fuller, Liddell Hart, and De Gaulle—but only the Nazis put it into practice.

The fact that the marvelous ingenuity of technology and military management resulted in such unexpected destruction of life and property produced a deep agony and revulsion in the world, in many ways deeper than that created by World War II. The unprecedented loss of life and the massive devastation of material civilization, compressed into a few years, intensified the psychological shock caused by the sharp contrast with prewar expectations of a quick, decisive, ex-hilarating contest. The wholesale inhumanity and suffering inflicted by modern nations geared to war seemed like a cruel refutation of the general optimism in the preceding decades that industrial-technological and sociopolitical progress marched together.

It is true that if one measures the destructiveness of war by economic and demographic statistics covering the immediate post-war period of recuperation was well as the war itself, World War I seems much less pernicious as a whole than its reputation—indeed, almost beneficent in some countries. For the same factors of modern civili-zation that made massive violence possible also facilitated a rapid restoration of population and national incomes. But this measure-ment, of course, is irrelevant to the lasting psychological and political effect of an immense, violent upheaval in modern civilization inflicted by man's own monstrous military machines running amuck.

A new dimension of force. Man's enthusiasm for war and the whole war system was deeply shaken by World War I, yet his underly-ing confidence in technological solutions to warfare was not under-mined. On the contrary, the war aroused hope that some single new weapon might prove overwhelming, that some technological breakthrough might simplify the problem of exerting calculable, decisive force. This hope centered above all on the strategic bomber, which promised to attain victory by striking directly at the enemy's homeland, avoiding massive, inconclusive encounters on the ground and obviating the travails of attrition.

Actually, although the development of strategic airpower greatly enhanced the peacetime effects of force, it showed as dramatically as World War I the difficulty of controlling the wartime effects of the volatile new technology. Indeed, the very characteristic of strategic

---

grew into a gigantic co-ordinated international effort including Canada and the U.S. A great part of this effort went into the perfection of weapons developed in previous wars; but new inventions—most notably radar, the proximity fuse, and the atomic bomb—played an even more significant role than in World War I.

airpower that enhanced its political impact short of war complicated
its control in war: its capacity to inflict sudden punishment directly
upon civilians at a range far beyond the battlefield. This characteristic, although analogous to the indirect punitive effect of the naval
blockade, distinguishes airpower from all other kinds of military
power.

In the midst of the stalemate during World War I, the development
of the military airplane inspired a small but influential group of advocates to propound a doctrine of strategic bombing long before the
bomber was technically capable of playing its purported role. The
doctrine promised victory by inflicting decisive damage of the basic
civilian sources of enemy power without having to defeat the enemy's
armed forces or occupy his territory.

In April, 1918, British political leaders, over the opposition of the
highest ranking military officers, succeeded in establishing a separate
Royal Air Force in their search for an alternative to sending the flower
of British manhood to "chew barbed wire in Flanders," as Churchill
put it. The public shock over the German attacks on London with
Zeppelins, and later Gotha bombers, provided the immediate impetus.
The prevailing strategic doctrine at the time contemplated the use of
bombers against military targets directly related to the war on the
ground, but the general impression that punitive air raids on cities
could exert great psychological effects injected a significant ambiguity
in the nascent doctrine of airpower. The heavy casualties inflicted by
the daylight raids on undefended London raised great popular and
professional expectations about the efficacy of strategic bombing. On
the basis of these casualties it was calculated that in a future war
London might be made almost uninhabitable in the first weeks of
bombing. Furthermore, the one-sided emphasis on offensive uses of
airpower in World War I fostered the conviction that there was no effective defense against such devastation except bombing the enemy's
bases and factories and inflicting reprisal damage upon his cities. These
assumptions and the strategic doctrine that was based upon them had a
powerful effect upon international politics after World War I.

In the years after the war the writings of the Italian prophet of airpower, Giulio Douhet, broadcast the doctrine of victory-through-
strategic-bombing throughout Europe and beyond. In essence this
doctrine held that victory depended first on obtaining "command of
the air," which in turn depended on destroying air bases and air factories, and then on shattering the enemy's will to fight by inflicting
maximum damage on his cities, transportation centers, and industries.
The doctrine assumed that war among major powers must aim at an-
nihilating the enemy before he annihilates you, that there would be no
defense against the bomber, and that victory would come quickly
(and, incidentally, therefore humanely) to the force that could strike
first by surprise and inflict the greatest damage in the shortest time.

The logical defense against this danger would be either to strike first in a pre-emptive or preventive attack or else to depend on the threat of reprisal to deter the enemy from striking first.

As in the case of prospective naval or ground attack, the supposition that a sudden first strike from the air could be decisive added an element of tension to international conflict and a new danger of pre-emptive or preventive attack. It also gave states a mighty instrument of intimidation and deterrence. With the integration of airpower into military establishments, the whole nation became the direct object as well as the source of military power—in peacetime as well as in war. In short, strategic bombing put the nation-in-arms in the front line. This further complicated the problem of calculating and controlling military power.

Success in exploiting military power for its psychological and political effects short of war depended heavily on the credibility of a government's and, indirectly, a whole nation's will to use its power of devastation, especially when the enemy was assumed to have the power of counter-devastation. But what determined credibility? It depended partly on the relative material capabilities of opposing air forces; but, because of the subjective nature of governmental and national will, the relation of capabilities to credibility was less direct and more complicated than in the case of weapons that exerted their effect only against armed forces.

Moreover, the estimate of air capabilities was also uncertain. Not only was the efficacy of untried weapons in doubt, but, as in the case of naval competition, plans and preparations for weapons that would be produced only years hence were a crucial factor in capabilities; yet these plans and preparations were obscured by secrecy and the diffuseness of the production process. Thus after the British decided in 1934 to seek air "parity" as a "deterrent" to German aggression, they discovered not only that parity was difficult to define in quantitative and qualitative terms but that attaining it required a rearmament effort based on quite uncertain and fallible estimates of Germany's rate of production, which in the early stages of German rearmament depended heavily on such obscure auxiliary preparations as the manufacturing of machine tools. In May, 1935, Prime Minister Baldwin publicly confessed that his government had completely underestimated the rate of German rearmament. Britain's task then became to expand her aircraft industry and rate of production so as to obtain parity with the air force that Germany was expected to have by 1940.

Britain's whole air rearmament program was based on the assumption that Germany could deliver a knockout blow against England. Baldwin's pronouncement that "the bombers will always get through" was taken as axiomatic. The fact that the Germans had no intention, plan, or capability for such an attack did not change the significance of the British assumption. Indeed, Germany capitalized on this psychological reality by encouraging British apprehensions of a knockout blow and by exploiting them to paralyze British diplomatic and military resistance to piecemeal aggression. Consequently, Britain's strategic doctrine stressed the deterrent effect of a capability for offensive reprisals against Germany, and her rearmament program stressed heavy bombers. Nevertheless, when the government belatedly discovered the magnitude of Germany's air superiority after 1938, it shifted from a strategy of massive civilian bombing to one of confining bombing to military objectives in the hope that Germany would spare British cities. Then, shortly before the war, the Air Staff, having previously failed to base air strategy on operational possibilities, discovered the limited penetration ability of bombers; so it shifted the strategic priority to defending France on the ground, although there were no concerted plans to fulfill this priority.

War itself was the great school of strategy and tactics, but wartime trial and error provided unexpected lessons. Strategic bombing turned out to be even more volatile and less subject to foresight and control than the contest between massive armies had been in World War I. At first both sides confined bombing to tactical and industrial targets. The air war demonstrated that both sides had unprecedented incentives for contrived reciprocal restraints. And for a while such restraints were practiced.[20] But, contrary to claims of great precision, the inaccuracy of bombing and the collateral civilian damage, combined with the unexpected vulnerability of bombers engaged in precision bombing, eventually broke down reciprocal restraints and led to raids designed chiefly to inflict terror and reprisals upon civilians and things of civilian value, culminating in the senseless bombing of cities like Dresden.

The actual effect of such bombing upon civilian morale and the national will to fight proved to be almost negligible in Germany, as in England, although similar attacks on Japanese cities were apparently more effective in helping to induce surrender. But in both cases civilian bombing signified that an ultimate stage had been reached in the expansion of military power—a stage in which the whole nation had become a direct target of psychological pressure and physical punishment. Before the nuclear age airpower revealed both the possible utility of modern force short of war and its potential uselessness in war. . . .

---

[20] In view of common assumptions about Hitler's "irrationality," it is interesting to note that he felt special incentives to avoid city bombing, such as the fear of the adverse effect of British retaliatory bombings on his domestic support; and that he was generally more anxious to preserve reciprocal restraints than the British. . . .

THE POLITICS OF FORCE

The changing attitude toward force. In the whole melancholy tale of misadventures accompanying the expansion of force through the period of two world wars, perhaps something as simple yet as imponderable as the prevailing attitude toward force and war affected international order more decisively than the structure and organization of power or the nature of military technology—although, of course, these factors were closely related.

The prevailing attitude toward force did not change as dramatically or as uniformly as military technology; yet there is a tremendous gap between the attitude of the eighteenth century and that of the period following World War I. In the eighteenth century when the instruments of force were inherently quite limited and power politics was no concern of national publics, war was largely taken for granted as a normal recourse of statecraft. Those who deplored war did so more for its wastefulness, its control by the aristocracy, its cruelty, and its irrationality than for its material destruction of civilian life and its threat to national survival. . . .

During the last quarter of the nineteenth century governments became very receptive to an influential group that exalted war, the military virtues, and national expansion. In a kind of reversion to preindustrial attitudes and in reaction to the rising spirit of bourgeois liberal pacifism, this movement extolled international conflict and war as instruments of progress and expressed a strong preference for "total" war and the all-out offensive in contrast to unheroic and inconclusive limited wars. But it is important to note that this glorification of war and the war system still assumed that war was either so quick and decisive as to be moderate in its destructiveness or else so intense as to be increasingly rare. . . .

The romanticization of the military ethic reached its ultimate political expression in imperialism, rationalized by the Darwinian doctrine of the survival of the fittest through constant struggle. Yet political Darwinism was really the dying, though vociferous, gasp of laissez faire in international theory. While the militant spirit continued to grow more popular and vocal, the liberal opposition to war and power politics also grew stronger. By the beginning of the twentieth century, the organized peace movement, now appealing directly to governments, had become a powerful voice in political life and diplomacy—witness the two Hague disarmament conferences and the active concern of governments with arbitration treaties. The argument about war's wastefulness and irrationality (by then called "obsolescence") had gained new force with the spectacular advance of industrialism and commerce and the growing interdependence of military preparedness and civilian economy.

To be sure, on the eve of World War I public spokesmen could still rattle the national sword with an exuberant spirit of military adventure and glory without being considered eccentric or evil. The patriotic thirst for military pageantry and excitement reached its height. Nations could face war with unabashed crusading zeal, exulting in the prospect and then in the reality with a passion more intense than was ever attained in the real Crusades. Yet this was probably the final spasm of massive military enthusiasm in the advanced democratic states. World War I killed the romance in war—except in a tragic or personal sense—and destroyed man's confidence in the beneficence of military laissez faire. The Fascist glorification of war was an evil aberration and seemed so at the time.

One should not depreciate the practical significance of the spreading popular aversion to force and the declining legitimacy of acquisitive war, which has been voiced so conspicuously since World War I, simply because of the continuing discrepancy between the ideal and reality of international politics. The widespread revulsion against the Religious Wars and the Napoleonic Wars probably had more to do with the moderation of war and politics in the eighteenth century and the resolution of crises short of war in the nineteenth than any of the so-called objective factors of international politics. Similarly, the widespread revulsion against war, international laissez faire, and military preparedness after World War I had a decisive impact upon international order. Its impact, unfortunately, was largely negative because it was accompanied by an aversion to the calculated management of force as an instrument of policy.

In the nuclear age preoccupation with the avoidance of war between nuclear powers and their allies has tempered the aversion to war with a novel respect for deterrence and the contrived control of force. It remains to be seen whether it has also created a more stable international order, or only the complacent illusion of self-sustaining order that has eventually proved the nemesis of every other period of equilibrium.

The Diplomacy of Violence

THOMAS C. SCHELLING

The usual distinction between diplomacy and force is not merely in the instruments, words or bullets, but in the relation between adversaries —in the interplay of motives and the role of communication, understandings, compromise, and restraint. Diplomacy is bargaining; it seeks outcomes that, though not ideal for either party, are better for both than some of the alternatives. In diplomacy each party somewhat controls what the other wants, and can get more by compromise, exchange, or collaboration than by taking things in his own hands and ignoring the other's wishes. The bargaining can be polite or rude, entail threats as well as offers, assume a status quo or ignore all rights and privileges, and assume mistrust rather than trust. But whether polite or impolite, constructive or aggressive, respectful or vicious, whether it occurs among friends or antagonists and whether or not there is a basis for trust and goodwill, there must be some common interest, if only in the avoidance of mutual damage, and an awareness of the need to make the other party prefer an outcome acceptable to oneself.

With enough military force a country may not need to bargain. Some things a country wants it can take, and some things it has it can keep, by sheer strength, skill, and ingenuity. It can do this *forcibly*, accommodating only to opposing strength, skill and ingenuity and without trying to appeal to an enemy's wishes. Forcibly a country can repel and expel, penetrate and occupy, seize, exterminate, disarm and disable, confine, deny access, and directly frustrate intrusion or attack. It can, that is, if it has enough strength. "Enough" depends on how much an opponent has.

There is something else, though, that force can do. It is less military, less heroic, less impersonal, and less unilateral; it is uglier, and has received less attention in Western military strategy. In addition to seizing and holding, disarming and confining, penetrating and obstructing, and all that, military force can be used *to hurt*. In addition to taking and protecting things of value it can *destroy* value. In

From *Arms and Influence* by Thomas C. Schelling. Copyright © 1966 by Yale University, pp. 1–10 and 12–34. Reprinted by permission of the publisher, Yale University Press. Portions of the text and some footnotes have been omitted.

101

addition to weakening an enemy militarily it can cause an enemy plain suffering.

Pain and shock, loss and grief, privation and horror are always in some degree, sometimes in terrible degree, among the results of warfare; but in traditional military science they are incidental, they are not the object. If violence can be done incidentally, though, it can also be done purposely. The power to hurt can be counted among the most impressive attributes of military force.

Hurting, unlike forcible seizure or self-defense, is not unconcerned with the interest of others. It is measured in the suffering it can cause and the victims' motivation to avoid it. Forcible action will work against weeds or floods as well as against armies, but suffering requires a victim that can feel pain or has something to lose. To inflict suffering gains nothing and saves nothing directly; it can only make people behave to avoid it. The only purpose, unless sport or revenge, must be to influence somebody's behavior, to coerce his decision or choice. To be coercive, violence has to be anticipated. And it has to be avoidable by accommodation. The power to hurt is bargaining power. To exploit it is diplomacy—vicious diplomacy, but diplomacy.

THE CONTRAST OF BRUTE FORCE WITH COERCION

There is a difference between taking what you want and making someone give it to you, between fending off assault and making someone afraid to assault you, between holding what people are trying to take and making them afraid to take it, between losing what someone can forcibly take and giving it up to avoid risk or damage. It is the difference between defense and deterrence, between brute force and intimidation, between conquest and blackmail, between action and threats. It is the difference between the unilateral, "undiplomatic" recourse to strength, and coercive diplomacy based on the power to hurt.

The contrasts are several. The purely "military" or "undiplomatic" recourse to forcible action is concerned with enemy strength, not enemy interests; the coercive use of the power to hurt, though, is the very exploitation of enemy wants and fears. And brute strength is usually measured relative to enemy strength, the one directly opposing the other, while the power to hurt is typically not reduced by the enemy's power to hurt in return. Opposing strengths may cancel each other, pain and grief do not. The willingness to hurt, the credibility of a threat, and the ability to exploit the power to hurt will indeed depend on how much the adversary can hurt in return; but there is little or nothing about an adversary's pain or grief that directly reduces one's own. Two sides cannot both overcome each other with superior strength; they may both be able to hurt each other. With strength they can dispute objects of value; with sheer violence they can destroy them.

And brute force succeeds when it is used, whereas the power to hurt is most successful when held in reserve. It is the *threat* of damage, or of more damage to come, that can make someone yield or comply. It is *latent* violence that can influence someone's choice—violence that can still be withheld or inflicted, or that a victim believes can be withheld or inflicted. The threat of pain tries to structure someone's motives, while brute force tries to overcome his strength. Unhappily, the power to hurt is often communicated by some performance of it. Whether it is sheer terroristic violence to induce an irrational response, or cool premeditated violence to persuade somebody that you mean it and may do it again, it is not the pain and damage itself but its influence on somebody's behavior that matters. It is the expectation of *more* violence that gets the wanted behavior, if the power to hurt can get it at all.

To exploit a capacity for hurting and inflicting damage one needs to know what an adversary treasures and what scares him and one needs the adversary to understand what behavior of his will cause the violence to be inflicted and what will cause it to be withheld. The victim has to know what is wanted, and he may have to be assured of what is not wanted. The pain and suffering have to appear *contingent* on his behavior; it is not alone the threat that is effective—the threat of pain or loss if he fails to comply—but the corresponding assurance, possibly an implicit one, that he can avoid the pain or loss if he does comply. The prospect of certain death may stun him, but it gives him no choice.

Coercion by threat of damage also requires that our interests and our opponent's not be absolutely opposed. If his pain were our greatest delight and our satisfaction his greatest woe, we would just proceed to hurt and to frustrate each other. It is when his pain gives us little or no satisfaction compared with what he can do for us, and the action or inaction that satisfies us costs him less than the pain we can cause, that there is room for coercion. Coercion requires finding a bargain, arranging for him to be better off doing what we want—worse off not only doing what we want—when he takes the threatened penalty into account.

It is this capacity for pure damage, pure violence, that is usually associated with the most vicious labor disputes, with racial disorders, with civil uprisings and their suppression, with racketeering. It is also the power to hurt rather than brute force that we use in dealing with criminals; we hurt them afterward, or threaten to, for their misdeeds rather than protect ourselves with cordons of electric wires, masonry walls, and armed guards. Jail, of course, can be either forcible restraint or threatened privation; if the object is to keep criminals out of mischief by confinement, success is measured by how many of them are gotten behind bars, but if the object is to *threaten* privation, success will be measured by how few have to be put behind bars and success then depends on the subject's understanding of the consequences. Pure damage is what a car threatens when it tries to hog the road or to keep its rightful share, or to go first through an intersection. A tank or a bulldozer can force its way regardless of others' wishes; the rest of us have to threaten damage, usually mutual damage, hoping the other driver values his car or his limbs enough to give way, hoping he sees us, and hoping he is in control of his own car. The threat of pure damage will not work against an unmanned vehicle.

This difference between coercion and brute force is as often in the intent as in the instrument. To hunt down Comanches and to exterminate them was brute force; to raid their villages to make them behave was coercive diplomacy, based on the power to hurt. The pain and loss to the Indians might have looked much the same one way as the other; the difference was one of purpose and effect. If Indians were killed because they were in the way, or somebody wanted their land, or the authorities despaired of making them behave and could not confine them and decided to exterminate them, that was pure unilateral force. If *some* Indians were killed to make *other* Indians behave, that was coercive violence—or intended to be, whether or not if was effective. The Germans at Verdun perceived themselves to be chewing up hundreds of thousands of French soldiers in a gruesome "meatgrinder." If the purpose was to eliminate a military obstacle— the French infantryman, viewed as a military "asset" rather than as a warm human being—the offensive at Verdun was a unilateral exercise of military force. If instead the object was to make the loss of young men—not of impersonal "effectives," but of sons, husbands, fathers, and the pride of French manhood—so anguishing as to be unendurable, to make surrender a welcome relief and to spoil the foretaste of an Allied victory, then it was an exercise in coercion, in applied violence, intended to offer relief upon accommodation. And of course, since any use of force tends to be brutal, thoughtless, vengeful, or plain obstinate, the motives themselves can be mixed and confused. The fact that heroism and brutality can be either coercive diplomacy or a contest in pure strength does not promise that the distinction will be made, and the strategies enlightened by the distinction, every time some vicious enterprise gets launched.

The contrast between brute force and coercion is illustrated by two alternative strategies attributed to Genghis Khan. Early in his career he pursued the war creed of the Mongols: the vanquished can never be the friends of the victors, their death is necessary for the victors' safety. This was the unilateral extermination of a menace or a liability. The turning point of his career, according to Lynn Montross, came later when he discovered how to use his power to hurt for diplomatic ends. "The great Khan, who was not inhibited by the usual mercies,

conceived the plan of forcing captives—women, children, aged
fathers, favorite sons—to march ahead of his army as the first potential victims of resistance.''[1] Live captives have often proved more
valuable than enemy dead; and the technique discovered by the Khan
in his maturity remains contemporary. North Koreans and Chinese
were reported to have quartered prisoners of war near strategic targets
to inhibit bombing attacks by United Nations aircraft. Hostages
represent the power to hurt in its purest form.

COERCIVE VIOLENCE IN WARFARE

This distinction between the power to hurt and the power to seize or
hold forcibly is important in modern war, both big war and little war,
hypothetical war and real war. For many years the Greeks and the
Turks on Cyprus could hurt each other indefinitely but neither could
quite take or hold forcibly what they wanted or protect themselves
from violence by physical means. The Jews in Palestine could not expel the British in the late 1940s but they could cause pain and fear and
frustration through terrorism, and eventually influence somebody's
decision. The brutal war in Algeria was more a contest in pure
violence than in military strength; the question was who would first
find the pain and degradation unendurable. The French troops
preferred—indeed they continually tried—to make it a contest of
strength, to pit military force against the nationalists' capacity for terror, to exterminate or disable the nationalists and to screen off the
nationalists from the victims of their violence. But because in civil war
terrorists commonly have access to victims by sheer physical propinquity, the victims and their properties could not be forcibly defended
and in the end the French troops themselves resorted, unsuccessfully,
to a war of pain.

Nobody believes that the Russians can take Hawaii from us, or
New York, or Chicago, but nobody doubts that they might destroy
people and buildings in Hawaii, Chicago, or New York. Whether the
Russians can conquer West Germany in any meaningful sense is questionable; whether they can hurt it terribly is not doubted. That the
United States can destroy a large part of Russia is universally taken
for granted; that the United States can keep from being badly hurt,
even devastated, in return, or can keep Western Europe from being
devastated while itself destroying Russia, is at best arguable; and it is
virtually out of the question that we could conquer Russia territorially
and use its economic assets unless it were by threatening disaster and
inducing compliance. It is the power to hurt, not military strength in
the traditional sense, that inheres in our most impressive military

---

[1] Lynn Montross, *War Through the Ages* (3rd ed., New York, Harper, and
Brothers, 1960), p. 146.

capabilities at the present time. We have a Department of *Defense* but emphasize *retaliation*—"to return evil for evil" (synonyms: requital, reprisal, revenge, vengeance, retribution). And it is pain and violence, not force in the traditional sense, that inhere also in some of the least impressive military capabilities of the present time—the plastic bomb, the terrorist's bullet, the burnt crops, and the tortured farmer.

War appears to be, or threatens to be, not so much a contest of strength as one of endurance, nerve, obstinacy, and pain. It appears to be, and threatens to be, not so much a contest of military strength as a bargaining process—dirty, extortionate, and often quite reluctant bargaining on one side or both—nevertheless a bargaining process.

The difference cannot quite be expressed as one between the *use* of force and the *threat* of force. The actions involved in forcible accomplishment, on the one hand, and in fulfilling a threat, on the other, can be quite different. Sometimes the most effective direct action inflicts enough cost or pain on the enemy to serve as a threat, sometimes not. The United States threatens the Soviet Union with virtual destruction of its society in the event of a surprise attack on the United States; a hundred million deaths are awesome as pure damage, but they are useless in stopping the Soviet attack—especially if the threat is to do it all afterward anyway. So it is worthwhile to keep the concepts distinct—to distinguish forcible action from the threat of pain—recognizing that some actions serve as both a means of forcible accomplishment and a means of inflicting pure damage, some do not. Hostages tend to entail almost pure pain and damage, as do all forms of reprisal after the fact. Some modes of self-defense may exact so little in blood or treasure as to entail negligible violence; and some forcible actions entail so much violence that their threat can be effective by itself.

The power to hurt, though it can usually accomplish nothing directly, is potentially more versatile than a straightforward capacity for forcible accomplishment. By force alone we cannot even lead a horse to water—we have to drag him—much less make him drink. Any affirmative action, any collaboration, almost anything but physical exclusion, expulsion, or extermination, requires that an opponent or a victim *do* something, even if only to stop or get out. The threat of pain and damage may make him want to do it, and anything he can do is potentially susceptible to inducement. Brute force can only accomplish what requires no collaboration. The principle is illustrated by a technique of unarmed combat: one can disable a man by various stunning, fracturing, or killing blows, but to take him to jail one has to exploit the man's own efforts. "Come-along" holds are those that threaten pain or disablement, giving relief as long as the victim complies, giving him the option of using his own legs to get to jail. . . .

The fact that violence—pure pain and damage—can be used or threatened to coerce and to deter, to intimidate and to blackmail, to demoralize and to paralyze, in a conscious process of dirty bargaining, does not by any means imply that violence is not often wanton and meaningless or, even when purposive, in danger of getting out of hand. Ancient wars were often quite "total" for the loser, the men being put to death, the women sold as slaves, the boys castrated, the cattle slaughtered, and the buildings leveled, for the sake of revenge, justice, personal gain, or merely custom. If an enemy bombs a city, by design or by carelessness, we usually bomb his if we can. In the excitement and fatigue of warfare, revenge is one of the few satisfactions that can be savored. . . . Pure violence, like fire, can be harnessed to a purpose; that does not mean that behind every holocaust is a shrewd intention successfully fulfilled.

But if the occurrence of violence does not always bespeak a shrewd purpose, the absence of pain and destruction is no sign that violence was idle. Violence is most purposive and most successful when it is threatened and not used. Successful threats are those that do not have to be carried out. By European standards, Denmark was virtually unharmed in the Second World War; it was violence that made the Danes submit. Withheld violence—successfully threatened violence—can look clean, even merciful. The fact that a kidnap victim is returned unharmed, against receipt of ample ransom, does not make kidnapping a nonviolent enterprise. The American victory at Mexico City in 1847 was a great success; with a minimum of brutality we traded a capital city for everything we wanted from the war. We did not even have to say what we could do to Mexico City to make the Mexican government understand what they had at stake. (They had undoubtedly got the message a month earlier, when Vera Cruz was being pounded into submission. . . .)

Whether spoken or not, the threat is usually there. . . .

THE STRATEGIC ROLE OF PAIN AND DAMAGE

Pure violence, nonmilitary violence, appears most conspicuously in relations between unequal countries, where there is no substantial military challenge and the outcome of military engagement is not in question. Hitler could make his threats contemptuously and brutally against Austria; he could make them, if he wished, in a more refined way against Denmark. It is noteworthy that it was Hitler, not his generals, who used this kind of language; proud military establishments do not like to think of themselves as extortionists. Their favorite job is to deliver victory, to dispose of opposing military force and to leave most of the civilian violence to politics and diplomacy. But if there is no room for doubt how a contest in strength will come out, it may be possible to bypass the military stage altogether and to proceed at once to the coercive bargaining.

A typical confrontation of unequal forces occurs at the *end* of a war, between victor and vanquished. Where Austria was vulnerable before a shot was fired, France was vulnerable after its military shield had collapsed in 1940. Surrender negotiations are the place where the threat of civil violence can come to the fore. Surrender negotiations are often so one-sided, or the potential violence so unmistakable, that bargaining succeeds and the violence remains in reserve. But the fact that most of the actual damage was done during the military stage of the war, prior to victory and defeat, does not mean that violence was idle in the aftermath, only that it was latent and the threat of it successful. . . .

. . . The Russians crushed Budapest in 1956 and cowed Poland and other neighboring countries. There was a lag of ten years between military victory and this show of violence, but the principle was the one [just] explained. . . . Military victory is often the prelude to violence, not the end of it, and the fact that successful violence is usually held in reserve should not deceive us about the role it plays.

What about pure violence during war itself, the infliction of pain and suffering as a military technique? Is the threat of pain involved only in the political use of victory, or is it a decisive technique of war itself?

Evidently between unequal powers it has been part of warfare. Colonial conquest has often been a matter of "punitive expeditions" rather than genuine military engagements. If the tribesmen escape into the brush you can burn their villages without them until they assent to receive what, in strikingly modern language, used to be known as the Queen's "protection." . . .

Pure hurting, as a military tactic, appeared in some of the military actions against the plains Indians. In 1868, during the war with the Cheyennes, General Sheridan decided that his best hope was to attack the Indians in their winter camps. His reasoning was that the Indians could maraud as they pleased during the seasons when their ponies could subsist on grass, and in the winter hide away in remote places. "To disabuse their minds from the idea that they were secure from punishment, and to strike at a period when they were helpless to move their stock and villages, a winter campaign was projected against the large bands hiding away in the Indian territory."[2]

These were not military engagements; they were punitive attacks on people. They were an effort to subdue by the use of violence, without a futile attempt to draw the enemy's military forces into decisive battle. They were "massive retaliation" on a diminutive scale, with

---

[2] Paul I. Wellman, *Death on the Prairie* (New York, Macmillan, 1934), p. 82.

local effects not unlike those of Hiroshima. The Indians themselves totally lacked organization and discipline, and typically could not afford enough ammunition for target practice and were no military match for the cavalry; their own rudimentary strategy was at best one of harassment and reprisal. Half a century of Indian fighting in the West left us a legacy of cavalry tactics; but it is hard to find a serious treatise on American strategy against the Indians or Indian strategy against the whites. The twentieth is not the first century in which "retaliation" has been part of our strategy, but it is the first in which we have systematically recognized it.

Hurting, as a strategy, showed up in the American Civil War, but as an episode, not as the central strategy. For the most part, the Civil War was a military engagement with each side's military force pitted against the other's. The Confederate forces hoped to lay waste enough Union territory to negotiate their independence, but hadn't enough capacity for such violence to make it work. The Union forces were intent on military victory, and it was mainly General Sherman's march through Georgia that showed a conscious and articulate use of violence. "If the people raise a howl against my barbarity and cruelty, I will answer that war is war. . . . If they want peace, they and their relatives must stop the war," Sherman wrote. And one of his associates said, "Sherman is perfectly right. . . . The only possible way to end this unhappy and dreadful conflict . . . is to make it terrible beyond endurance."[3]

Making it "terrible beyond endurance" is what we associate with Algeria and Palestine, the crushing of Budapest, and the tribal warfare in Central Africa. But in the great wars of the last hundred years it was usually military victory, not the hurting of the people, that was decisive; General Sherman's attempt to make war hell for the Southern people did not come to epitomize military strategy for the century to follow. To seek out and to destroy the enemy's military force, to achieve a crushing victory over enemy armies, was still the avowed purpose and the central aim of American strategy in both world wars. Military action was seen as an *alternative* to bargaining, not a *process* of bargaining.

The reason is not that civilized countries are so averse to hurting people that they prefer "purely military" wars. (Nor were all of the participants in these wars entirely civilized.) The reason is apparently

[3] J. F. C. Fuller reproduces some of this correspondence and remarks, "For the nineteenth century this was a new conception, because it meant that the deciding factor in the war—the power to sue for peace—was transferred from government to people, and that peace-making was a product of revolution. This was to carry the principle of democracy to its ultimate stage. . . ." *The Conduct of War: 1789-1961* (New Brunswick, Rutgers University Press, 1961), pp. 107-12.

that the technology and geography of warfare, at least for a war between anything like equal powers during the century ending in World War II, kept coercive violence from being decisive before military victory was achieved. Blockade indeed was aimed at the whole enemy nation, not concentrated on its military forces; the German civilians who died of influenza in the First World War were victims of violence directed at the whole country. It has never been quite clear whether blockade—of the South in the Civil War or of the Central Powers in both world wars, or submarine warfare against Britain—was expected to make war unendurable for the people or just to weaken the enemy forces by denying economic support. Both arguments were made, but there was no need to be clear about the purpose as long as either purpose was regarded as legitimate and either might be served. "Strategic bombing" of enemy homelands was also occasionally rationalized in terms of the pain and privation it could inflict on people and the civil damage it could do to the nation, as an effort to display either to the population or to the enemy leadership that surrender was better than persistence in view of the damage that could be done. It was also rationalized in more "military" terms, as a way of selectively denying war material to the troops or as a way of generally weakening the economy on which the military effort rested.

But terrorism—as violence intended to coerce the enemy rather than to weaken him militarily—blockade and strategic bombing by themselves were not quite up to the job in either world war in Europe. (They might have been sufficient in the war with Japan after straightforward military action had brought American aircraft into range.) Airplanes could not quite make punitive, coercive violence decisive in Europe, at least on a tolerable time schedule, and preclude the need to defeat or to destroy enemy forces as long as they had nothing but conventional explosives and incendiaries to carry. Hitler's V-1 buzz bomb and his V-2 rocket are fairly pure cases of weapons whose purpose was to intimidate, to hurt Britain itself rather than Allied military forces. What the V-2 needed was a punitive payload worth carrying, and the Germans did not have it. Some of the expectations in the 1920s and the 1930s that another major war would be one of pure civilian violence, of shock and terror from the skies, were not borne out by the available technology. The threat of punitive violence kept occupied countries quiescent; but the wars were won in Europe on the basis of brute strength and skill and not by intimidation, not by the threat of civilian violence but by the application of military force. Military victory was still the price of admission. Latent violence against people was reserved for the politics of surrender and occupation.

The great exception was the two atomic bombs on Japanese cities. These were weapons of terror and shock. They hurt, and promised more hurt, and that was their purpose. The few "small" weapons we had were undoubtedly of some direct military value, but their enormous advantage was in pure violence. In a military sense the United States could gain a little by destruction of two Japanese industrial cities; in a civilian sense, the Japanese could lose much. The bomb that hit Hiroshima was a threat aimed at all of Japan. The political target of the bomb was not the dead of Hiroshima or the factories they worked in, but the survivors in Tokyo. The two bombs were in the tradition of Sheridan against the Comanches and Sherman in Georgia. Whether in the end those two bombs saved lives or wasted them, Japanese lives or American lives; whether punitive coercive violence is uglier than straightforward military force or more civilized; whether terror is more or less humane than military destruction; we can at least perceive that the bombs on Hiroshima and Nagasaki represented violence against the country itself and not mainly an attack on Japan's material strength. The effect of the bombs, and their purpose, was not mainly the military destruction they accomplished but the pain and shock and the promise of more.

THE NUCLEAR CONTRIBUTION TO
TERROR AND VIOLENCE

Man has, it is said, for the first time in history enough military power to eliminate his species from the earth, weapons against which there is no conceivable defense. War has become, it is said, so destructive and terrible that it ceases to be an instrument of national power. "For the first time in human history," says Max Lerner in a book whose title, *The Age of Overkill*, conveys the point, "men have bottled up a power . . . which they have thus far not dared to use." And Soviet military authorities, whose party dislikes having to accommodate an entire theory of history to a single technological event, have had to re-examine a set of principles that had been given the embarrassing name of "permanently operating factors" in warfare. Indeed, our era is epitomized by words like "the first time in human history," and by the abdication of what was "permanent."

For dramatic impact these statements are splendid. Some of them display a tendency, not at all necessary, to belittle the catastrophe of earlier wars. They may exaggerate the historical novelty of deterrence and the balance of terror.[4] More important, they do not help to iden-

---

[4] Winston Churchill is often credited with the term, "balance of terror," and the following quotation succinctly expresses the familiar notion of nuclear mutual deterrence. This, though, is from a speech in Commons in November 1934. "The fact remains that when all is said and done as regards defensive methods, pending some new discovery the only direct measure of defense upon a great scale is the certainty of being able to inflict simultaneously upon the enemy as great damage as he can inflict upon ourselves. Do not let us undervalue the efficacy of this procedure. It may well prove in

tify just what is new about war when so much destructive energy can be packed in warheads at a price that permits advanced countries to have them in large numbers. Nuclear warheads are incomparably more devastating than anything packaged before. What does that imply about war?

It is not true that for the first time in history man has the capability to destroy a large fraction, even the major part, of the human race. Japan was defenseless by August 1945. With a combination of bombing and blockade, eventually invasion, and if necessary the deliberate spread of disease, the United States could probably have exterminated the population of the Japanese islands without nuclear weapons. . . .

It is a grisly thing to talk about. We did not do it and it is not imaginable that we would have done it. We had no reason; if we had had a reason, we would not have had the persistence of purpose, once the fury of war had been dissipated in victory and we had taken on the task of executioner. If we and our enemies might do such a thing to each other now, and to others as well, it is not because nuclear weapons have for the first time made it feasible.

Nuclear weapons can do it quickly. . . . To compress a catastrophic war within the span of time that a man can stay awake drastically changes the politics of war, the process of decision, the possibility of central control and restraint, the motivations of people in charge, and the capacity to think and reflect while war is in progress. It *is* imaginable that we might destroy 200,000,000 Russians in a war of the present, though not 80,000,000 Japanese in a war of the past. It is not only imaginable, it is imagined. It is imaginable because it could be done "in a moment, in the twinkling of an eye, at the last trumpet."

This may be why there is so little discussion of how an all-out war might be brought to a close. People do not expect it to be "brought" to a close, but just to come to an end when everything has been spent. It is also why the idea of "limited war" has become so explicit in recent years. Earlier wars, like World Wars I and II or the Franco-Prussian War, were limited by *termination*, by an ending that occurred before the period of greatest potential violence, by negotiation that brought the *threat* of pain and privation to bear but often precluded the massive *exercise* of civilian violence. With nuclear weapons available, the restraint of violence cannot await the outcome of a contest of military strength; restraint, to occur at all, must occur during war itself.

This is a difference between nuclear weapons and bayonets. It is not in the number of people they can eventually kill but in the speed

---

practice—I admit I cannot prove it in theory—capable of giving complete immunity. If two Powers show themselves equally capable of inflicting damage upon each other by some particular process of war, so that neither gains an advantage from its adoption and both suffer the most hideous reciprocal injuries, it is not only possible but it seems probable that neither will employ that means. . . ."

with which it can be done, in the centralization of decision, in the divorce of the war from political processes, and in computerized programs that threaten to take the war out of human hands once it begins.

That nuclear weapons make it *possible* to compress the fury of global war into a few hours does not mean that they make it *inevitable*. We have still to ask whether that is the way a major nuclear war would be fought, or ought to be fought. Nevertheless, that the whole war might go off like one big string of firecrackers makes a critical difference between our conception of nuclear war and the world wars we have experienced.

There is no guarantee, of course, that a slower war would not persist. The First World War could have stopped at any time after the Battle of the Marne. There was plenty of time to think about war aims, to consult the long-range national interest, to reflect on costs and casualties already incurred and the prospect of more to come, and to discuss terms of cessation with the enemy. The gruesome business continued as mechanically as if it had been in the hands of computers (or worse: computers might have been programmed to learn more quickly from experience). One may even suppose it would have been a blessing had all the pain and shock of the four years been compressed within four days. Still, it was terminated. And the victors had no stomach for doing then with bayonets what nuclear weapons could do to the German people today.

There is another difference. In the past it has usually been the victors who could do what they pleased to the enemy. War has often been "total war" for the loser. With deadly monotony the Persians, Greeks, or Romans "put to death all men of military age, and sold the women and children into slavery," leaving the defeated territory nothing but its name until new settlers arrived sometime later. But the defeated could not do the same to their victors. The boys could be castrated and sold only after the war had been won, and only on the side that lost it. The power to hurt could be brought to bear only after military strength had achieved victory. The same sequence characterized the great wars of this century; for reasons of technology and geography, military force has usually had to penetrate, to exhaust, or to collapse opposing military force—to achieve military victory—before it could be brought to bear on the enemy nation itself. The Allies in World War I could not inflict coercive pain and suffering directly on the Germans in a decisive way until they could defeat the German army; and the Germans could not coerce the French people with bayonets unless they first beat the Allied troops that stood in their way. With two-dimensional warfare, there is a tendency for troops to confront each other, shielding their own lands while attempting to press into each other's. Small penetrations could not do major damage to the people; large penetrations were so destructive of military organization that they usually ended the military phase of the war.

Nuclear weapons make it possible to do monstrous violence to the enemy without first achieving victory. With nuclear weapons and today's means of delivery, one expects to penetrate an enemy homeland without first collapsing his military force. What nuclear weapons have done, or appear to do, is to promote this kind of warfare to first place. Nuclear weapons threaten to make war less military, and are responsible for the lowered status of "military victory" at the present time. *Victory is no longer a prerequisite for hurting the enemy.* And it is no assurance against being terribly hurt. One need not wait until he has won the war before inflicting "unendurable" damages on his enemy. One need not wait until he has lost the war. There was a time when the assurance of victory—false or genuine assurance—could make national leaders not just willing but sometimes enthusiastic about war. Not now.

Not only *can* nuclear weapons hurt the enemy before the war has been won, and perhaps hurt decisively enough to make the military engagement academic, but it is widely assumed that in a major war that is *all* they can do. Major war is often discussed as though it would be only a contest in national destruction. If this is indeed the case—if the destruction of cities and their populations has become, with nuclear weapons, the primary object in an all-out war—the sequence of war has been reversed. Instead of destroying enemy forces as a prelude to imposing one's will on the enemy nation, one would have to destroy the nation as a means or a prelude to destroying the enemy forces. If one cannot disable enemy forces without virtually destroying the country, the victor does not even have the option of sparing the conquered nation. He has already destroyed it. Even with blockade and strategic bombing it could be supposed that a country would be defeated before it was destroyed, or would elect surrender before annihilation had gone far. In the Civil War it could be hoped that the South would become too weak to fight before it became too weak to survive. For "all-out" war, nuclear weapons threaten to reverse this sequence.

So nuclear weapons do make a difference, marking an epoch in warfare. The difference is not just in the amount of destruction that can be accomplished but in the role of destruction and in the decision process. Nuclear weapons can change the speed of events, the control of events, the sequence of events, the relation of victor to vanquished, and the relation of homeland to fighting front. Deterrence rests today on the threat of pain and extinction, not just on the threat of military defeat. We may argue about the wisdom of announcing "unconditional surrender" as an aim in the last major war, but seem to expect "unconditional destruction" as a matter of course in another one.

Something like the same destruction always *could* be done. With nuclear weapons there is an expectation that it *would* be done. . . .

What is new is . . . the idea that major war might be just a contest in the killing of countries, or not even a contest but just two parallel exercises in devastation.

That is the difference nuclear weapons make. At least they *may* make that difference. They also may not. If the weapons themselves are vulnerable to attack, or the machines that carry them, a successful surprise might eliminate the opponent's means of retribution. That an enormous explosion can be packaged in a single bomb does not by itself guarantee that the victor will receive deadly punishment. Two gunfighters facing each other in a Western town had an unquestioned capacity to kill one another; that did not guarantee that both would die in a gunfight—only the slower of the two. Less deadly weapons, permitting an injured one to shoot back before he died, might have been more conducive to a restraining balance of terror, or of caution. The very efficiency of nuclear weapons could make them ideal for starting war, if they can suddenly eliminate the enemy's capability to shoot back.

And there is a contrary possibility: that nuclear weapons are not vulnerable to attack and prove not to be terribly effective against each other, posing no need to shoot them quickly for fear they will be destroyed before they are launched, and with no task available but the systematic destruction of the enemy country and no necessary reason to do it fast rather than slowly. Imagine that nuclear destruction *had* to go slowly—that the bombs could be dropped only one per day. The prospect would look very different, something like the most terroristic guerrilla warfare on a massive scale. It happens that nuclear war does not have to go slowly; but it may also not have to go speedily. The mere existence of nuclear weapons does not itself determine that everything must go off in a blinding flash, any more than that it must go slowly. Nuclear weapons do not simplify things quite that much.

In recent years there has been a new emphasis on distinguishing what nuclear weapons make possible and what they make inevitable in case of war. The American government began in 1961 to emphasize that even a major nuclear war might not, and need not, be a simple contest in destructive fury. Secretary McNamara gave a controversial speech in June of 1962 on the idea that "deterrence" might operate even in war itself, that belligerents might, out of self-interest, attempt to limit the war's destructiveness. Each might feel the sheer destruction of enemy people and cities would serve no decisive military purpose but that a continued *threat* to destroy them might serve a purpose. The continued threat would depend on their not being destroyed yet. Each might reciprocate the other's restraint, as in limited wars of lesser scope. Even the worst of enemies, in the interest of reciprocity, have often not mutilated prisoners of war; and citizens might deserve comparable treatment. The fury of nuclear attacks might fall mainly on each other's weapons and military forces.

"The United States has come to the conclusion," said Secretary McNamara,

> that to the extent feasible, basic military strategy in a possible general war should be approached in much the same way that more conventional military operations have been regarded in the past. That is to say, principal military objectives . . . should be the destruction of the enemy's military forces, not of his civilian population . . . giving the possible opponent the strongest imaginable incentive to refrain from striking our own cities.[5]

This is a sensible way to think about war, if one has to think about it and of course one does. But whether the Secretary's "new strategy" was sensible or not, whether enemy populations should be held hostage or instantly destroyed, whether the primary targets should be military forces or just people and their source of livelihood, this is not "much the same way that more conventional military operations have been regarded in the past." This is utterly different, and the difference deserves emphasis.

In World Wars I and II one went to work on enemy military forces, not his people, because until the enemy's military forces had been taken care of there was typically not anything decisive that one could do to the enemy nation itself. The Germans did not, in World War I, refrain from bayoneting French citizens by the millions in the hope that the Allies would abstain from shooting up the German population. They could not get at the French citizens until they had breached the Allied lines. Hitler tried to terrorize London and did not make it. The Allied air forces took the war straight to Hitler's territory, with at least some thought of doing in Germany what Sherman recognized he was doing in Georgia; but with the bombing technology of World War II one could not afford to bypass the troops and go exclusively for enemy populations—not, anyway, in Germany. With nuclear weapons one has that alternative.

To concentrate on the enemy's military installations while deliberately holding in reserve a massive capacity for destroying his cities, for exterminating his people and eliminating his society, on condition that the enemy observe similar restraint with respect to one's own society, is not the "conventional approach." In World Wars I and II the first order of business was to destroy enemy armed forces because that was the only promising way to make him surrender. To fight a purely military engagement "all-out" while holding in reserve

---

[5] Commencement Address, University of Michigan, June 16, 1962.

a decisive capacity for violence, on condition the enemy do likewise, is not the way military operations have traditionally been approached. Secretary McNamara was proposing a new approach to warfare in a new era, an era in which the power to hurt is more impressive than the power to oppose.

FROM BATTLEFIELD WARFARE TO THE DIPLOMACY OF VIOLENCE

Almost one hundred years before Secretary McNamara's speech, the Declaration of St. Petersburg (the first of the great modern conferences to cope with the evils of warfare) in 1868 asserted, "The only legitimate object which states should endeavor to accomplish during war is to weaken the military forces of the enemy." And in a letter to the League of Nations in 1920, the President of the International Committee of the Red Cross wrote; "The Committee considers it very desirable that war should resume its former character, that is to say, that it should be a struggle between armies and not between populations. The civilian population must, as far as possible, remain outside the struggle and its consequences."[6] His language is remarkably similar to Secretary McNamara's.

The International Committee was fated for disappointment, like everyone who labored in the late nineteenth century to devise rules that would make war more humane. When the Red Cross was founded in 1863, it was concerned about the disregard for noncombatants by those who made war; but in the Second World War noncombatants were deliberately chosen as targets by both Axis and Allied forces, not decisively but nevertheless deliberately. The trend has been the reverse of what the International Committee hoped for.

In the present era noncombatants appear to be not only deliberate targets but primary targets, or at least were so taken for granted until about the time of Secretary McNamara's speech. In fact, noncombatants appeared to be primary targets at both ends of the scale of warfare; thermonuclear war threatened to be a contest in the destruction of cities and populations; and, at the other end of the scale, insurgency is almost entirely terroristic. We live in an era of dirty war.

Why is this so? Is war properly a military affair among combatants, and is it a depravity peculiar to the twentieth century that we cannot keep it within decent bounds? Or is war inherently dirty, and was the Red Cross nostalgic for an artificial civilization in which war had become encrusted with etiquette—a situation to be welcomed but not expected?

---

[6] International Committee of the Red Cross, *Draft Rules for the Limitation of the Dangers Incurred by the Civilian Population in Time of War* (2nd ed., Geneva, 1958), pp. 144, 151.

To answer this question it is useful to distinguish three stages in the involvement of noncombatants—of plain people and their possessions —in the fury of war. These stages are worth distinguishing; but their sequence is merely descriptive of Western Europe during the past three hundred years, not a historical generalization. The first stage is that in which the people may get hurt by inconsiderate combatants. This is the status that people had during the period of "civilized warfare" that the International Committee had in mind.

From about 1648 to the Napoleonic era, war in much of Western Europe was something superimposed on society. It was a contest engaged in by monarchies for stakes that were measured in territories and, occasionally, money or dynastic claims. The troops were mostly mercenaries and the motivation for war was confined to the aristocratic elite. Monarchs fought for bits of territory, but the residents of disputed terrain were more concerned with protecting their crops and their daughters from marauding troops than with whom they owed allegiance to. They were, as Quincy Wright remarked in his classic *Study of War*, little concerned that the territory in which they lived had a new sovereign.[7] Furthermore, as far as the King of Prussia and the Emperor of Austria were concerned, the loyalty and enthusiasm of the Bohemian farmer were not decisive considerations. It is an exaggeration to refer to European war during this period as a sport of kings, but not a gross exaggeration. And the military logistics of those days confined military operations to a scale that did not require the enthusiasm of a multitude.

Hurting people was not a decisive instrument of warfare. Hurting people or destroying property only reduced the value of the things that were being fought over, to the disadvantage of both sides. Furthermore, the monarchs who conducted wars often did not want to discredit the social institutions they shared with their enemies. Bypassing an enemy monarch and taking the war straight to his people would have had revolutionary implications. Destroying the opposing monarchy was often not in the interest of either side; opposing sovereigns had much more in common with each other than with their own subjects, and to discredit the claims of a monarchy might have produced a disastrous backlash. It is not surprising—or, if it is surprising, not altogether astonishing—that on the European continent in that particular era war was fairly well confined to military activity.

One could still, in those days and in that part of the world, be concerned for the rights of noncombatants and hope to devise rules that both sides in the war might observe. The rules might well be observed because both sides had something to gain from preserving social order

---

[7] Chicago, University of Chicago Press, 1942, p. 296.

and not destroying the enemy. Rules might be a nuisance, but they restricted both sides the disadvantages might cancel out.

This was changed during the Napoleonic wars. In Napoleon's France, people cared about the outcome. The nation was mobilized. The war was a national effort, not just an activity of the elite. It was both political and military genius on the part of Napoleon and his ministers that an entire nation could be mobilized for war. Propaganda became a tool of warfare, and war became vulgarized.

Many writers deplored this popularization of war, this involvement of the democratic masses. In fact, the horrors we attribute to thermonuclear war were already foreseen by many commentators, some before the First World War and more after it; but the new "weapon" to which these terrors were ascribed was people, millions of people, passionately engaged in national wars, spending themselves in a quest for total victory and desperate to avoid total defeat. Today we are impressed that a small number of highly trained pilots can carry enough energy to blast and burn tens of millions of people and the buildings they live in; two or three generations ago there was concern that tens of millions of people using bayonets and barbed wire, machine guns and shrapnel, could create the same kind of destruction and disorder.

That was the second stage in the relation of people to war, the second in Europe since the middle of the seventeenth century. In the first stage people had been neutral but their welfare might be disregarded; in the seond stage people were involved because it was *their* war. Some fought, some produced materials of war, some produced food, and some took care of children; but they were all part of a war-making nation. When Hitler attacked Poland in 1939, the Poles had reason to care about the outcome. When Churchill said the British would fight on the beaches, he spoke for the British and not for a mercenary army. The war was about something that mattered. If people would rather fight a dirty war than lose a clean one, the war will be between nations and not just between governments. If people have an influence on whether the war is continued or on the terms of a truce, making the war hurt people serves a purpose. It is a dirty purpose, but war itself is often about something dirty. The Poles and the Norwegians, the Russians and the British, had reason to believe that if they lost the war the consequences would be dirty. This is so evident in modern civil wars—civil wars that involve popular feelings—that we expect them to be bloody and violent. To hope that they would be fought cleanly with no violence to people would be a little like hoping for a clean race riot.

There is another way to put it that helps to bring out the sequence of events. If a modern war were a clean one, the violence would not be ruled out but merely saved for the postwar period. Once the army has been defeated in the clean war, the victorious enemy can be as brutally coercive as he wishes. A clean war would determine which side gets to use its power to hurt coercively after victory, and it is likely to be worth some violence to avoid being the loser.

"Surrender" is the process following military hostilities in which the power to hurt is brought to bear. If surrender negotiations are successful and not followed by overt violence, it is because the capacity to inflict pain and damage was successfully used in the bargaining process. On the losing side, prospective pain and damage were averted by concessions; on the winning side, the capacity for inflicting further harm was traded for concessions. The same is true in a successful kidnapping. It only reminds us that the purpose of pure pain and damage is extortion; it is *latent* violence that can be used to advantage. A well-behaved occupied country is not one in which violence plays no part; it may be one in which latent violence is used so skillfully that it need not be spent in punishment.

This brings us to the third stage in the relation of civilian violence to warfare. If the pain and damage can be inflicted during war itself, they need not wait for the surrender negotiation that succeeds a military decision. If one can coerce people and their governments while war is going on, one does not need to wait until he has achieved victory or risk losing that coercive power by spending it all in a losing war. General Sherman's march through Georgia might have made as much sense, possibly more, had the North been losing the war, just as the German buzz bombs and V-2 rockets can be thought of as coercive instruments to get the war stopped before suffering military defeat.

In the present era, since at least the major East-West powers are capable of massive civilian violence during war itself beyond anything available during the Second World War, the occasion for restraint does not await the achievement of military victory or truce. The principal restraint during the Second World War was a temporal boundary, the date of surrender. In the present era we find the violence dramatically restrained during war itself. The Korean War was furiously "all-out" in the fighting, not only on the peninsular battlefield but in the resources used by both sides. It was "all-out," though, only within some dramatic restraints: no nuclear weapons, no Russians, no Chinese territory, no Japanese territory, no bombing of ships at sea or even airfields on the United Nations side of the line. It was a contest in military strength circumscribed by the threat of unprecedented civilian violence. Korea may or may not be a good model for speculation on limited war in the age of nuclear violence, but it was dramatic evidence that the capacity for violence can be consciously restrained even under the provocation of a war that measures its military dead in tens of thousands and that fully preoccupies two of the largest countries in the world.

A consequence of this third stage is that "victory" inadequately expresses what a nation wants from its military forces. Mostly it wants, in these times, the influence that resides in latent force. It wants the bargaining power that comes from its capacity to hurt, not just the direct consequence of successful military action. Even total victory over an enemy provides at best an opportunity for unopposed violence against the enemy population. How to use that opportunity in the national interest, or in some wider interest, can be just as important as the achievement of victory itself; but traditional military science does not tell us how to use that capacity for inflicting pain. And if a nation, victor or potential loser, is going to use its capacity for pure violence to influence the enemy, there may be no need to await the achievement of total victory.

Actually, this third stage can be analyzed into two quite different variants. In one, sheer pain and damage are primary instruments of coercive warfare and may actually be applied to intimidate or to deter. In the other, pain and destruction *in* war are expected to serve little or no purpose but *prior threats* of sheer violence, even of automatic and uncontrolled violence, are coupled to military force. The difference is in the all-or-none character of deterrence and intimidation. Two acute dilemmas arise. One is the choice of making prospective violence as frightening as possible or hedging with some capacity for reciprocated restraint. The other is the choice of making retaliation as automatic as possible or keeping deliberate control over the fateful decisions. The choices are determined partly by governments, partly by technology. Both variants are characterized by the coercive role of pain and destruction—of threatened (not inflicted) pain and destruction. But in one the threat either succeeds or fails altogether, and any ensuing violence is gratuitous; in the other, progressive pain and damage may actually be used to threaten more. The present era, for countries possessing nuclear weapons, is a complex and uncertain blend of the two.

Coercive diplomacy, based on the power to hurt, was important even in those periods of history when military force was essentially the power to take and to hold, to fend off attack and to expel invaders, and to possess territory against opposition—that is, in the era in which military force tended to pit itself against opposing force. Even then, a critical question was how much cost and pain the other side would incur for the disputed territory. The judgment that the Mexicans would concede Texas, New Mexico, and California once Mexico City was a hostage in our hands was a diplomatic judgment, not a military one. If one could not readily take the particular territory he wanted or hold it against attack, he could take something else and trade it. Judging what the enemy leaders would trade—be it a capital city or national survival—was a critical part of strategy even in the past. Now we are in an era in which the power to hurt—to inflict pain and shock and privation on a country itself, not just on its military forces—is commensurate with the power to take and to hold, perhaps more than commensurate, perhaps decisive, and it is even more necessary to think of warfare as a process of violent bargaining. This is not the first era in which live captives have been worth more than dead enemies, and the power to hurt has been a bargaining advantage; but it is the first in American experience when that kind of power has been a dominant part of military relations.

The power to hurt is nothing new in warfare, but for the United States modern technology has drastically enhanced the strategic importance of pure, unconstructive, unacquisitive pain and damage, whether used against us or in our own defense. This in turn enhances the importance of war and threats of war as techniques of influence, not of destruction; of coercion and deterrence, not of conquest and defense; of bargaining and intimidation.

Quincy Wright, in his *Study of War*, devoted a couple of pages (319–320) to the "nuisance value" of war, using the analogy of a bank robber with a bomb in his hand that would destory bank and robber. Nuisance value made the threat of war, according to Wright, "an aid to the diplomacy of unscrupulous governments." Now we need a stronger term, and more pages, to do the subject justice, and need to recognize that even scrupulous governments often have little else to rely on militarily. It is extraordinary how many treatises on war and strategy have declined to recognize that the power to hurt has been, throughout history, a fundamental character of military force and fundamental to the diplomacy based on it.

War no longer looks like just a contest of strength. War and the brink of war are more a contest of nerve and risk-taking, of pain and endurance. Small wars embody the threat of a larger war; they are not just military engagements but "crisis diplomacy." The threat of war has always been somewhere underneath international diplomacy, but for Americans it is now much nearer the surface. Like the threat of a strike in industrial relations, the threat of divorce in a family dispute, or the threat of bolting the party at a political convention, the threat of violence continuously circumscribes international politics. Neither strength nor goodwill procures immunity.

Military strategy can no longer be thought of, as it could for some countries in some eras, as the science of military victory. It is now equally, if not more, the art of coercion, of intimidation and deterrence. The instruments of war are more punitive than acquisitive. Military strategy, whether we like it or not, has become the diplomacy of violence.

Deterrence and Defense

GLENN H. SNYDER

National security still remains an "ambiguous symbol," as one
scholar described it almost a decade ago.[1] Certainly it has grown more
ambiguous as a result of the startling advances since then in nuclear
and weapons technology, and the advent of nuclear parity between the
United States and the Soviet Union. Besides such technological complications, doctrine and thought about the role of force in international politics have introduced additional complexities. We now have,
at least in embryonic form, theories of limited war, of deterrence, of
"tactical" vs. "strategic" uses of nuclear weapons, of "retaliatory"
vs. "counterforce" strategies in all-out war, of "limited retaliation,"
of the mechanics of threat and commitment-making, of "internal
war," "protracted conflict," and the like. Above all, the idea of the
"balance of terror" has begun to mature, but its relation to the older
concept of the "balance of power" is still not clear. We have had a
great intellectual ferment in the strategic realm, which of course is all
to the good. What urgently remains to be done is to tie together all of
these concepts into a coherent framework of theory so that the end-
goal of national security may become less ambiguous, and so that the
military means available for pursuance of this goal may be ac-
cumulated, organized, and used more efficiently. This book can claim
to make only a start in this direction.

The central theoretical problem in the field of national security
policy is to clarify and distinguish between the two central concepts of
deterrence and *defense*. Essentially, deterrence means discouraging
the enemy from taking military action by posing for him a prospect of
cost and risk outweighing his prospective gain. Defense means reducing our own prospective costs and risks in the event that deterrence
fails. Deterrence works on the enemy's *intentions*; the *deterrent value*

From *Deterrence and Defense: Toward a Theory of National Security* by Glenn H.
Snyder, pp. 3–16, 31, 33–40, 50, 97–109. Copyright © 1961 by Princeton University
Press. Reprinted by permission of Princeton University Press. Portions of the text and
some footnotes have been omitted.
    [1] Arnold Wolfers, " 'National Security' as an Ambiguous Symbol," *Political
Science Quarterly*, Vol. LXVII, No. 4 (December 1952), pp. 481ff.

of military forces is their effect in reducing the likelihood of enemy military moves. Defense reduces the enemy's *capability* to damage or deprive us; the *defense value* of military forces is their effect in mitigating the adverse consequences for us of possible enemy moves, whether such consequences are counted as losses of territory or war damage. The concept of "defense value," therefore, is broader than the mere capacity to hold territory, which might be called "denial capability." Defense value is denial capability plus capacity to alleviate war damage.

It is commonplace, of course, to say that the primary objectives of national security policy are to deter enemy attacks and to defend successfully, at minimum cost, against those attacks which occur. It is less widely recognized that different types of military force contribute in differing proportions to these two objectives. Deterrence does not vary directly with our capacity for fighting wars effectively and cheaply; a particular set of forces might produce strong deterrent effects and not provide a very effective denial and damage-alleviating capability. Conversely, forces effective for defense might be less potent deterrents than other forces which were less efficient for holding territory and which might involve extremely high war costs if used.

One reason why the periodic "great debates" about national security policy have been so inconclusive is that the participants often argue from different premises—one side from the point of view of deterrence, and the other side from the point of view of defense. For instance, in the famous "massive retaliation" debate of 1954, the late Secretary of State Dulles and his supporters argued mainly that a capacity for massive retaliation would deter potential Communist mischief, but they tended to ignore the consequences should deterrence fail. The critics, on the other hand, stressed the dire consequences should the threat of massive retaliation fail to deter and tended to ignore the possibility that it might work. The opposing arguments never really made contact because no one explicitly recognized that considerations of reducing the probability of war and mitigating its consequences must be evaluated simultaneously, that the possible consequences of a failure of deterrence are more or less important depending on the presumed likelihood of deterrence. Many other examples could be cited.

Perhaps the crucial difference between deterrence and defense is that deterrence is primarily a peacetime objective, while defense is a wartime value. Deterrent value and defense value are directly enjoyed in different time periods. We enjoy the deterrent value of our military forces prior to the enemy's aggressive move; we enjoy defense value after the enemy move has already been made, although we indirectly profit from defense capabilities in advance of war through our knowledge that if the enemy attack occurs we have the means of mitigating its consequences. The crucial point is that *after* the enemy's attack takes place, our military forces perform different functions and yield wholly different values than they did as deterrents prior to the attack. As deterrents they engaged in a psychological battle—dissuading the enemy from attacking by attempting to confront him with a prospect of costs greater than his prospective gain. After the enemy begins his attack, while the psychological or deterrent aspect does not entirely disappear, it is partly supplanted by another purpose: to resist the enemy's onslaught in order to minimize *our* losses or perhaps maximize *our* gains, not only with regard to the future balance of power, but also in terms of intrinsic or non-power values. That combination of forces which appeared to be the optimum one from the point of view of deterrence might turn out to be far inferior to some other combination from the point of view of defense should deterrence fail. In short, maximizing the enemy's cost expectancy may not always be consistent with minimizing our own. Thus we must measure the value of our military forces on two yardsticks, and we must find some way of combining their value on *both* yardsticks, in order accurately to gauge their aggregate worth or "utility" and to make intelligent choices among the various types of forces available.

Before launching into a theoretical analysis of the concepts of deterrence and defense, it may be useful to present a sampling of policy issues involving a need to choose between deterrence and defense; the examples will be treated in more detail in subsequent chapters.

EXAMPLES OF CHOICES AND CONFLICTS BETWEEN
DETERRENCE AND DEFENSE

A strategic retaliatory air force sufficient only to wreak minimum "unacceptable" damage on Soviet cities—to destroy, say, 20 cities—after this force has been decimated by a surprise Soviet nuclear attack, would have great value for deterring such a surprise attack and might be an adequate deterrent against that contingency. But if deterrence were to fail and the Soviet attack took place, it would then not be rational to *use* such a minimum force in massive retaliation against Soviet cities, since this would only stimulate the Soviets to inflict further damage upon us and would contribute nothing to our "winning the war." If we are interested in defense—i.e., in winning the war and in minimizing the damage to us—as well as in deterrence, we may wish to have (if technically feasible) a much larger force and probably one of different composition—a force which can strike effectively at the enemy's remaining forces (thus reducing our own costs) and, further, either by actual attacks or the threat of attacks, force the enemy to surrender or at least to give up his territorial gains.

The threat of massive nuclear retaliation against a Soviet major ground attack in Western Europe may continue to provide considerable deterrence against such an attack, even if actually to carry out the threat would be irrational because of the enormous costs we would suffer from Soviet counterretaliation. Strategic nuclear weapons do not provide a rational means of defense in Western Europe unless they not only can stop the Russian ground advance but also, by "counterforce" strikes, can reduce to an acceptable level the damage we would suffer in return. We may not have this capability now and it may become altogether infeasible as the Soviets develop their missile technology. For a means of rational defense, therefore, NATO may need enough ground forces to hold Europe against a full-scale attack by Soviet ground forces. This does not mean, however, that we necessarily must maintain ground forces of this size. If we think the probability of attack is low enough, we may decide to continue relying on nuclear deterrence primarily, even though it does not provide a rational means of defense. In other words, we might count on the Soviet uncertainties about whether or not nuclear retaliation is rational for us, and about how rational we are, to inhibit the Soviets from attacking in the face of the terrible damage they *know* they would suffer if they guessed wrong.

An attempt to build an effective counterforce capability, in order to have both a rational nuclear defense and a more credible nuclear deterrent against ground attack in Europe, might work against the *deterrence* of direct nuclear attack on the United States. Since such a force, by definition, would be able to eliminate all but a small fraction of the Soviet strategic nuclear forces if it struck first, the Soviets might, in some circumstances, fear a surprise attack and be led to strike first themselves in order to forestall it.

Tactical nuclear weapons in the hands of NATO forces in Europe have considerable deterrent value because they increase the enemy's cost expectation beyond what it would be if these forces were equipped only with conventional weapons. This is true not only because the tactical weapons themselves can inflict high costs on the enemy's forces, but also because their use (or an enemy "preemptive" strike against them) would sharply raise the probability that the war would spiral to all-out dimensions. But the defense value of tactical nuclear weapons against conventional attack is comparatively low against an enemy who also possesses them, because their use presumably would be offset by the enemy's use of them against our forces, and because in using such weapons we would be incurring much greater costs and risks than if we had responded conventionally.

For deterrence, it might be desirable to render automatic a response which the enemy recognizes as being costly for us, and communicate the fact of such automation to the enemy, thus reducing his doubts that we would actually choose to make this response when the occasion for it arose. For example, a tactical nuclear response to conventional aggression in Europe may be made semi-automatic by thoroughly orienting NATO plans, organization, and strategy around this response, thus increasing the difficulty of following a non-nuclear strategy in case of a Soviet challenge. But such automation would not be desirable for defense, which would require flexibility and freedom to choose the least costly action in the light of circumstances at the time of the attack.

The Continental European attitude toward NATO strategy is generally ambivalent on the question of deterrence vs. defense; there is fear that with the Soviet acquisition of a substantial nuclear and missile capability, the willingness of the United States to invoke massive retaliation is declining, and that therefore the deterrent to aggression has weakened. Yet the Europeans do not embrace the logical consequence of this fear: the need to build up an adequate capacity to defend Europe on the ground. A more favored alternative, at least in France, is the acquisition of an independent strategic nuclear capability. But when European governments project their imaginations forward to the day when the enemy's divisions cross their borders, do they really envisage themselves shooting off their few missiles against an enemy who would surely obliterate them in return? One doubts that they do, but this is not to say that it is irrational for them to acquire such weapons; they might be successful as a deterrent because of Soviet uncertainty as to whether they would be used, and Soviet unwillingness to incur the risk of their being used.

Further examples easily come to mind. For the sake of deterrence in Europe, we might wish to deploy the forces there as if they intended to respond to an attack with nuclear weapons; but this might not be the optimum deployment for defense once the attack has occurred, if the least-cost defense is a conventional one. For deterrence of limited aggressions in Asia, it might be best to deploy troops on the spot as a "plate-glass window." But for the most efficient and flexible defense against such contingencies, troops might better be concentrated in a central reserve, with transport facilities for moving them quickly to a threatened area.

As Bernard Brodie has written,[2] if the object of our strategic air forces is only deterrence, there is little point in developing "clean" bombs; since deterrence is to be effected by the threat of dire punishment, the dirtier the better. But if we also wish to minimize our own costs once the war has begun, we might wish to use bombs producing minimum fall-out, to encourage similar restraint in the enemy.

---

[2] Bernard Brodie, *Strategy in the Missile Age*, Princeton: Princeton University Press, 1959, p. 295.

For deterrence, it might be desirable to disperse elements of the Strategic Air Command to civilian airfields, thus increasing the number of targets which the enemy must hit if he is to achieve the necessary attrition of our retaliatory power by his first strike. However, this expedient might greatly increase the population damage we would suffer in the enemy's first strike, since most civilian airfields are located near large cities, assuming that the enemy would otherwise avoid hitting cities.

THE TECHNOLOGICAL REVOLUTION

The need to *choose* between deterrence and defense is largely the result of the development of nuclear and thermonuclear weapons and long-range airpower. Prior to these developments, the three primary functions of military force—to *punish* the enemy, to *deny* him territory (or to take it from him), and to *mitigate damage* to oneself— were embodied, more or less, in the same weapons. Deterrence was accomplished (to the extent that military capabilities were the instruments of deterrence) either by convincing the prospective aggressor that his territorial aim was likely to be frustrated, or by posing for him a prospect of intolerable cost, or both, but both of these deterrent functions were performed by the *same* forces. Moreover, these same forces were also the instruments of defense if deterrence failed.

Long-range airpower partially separated the function of punishment from the function of contesting the control of territory, by making possible the assault of targets far to the rear whose relation to the land battle might be quite tenuous. Nuclear weapons vastly increased the relative importance of prospective *cost* in deterring the enemy and reduced (relatively) the importance of frustrating his aggressive enterprise. It is still true, of course, that a capacity to deny territory to the enemy, or otherwise to block his aims, may be a very efficient deterrent. And such denial *may* be accomplished by strategic nuclear means, though at high cost to the defender. But it is now conceivable that a prospective aggressor may be deterred, in some circumstances at least, solely or primarily by threatening and possessing the capability to inflict extreme punishment on his homeland assets and population, even though he may be superior in capabilities for contesting the control of territory. Nuclear powers must, therefore, exercise a conscious choice between the objectives of deterrence and defense, since the relative proportion of "punishment capacity" to "denial capacity" in their military establishments has become a matter of choice.

This is the most striking difference between nuclear and prenuclear strategy: the partial separation of the functions of pre-attack deterrence and post-attack defense, and the possibility that deterrence may now be accomplished by weapons which might have no rational use for defense should deterrence fail.

DETERRENCE

Deterrence, in one sense, is simply the negative aspect of political power; it is the power to dissuade as opposed to the power to coerce or compel. One deters another party from doing something by the implicit or explicit threat of applying some sanction if the forbidden act is performed, or by the promise of a reward if the act is not performed. Thus conceived, deterrence does not have to depend on military force. We might speak of deterrence by the threat of trade restrictions, for example. The promise of economic aid might deter a country from military action (or any action) contrary to one's own interests. Or we might speak of the deterrence of allies and neutrals as well as potential enemies—as Italy, for example, was deterred from fighting on the side of the Dual Alliance in World War I by the promise of substantial territorial gains. In short, deterrence may follow, first, from any form of control which one has over an opponent's present and prospective "value inventory"; secondly, from the communication of a credible threat or promise to decrease or increase that inventory; and, thirdly, from the opponent's degree of confidence that one intends to fulfill the threat or promise.

In an even broader sense, however, deterrence is a function of the *total* cost-gain expectations of the party to be deterred, and these may be affected by factors other than the apparent capability and intention of the deterrer to apply punishments or confer rewards. For example, an incipient aggressor may be inhibited by his own conscience, or, more likely, by the prospect of losing moral standing, and hence political standing, with uncommitted countries. Or, in the specific case of the Soviet Union, he may fear that war will encourage unrest in, and possibly dissolution of, his satellite empire, and perhaps disaffection among his own population. He may anticipate that his aggression would bring about a tighter welding of the Western alliance or stimulate a degree of mobilization in the West which would either reduce his own security or greatly increase the cost of maintaining his position in the arms race. It is also worth noting that the benchmark or starting point for the potential aggressor's calculation of costs and gains from military action is not his *existing* value inventory, but the extent to which he expects that inventory to be changed if he refrains from initiating military action. Hence, the common observation that the Russians are unlikely to undertake overt military aggression because their chances are so good for making gains by "indirect" peaceful means. Conceivably the Soviets might attack the United States, even though they foresaw greater costs than gains, if the alternative of not attacking seemed to carry within it a strong possibility that the United States would strike them first and, in doing so, inflict greater costs on the Soviet Union than it could by means of retaliation after the Soviets had struck first. In a (very abstract) nutshell, the potential aggressor presumably is deterred from a military move not simply when his expected cost exceeds his expected gain, but when the net gain is less or the net loss is more than he can expect if he refrains from the move. But this formulation must be qualified by the simple fact of inertia: deliberately to shift from a condition of peace to a condition of war is an extremely momentous decision, involving incalculable consequences, and a government is not likely to make this decision unless it foresees a very large advantage in doing so. The great importance of *uncertainty* in this context will be discussed below.

In a broad sense, deterrence operates during war as well as prior to war. It could be defined as a process of influencing the enemy's *intentions*, whatever the circumstances, violent or non-violent. Typically, the outcome of wars has not depended simply on the clash of physical capabilities. The losing side usually accepts defeat somewhat before it has lost its physical ability to continue fighting. It is deterred from continuing the war by a realization that continued fighting can only generate additional costs without hope of compensating gains, this expectation being largely the consequence of the previous application of force by the dominant side. In past wars, such deterrence usually has been characteristic of the terminal stages. However, in the modern concept of limited war, the intentions factor is more prominent and pervasive; force may be threatened and used partly or even primarily, as a bargaining instrument to persuade the opponent to accept terms of settlement or to observe certain limitations. Deterrence in war is most sharply illustrated in proposals for a strategy of limited retaliation, in which initial strikes, in effect, would be *threats* of further strikes to come, designed to deter the enemy from further fighting. In warfare limited to conventional weapons or tactical nuclear weapons, the strategic nuclear forces held in reserve by either side may constitute a deterrent against the other side's expanding the intensity of its war effort. Also, limited wars may be fought in part with an eye to deterring future enemy attacks by convincing the enemy of one's general willingness to fight.

The above observations were intended to suggest the broad scope of the concept of deterrence, its non-limitation to military factors, and its fundamental affinity to the idea of political power. In the discussion following, we shall use the term in a narrower sense, to mean the discouragement of the *initiation* of military aggression by the threat (implicit or explicit) of applying military force in response to the aggression. We shall assume that when deterrence fails and war begins, the attacked party is no longer "deterring" but rather "defending." Deterrence in war and deterrence, by military action, of subsequent aggressions will be considered as aspects of defense and will be treated later in this chapter.

The logic of deterrence. The object of military deterrence is to reduce the probability of enemy military attacks, by posing for the enemy a sufficiently likely prospect that he will suffer a net loss as a result of the attack, or at least a higher net loss or lower net gain than would follow from his not attacking. If we postulate two contending states, an "aggressor" (meaning potential aggressor) and a "deterrer," with other states which are objects of conflict between these two, the probability of any particular attack by the aggressor is the resultant of essentially four factors which exist in his "mind." All four taken together might be termed the aggressor's "risk calculus." They are (1) his valuation of his war objectives; (2) the cost which he expects to suffer as a result of various possible responses by the deterrer; (3) the probability of various responses, including "no response"; and (4) the probability of winning the objectives with each possible response. We shall assume, for simplicity's sake, that the deterrer's "response" refers to the deterrer's entire strategy of action throughout the war precipitated by the aggressor's move—i.e., not only the response to the initial aggressive move, but also to all subsequent moves by the aggressor. Thus the aggressor's estimate of costs and gains is a "whole war" estimate, depending on his image of the deterrer's entire sequence of moves up to the termination of the war, as well as on his own strategic plans for conducting the war, plans which may be contingent on what moves are made by the deterrer during the war.

Obviously, we are dealing here with factors which are highly subjective and uncertain, not subject to exact measurement, and not commensurate except in an intuitive way. Nevertheless, these are the basic factors which the potential aggressor must weigh in determining the probable costs and gains of his contemplated venture.

Certain generalizations can be made about the relationship among these factors. Factor 3 in the aggressor's calculus represents the "credibility" of various possible responses by the deterrer. But credibility is only one factor: it should not be equated with the deterrent *effectiveness* of a possible or threatened response, which is a function of all four factors—i.e., the net cost or gain which a response promises, discounted by the probability (credibility) of its being applied. An available response which is very low in credibility might be sufficient to deter if it poses a very severe sanction (e.g., massive retaliation) or if the aggressor's prospective gain carries very little value for him. Or a threatened response that carries a rather high credibility but poses only moderate costs for the aggressor—e.g., a conventional response, or nuclear retaliation after the aggressor has had the advantage of the first strategic strike—may not deter if the aggressor places a high value on his objective and anticipates a good chance of attaining it.

THEORIES ABOUT THE USE OF FORCE

The credibility factor deserves special attention because it is in terms of this component that the risk calculus of the aggressor "interlocks" with that of the deterrer. The deterrer's risk calculus is similar to that of the aggressor. If the deterrer is rational, his response to aggression will be determined (within the limits, of course, of the military forces he disposes) largely by four factors: (1) his valuation of the territorial objective and of the other intangible gains (e.g., moral satisfaction) which he associates with a given response; (2) the estimated costs of fighting; (3) the probability of successfully holding the territorial objective and other values at stake; and (4) the change in the probability of future enemy attacks on other objectives which would follow from various responses. Variations on, and marginal additions to, these factors may be imagined, but these four are the essential ones. The deterrer will select the response which minimizes his expectation of cost or maximizes his expectation of gain. (As in the case of the aggressor's calculus, we assume that the deterrer's estimates of cost and gain are "whole war" estimates—i.e., the aggregate effects not only of the deterrer's initial response, but also of all the aggressor's countermoves, combined with the deterrer's counter-countermoves, over the entire progress of the war.) The credibility of various possible responses by the deterrer depends on the aggressor's image of the deterrer's risk calculus—i.e., of the latter's net costs and gains from each response—as well as on the aggressor's assessment of the deterrer's capacity to act rationally.

The aggressor, of course, is not omniscient with respect to the deterrer's estimates of cost and gain. Even the deterrer will be unable to predict in advance of the attack how he will visualize his cost-gain prospects and, hence, exactly what response he will choose once the aggression is under way. (Witness the United States response to the North Korean attack in 1950, which was motivated by values which apparently did not become clear to the decision-makers until the actual crisis was upon them.) Nor can the aggressor be sure the deterrer will act rationally according to his own cost-gain predictions. Because of these uncertainties, the aggressor's estimate of credibility cannot be precise. More than one response will be possible, and the best the aggressor can do is attempt to guess how the deterrer will visualize his gains and losses consequent upon each response, and from this guess arrive at a judgment about the likelihood or probability of each possible response.

The deterrer evaluates the *effectiveness* of his deterrent posture by attempting to guess the values of the four factors in the aggressor's risk calculus. In estimating the credibility factor, he attempts to guess how the aggressor is estimating the factors in *his* (the deterrer's) calculus. He arrives at some judgment as to whether the aggressor is likely to expect a net cost or net gain from the aggressive move and, using this judgment and his degree of confidence in it as a basis, he determines the probability of aggression. Happily, the spiral of "guesses about the other's guesses" seems to stop here. In other words, the aggressor's decision whether or not to attack is not in turn affected by his image of the deterrer's estimate of the likelihood of attack. He knows that once the attack is launched the deterrer will select the response which promises him least cost or greatest gain—at that point, the deterrer's previous calculations about "deterrence" of that attack become irrelevant.

Denial vs. punishment. It is useful to distinguish between deterrence which results from capacity to deny territorial gains to the enemy, and deterrence by the threat and capacity to inflict nuclear punishment. Denial capabilites—typically, conventional ground, sea, and tactical air forces—deter chiefly by their effect on the fourth factor in the aggressor's calculus: his estimate of the probability of gaining his objective. Punishment capabilities—typically, strategic nuclear power for either massive or limited retaliation—act primarily on the second factor, the aggressor's estimate of possible costs, and may have little effect on his chances for territorial gain. Of course, this distinction is not sharp or absolute; a "denial" response, especially if it involves the use of nuclear weapons tactically, can mean high direct costs, plus the risk that the war may get out of hand and ultimately involve severe nuclear punishment for both sides. This prospect of cost and risk may exert a significant deterring effect. A "punishment" response, if powerful enough, may foreclose territorial gains, and limited reprisals may be able to force a settlement short of complete conquest of the territorial objective. However, there are some differences worth noting between these two types or strategies of deterrence.

Apart from their differential impact on the cost and gain elements of the aggressor's calculations, the two types of response are likely to differ also in their credibility or probability of application. As a response to all-out nuclear attack on the deterrer, the application of punishment will be highly credible. But for lesser challenges, such as a conventional attack on an ally, a threat to inflict nuclear punishment normally will be less credible than a threat to fight a "denial" action —assuming, of course, that denial capabilities are available. While the making of a *threat* of nuclear punishment may be desirable and rational, its *fulfillment* is likely to seem irrational after the aggressor has committed his forces, since punishment alone may not be able to hold the territorial objective and will stimulate the aggressor to make counterreprisals. The deterrer therefore has a strong incentive to renege on his threat. Realizing this in advance, the aggressor may not think the threat a very credible one. A threat of denial action will seem more credible on two counts: it is less costly for the deterrer and it may be effective in frustrating the aggressor's aims, or at least in reducing his gains. A denial response is more likely than resprisal action to promise a rational means of *defense* in case deterrence fails; this consideration supports its credibility as a deterrent.

A related difference is that the threat of denial action is likely to be appraised by the aggressor in terms of the deterrer's *capabilities*; threats of nuclear punishment require primarily a judgment of *intent*. It is fairly certain that the deterrer will fight a threatened denial action if he has appropriate forces;[3] the essential question for the aggressor, therefore, is whether these forces are strong enough to prevent him from making gains. In the case of nuclear reprisals, however, the capability to inflict unacceptable punishment is likely to be unquestioned, at least for large nuclear powers; here the aggressor must attempt to look into the mind of the deterrer and guess whether the will to apply punishment exists. Thus a denial threat is much more calculable for the aggressor than a reprisal threat—assuming that a comparison of military capabilities is easier than mind-reading. This may make a denial strategy the more powerful deterrent of the two if the deterrer has strong denial forces; but if he obviously does not have enough ground and tactical forces to block conquest, the threat may be weaker than a nuclear reprisal threat. Even if there is doubt in the aggressor's mind that the reprisals will be carried out, these doubts may be offset by the possible severity of his punishment if he miscalculates and the threat is fulfilled. . . .

DEFENSE[4]

The deterrer, in choosing his optimum military and threat posture in advance of war, must estimate not only the effectiveness of that posture for deterrence, but also the consequences for himself should deterrence fail. In short, he is interested in defense as well as in deterrence; his security is a function of both of these elements. Capabilities and threats which produce a high level of deterrence may not yield a high degree of security because they promise very high costs and losses for the deterrer should war occur. . . .

Strategic value and deterrent value. Much of the inconclusiveness of the recurring "great debates" about military policy might be avoided if the concept of "strategic value" could be clarified and clearly separated from the deterrent effects of military action. The strategic

---

[3] It is possible that the aggressor may be able to deter "denial" resistance t threatening to take punitive action if resistance occurs. This is perhaps most feasible with respect to allies of the country attacked whose troops are not deployed on the territory of the victim.

[4] The reader is reminded that I am using the word "defense" in a rather special sense, which is narrower than one ordinary usage of the term and broader than another. Obviously it is narrower than the usage which makes "defense" synonymous with all military preparedness. It is broader, however, than "capacity to hold territory in case of attack," which I would prefer to call "denial capability."

value of a particular piece of territory is the effect which its loss would have on increasing the enemy's *capability* to make various future moves, and on decreasing our own capacity to resist further attacks. The deterrent value of defending or attempting to defend that piece of territory is the effect of the defense on the enemy's *intention* to make future moves. The failure to recognize this distinction contributed to the apparent about-face in United States policy toward South Korea, when we decided to intervene after the North Korean attack in June 1950. Earlier, the Joint Chiefs of Staff had declared that South Korea had no strategic value—apparently meaning that its loss would have no significant effect on the U.S. capacity to fight a general war with the Soviet Union. This determination was thought to justify—or at least was used as a rationalization for—the withdrawal of U.S. combat forces from the Korean peninsula in 1948 and 1949. Secretary of State Dean Acheson strengthened the impression that "no strategic value" meant "no value" when, in a speech early in 1950, he outlined a U.S. "defense perimeter" in the Far East which excluded Korea. Then when the North Koreans, perhaps encouraged by these high-level U.S. statements, attacked in June 1950, the United States government suddenly discovered that it had a deterrent interest, as well as strong political and intrinsic interests, in coming to the rescue of South Korea. The dominant theme in the discussions leading up to the decision to intervene was that if the Communists were "appeased" this time, they would be encouraged to make further attacks on other areas.[5] The chief motive behind the intervention was to prevent such encouragement from taking place, and positively to deter similar attempts in the future.

[5] As former President Truman has stated: "Our allies and friends abroad were informed through our diplomatic representatives that it was our feeling that it was essential to the maintenance of peace that this armed aggression against a free nation be met firmly. We let it be known that we considered the Korean situation vital as a symbol of the strength and determination of the West. Firmness now would be the only way to deter new actions in other portions of the world. Not only in Asia but in Europe, the Middle East, and elsewhere the confidence of peoples in countries adjacent to the Soviet Union would be very adversely affected, in our judgment, if we failed to take action to protect a country established under our auspices and confirmed in its freedom by action of the United Nations. If, however, the threat to South Korea was met firmly and successfully, it would add to our successes in Iran, Berlin and Greece a fourth success in opposition to the aggressive moves of the Communists. And each success, we suggested to our allies, was likely to add to the caution of the Soviets in undertaking new efforts of this kind. Thus the safety and prospects for peace of the free world would be increased." Harry S. Truman, *Years of Trial and Hope*, New York: Doubleday and Co., 1956, pp. 339–40.
The primary political value of the intervention, as U.S. decisionmakers saw it, was that it would give other free nations confidence that they could count on U.S. aid in resisting aggression. The most salient intrinsic values were moral value in opposing the aggressive use of force, support for the "rule of law" in international affairs, support for the collective security system embodied in the United Nations Charter, and the special responsibility the United States felt for the Republic of Korea, whose government it had played a major role in establishing. "Support for the collective security system" of course had deterrent and political as well as moral overtones.

Another case in point was the debate about the desirability of a United States commitment to defend the Chinese offshore islands of Quemoy and Matsu. Those who took the negative in this debate stressed that these two small islands held no "strategic value" for the United States, that they were not "vital" to the defense of Formosa, etc. Former Secretary of State Dean Acheson declared that the islands were not worth a single American life.[6] Administration spokesmen, on the other hand, emphasized the political and deterrent value of defending Quemoy and Matsu. President Eisenhower, for example, said that this country's allies "would be appalled if the United States were spinelessly to retreat before the threat of Sino-Soviet armed aggression."[7] Secretary of State Dulles asserted that the stakes were not "just some square miles of real estate," but the preservation of confidence in other countries—both allies and enemies—that the United States would resist aggression. It was better to meet the challenge at the beginning, Mr. Dulles said, than after "our friends become disheartened and our enemies overconfident and miscalculating."[8]

Power values are sometimes discussed in terms of the "falling domino" theory. According to this reasoning, if one objective is lost to the enemy, other areas contiguous to the first one inevitably will be lost as well, then still additional areas contiguous to these, etc., as a whole row of dominoes will fall when the first one is knocked over.[9] In its extreme form, the domino thesis would value any objective, no matter how small, as dearly as the value which the United States placed on the continued independence of all other non-Communist countries. Thus we should be as willing to fight for one place as another, since a failure to resist once inevitably means future losses. The important thing is to "draw a line" and resist violations of the line, whatever their dimensions and wherever and whenever they may occur.

The domino theory tends to overstate power values: since the enemy may have limited aims and may be satisfied with a small gain, his increase in capability from a single small conquest may not significantly shift the balance of capabilities in his favor, and the loss of single small areas may not have adverse political effects among

---

[6] *New York Times,* October 3, 1958, p. 3.

[7] *Ibid.,* October 5, 1958, p. 1.

[8] *Ibid.,* September 26, 1958, p. 1.

[9] Apparently the domino theory was first given public expression by President Eisenhower on April 7, 1954, when he said, in reply to a request that he explain the strategic value of Indo-China to the United States: "You had a row of dominoes set up, and you knocked over the first one, and what would happen to the last one was the certainty that it would go over very quickly. So you could have a beginning of a disintegration that would have the most profound influences." The President then referred to "the possible sequence of events, the loss of Indo-China, of Burma, of Thailand, of the peninsula, and Indonesia following." *Ibid.,* April 8, 1954, p. 18.

neutrals and allies.[10] Nevertheless, the domino image does highlight an important truth: the strategic and intrinsic value of the immediate territorial prize is not a sufficient criterion for evaluating the wisdom of resisting aggression, or for estimating the forces necessary for successful resistance. The enemy's possible ultimate objective must also be considered, as well as the effect of resistance in discouraging him from attempting further progress toward that objective, and in forestalling political changes among other countries which would tend to further that ultimate objective.

There is a relationship between the strategic, political, and intrinsic value which the enemy believes one attaches to a given objective, and the deterrent value which can be realized by responding to an attack on that objective. For example, a failure to resist effectively a Communist attack on the offshore islands of Quemoy and Matsu might not increase perceptibly the chances of Chinese Communist attacks on other non-Communist countries in Asia, if the Communists did not believe we placed a high intrinsic and strategic value on these islands. On the other hand, it could be argued that a determined and costly response to an attack on an objective which the enemy thinks means little to us in strategic and intrinsic terms is likely to give him greater pause with respect to his future aggressive intentions. Thus, if the objective is to "draw a line" to deter future aggression, perhaps the best place to draw it is precisely at places like Quemoy and Matsu. The enemy would reason that if the United States were willing to fight for a place of such trivial intrinsic and strategic value to itself, it must surely be willing to fight for other places of greater value. Thus, the deterrent value of defending any objective varies inversely with the enemy's perception of its value to us on other accounts. There is a further consideration: if it is thought necessary to fight a certain amount of war, or risk a certain amount of war, to convince the other side of our willingness to fight generally, what better place to do it than at places like Quemoy and Matsu, where it is least likely that the war will spiral to all-out dimensions?

Mutually shared expectations are extremely important in determining the deterrent value of military actions. The United States did not lose much in deterrent utility by failing to intervene in Hungary in 1956, because both sides regarded Hungary as part of the Communist camp. But a failure to defend Berlin would severely undermine the U.S. capability to deter future Communist incursions in Europe or elsewhere.

---

[10] It is hard to believe, for example, that a Communist Chinese conquest of Quemoy and Matsu would have reduced the confidence of the European allies in the willingness of the United States to defend Europe. The solidarity of NATO might have been weakened by a U.S. attempt to defend the islands.

The consequences of enemy moves, and the defense value of forces for resisting them, are subject to modification by policy declarations. Threats and commitments may involve one's honor and prestige in a particular area or objective, and this involvement increases the deterrent, political, and intrinsic value of defending such places and the value of forces which are able to defend. Thus the adverse consequences of an unresisted Communist attack on Quemoy and Matsu were increased by the various official statements, including the Formosa Resolution passed by Congress, to the effect that these offshore islands were "related" to the defense of Formosa. But these consequences were not increased as much as they might have been, had the United States made an unequivocal commitment to defend the islands.

Of course, losses of power values through the loss of an ally or neutral to the enemy may be offset by increased mobilization of domestic resources. The cost of the additional mobilization required might be taken as a measure of the power value of the territory in question. Thus the defending power might ask itself: "If I let this piece of territory or this ally be taken over by the enemy, how many additional resources will I have to spend for military weapons to have the same degree of security I have been enjoying?"

Once war is entered into, consideration of deterrent possibilities may call for a different strategy than would be the case if we were interested only in the strategic and intrinsic values of the particular area attacked. If the latter were our only interest, our war aims might be limited to restoration of the *status quo ante*; deterrence of future aggressions, however, might dictate more ambitious aims. In the Korean War, for example, it is possible that if closer consideration had been given to deterrent benefits, the U.N. armies might have pushed on farther than they did—if not to the Yalu, then perhaps at least to the "narrow neck" of the Korean peninsula. The opportunity was not taken to show the Communists that their aggressions were likely to result in losses not only of manpower but also of territory; that in future limited wars they could not hope to end up at least where they started.

In general, we will be willing to suffer higher costs in fighting a limited war if deterrence is an objective than if it is not. In other words, it may be desirable to fight on longer and in the face of a higher cost expectancy if an important objective is to assure the enemy of our willingness to suffer costs in future contingencies.

The objective of deterrence may call for the use of different weapons than would the simple objective of blocking enemy conquest of an area at least cost. Our use of nuclear weapons probably would support the Communist estimate of our willingness to use them in the future; and, conversely, to refrain from using them when such use would be militarily advantageous would weaken that estimate.

GLENN H. SNYDER   139

However, as in the decision whether or not to fight at all, the strategic
and intrinsic value of the immediate objective is relevant to the deterrent effects: the use of nuclear weapons to defend highly valued objectives might support but little the probability that they would be used to
meet lesser challenges;[11] the failure to use them when the prize was
small would not necessarily signal a reluctance to do so when the object of the conflict was vital.

Finally, for deterrent reasons it might be desirable to *attempt*
resistance against a particular limited enemy attack even though we
knew in advance that our resistance would fail. The purpose would be
to inform the enemy, for future reference, that although he could expect to make gains from limited aggression in the future, these gains
could be had only at a price which (we hoped) the enemy would not
want to pay. Proposals for limited nuclear retaliation against one or a
few enemy cities in response to limited ground aggression may draw
on this kind of reasoning.

Of course, the concept of "deterrence by action" has no relevance
in determining the appropriate response to a direct thermonuclear attack on the United States, or in valuing the forces for the response. In
that event there would be no future contingencies which would seem
worth deterring or worrying about at all, compared with the
magnitude of the catastrophe which had already taken place. The
primary values would be intrinsic values associated with reducing war
damage, perhaps limiting the enemy's territorial gains in Eurasia, and
preserving the independence of the United States itself.[12]

Power values lost by the defender represent power values gained by
the attacker, although the values may not be equally important to each
side. For example, the Middle East has strategic value for the United
States because its geographic location and resources add significantly
to the West's capacity to fight limited war in Europe and elsewhere,
and because the area, in the hands of the Soviets, would increase the
Soviets' capacity to fight such wars—because of its position athwart
vital transportation routes if not because of its oil resources. Our
strategic loss if the Middle East should fall under Communist control
would be the sum of the deprivation to the West's future military
capabilities and the increment to the Soviet capabilities. Similarly, the
strategic gain to the Soviets would be the sum of their own direct gain
in military resources plus the losses for the West.

[11] On the other hand, any use of nuclear weapons would set a precedent. The symbolic or psychological barrier to their use which had rested on their previous non-use
would be eroded. The Russians might believe, after they had been used once, that the
probability of their use in *any* future conflict had increased.

[12] We might, of course, attempt to "deter" the enemy from continuing his attacks,
thus reducing our war costs and perhaps preserving our independence and the essential
fabric of our society, by a discriminating use of the weapons we had left after absorbing
a surprise attack, accompanied by appropriate bargaining tactics. . . .

It is less obvious that deterrent values also have this reciprocal character. When, by fighting in Korea, we demonstrated our willingness to defend free institutions in Asia, not only did we gain "deterrent value" with respect to other possible Communist moves in Asia; the Communists lost something analogous to it in their own value system. Presumably they became less confident that overt aggression could be attempted again without U.S. intervention. Their "expected value" from future aggressive moves declined perhaps below what it was before Korea, and certainly below what it would have been if the North Korean aggression had been unopposed by the United States.

When an aggressor state successfully completes a conquest, or has its demands satisfied short of war, its willingness in the future to make war, or to make demands at the risk of war, presumably is strengthened by the reduction of expected cost or risk which it perceives in such future moves. This reduction in the perceived chances of being opposed in the future we might label "expectation value," to differentiate it from "deterrent value," which is peculiarly associated with *status quo* powers. Deterrent and expectational values are in obverse relationship—i.e., when the defender loses deterrent value by failing to fight or to carry out a threat, the aggressor gains expectational value, and vice versa—although again the gain or loss may have a stronger psychological impact on one side than on the other, since the value in question is highly subjective.

This distinction is similar to Thomas Schelling's distinction between "compellent" and "deterrent" threats.[13] A compellent threat is used in an aggressive way; it is designed to persuade the opponent to give up some value. A deterrent threat, on the other hand, is intended to dissuade the opponent from initiating some positive action. A successful conquest would increase an aggressor's compellent power with respect to other possible victims, especially if the fighting had included the use of nuclear weapons; other countries would lose deterrent power, since their psychological capacity to resist demands would be weakened by the aggressor's demonstration of willingness to risk or to undertake nuclear war.

Strategic gains by the Soviets might appear in their risk calculus as an increased probability that future attacks on other areas would be successful, or perhaps as a decreased expectation of cost in making future conquests. Gains in expectational value would appear as a decreased probability of resistance to future attacks, or perhaps as a reduced probability of a high-cost response by the defender or its allies. The aggregate of strategic gains and expectational gains pro-

[13] Thomas C. Schelling, *The Strategy of Conflict*, Cambridge: Harvard University Press, 1960, pp. 195-196.

duces an increase in "expected value" to be gained from future moves (or a reduction in "expected cost").

This might not always be the case if the consequence of a successful aggression were to stimulate an increased level of military mobilization by the United States and its allies and/or an increased determination to resist future attacks. Thus a successful limited attack might backfire and *reduce* the Soviets' strategic position as well as their expectational value, although of course they would retain whatever intrinsic values they had gained by their conquest. . . .

THE NEW BALANCE OF POWER

 . . . The existence of a balance of power, or the capabilities requirements for balancing, can hardly be determined without attempting to look into the "mind" of the enemy. One might say that a subjective "balance of intentions" has become at least as important as the more objectively calculable "balance of capabilities."

A corollary of the increased relative importance of intentions is that methods of communicating intent have become more important *means* in the balancing process than they have been in the past. First, nations are becoming more sensitive to what they say to each other about their intentions; the psychological importance of threats and other declarations is on the increase. Secondly, the function of military forces themselves may be shifting in the direction of a demonstrative role: the signaling of future intentions to use force in order to influence the enemy's intentions, as opposed to being ready to use, or using force simply as a physical means of conquest or denial. Hence the enhanced importance of *deterrence* in the modern balance of power as compared with *defense*. We are likely to see more imaginative and subtle uses of "force demonstration" in time of peace. . . . Warfare itself may in the future become less a raw physical collision of military forces and more a contest of wills, or a bargaining process, with military force being used largely to demonstrate one's willingness to raise the intensity of fighting, with the object of inducing the enemy to accept one's terms of settlement. While direct conflict or competition is going on at a low level of the spectrum of violence, selective force demonstrations using means appropriate to higher levels may take place as threats to "up the ante." . . .

Massive Retaliation

JOHN FOSTER DULLES

. . . As a loyal member of the United Nations, we had responded with force to repel the Communist aggression in Korea. And when that effort exposed our military weakness, we rebuilt rapidly our military establishment, and we helped to build quickly new strength in Western Europe.

KOREA

These were the acts of a nation which saw the danger of Soviet communism; which realized that its own safety was tied up with that of others; and which was capable of responding boldly and promptly to emergencies. These are precious values to be acclaimed. And also, we can pay tribute to the congressional bipartisanship which puts politics second and the nation first.

But we need to recall that what we did was in the main emergency action, imposed on us by our enemies.

Let me illustrate.

We did not send our Army into Korea because we judged, in advance, that it was sound military strategy to commit our Army to fight land battles in Asia. Our decision had been to pull out of Korea. It was a Soviet-inspired decision that pulled us back.

We did not decide in advance that it was wise to grant billions annually as foreign economic aid. We adopted that policy in response to the Communist efforts to sabotage the free economies of Western Europe.

We did not build up our military establishments at a rate which involved huge budget deficits, a depreciating currency and a feverish economy because this seemed, in advance, to be good policy. Indeed, we decided otherwise until the Soviet military threat was clearly revealed. . . .

. . . It is necessary also to say that emergency measures—however good for the emergency—do not necessarily make good permanent policies. Emergency policies are costly, they are superficial and they

Excerpts from a speech delivered before the Council on Foreign Relations, New York City, January 12, 1954.

imply that the enemy has the initiative. They cannot be depended upon to serve our long-time interests.

Now this "long time" factor is of critical importance.

SOVIET PLANS

The Soviet Communists are planning for what they call "an entire historical era," and we should do the same. They seek through many types of maneuvers gradually to divide and weaken the free nations by over-extending them in efforts which, as Lenin put it, are "beyond their strength, so that they come to practical bankruptcy." Then, said Lenin, "our victory is assured." Then, said Stalin, will be "the moment for the decisive blow."

In the face of such a strategy, our own measures cannot be judged adequate merely because they ward off an immediate danger. That, of course, needs to be done. But it is also essential to do this without exhausting ourselves.

And when the Eisenhower Administration applied this test, we felt that some transformations were needed.

It is not sound military strategy permanently to commit United States land forces to Asia to a degree that gives us no strategic reserves.

It is not sound economics to support permanently other countries; nor is it good foreign policy, for in the long run, that creates as much ill will as good.

It is not sound to become permanently committed to military expenditures so vast that they lead to what Lenin called "practical bankruptcy."

Change was imperative to assure the stamina needed for permanent security. But also it was imperative that change should be accompanied by understanding of what were our true purposes. There are some who wanted and expected sudden and spectacular change. That could not be. That kind of change would have created a panic among our friends, and our enemies might have miscalculated and misunderstood our real purposes and have assumed that we were prepared to tolerate their aggression.

So while we had to change also we had to change carefully.

We can, I believe, make a good report in these respects.

NATIONAL SECURITY

Take first the matter of national security. We need allies and we need collective security. And our purpose is to have them, but to have them on a basis which is more effective and on a basis which is less costly. How do we do this? The way to do this is to place more reliance upon community deterrent power, and less dependence upon local defensive power.

This is accepted practice so far as our local communities are concerned. We keep locks on the doors of our homes; but we do not have armed guards in every home. We rely principally on a community security system so well equipped to catch and punish any who break in and steal that, in fact, would-be aggressors are generally deterred. That is the modern way of getting maximum protection at bearable cost.

INTERNATIONAL SECURITY

What the Eisenhower Administration seeks is a similar international security system. We want for ourselves and for others a maximum deterrent at bearable cost.

Local defense will always be important. But there is no local defense which alone will contain the mighty land power of the Communist world. Local defense must be reinforced by the further deterrent of massive retaliatory power.

A potential aggressor must know that he cannot always prescribe the battle conditions that suit him. Otherwise, for example, a potential aggressor who is glutted with manpower might be tempted to attack in confidence that resistance would be confined to manpower. He might be tempted to attack in places where his superiority was decisive.

The way to deter aggression is . . .

MORE SECURITY, LESS COST

. . . To depend primarily upon a great capacity to retaliate instantly by means and at places of our choosing. . . . Now the Department of Defense and the Joint Chiefs of Staff can shape our military establishment to fit what is our policy instead of having to try to be ready to meet the enemy's many choices. And that permits of a selection of military means instead of a multiplication of means. And as a result it is now possible to get, and to share, more security at less cost.

Now let us see how this concept has been practically applied to foreign policy, taking first the Far East. In Korea this Administration effected a major transformation. The fighting has been stopped on honorable terms.

That was possible because the aggressor, already thrown back to and behind his place of beginning, was faced with the possibility that the fighting might, to his own great peril, soon spread beyond the limits and the methods which he had selected.

The cruel toll of American youth, and the nonproductive expenditure of many billions has been stopped. Also our armed forces are no longer committed to the Asian mainland. We can begin to create a strategic reserve which greatly improves our defensive posture.

This change gives added authority to the warning of the members of the United Nations which fought in Korea that if the Communists renewed the aggression, the United Nations' response would not necessarily be confined to Korea.

I have said, in relation to Indo-China, that if there were open Red Chinese aggression there, that would have "grave consequences which might not be confined to Indo-China."

I expressed last month the intention of the United States to maintain its position in Okinawa. This is needed to ensure adequate striking power to implement our new collective security concept.

All this is summed up in President Eisenhower's important statement of Dec. 26. He announced the progressive reduction of the United States ground forces in Korea. And in doing so, he pointed out that United States military forces in the Far East will now feature "highly mobile naval, air and amphibious units"; and he said that in this way, despite some withdrawal of land forces, the United States will have a capacity to oppose aggression "with even greater effect than heretofore."

The bringing home of our land forces also provides a most eloquent rebuttal to the Communist charges of "Western imperialism" in Asia.

EUROPEAN SECURITY

Let us turn now to Europe. . . .

Last April, when we went to the meeting of the NATO Council, the United States put forward a new concept which is now known as that of the "long haul." That meant a steady development of defensive strength at a rate that will preserve and not exhaust the economic strength of our allies and ourselves. This defensive strength would be reinforced by the striking power of strategic air based upon internationally agreed positions.

At this April meeting our ideas met with some skepticism. But when we went back as we did last month, December, we found that there had come about general acceptance of this "long haul" concept, and recognition that it better served the probable needs than an effort to create full defensive land strength at a ruinous price. . . .

FOREIGN AID

Turning now to foreign aid we see that new collective security concepts reduce nonproductive military expenses of our allies to a point where it is desirable and practicable also to reduce economic aid. There was need of a more self-respecting relationship, and that, indeed, is what our allies wanted. Trade, broader markets and a flow of investments are far more healthy than intergovernmental grants-in-aid.

There are still some strategic spots where local governments cannot maintain adequate armed forces without some financial help from us. In these cases we take the judgment of our military advisers as to how to proceed in the common interest. For example, we have contributed largely, ungrudgingly, and I hope constructively, to help to end aggression and advance freedom in Indo-China.

We do not, of course, claim to have found some magic formula that insures against all forms of Communist successes. It is normal that at some times at some places there may be setbacks to the cause of freedom. What we do expect to insure is that any setbacks will only be temporary and local because they will leave unimpaired those free world assets which in the long run will prevail.

If we can deter such aggression as would mean general war, and that is our confident resolve, then we can let time and fundamentals work for us. Under these conditions we do not need self-imposed policies which sap our strength.

Mutual Deterrence

NIKITA S. KHRUSHCHEV

While visiting the USA we became convinced that the most farsighted statesmen, businessmen, representatives of the American intelligentsia —not to speak of workers and farmers—desire not a continuation of the armament race, not a further increase in nervous tension, but calm and peace.

After the launching of the Soviet artificial satellites and cosmic rockets which demonstrated the possibilities of modern technology, the fact that the USA is now by no means less vulnerable in the military sense than any other country has firmly entered the mind of the American people.

I believe that nobody will suspect me of the intention of intimidating anybody by such words. No, this is the actual state of affairs, and

Excerpt of an address to the Supreme Soviet, January 14, 1960 it is evaluated in this way not only by us but also by Western statesmen of the USA herself. . . .

We cannot as yet give up completely the production of nuclear arms. Such decisions must be the result of an agreement among countries possessing nuclear arms.

Our state has at its disposal powerful rocket equipment. The air force and navy have lost their previous importance in view of the modern development of military equipment. This type of arms is not being reduced but replaced.

Almost the whole of the air force is being replaced by rocket equipment. We have by now cut down sharply and it seems will continue to cut down and even discontinue the manufacture of bombers and other obsolete machinery.

In the navy, the submarine fleet assumes great importance, whilst abovewater ships can no longer play the part they did in the past.

In our country, the armed forces have been to a considerable extent transferred to rocket and nuclear arms. These arms are being perfected and will continue to be perfected until the time they are banned.

The proposed reduction will in no way reduce the firepower of our armed forces, and this is the main point.

I am emphasizing once more that we already possess so many nuclear weapons, both atomic and hydrogen, and the necessary rockets for sending these weapons to the territory of a potential aggressor, that should any madman launch an attack on our state or on other Socialist states we would be able literally to wipe the country or countries which attack us off the face of the earth.

The Central Committee of the Communist Party and the Soviet Government can inform you, Comrade Deputies, that, though the weapons we have now are formidable weapons indeed, the weapon we have today in the hatching stage is even more perfect and more formidable.

The weapon, which is being developed and is, as they say, in the portfolio of our scientists and designers, is a fantastic weapon.

The following question arises, however, inevitably: if the possibility is not excluded that some capitalist countries will draw level with us in the field of contemporary armament, will they not, possibly, show perfidy and attack us first in order to make use of the factor of the unexpectedness of attack with such a formidable weapon as the rocket-atomic one and thus have an advantage to achieve victory?

No. Contemporary means of waging war do not give any country such advantage.

The "No-Cities" Doctrine

ROBERT S. MC NAMARA

. . . What I want to talk to you about here today are some of the concrete problems of maintaining a free community in the world today. I want to talk to you particularly about the problems of the community that bind together the United States and the countries of Western Europe. . . .

Today, NATO is involved in a number of controversies, which must be resolved by achieving a consensus within the organization in order to preserve its strength and unity. . . .

It has been argued that the very success of Western European economic development reduces Europe's need to rely on the U.S. to share in its defenses.

It has been argued that the increasing vulnerability of the U.S. to nuclear attack makes us less willing as a partner in the defense of Europe, and hence less effective in deterring such an attack.

It has been argued that nuclear capabilities are alone relevant in the face of the growing nuclear threat, and that independent national nuclear forces are sufficient to protect the nations of Europe.

I believe that all of these arguments are mistaken. . . . In our view, the effect of the new factors in the situation, both economic and military, has been to increase the interdependence of national security interests on both sides of the Atlantic, and to enhance the need for the closest coordination of our efforts.

A central military issue facing NATO today is the role of nuclear strategy. Four facts seem to us to dominate consideration of that role. All of them point in the direction of increased integration to achieve our common defense. First, the Alliance has over-all nuclear strength adequate to any challenge confronting it. Second, this strength not only minimizes the likelihood of major nuclear war, but it makes possible a strategy designed to preserve the fabric of our societies if war should occur. Third, damage to the civil societies of the Alliance resulting from nuclear warfare could be very grave. Fourth, improved non-nuclear forces, well within Alliance resources, could enhance deterrence of any aggressive moves short of direct, all-out attack on Western Europe.

Excerpts from a speech delivered at the Commencement Exercises, University of Michigan, Ann Arbor, Michigan, June 16, 1962.

Let us look at the situation today. First, given the current balance of nuclear power, which we confidently expect to maintain in the years ahead, a surprise nuclear attack is simply not a rational act for any enemy. Nor would it be rational for an enemy to take the initiative in the use of nuclear weapons as an outgrowth of a limited engagement in Europe or elsewhere. I think we are entitled to conclude that either of these actions has been made highly unlikely.

Second, and equally important, the mere fact that no nation could rationally take steps leading to a nuclear war does not guarantee that a nuclear war cannot take place. Not only do nations sometimes act in ways that are hard to explain on a rational basis, but even when acting in a "rational" way they sometimes, indeed disturbingly often, act on the basis of misunderstandings of the true facts of a situation. They misjudge the way others will react, and the way others will interpret what they are doing. We must hope, indeed I think we have good reason to hope, that all sides will understand this danger, and will refrain from steps that even raise the possibility of such a mutually disastrous misunderstanding. We have taken unilateral steps to reduce the likelihood of such an occurrence. . . .

For our part, we feel and our NATO allies must frame our strategy with this terrible contingency, however remote, in mind. Simply ignoring the problem is not going to make it go away.

The U.S. has come to the conclusion that to the extent feasible, basic military strategy in a possible general nuclear war should be approached in much the same way that more conventional military operations have been regarded in the past. That is to say, principal military objectives, in the event of a nuclear war stemming from a major attack on the Alliance, should be the destruction of the enemy's military forces, not of his civilian population.

The very strength and nature of the Alliance forces make it possible for us to retain, even in the face of a massive surprise attack, sufficient reserve striking power to destroy an enemy society if driven to it. In other words, we are giving a possible opponent the strongest imaginable incentive to refrain from striking our own cities.

The strength that makes these contributions to deterrence and to the hope of deterring attack upon civil societies even in wartime does not come cheap. . . .

. . . Relatively weak national nuclear forces with enemy cities as their targets are not likely to be sufficient to perform even the function of deterrence. If they are small, and perhaps vulnerable on the ground or in the air, or inaccurate, a major antagonist can take a variety of measures to counter them. Indeed, if a major antagonist came to believe there was a substantial likelihood of it being used independently, this force would be inviting a pre-emptive first strike against it. In the event of war, the use of such a force against the cities of a major

nuclear power would be tantamount to suicide, whereas its employment against significant military targets would have a negligible effect
on the outcome of the conflict. Meanwhile, the creation of a single additional national nuclear force encourages the proliferation of nuclear
power with all of its attendant dangers.

In short, then, limited nuclear capabilities, operating independently, are dangerous, expensive, prone to obsolescence, and lacking
in credibility as a deterrent. Clearly, the United States nuclear contribution to the Alliance is neither obsolete nor dispensable.

At the same time, the general strategy I have summarized magnifies
the importance of unity of planning, concentration of executive
authority, and central direction. There must not be competing and
conflicting strategies to meet the contingency of nuclear war. We are
convinced that a general nuclear war target system is indivisible, and
if, despite all our efforts, nuclear war should occur, our best hope lies
in conducting a centrally controlled campaign against all of the
enemy's vital nuclear capabilities, while retaining reserve forces, all
centrally controlled.

We know that the same forces which are targeted on ourselves are
also targeted on our allies. Our own strategic retaliatory forces are
prepared to respond against these forces, wherever they are and
whatever their targets. This mission is assigned not only in fulfillment
of our treaty commitments but also because the character of nuclear
war compels it. More specifically, the U.S. is as much concerned with
that portion of Soviet nuclear striking power that can reach Western
Europe as with the portion that also can reach the United States. In
short, we have undertaken the nuclear defense of NATO on a global
basis. . . .

Limited Nuclear Options

JAMES SCHLESINGER

THE NEED FOR OPTIONS

President Nixon underlined the drawbacks to sole reliance on
assured destruction in 1970 when he asked:

"Should a President, in the event of a nuclear attack, be left with the single option of ordering the mass destruction of enemy civilians, in the face of the certainty that it would be followed by the mass slaughter of Americans? Should the concept of assured destruction be narrowly defined and should it be the only measure of our ability to deter the variety of threats we may face?"

The questions are not new. They have arisen many times during the nuclear era, and a number of efforts have been made to answer them. We actually added several response options to our contingency plans in 1961 and undertook the retargeting necessary for them. However, they all involved large numbers of weapons. In addition, we publicly adopted to some degree the philosophies of counterforce and damage-limiting. Although differences existed between those two concepts as then formulated, particularly in their diverging assumptions about cities as likely targets of attack, both had a number of features in common.

—Each required the maintenance of a capability to destroy urban-industrial targets, but as a reserve to deter attacks on U.S. and allied cities rather than as the main instrument of retaliation.

—Both recognized that contingencies other than a massive surprise attack on the United States might arise and should be deterred; both argued that the ability and willingness to attack military targets were prerequisites to deterrence.

—Each stressed that a major objective, in the event that deterrence should fail, would be to avoid to the extent possible causing collateral damage in the USSR, and to limit damage to the societies of the United States and its allies.

—Neither contained a clear-cut vision of how a nuclear war might end, or what role the strategic forces would play in their termination.

—Both were considered by critics to be open-ended in their requirement for forces, very threatening to the retaliatory capabilities of the USSR, and therefore dangerously stimulating to the arms race and the chances of pre-emptive war.

—The military tasks that each involved, whether offensive counterforce or defensive damage-limiting, became increasingly costly, complex, and difficult as Soviet strategic forces grew in size, diversity, and survivability.

Of the two concepts, damage-limiting was the more demanding and costly because it required both active and passive defenses as well as a counterforce capability to attack hard targets and other strategic delivery systems. Added to this was the assumption (at least for planning purposes) that an enemy would divide his initial attack between our cities and our retaliatory forces, or switch his fire to our cities at some later stage in the attack. Whatever the realism of that assumption, it placed an enormous burden on our active and passive defenses—and particularly on anti-ballistic missile (ABM) systems—for the limitation of damage.

With the ratification of the ABM treaty in 1972, and the limitation it imposes on both the United States and the Soviet Union to construct no more than two widely separated ABM sites (with no more than 100 interceptors at each), an essential building-block in the entire damage-limiting concept has now been removed. As I shall discuss later, the treaty has also brought into question the utility of large, dedicated anti-bomber defenses, since without a defense against missiles, it is clear that an active defense against bombers has little value in protecting our cities. The salient point, however, is that the ABM treaty has effectively removed the concept of defensive damage limitation (at least as it was defined in the 1960s) from the contention as a major strategic option.

Does all of this mean that we have no choice but to rely solely on the threat of destroying cities? Does it even matter if we do? What is wrong, in the final analysis, with staking everything on this massive deterrent and pressing ahead with a further limitation of these devastating arsenals?

No one who has thought much about these questions disagrees with the need, as a minimum, to maintain a conservatively designed reserve for the ultimate threat of large-scale destruction. Even more, if we could all be guaranteed that this threat would prove fully credible (to friend and foe alike) across the relevant range of contingencies—and that deterrence would never be severely tested or fail—we might also agree that nothing more in the way of options would ever be needed. The difficulty is that no such guarantee can be given. There are several reasons why any assurance on this score is impossible.

Since we ourselves find it difficult to believe that we would actually implement the threat of assured destruction in response to a limited attack on military targets that caused relatively few civilian casualties, there can be no certainty that, in a crisis, prospective opponents would be deterred from testing our resolve. Allied concern about the credibility of this particular threat has been evident for more than a decade. In any event, the actuality of such a response would be utter folly except where our own or allied cities were attacked.

Today, such a massive retaliation against cities, in response to anything less than an all-out attack on the U.S. and its cities, appears less and less credible. Yet . . . deterrence can fail in many ways. What we need is a series of measured responses to aggression which bear some relation to the provocation, have prospects of terminating hostilities before general nuclear war breaks out, and leave some possibility for restoring deterrence. It has been this problem of not having sufficient options between massive response and doing nothing, as the Soviets built up their strategic forces, that has prompted the President's concerns and those of our Allies.

Threats against allied forces, to the extent that they could be deterred by the prospect of nuclear retaliation, demand both more limited responses than destroying cities and advanced planning tailored to such lesser responses. Nuclear threats to our strategic forces, whether limited or large-scale, might well call for an option to respond in kind against the attacker's military forces. In other words, to be credible, and hence effective over the range of possible contingencies, deterrence must rest on many options and on a spectrum of capabilities (within the constraints of SALT) to support these options. Certainly such complex matters as response options cannot be left hanging until a crisis. They must be thought through beforehand. Moreover, appropriate sensors to assist in determining the nature of the attack, and adequately responsive command-control arrangements, must also be available. And a venturesome opponent must know that we have all of these capabilities.

Flexibility of response is also essential because, despite our best efforts, we cannot guarantee that deterrence will never fail; nor can we forecast the situations that would cause it to fail. Accidents and unauthorized acts could occur, especially if nuclear proliferation should increase. Conventional conflicts could escalate into nuclear exchanges; indeed, some observers believe that this is precisely what would happen should a major war break out in Europe. Ill-informed or cornered and desperate leaders might challenge us to a nuclear test of wills. We cannot even totally preclude the massive surprise attack on our forces which we use to test the design of our second-strike forces, although I regard the probability of such an attack as close to zero under existing conditions. To the extent that we have selective response options—smaller and more precisely focused than in the past—we should be able to deter such challenges. But if deterrence fails, we may be able to bring all but the largest nuclear conflicts to a rapid conclusion before cities are struck. Damage may thus be limited and further escalation avoided.

I should point out in this connection that the critics of options cannot have the argument both ways. If the nuclear balance is no longer delicate and if substantial force asymmetries are quite tolerable, then the kinds of changes I have been discussing here will neither perturb the balance nor stimulate an arms race. If, on the other hand, asymmetries do matter (despite the existence of some highly survivable forces), then the critics themselves should consider seriously what responses we should make to the major programs that the Soviets currently have underway to exploit their advantages in numbers of missiles and payload. Whichever argument the critics prefer, they should recognize that:

—inertia is hardly an appropriate policy for the United States in these vital areas;

—we have had some large-scale pre-planned options other than attacking cities for many years, despite the rhetoric of assured destruction;

—adding more selective, relatively small-scale options is not necessarily synonymous with adding forces, even though we may wish to change their mix and improve our command, control, and communications.

It is worth stressing at this point . . . that targets for nuclear weapons may include not only cities and silos, but also airfields, many other types of military installations, and a variety of other important assets that are not necessarily collocated with urban populations. We already have a long list of such possible targets; now we are grouping them into operational plans which would be more responsive to the range of challenges that might face us. To the extent necessary, we are retargeting our forces accordingly.

Which among these options we might choose in a crisis would depend on the nature of any enemy's attack and on his objectives. Many types of targets can be pre-programmed as options—cities, other targets of value, military installations of many different kinds, soft strategic targets, hard strategic targets. A number of so-called counterforce targets, such as airfields, are quite soft and can be destroyed without pinpoint accuracy. The fact that we are able to knock out these targets—counterforce though it may be—does not appear to be the subject of much concern.

In some circumstances, however, a set of hard targets might be the most appropriate objective for our retaliation, and this I realize is a subject fraught with great emotion. Even so, several points about it need to be made.

—The destruction of a hardened target is not simply a function of accuracy; it results from the combined effects of accuracy, nuclear yield, and the number of warheads applied to the target.

—Both the United States and the Soviet Union already have the necessary combinations of accuracy, yield, and numbers in their missile forces to provide them with some hard-target-kill capability, but it is not a particularly efficient capability.

—Neither the United States nor the Soviet Union now has a disarming first strike capability, nor are they in any position to acquire such a capability in the foreseeable future, since each side has large numbers of strategic offensive systems that remain untargetable by the other side. Moreover, the ABM Treaty forecloses a defense against missiles. As I have already noted in public: "The

Soviets, under the Interim Offensive Agreement, are allowed 62 submarines and 950 SLBM launchers. In addition, they have many other nuclear forces. Any reasonable calculation would demonstrate, I believe, that it is not possible for us even to begin to eliminate the city-destruction potential embodied in their ICBMs, let alone their SLBM force.''

The moral of all this is that we should not single out accuracy as some sort of unilateral or key culprit in the hard-target-kill controversy. To the extent that we want to minimize unintended civilian damage from attacks on even soft targets, as I believe we should, we will want to emphasize high accuracy, low yields, and airburst weapons.

To enhance deterrence, we may also want a more efficient hard-target-kill capability than we now possess: both to threaten specialized sets of targets (possibly of concern to allies) with a greater economy of force, and to make it clear to a potential enemy that he cannot proceed with impunity to jeoparize our own system of hard targets.

Thus, the real issue is how much hard-target-kill capability we need, rather than the development of new combinations of accuracy and yield per se. Resolution of the quantitative issue, as I will discuss later, depends directly on the further evolution of the Soviet strategic offensive forces and on progress in the current phase of the Strategic Arms Limitation Talks. . . .

With a reserve capability for threatening urban-industrial targets, with offensive systems capable of increased flexibility and discrimination in targeting, and with concomitant improvements in sensors, surveillance, and command-control, we could implement response options that cause far less civilian damage than would now be the case. For those who consider such changes potentially destabilizing because of their fear that the options might be used, let me emphasize that without substantially more of an effort in other directions than we have any intention of proposing, there is simply no possibility of reducing civilian damage from a large-scale nuclear exchange sufficiently to make it a tempting prospect for any sane leader. But that is not what we are talking about here. At the present time, we are acquiring selective and discriminating options that are intended to deter another power from exercising any form of nuclear pressure. Simultaneously . . . we and our allies are improving our general purpose forces precisely so as to raise the threshold against the use of any nuclear forces.

The Countervailing Strategy

HAROLD BROWN

A significant achievement in 1980 was the codification of our evolving strategic doctrine, in the form of Presidential Directive No. 59. In my Report last year, I discussed the objectives and the principal elements of this countervailing strategy, and in August 1980, after P.D. 59 had been signed by President Carter, I elaborated it in some detail in a major policy address. Because of its importance, however, the countervailing strategy warrants special attention in this Report as well.

Two basic points should underlie any discussion of the counter-vailing strategy. *The first is that, because it is a strategy of deterrence, the countervailing strategy is designed with the Soviets in mind.* Not only must we have the forces, doctrine, and will to retaliate if attacked, we must convince the Soviets, *in advance,* that we do. Because it is designed to deter the Soviets, our strategic doctrine must take account of what we know about Soviet perspectives on these issues, for, by definition, deterrence requires shaping Soviet assessments about the risks of war—assessments they will make using their models, not ours. We must confront these views and take them into account in our planning. We may, and we do, think our models are more accurate, but theirs are the reality deterrence drives us to consider.

Several Soviet perspectives are relevant to the formulation of our deterrent strategy. First, Soviet military doctrine appears to contemplate the possibility of a relatively prolonged nuclear war. Second, there is evidence that they regard military forces as the obvious first targets in a nuclear exchange, not general industrial and economic capacity. Third, the Soviet leadership clearly places a high value on preservation of the regime and on the survival and continued effectiveness of the instruments of state power and control—a value at least as high as that they place on any losses to the general population, short of those involved in a general nuclear war. Fourth, in some contexts, certain elements of Soviet leadership seem to consider Soviet victory in a nuclear war to be at least a theoretical possibility.

From Report of the Secretary of Defense to the Congress on the FY 1982 Budget, FY 1983 Authorization Request and FY 1982–1986 Defense Programs, pp. 38–43. January 19, 1981.

All this does not mean that the Soviets are unaware of the destruction a nuclear war would bring to the Soviet Union; in fact, they are explicit on that point. Nor does this mean that we cannot deter, for clearly we can and we do.

The second basic point is that, because the world is constantly changing, our strategy evolves slowly, almost continually, over time to adapt to changes in U.S. technology and military capabilites, as well as Soviet technology, military capabilities, and strategic doctrine. A strategic doctrine that served well when the United States had only a few dozen nuclear weapons and the Soviets none would hardly serve as well unchanged in a world in which we have about 9,000 strategic warheads and they have about 7,000. As the strategic balance has shifted from overwhwelming U.S. superiority to essential equivalence, and as ICBM accuracies have steadily improved to the point that hard target kill probabilities are quite high, our doctrine must adapt itself to these new realities.

This does not mean that the objective of our doctrine changes; on the contrary, deterrence remains, as it always has been, our basic goal. Our countervailing strategy today is a natural evolution of the conceptual foundations built over a generation by men like Robert McNamara and James Schlesinger.

The United States has never—at least since nuclear weapons were available in significant numbers—had a strategic doctrine based simply and solely on reflexive, massive attacks on Soviet cities and populations. Previous administrations, going back almost 20 years, recognized the inadequacy as a deterrent of a targeting doctrine that would give us too narrow a range of options. Although for programming purposes, strategic forces were sometimes measured in terms of ability to strike a set of industrial targets, we have always planned both more selectively (for options limiting urban-industrial damage) and more comprehensively (for a wide range of civilian and military targets). The unquestioned Soviet attainment of strategic parity has put the final nail in the coffin of what we long knew was dead—the notion that we could adequately deter the Soviets solely by threatening massive retaliaton against their cities. . . .

Our countervailing strategy—designed to provide effective deterrence—tells the world that no potential adversary of the United States could ever conclude that the fruits of his aggression would be worth his own costs. This is true whatever the level of conflict contemplated. To the Soviet Union, our strategy makes clear that no course of aggression by them that led to use of nuclear weapons, on any scale of attack and at any stage of conflict, could lead to victory, however they may define victory. Besides our power to devastate the full target system of the USSR, the United States would have the option for more selective, lesser retaliatory attacks that would exact a prohibitively high price from the things the Soviet leadership prizes most—political and military control, nuclear and conventional military force, and the economic base needed to sustain a war.

Thus, the countervailing strategy is designed to be fully consistent with NATO's strategy of flexible response by providing options for appropriate response to aggression at whatever level it might occur. The essence of the countervailing strategy is to convince the Soviets that they will be successfully opposed at any level of aggression they choose, and that no plausible outcome at any level of conflict could represent "success" for them by any reasonable definition of success.

Five basic elements of our force employment policy serve to achieve the objectives of the countervailing strategy.

A. *Flexibility*

Our planning must provide a continuum of options, ranging from use of small numbers of strategic and/or theater nuclear weapons aimed at narrowly defined targets, to employment of large portions of our nuclear forces against a broad spectrum of targets. In addition to pre-planned targeting options, we are developing an ability to design other employment plans—in particular, smaller scale plans—on short notice in response to changing circumstances.

In theory, such flexibility also enhances the possibility of being able to control escalation of what begins as a limited nuclear exchange. I want to emphasize once again two points I have made repeatedly and publicly. First, I remain highly skeptical that escalation of a limited nuclear exchange can be controlled, or that it can be stopped short of an all-out, massive exchange. Second, even given that belief, I am convinced that we must do everything we can to make such escalation control possible, that opting out of this effort and consciously resigning ourselves to the inevitability of such escalation is a serious abdication of the awesome responsibilities nuclear weapons, and the unbelievable damage their uncontrolled use would create, thrust upon us. Having said that, let me proceed to the second element, which is escalation control.

B. *Escalation Control*

Plans for the controlled use of nuclear weapons, along with other appropriate military and political actions, should enable us to provide leverage for a negotiated termination of the fighting. At an early stage in the conflict, we must convince the enemy that further escalation will not result in achievement of his objectives, that it will not mean "success," but rather additional costs. To do this, we must leave the enemy with sufficient highly valued military, economic, and political resources still surviving but still clearly at risk, so that he has a strong incentive to seek an end to the conflict.

C. *Survivability and Endurance*

The key to escalation control is the survivability and endurance of our nuclear forces and the supporting communications, command and control, and intelligence (C³I) capabilities. The supporting C³I is critical to effective deterrence, and we have begun to pay considerably more attention to these issues than in the past. We must ensure that the United States is not placed in a "use or lose" situation, one that might lead to unwarranted escalation of the conflict. That is a central reason why, while the Soviets cannot ignore our *capability* to launch our retaliatory forces before an attack reaches its targets, we cannot afford to rely on "launch on warning" as the long-term solution to ICBM vulnerability. . . . Survivability and endurance are essential prerequisites to an ability to adapt the employment of nuclear forces to the entire range of potentially rapidly changing and perhaps unanticipated situations and to tailor them for the appropriate responses in those situations. And, without adequate survivability and endurance, it would be impossible for us to keep substantial forces in reserve.

D. *Targeting Objectives*

In order to meet our requirements for flexibility and escalation control, we must have the ability to destroy elements of four general categories of Soviet targets.

1. *Strategic Nuclear Forces*

The Soviet Union should entertain no illusion that by attacking our strategic nuclear forces, it could significantly reduce the damage it would suffer. Nonetheless, the state of the strategic balance after an initial exchange—measured both in absolute terms and in relation to the balance prior to the exchange—could be an important factor in the decision by one side to initiate a nuclear exchange. Thus, it is important—for the sake of deterrence—to be able to deny to the potential aggressor a fundamental and favorable shift in the strategic balance as a result of a nuclear exchange.

2. *Other Military Forces*

"Counterforce" covers much more than central strategic systems. We have for many years planned options to destroy the full range of Soviet (and, as appropriate, non-Soviet Warsaw Pact) military power, conventional as well as nuclear. Because the Soviets may define victory in part in terms of the overall post-war military balance, we will give special attention, in implementing the countervailing strategy, to more effective and more flexible targeting of the full range of military capabilities, so as to strengthen deterrence.

3. *Leadership and Control*

We must, and we do, include options to target organs of Soviet political and military leadership and control. As I indicated earlier, the regime constituted by these centers is valued highly by the Soviet leadership. A clear U.S. ability to destroy them poses a marked challenge to the essence of the Soviet system and thus contributes to deterrence. At the same time, of course, we recognize the role that a surviving supreme command could and would play in the termination of hostilities, and can envisage many scenarios in which destruction of them would be inadvisable and contrary to our own best interests. Perhaps the obvious is worth emphasizing: possession of a capability is not tantamount to exercising it.

4. *Industrial and Economic Base*

The countervailing strategy by no means implies that we do not—or no longer—recognize the ultimate deterrent effect of being able to threaten the full Soviet target structure, including the industrial and economic base. These targets are highly valued by the Soviets, and we must ensure that the potential loss of them is an ever-present factor in the Soviet calculus regarding nuclear war. Let me also emphasize that while, as a matter of policy, we do not target civilian population *per se*, heavy civilian fatalities and other casualties would inevitably occur in attacking the Soviet industrial and economic base, which is collocated with the Soviet urban population. I should add that Soviet civilian casualties would also be large in more focused attacks (not unlike the U.S. civilian casualty estimates cited earlier for Soviet attacks on our ICBM silos); indeed, they could be described as limited only in the sense that they would be significantly less than those resulting from an all-out attack.

E. *Reserve Forces*

Our planning must provide for the designation and employment of adequate, survivable, and enduring reserve forces and the supporting C³I systems both during and after a protracted conflict. At a minimum, we will preserve such a dedicated force of strategic weapon systems.

Because there has been considerable misunderstanding and misinterpretation of the countervailing strategy and of P.D. 59, it is worth restating what the countervailing strategy is *not*.

—It is *not* a new strategic doctrine; it is *not* a radical departure from U.S. strategic policy over the past decade or so. It *is* a refinement, a re-codification of previous statements of our strategic policy. It *is* the same essential strategic doctrine, restated more clearly and related more directly to current and prospective conditions and capabilities—U.S. and Soviet.

—It does *not* assume, or assert, that we can "win" a limited nuclear war, nor does it pretend or intend to enable us to do so. It *does* seek to convince the Soviets that they could not win such a war, and thus to deter them from starting one.

—It does *not* even assume, or assert, that a nuclear war could remain limited. I have made clear my view that such a prospect is highly unlikely. It *does,* however, prepare us to respond to a limited Soviet nuclear attack in ways other than automatic, immediate, massive retaliation.

—It does *not* assume that a nuclear war will in fact be protracted over many weeks or even months. It *does,* however, take into account evidence of Soviet thinking along those lines, in order to convince them that such a course, whatever its probability, could not lead to Soviet victory.

—It does *not* call for substituting primarily military for primarily civilian targets. It *does* recognize the importance of military and civilian targets. It does provide for increasing thè number and variety of options available to the President, covering the full range of military and civilian targets, so that he can respond appropriately and effectively to any kind of an attack, at any level.

—It is *not* inconsistent with future progress in arms control. In fact, it *does* emphasize many features—survivability, crisis stability, deterrence—that are among the core objectives of arms control. It does *not* require larger strategic arsenals; it *does* demand more flexibility and better control over strategic nuclear forces, whatever their size.

—Lastly, it is *not* a first strike strategy. Nothing in the policy contemplates that nuclear war can be a deliberate instrument for achieving our national security goals, because it cannot be. The premise, the objective, the core of our strategic doctrine remains unchanged—deterrence. The countervailing strategy, by specifying what we would do in response to any level of Soviet attack, serves to deter any such attack in the first place.

The Impossibility of
Limited Nuclear War

LEONID BREZHNEV

Q. Can a nuclear war be considered winnable?

A. Western political and military writers contend that Soviet military doctrine is based exclusively on the belief that a world nuclear war can be won. But that is a simplistic and distorted view of our approach. In fact, the Soviet Union holds that nuclear war would be a universal disaster and that it would most probably mean the end of civilization. It may lead to the destruction of all humankind. There may be no victor in such a war, and it can solve no political problems. As Leonid Brezhnev pointed out in his reply to a Pravda correspondent on 21 October 1981: "Anyone who starts a nuclear war in the hope of winning it has thereby decided to commit suicide. Whatever strength the attacker may have and whatever method of starting a nuclear war he may choose, he will not achieve his aims. Retaliation is unavoidable. That is our essential point of view."

AVERTING WAR BY ALL MEANS

Soviet people are not thinking in terms of winning a nuclear war but of averting such a war by all means. They take into account the changing relevance of armed forces as an instrument of politics. Here is how Leonid Brezhnev put it: "By and large, it is probably safe to say that people are gradually coming to understand that none of the problems in the world can be solved from positions of strength, by any sabre-rattling." (Speech in Alma-Ata, 29 August 1980.) Armed force, and doubly so nuclear force, is acquiring new functions. In this sense, we see eye to eye with Rear Adm. Gene LaRocque, director of the U.S. Center for Defense Information, who says neither side could eventually consider itself a victor in the event of a major nuclear war between the U.S.S.R. and the U.S.A. More than a hundred million people would perish on either side, and up to three-quarters of the two countries' economic potentials would be destroyed.

From *The New York Times,* Saturday, November 21, 1981, Leonid Brezhnev, "Excerpts from a Soviet Booklet on Nuclear War" *The Threat to Europe.*

'LIMITED NUCLEAR WAR'

The same applies to the idea of a "limited nuclear war" in Europe or elsewhere as conceived in U.S. Presidential Directive 59 of 25 July 1980. One might discourse on "limited nuclear war" in theory only, but on the practical plane it is nothing less than unrealistic.

Q. In the West one hears now and then that Soviet military doctrine is of an aggressively offensive nature, considers a first strike possible and includes plans for a sudden, blitzkrieg-style invasion of Western Europe. Is this true?

A. That is another popular theme in Western military and political propaganda. They use a very simple ruse to adduce that Soviet doctrine is aggressively offensive. They do so by quoting from works of Soviet military theorists devoted not to doctrine or military policy but to particular aspects of combat, such as tactics in the battlefield. These quotes are passed off as Soviet doctrine, though that is a deliberately incorrect and specious approach. It gives not the slightest idea of Soviet doctrine, which is defensive but, of course, necessarily envisages the training of soldiers for various actions in the field of battle.

Soviet military doctrine is of a purely defensive nature. "We never had and never will have any strategic doctrine other than a defensive one," says the declaration of the Warsaw Treaty states of 15 May 1980. It does not admit of either a first or pre-emptive strike or of any "lightning" invasion of Western Europe. In so doing it follows definite political, ethical and military principles. There is no aggressive element in Soviet military doctrine because the Soviet Union has no political, economic, social or military aims in Europe or anywhere else that it intends to secure by armed force.

Q. Why then do Soviet theoretical works on military strategy of, say, the early 60's refer to offensive action, to building up a military advantage? Doesn't this prove that Soviet military strategy reposes on these principles even today?

A. No, it proves no such thing. Soviet military strategy is neither immutable nor everlasting. It changes with the changing world. The same happens in the United States, where the strategy of flexible response and thereupon that of realistic deterrence replaced a doctrine of massive retaliation. Soviet theoretical works of the early 60's reflected the views of their time. And it was a time when the United States commanded a considerable nuclear-missile advantage, when it threatened the Soviet Union with massive nuclear strikes and declared that a nuclear war against the U.S.S.R. was winnable.

EMERGENCE OF DÉTENTE

The equilibrium of strategic forces that shaped up between the U.S.S.R. and the U.S.A. compelled the latter to accept détente, which made considerable headway in the 70's and slackened the war danger.

Technological advances and growth of nuclear weapons stockpiles had made nuclear war altogether senseless. Soviet military doctrine, which has always reposed on the principle of retaliatory, that is, defensive, action, says nothing at all in the new conditions of the 70's and early 80's of nuclear war being winnable and, more, lays the accent still more emphatically than before on preventing it, on maintaining the military equilibrium and on lowering the level of military confrontation by means of military détente. "There is no task that we intend to accomplish by armed force," Leonid Brezhnev said in an interview to Vorwärts, the weekly of the Social Democratic Party of Germany.

Q. It is said that the numerical strength of the Soviet armed forces is far greater than the country needs for defense. Is that true?

A. The strength of the Soviet armed forces is not greater than needed for defense. It matches the defensive needs. To see this you must consider at least two pertinent factors: the regional strength balances and the geostrategic factor.

SPECIAL SOVIET SITUATION

The Soviet Union's strategic situation compels it, for purposes of defense, to insure not only a general equilibrium of strength between it and the U.S.A., and between the Warsaw Treaty countries and NATO, but also a regional equilibrium in separate theaters, each with its own military specifics. To begin with, the strength of the armed forces of the Soviet Union and its allies must match the area of the territory they defend, the overall length of frontiers and the nature of the potential dangers. No other country in the world has anything even remotely equal or similar to these factors. The armies of the Warsaw Treaty countries have a territory of 23,500,000 square kilometers to defend, out of which 22,500,000 square kilometers are Soviet territory. This is more than the area of the United States, Europe and China combined. The NATO armies have only 2 million square kilometers, or one-eleventh of that area, to defend.

Faced in the West by the NATO bloc, which includes three nuclear powers, the Soviet Union is simultaneously exposed to danger in the east from two American Pacific nuclear fleets and from China, with its growing nuclear potential and the world's most numerous army. Furthermore, the deployment of U.S. Naval nuclear forces in the northern sector of the Indian Ocean within reach of southern regions of the Soviet Union combines with the string of U.S. military bases stretching from the Mediterranean across the Middle East to Pakistan and countries in Southeast Asia. In effect, the Soviet Union is compelled to reckon with the likelihood of a blockade being put up around it. This is being made increasingly apparent, among other things, by the growing political and military cooperation between the United States and China.

AN AMERICAN ADVANTAGE

Further, it ought to be borne in mind that by virtue of its favorable geographical situation, the United States can insure the defense of its own national frontiers by a minimal force. The Soviet Union, on the other hand, is compelled to guarantee proper balance and dependable defense by distributing its forces along the entire length of its borders and, moreover, insuring a rough equilibrium in the world ocean where it is exposed to growing dangers from the U.S. nuclear Navy. Lastly, we ought to remember that the United States can add freely to its troop strength in Europe and Asia by moving reserves and weaponry stationed in its national territory, where they are not pinned down by anyone and in no way hemmed in. In this sense, the Soviet Union would be in a far less favorable position in the event of a conflict.

It is therefore completely wrong to compare the aggregate strength of the Soviet armed forces to the strength of NATO troops in Europe, as this is often done in the West, and to overlook the radical distinctions in the geostrategic position of the U.S.S.R. and the U.S.A., the Warsaw Treaty organization and NATO. It is clear that the more complicated global geostrategic situation of the Soviet Union makes its position in the European theater less favorable than that of the United States. This is proof enough that Soviet troop strength balances with the real defensive needs of the country as a whole and does not exceed these needs.

Q. Isn't the military balance steadily tipping in favor of the Soviet Union? This can't help creating alarm in the West.

A. During the first roughly 20 years after the war, the United States had a strategic nuclear advantage over the U.S.S.R. At the turn of the 70's, the defensive efforts of the Soviet Union ended this superiority. Since then, there has been military-strategic equilibrium.

COMMENTS OF AMERICANS

This is acknowledged by the Soviet Union and by Western statesmen as well.

President Carter, for example, said on 25 April 1979 that the strategic forces of the United States and the Soviet Union today are essentially equivalent. The same was said on 5 April 1979 by Harold Brown, who acknowledged that despite the Russian military achievements, the Soviet Union has no military superiority in the nuclear field and that today there is a strategic balance; the United States, he said, is not likely to be strategically behind in 1985.

Part II
Case Studies
in the Innovation,
Obsolescence, and
Application of Force

The ten studies in Part II are taken from the twentieth century and are arranged in chronological order. Seven of the selections illustrate the general principles explained in Part I. They deal with different types of military technologies, ranging from chemical to nuclear weapons, and treat the use of military force in both wartime and peacetime. In all of the examples, military power was essential to the successful pursuit of national goals or was thought to be so. Each of these selections either demonstrates a specific way of using military power—in an offensive, defensive, or deterrent fashion—or identifies the factors that restrained states in their use of force.

Frederic J. Brown explains why restraint prevailed in the use of chemical weapons in World Wars I and II. George H. Quester explores the effects that fears of strategic bombing had on foreign policy in Europe in the 1930s and shows why these fears were not realized in the first few years of World War II. Sir George Sansom explains why the Japanese decided to launch what they considered to be a preventive war against the United States and indicates why their strategic calculations were faulty. Louis Morton discusses the reasons why the United States used the atomic bomb against Japan. Morton H. Halperin describes the evolution of a system of mutual restraints in the American and the Chinese use of force during the Korean War and speculates on why the two countries accepted the restraints. Albert and Robert Wohlstetter discuss the reasons why the Soviet Union put missiles into Cuba in September of 1962 and why it took them out in October and November of the same year. John Lewis Gaddis tests the strategy of flexible response in its application to Vietnam by the Kennedy and Johnson administrations.

Three of the studies in Part II deal with two of the perennial tasks involved in using military power. The first task is to discover how to use a new weapon effectively; the second, to determine when an old weapon has become obsolete. These two tasks are not easy for strategists and political leaders to perform. Because of the nature of their work strategists come to believe firmly in certain doctrines. The difficulty they have in adjusting strategy to capability depends in part on just how tenaciously they hold to those doctrines. If they become committed to fixed paths, they will not be receptive either to experimentation with new weapons or to elimination of old ones. Political leaders sometimes press for the adoption of new weapons and strategies and sometimes oppose them. Which weapons and strategies political leaders favor depends on their domestic political interests, on their security requirements, and on their image of the nation.

Robert J. Art shows how weapons innovation is related to the interests of military organizations and to the purposes of political leaders. Edward L. Katzenbach, Jr., describes the innumerable rationalizations used to extend the life of the horse cavalry well into the twentieth century. Art and Stephen E. Ockenden show why the intervention of political leaders was required to overcome the resistance of the American military services to the cruise missile.

The Influence of
Foreign Policy on Seapower:
New Weapons and Weltpolitik
in Wilhelminian Germany

ROBERT J. ART

INTRODUCTION

In researching for this piece, I began with the following question: what caused the German navy in the early months of World War I to proclaim so rapidly and so vociferously the potential of the U-boat when, for at least ten years before that time, the very same Navy had scoffed at the submarine and treated it with "benign neglect?" Why in a matter of months did the Navy herald a weapon that for years it had downplayed? I soon realized that I could not emphasize the rapidity *and* the profundity of the change that occurred in naval thinking during these few months unless I could show how firmly fixed and lowly placed were submarines in German naval thought before World War I. What thus began as a short piece on the change in German naval thinking from August through December of 1914 quickly blossomed into a search for the causes of the earlier benign neglect.

I therefore found it necessary to immerse myself, not only in German naval thinking from 1895 to 1915, but also in German foreign policy during the same period. For as the title testifies, German foreign policy had a signal influence on German naval power. The aims and tactics of Germany's rulers—on the one hand, their pursuit of *Weltpolitik* (a world policy) and their desire for coequal status with England; and on the other, their resort to military threats and their penchant for direct confrontation—determined the types of weapons the navy developed, the ones it chose to concentrate resources on, and the ways it planned to use them. But because the thrust of German

This chapter is adapted from Robert J. Art *The Influence of Foreign Policy on Seapower,* Sage Professional Papers in International Studies, Copyright © 1973 by Sage Publications, Inc.

To save space, all footnotes have been omitted. For full documentation, see original.

AUTHOR'S NOTE: *I would like to thank the following people for the valuable comments they gave me on this monograph: Vincent Davis, Robert Erwin, Lawrence Finklestein, Robert Jervis, William Kaufmann, James Kurth, George Quester, Thomas Schelling, Richard Ullman, Kenneth Waltz, and Samuel Williamson. I would also like to thank the Center for International Affairs, Harvard University, under whose auspices this work was written, for continuing research support; and the Council on Foreign Relations, for the time off they so graciously gave me as an International Affairs Fellow for 1971-1972.*

foreign policy from the mid 1890s onward was to challenge Britain's preeminent world position, the way Germany's rulers envisioned using their seapower was almost entirely dependent upon their image of *England's* political and naval leaders' image of what counted in seapower and naval warfare. The benign neglect of submarines and the fixation on battlefleets that characterized German naval development in the twenty years before Sarajevo occurred precisely because the British played up the latter and downgraded the former. The two decades before 1914 can be aptly termed "compellence before Sarajevo" when describing the use Germany made of her seapower vis-à-vis England. One intent of this piece, then, is to do for seapower from 1895 to 1915 what George Quester did for airpower from 1919 to 1945 in his fine study *Deterrence before Hiroshima*—namely, to show that the post 1945 strategic concepts and style of analysis generated by nuclear strategists were in use at a much earlier time, even if the present-day terminology was not then in vogue.

A second intent of this piece is to demonstrate by example the determinative role that intangible factors often play in international politics. A lust for greatness, an aggressiveness born of feeling second-best, a dogged determination to swagger on the world's stage, a revengeful pique at England's refusal to accord Germany a position her leaders felt her entitled to—these factors were as important, if not more so, than were any economic necessities or domestic political considerations for setting the course of German foreign policy from 1895 onward. In stressing the role of these intangibles, I have, by counter-example, taken issue with, but by no means invalidated, two approaches currently popular among international relations students: the bureaucratic politics school and the misperception theorists. Neither of these groups will find much support for their viewpoints here.

The outstanding lesson for the bureaucratic politics school is that bureaucratic politics made little dent on German foreign policy and naval doctrine before August, 1914. Wilhelm II did not control foreign policy as tightly as Bismarck had; but from 1897 until Sarajevo, his voice, his perceptions, his perspectives, his desires, and his indiscretions largely set the course of German foreign policy. Tirpitz did not run the navy without opposition to his program, but at every significant point, because he had the support of the Kaiser, he crushed all his opponents. The ability of the Kaiser and Tirpitz to impose their conceptions of foreign policy and seapower on their subordinates gives evidence of the utility of what Graham Allison has termed "the rational actor model." There is great economy and hence validity in viewing Germany's foreign policy, naval doctrine, and interaction with Britain in these twenty years in terms of Germany as a unitary purposive actor. Bureaucratic politics is important for explaining why the navy rapidly reversed its position after Sarajevo and argued for all-out submarine warfare against England's commerce. But, even here, we cannot ignore the change in structural conditions: battleships were best suited for "compellence" in peacetime; U-boats, for victory in war. A radical alteration in environment changed the terms under which pro- and anti-submarine partisans would wage their bureaucratic struggles. In this case bureaucratic politics makes sense *only* when viewed in light of the systemic perspective. (I suspect that this proposition holds true for most other important cases in modern international relations.)

Similarly, misperception theorists (see, for example, Robert Jervis' forthcoming *Misperception and International Relations*) will find little evidence for their viewpoint, if by the term "misperception" they mean misunderstandings based on intentions incorrectly inferred from the actions of others. There are two difficulties with this approach, one theoretical and the other empirical. First, the intentions of statesmen, although not inscrutable, will never possess the air of finality that their actions have. If a statesman can never be certain of the intentions of others, he can never be certain that he is misperceiving the intent of their actions. Furthermore, in a fundamental sense, misperception is endemic to international relations: it is rooted in the very structure of international politics. Anarchy breeds a bias in statesmen toward conservativism, toward planning for the most disastrous (even if it be the least likely) event, and toward being capability- not intention-oriented. In an environment that puts a premium on self-help, there is no responsible alternative to being skeptical and cautious about the actions of others. We are thus faced with one or both of two uncomfortable conclusions: either statesmen always misperceive the actions of others (in which case we should ask the misperception theorists to tell us, not why statesmen misperceive, but why they sometimes correctly guess the intent of others); or they can never know if they are doing so. The only escape for the political actor is to concentrate on the *consequences* of other statesmen's actions, not on their intent.

What stands out starkly in Anglo-German relations from 1895 to 1914 is precisely this concentration by elites in both countries on the consequences for their country's position of the other's actions.

Second, to the extent that we can plumb the intentions of statesmen, what also stands out in this period is—not each elite's wrongly conceived beliefs about the other—but the clarity and correctness of the perceptions that leaders at the top had of the other's goals and of the challenges and dangers that each presented to the other. Anglo-German perceptions of one another were rooted, not only in the structure of pre-World War I international politics, but also in the substance of German and British aims in the world at large. There were various misunderstandings and miscalculations at certain points, but the central aspect around which Anglo-German relations turned was never in doubt—that each wished to be "top dog" and that neither could tolerate the other's being so. There were no misperceptions on this score in Berlin or London.

A third intent of this piece is to illustrate by example the reactions of military organizations to major innovations in weaponry. Given the fact that there is an indeterminate relation between the technological capability of a weapon and its use, that what a weapon can do does not predetermine how it will be used, what are the other factors that determine how it will be employed? The basic conclusion of this piece is that military organizations are terribly conservative in adapting radically new weapons into their contingency planning. They try to fit these radically new weapons into their preexisting images of war; they do not readily alter these images to take account of major innovations unless forced to do so by political pressures or exigencies of war. Organization theorists will find evidence for their thesis that crises are necessary in order to shatter military "mind-sets."

The final intent of this paper is to satisfy one of my long-standing desires, born out of an equally long-standing frustration with both diplomatic historians and international relations theorists. I view this piece as an exercise in "analytic history"—to serve as a model for diplomatic historians who too often have no theoretical framework from which to interpret events and for international relations theorists who too often know nothing of diplomatic history. To quote Immanuel Kant: "Experience without theory is blind, but theory without experience is mere intellectual play." I hope that this piece combines both.

NEW WEAPONS: THE GAP BETWEEN CAPABILITY AND USE

Nations often use new military weapons in ways quite different from what had been planned. Hindsight reveals an oft-recurring difference between what could or should have been done with new weapons and what was done with them. Many reasons can be given to explain the difference between capability and use. One is of particular concern here: namely, the indeterminate nature of the relation between technological capability and effective use. What can be done with aggregate forces or with particular types of weapons does not necessarily prescribe what should be done with them. Capabilities created by technology do not automatically yield guidelines either for the tactics of the battlefield or for the strategy of a war. The relation between technological capability and effective use is indeterminate simply because a single military instrument can have multiple uses. Because many choices are possible, good choices are difficult. The opportunity to do many things with a weapon makes it hard to decide a priori which ones of them are among the more effective.

The problem of choice becomes acute when strategists and

statesmen must cope with major innovations in weaponry. In these cases their past experience does not necessarily show them how new capabilities can be most effectively used in pursuit of their foreign and military policies and can in fact cause them to misuse the new capabilities at their disposal. In attempting to devise the tactics and the strategies with which to exploit new weaponry, these men find themselves in a terrible bind. They are forced to engage in the worst sort of crystal ball-gazing: trying to figure out how to make best use of something that has never been used (or with which there is very limited experience) in future conditions, the shape of which no one is or can be certain.

In such circumstances, national leaders can easily err in the plans they make and actions they take. The cases of error are legion. One has been chosen to illustrate the point: the use the German navy contemplated for the U-boat before 1914. Before World War I, the German navy regarded the U-boat as an experimental weapon, one whose role in the navy's overall strategy was at best marginal. Very early in the war, however, the German navy quickly reversed its position and held out to the civilian officials of the government and to the army High Command the U-boat's great promise. Later on in the war, the U-boat proved to be one of Germany's most effective weapons.

The case of Germany and the U-boat is a rich one for study because it illustrates four important lessons: first, that strategists will often resist making the changes in strategic doctrine that would be necessary to accommodate a new weapon; second, that the foreign policy goals that strategists have accepted and the strategic theories that they have developed to support these goals profoundly affect the ways that new weapons will be viewed and used; third, that "brand loyalty"—a strongly held and an emotionally felt attachment to a particular strategic theory—can blind strategists to the possibilities inherent in new weapons; and, fourth, that the exigencies of war shatter expectations and thereby create the political and the psychological conditions conducive to the exploitation of new military capabilities.

THE U-BOAT'S PROMISE AND POWER

On the eve of World War I, Sir Percy Scott, the man who had fathered the gunnery revolution at sea in the late 1890s, declared that the era of the battleship was over. In a famous letter to the London *Times* he wrote:

> I do not think that the importance of submarines has been fully recognized, neither do I think that it has been realized how completely their advent has revolutionized naval warfare. . . .
> The . . . function of a battleship is to attack an enemy's fleet, but there will be no fleet to attack, as it will not be safe for a fleet to put to sea. . . . now that submarines have come in battleships are of no use whether for

defensive or offensive purposes. . . . Not only is the open sea unsafe; a battleship is not immune from attack even in a closed harbor. . . .
    . . . as the motor-vehicle has driven the horse from the road, so has the submarine driven the battleship from the sea [Scott, 1914: 10].

Scott was not alone in dire predictions about the submarine's effects on sea warfare. Equally pessimistic, though for different reasons, was Sir John Fisher, First Sea Lord from 1904 to 1910. In a memorandum of January, 1913, to Winston Churchill, then First Lord of the Admiralty, Fisher prophetically described the effects the submarine would have on Britain:

> [The submarine] cannot capture the merchant ship; she has no spare hands to put a prize crew on board; little or nothing would be gained by disabling her engines or propeller; she cannot convoy her into harbor; and, in fact, it is impossible for the submarine to deal with commerce in the light and provisions of accepted international law. . . . There is nothing else the submarine can do except sink her capture. . . . This submarine menace is a terrible one for British commerce and Great Britain alike, for no means can be suggested at present of meeting it except by reprisals [quoted in Marder 1966: 363].

To Scott the submarine was a counterforce weapon that rendered the battleship highly vulnerable to attack; to Fisher the submarine was a terror weapon that threatened Great Britain with mass starvation. Neither of these conceptions, however, gained much currency in the British royal navy in the decade before World War I. During that period the Admiralty continued to cast the submarine in a decidedly defensive role: its primary task was to serve as the "final insurance against invasion" by patrolling the coastal waters along with the older destroyer flotillas (Marder, 1966: 334; Hurd, 1918: 187–197; Keyes, 1934: 19–39; and Smith, 1964: 8–24). Even Sir Roger Keyes, Inspecting Captain of Submarines and a submarine enthusiast, dismissed as "impossible and unthinkable" the idea that the Germans would use the submarine to sink merchantmen without warning and without regard to the safety of their crews. In reply to Fisher's 1913 Memorandum, Churchill wrote that "on the question of the use of submarines to sink merchant vessels . . . I do not believe this would ever be done by a civilized Power (Keyes, 1934: 53; Churchill, 1923: 280). Not considering the submarine a significant weapon, nor one likely to be used widely against either merchant or war ships, the royal navy spent little time and effort devising offensive and defensive tactics for it. As a consequence, Britain entered World War I without the royal navy's having developed a single weapon effective against the submarine.
    The German navy shared the British royal navy's skepticism about the submarine. As a consequence of its attitude, the German navy

entered the war without any definite idea of what to do with the U-boat and without any expectation that it would be of great value. And yet, soon after the war began, the German navy became an ardent proponent of using the U-boat against Britain's merchant shipping and overseas trade. The navy succeeded in converting the Kaiser and the government to its point of view: on February 4, 1915, Germany announced to the world that she had adopted a *Handelskrieg* (commerce war) policy. She declared that beginning with the eighteenth of the month, the waters around Britain and Ireland would constitute a war zone and that "every enemy merchant ship found in this area would be destroyed" (Foreign Office dispatch quoted in May, 1959: 122). By 1916, even the U-boat's greatest skeptic, Admiral Alfred von Tirpitz, who also happened to be the creator of Germany's modern navy, was praising the U-boat. Trying to convince Chancellor Bethmann-Holweg to drop his resistance to the unrestricted use of the U-boat, Tirpitz wrote in support of the Handelskrieg policy:

> The most important and surest means which can be adopted to bring England to her knees is the use of our U-boats at the present time. We shall not be able to defeat England by a war on land alone. . . . England will be cut to the heart by the destruction by U-boats of every ship which approaches the English coast. The ocean's commerce is the very elixir of life for England, its interruption for any length of time a deadly danger, its permanent interruption absolutely fatal within a short time. . . . The more the losses take place with merciless regularity at the very gates of the island kingdom, the more powerful will be the moral effect on the English people. . . . a timely U-boat war is . . . , if vigorously carried on, the form of warfare which will unconditionally decide the war to England's disadvantage.

Tirpitz's expectations were never fully realized. Germany did, however, come within a shade of knocking Britain out of the war after she began unrestricted submarine warfare on January 8, 1917. In April of that year alone, 881,000 tons of allied and neutral shipping were sunk. Out of every hundred ships that left Britain in the spring and summer of 1917, twenty-five never came back. The unrestricted U-boat war was also highly effective against the royal navy, though indirectly. At one point the heavy losses of British tankers reduced the usual six to eight month's reserve of fuel oil to eight weeks. This shortage in turn required that restrictions be placed on the movements of the Grand Fleet (Brodie, 1944: 317). Only American entry into the war, shortage of U-boats due to the lack of a crash building program, and development of convoying and other antisubmarine techniques narrowly saved Britain from disaster.

U-BOATS BEFORE THE HANDELSKRIEG

The contrast between the use Germany made of the U-boat after February of 1915 and the use she had previously envisioned is striking. Before the war no one at the top levels of naval command had seriously thought of using the U-boat against Britain's commercial shipping (Scheer, 1920: 224, Spindler, 1932: 1–4, 153; Spindler, 1926: 837–838). In September, 1914, the German High Command had rejected any such plan. Even as late as October 13, 1914, Admiral von Pohl, Chief of the Admiralty, refused to accept it. Only in early November did support for a Handelskieg sweep through the top echelons of the navy (Birnbaum, 1958: 22–25; Spindler, 1932: 8–10, 27–28). The pressure of events, not careful planning beforehand, converted the navy. Almost by accident and almost as an afterthought did the German navy become converted to the Handelskrieg strategy.

If Germany did not seriously contemplate a U-boat commerce-war against Britain before November of 1914, what did she plan to do with her submarines? Over this question the German navy was divided. One group had little faith in the new weapon and thought that it would be useful primarily for reconnaissance. Another group was more optimistic: perhaps the U-boat could be used in conjunction with the high seas fleet to achieve superiority over the British battlefleet and thereby gain control of the seas. Even this group, however, envisioned an auxiliary, counterforce role for the U-boat. Its function would be to cooperate with the high seas fleet in engaging and in destroying portions of the enemy fleet at a time. In this manner the fleet could at some point risk a decisive encounter with the main British force (Brodie, 1944: 297–298; Scheer, 1920: 20–25, 29; Spindler, 1932: 151–152; Tirpitz, 1919: II, 412–417).

In the decade before 1914, Germany's U-boat building program reflected the navy's estimate of its limited utility. A larger amount was spent during these ten years on torpedo boats than on U-boats, and both amounts were small. At the beginning of the war, the German navy had 28 submarines, of which only ten were capable of long distance operations (Spindler, 1932: 151).

That the building program reflected the limited, counterforce role conceived for the U-boat becomes even clearer if the small number of submarines that Germany had in 1914 is contrasted with her own estimate of what she would have required in order to engage successfully in a commerce war. The estimate was made in March of 1914 by one of Germany's best technical experts on the U-boat, Lieutenant-Captain Blum who also happened to be one of the country's few vigorous proponents of U-boat warfare. Blum calculated that Germany would need 222 long-range U-boats in order to maintain an effective blockade of Great Britain (Spindler, 1932: 153–154). He had

arrived at this figure after his superior had told him to determine how
many U-boats the German navy would require in case of war; his conclusions were then to be used as the basis for a new U-boat construction program. Blum's enthusiasm for the U-boat far surpassed that of
his superiors: they accepted neither his figure of 222 nor the plans
accompanying it. By refusing to implement Blum's recommendations,
the navy had clearly rejected a commerce-war strategy and made
definite its intent to relegate the U-boat to an auxiliary role.

Before 1913, such a decision would have been sensible. Between
1906 (when Germany completed construction of her first U-boat) and
1913 (when she installed the first diesel engines on the U-19), the
primitive technical state of U-boat development dictated, not
necessarily a modest investment in the submarine, but certainly a
modest submarine force (Spindler, 1932: 149). To have built many
U-boats would have been wasteful because, before 1913, they suffered
from two debilitating deficiencies:

(1) Their range was so severely restricted that any effective blockade along
the entire English coast was impossible to carry out.

(2) Because their engines were gasoline-burning, these U-boats were rather
risky to serve on. The engines not only emitted toxic fumes within the
vessel, but they also expelled such huge clouds of exhaust that discovery
by enemy destroyers was made easy (Brodie, 1944: 296–297; Tirpitz,
1919: II, 404–417).

In view of such deficiencies, one can understand Admiral Tirpitz saying, "I refused to throw away money on submarines so long as they
could only cruise in home waters, and therefore be of no use to us"
(Tirpitz, 1919: II, 179–180). One of Tirpitz's confirmed rules was
never to adopt a new weapon fully until after its military usefulness
had clearly been shown. This rule may also account for his failure to
invest more money at an earlier date in U-boat development so as to
improve its range.

STRATEGY AND TECHNOLOGY: THE COMPLEX RELATIONSHIP

The state of U-boat development until 1913 helps to explain why
the German navy relegated the submarine to a secondary role and
chose to build only a small number of them. Beginning in 1913,
however, diesel engines were installed on the U-19 and on all subsequent boats (Tirpitz, 1919: II, 406). The effects were dramatic: range
and safety both increased. For the first time since she began building
U-boats in 1904, Germany had a submarine capable of sustained,
long-distance activities. And yet, the improvement did not alter the
role cast for the U-boat by the German navy. The navy continued to

reject the use of the submarine for any kind of solo, long-distance mission—except perhaps for reconnaissance—right up until the war. It continued to cast the U-boat in an auxiliary, counterforce role. And by its rejection of the Blum building program, it had clearly rejected the Handelskrieg strategy. To explain why the navy continued to think in pre-1913 terms about the U-boat from 1913 on—to explain why she poured resources into dreadnoughts once they were "discovered" but not U-boats once they were improved—we must turn from the U-boat's technological development to the German navy's grand strategy. To do so is to see the importance of predispositions—to see how strategic doctrine can affect, not only the uses to which new technology is put, but also the rapidity with which new technology will be developed.

CRUISERS OR BATTLESHIPS?

Before the war, in essence, submarines were denigrated because battleships were worshipped. Tirpitz, the Kaiser, and the officers of the high seas fleet had all locked onto the strategy that Tirpitz himself had devised seventeen years earlier. In June of 1897, after having assumed the position of State Secretary of the Imperial Naval Office, Tirpitz sent to the Kaiser a long memorandum in which he set forth the outlines of the strategy that was to dominate German naval thinking until November, 1914. The strategy, as simple as it was revolutionary, was built upon these four principles:

(1) The naval force should be built for the worst-case contingency, because "that . . . naval force which meets the most difficult situation will be seen to be sufficient for all other situations."

(2) The naval force should be aimed against Great Britain, not only because England was "the most dangerous naval enemy at the present time," but also "it is . . . the enemy against which we most urgently require a certain measure of naval force as a political power factor."

(3) The naval force must be concentrated in home waters, because then "it can unfold its greatest military potential between Heligoland and the Thames."

(4) The naval force should consist of battleships, not cruisers, because "the military situation against England demands battleships in as great a number as possible."

The type of navy Tirpitz desired was determined by the type of goal he held. Tirpitz wanted a navy that could be used to compel Britain to come to terms with Germany. Germany's terms were Britain's acceptance of Germany's colonial aspirations, maritime interests, and expanding overseas trade and investment—in short, Britain's acquiescence in Germany's challenge to British economic and political predominance throughout the world. Tirpitz argued that "the flag had to follow trade" and that German "development on the broad back of British Free Trade and the British world-empire would continue only *until it was stopped.*" The navy was never "an end in itself, but always a function of these maritime interests." "Without seapower," declared Tirpitz (1919: I, 77–78, 254, 274), "Germany's position in the world resembled a mollusc without a shell." Tirpitz held to "the old principle that only through '*Macht*' [Might] can a great people be secure . . . [because as] long as the earth is peopled with men, it must stand in the life of the people before 'Right'" (quoted in Graham, 1938: 307).

For Tirpitz the game was thus great power rivalry; the stakes, world preeminence; the resources, ships. To be a great power, a nation had to have a powerful navy. To be a world power, a nation had to have the means to make its influence felt and its will obeyed all over the globe. To challenge the world's greatest power, a nation had to imitate its sources of strength. To be a great power or a world power or the world's greatest power thus required that Germany build a formidable navy.

What kind of navy should Germany build? One, answered Tirpitz, that would enable Germany to make credible threats. If Britain were to take the German threat seriously, then Germany had to be capable of seriously threatening Britain. Tirpitz therefore argued that successful sea warfare (or credible threats to go to war) required a navy's weapons to be *similar* to those of its potential opponent. Because Britain had built a battleship fleet, so must Germany: only battleships could fight battleships with any hope of success. He argued, furthermore, that German battleships had to match British battleships in quality. If British battleships, for example, had guns with a range of ten miles and German battleships had guns with a range of only five miles, then the British fleet could sink the German fleet before its guns had had an opportunity to fire (Tirpitz, 1919: I, 75–87, 119–120; see also Churchill, 1951: 125–133, and Steinberg, 1965: 65–66). Through his experience in the Far East, Tirpitz had thus reached the same conclusion about seapower that Mahan had arrived at through his study of British naval history: "the natural purpose of a fleet is the strategic offensive" (Tirpitz, quoted in Langer, 1960: 431).

By choosing to concentrate on building battleships instead of cruisers, Tirpitz was clearly rejecting the other major strand of naval thinking in the late nineteenth century: the cruiser-commerce-raiding strategy. The theory of cruiser warfare attained its greatest degree of acceptance in France and was fully developed there by Admiral Théophile Aube and the *Jeune École*. According to this school of naval strategy, steam engines had made sea battles like Trafalgar relics of the past. France had fought at Trafalgar in order to break the British blockade. Now, no longer dependent upon the whims of the wind, a nation could easily slip its ships through an enemy's blockade and thereby render it ineffective or, by concentrating its own forces at selective points, smash the blockade. The swiftness of modern war, moreover, had rendered blockades obsolete: the next war, like those of 1859, 1866, and 1870, would be over long before the pressure of a blockade could make itself felt. Furthermore, rather than seeking combat with the stronger sea power's main fleet, the weaker power would keep its main fleet from action, either by fleeing from its stronger opponent on the high seas or by remaining at rest at base.

Instead of challenging his adversary's battlefleet, the weaker power would raid and destroy his commerce and thereby ruin him (Ropp, 1966: 446-447, 1962: 208-209, 1937: 258-262, 273-275; and Langer, 1960: 420-421). The purpose of commerce-raiding was not to starve the opponent or to prevent him from importing all of the goods necessary to carry on the war, but rather to produce an economic panic that would in turn bring about a social collapse (Ropp, 1937: 269; Z. and Montechant, 1893: 71-89, 136-155, 322-364). The strategy was to destroy only that amount of his commerce necessary to produce a collapse from within. The focus was on the enemy's morale rather than upon his material.

For effective commerce-raiding, cruisers and torpedo boats would suffice. For the cost of one battleship, many cruisers and scores of torpedo boats could be built. Battleships were therefore not "cost-effective"—they surpassed the requirements for the task at hand and consequently entailed too many opportunity costs. Battleships were also highly vulnerable to attack by torpedo boats: the modern-day "Davids" would literally swarm around these monoliths and swiftly send them to the bottom (Ropp, 1937: 263-267, 275). Aube argued that it was insane to invest huge sums of money in a weapon so vulnerable to attack and to do so with the knowledge that such investments would preclude the purchase of enough of the weapons that would really count in a war with a major naval power.

The cruiser-warfare theory was clearly a countervalue, not a counterforce, strategy: its ultimate target was the enemy's civilian population and its will to fight, not the enemy's physical ability to do so. The cruiser-warfare theory was the strategy of an inferior naval power. The Jeune École strategists knew that France could never hope to build as many battleships as England had. Since that was not possible, why not assert that France need not do so? By arguing that France should build cruisers and torpedo boats to raid commerce, instead of battleships to fight battleships, the Jeune École declared that the only alternative open to France was also the most effective. The Jeune

École, in short, argued that the only way to defeat England at sea was to build weapons that were *not* similar to those of the royal navy. In the words of one member of this school: "Let us be better, if that be possible, but in any case, *we must be different*, in the adaptation to rejuvenate methods of war, of new engines, judiciously conceived, and rapidly executed (quoted in Ropp, 1937: 273).

The Jeune École's doctrines enjoyed widespread popularity in France because of the country's conviction, first, that she could not live without colonies and, second, that Britain would not give up her monopoly of the seas without a struggle. The Jeune École gave to France the hope that she might prevail in that struggle. Until 1900, the commerce-raiding school of naval warfare profoundly altered French naval construction, with the emphasis put upon craft other than battleships.

In the mid 1890s, German naval strategists were divided over the value of cruisers and commerce-raiding. Under the direction of Admiral Hollman, the Imperial Naval Office favored a large cruiser-building program, but for the defensive purposes of protecting Germany's coasts and maritime trade rather than for the offensive purposes of attacking the enemy's commerce. The Kaiser tended to support Hollman. Under the direction of Admiral von Knorr, the High Command of the navy pushed for a large battleship-building program. The Imperial Naval Office was responsible for preparing the budget, for presenting it to the Reichstag, and, consequently, for overseeing ship construction; the High Command, for developing strategy. As a result of the cruiser-battleship debate that persisted until 1897, the German navy found itself in a real predicament: the Naval Office built ships for which there was no strategy, while the High Command formulated strategy for which there were no ships (see Steinberg, 1965: 61–97 and Tirpitz, 1919: I, 75–77, 118–122, 128–129).

DOMESTIC POLITICS, WELTPOLITIK AND THE "RISK THEORY"

During the early and middle 1890s, Tirpitz sided with the High Command. He was the one, in fact, who, after his appointment in 1892 as Chief of Staff to von Knorr, had transformed the thinking of the High Command and shifted its emphasis from cruisers to battle-ships as the navy's mainstay and from France and Russia to Great Britain as the major naval threat (Steinberg, 1965: 70–71). The struggle to win over both the Kaiser and the Reichstag to his point of view was an exceedingly tough one for Tirpitz, one he thought he had lost for good in 1896. For at that time, Hollman had managed to convince the Reichstag that no large expansion of the navy was being contemplated. The Reichstag had then overwhelmingly approved Hollman's modest program to build one battleship and three cruisers. Unwilling to dismiss Hollman after his vote of confidence, the Kaiser had no choice but to make Tirpitz the "imperial scapegoat;" he left Berlin to assume command of the cruiser squadron in the China Sea (Steinberg, 1965: 95).

Within one year, however, Tirpitz was back in Berlin with the post that Hollman had held: State Secretary of the Imperial Naval Office. During his year abroad, the High Command had waged a vigorous campaign against Hollman and had developed a coherent strategy that called for the building of a battlefleet and for its concentration in home waters. The Kaiser, too, had not been idle. Faced with a dispute between the Naval Office and the High Command that was debilitating the navy, he had created an imperial committee to resolve the dispute. In the meantime Hollman had developed an ambitious budget for the navy, but one that called mostly for a great variety of light craft. Hollman's position, however, had become untenable: the Reichstag was balking at the idea of a big fleet, while the Kaiser, who was primarily interested in getting more ships—never mind whether they were mostly cruisers or battleships—consequently began to lose confidence in Hollman. When the Reichstag in March, 1897, sharply cut the naval estimates, Hollman's usefulness had ended. The Kaiser ordered Tirpitz home and officially named him State Secretary of the Imperial Naval Office on June 17 (Steinberg, 1965, 97–124).

In such a political climate, faced with a hostile Reichstag, a Kaiser anxious to get on with building his navy, and a public that had begun to doubt the wisdom and the stability of its naval authorities, Tirpitz took office. Through his great political skills and through the force of his arguments, Tirpitz succeeded in persuading first the Kaiser, then the Reichstag, and finally the German public to accept *his* kind of German navy. But although Tirpitz's assumption of power was essential to the building of a battlefleet, he alone was not sufficient to insure its construction. His role was crucial, but it must be viewed in the broader context of political developments within Germany in the 1890s.

Tirpitz took office at a turning point in German history. The month of June, 1897, marked the date when the Kaiser consolidated his personal control over the imperial German government. William II succeeded in obtaining a type of rule over all of Germany that came much closer to, but did not reach, that which he held in Prussia. The Kaiser by no means became an absolute monarch within Germany, but he subsequently continued to be "the decisive figure in the German Executive" (Röhl, 1967: 272). Tirpitz took office precisely because the Kaiser had won a seven-year struggle between the court party and the constitutional party for the right to speak for the imperial government and to set the direction of policy. The court party consisted of the Kaiser, the chiefs of his civil, military, and naval cabinets, and his retinue of cronies (mostly military figures) who served as his informal advisors. The Reich Chancellor and the various ministers attached to his office made up the constitutional party. The years from 1890 to 1897 witnessed a steady dimunition in the authority of the Chancellor vis-à-vis the Kaiser.

The coup de grâce came in June of 1897 when Hohenlohe dismissed his most trusted advisors and replaced them with men who were closely identified with William II and who shared his outlook. Bülow became Foreign Secretary; Miquel assumed control over internal affairs; Tirpitz took charge of the navy. Each of these men pursued policies that the Kaiser had long favored, but that had been resisted by the Reich Chancellor or his ministers. Bülow pushed *Weltpolitik*, a world policy; Miquel, *Sammlungspolitik*, the restoring of harmony between the conservative landowners of the east and the big industrialists of the west and the rallying of these two groups and the masses around the throne; Tirpitz, *Flottenpolitik*, constructing the Grand Fleet (Röhl, 1967: 246–258, 276–277). The era of "personal rule" began in June of 1897; after that date the Kaiser's right to dismiss or appoint Reich ministers was no longer questioned.

The "turn to the right" internally was therefore accompanied by an aggressive external stance. The two went together because the Kaiser and the new men around him viewed each policy as necessary to the success of the other. In order to pursue a more aggressive world policy, the Kaiser had to remove the centers of opposition to it, to establish his right of personal rule. But in order to win acceptance at home for a more active throne, in particular to undercut the appeal of the Social Democrats and thwart a turn to the left and toward parliamentarianism, the Kaiser needed dramatic successes abroad. Bülow put it thus in December of 1897:

> I am putting the main emphasis on foreign policy. Only a successful foreign policy can help to reconcile, pacify, rally, unite.
> If the German people had gone on thinking only of the Courts Martial Reform Bill and the Tausch trial, the domestic situation in the Reich would rapidly have deteriorated to the Austrian level [quoted in Röhl, 1967: 252].

The pursuit of adventures overseas in order to build support at home was certainly not new in Germany; Bismarck had resorted to this tactic. What was new now was the vengeance and single-mindedness with which it was employed (see Carroll, 1966: chs. 8, 9; and Sontag, 1964: chs. 6, 8, 10). The Kaiser and his previous advisors had failed to establish internal harmony through other means; now the Kaiser and his new advisors would buy unity at home through "concerted action against the world outside" (Sontag, 1964: 320). In June, 1897, Germany had chosen to export her internal difficulties.

The Kaiser's consolidation of his personal rule explains why the turn outward occurred when it did, but not why the German people supported Weltpolitik in the first place. Opposition to such a policy certainly did exist. It came from the army because of the diversion of funds away from it and the tension with England that would ensue, from the agrarian interests because of the favoritism that such a policy would bestow on the industrialists, and from the Social Democrats because of the increase in popularity that would accrue to the imperial government. Support for the policy of imperialism and navalism, however, was intense and broad-based and came primarily from the Pan-Germans, the university professors and intellectuals, the growing middle class, and the big industrialists. Increasingly since 1890 colonialism had proved to have widespread appeal with the masses; even Bismarck had been forced earlier to respond to the popular clamor for colonies. The doctrine of social Darwinism as applied to international politics and the belief that "not to expand is to die" gave an intellectual rigor and justification to Weltpolitik. The phenomenal growth of German industry, trade, and overseas investment (Feis, 1964: 60–68; Hoffman, 1933: 73–79, 279–280), moreover, seemed to be dramatic proof for the Kaiser's statement that "The German Empire has become a world empire" (quoted in Steinberg, 1964: 102). Germany in the 1890s was ripe for an outward-looking policy. Acceptance of it was by no means automatic, but many groups within German society were ready to support it if properly mobilized and led.

Tirpitz was clearly the right man in the right place at the right time. He provided the necessary leadership; he crystallized the available support; he wheeled and dealed with the Reichstag; he popularized the cause of navalism. The ultimate key to this success, however, was that he convinced the German people, not only that a bigger navy would be of benefit to them, but also that *they could afford it*. The political acceptability of a bigger navy depended on its not being too expensive. In order to persuade the Reichstag of this fact, Tirpitz resorted to two devices: outright deception and the "risk theory." He obtained from the Reichstag a naval law that fixed the strength of the fleet, but that did not specify what type of ships would be built (Steinberg, 1965: 170). Tirpitz knew he would construct battleships, but the law disguised this fact. He secured a binding commitment to the size of a new navy without having to tell what would be its ultimate cost!

The second device, the risk theory, offered to Germans world status and power "on the cheap." Domestic constraints gave birth to a strategic theory that promised tremendous political leverage would be obtained from a permanently inferior force. Tirpitz had argued, as seen above, that the threat value of a German navy would lay in its ability to go out and do battle with the royal navy. For this battleships were required. But how many battleships would Germany need? If it were necessary for the German navy to fight the entire royal navy, then Germany could not plan to use her battlefleet in order to obtain political leverage against Britain, for she could never hope to match the British navy in numbers because of its overwhelming superiority. A battlefleet equal in quality but decidedly inferior in quantity would not constitute a force that could seriously threaten the royal navy. With her overwhelming superiority Britain could concentrate her battlefleet, achieve a devastating superiority in numbers of long-range guns, and, by directing massive and concentrated fire in turn on portions of the German fleet, totally obliterate it. Because victory in sea warfare required taking the offensive, parity in quantity was as much a prerequisite for success as was parity in quality (Churchill, 1951: 125-133; Hoag, 1962: 391-393). But because such quantitative matching was beyond the means of Germany, Tirpitz was forced to make a virtue out of necessity. He simply argued that such matching was not required: Britain's worldwide commitments would prevent her from concentrating her entire fleet in home waters. The threat value of the German fleet would lay, therefore, in the risk it posed to a much smaller British *home fleet,* one that Germany could match in numbers and perhaps surpass in quality.

Tirpitz's risk theory ruled out, not only the need to match the entire royal navy in numbers, but also the the necessity to achieve a decisive victory over the home fleet. Tirpitz's proposed battlefleet would pose a threat to Britain, not directly by challenging her supremacy on the seas, but indirectly by undermining the two-power standard that she had adopted in 1889. Alarmed by the vigorous French and Russian naval building programs of the 1880s, Britain had decided to maintain a naval strength equal in fighting power to that of the next two largest powers combined. To subsequent Liberal and Conservative governments, equality in fighting power meant numerical equality in battleships to the combined strength of the second- and third-ranked European naval powers. To the Admiralty, equality in fighting power meant, not a fleet equal in numbers to the combined fleets of France and Russia, but rather one "equal to beating them" (Marder, 1940: 106-107). Equality thus became superiority, and the Admiralty lobbied for a 5:3 ratio in battleships between England and the next two powers. Whether the lower or the higher interpretation was accepted, the Admiralty and the governments of both parties agreed the numerical equality to the combined strength of the next two European navies was "the *minimum* standard of security which the country demands and expects."

Tirpitz formulated his risk theory with the two-power standard in mind, but he was also able to capitalize upon diplomatic developments within and without Europe. Overseas, France and Russia together were contesting British predominance in China; and, separately,

Russia was doing so in Persia and France in Sudan. The challenge abroad that the two powers presented to Britain's imperial interests was magnified by the military alliance that they had concluded in 1894. Although the Franco-Russian alliance was directed against Germany in Europe, Britain had to reckon that the alliance could be directed against British interests overseas. The Franco-Russian alliance increased the probability that the French and Russian fleets would cooperate in the event of a war with England and therefore that the royal navy would simultaneously face the combined strength of her next two competitors. It thereby reinforced Britain's need to adhere to the two-power standard.

The Franco-Russian alliance also made more credible the naval threat that Tirpitz proposed to direct against England. The risk that the German navy could pose would be to sink enough ships of the British home fleet in battle, even if defeat for Germany were to follow, such that British strength would be reduced below the level required by the two-power standard. Even in defeat the German navy could cripple Britain. The two-power standard, together with the Franco-Russian alliance, would enable Germany to achieve a degree of political leverage from its battlefleet that was much larger than that which the fleet's size would in isolation warrant. Germany would, in short, enjoy a "multiplier effect" from her fleet. Tirpitz concluded that Britain would prefer to accommodate Germany rather than run the risk of a collision with her fleet.

ENTENTES, DREADNOUGHTS, AND THE "RISK THEORY"

Tirpitz's goal was to compel Great Britain to come to terms with Germany—to accept not only German predominance on the continent, but also German equality with Britain overseas. His strategy backfired: it succeeded in strengthening England's ties with France and hastening the development of those with Russia. First the Entente Cordiale and then the Triple Entente undermined the threat value of the German fleet. Beginning in late 1904, the British Admiralty began to redistribute the fleet in order to increase the number of ships in home waters. After 1904, Germany could no longer count on Britain's inability to prevent the dispersal of her fleet. The closer Britain came to France and Russia the more she could concentrate her fleet in home waters, and the smaller the threat posed by the German fleet.

From 1904 onward, changes in European diplomatic realignments destroyed the threat value of a German navy as Tirpitz had originally conceived it. From 1906 onward, however, changes in naval technology resurrected the threat value of a German navy, but not the type of navy that Tirpitz had planned for. A navy equal to that of Britain in quality, but inferior in quantity, was Tirpitz's original design. Britain's introduction of the dreadnought in 1906 changed all that. The dreadnought marked a significant advance in naval weaponry: it was the first "all-big-gun" battleship, having a main battery of ten 12-inch guns in contrast to the four 12-inch and the ten 9.2-inch guns of the "Lord Nelsons," Britain's last pre-dreadnought class (Marder, 1966: I, 43). With superiority in both armament and speed, the dreadnought made all pre-dreadnought battleships obsolete. Battleships had been built to engage and sink other battleships. The "virtue" of the dreadnought was that it was more suited than its predecessors to the purpose that the battleship was intended to serve: it was more effective in destroying other battleships. Six of its guns could fire ahead; eight, on either broadside. The "Lord Nelsons" could fire only two ahead and four on either broadside. When firing broadside, therefore, a line of ten dreadnoughts equalled a line of twenty "Lord Nelsons;" when firing ahead, one dreadnought equalled three "Lord Nelsons" (Woodward, 1966: 106).

By rendering all previous battleships obsolete, the dreadnought made possible a German battlefleet equal to that of Britain in both quality and quantity. The dreadnought began the naval contest anew, with both of the participants being more nearly equally positioned than before. By introducing the dreadnought, Britain had effectively wiped out her lead in pre-dreadnought battleships. But, by being the first to introduce the dreadnought, she had gained the inside track. With a vigorous building program, however, Germany could dangerously narrow the lead and perhaps even close the gap. The dreadnought thus changed the nature of the naval contest between Germany and Britain. It converted a defined, limited competition between a superior participant and hopelessly inferior one to an all-out struggle between two adversaries, each of which aimed at supremacy over the other. The Anglo-German naval "race" really began in 1906, not in 1897.

With a change in the type of navy Germany could build came a change in the type of threat she could pose. The possibility of matching the British in numbers of dreadnoughts meant that the German navy would now constitute a direct, not an indirect, threat to the royal navy. Britain recognized this when she scrapped the two-power standard in April 1909, as the measure by which to judge the navy's requirements; she replaced it by direct comparisons with the number of German dreadnoughts. The effect of doing so was to place Germany in the position of being the prime threat to Britain's security, a position she had not occupied before.

General political differences and conflicting foreign policy goals had initially given rise to an Anglo-German naval competition. The introduction of the dreadnought created an Anglo-German naval race; and because the dreadnought obscured the political differences between the two countries, it raised the naval question to a position of central importance in Anglo-German relations. Germany continued to insist that a political settlement with the British must precede any agreement over the relative sizes of their fleets. Britain continued to insist that a naval agreement must precede any political settlement. By putting a naval before a political agreement, the British convinced the Germans that Britain intended to encircle her and to keep her permanently in the position of a second-rank power. By putting a political before a naval agreement, the Germans convinced the British that Germany intended to attack her or isolate her. Germany viewed her own stance as one that her economic and military power entitled her to take. Britain viewed her own stance as defensive and as one that her special geographic location and world interests entitled her to take. Each, however, viewed the stance of the other as aggressive. The dreadnought did not create an Anglo-German conflict, but it certainly did intensify and complicate one that was already there.

Changes in both battleship technology and diplomatic alignments did not alter either the method that Tirpitz employed or the goal that he and the Kaiser pursued. Each change in fact had the effect of reconfirming and strengthening their commitment to both the method and the goal that they had chosen. The goal continued to be to coerce Britain into accepting Germany's political terms; the means, the threat of a German battlefleet. After 1906, as before, great power status required a great battlefleet. The possibility of matching the British navy in the number of dreadnoughts did not change the need to build battleships, but only the number that should be built. Until World War I, Germany continued to hold fast to the basic Tirpitz strategy: use the threat of a German battlefleet in order to bring about a British accommodation to Germany's desires.

SUBMARINES IN THE GREAT WAR

In light of the above developments, the submarine understandably played only a marginal role in German naval thinking until November of 1914. They were experimental, untested in combat, and, until very late, unreliable and of limited range. The building of a large submarine fleet also involved opportunity costs: more submarines meant fewer battleships. In the competition for scarce resources, submarines lost out. Submarines, moreover, did not fit well, if at all, into the grand strategy. If the purpose of building a German navy was to pose a threat to the English navy, then a large U-boat fleet would be useless. How could Germany create the type of threat to the English navy that Tirpitz thought was necessary if she built a fleet of naval craft that the *English* navy considered to be "local defense vessels" and "the weapons of the weaker power?" To make a credible threat required that Germany accept England's conception of what was credible and threatening. Battleships and dreadnoughts were included in that conception; submarines were not. Even the dramatic increase in operating range in 1913 did not alter Tirpitz's outlook. He was too enamoured with, and too fixed upon, the battlefleet to consider using the U-boat in an offensive, counterforce role. The fashion-setter was Great Britain. She had built a great battlefleet. To challenge the leader, one had first to ape him.

U-BOATS AND THE BRITISH BATTLEFLEET

War brings change; World War I was no exception. Although it had denigrated the submarine before the war, the British navy came to fear it at a very early stage in the war. Perhaps the greatest irony in the story of the U-boat was the series of actions taken by the royal navy in September, October, and November of 1914, as a consequence of its fears of submarine attack. Not German dreadnoughts, but German U-boats succeeded in disrupting Britain's entire naval strategy in the first months of hostilities. On September 1, the entire grand fleet sped out to sea from anchorage at Scapa Flow after it had received a report of a U-boat sighting at the base. A few days later the fleet took up anchorage at Loch Ewe on England's northwestern coast because that base was considered to be more secure from the submarine threat than was Scapa Flow. A report of a German submarine inside Loch Ewe on October 7 once again chased the fleet out to sea (Jellicoe, 1919: 117, 118, 139). On October 17, Admiral Sir John Jellicoe, Commander-in-Chief of the Grand Fleet, ordered the entire fleet to take up temporary anchorage at Loch Swilly in Northen Ireland until the submarine defenses at Scapa Flow were completed. Jellicoe chose Loch Swilly because "the water was so shallow as to make it difficult for a submarine to enter submerged" (Jellicoe, 1919: 144–145).

Jellicoe's fears of the submarine threat may have been exaggerated. Until September, 1914, no one in the royal navy had "seriously contemplated hostile submarines in time of war entering the war harbors of either side and attacking the ships at anchor" (Churchill, 1951: 414). The difficulties in doing so were calculated to be so great that successful attack was unlikely. "No trace of a submarine" was detected at Scapa Flow immediately after the September 1 sighting, and a subsequent investigation showed that the alarm may have been false (Jellicoe, 1919: 118). The threat, nevertheless, was presumed to be real; the fears certainly were. In his World War I memoirs, Churchill vividly portrays those fears that initially swept through the royal navy:

> Everything depended upon the Fleet, and during these same months of October and November the Fleet was disquieted about the very foundations of its being. . . . The Grand Fleet was uneasy. She could not find a resting place except at sea. Conceive it, the *ne plus ultra,* the one ultimate sanction of our existence, the supreme engine which no one had dared to brave, whose authority encircled the globe no longer sure of itself. The idea had got round—"*the German submarines were coming after them into their harbours*" (Churchill, 1951: 413–414).

After the U-boat sightings off the northeastern and northwestern English coasts, the royal navy realized it had grievously miscalculated: the range and hence radius of action of German submarines were much greater than had been previously estimated (Jellicoe, 1919: 16–18). The Admiralty had to reckon that submarine attacks on the grand fleet while at anchorage at Scapa Flow had become possible. Because it had previously considered such attacks unlikely, the Admiralty had decided not to fortify the base against them. Until Scapa Flow could be so fortified, both Churchill and Jellicoe agreed that the central aim was "to secure the safety of the British Fleet during the long and indefinite period of waiting for a general action" (Churchill, 1951: 418). What had thus happened, in the words of two careful observers of British naval history, was that

> a few submarines had forced the most powerful battle-fleet in history to abandon its base [Scapa Flow] and retreat to a second base [Loch Ewe], and then to a third [Loch Swilly], each being progressively more remote from the main theatre of naval hostilities—the North Sea. . . .
>
> The whole of the East Coast was left perilously exposed to hostile attack: the naval forces in these waters were left unsupported. In a word, the bottom of the whole strategical situation was knocked out for a time by the German U-boats (Gibson and Prendergast, 1931: 14–15).

England was spared the innumerable disasters that could have flowed from the forced redeployment of the grand fleet only because the Germans were completely ignorant of what had happened. For a time they had gained full freedom of operations in the North Sea, but they did not know they had it! The English fleet had retreated in the face of a threat that it had not expected; the German fleet, meanwhile, continued to remain bottled up in the Baltic and close to the river entrances to the North Sea in the face of a threat that was no longer there.

U-BOATS AND THE HANDELSKRIEG

The final twist to the tale is the abrupt reversal made by the German navy over the use of its U-boats. The navy had definitely rejected a building program requisite for such a strategy in March of 1914, had clearly refused to adopt the strategy in September, and had rejected it again in early October. But by November, the high seas fleet and the Chief of the Admiralty, von Pohl, were vigorously pushing for the Handelskrieg. What had happened during the first four months of the war to change the navy's mind? The answer lies with the grand strategies pursued by the British and German navies. Before the war and during its first few weeks, both navies had expected a major encounter, perhaps even a decisive one, to occur between the two fleets. In anticipation of such an encounter, each navy had concentrated its battlefleet: the grand fleet cruising off Scapa Flow and the Orkney

Islands, and with the high sea fleet lying between the Heligoland Bight and Wilhelmshaven. Both navies expected the North Sea to be the main arena of battle.

Such an encounter, however, failed to materialize because each navy refused to wage battle unless it could do so on its own terms. Each was not shunning offensive action, but each was refusing to initiate it if that meant fighting far from its home base. Each, therefore, was trying to entice the other to fight far from its home base. The British Admiralty wanted to fight off the coast of northern England; the German Naval Staff, as close as possible to the Heligoland Bight. Each was waiting on opposite sides of the North Sea for the other. Both, moreover, were pursuing the strategies that the sizes of their fleets dictated. As the country with the superior navy, Britain wanted to engage the entire high seas fleet, but only when she could be certain of capitalizing upon her superiority—only, that is, when she had the entire grand fleet at hand. As the country with the inferior navy, Germany wanted to engage only portions of the British fleet at a time, the strategy being to whittle down Britain's numerical superiority to the point where a decisive encounter between both fleets could be risked with a good chance of success (Churchill, 1951: 149–160; Hurd, 1918: 46–89; Jellicoe, 1919: 12–33; Scheer, 1920: 13–41; Tirpitz, 1919: II, 22–32; and Weniger, 1930: 1–10). The British were pursuing (in Jellicoe's phrase) "a watching policy from a distance"; the Germans (in Scheer's phrase), "guerrilla warfare."

In the decade before the war, each nation had spent great sums in order to build a formidable battlefleet. The rationale for doing so was that only battleships could take on battleships. Now, when war had come, both shrank from risking their investments. The rationale for doing so was that because only battleships could take on battleships, the battlefleet should not fight unless the prospects for success looked very promising.

Each country was clearly worried about its pre-attack and post-attack positions relative to the other. Because parity in the number of battleships was deemed the minimum essential for victory, neither wished to risk battle with the other unless forces were at least equal; each preferred to have a decisive superiority in order to make victory certain. If one side suffered losses much larger than the other during an encounter, then it would face future battles either from a weakened position and with a reduced chance of success, or from a hopelessly inferior position and with no chance of success. If England sustained the disproportionately larger losses, its position would be weakened; if Germany did so, its position would become hopeless. The fear of having the smaller number of battleships both before and after attack caused each country to hold back its battlefleet from action. Victory in sea warfare may in fact require taking the offensive, but in 1914, the prospects associated with an untimely offensive inhibited each country from initiating one against the other.

Because of the German navy's reluctance to risk battle with the entire grand fleet and because of the royal navy's deliberate decision not to send portions of the grand fleet out to do battle, the high seas fleet remained relatively inactive. The consequence of inaction was that the German navy became, day by day, increasingly restless. Its prestige and its pride were suffering. Its morale was at low ebb. The army was getting all the glory and bearing the full burden. The future effects of present inaction were also troubling the navy. In a letter to Ingenohl, Commander-in-Chief of the high seas fleet, on September 16, 1914, Tirpitz (1919: II, 96) revealed his concern over the Navy's future:

> If we come to the end of a war so terrible as that of 1914 without the fleet having bled and worked, we shall get nothing more for the fleet, and all the scanty money that there may be will be spent on the Army. The great efforts of His Majesty The Emperor to make Germany a naval power will have been all in vain.

The navy, moreover, was chafing under the subordinate role that the General Staff's strategy had required it to take. The Schlieffen Plan called for a rapid movement of the bulk of the German army through Belgium and down through northern France, while the remainder of the army carried on holding operations on the southern Franco-German border and in the east. The goal was to knock France quickly out of the war through a swift offensive and then to move forces to the eastern front where a defensive war would be waged against the Russians. The concentration of forces in the west left the eastern front weakly defended. The gamble was that France could be defeated and German troops redeployed to the eastern front before Russia had fully mobilized and fielded her forces. The navy's role was to support the defensive holding operation in the east until France was defeated and to do so by preventing the Russians from landing troops on the coast of Pomerania. The main function of the high seas fleet was to command the Baltic in order to secure the rear of the eastern front. To perform this function, the high seas fleet had to remain in being and at full strength.

Thus, while the superiority of the grand fleet made a "guerrilla policy" prudent, the Schlieffen Plan made the "fleet-in-being" policy essential. Both policies required that the navy do the same thing: avoid engaging either the grand fleet or the Russian Baltic fleet. Each policy reinforced the logic of the other. The cost of destroying the Russian fleet would be to weaken the high seas fleet vis-à-vis the grand fleet. The cost of engaging the grand fleet would be to weaken the high seas fleet vis-à-vis the Russian fleet. The consequence of weakening the Fleet in either fashion would be to lay the northern coasts of Germany open to attack by the Russians or by the British or by both simultaneously. The navy and the General Staff calculated that neither cost could be incurred. The high seas fleet could not even attempt to hinder the passage of British troop transports across the channel to France because "we could only interfere with it at the price of a decisive battle with the English Fleet" (Scheer, 1920: 18–21; Weniger, 1930: 7–8). That, of course, could not at present be risked. The navy had an important role to play, but it could do so only if it avoided a major battle. Its function was to prevent troop landings by intimidating the Russians and by deterring the British. Its ability to intimidate and to deter depended upon the respect its enemies had for its power. That power had to be conserved, not expended, if the respect were to be maintained. *The paradox for the high seas fleet was that it could be most useful to the war effort only if it did not fight.*

This role was a difficult one for the navy to accept, no matter how sound the logic that lay behind it. For fifteen years the navy and the nation had been subjected to Tirpitz's and the Kaiser's continual utterances about the need for a battlefleet. For fifteen years the Navy League had been praising the merits and strengths of the navy. For fifteen years the raison d'etre of the fleet had been the damage it could do to the royal navy in battle. For fifteen years expectations had been geared to fighting. Now that war had come, the fleet was not being permitted to fulfill its destiny. Tirpitz (1919: II, 114) captured the sentiments of many naval officers when he asked, "How could a nation build a fleet, and not send it to battle in its fight for existence?" The navy was understandably anxious to take action, to do *something*.

Before the war the U-boat had played only a marginal role in German naval thinking because the focus had been put upon the battlefleet. In the early months of the war, after the high seas fleet found itself stymied, the fortunes of the U-boat began to rise. The new role that the U-boat was to play began inauspiciously. On August 6, at the urging of the commander in charge of submarines, the commander-in-chief of the high seas fleet authorized ten U-boats to proceed to the Orkney Islands on a six-day mission against English battleships. In terms of relative losses, the mission was a failure: two U-boats never came back, and no British battleships were sunk. In terms of the U-boat's future, however, the mission was an unqualified success: for the first time and under actual combat conditions, the U-boat's abilities to remain at sea for long periods and to travel great distances were clearly demonstrated. Germany's "naval operations took a decisive turn as a result of this cruise": with this mission began the transformation of the submarine "from being merely a coastal-defense machine, as was originally planned, . . . [to being] the most effective long-range weapon" that the navy had (Scheer, 1920: 36). For the next three months, the U-boat operated with considerable success against the royal navy's cruisers and battleships; but the German navy was not aware of the disruption that fears of U-boat attack had wrought in the British Admiralty's grand strategy.

Ignorant of this degree of success, the navy continued to search for other ways to aid the war effort. An unauthorized sinking of a merchant steamer (the *Glitra*) by a U-boat on October 20 provided dramatic support for those lower-ranking naval officers who had been urging their superiors to opt for U-boat attacks on merchant shipping. The timing of the *Glitra* attack was fortuitous but fortunate: by late October, the high seas fleet was receptive to a new strategy. Three months of operations against the royal navy had conclusively proven that the U-boat could operate effectively at long distances from its bases, the minimum condition for offensive activity. The failure of the army's Schlieffen Plan to defeat France swiftly meant that the war would be a long one and consequently that the endurance of the belligerents' economies would be crucial to their war efforts. The Schlieffen Plan's failure thus made a U-boat war on commerce extremely attractive: such attacks might cripple England's economy and bring an earlier victory to Germany. Finally, the type of blockade that Britain had imposed on Germany revealed that England was in fact attempting to do against Germany precisely what the German navy was now contemplating doing against England (see Churchill, 1951: 149–160). To Germany, the British blockade meant that England was trying to starve her out.

After England had built a great battlefleet and concentrated it in home waters, the Admiralty had not abandoned its long-standing commitment to the blockade, but had modified the manner in which it was to be carried out. The development of modern naval defenses—submarines, torpedo boats, and long-range coastal artillery—had rendered the traditional "close blockade" of the enemy's ports too dangerous and had forced the Admiralty to resort to the "distant blockade." The Admiralty based the latter's effectiveness upon the grand fleet's power to command the approaches to the North Sea and Atlantic Ocean and thereby to block the entry and exit of goods to and from Germany (Spindler, 1932: 1–10, 26–29). Because goods destined for Germany could no longer be seized right at her ports of entry, the royal navy stopped all neutral ships before they penetrated very far into the channel or North Sea and then brought them back to English ports where they were searched for contraband goods. Any that could be of use to Germany's war effort were seized on the pretext that if they could be of use to Germany, then they would find their way into Germany. With the distant blockade thus came the doctrine of "continuous voyage," which said that the ultimate rather than the initial destination of contraband goods was the criterion determining whether such goods would be seized. Unable to blockade Germany's ports, England chose to blockade all the Baltic ports. The policy of distant blockade and the doctrine of continuous voyage brought an end to Germany's merchant trade and shipping, an expanding list of what England considered contraband, and an increasing control exerted by England over neutral trade. Both of those measures fitted in well with the primary goal of the grand fleet—namely, to do battle with and destroy the high seas fleet. The Admiralty hoped that the pressure exerted on Germany by the blockade would force the high seas fleet to come into the North Sea where the grand fleet possessed all the advantages (Marder, 1966: I, 367–383).

England's resort to this type of blockade clinched the high seas fleet's commitment to the Handelskrieg. When the British declared the North Sea a war zone and off-bounds to neutral shipping on November 2, the last major center of resistance in the navy to the strategy collapsed. Admiral von Pohl had become convinced that Britain fully intended to starve Germany by blockade (Spindler, 1932: 9–10). He at once began a vigorous campaign to persuade the Kaiser and Chancellor that Germany must follow suit and retaliate in kind. The means, though, had to be different and brutal. Because the battlefleet could not risk an encounter, U-boats must be used. Because they were too fragile to risk warning and too small to take on survivors, their attacks must take place by surprise and without regard to loss of life. That the German navy firmly believed it would only be following the precedent set by England is reflected in the formal proposal presented by the high seas fleet to von Pohl:

> As England is trying to destroy our trade it is only fair if we retaliate by carrying on the campaign against her trade by all possible means. Further, as England completely disregards International Law in her actions, there is not the least reason why we should exercise any restraint in our conduct of the war. We can wound England most seriously by injuring her trade. By means of the U-boat we should be able to inflict the greatest injury. We must therefore make use of this weapon, and do so, moreover, in the way most suited to its peculiarities. . . . Consequently a U-boat cannot spare the crews of steamers, but must send them to the bottom with their ships. (quoted in Scheer, 1920: 222).

Thus, unaware of the magnitude of success that the submarine had achieved in September and October as a counterforce weapon, the navy by November of 1914 was seized by the promise of using U-boats to cripple Britain's trade. The adoption of the Handelskrieg policy was not automatic; the U-boat was not the navy's first choice, but clearly her second. Only after "the great hopes centered in the High Seas Fleet" had not been realized did the German navy begin to look elsewhere. Only after the British had made it clear that they were not going to engage the high seas fleet on its terms did the German navy turn to the U-boat. Only after the British had imposed their blockade did the German navy begin to think along similar lines. Only after the Schlieffen Plan had clearly failed to work could the German navy argue that a new strategy—this time, one at sea—was needed. Accident, prestige, service pride, internal politics, British naval strategy, and the course of the land war—all had a hand in bringing the German navy to opt for the Handelskrieg by the fourth month of World War I.

NEW WEAPONS, STRATEGIC DOCTRINE, AND FOREIGN POLICY

In the case of the U-boat, wartime experience contradicted peacetime expectations. Within both the British and German navies, few people thought the U-boat would be as fearsome a weapon as it proved to be. The predictions of those who warned of its potentialities went unheeded. With such expectations, few were willing to invest great sums in it before the war either to improve its technology or to build large numbers of them. As a consequence, Germany had only ten U-boats capable of operating in the waters around England when the blockade was declared in February, 1915. In prewar Germany, U-boats suffered because battleships prospered.

THE MILITARY USE OF THE FLEET

Battleships were what the risk theory called for. The irony of German naval thinking, however, was that the risk theory did not call for enough battleships in order to make the seventeen-year investment worth the cost. The theory had posited that the smaller German fleet would pose a risk in battle to the British home fleet only because England would never be able to concentrate her entire navy, or even the bulk of it, in home waters. The extent of damage the German fleet could wreak on the British fleet hung heavily on the disparity in numbers between the two. Because of the advantages in firepower that accrued to the superior force, the greater the disparity, the smaller the damage the inferior fleet could be expected to inflict. If the disparity became too great, the inferior fleet could not risk battle because, while defeat would be certain, the enemy's losses would prove too small. The only point of battle in the face of certain annihilation by a superior force was to weaken it fatally. Once that possibility had passed, the only result of such a battle was annihilation.

Before 1904, the disparity between the two home fleets was still small enough to warrant battle and hence to validate the risk theory; after 1904, this condition ceased to hold. In late 1904, the royal navy began to concentrate in home waters. The renewal of the Anglo-Japanese Alliance in 1905, the strengthening of the Anglo-French Entente in 1905–1906, and the conclusion of the Anglo-Russian

Entente in 1907 facilitated a further concentration of the royal navy. By 1908, the disparity between the two fleets had reached the point where battle under the proper conditions posed little "risk" to the grand fleet. The dreadnought did not alter this condition because Britain had seized the lead in construction and continued to maintain it. By 1908, the central assumption of the risk theory had crumbled; and consequently, its strategic rationale vanished.

In the face of such a development, what could be expected of the high seas fleet? The "gut feeling" of most officers was, of course, to wage glorious battle. But when the Admiralty Office, the body charged with formulating war plans, began to consider the question more closely, the gut reaction slowly dissipated; in its place, hesitation, vacillation, and confusion set in. In 1904, the Admiralty Office was still committed to the offensive in order to do as much damage against the British fleet as possible. From 1905 to 1909, the war plans called for avoidance of a major encounter with the superior British fleet unless the high seas fleet could be assured of success. From 1909 to 1912, the Admiralty recommitted the fleet to the all-out offensive. From 1912 until the outbreak of war, the contingency plans contained all the elements of the previous eight years: the desire to take the offensive against the British fleet; the recognition that it would be a disaster to do so if the entire fleet had to be confronted; and the stipulation that the offensive could be assumed only when "conditions" would warrant it (Weniger, 1930: 1–10). By 1912, the high seas fleet was no longer committed to the offensive the risk theory had called for.

The restrictions placed on the battlefleet's activity by the Admiralty were matched by Tirpitz's own muddled ideas about what the fleet should do. In his Service Memorandum 9 of 1894, he had written that command of the seas could be seized only by the strategic offensive, which required a numerical superiority of at least one-third over the opponent (see Rosinski, 1945: 130–132). In his memorandum of 1897, he still argued for the offensive; but since the enemy was now England, not France and Russia, he had to settle for numerical equality or even inferiority. By 1911, even Tirpitz had been forced to conclude that Britain's superiority was so great that the all-out offensive had to be abandoned for the "fair defensive chance." According to this theory, the two fleets would do battle near Heligoland where mine fields, torpedo boats, U-boats and coastal artillery could be used to offset Germany's numerical disadvantage (Ritter, 1970: 152–153; Rosinski, 1945: 133). Even here Tirpitz was inconsistent. Only Britain's continued use of the close-in blockade would put her fleet near enough to Heligoland in order that the German fleet could so engage it. As early as 1909, however, Tirpitz had reasoned that Britain might abandon the close-in blockade for the distant blockade precisely because of the dangers posed by torpedo boats, U-boats, and long-range coastal artillery. If Britain did so, then the high seas fleet could not engage the British in the area where it held the advantage. In May of 1914, Tirpitz is reputed to have asked Ingenhol, the Commander of the high seas fleet, what the fleet would do if the British did not show up. Ingenhol had no answer. Nor did Tirpitz.

From 1909 onwards, German naval strategy was thus bankrupt. Tirpitz continued to believe that a decisive battle would take place near Heligoland, but he had also concluded that the British fleet would not risk the type of blockade necessary to put it there. The Admiralty did not think the high seas fleet could risk a decisive battle on the open seas, but neither did it really believe the British would abandon the close-in blockade. Tirpitz had no strategy to entice the British fleet to where it could be "safely" fought; the Admiralty had no plans to deal with a distant blockade. The situation had reverted to that existing in the mid-1890s before Tirpitz took over: ships were being built for which no coherent war plans existed to guide their use.

POLITICAL USE OF THE FLEET

Clearly no one within the German navy could devise a sound plan for the battlefleet in war. Why, then, did Germany continue to build it? The answer to the question lies deeply imbedded in the nature of German foreign policy from 1895 to 1914. Not in the use contemplated for it during war, but in that made of it during peace do we find the rationale for the fleet.

In the twenty years before the war, German foreign policy was blundering, often formulated and implemented by third-rate men, uncoordinated, subject to the personal whims of the Kaiser, grossly mistaken about the effects that its policies would have on the other great powers, and sometimes hazy about exactly what Germany wanted from the other powers. But, although the means chosen were often ill-suited to realize the goals sought and although the goals were often vaguely put, there was, nonetheless, some degree of consistency in both the means and the ends of Germany's foreign policy. With respect to means, Germany's tactics were characterized by bluster, provocation, confrontation, overreliance on threats to use force, overconfidence in the utility of military power, and overestimation of German military power. With respect to ends, Germany's goals were characterized by a yearning to swagger on the world's stage, a demand to be consulted on all matters, a desire to be accepted as a world power of the first rank, and a determination to force from England an acceptance of coequality. Weltpolitik was thought best served by being aggressive towards others and difficult to work with. "Reputation for power is power" said Hobbes; Germany's leaders sought for their nation the "reputation for power" that they felt Germany's actual economic and military strength entitled her to have. Bülow best captured the spirit, if not the substance, of Germany's goal in a speech before the Reichstag on December 6, 1897:

The days are past when the German left to one neighbor the earth, to another the sea, and reserved for himself the air. . . . We do not wish to place anyone in the shadow, but we demand also our place in the sun (quoted in Anderson, 1966: 56).

From 1895 to 1914, the substance of German foreign policy falls into two distinct periods: the era of the "free hand" (1895-1904) and the drive to break out of "encirclement" (1905-1914). The earlier period was marked by the following: first, by the premise that England could never come to terms with France and Russia; second, by the calculation, therefore, that the Franco-Russian Alliance could be turned to Germany's advantage; third, by the belief that Germany need not hurry to settle with England because she would be forced to come to Germany; and fourth, by the pursuit of a policy of waiting without making specific commitments to either Russia or England unless Germany's full terms were met. The second period was marked by the following: first, by the recognition that Germany was being slowly isolated; second, by the recognition that the Triple Alliance was weaker now than ever before; and third, by the pursuit of a policy calculated to break encirclement by forcing England to reach an accord with Germany. In the earlier period, Germany's statesmen felt secure in the knowledge of German military prowess and experienced no sense of urgency about her diplomatic position. In the later period, they felt increasingly insecure and struggled frantically to reach an accord with Russia in 1904-1905 and doggedly with England from 1908 until 1914. In the first period, Germany's leaders reasoned they could afford to await developments; in the second, they tried to determine them.

The spirit and substance of Germany's foreign policy demonstrate why her statesmen thought the battlefleet so important and why they clung to it long after anyone was clear about how to use it in war. The perceived *political* utility of the high seas fleet explains the continuing commitment to its construction. The battlefleet was not the only tool of German statecraft, but it was one of the central ones and was considered crucial to Germany's aims in both periods. From 1895 to 1904, the fleet was used to heighten Germany's prestige, to protect and increase her overseas commerce, to transform her from a continental to a world power, and to enhance her "alliance value." This latter use could work one of two ways: because she had a powerful fleet, an alliance with Germany would appear more attractive to France and Russia in their imperial struggles with England; or because the fleet posed a significant threat to the royal navy, Britain would have to conclude an alliance with Germany in order either to neutralize her or to secure her aid in the overseas rivalry with France and Russia. In either instance, the battlefleet would serve the "free hand" policy: by preserving Germany's diplomatic flexibility and by forcing the others to come to her, the fleet would enable Germany to conclude settlements on her own terms.

From 1906 until 1914, Germany's statesmen used the fleet in order to try to shatter the Triple Entente. After Germany had failed in 1904 to reach an accord with England (as France had), after she had failed in 1905 to secure an alliance from Russia and through her to reach France, after she had failed in 1905–1906 to break up the Entente Cordiale by challenging France over the question of Morocco—Germany's leaders turned finally toward England.

After 1906, Germany came to view England as the central obstacle to regaining the free hand. From 1909 until 1914, Bethmann-Hollweg actively used the fleet in an attempt to wrest a neutrality pact from the British Cabinet. He tried to do with the fleet what Bülow had failed to achieve at Björko and Algeciras: to end Germany's isolation. In this sense, Algeciras, Agadir, the Anglo-German naval talks, and the use made of Sarajevo all have this thread in common: they were attempts to regain the diplomatic initiative for Germany. Thus the point of building an ever larger fleet after 1906 was to coerce England into Germany's arms. Tirpitz argued, the Kaiser agreed, and Bethmann-Hollweg reluctantly went along with them, that the stronger the fleet became, the smaller the chance of war because the more hesitant would Britain be to attack Germany. In this political sense was the risk theory applied: offensive preparations (building battleships) would enhance the prospects for peace; defensive preparations (torpedo and U-boats) would decrease them. Tirpitz and the Kaiser even conceded that Britain could have the superior fleet; what they thought they could do was to bleed Britain financially into an alliance.

But whether the focus be before or after 1905, the leaders of Wilhelminian Germany pursued this central goal: to dislodge England from her position of supremacy. Before the Entente Cordiale, in order to achieve this goal, Germany challenged Britain overseas; after the Entente was formed, Germany challenged her in Europe. The change in the focus of the German challenge was reflected by the change in the preoccupations of the British Cabinet: before 1905, they were imperial; after 1905, they became continental. World War I can be viewed as a security war for both Britain and Germany, but that should not cause us to lose sight of why each saw it that way. After 1905, Germany's security on the continent and coequal status with Britain overseas were both served by breaking up the Triple Entente. By detaching England from the Triple Entente, Germany would not only have ended her own encirclement, but also brought about England's isolation. And a Britain detached from her allies would have had to settle with Germany.

Thus the risk theory was a strategic doctrine devised to challenge, threaten, and ultimately isolate England. The doctrine determined the manner in which the navy viewed battleships and submarines. War was necessary to shatter preconceptions, to drive home the military futility of an inferior fleet, but most important of all, to change the prime goal of Germany from "compellence" in peacetime to victory in war. Once hostilities occurred, the offensive capabilities of the U-boat came into full view.

CONCLUSIONS AND EXTENSIONS

Out of this study of prewar Germany naval thinking emerge two conclusions that apply, not only to battlefleets from 1880 to 1915, but also to airpower from 1919 to 1939 and to nuclear-tipped missile power from the mid-1950s to the present—conclusions, that is, that apply to the three successive "dominant weapons" (in J.F.C. Fuller's sense) of the last one hundred years. The conclusions are:

(1) that in the absence of a strong external stimulus (exigencies of war, peacetime crises, or pressures from political leaders), a military organization will usually relegate costly, potentially revolutionary new weapons to marginal, auxiliary, or supportive roles (ones that do not threaten the raison d'etre of the organization or the supremacy of its prime weapon); and

(2) that in peacetime a military organization's acceptance of such a weapon as central to its function will depend mainly upon how vital political leaders think that weapon is to the realization of the foreign policy goals they are pursuing.

In short, a peacetime military organization will fit a new weapon into its existing image of war, not adapt the image to the weapon; and in peacetime, political leaders, not military brass, determine to what extent the newest dominant weapon will be used.

The validity of these two conclusions stems from the structure and task of military organizations: they are tight hierarchies and their function involves high risk. Those who have risen to the top have fixed views of how to wage war. They have risen to the pinnacles of power precisely because of their personal successes in wars in which they fought, or because of the lessons they read from wars in which they did not fight, or because of their championing of a new weapon that finally became fully incorporated into the standard weaponry inventory. For whatever the reason, those at the top have an enormous personal commitment to, and investment in, particular doctrines and weapons. New doctrines and weapons represent potential challenges to their prestige and predominance; acceptance of them could very well mean loss of face, if not command, but certainly dilution of power. Those in the middle or lower ranks who advocate changes thus face superiors with set attitudes and with the power to enforce them.

Centralized, tightly controlled bureaucracies do not readily accept innovations (see Davis, 1967; Morton, 1969; Ransom, 1958; Thompson, 1965; Wilson, 1966; and Wolff, 1970).

Not only the way military organizations are structured, but also the function they perform explains their resistance to change in peacetime. For the soldier, war involves risk of death; for the nation, perhaps its continued existence. Because the stakes of combat are so high and the uncertainties so numerous, the pressures to fix upon the known and the familiar are great; the inclinations to stick with the tried and the proven, strong; the willingness to rely upon the "untested," therefore, small. Because matters of warfare are judgmental, not scientific, military figures tend to be historically oriented: they cope with the uncertain present and the unforeseeable future by retreating into the familiar past for guidelines to action. A paradox therefore occurs when peacetime military organizations choose the weapons they will rely on in order to wage war. They will select the newest *version* of a familiar weapon because the increment in performance can make the difference between success or failure, but they will reject the *newest weapon* because they do not want to gamble in order to find out how useful it can be. Thus, because by nature military organizations are conservative, when radical peacetime changes in structure or doctrine occur, they are usually imposed from without.

The cases of seapower, airpower, and nuclear-tipped missile power illustrate, not only the inertia of military organizations, but also how the goals political superiors pursue determine the ways new weapons will be used. In the case of seapower from 1880 to 1915, most navies considered battleships the prime weapons and U-boats the auxiliary ones because political leaders saw world status and rank symbolized by big, powerful-looking ships, not by small, largely invisible ones. In Germany Weltpolitik required prestigious weapons; in Britain a world empire required a powerful navy. In the United States the requirements of the strategic defensive and the widespread acceptance of Mahan's linkage of seapower to world power led Americans to cast off cruiser-commerce theories and opt for a large navy composed of battleships (see Sprout and Sprout, 1966: chs. 11–13; Grenville and Young, 1966: chs. 1, 8, 11). For a while, France deviated from the pattern; but by 1900, even she returned to the emphasis on battlefleets. All these powers did invest resources in submarines, but the amounts were insignificant compared to those invested in their battlefleets.

In the interwar years, the use contemplated for airpower—whether it would be integral or auxiliary to a nation's forces in war—depended upon the foreign policy goals a nation pursued. In England and Italy, airpower achieved equal status with land and seapower; in the United States, airpower remained to land and seapower what submarines had earlier been to battleships—marginal and auxiliary (Ransom, 1958). The experience with airpower in World War I, together with an outlook (ingrained by the long years of reliance on seapower) that held that protective forces were to engage the enemy far away from the homeland, led the British to accord great value to airpower. An ambitious foreign policy, together with a desire to dominate the Mediterranean, led Mussolini to regard airpower as a natural offensive weapon. An isolationist foreign policy, together with a long distance from Europe and Japan, a defensively-oriented posture, and an acceptance of the navy as the first line of defense, led the Americans to see little value in a device heralded as the offensive weapon of the future.

In the case of nuclear-tipped missile power, in the United States, for example, neither the air force nor the navy readily pushed intercontinental ballistic missile programs. The air force wanted to deliver nuclear weapons with aircraft based at home and overseas; the navy, with aircraft flown from supercarriers. The air force scrapped an ICBM program in the late 1940s and continued to build bombers. The navy, after it had lost the battle for the supercarrier, continued with the "regular" aircraft carrier and also began to develop the atomic-powered submarine; but even in this case the navy viewed it, not as a strategic missile launcher, but as a submarine better equipped to do what submarines had always done, namely to sink other ships. Not until the Eisenhower administration switched American strategic policy from a war-fighting to a war-deterring posture did the air force (and army) crash missile programs begin. Not until after Sputnik did the navy begin in earnest to develop a missile capability for its atomic submarines; and even as late as 1957, it still saw the submarine's missiles attacking other enemy submarine bases, not his cities or aircraft. Only as the prime security goal shifted from defense and victory in a general war to deterrence of it did the construction and maintenance of a second-strike nuclear capability become the central concern of America's military leaders. Much the same thing has occurred within the Soviet Union in the 1960s.

One final point remains to be made. Because dominant weapons can perform, not only a security function, but also a "swagger" function, the likelihood that political leaders will want really large numbers of them will depend upon just how expansive their foreign policy goals are. At least twice in the last one hundred years has the challenger to the world's greatest power aped him. In this respect, the Soviet Union has done in the 1960s what Germany did three generations ago: challenged the leader's supremacy by building a military force nearly equal to, and akin to, his. The security dilemma will cause nations to spend more in order to remain where they were, but sometimes statesmen may act initially or even later on, not merely from a concern for security, but also from a desire for greatness. Sir Edward Grey, Britain's Foreign Secretary before the Great War and man not noted for his pro-German sentiments, spoke to the House of

Commons on July 25, 1912 with Germany in mind, but his words have equal merit today: "A great and growing nation generates power not necessarily for aggression, and with no special design, but because it wishes to be powerful" (quoted in Woodward, 1966: 374). Schumpeter said the root cause of imperialism is expansion for the sake of expansion. May not the same hold true for nations that build tremendous numbers of the dominant weapons—that perhaps they accrete power for the sake of being powerful?

The Horse Cavalry
in the Twentieth Century

EDWARD L. KATZENBACH, JR.

THE PROBLEM

Lag-time, that lapsed period between innovation and a successful institutional or social response to it, is probably on the increase in military matters. Moreover, as the tempo of technological change continues to quicken, it is likely that lag-time will increase as well. . . .

Of course, at first there would seem to be a paradox here. As weapons systems have become more complex, the lead-time needed to bring them from the drawing board to the assembly line has become markedly longer. On the basis of the longer lead-time one might hypothesize that the institutional lag might lessen inasmuch as prior planning would seem eminently more possible. It might even be surmised that the institutional response might be made to coincide with the operational readiness of new weapons. To date, however, military institutions have not been able to use this lead-time effectively because real change has so outdistanced anticipated change. Moreover, there is not the urgency that there should be in the military to make major institutional adjustments in the face of the challenge of new weapons

From Public Policy, 1958, pp. 120–149. Copyright © 1958 by John Wiley & Sons, Inc. Reprinted by permission of John Wiley & Sons, Inc. Portions of the text and some footnotes have been omitted.

systems, if for no other reason than that the problem of testing is so difficult. . . . It is quite impossible to *prove* that minor adjustments in a traditional pattern of organization and doctrine will not suffice to absorb technological innovations of genuine magnitude.

Furthermore the absence of any final testing mechanism of the military's institutional adequacy short of war has tended to keep the pace of change to a creep in time of peace, and, conversely, has whipped it into a gallop in time of war. The military history of the past half century is studded with institutions which have managed to dodge the challenge of the obvious. . . . The most curious of all was the Horse Cavalry which maintained a capacity for survival that borders on the miraculous. The war horse survived a series of challenges each of which was quite as great as those which today's weapons systems present to today's traditional concepts. . . . It continued to live out an expensive and decorous existence with splendor and some spirit straight into an age which thought it a memory. . . .

The horse cavalry has had to review its role in war four times since the end of the nineteenth century in the face of four great changes in the science of war: the development of repeating automatic and semi-automatic weapons, the introduction of gasoline and diesel-fueled engines, the invention of the air-borne weapon, and the coming of the nuclear battlefield. Each new challenge to the horse has been, of necessity, seriously considered. Each has demanded a review of doctrine, a change in role and mission. And in each review there have been, of necessity, assumptions made as to the relevance of experience to some pattern of future war . . . [for] the paradox of military planning is that it must be reasonably precise as to quite imprecise future contingencies.

THE WEAPONS PROBLEM

By the year 1900, or thereabouts, the clip-fed breech-loading repeating rifle was in the hands of the troops of all the major powers. . . . Self-firing automatic weapons were also on the assembly lines of the world's armament makers. Hiram Maxim had registered the last of a famous series of machine gun patents in 1885. By the time (1904–1905) of the Russo-Japanese War the guns of Maxim and Hotchkiss were in national arsenals everywhere, or almost everywhere, for the expense of new weapons was rapidly shrinking the ranks of those powers which could be considered "great." At roughly the same time it had been found that the use of glycerine in the recoil mechanism of artillery pieces enabled these to remain aimed after being fired. This in turn meant that the artillery piece itself became a rapid fire (20 rounds per minute) weapon. . . . Firepower, in short, had a new meaning.

For the elite of the armies of the world, the cavalry, each of these developments would seem to have been nothing short of disaster. For that proud and beautiful animal, the horse, has a thin skin and a high silhouette, and its maximum rate of speed on the attack is only 30 m.p.h. Especially in conjunction with barbed wire, automatically manufactured since 1874 and in military use at the end of the century, it is difficult to imagine a target more susceptible to rapid fire.

The cavalry had always considered itself to have a variety of missions. The cavalry was the good eye of the infantry. It was taught to collect, and if necessary to fight for information about the enemy. The cavalry protected friendly, and harried enemy flanks and rear. It covered any necessary withdrawal. It was used in pursuit of defeated enemy. And above and beyond all else, the cavalry was used to charge the faltering, the weary, or the unwary, to deliver the *coup de grâce* with the *arme blanche:* with cold steel, with saber or lance, to "crown victory" as the proud phrase went.

It was clear that the introduction of the automatic and the semi-automatic weapon would make some cavalry missions more difficult. But there was no doubt in any cavalryman's mind, and there was little doubt in the minds of most others, that most cavalry missions would have to continue simply because there was no viable substitute. The horse was transport, and the horse was mobility. A group of horsemen could cover a hundred miles in twenty-four hours with a load of around 225–250 pounds. The beast was reasonably amphibious; at least it could swim rivers. To scout, to patrol, to cover flank, rear and withdrawal, to raid—these missions remained untouched.

There remained, however, one really great problem area. Did automatic fire relegate the horse to a transport role or should it still be considered as part of a weapons system? At the time the problem was never stated quite this simply. Indeed it was never stated simply at all, but in essence this was the issue from roughly the end of the Boer War until World War I. The reason why the question so divided men was this: Cavalry as an arm was an integrated weapon made up of horse, man and cold steel fighting as one. If horses were to be considered simply as transportation, and if man and horse were to be separated for the fire fight, then the cavalry as an arm would no longer exist. Only mounted infantry would remain.[1]

On the issue of the relationship between horse and man hung a number of subsidiary issues. Should the horseman be armed with the new automatic weapons? If so, he would have to be dismounted in

---

[1] Perhaps this will be better understood if a modern analogy is cited—the substitution of missile for manned aircraft, for example.

action, for the horse, as differentiated from the elephant, is a most unsatisfactory gun platform. Yet to deprive cavalry of the new weapons
would be to deprive the weapons of mobility. And if the horse could
no longer be used to charge the new guns, then of what possible use
was honed steel, e.g., lance and sword, even if one took into serious
account the last ditch defense of it, to wit that it was "always
loaded"? Finally, and here one comes to the most burning question in
any issue of military policy—the effect of change on morale. If the
cavalry were deprived of its cold steel, would it lose that fine edge of
morale, that élan without which of course it would not be "cavalry,"
no matter what its mission?

There should have been some way to learn through experience just
what could and could not be done with the cavalry with and against
the new weapons. There were, after all, two wars of some importance
during the period under consideration—the Boer War (1898–1901)
and the Russo-Japanese (1904–1905). In both, cavalry and repeating
and automatic weapons were used. Each fall, moreover, there were
great maneuvers in each country of Europe. Present at each were
foreign observers with, at least by modern standards, a free run of the
field of action. Why was it then that there could be no final decisions
on these matters?

The answer lies in the number of variables. For instance, before the
problem of the cavalry armament could even be tackled, the difficult
question had to be answered as to what the rapid-fire weapons could
do and should be doing.

. . . For each demonstrable fact there was an awkwardly intangible
"if" which could neither be properly accounted for nor possibly
forgotten. If into the balance of judgment concerning the machine
gun was thrown the urgent problem of its resupply and its vulnerability
to long-range artillery fire, then a rational conclusion might be reached
that the weapon was primarily defensive in character and should be
dug into the earth, into a well sandbagged bunker, there to pour forth
its withering fire into an attacking force. Yet if, on the other hand, it
was concluded that the withering fire of the weapon made it ideal to
use on the surprise target, the target of opportunity on the enemy
flank, then the weapon became offensive. If an offensive weapon,
then the machine gun could well be designated a cavalry weapon. If
defensive, then was it not an infantry, or even an artillery weapon? Of
course this initial decision was a serious one for it might well determine the future of the weapon. Once assigned to an organization, a
branch or arm of a service, it was at least likely that the weapon's
development would be stunted except in line with the mission of the
unit to which it was assigned.

Within the military staff of all nations the machine gun raised
many more problems than it solved—as can be expected of any new

weapons system. These problems were, furthermore, broadly intellectual rather than narrowly technical. Indeed the mechanical improvement of a given weapons system is usually less urgent and almost always less baffling than deciding a proper and fitting target for it, and then solving the galaxy of problems of organization and control which hinge on this basic decision. . . .

So in the period between 1900 and 1914 the immediate problem was to conceptualize the mission or missions of the machine gun and the tactics of the new clip-fed, bolt-action rifle and the automatic gun. The second problem was to decide the future tactics and armament of cavalry in view of the concept arrived at. What actually happened was that the new was absorbed into old organizational and tactical concepts, and nothing of the old was rejected. The reasoning from country to country may, however, be of lasting interest. The matter of the cavalry *charge* provides an excellent focal point.

THE CHARGE

It is hard to see where there was room for claim and counterclaim in so substantive an issue as this—the charge of a wave of horsemen, gaily colored (except in the United States), helmets shining, plumes flying, sabers drawn or lances at the ready. Surely a comprehensive and conclusive study of the charge and its role, if any, in modern war was not outside the bounds of logical possibility. Yet just as it was impossible in the 1930s to analyze the role of the battleship in the air age and is now impossible to assess the relationship between the naval aircraft carrier and the nuclear bomber, so it was impossible to evaluate the charge—and for much the same reasons.

The reasons why the charge was continued varied from one country to another. But basically it was continued because the cavalry liked it. In virtually all countries the cavalry was a club, an exclusive one, made up at the officer level of those who could afford to ride when young, hunt, dress and play polo when older. The impression that one absorbs from contemporary cavalry reviews, from the pictures, the social columns, the interests expressed in the less than serious articles, together with the portrait of the cavalryman in the contemporary novel, is of a group of men who were at once hard-riding, hard-drinking, and hard-headed. Its leadership was derived from the countryside rather than from the city. The cavalry was the home of tradition, the seat of romance, the haven of the well-connected. New York City's Squadron A, the proud majors in the Prussian Cavalry Reserve, the French Horse Breeders' Association, all had a built-in loyalty to the cavalry, and if the Chief of Cavalry said that the charge was still feasible, he had important backing. So it was that in Europe the charge was still considered not only feasible, but a future way of war.

American cavalrymen, however, thought that European cavalry had much to learn. And in many respects the U.S. "Red Necks" were quite the most realistic of the world's cavalries in the period just prior to World War I. To be sure, they retained the saber charge, executing it with the same straight saber, a thrust weapon, used by the Canadian cavalry. But in the years just before World War I until just after World War II the U.S. Cavalry preferred to practice the charge with the Colt semi-automatic .45 pistol. (The pistol charge was never actually used in battle. The last battle charge of the U.S. Cavalry seems to have been in the Philippines during the insurrection of 1901.) Of course it might be argued that to put a .45 in the hands of a man on a horse was simply to mount the inaccurate on the unstable, but given the argument that the essence of the charge was its psychological impact, the sound of the .45 might have had an effect comparable to the sight of saber or lance.

But what the U.S. Cavalry did have that the others did not was a genuine appreciation of the importance of dismounted action. It is this which is given the more elaborate treatment in the regulations, and it is this that the trooper really expected to be the rule in combat. But was this the result of a thoughtful analysis of the new weapons or something else?

Certainly the articles in the *Journal of the U.S. Cavalry Association* are the most sophisticated in regard to the new repeating arms and their impact on cavalry. In the years just after the turn of the century the great argument in U.S. Cavalry circles was whether or not the saber should be retained at all. But it seems to have been generally admitted that while "Mounted charges may yet be used on rare occasions when the enemy is demoralized, out of ammunition, or completely taken by surprise . . .," nonetheless "for cavalry to make a mounted charge against enemy troops who are dismounted and armed with the present magazine gun, would be to seek disaster." The corollary that ". . . the trooper must bear in mind that in fighting his carbine is his main reliance"[2] was also accepted.

Were it not that certain European cavalry groups were at the time tending to reject the thesis to which the U.S. subscribed, there would be nothing in any way remarkable about the U.S. position, so patently obvious and right does it seem in retrospect. Yet in the early nineteen hundreds U.S. doctrine was different, and hence needs a word of explanation.

The U.S. cavalryman had a tradition quite different from that of any of the Europeans. He had always done the bulk of his fighting on his feet. Therefore there was no break in tradition for him to recognize

---

[2] "Comment and Criticism," *Journal of the U.S. Cavalry Association (JUSCA)*, Vol. 13, No. 48, April 1903, pp. 720, 721.

the revolution in firepower for the great change it was. Cavalry during the Civil War most frequently fought dismounted, although clashes between cavalry were fought with the sword, and in the wars against the Indians cavalrymen also dismounted to fight with the aimed accurate fire quite unattainable on horseback. Horses were considered transportation, and the ground was considered a respectable substance on which to fight a battle. U.S. cavalrymen did not feel morally obligated to die on a horse—which European cavalrymen did. In short, the U.S. Cavalry reacted to the new firepower as it did because its history and its tradition made it quite natural for it to do so. In Europe the cavalry history of the U.S. Civil War was scarcely known until the very late nineteen hundreds, and hence the relevance of that war to cavalry problems was largely overlooked. Or given European experience and tradition, would a study of the Civil War have made any real difference?

Of all the cavalry arms of the world that which seems in retrospect to have been the furthest behind the times was that of the German Empire. The German Cavalry had adopted the lance for all ninety-three of its cavalry regiments in 1890 instead, as was true in the mid-nineteenth century, of having only one in four so armed. The lance was, of course, much more than a shaft of wood taller than a man, one tipped with steel and pennant decked: a lance was a state of mind. And it was a reminder that those who carried it still believed that the cavalry really was an arm to be reckoned with. . . .

Why was it that such serious students of war as the Germans are reputed to have been were in general quite so oblivious to the impact of the new firepower? There seem to have been several reasons. The first and most important was the attitude of Emperor William II towards cavalry. A young U.S. Cavalry lieutenant who witnessed German maneuvers in the fall of 1903 was frankly appalled by it. He noted the total lack of realism in the great rolling charges of the cavalry against both rifle and artillery. And he noted too the fact that the Kaiser was so proud of his cavalry that his umpires, knowing their place, pronounced the charges successful!! In Germany, in short, the well-known penchant of the Emperor for the charge undoubtedly did much to insulate the Germans from any serious thought of change.

There was, however, another reason as well. Even after seeing machine guns fired in the late 1880s, the German General Staff refused to take them seriously. Their reason lay in their mis-reading of their own experience with the *mitrailleuses* during the war of 1870–71 when these were badly misused. The fact that past experience happened to be irrelevant did not make it any less important, however, and it was not until 1908 that the machine gun was given the serious attention in Germany that it so obviously deserved. Even then it was only the infantry that recognized the importance of the new automatic weapons. Cavalry units, although armed with them, did not take them very seriously. German cavalry went trotting off to war in 1914, pennons flying from their lances, just as units of French infantry went off to war in red trousers, and for much the same reason: psychological effect. For the real effect of cavalry was, when on the charge, a psychological one, and was generally admitted as such. It was the role of the charge to break the enemy's will, and what could do this more effectively than a charge by lancers? The same argument was used by those who wanted to keep the infantry in red pants. They advanced the proposition that the sense of belonging was the essence of group spirit, and group spirit in turn was the touchstone of the will to fight, the ingredient that won battles. They added the corollary that nothing gave units the sense of oneness that did red trousers, and that therefore camouflaged material would actually sabotage national security. . . .

So tradition, personal predilection, and misinterpreted past experience kept the cavalry charge alive in Germany. The experience of the British after the Boer War likewise suggests how difficult it is to test the relevance of one's own experience in war.

THE RELEVANCE OF EXPERIENCE

From the end of the Boer War to the beginning of World War I the great debate in the British Cavalry, as in other countries, dealt with the retention of the lance and the charge. The arguments put forward for their retention inevitably raise the question of whether faith was not interfering with reason. . . .

A U.S. Cavalry officer noted on a trip to Aldershot in 1903 that "Every change is made entirely with reference to the Boer War and the Boer country, as though future wars would be fought under the same conditions."[3] But what this observer should also have noted was that there was a wide division of opinion as to just what that war proved, and how genuinely relevant it really was. . . .

Like other modern wars the Boer War was made up of a series of actions no one of which was decisive. The Boers, fine shots and fine horsemen, used their horses as transportation. In effect they fought as mounted infantry, employing the mobility of the horse in combination with the aimed firepower of infantry. They possessed all the advantages of great space and a friendly and embattled population, and the British were hard put to it to bring them to terms. But these were virtually the only points on which there was any agreement whatsoever. What did the facts mean, if anything?

Two of Great Britain's best known military figures, Lord Roberts,

[3] Frank R. McCoy, "Notes of the German Maneuvers," *JUSCA*, Vol. 14, No. 49, January 1904, pp. 30, 31.

the British Chief of Staff, and Field-Marshal Sir John D. P. French, Cavalry Commander in Africa and, in 1914, Commander-in-Chief of the British Expeditionary Forces, led two factions within the army whose views of the future of cavalry were in direct opposition.

The Right Honorable Field-Marshal Earl Roberts placed the *imprimatur* of his authority on a book called *War and the Arme Blanche* by one Erskine Childers. In his introduction to this book Lord Roberts set forth his basic beliefs. . . . Lord Roberts believed simply that the "main lesson" to be learned from the Boer War and the Russo-Japanese War was that "knee to knee, close order charging is practically a thing of the past." He qualified his opinion somewhat. "There may be, there probably will be, mounted attacks, preferably in open order against Cavalry caught unawares, or against broken Infantry," he wrote. But even these mounted attacks, he said, should be carried out with the rifle, rather than with steel.[4] These ideas he actually wrote into the British regulations, *Cavalry Training*, in 1904.

. . . The general argument, as one can imagine, was first that lances and sabers were not killing men in war, and second, that infantry and mounted infantry were killing, when dismounted, cavalrymen. Three wars, the U.S. Civil War, the Boer War, and the Russo-Japanese War, were cited as proof of the contention. In retrospect this point of view hardly needs explanation. It seems quite obvious to think that the armaments which took the warrior off his feet and put him on his belly would by the same token take him off his charger and put him on the ground.

For a time Lord Roberts was Commander-in-Chief of the British Army, and his views were thus imposed for a brief moment on the generals. What this meant in effect was that the lance disappeared in Britain between 1903 and 1906. But Lord Roberts proved unpopular, and as is the way with unpopular leaders, he was eased gently out of office in quite short order, to become a disturbing shadow amongst their eminences in the House of Lords. And the lance came back into use in 1906 to remain for better than two decades—until 1927, to be precise.

Sir John French, an officer whom one of the most distinguished of Great Britain's War Secretaries, Lord Haldane, called "a real soldier of the modern type"[5] was an old Hussar. He had entered the army through the Militia and had thus avoided Sandhurst and the mental training this would have involved. For Sir John the experience of the Boer War was disturbing only because a number of his colleagues had been disturbed by it. As he thought over this experience, his final

[4] Erskine Childers, *War and the Arme Blanche* (London, 1910). With an introduction by the Right Hon. Field-Marshal Earl Roberts, V.C., K.G., p. xii.
[5] Richard Burdon Halden, *An Autobiography* (London, 1929), p. 295.

assessment as of the very eve of World War I was that "It passes comprehension that some critics in England should gravely assure us that the war in South Africa should be our chief source of inspiration and guidance, and that it was not normal."[6]

The Field-Marshal's reasoning was very simple. First, he said, "The composition and tactics of the Boer forces were as dissimilar from those of European armies as possible," and he added that "Such tactics in Europe would lead to the disruption and disbandment of any army that attempted them."[7] Second, he noted that in South Africa both unlimited space and the objective of complete submission of the enemy made it a most unusual war. Third, he maintained that the British had not at the time developed proper means for remounting the cavalry with trained horses. But to say this is really to say nothing at all. It is only by uncovering Sir John's basic premises that there is really any possibility of understanding his view of his own experience.

Perhaps Sir John summarized his own thinking best when he wrote sometime during the course of 1908 that "The Boers did all that could be expected of Mounted Infantry, but were powerless to crown victory as only the dash of Cavalry can do."[8] It was the "dash of Cavalry" of which Sir John was thinking. There is ample evidence to document the point. If cold steel were thrown away as "useless lumber," he wrote, ". . . we should invert the role of cavalry, turn it into a defensive arm, and make it a prey to the first foreign cavalry that it meets, for good cavalry can always compel a dismounted force of mounted riflemen to mount and ride away, and when such riflemen are caught on their horses they have power neither of offence nor of defence and are lost."[9] Based on this analysis of the effect of rapid fire on mounted cavalry action, he deduced that the proper role of cavalry was first to fight the battlefield's greatest threat, i.e., the enemy cavalry. "The successful cavalry fight confers upon the victor command of the ground."[10] This, he said, was a job for cold steel. Only when the enemy cavalry was out of action did he think that the cavalry would rely more on the rifle than on steel—which is not to say that he ruled "out as impossible, or even unlikely, attacks by great bodies of mounted men against other arms on the battlefield."[11]

So it was that Sir John and his followers decided that the experience of recent wars was irrelevant. The Boer War was not relevant because

---

[6] General Friedrich von Bernhardi, *Cavalry* (New York, 1914), with a preface by Field-Marshal Sir J. D. P. French, p. 9.

[7] *Ibid.*, p. 9.

[8] From his introduction to the English edition of Lt. Gen. Friedrich von Bernhardi, *Cavalry in Future Wars* (London, 1909), p. x.

[9] Bernhardi, *Cavalry, op. cit.*, p. 11.

[10] *Ibid.*, p. 13.

[11] *Ibid.*, p. 15. See also A. P. Ryan, *Mutiny at the Curragh* (London, 1956), pp. 97–100 for a further elaboration of Sir John's views.

it had not been fought in Europe and because the Boers had not been armed with steel as were cavalries in Europe. The war in Manchuria between the Russians and the Japanese was irrelevant not only because it had not been fought in Europe, but also because the cavalry used there had been badly mounted, rode indifferently, and, above all, were poorly trained, i.e., in dismounted principles. "They were," wrote Sir John, "devoid of real Cavalry training, they thought of nothing but of getting off their horses and shooting. . . ."[12] From one principle, note, Sir John never deviated: *Unless the enemy cavalry was defeated, the cavalry could not carry out its other responsibilities.* And there was a corollary of this, to wit: "*Only cavalry can defeat cavalry*," cavalry being defined of course as "a body of horsemen armed with steel."

Sir John, however wrong he may have been in his estimate of the firepower revolution of his day, made one point of real consequence when he insisted that the cavalry should keep its mind on a war likely to be fought—which a war in Manchuria, the United States, or South Africa was not. To talk about wars which are likely seems eminently sensible, although there are times when the unlikely ones are given rather more attention than they warrant depending on what set of premises are in search of some wider acceptance. To cite a recent example, the war in Korea in 1950–1952 provided what seemed to the U.S. Air Force to be irrelevant experience because bombers were not effectively used. To the U.S. Navy and Marine Corps, on the other hand, it seemed very relevant indeed because Korea was a peninsula admirably suited to the projection of naval power. To the U.S. Army it presented a whole new way of thinking: that limited war involving ground troops might well be the way of the future despite and because of the horrors of nuclear exchange.

THE LIMITS OF A WEAPONS SYSTEM EVALUATION

But even if history in terms of recent war experience seemed irrelevant for one reason or another to the problem of the charge, it is hard to believe that war is a science so limited that means could not be found to test in practice the effectiveness of the charge, that a conclusive study could not be made of charges made in a variety of patterns, in different formations, and with different weapons against simulated "enemy formations." But the simple truth is that nothing is more difficult to test than a weapon's effectiveness. . . .

There is a grievously large number of intellectual stumbling blocks in first setting up and then later evaluating any test experience. For example, during the summer of 1936[13] the U.S. Infantry maneuvered

[12] Bernhardi, *Cavalry in Future Wars*, *op. cit.* p. xxiii.
[13] The story is from eye-witness reports and there is a date problem.

against the U.S. Cavalry at Fort Benning, Georgia. As the problem started, the cavalry rode and the infantry trucked to the given maneuver area. The motor vehicles being rather faster than the horses the infantry had ample time to get into position first. This proved a most frightening advantage. The infantry, well camouflaged, waited with some excitement while the cavalry were allowed to pass concealed forward infantry units. Only when the advance units of cavalry hit the main units of infantry did the infantry's stratagem become apparent. It was at that moment that the infantrymen rose shouting from entrenched positions waving bed sheets. The horses thought their Day of Judgment had arrived as ghosts rose over the battlefield, and what followed is best left to the imagination.

To infantrymen the maneuver proved conclusively that trucks gave the infantry a mobility with which the cavalry could not hope to compete and that when minus multicolored uniforms and not drawn up in drill formation, the infantry made unsatisfactory cavalry targets. Yet to the cavalrymen—and this raised a furor that still stays in men's minds—the whole exercise only proved that infantrymen were practical jokers. The problem, that is to say, of "proving out" doctrine in the field of maneuver is distressingly difficult.

Essentially the problem lies in one's estimate of that appalling obscurity, "the nature of man." The cavalryman knows, as he charges "the enemy designate," that if this were really the enemy, he would be quite too frightened to fire accurately. And he knows this because it is part of a credo without which he would never be induced to charge in the first place. Therefore the "effect of fire" becomes a subjective instead of an objective judgment, mitigated by one's belief in a concatenation of other effects—of surprise, of fear, of the use of the defilade. So while all will call for more realism in testing, getting a consensus as to what "realism" is, more frequently than not, quite outside the realm of possibility.

FACTORS IN INSTITUTIONAL SURVIVAL

The role of history. On the morrow of victory after World War I, a member of the House of Commons rose to criticize the Secretary of War, Mr. Winston Churchill. He noted that the cavalry was at "practically the same figure as before the war, and yet if I should have thought anything had been proved by the War, it was that cavalry was less useful (than) we had previously thought it was going to be."[14]

Shortly thereafter, in 1930 to be precise, there appeared a history of the French Cavalry in the World War by a Professor of Tactics at l'École Militaire et d'Application du Génie, a most prolific writer by the name of Capitaine F. Gazin. The next to the last paragraph reads as follows:

[14] *125 H.C. Deb. 25*, pp. 1366 ff.

Today, really more than yesterday, if the cavalry is to have power and
flexibility, following along with technical progress, it must have horses with
better blood lines, cadres filled with burning faith, and above all well trained
troops conscious of the heavy weight of past glory.[15]

There would seem to be no reasonable doubt but that in the minds
of the doughboy, the *poilu* or Tommy Atkins, the day of the horse
was over. The cavalryman had been called a number of things during
the war, "Pigsticker," the "Rocking Horseman," etc., which indicated what the infantry thought of his contribution. But to the
cavalryman himself the cavalry was not dead, and the history of the
Great War was never written really in meaningful terms. To him the
role of the horseman in the victory became swollen with the yeast of
time. Indeed, in cavalry historiography, the role of the horse in World
War I was most emphasized at that moment in time when the cavalry
was most threatened in army reorganization plans, between 1934 and
1939.

The cavalry had been used in the First World War. The Germans
used it extensively on that last stronghold of the cavalryman, the
eastern frontier. The British and French used it extensively in 1914
during the retreat from Le Mans during late August and early
September. Indeed the largest item of export from Great Britain to its
forces on the Continent for the war as a whole was horse fodder. . . .
For the most part the cavalry fought dismounted, but it did fight
mounted as well. It did charge machine guns. In one case the Canadians charged a group of German machine guns, and came out
unscathed, so great was the surprise achieved when the horsemen
charged, blades bared. And it was used mounted as late as 1918. Indeed this claim has been made for its work at that time—by a
cavalryman: "It may or may not be true to say that we (the allies)
should have defeated the Germans just the same in the autumn of
1918, even without our cavalry. But it is certainly true that, had it not
been for that same cavalry, there would have been no autumn advance
at all for the Germans would have defeated us in the spring."[16]

But the campaign which did more to save the horse cavalry than
any other was not fought in Europe at all. It was fought on the sands
of Palestine, at Gaza, at Beersheba, at Jerusalem, and it was fought in
part, and indeed in large part, with the lance. It was as dashingly
romantic as anything that happened during that singularly drab war,
and strong drink it was to the cavalry. In a sense, it kept the cavalry
going for another quarter century. There was irony in this for the most
eager of the cavalrymen, men of the stamp of Sir John French, had

[15] F. Gazin, *La Cavalerie dans la Guerre Mondiale* (Paris, 1930), p. 325.
[16] Lt. Col. T. Preston, "Cavalry in France," *Cavalry Journal* (British), No. 26
(1936), p. 19.

for a decade defended the cavalry regulations of the basis of the forecast of their utility for the big war on the continent, only to have the cavalry successfully used only on the periphery of the great battlefields.

So experience, that most revered of teachers, continued to couch the "lessons" of war in a certain studied ambiguity. The horse retained that place in warfare which it had had for a thousand years—in the minds of its military riders.

Mission justification for the future, 1920–1940. On the eve of World War II the General Officers of the U.S. Army were, next to those of Poland, Rumania and possibly the USSR, most convinced of the continuing utility of the horse. The French had four divisions of mixed horse and mechanized cavalry. The Germans had a debated number of horses and mechanized cavalry, for use largely as reconnaissance. The British were converting from oats to oil as rapidly as possible.

A number of problems immediately present themselves. A first very general question must be asked of the cavalrymen themselves: What did they consider their mission to be in the period between 1920 and roughly 1935 when the development of both plane and tank had reached the stage at which their future development could be foreseen with some clarity, and at which therefore some reasonable readjustment of forces to the fact of their existence could be expected? How can one account for those great differences in thinking between the responsible staffs of the larger nations during the years between 1935 and the outbreak of war in 1939? . . .

The basic argument of the cavalrymen in their journals and in their manuals in the period between the great wars was an absolutely sound one. They argued in essence that new weapons obviated only those with like characteristics. They argued that while a better tank scrapped a worse one, the tank as a weapons system could not replace the horse until such time as it could perform all the missions of a horse. Whether these missions were worthwhile was seldom considered.

Many of the arguments which cavalrymen of all nations advanced to substantiate their claims as to their future role in war will be recognized by any student of recent military history as a version of what one can only describe as standardized clap-trap. One was the argument that, since most of the world was roadless, "To base our transportation needs solely upon conditions existent in the comparatively tiny proportion of the earth's surface containing roads . . . is putting too many eggs in the same basket."[17] This will be recognized as a cavalry variant on the navy contention that "since the world is 60 per cent water . . .," and the air contention that "since air surrounds

[17] Major Malcolm Wheeler-Nicholson, *Modern Cavalry* (New York, 1922), p. vii.

the earth and the shortest distance between two points. . . ." Another argument familiar to all military historians came up again and again in the journals. This one was to the effect that mechanical aids and auxiliaries end by neutralizing each other, an argument which in its most outrageous form had the anti-tank weapon returning the battlefield to the horse.[18] "It is quite within the bounds of possibility that an infantry anti-tank weapon may be produced which will make tanks useless as weapons of attack," wrote one enthusiast[19] in a vein not unlike that used by airmen against seamen at roughly the same moment in time. The difficulty of supplying tanks was brought up as the supply problem is brought up as a limitation on each new weapons system.[20] And, of course, the essentially experimental nature of tanks—"as yet untried" is the term—raised its head perennially and everywhere.

But there were other problems and more serious ones. If the tank could be made to replace the cavalry on the charge, did that mean that the tank could take over all the other cavalry missions: reconnaissance, raids, flank protection in rough country? Could the plane be made to supplement the tank in such a way that the two used in combination could effectuate a complete substitution for the horse? Or would some kind of combination of horse and tank, and plane and tank be a future necessity? And if this were so with whom would the control lie, with tankmen or horsemen or pilots? And finally if this was a problem of phasing out the horse, what factors should govern the timing of this phasing?

These questions do not seem to have been asked with any precision largely perhaps because they edged too closely on the emotion-packed matter of prestige, on the one hand, and on an essentially insoluble organizational problem on the other. Naturally armor wanted maximum independence as do those who service and fire any weapon. The tankman wanted a command of his own, just as the machinegunner wanted his own battalion, the artillery its own regiment, the horse cavalry its own division and the airman his own service. And this is logical for in a decentralized structure growth is faster as imagination is given a freer rein. But the difficulty is that, war being all of one cloth, each weapon component also wishes to control elements of the others. And this is why the sparks flew between arms in the period between the World Wars, and before the First and after the Second. Where, as in Germany and Great Britain, armor was given its independence, it thrived. Where, as in the United States and Poland, the

[18] Anonymous, "Oil and Oats," *Cavalry Journal* (British), Vol. 28, No. 107, Jan. 1938, p. 31; Col. Sir Hereward Wake, "The Infantry Anti-Tank Weapon," *Army Quarterly*, Vol. 17, No. 2, Jan. 1929.

[19] Wake, *op. cit.*, p. 349.

[20] Lt. F. A. S. Clark, "Some Further Problems of Mechanical Warfare," *Army Quarterly*, Vol. 6, No. 2, July 1923, p. 379.

Cavalry (Horse) remained in control, tank doctrine never grew roots. But where, as in France, mechanized and horse were joined together in what at first blush seemed to be a happy marriage, a unity was forced which was pitifully inadequate from every standpoint.

For the man on the horse there was much greater difficulty in understanding the tank than in understanding the rapid fire weapon. Perhaps this could be expected since tank and horse were competitors for the same missions. Certainly the limpid eye and high spirit of the one and the crass impersonal power of the other was enough to render partisans of the one quite helpless when it came to understanding the military views of the other, quite as helpless indeed as the seabased fighter is to understand the landbased or the airbased and their view of world geography.

Practicality and the concept of the balanced force. One finds the horse cavalryman making the same points over and over again. He stressed the tanks' need for spare parts, without taking into consideration that one of the greatest difficulties of the cavalry was that horses do not have spare parts. He stressed the lack of mobility of the tank along mountain trails without mention of the appalling problem of getting horses overseas—they have a tendency to pneumonia, together with a soft breast which becomes raw and infected with the roll and pitch of the ship. Whereas the point was occasionally made that the Lord took care of the resupply of horses—i.e., that while factories could be bombed out, sex could not—no mention was ever made that in wartime as in peace He still took four or five years to produce each animal. And, finally, although the horse was claimed to have certain immunities to gas warfare, the peculiar problems of getting gas masks on the poor beasts were omitted.

Yet whether partisans were ankle deep in the sands of prejudice or not, there were certain aspects of the relationship between horses and planes, and horses and tanks which were so obvious that they could hardly be missed. However low and slow it flew, the plane would not be a substitute for a still lower and still slower man on a horse. And the plane could not penetrate forests and neither, within limits, could tanks. So there was, and indeed there still is, a gap between what the horse can do and what the plane and tank can do. But admitting the gap, there still remained the most vexing problem of all, to wit whether that gap was worth filling and if so how. And this was something which each general staff decided somewhat differently and for itself.

The U.S. Cavalry was, in retrospect, as retrogressive in 1940 as it had been progressive in the years before World War I. It had never crossed the sea during World War I due to transportation difficulties, and spent its war chasing Mexicans. But it shared every confidence that its future role would be everything that it had not been in the recent past. As of 1940 it labored under the most embarrassing of illusions. The U.S. Cavalry believed that it had modernized itself. And it defended its horse cavalry on the sacred ground of "balanced force." "Each arm has powers and limitations," explained Major General John K. Herr, Chief of Cavalry, before the Subcommittee on Military Affairs of the House Committee on Appropriations on March 11, 1940. "The proper combination is that which arranges the whole so that the powers of each offset the limitations of the others." It was because the Poles did not have that balance that they were, said General Herr, overrun by the Germans.

> Judging from Spain, had Poland's cavalry possessed modern armament in every respect and been united in one big cavalry command with adequate mechanized forces included, and supported by adequate aviation, the German light and mechanized forces might have been defeated.

Then General Herr went on to add these words of comfort:

> Mechanized cavalry is valuable and an important adjunct but is not the main part of the cavalry and cannot be. Our cavalry is not the medieval cavalry of popular imagination but is cavalry which is modernized and keeping pace with all developments.[21]

Yet is certainly does not seem that the U.S. cavalry was "keeping pace with all developments." Putting horses in trucks to give them mobility (this was the so-called "portée cavalry"), and adding inadequate anti-tank batteries can hardly be called modernizing. Is there any reasonable explanation for the illusion?

Concepts of modernization. One cannot help but be impressed with the intellectual isolation in which the U.S. armed forces operated in the 1930's. *The Journal of the U.S. Cavalry Association* paid almost no attention to mechanization throughout the period. Compared to the military periodicals on the continent, the U.S. journal seems curiously antiquated. And because there was so little critical thinking going on within the service, it is not surprising that there was virtually no thinking going on in Army ordnance either, for ordnance, after all, works on a demand basis and if there is no demand, there is likely to be no new hardware. In the United States there was in short no intellectual challenge.

Not only were there no pressures to change cavalry thinking from inside the arm, there were no pressures from outside either. United

---

[21] The text of General Herr's testimony before Congress may be found reprinted in *JUSCA,* Vol. 49, No. 3, May–June 1940. See p. 206. . . .

States industry was never anxious to sell to the services during the depression years or before. They were no more willing to put money into military research and development than were the services or the Congress. The few Secretaries of War who can be considered adequate were interested in the managerial aspects of their office and not in matters which they considered "purely military." And finally there was a not inconsiderable pressure for the *status quo* in the Congress. The U.S. had some ten millions of horses, and government spending in this direction, little though it was, was a chief source of revenue to all the many horse breeders, hay growers, and saddlemakers.

In Great Britain, the situation was markedly different. Although the British had their branch journals,—the tankers founded their own in 1937—they also had great advantage in having two journals which were more generally read. The first was the *Army Quarterly* which published on all topics of concern to the army as a whole, and the other was *The Journal of the Royal United Service Institution* which crossed service lines. Into these journals there poured articles from a singularly able, and remarkably prolific and dedicated group of publicists of whom J. F. C. Fuller and Captain Basil H. Liddell Hart are simply the best known. Officers in the British Empire were simply unable to escape, as were U.S officers, from challenge. Thus from 1936 onwards there was an increasingly strong movement in favor of conversion to oil. Furthermore this was helped rather than hindered by the stand taken by many in Parliament. For Parliament was at least conscious of *The Times* military correspondent, Liddell Hart, and the battle he was waging for mechanized warfare, a form of warfare which would, so he thought, limit and shorten future wars by making them more rapid, hence shorter and cheaper than the war of the trenches. To be sure there were those who, like Admiral of the Fleet Sir Roger Keyes, took a position against the reduction of cavalry. But they were in the minority. Most felt that the Household Cavalry and two mounted regiments still left in Egypt in 1939 were probably two too many. . . .

After World War II the French, as is the wont of democracies, held an inquiry into the military disasters of some five years before. But the questions which were put to the generals and the questions which they wanted to answer were all in terms of why they had not understood and appreciated the role of the tank and the plane. Never does the question seem to have been asked in the converse, i.e., why was the horse thought to have been so useful circa 1939? It would have been interesting to know too what thinking had been done as to the circumstances under which Cavalry divisions, offensive forces, were to be used in conjunction with the Maginot Line, a defensive ideal. Perhaps they were to have been used in the second phase of the struggle in a counter-offensive after the enemy had partially defeated himself by throwing his troops against the defensive fires of the Line. . . .

However the overall development of French cavalry thinking between the wars is plain enough. What they did was to absorb the new machines of war into old doctrine. Instead of allowing the characteristics of new weapons to create new doctrine, the French General Staff simply gave them missions to fulfill that were within the old framework. Thus tanks were made subordinate and supporting weapons to the infantry, and subordinate and supporting weapons to the cavalry. In a sense the French achieved what General Herr of the U.S. Cavalry wanted to achieve, except that the French did look forward to complete mechanization at some future date, which Herr did not. And the *Revue de Cavalerie*, a strange hodge-podge of oats, history and oil, reflects that point of view.

The German experience was somewhat different again. Whereas the French looked back to the stalemate at Verdun, the great achievement of defensive weapons, the Germans looked back to the great offensives of 1918 and to the very near miss of the Schlieffen plan in 1914. Particularly in the case of the younger officers the great objective was regaining the lost means of offensive. A defeated army, the Germans were in a position to start once more from the beginning. To be sure there was a very difficult period of struggle with German horse cavalrymen, but those in Germany with an interest in tanks had an advantage which those in the democracies did not. They had the interest of the Chief of State. When Hitler saw Panzer units in action, he said repeatedly, "That's what I need! That's what I want to have!"[22] To Hitler they were the keystone in a concept of total war.

The *Revue de Cavalerie* stopped publication during the war and never appeared again. The British *Cavalry Journal* disappeared forever as well. Only the *Journal of the U.S. Cavalry Association* continued to appear. Its heroes were the horse-drawn artillery which landed on Guadalcanal, the animals flown over the Burma "Hump" into China, the U.S. units which were remounted on Italian Cavalry horses in Italy and German horses in Germany; the great heroes were the only real cavalry left—the Cossacks. Duly noted was how greatly needed were horse cavalry during the battles in Normandy and elsewhere.

In his closing chapter of *He's in the Cavalry Now*, Brig. Gen. Rufus S. Ramey, a former commander of the U.S. Cavalry School, concluded in 1944, "Currently we are organizing and training adequate mechanized horse cavalry for field employment."[23] His was the final testament. The last old Army mule, except for the West Point Mascot, was retired in 1956. The horse cavalry had been disbanded five years before.

New Item. In 1956 the Belgian General Staff suggested that for the kind of dispersed war which low yield atomic weapons necessarily

[22] General Heinz Guderian, *Panzer Leader* (New York, 1952), p. 30.
[23] Brig. Gen. Rufus S. Ramey, *He's in the Cavalry Now* (New York, 1944), p. 190. There were 60,170 animals in the U.S. Forces on December 31, 1943.

create, the horse, which in Europe could be independent of depots, should be reintroduced into the weapons system.[24]

CONCLUSION

The military profession, dealing as it does with life and death, should be utterly realistic, ruthless in discarding the old for the new, forward-thinking in the adoption of new means of violence. But equally needed is a romanticism which, while perhaps stultifying realistic thought, gives a man that belief in the value of the weapons system he is operating that is so necessary to his willingness to use it in battle. Whether a man rides a horse, a plane or a battleship into war, he cannot be expected to operate without faith in his weapons system. But faith breeds distrust of change. Furthermore there is need for discipline, for hierarchy, for standardization within the military structure. These things create pressures for conformity, and conformity too is the enemy of change. Nor is there generally the pressure for the adoption of the new that is found in other walks of life. There is no profit motive, and the challenge of actual practice, in the ultimate sense of war, is very intermittent. Finally, change is expensive, and some part of the civilian population has to agree that the change is worth the expense before it can take place. What factors then make for change in situations short of war?

Surely the greatest instigation of new weapons development has in the past come from civilian interest plus industrial pressure. The civilian governors get the weapons system *they* want. Hitler gets his tanks, the French public their line of forts. When society shows an interest in things military, weapons are adopted—apparently in great part because of the appeal they make to a set of social values and economic necessities. The abolition of the horse cavalry came about first in those countries which could not afford to raise the horses and in which there were those with a hungry intellectual interest in the ways of war. When there was no interest in the military, as in the United States, there was no pressure to change and the professional was given tacit leave to romanticize an untenable situation. Thus the U.S. Horse Cavalry remained a sort of monument to public irresponsibility in this, the most mechanized nation on earth.

[24] "Belgians Hit U.S. Concept of Atomic War," *Christian Science Monitor*, August 25, 1956.

Chemical Warfare:
A Study in Restraints

FREDERIC J. BROWN

. . . [World War I] was [a] war without limits—the brains and muscle of modern industrial nations applied without restriction to the art of war. In the minds of expert and layman alike, World War I was about to pass a threshold into new levels of violence when it ended. It was the mind that could speculate not the eye that had seen which would project World War I as it could have been in 1919.

MILITARY PERSPECTIVES

Speculation would play a significant role in determining the future of gas warfare; however, there were more substantial factual inputs that would influence subsequent decision-makers—the lessons learned from the experiences of World War I.

Tactical characteristics. The tactical military lessons were mixed, a potpourri of individual or unit experiences extremely difficult to evaluate in the aggregate in order to rate gas as "effective" or "noneffective." More important to military analysts than an imprecise evaluation of effectiveness were the characteristics of poison gas as observed on the battlefield. By November 1918, it was apparent that chemical warfare had three central characteristics: it was an extremely versatile weapon, tractable to almost any tactical situation; the logistic requirements complicated the battlefield enormously; and its employment demanded unprecedented sophistication of individual and unit training.

The tactical versatility of gas was derived from the diverse properties of the gases employed. Gas could be persistent or nonpersistent over a wide range of lethality—from an extremely toxic cyanic compound to a nonlethal, harassing tear or sneezing gas. The effect of the gas could be immediate or delayed for several hours.

These properties gave chemical warfare a role in the offensive or defensive, in mobile or position warfare. A lethal, nonpersistent agent could be placed on enemy positions just before attack and it would be

From *Chemical Warfare: A Study in Restraints* by Frederic J. Brown, pp. 32–48 and 290–298. Copyright © 1968 by Princeton University Press. Reprinted by permission. Portions of the text and some footnotes have been deleted.

dissipated before friendly troops arrived. A persistent agent such as mustard could be placed to protect a flank during an attack, to deny an area to the enemy, or as a very effective barrage in front of a defensive position. Such flexibility applied, of course, to all belligerents, provided that each could support the logistic requirements of gas warfare.

The logistic demands were enormous. Gas substituted for nothing. Its requirements were an additional load to an already overloaded battlefield. To be effective, a high concentration of gas had to be maintained over the enemy position. The Germans found that 12,000 kilograms of Green Cross [nonpersistent] shells were necessary to gas an area one kilometer square. Similar consumption figures were experienced by other belligerents.[1]

Graver problems were presented to both logisticians and tacticians by the requirements for individual and collective protection in a toxic environment. In addition to the other stresses and dangers of war, the very air the soldier breathed and the harmless inanimate objects he touched had become potential weapons against him. The range of problems posed was infinite: How would the soldier eat, drink, sleep, perform bodily functions, use his weapon, give and receive commands; how would he protect horses, pigeons, and watch dogs; how would he know when his immediate area was contaminated? By November 1918, many of these issues had been broached but they had not been solved. The battlefield had experienced a quantum jump in sophistication; it had become too "complicated."

Nothing indicated the spectrum of new problems better than the gas mask. A highly personal symbol of gas warfare, it was awkward, heavy to carry, and uncomfortable to wear. An officer in the 3rd Division, AEF, described it:

> The mask is safe but it is the most uncomfortable thing I ever experienced. If . . . [anyone wants to] know how a gas mask feels, let him seize his nose with a pair of fire tongs, bury his face in a hot feather pillow, then seize a gas pipe with his teeth and breathe through it for a few hours while he performs routine duties. It is safe, but like the deadly poison which forced its invention, it is not sane.[2]

It was not just that the mask was uncomfortable. The survival of the individual was determined by the quality of the mask. Either it worked

[1] . . . High ammunition expenditure rates were not unique to gas; however, gas required a special infrastructure—meteorological stations, special purpose units with specialized training, etc.—that was not required for conventional warfare.

[2] R. Cochrane, *Gas Warfare in World War I*, 20 Studies (Army Chemical Center: Chemical Corps Historical Office, 1957–1960), Study 14, p. 34. . . . The mask also reduced vision and muffled the voice—two essential requirements to command on the battlefield. . . .

faultlessly or the soldier died. Life was dependent upon 100 per cent reliability. This unique and disquieting reliance on science and industry, was not the only psychological problem related to wearing the mask. There was the added trauma of divorcement from the external environment. The gas mask "makes the soldier blind and deaf when he enters into material warfare, despoils him of his feed and drink, his nicotine and alcohol, and then makes war a fearful means for the destruction of morale."[3]

As well as indirect psychological effects derived from protective measures, fears of gas warfare produced other reactions. One was a psychoneurosis, "Gas Fright." Soldiers, hearing a report that gas was in the area, would acquire all of the symptoms of gas poisoning although they had not been gassed. Gas could induce severe morale problems among troops already fatigued and dispirited by a difficult tactical situation. The First Army of the AEF was in such a situation facing the Kriemhilde Stellung in October 1918. The history of the 42nd Division commented:

> . . . an important cause of the low morale was the mounting fear of the enemy's use of gas . . . it was largely responsible for creating so great a straggler problem that, as Bullard said, a solid line of MP's back of the fighting front had become necessary to keep the men in the line. The basis of that fear was the gas atmosphere that the enemy maintained over much of the front by his regulated gas fire each day. When it did not cause real casualties, it supported apprehension and panic, and hastened the onset of battle fatigue and gas mask exhaustion.[4]

The combined effects of tactical flexibility, logistical complexity, and adverse psychological response to an alien environment required highly trained units. For front-line troops, instantaneous reaction was required twenty-four hours per day. If the unit was not properly trained, it suffered debilitating casualties.[5]

In summary, chemical warfare was an enigma from the perspective of tactical military employment. If it could be used unilaterally, there was no question that it was effective. Unfortunately, however, it could not be used unilaterally. Once the enemy retaliated, the game did not appear worth the candle. No transitory advantage justified the difficulties of a chemical battlefield. The problems of fighting in an alien

[3] Maj. G. Soldan, *Der Mensch und die Schlacht der Zunkuft* (Oldenberg: Verlag Stalling, 1925). . . .
[4] Cochrane, *op. cit.*, Study 17, pp. 40–41. . . .
[5] All armies experienced roughly equivalent gas-casualty rates, dependent upon the training of troops. Casualties at Ypres in 1915 were estimated at over 30 per cent. Later in the year, the gas-casualty rate declined to less than 3 per cent as training improved. Yet the first attack on U.S. troops in 1918 produced over 30 per cent casualties—not a glowing testimonial to U.S. preparations. . . .

environment appeared insoluble. Science and technology might develop an answer but this was a mixed blessing at best.

Science and technology. If it can be said that science and the industrial revolution approached the battlefield in the American Civil War, it can be said to have arrived during World War I. In no other area was this as apparent as chemical warfare. A General could improve upon or detract from the capabilities of the chemical warfare equipment given to him; but the life and death decisions of strategic magnitude were made in laboratories and industrial plants.

Throughout the war there was a scientific race between belligerents. The Germans seized the initiative when they introduced chlorine gas at Ypres in April 1915; six months passed before the Allies could retaliate. In July 1917, the Germans introduced mustard gas; it was June 1918 before the Allies could retaliate in kind,[6] and not until the last month of the war that they had sufficient stocks of mustard gas. This provided a significant advantage to the Germans in the spring-summer offenses of 1918.

Thirty different chemical substances were tested in combat during the war,[7] each of which posed a unique problem for defense. Since no army could afford to find itself in a defenseless position due to a new enemy gas, there were continual efforts at improvement. The British alone issued 7 different masks to their troops—a total of 50 million masks. . . .

The role of science was equal to if not greater than the traditional value of physical courage in determining success on the battlefield. As toxic agents and their methods of delivery became more sophisticated in 1917 and 1918, the necessity for professional-military assimilation of science and technology became more pronounced. It was not a comforting thought to realize that an enemy with a superior technical expertise and industrial capability could introduce a weapon which would overcome one's own superior training and leadership. This was a disturbing reality that the military profession faced in looking back at World War I. Chemical warfare was the most striking example.

A question of honor. However, there was more to disturb the military profession than science and technology. Chemical warfare did not fall within the limits of the honor of the profession. The code of war was unwritten, but it was understood. Essentially based upon the code of chivalry, it had varied as mores changed and as the increasing range of weapons changed the nature of the battlefield. In 1914, it was represented by the Rules of Land Warfare in the Hague Conventions. Violation could be tolerated only through necessity of

[6] Due to a brilliant manufacturing feat of the French. The British did not have mustard gas until September 1918.

[7] . . . Over 3,000 substances were investigated for war use.

war and even here the accountability rested with the Head of State.

Two hallmarks of the profession were that war would be limited in its efforts to combatants only, and that the most honorable and heroic way to defeat the enemy was in hand-to-hand combat. In the minds of certain World War I military leaders, gas violated these customs and typified the contemporary degeneration of the profession in the face of unlimited war.

General Peyton March, the Chief of Staff of the United States Army during and after the war, recalled a visit to a hospital in France:

> [The hospital contained] . . . over one hundred French women and children who had been living in their homes in rear of and near the front and who were gassed. The sufferings of these children, particularly, were horrible and produced a profound impression on me. War is cruel at best, but the use of an instrument of death, which once launched, cannot be controlled, and which may decimate noncombatants—women and children—reduces civilization to savagery.[8]

While March was primarily concerned about the gassing of non-combatants, two general officers more closely connected with the initiation at Ypres condemned the effect on troops. General von Deimling, Commanding General of a German Corps at Ypres, commented: "I must confess that the commission for poisoning the enemy just as one poisons rats struck me as it must any straightforward soldier; it was repulsive to me."[9] Lord French, the British Commander in France, expressed the "deepest regret and some surprise" that the German Army claiming to be "the chief exponent of the chivalry of war should have stooped to employ such devices against brave and gallant foes. . . ."[10] Reactions such as these would be reinforced with time as the rationale of wartime necessity faded from view. A sense of guilt for past actions combined with the natural desire to enhance the image of one's profession could make gas an exceedingly unpopular subject for military discussion.

At the end of World War I, the prospects of military acceptance of chemical warfare were unfavorable. On balance, the military characteristics of gas warfare did not justify its use unless the situation ensured unilateral employment. Unless some nation made a significant technological breakthrough in protection, a mutual exchange of gas would create a toxic battle environment causing more problems to

---

[8] Gen. P. March, *The Nation at War* (Garden City, N.Y.: Doubleday-Doran, 1932), p. 333. This passage was written in 1931, but it was not inconsistent with his immediate postwar attitude.

[9] Gen. von Deimling, *Reminiscences* (Paris: Montaigne, 1931). . . .

[10] *The Despatches of Lord French* (London: Chapman and Hull Ltd., 1917), p. 360. In the British Army, the Gas Brigade and gas itself were referred to as "frightfulness. . . ."

be raised than could be solved. Nevertheless, the rewards for a breakthrough would be high. . . .

The question was complicated, however, by the side issues that gas introduced. Gas symbolized the encroachment of science and technology into military decision-making, and became "an affair of honor" to the military profession. If the military continued to view gas from these perspectives, its future would not be promising.

FEARS FOR THE FUTURE—ESCALATION

The issues that gas posed to the military were dwarfed by the problems it presented to the makers of national security policy. The history of the use of toxic agents in World War I made a near perfect model of escalation: escalation of delivery systems, of weapon capabilities, and of targets selected. . . .

By the time of the 1918 offensive, at least 50 per cent of the artillery shells fired by the Germans were gas shells. The last ominous increment to delivery capability was never employed. In 1918, the British contracted for 250 bombing aircraft each with a 7,500-pound bomb load. . . .

The last and most foreboding input to the model of escalation was target selection. The initial use of gas was confined to a military target, but as the war developed and the use of gas increased in intensity, it was impossible to avoid noncombatants. One of the objections to the release of clouds of gas from cylinders was that the size of the cloud produced significant gas concentrations at undesired locations. In discussing this problem, Hanslian referred to effects as far as 20 kilometers behind the front and deaths at a distance of 15 kilometers. There is no indication, however, that the belligerents did not tacitly agree that a certain "spillover" of gas into towns was an inevitable accompaniment to its tactical use in a congested countryside.

The strategic use of gas was an entirely different question. The delivery system could only be by airplane and the implications were truly frightening. The Germans initiated strategic bombing on Christmas Eve 1914—one aircraft with one bomb. The bombing effort gradually escalated to two serious raids on London (June 13, 1917 and July 7, 1917) causing 832 casualties. After the July 7th raid, the English War Cabinet appointed a committee headed by Jan Christian Smuts to study the air defense of the United Kingdom. In its report, this committee gave serious consideration to the "probability" of the Germans using gas to attack London. Thus by the fall of 1917, the Germans had initiated unrestricted city bombing and the British had matched the capability of gas with the potential of the airplane, at least in defensive contingency planning.

By late 1918, the potential of the airplane was becoming real capability. The bomber force would be available in 1919. There was no shortage of toxic agent. The Allies were prepared.[11] As the capability was being gathered, the Allies made plans for the forthcoming air offensive. The order called for unrestricted bombing. In addition to authorizing the use of high explosives, the order provided a ready case for gas bombing.

There is no indication that a decision was ever made to initiate strategic gas bombing. The mere fact that it had quite obviously been seriously considered was enough to complete a rather terrifying model of escalation that would haunt the makers of postwar policy.

During the war there had been two attempts to halt the spiral of escalation. The first was offered by the United States in May 1915—after German initiation at Ypres but before British retaliation at Loos. President Wilson proposed that Germany discontinue submarine warfare against merchant ships and the use of poison gas, while England would terminate the blockade of neutral ports. The offer was refused by both powers.[12]

The other attempt was an appeal against the use of gas by the International Committee of the Red Cross on February 6, 1918. The Red Cross put its finger on the root of the problem when it predicted that the use of gas "threatens to increase to a never foreseen extent."[13] The appeal was rejected by both sides in notes designed more for propaganda effect than for serious negotiation. The atmosphere of distrust could not be overcome despite a mutual interest in terminating gas warfare.

Viewed in retrospect, the image of gas was no more encouraging to the decision-maker than it was to the military professional. The other group whose impressions would influence the future of poison gas was the general public. It will be recalled that the Allies had changed the focus of gas propaganda several times during the war. By 1918, poison gas was being represented as an unwanted but German-introduced feature of the war in which Allied science and technology were proving their superiority.

---

[11] In the spring of 1918, Colonel Fries suggested to General Pershing that the Allies deliver gas by airplane. As the incident was related by General Harbord, Chief of Staff, AEF, General Pershing refused the idea because the AEF would not initiate and "at that time" the enemy was not using gas against civilian populations, although the situation could change. "While our aviators were not allowed to initiate such warfare, *we were not unprepared to retaliate if it came to that*" (Maj. Gen. J. Harbord, *The American Army in France, 1917-1919* [Boston: Little, Brown, 1936], p. 223 [italics mine]).

[12] E. Franklin, "Chemical Warfare—Its Possibilities and Probabilities," *International Conciliation*, No. 248 (March 1929), p. 57.

[13] Comité International de la Croix-Rouge (CICR), *Documents relatifs à la Guerre Chimique et Aérienne* (Genéve: CICR, 1932), p. 6. Trans. by author.

Under the circumstances, gas was being presented quite rationally, and it apparently was not the subject of any more unfavorable reaction than that directed at all the new weapons of war. The situation could change rapidly, however, if interest groups, including decision-makers and the military, desired to use gas as a *cause célèbre* to promote a particular want.

Only the future would tell. . . .

SUMMARY AND CONCLUSIONS

To advocates of chemical warfare, World War II repeated the pattern of World War I. Toxic agents had been on the verge of acceptance as a major strategic weapons system but then were not employed. In both cases, the war ended before chemical warfare had the opportunity to display its potential. In the former case, realization of the potential effectiveness of gas was impeded due to the unavailability of a delivery system (the long-range bomber) commensurate with the capabilities of the weapon.

The situation was totally different in World War II. The supporting infrastructure required for effective employment had been developed. Non-use resulted from the interaction of a variety of objective and subjective restraints. For the first time since the advent of the nation at arms a major weapon employed in one conflict was not carried forward to be used in a subsequent conflict. Can this be considered a favorable indicator of inhibitions on the employment of nuclear weapons in general war, or is it an accident unlikely to recur?

It is extremely difficult to predict the future employment of nuclear weapons. Nevertheless, I believe that a study of American chemical warfare policy can provide an understanding of the nature of restraints which should prove as valid in the present and future as it has in the past. . . .

Three general areas of restraint have emerged in this study. First, there are those forces which were expected to restrain but which were proven generally ineffective in the heat of war. Second, there is the problem of non-assimilation by the professional military—a significant but little-appreciated subjective inhibition on employment. Last are the agreed components of deterrence—cost, capability, and credibility; this study evaluates their effectiveness as an element of restraint and emphasizes several critical aspects of deterrence developed from the study of chemical warfare.

Overestimation of the influence of public opinion was a serious fallacy of interwar prognostication. In the belief that adverse public sentiment was a major hope of preventing war, the United States actively encouraged anti-gas propaganda in the immediate post-World War I period. During World War II, however, this restraint was ineffective. Without government encouragement, American public attitudes toward the employment of gas shifted from opposition to passive acceptance if not support of initiation. The combination of bitter, costly island invasions in the Pacific Theater, and the identification of the entire enemy population as evil created an environment wherein the primary criterion for weapon use was rapid termination of the conflict rather than the "humanity" of a particular weapon.

Although public opinion per se was not a direct restraint on the use of gas, indirect effects of public attitudes in the interwar period were operative throughout the war. Due in significant measure to its awareness of the abhorrence with which the public viewed gas during the twenties and thirties, the Army never seriously pressed for gas warfare readiness; an Army desiring integration into the mainstream of American life would not burnish its image by meaningful support of a weapon so distasteful to the public. Public opinion, therefore, contributed to the nation's low state of readiness for chemical warfare at the outbreak of war.

Public opinion also had an impact on the decision-making elite of World War II. Profoundly influenced by the anti-gas propaganda, President Roosevelt would not even consider the possibilities of American initiation or preparation beyond the minimum amount required for retaliation. Anti-gas propaganda conditioned the attitudes of other leaders, both military and civilian, as well. Chemical warfare was consistently associated with a normative qualifying expression. State Department as well as JCS* papers on chemical warfare referred to "this inhuman method of warfare" or "this particularly inhuman form of warfare."

The other great hope of opponents of gas warfare lay in the creation of legal restraints, which turned out to have no greater direct effect than had public opinion. No power considered any treaty restriction or limiting declaration of a belligerent to be more than a statement of intent, which could be violated if the exigencies of unlimited war required.

The legal restraint was moderately effective; but in an unanticipated sense. The numerous interwar attempts to codify prohibition served to focus public and elite group attention on the problems and prospects of chemical warfare. Due to extensive conferences, specific national decisions had to be made on chemical warfare policy at times when national capability and popular sentiment created environments of unreality. Particularly in the United States, ratification of the chemical warfare prohibition of the Washington Conference established a questionable precedent for future negotiation and made it exceedingly difficult to promote actual chemical warfare readiness.

---

* [*Editors' note:* Joint Chiefs of Staff.]

A comparable effect developed in Germany. Readiness was impeded by the legal prohibition of Versailles and the Geneva Protocol; in addition, there were the specific arms control measures of the Peace Treaty. The Germans lost ten years in the international race to develop more effective chemical warfare weapons, and this hiatus provoked a serious "crisis of confidence." Ironically, the Germans made the major offensive chemical warfare breakthrough of the interwar period—nerve agents—yet forfeited the advantage by presuming that the Allies had made a similar advance. Thus, a former legal restraint helped indirectly to negate a major technological breakthrough.

Similar to the case with public attitudes, the legal restraint gained its limited effectiveness in an indirect and unanticipated manner. Based upon this experience, it would appear that the primary value of the legal restraint rests in its tendency to reinforce other existing restraints. Treaty prohibition, though imperfect, reinforced both public and military dislike and fear of chemical warfare and provided a ready excuse for lack of substantive preparation. Any legal restraint derived from custom or a general principle of law prohibiting weapons causing unnecessary suffering—if such exists and can be applied—should be even more effective, in that each would represent a more universal consensus of expert and lay attitudes.

Acceptance of a weapon within the military establishment is a prerequisite to employment. Influenced by the counter-propaganda writings of articulate military proponents of chemical warfare, most civilians assumed that the military accepted and was eager to employ chemical weapons. This assumption was false. Aside from those military leaders institutionally committed to toxic agents, the military establishment as a whole was opposed to their use. As an area weapon developed by scientists to strike insidiously and from afar, gas did not accord with the honor of the profession. In addition, the immense logistical and training burden unique to gas warfare required greater battlefield effect than could be attained with other weapons in order to justify resort to such a high-cost weapon. It could not be proven that the use of gas would provide any quantum jump in probability of battlefield success, particularly when the enemy could be expected to retaliate in kind. With major financial restraints imposed throughout the Depression, no national military establishment was inclined to emphasize weapons of doubtful effectiveness when Artillery, Infantry, and the Air Force were faced with acute shortages in conventional weapons.

Since gas warfare was not assimilated into the military establishment of any major power, its use was precluded in World War II. Without professional support for meaningful gas warfare readiness, no nation was prepared to employ toxic agents when it entered the war. For the Axis Powers, during the successful first half of the war, there was no incentive to commit the resources required for increased chemical warfare preparedness when other weapons of proven utility were in constant demand. The same logic, albeit reversed in its time sequence, applied to the Allied Powers.

This lack of assimilation was particularly evident in the United States response to the extreme asymmetry of readiness existing between the United States and Japan toward the end of World War II. Despite its awareness that the Japanese could not retaliate, the United States did not employ toxic agents. The central reason for this lay in the general military disinterest in gas which had retarded readiness sufficiently to preclude timely, serious consideration of initiation. Decades of conditioning to a second-strike philosophy prevented such logistic preparedness in the forward areas which could have provided an incentive to striking the first blow.

The implication here is that lack of assimilation is a more fundamental inhibition to initiation than fear of retaliation. No major belligerent in World War II accepted gas warfare. As a result, a defensive aura surrounded the entire area of toxic chemical warfare. Aside from Japan, each nation maintained a credible retaliatory capability, yet the capability was in each case more potential than real. There was never sufficient readiness to provide the incentive for immediate initiation.

Even if any nation had developed a material capability adequate to make initiation feasible, fear of the costs of enemy retaliation would have remained as a restraint sufficient to deter it. Whether the prospective victim actually possessed sufficient retaliatory capability to inflict intolerable levels of punishment is essentially irrelevant. Partially due to poor chemical warfare intelligence on the part of all belligerents, which credited the enemy with a capability commensurate with the assumed diabolical nature of his intentions, each nation saw asymmetrical chemical warfare capabilities as favoring the enemy. When the potential initiator realized his superiority and his invulnerability to direct enemy retaliation, as was the case of the United States, in the last stages of the Pacific War, initiation was deterred by threat of retaliation against an ally, China. In World War II, the restraint of enemy retaliation was magnified in effect by the demands of coalition warfare. The presence of allies that were hostages for the good conduct of the coalition leader increased the stability of mutual deterrence.

These restraints, proven in war, varied considerably from interwar predictions. Neither public opinion nor legal restriction was directly effective; but, on the other hand, lack of assimilation and fear of retaliation proved to be significant restraints. In World War II, the lesson was clear; the loci of decision-making with respect to gas warfare lay within the professional military establishments themselves. Military lack of interest kept the issue of initiation from reaching civilian elite groups.

American experience with toxic agents during World War II revealed several general characteristics of successful deterrence. Readiness to retaliate was communicated through statements of heads of government backed up with overt chemical warfare preparations. The unrestricted nature of war, exemplified by the unlimited bombing policy, gave credibility to the threat to employ toxic agents in response to enemy initiation. No nation doubted that the potential target nation possessed a retaliatory capability sufficient to punish the initiator, directly, or indirectly, through a coalition partner, and general military dislike of toxic agents was sufficient to restrain any inclination to develop a possible disarming first-strike capability.

Each belligerent saw escalation of toxic agent employment as an inevitable effect of initiation. Once World War II began, there does not appear to have been any serious consideration of initiation solely for tactical success. It was tacitly assumed that any use of gas would immediately escalate to the strategic level and, therefore, that any initiation should itself be at the strategic level. Essentially the same logic applied to the choice of chemical agents. It was assumed that there was no effective limiting point between the employment of nonlethal and lethal agents. For this reason, nontoxic chemical agents were not employed in a combat environment.

Based upon Japanese actions, however, the validity of both assumptions is questionable. The Japanese employed nontoxic and toxic agents against the Chinese both before and after United States entry in the war, yet the United States ignored the situation. Due to lack of readiness and unwillingness to employ, the United States preferred to overlook a situation that, in terms of declaratory policy, would have required retaliation. As long as Japanese violation of tacitly agreed limits did not affect a core interest of the United States as defined by decision-makers or by reaction of the general public, there was no automaticity of escalation. The effect of this American response was to diminish the credibility of the American policy which enabled the Japanese to reallocate their chemical warfare readiness resources.[14]

World War II also saw in the United Kingdom and Germany the establishment of the most extensive and costly passive defense systems yet developed. In neither case did civil defense measures act as a destabilizing element in the maintenance of mutual deterrence. Each accepted civil protection as a necessary component of readiness for a nation continuously under the threat of surprise strategic attack. If it had any specific effect, the existence of effective civil defense acted as

---

[14] There is no indication that, despite attendance at interwar international conferences, the Japanese thought that in initiating they were doing anything other than field testing a new weapon. One can only speculate that it was their inexperience with chemical warfare which prevented them from realizing the implications of initiating employment.

a stabilizing element by reducing the expected reward, and thus incentive, for a surprise first strike.

A further element of restraint demonstrated in the Second World War was the impact on decision-making of an irrational leader. Hitler was accepted by the Allied Powers as a national leader likely to make irrational decisions. This image was in itself a stimulant to British preparations for gas warfare and thus indirectly contributed to deterrence. With his back to the wall, Hitler apparently decided to initiate gas warfare, but the inevitability of defeat was so obvious by early 1945 that he had lost authority over his key military subordinates. The result was failure to implement his decision.

This development would suggest that the critical time for one belligerent's initiation of a mass-casualty weapon is during that period when it is becoming obvious that eventual victory is improbable unless a new element is introduced into the war to restore the momentum of the offensive, but before it is obvious to the military establishment that the initiative has passed to the enemy and that eventual defeat is certain. In short, the decision would have to be made before the national leader has, by failure, undermined his power to have such a momentous decision implemented.

It remains one of the ironies of the Second World War that toxic agents, considered sufficiently humane to be used for the execution of convicted prisoners, were not employed in a war which saw the extensive use of another weapon with enormous destructive powers—the atomic bomb. The heritage of World War I was responsible—poison gas was a weapon too technologically demanding and psychologically disquieting to be assimilated by the military profession. It was an unacceptable anachronism, born too early out of a unique marriage of science and war. Added to this primary and most effective restraint of nonassimilation was mutual possession of a credible deterrent force. . . .

*Strategic Bombing
in the 1930's and 1940's*

GEORGE H. QUESTER

THE CONTEST FOR BOMBER SUPERIORITY, 1933–1937

The Nazi assumption of power in January of 1933 forced an almost immediate shift of Britain's attention from the more hypothetical French air threat to the real menace of Germany. An increasingly visible German air potential, coupled with the open Nazi challenge to the settlements of 1919, made an upward revision of British air procurement plans almost inevitable. Yet the failure of the British government to fully underwrite aircraft development in the 1920's or to implement the expansion plans of 1923 left the RAF with great technological obstacles in its rearmament schemes, which were to be seen as a real handicap to any staving off of German equality or superiority.

For the ensuing six years, three broad observations hold true. First, British air expenditures, for reasons of economy, and for lingering hope of some accommodation with Germany, were never to satisfy the requests of the RAF leadership, although these expenditures were, in fact, to rise markedly through this period. Second, the RAF thus found itself, by Allied intelligence estimates, steadily falling behind the supposed strength of its opponent, the German Luftwaffe. Third, these intelligence estimates were generally exaggerated, to the point that the RAF was never in anything like the supposed position of inferiority. . . .

. . . At no time was the German potential to be what British observers feared it to be. The German aircraft industry was never rationalized until 1943 and 1944, and even the major retooling for the production of World War II quality aircraft did not occur until 1937 and 1938. Such German effort as was expended, moreover, was not channeled into a really strategic weapon. Proponents of a broad strategic development in the German Air Force, such as Milch and Wever, were overruled by Goering and Hitler, and the long-range bomber, in which Germany might have moved ahead of Britain in 1937, was canceled in that year, as the interest of the Luftwaffe leadership shifted to tactical support and dive bombers. . . .

From *Deterrence Before Hiroshima* by George Quester. Reprinted by permission of the publisher, John Wiley and Sons, Inc., pp. 82–122. Portions of the text and some footnotes have been omitted.

[In Britain] the general issue of instability and pre-emption was again a source of some concern. Philip Noel Baker, a leading Labor spokesman on disarmament in the 1920's, now warned that the offensive efficacy of large bomber forces would increase the likelihood of their use, since pre-emption would seem so necessary if war threatened. The larger the matching bomber forces, the greater would be the incentive to striking first rather than second, and the greater the destruction when war came. . . .

Thus, continued effort to achieve a reliable reduction or abolition of air weapons (and of offensive bombers in particular) was held to be desirable. Analysts concerned about strategic stability in the 1930's once more urged the transfer of funds from great inventories of bombers (which were threatening to Germany) to active or passive defenses (which would cancel the threat from Germany). This position, in many ways consistent with that of the appeasement school, implied that German military growth was somewhat justified, and that the British response should not be such as to bait the Germans into fears which would force further growth. By such a policy, a mutual deterrence was sought, based both on the painfulness and on the fruitlessness of air war. In the words of a persistent British critic of bomber procurement, Jonathan Griffin, whose language is impressively modern:

> One is the fact that war is becoming so destructive as to be its own deterrent: so much so that already even the rashest of rulers are coming to see that only a short war can pay anyone. This gives us a new chance of permanent peace, if we will use it; for by making a successful short war clearly impossible we can make any war highly improbable. The way to do this is for each country that wants peace—but especially for Great Britain—to concentrate mainly on making itself less vulnerable to attack from the air, not (as now) on competitive counter-measures.[1]

The maintenance of deterrence was seen to require some inhibition of the bomber's offensive advantage, since this advantage in symmetrical confrontations was likely to offer both sides the prospect of quick victory, or more importantly, threaten them both with an apparently quick defeat.

> . . . Even if all the countries were equally vulnerable and if all were neglecting home front defence, still to concentrate on bombers would be folly, because bombers, though they may in time deter, must in the end precipitate attack. Competitive rearmament concentrating mainly on weapons of unprecedented power for sudden devastation at long ranges will, if it goes on, create a situation in which every country is defenceless,

---

[1] Jonathan Griffin, *Glass Houses and Modern War* (London: Chatto and Windus, 1938), p. 3.

yet has one chance of a decisive victory—to get in first with a knockout blow from the air. There may be cases where in the short run this or that country by rearming mainly with weapons of offence will lessen the risk of war; but when all the Great Powers vie hysterically in mainly menacing rearmament, the upshot is bound to be an explosive situation, even if each of them means to use those terrific armaments against aggression only.[2]

Any attempt at a deterrence based primarily on threats of retaliation was seen to be too precarious, when the means of retaliation also threatened to be a means of violent disarmament, and when the "retaliatory" city-bombing tools could be used to pre-empt and cripple an enemy's war machine. A "balance of terrors," according to Griffin, could not be a stable one:

> It would be a balance of terrors—for that is what the balance of power, loaded with bombs, should truly be called. In the end one group must strike.[3]

An equality of large bombing forces would not be as stable as an equality of small forces coupled with the bolstering of the domestic societies involved. An assumption was again made that the disabling capability or offensive superiority is enhanced as bomber forces increase in size.

> Deadly mutual menaces are more likely to deter attack in proportion as neither side is reasonably sure of getting in first with a crushing offensive and making retaliation impossible. From this it is often concluded that it will be enough to get equality between the air forces of the Great Powers. Such thinking is hasty; it leaves out several steps—steps which lead to a far different conclusion. In the first place, with the scale and swiftness of air forces already so great and growing so quickly, an aggressor may soon find half his air force enough to crush the cities, leaving the other half free to damage and delay the opposing air-power.[4]

. . . The strengthening of defenses, with resources drawn away from the offensive, was thus held to be the ideal over-all policy; an essentially unilateral act would suffice both for the protection of national sovereignty and for the prevention of war. If defensive research removed the destabilizing influence of air weapons, it would make possible a safe reduction of total retaliatory forces in an early version of a "finite deterrence" policy.

Awesome bombing capabilities for aircraft were almost taken for

---

[2] *Ibid.,* p. 178.
[3] Jonathan Griffin, *Alternative to Rearmament* (London: Macmillan and Co., 1936), p. 75.
[4] *Ibid.,* pp. 62–63.

granted now; relatively few observers felt driven to scrutinize these pessimistic assumptions more closely, or to doubt that war would indeed be so horrible as to be unthinkable. . . .

THE ALLIED ACCEPTANCE OF INFERIORITY, 1937–1939

As the months rolled on and Axis air strength seemed to grow, some alteration, almost inevitably, had to come in the RAF operational strategy which had been based for so long on 1918 force ratios. By early 1937, a significant slippage had begun to show itself, as relatively abstract airpower theories were compared with real aircraft inventories; in May of that year the Air Staff expressed grave doubts as to whether a "knockout blow" against Germany could still be possible, if only because no city in Germany now seemed to hold the great significance that London apparently held for Great Britain.

> Any attempt to demoralise the German people before German air attacks could demoralise our own people would operate under severe handicap. London is an objective of far greater national importance than Berlin, and for many reasons presents an easier and more effective target for German attack than Berlin does for the Allied air forces. . . . Germany covers twice the geographical area of Great Britian, so that opportunities for dispersion are correspondingly greater. German preparations to meet air attack are much in advance of our own. Moreover, a military dictatorship is likely to be less susceptible to popular outcry than a democratic Government. It is, consequently, unsafe to assume that under our present programme our air force, even with the co-operation of the French, will be able, by attacking the morale of the German people, to produce an effect in any way comparable with that which would result from German air attack against our own.[5]

The RAF bomber force was now rated as being so weak that its bases could not even draw the expected German air assault away from British cities, no matter what the British bombers were trying to do over Germany.

> So far, we have been unable to discover any air objective to attack which would be likely to force Germany to divert her own air offensive from the relatively more vulnerable points in our own organisation. Unless, therefore, we discover some unexpected weakness in Germany, it is certain that mutual air attack, even at equal intensity, upon each other's vulnerable points would only lead to a far quicker reduction of the war effort in England than in Germany.[6]

[5] Text in Charles Webster and Noble Frankland, *The Strategic Air Offensive Against Germany* (London: H.M.S.O., 1961), IV, p. 89.
[6] *Ibid.*

Counterforce raids against the strictly "military" German air bases would now replace attacks on the enemy's civilian "heart." Such a shift might spare German civilians and thus leave some unspoiled "value" to the German government; more importantly, this shift offered the only physically significant prospect—mere damage limitation for British cities, hardly an optimistic outlook:

> While we are forced to admit that there seems to be no satisfactory answer to the problem on such *premises*, nevertheless we are here concerned with doing the best we can with the forces we have presumed to be at our disposal.
> It appears that in these circumstances we should be forced . . . to direct the bulk of our counter air offensive against the enemy's air striking force and its maintenance organisation as the most immediate method of reducing, however inadequately, the scale of enemy air attack.[7]

While the British government had been expanding its air programs steadily since the advent of Hitler's power, it had not, at any time, appropriated as much as the RAF leadership had requested. Operational plans that might have been appropriate on the basis of a once-achievable RAF bomber superiority now had to be dropped, with a dramatic descent, in fact, to the alarmist assumption of a marked German bomber superiority. The increasing anxiety of the British civilian leadership made greater resources now available at last, but these had for the time to flow into a quite different and more restricted strategy—into a large step-up in British active and passive defenses. The apparent shift in bomber superiority would indeed be politically significant.

As the prospect of German territorial expansion became more immediately threatening, with the seizure of Austria in 1938, the development and procurement of interceptor fighters were now accelerated. Shelter and gas mask programs were also set in motion, and plans were made again for the evacuation of cities.[8] Remembering the disorders of 1917, British planners expected a panicky and disorderly mass exodus from cities, the control of which would require a substantial reserve of police manpower. Steps had to be taken both to spare the British people unnecessary suffering and to keep such suffering from hamstringing the government. By June of 1938, the British Prime Minister had publicly announced to Parliament that in the event of war the RAF would bomb only such German targets as were separate from civilian residences. As a crisis developed in the ensuing months over German claims on the Sudetenland, the RAF command remained resigned to the limitations implied by such

[7] *Ibid.*, p. 90 (italics in original).
[8] Terence H. O'Brien, *Civil Defence* (London: H.M.S.O., 1955), pp. 117–19; R. M. Titmuss, *Problems of Social Policy* (London: H.M.S.O., 1950), pp. 16–22.

announcements, in the face of its supposed inability to deliver a serious blow against the heart of Germany or to blunt a Luftwaffe attack; implicitly, therefore, the counterforce blow at Luftwaffe bases would only come if (and *after*) air raids on Britain were begun.[9]

Similarly intense fears of German bombing capability began to be expressed at this time in the French Cabinet. For causes not traceable to any particular government, France had completely lost her earlier advantage in air strength, as she passed through a series of eleven air force reorganizations in ten years; moreover, the nationalization of the aircraft industry in 1936 had proved disastrously disruptive to aircraft production. The reports of British liaison officers in Paris, at the time of Munich, pointed to the threat of German bombing as the primary deterrent to any French aid for the Czechs. French estimates of German bombing capability seem to have been as extravagant as those of the British intelligence estimates, having been inflated in part by the pessimistic reports of Charles Lindbergh.

> But pointed at Paris (and at London) is the threat of the German Air Force, and the Fuhrer found a most convenient ambassador in Colonel Lindbergh, who appears to have given the French an impression of its might and preparedness which they did not have before, and who at the same time confirmed the view that the Russian Air Force was worth almost exactly nothing.
> . . . Colonel Gauche replied, "Of course there will be no European War, since we are not going to fight." He went on to say that they could not face the risk of the German air threat—since their material was so superior that they (the French) were powerless to deal with it.
> To sum up, then, the military situation is that the German Army is mobilised, and that it has completed its concentration against Czechoslovakia. The "couverture" in the West is very thin because Hitler is convinced, in spite of all statements to the contrary, that the threat of his Air Force is sufficient to keep the French, and consequently ourselves, quiet under all circumstances.[10]

> I said "What then, since you don't intend to fight?" and went on to suggest that the situation had deteriorated since Colonel Lindbergh's visit and his stories of the German Air Force. General Dentz did not react; he merely pointed out that French cities would be laid in ruins and that they had no means of defence. They were now paying the price of years of neglect of their Air Force.[11]

Aerial bombardment was thought to threaten a demoralization of the French civilian population, or even some sort of a revolt. . . .

[9] Webster and Frankland, *op. cit.*, I, pp. 99–100.
[10] *Documents on British Foreign Policy* (Third Series, Vol. II [London: H.M.S.O., 1949]), p. 439.
[11] *Ibid.,* p. 474.

While France had set little store by airpower when she was pre-occupied with tactical victory at the front, the security of the Maginot Line and the stalemate it promised had now allowed the French imagination to wander to the air, precisely at a time when French air superiority seemed irretrievably lost.

Both Britain and France thus went into September of 1938 quite concerned about the German air threat. During the Munich crisis itself, trenches were dug in London parks, and nearly a third of the population of Paris evacuated the city. Yet the evacuations could promise to reduce civilian suffering only somewhat, and the willingness of both Allies to accede to Hitler's demands reflected the continuing concern about the Luftwaffe's potential. When the possibility arose that Czech intransigence or Hitler's bellicosity might still produce war, Chamberlain pleaded with Hitler to spare Prague. Hitler responded with promises that no air attack would be made on that city and reaffirmed a general feeling that cities should not be bombed at all.

> *Mr. Chamberlain:* . . . in particular, he trusted that there would be no bombardment of Prague or killing of women and children by attacks from the air.
>
> *Herr Hitler:* Before answering that specific question, he would like to say something on a point of principle. Years ago he made proposals for the restriction of the use of the air arm. He himself fought in the Great War and has a personal knowledge of what air bombardment means. It had been his intention, if he had to use force, to limit air action to front line zones as a matter of principle, but even if the Czechs were mad enough to reject the terms and he had consequently to take forcible action, he would always try to spare the civilian population and to confine himself to military objectives. He hated the thought of little babies being killed by gas bombs.[12]

Hitler reiterated a proposal he had first advanced in 1935 for a combat zone or artillery range limitation on air raids, while suggesting the more general abolition of all bombers, where other nations could, somehow, be brought to comply.

> It would be just the same if one tried to abolish bombing aircraft. It could only be accepted if all did the same. He himself had proposed years ago—
>   1. The abolition of bombing aircraft;
>   2. If *1* could not be accepted, the abolition of bombing outside a zone of 15 to 20 km from the front line;
>   3. If neither *1* nor *2* were accepted, the limitation of bombing to a zone which could be reached by heavy artillery.
>
> He himself was particularly attached to *1*, which was, in his view, in line with the Geneva Agreement providing for the exemption of non-

[12] *Ibid.,* pp. 636–38.

combatants from the effects of warfare. The development of bombing from the air extends the horrors of war to the non-combatant population and is therefore a barbarism.[13]

While German endorsements of abstentions from terror bombing had not been lacking, in fact, after the Nazi ascendance to power, relatively little significance had been attached to such declarations by observers monitoring the supposedly burgeoning Luftwaffe, especially since Goering and others still were fond of boasting that Germany had a decisive "knockout blow" capability that could be directed against any of its neighbors. In actuality, the Luftwaffe planners saw no such possibilities in the 1930's, the potential of long-range bombardment now having been considerably more soberly appraised than it had been by the Zeppelin officers at the outbreak of World War I. At the time of the Munich crisis, Hitler's contingency directives to his air force had clearly forbidden any attack on Czech cities until he should direct such an attack;[14] as late as 1939, Hitler privately expressed his continuing skepticism about the possibility of any victory through air attack alone, refusing to believe that bombing could completely incapacitate an enemy's war-making potential.

> If the German Air Force attacks English territory, England will not be forced to capitulate in one day. But if the fleet is destroyed, immediate capitulation will be the result.
> A country cannot be brought to defeat by an Air Force. It is impossible to attack all objectives simultaneously and the lapse of time of a few minutes would evoke defensive counter-measures.[15]

Despite its independent status and a tendency to revel in its aerial accomplishments, the Luftwaffe, in actuality, was now satisfied with the functions of close support to ground forces, and of the maintenance of tactical air superiority. It saw little more to be achieved by air. Moreover, as the German leadership did not believe in the feasibility of the counterforce knockout blow against its enemies, it similarly did not fear any such blow against Germany. Yet Hitler was, nevertheless, very anxious to avoid any bombing of Germany at all, not for fear of the total military breakdown envisaged in London and Paris, but because of his personal desire to spare Germany all possible wartime hardship, and because of his fear that the enthusiasm of the German people for his regime might not survive the rigors of war. Hitler's policies on the production of consumer goods and on the mobilization of women show a great unwillingness to impose a real

[13] *Ibid.,* p. 638.
[14] *Nazi Conspiracy and Aggression* (Washington: U.S.G.P.O., 1946), III, p. 388.
[15] *Nazi Conspiracy and Aggression* (Washington: U.S.G.P.O., 1946), VII, pp. 852–53.

austerity on Germany, and his aversion to an aerial exchange of strategic attacks sprang from the same motive. Anxious, therefore, to avoid an actual exchange of blows, the German leadership strove to build up the deterring fears of the Allies, fears which the Luftwaffe did not feel itself capable of fulfilling.

Nonetheless, the possibility was left open to the world that foreign cities might yet come to be bombed even if German cities had not already been attacked. For reasons of personal psychological satisfaction, it may well have suited Hitler and Goering to play with, and be the object of, fears that lacked real justification; more rationally such vague allusions to a strategic instability could, in fact, be exploited for minor diplomatic victories. Aggressive German initiatives, until Munich, were often accompanied by subtle references to "total destruction" inevitably raining down from the air, if German demands should be militarily resisted; during the final takeover of Bohemia-Moravia, the threat (entirely a bluff) of a bombing of Prague was conveyed to Dr. Hacha, with significant influence on his decision not to resist. While Hitler thus saw little possibility of victory in an aerial assault on the population centers of the Allies, and, for several reasons, was extremely reluctant to have his own population centers bombed, we find, nonetheless, the German leadership until 1939 playing the somewhat dangerous game of predicting a course of events which it, in fact, hoped to avoid.

Since bombers could not be totally abolished (even though Germany had been responsive to this proposal), they could be harnessed by Hitler to deter both all-out war *and* any more-restrained resistance. If such a restrained conflict should break out, however, the German advantage would lie again with a limited bombing zone immediately along the line of combat, which would mean that only foreign towns would be damaged when the Germans were on the offensive. Such a set of limits still had some hope of acceptance because of its resemblance to the traditional rules of international law limiting damage to "combat areas," and because the initiative of any escalation from this level could be thrown to the defending Allied nations, who had now lost confidence in their ability to terrorbomb Germany into submission. The German operational assumption, here, seemed to be that the use of aircraft in a limited sense would favor the tactical offense, and would (if kept restrained) be preferable even to an absolute ban on bombing.

Thus, we have three simultaneous Nazi objectives: to deter any Allied conventional military operations by issuing warnings of strategic instability; to deter any Allied all-out air attack, by promises of restraint and threats of retaliation; but to allow for German combat zone air attack if any Allied military resistance did arise. The interaction of these goals created an obscurity which may have later contributed to Germany's undoing.

The aftermath of Munich saw no relaxation of Britain's air augmentation, but rather an intensification of the program. Partially because the chances of striking a real blow at Germany had come to be seen as depending on a tremendous and temporarily unachievable bomber force, and because of the extreme exposure of Britain to air attack, the emphasis was now predominantly shifted to the buildup of fighter forces. The lingering argument that a bomber expansion would provoke Germany still drew some support; but more important were the assumptions that no strikes against Germany itself could be powerful enough in the near future to blunt an attack on London, and that defenses at the site might be more helpful to the city against an attack now rated as quite likely to come. . . .

Where Germany could expand against minor satellites of France, the military initiative could be thrown back to the presumably deterred Allies; yet, while this stratagem worked in 1938, it failed in 1939 when the Allies decided to risk all-out air war rather than to acquiesce in the demise of Poland.

In light of the vague German threats and of the earlier British strategic theories, it is not surprising that the Allies did indeed expect an offensive against their cities as the likely price of military action in the Munich crisis and later. But the apparently overwhelming superiority of the German Air Force left few advantages to a preemptive Allied air attack; it was not high hopes of wartime German abstinence that held back the French and British bomber forces, but an awareness of these forces' impotence, which made even a small hope of German restraint seem preferable to the meager projected results of any bombing of Germany.

The years up to 1939, therefore, are remarkable for the abandonment of some implicit assumptions of post-1918 airpower theorists. On the German side there is a realistic skepticism about the preemptive panacea of aerial bombardment; on the Allied side one finds an acceptance of a numerical inferiority, which similarly invalidated the preemptive strategies of the past. Yet the Allies still had to fear the imaginary Luftwaffe offensive strategy. Hitler's awareness of these Allied fears, and his willingness to exploit such fears, completed the setting for the war that was about to ensue.

THE PHONEY WAR: SEPTEMBER, 1939–MAY, 1940

It is clear that Hitler was disappointed when his aggression against Poland of September 1, 1939 led to British and French declarations of war, and thus to World War II. The German leadership had hoped that the dismemberment of Poland might yet be so handled that the Allies would prefer continued peace to intervention, with the threat of air attack perhaps solidifying their preference for peace.

But Hitler's hopes may not have been so unrealistic. At Munich the Allied leaders had rejected intervention on the side of Czechoslovakia, even when their civil defense measures and some evacuations had been implemented to reduce the costs of an all-out air war. By the summer of 1939, some further progress had presumably been made in these preparations for the protection of Allied populations; but this could not have sufficed to change the Allied expectation that the inevitable wartime German city busting would be very painful. If the Allied aversion to war was now less pronounced, therefore, it was only because Hitler's territorial appetites seemed so very much less appeasable than before.

The German invasion of Poland had been scheduled for August 25, and then postponed, as Hitler strove to ease Britain and France out of their commitments to the Poles. Evacuations of Paris and London were begun. As the German invasion began, at last, on September 1, the Allied response was certainly not immediate; Italian suggestions for mediation were examined, warnings delivered, and positions coordinated; several days passed with declarations of war coming neither from Britain nor France. It was without enthusiasm that Chamberlain at last delivered his final ultimatum and declaration of war on September 3, after much of his Parliament had in fact feared that he would again concede to Hitler. The French government had pleaded again for a delayed ultimatum, for time to complete the evacuation of its cities, and, perhaps, to negotiate. Expecting severe bombing as the price of intervention, the British and French leaderships declared war without eagerness or haste, and might well not have done so had Hitler staged his Polish operation more carefully. No Allied land or air offensives were set in motion; the Allied governments, having resolved to risk declaration of war, braced themselves now for the initiative they had felt forced to concede to the Luftwaffe.

Despite the many dire prewar predictions of a terroristic conflict, leaving no sanctuary for civilian populations, and despite these British expectations of an immediate "knockout blow" attempt by the Luftwaffe, the opening rounds of World War II now witnessed no bombing raids at all on the populated areas of Britain and France or of Germany.

On September 1, 1939, President Roosevelt had addressed an appeal to the belligerent powers for a restriction of aerial warfare to strictly military targets, the formal acceptance of which appeal was announced on the 2nd by the Allies and, on September 18 by the German government. But orders to this effect had been issued to each of the air forces in question even before the appeal; while many expected otherwise, Luftwaffe operations against Britain and France were forbidden by Hitler himself. . . .

THE BLITZ: AUGUST, 1940–MAY, 1941*

. . . The "Blitz" was now about to be triggered. On August 24, 1940, the Luftwaffe, still concentrating its daytime attack on the installations and supporting industries of the RAF, added a series of night attacks on aircraft factories and other industrial targets in cities around England. Although London was not programmed as a target, navigation and accuracy inevitably suffered at night, and several planes (by any account less than twelve) did drop bombs on London unintentionally on the 24th (London had, in fact, been accidentally bombed before, as early as June 18).[16] The extension and change in form of the Luftwaffe raids once more increased the exposure of the British populace to aerial attack, if only because of the lesser accuracies of night bombing. . . .

On August 25, however, 95 aircraft of RAF Bomber Command were dispatched on the first mission against Berlin (of which 81 found the target), a mission executed as usual by night, described, nonetheless, as a precision bombing of industrial targets.[17] Berlin was now on the regular target list alongside the invasion ports and the Ruhr, and five similar raids were flown against the German capital in the succeeding two weeks. The German response came soon. On September 7, the Luftwaffe halted most of its attack on the airdromes and began a heavy assault on the city of London, an assault which was to continue for two months, until the middle of November. While the orders to the German crews were still to bomb carefully and not indiscriminately, the sheer weight of the night attacks tended to mitigate the effects of such orders. After November 14, attacks were extended again to areas outside of London. Targets and aiming points still were

*[*Editors' note:* Prior to the "Blitz," air warfare went through three phases: (1) The Phoney War, September, 1939–May, 1940; (2) The Fall of France, May–June, 1940; and (3) The Battle of Britain, June–August, 1940. In the first phase mutual restraints were observed, and bomber missions were confined to reconnaissance. In the second phase bomber operations on both sides expanded but were confined to military targets. The Germans spared Paris from bombing and made only a few raids on RAF fighter strips in southeastern England. Beginning May 15, the British began to bomb selected military targets at night in and around northwestern German cities. In the third phase the restraints on bomber operations weakened still more. The Germans continued to observe a "no-cities" policy, but began a heavy assault on English coastal shipping, RAF airfields, and the British aircraft industry. In effect, the Germans were pursuing a counterforce campaign to destroy British air power. The Blitz begins the fourth major phase of the bomber war when all restraints were ended.]

[16] Accounts of the August 24th bombing of London are not very clear. All now agree that London was not intended as a target, but the number of planes participating is left vague. Apparently, twelve planes were programmed for targets near London, and *some* of these dropped bombs within the city limits. . . .

[17] Arthur Bryant, *The Turn of the Tide* (London: Collins, 1957), p. 213; B. Collier, *The Defence of the United Kingdom* (London: H.M.S.O., 1957), p. 234.

chosen for industrial potential as the new phase opened with a severe raid on Coventry. Intensive raids alternating between London and the lesser cities of Britain continued through the winter and spring, until the middle of May of 1941, with close to 40,000 British civilians losing their lives.

Over the period of the "Blitz," Bomber Command continued to hit an assortment of targets including the Ruhr, northern Italy, Berlin, invasion shipping, German naval bases, and various special industrial sites around northwestern Germany. On October 30, 1940, it was decided, moreover, to seek targets with a supplementary effect for stray bombs, that is, targets surrounded by populated areas. On December 12, an attack experimentally designed to inflict maximum destruction on a German town was ordered, the "area bombing" attack being executed on Mannheim on the night of the 16th, with disappointing results. Early 1941 saw attacks on German U-boat bases, and another area attack on Bremen, followed by similar attacks on a series of German North Sea ports through the rest of the spring. Yet as British bomber forces were drawn away to the Middle East and to anti-submarine patrols at sea, the British bombload of 15,000 tons in this period failed to match the 67,000 tons of the German assault.

The winter of 1940–1941 thus saw all possible military and industrial targets opened to attack in both Britain and the Axis homelands. No deliberate "terror-maximizing" attacks had as yet been launched against Britain, and only a few with limited resources had as yet been launched against Germany, but the inaccuracies of navigation and bombardment on night flights made the results of "terror" attacks seem not very different from "discriminate" or "precision" attacks. Meaningful limits on the air war were at an end, and the explanation is not so obvious.

Winston Churchill in his memoirs cites the bombs dropped on London on August 24, 1940 as his moral justification for the British raids beginning on the 25th, and he further indicates that he expected a serious German assault on London sooner or later in any event:

> The sporadic raiding of London towards the end of August was promptly answered by us in a retaliatory attack on Berlin. . . . He [Hitler] took, of course, full advantage of our reprisal on Berlin, and publicly announced the previously settled German policy of reducing London and other British cities to chaos and ruin.[18]

But it was clear that the bombs dropped on the 24th were not the all-out Luftwaffe terror attack for which Britain had been braced

---

[18] Winston Churchill, *Their Finest Hour* (Boston: Houghton Mifflin Co., 1949), p. 342.

since 1939, and a serious German assault on London, in the absence of provocation, could by no means be a certainty. If Churchill was writing off further German restraints, he was writing off quite a lot, for most of London still stood untouched. There was, therefore, a reason why Churchill took the step which indeed made an early German attack on London more likely, and it was not simply a desire for revenge for the stray bombs that had fallen; it is remarkable how even the words of 1914 are echoed:

> *Far more important to us than the protection of London* from terror-bombing was the functioning and articulation of these airfields and the squadrons working from them. In the life-and-death struggle of the two air forces, this was a decisive phase. We never thought of the struggle in terms of the defence of London or any other place, but only who won in the air.
>
> The War Cabinet were much in the mood to hit back, to raise the stakes, and to defy the enemy.
>
> It was therefore with a sense of relief that Fighter Command felt the German attack turn on to London on September 7, and concluded that the enemy had changed his plan.
>
> The night attacks on London for ten days after September 7 struck at the London docks and railway centres, and killed and wounded many civilians, but they were in effect for us a breathing space of which we had the utmost need.[19]

In fact, Churchill's decision to bomb Berlin almost certainly was a conscious effort to bait Hitler into an immediate shifting of the Luftwaffe attack on to London, away from the RAF Fighter Command bases which were beginning to collapse under the strain. The decision was made in the context of the threat of a German invasion, which was, indeed, expected momentarily. A continuing Luftwaffe assault on the airdromes threatened not only to weaken the bases as flying strips, but also to destroy enough on-base communications and control centers (the "Sector-Stations," which digested radar information and guided the fighter groups in the air) to make southern England untenable for the RAF. A withdrawal of the RAF to the north would have given the Luftwaffe the superiority it needed over the Channel to support an invasion. Churchill's assessment, therefore, of the value of sparing London from attack may not have declined seriously from May to August, but his estimation of the value of inducing Hitler to bomb London instead of the airdromes had risen, indeed.

Churchill admits his desire, in late August, for an immediate shifting of the massive Luftwaffe offensive from the RAF airstrips to London, and he admits his personal responsibility for the bombings of

---

[19] *Ibid.,* pp. 330–331, 331 (italics added) 342. . . .

Berlin, begun on August 25; it seems quite likely that he was aware of the probable connection between the two. While the RAF Air Staff opposed the bombing of Berlin on military grounds, since strikes at the invasion ports seemed far more pressing at this crucial moment, Churchill himself overruled its objections.

Before the war, the RAF had contemplated using its bombers to draw the expected German assault on to its air bases, away from London; now, ironically, it was directed to divert the Germans in exactly the opposite direction. Similarly, while efforts had earlier been made to separate British defense industries from cities, the closeness of "legitimate" Luftwaffe targets to London now had given Churchill the pretext for an escalation.

The German reaction to the attacks on Berlin was not long in coming. Hitler had desired to deter all air attacks on German cities, and he had, by his restraining directives to the Luftwaffe, been bargaining since May for an end to the Bomber Command offensive. As the program of conquering Britain got under way, some of these restraints began to be deferred (at least for a time) to the requirements of winning superiority over RAF Fighter Command, and the decision prior to the 24th to open a German night offensive was such a deferment. But a great deal of the bargaining restraint was still in effect; Berlin, in particular, was of great value to Hitler, for while the minor raids being executed in the Ruhr could be ignored or explained away, a bombing of Berlin would spoil completely the illusion of "perfect safety" for the German people, an illusion for which Hitler still showed himself willing to spare London. While the attack on the German capital was not the only factor in the assault on London, it was, therefore, the critical factor, and Hitler made his decision on the morning after Berlin was first bombed.

Since the real weakness of Fighter Command was not, however, known to the Germans, the decision to bomb London cannot be viewed merely as an instance of the revenge motive (or "punishing of a contract-breaker") irrationally overriding all other practical considerations. The Luftwaffe command was not, in fact, aware of the critical state of Fighter Command's communications, and it had been hitting the "Sector-Station" communication centers as part of its general bombardment of RAF airdromes. The invasion of Britain still was pending, still requiring the achievement of air superiority over the coasts, but the Luftwaffe command was far from agreement on tactical policy at this time; some planners had been advocating raids on London as a means of forcing a British commitment of Fighter Command's remaining reserves, while others urged a continued bombing of the airdromes to catch fighters on the ground.

By removing the sparing of Berlin from the German prospects, Churchill tipped the scales in the multi-elemented German calculations and induced a shifting of attack which spared Fighter Command. By exposing London to attack, he led the Germans to see a net advantage where they did not have one, and to miss the real opportunity available to them.

The German motives in continuing the bombing of London, after the "Operation Sea Lion" invasion plan was finally given up on September 17, hinged on the possibility (now, for the first time seriously contemplated by the Luftwaffe) that painful air attack, alone, might induce the British to surrender. Yet this assumption was accepted only with strong reservations, reservations which, in fact, required that bombing continue to be programmed for industrial targets, regardless of what effects on the national will were expected, reservations which, moreover, still could allow the attack to be labeled as less than a deliberate antipopulation "terror" assault, for fear of more severe British retaliation. Having moved up to a strategically significant counterforce operation, the originally "tactical" Luftwaffe now moved on to a morale campaign, but still with some show of restraint.

The British reaction to the heavier bombings (especially of London and Coventry) was nonetheless to interpret them as meaningfully equivalent to all-out terror attacks, which seemed to leave little prospects of gain in any further RAF restraints. At about the same time (although for reasoning processes which now seem slightly suspect), British target planners began again to speculate that German morale might be the key target whose significance had been overlooked, and that an "area" bombing offensive might in any event be more effective than a precision attack, on purely practical considerations. This conclusion, still quite tentative, stemmed largely from the disappointing accuracies shown in missions against precision targets, and also from a flood of advice that German morale would never equal the performance of the British under the Blitz, and that heavy bombing of the German populace might lead to a breakdown of German civilian life, or even to a revolt.

> The evidence at our disposal goes to show that the morale of the average German civilian will weaken quicker than that of a population such as our own as a consequence of direct attack. The Germans have been undernourished and subjected to a permanent strain equivalent to that of war conditions during almost the whole period of Hitler's regime, and for this reason also will be liable to crack before a nation of greater stamina. . . .
>
> Morale as a main target is one which it may prove profitable to turn to as a long-term objective for our expanded bomber force, and when the

state of German morale is less robust than it is at the moment. We think that there is not sufficient justification to concentrate upon it with our present strength, although we believe that the undermining of enemy morale must be an aim which we must always keep in mind.[20]

Yet British capabilities were still to be so limited as to preclude any really effective "terror raids," and the paradoxical result thus obtained that neither side correctly interpreted the other's intentions of attack in 1941, the German "limited" attack not being seen as such in Britain because of its inaccuracy by night, and the few British "terror" or "area" attacks being misinterpreted because of their weakness.

The "Blitz" thus represented the end of effective bargaining on the question of aerial bombardment, for while certain later German moves could possibly be interpreted as "feelers" aimed at re-establishing restraints for the exchange, September of 1940 marked the end of British desires for such restraints. A bargain, to be consummated, requires that both partners see themselves as better off by it; after September of 1940 this could not be the case.

As the bombings went on through the winter of 1940–1941, the British government slowly resigned itself to a complete destruction of London and the other cities of southern England. British civilian life made its adjustment to the bombings far more successfully than it had in 1917. The contrast between the two world wars is remarkable in this regard. Enthusiasm for a quick successful war had been manifest in both Germany and Britain in 1914, and the prolonged suffering endured thereafter had come as an unpleasant shock. In 1939, by contrast, inhabitants of all major cities in Europe had expected a severe punishment. In Britain, the worst fears were not realized. The need for hospital beds, the number of casualties, the destruction of cities, all had been overestimated, and these over-estimates widely circulated and accepted. When the expected pain clearly did not materialize, the public proved to be more able to bear the suffering actually inflicted. Some planners began almost cheerfully to contemplate the complete urban redevelopment of the British capital. With no prospect for an end to the bombings in sight, this prospect ceased to be a powerful incentive for any British concessions.

It is probably fair to say that Nazi Germany held an interest in limits to aerial warfare longer than Britain did. Unfortunately, for the Germans, their bargaining for such limits had been poorly executed. German propaganda under Goebbels had not been fully enough harnessed to the communication of the nation's intent; Luftwaffe complaints of misinterpretations and distortions of its campaigns were recurrent, and on crucial questions of fine distinction, such as Warsaw

---

[20] Text in Webster and Frankland, *op. cit.,* IV, p. 190.

and Rotterdam, broadcasts threatening other cities with similar imminent fates served to undermine the general German purpose. The deliberate prewar tendency (in pursuit of lesser objectives) to hint at all-out air attack if German wishes were not granted similarly had made dangerously ambiguous the wartime German intention to abstain from such attack except in retaliation.

Beyond the distortions of propaganda, however, the German decision at several points to interpret borderline opportunities in their own favor was incautious, for these opportunities did not seem "tactical" or "strictly military" to the other side. For a nation as averse to bombing as Germany, the severity of the final raid on Warsaw and the dive-bomber attack on Rotterdam were precarious moves, as was the decision to add a night offensive against Britain, based, as it was, on a serious overestimation of bombing accuracy and of the separability of "military" and "civilian" targets.

If the Germans still hoped to limit the war, after they had seemed to acquire a chance to eliminate RAF's Fighter Command, a more careful measure of the values of their opponent had to be taken. While France proved willing to surrender before expanding the air war, Britain preferred, under Churchill, to drop limits when military force survival (and the national existence) were threatened, when a dropping of such limits offered a contribution to force survival. By threatening to disarm or to invade Britain, Germany exposed herself to air assault.

Finally, since the German ability to restrain the war depended so much on a British fear of the Luftwaffe, it was unwise to demonstrate the limits of its capabilities. Indeed, if the British had known in 1938 what the Blitz would be like, it seems unlikely that they would have been restrained by fear of air attack.

In the battle of Britain and the Blitz, some 67,000 tons of bombs were delivered to England by the Luftwaffe, considerably less than had been expected, but still roughly 2500 times as much as had been delivered in all of World War I. Much more physical damage was now inflicted on the city, and 30 times as many people were killed. The inaccuracy of the forecast linear relationship of casualties to bomb tonnage is interesting here; yet the psychological effects on the British public in fact were *absolutely* less than in 1916 and 1917, and this is much more remarkable.

The severity of the later Allied air offensive was to come as a surprise to Hitler, and would greatly overshadow the tonnage and casualty figures of the Blitz. Perhaps the German aversion to air attack would indeed have been fortified if there had been foreknowledge of its actual severity, and perhaps the bargaining for limits might then have been conducted with more care. As it was, the Germans had sought restraints fairly consistently, but also quite ineptly.

The first year of the war thus saw two factors push the powers into a campaign of all-out air attack; the German tendency to misjudge the values of Britain, and then the emergence of an apparently decisive opportunity for the Luftwaffe to disarm the RAF. The knowledge that this last opportunity might not quite be decisive still imposed some caution on the Germans, but apparently not enough.

Japan's Fatal Blunder

SIR GEORGE SANSOM

In the light of what we know today the decision of the leaders of Japan to make war upon the United States appears as an act of folly, by which they committed themselves to a hopeless struggle against a Power with perhaps ten times their own potential industrial and military strength. But was that decision in fact as reckless as it now seems, or can it be regarded as the taking of a justifiable risk in the circumstances in which it was made?

Perhaps it is too soon to expect a complete answer to this question, but there is already available a good deal of useful information upon which a preliminary judgement can be based. There is, for instance, an interesting series of reports published by the United States Strategic Bombing Survey,* which was conducted (by civilians) primarily for the purpose of ascertaining the degree to which air-power contributed to the defeat of Japan. During this enquiry there was collected a mass of statistical and other information regarding political and economic conditions in Japan prior to and during the war. These studies, together with two volumes of Interrogations compiled by the United States Navy,† include valuable data based upon oral and documentary

Reprinted by permission from *International Affairs,* October 1948, pp. 543–555. One footnote has been omitted.

* [*Editors' note:* United States Strategic Bombing Survey, *Japan's Struggle to End the War* (Washington, D.C.: Government Printing Office, 1946).]

† [*Editors' note:* United States Strategic Bombing Survey, *Interrogations of Japanese Officials,* 2 vols. (Washington, D.C.: Government Printing Office, 1946).]

evidence obtained in Japan in 1945, not long after the surrender, when memories were fresh. It should be understood that the answers elicited by interrogations cannot all be taken at face value. Allowance must be made for certain factors of error. Thus, the "Summaries" of the Bombing Survey, in which general conclusions are drawn, naturally tend to place emphasis on the part played by aircraft in reducing Japan to the point of surrender and, by implication, to underestimate the importance of the general strategic conduct of the war and the particular effectiveness of submarine action on vital Japanese lines of communication by sea. Moreover, the interrogations were not always skillfully conducted and the replies sometimes betray a desire to please the questioners, if not to mislead them. Different and more reliable results might have been obtained from really searching cross-examination by experienced persons. Nevertheless, the documents are extremely interesting and suffice to establish beyond reasonable doubt a number of important facts. The following tentative appraisal draws freely upon information which they contain, though it is supplemented at a few points by knowledge derived by the writer from other sources during a visit to Japan early in 1946.

There is no doubt that Japan was preparing for war at least a decade before 1941, but this does not necessarily mean that she had decided before that year to make war upon the United States or the British Commonwealth. The most that can be safely said is that certain influential army leaders and their civilian supporters contemplated war if the European situation should so develop as to make it feasible and advantageous. There was no concealment of Japan's intention to get ready for war. But during 1940 there was still no agreement in influential circles as to the course which Japan should take in international affairs, or even as to the lines upon which her economy should be further developed and controlled. The full powers which the Government had progressively acquired in preceding years were exercised only partially; a medley of State controls existed side by side with autonomous direction in separate branches of production and trade; and, in general, conflict between the military and the leaders of industry and finance continued unabated and unresolved.

It is sometimes stated by British and American writers that Big Business in Japan—the so-called *Zaibatsu*—co-operated enthusiastically in preparations for war or at least meekly gave way to military pressure. The evidence for this view is poor. On the contrary, during the early part of 1940 the influential Economic Federation of Japan (*Nihon Keizai Remmei*) resisted the Government's plans for industrial expansion, arguing that they were basically unsound. Their opposition was, it is true, based on technical rather than political grounds, but it cannot be said that they co-operated freely with the military leaders in the development of an economy designed for warlike purposes.

In fact, under the Yonai Government, which was in power until July 1940, there were still elements in the Cabinet that favoured a cautious if not a pacific foreign policy, and were inclined to take the side of the industrialists in resisting totalitarian trends. It was at this point that the military used their strongest political weapon. By withdrawing the War Minister, they forced the resignation of the Yonai Cabinet, in which the relatively liberal Mr. Arita was Foreign Minister. The second Konoye Cabinet was then formed, with Tojo, a convinced expansionist, as War Minister. Its announced policy was the development of a highly organized National Defence State and the consolidation of an Asiatic "Co-Prosperity Sphere." This was definitely a war Cabinet, and its immediate purpose was to bring the industrialists to heel. Once the Government reached a firm decision the resistance of the industrialists was sooner or later bound to collapse. The close concentration of industrial power in Japan, having historically been achieved largely under offical direction or with official support, had never acquired true independence or substantial political strength. It could struggle against this measure or that, but in matters of high policy it could not successfully challenge the authority of the bureaucracy with which it was so organically related.

In September 1940, Tojo let it be known that national mobilization required an intensified control which was inconsistent with the old liberal economic structure. But still the struggle continued and, surprisingly, the resistance of the industrial and financial leaders, represented by the Economic Federation, increased rather than diminished. The planned economy which was the object of Hoshino and Ohashi—two officials who had gained experience in Manchuria—was fought with some success by members of the *Zaibatsu* who, whatever their views as to war and peace, realized the limitations of the Japanese economy. But they were at length forced to execute plans in which they had little faith.

These facts are cited as showing that as late as 1941, despite long preparation, there was yet no effective centralized control of the Japanese industrial structure; and, quite apart from the conflict between Government and private enterprise, there was another defect in the country's war-making capacity, for the administrative machine, seemingly so efficient in normal times, turned out to be rigid and unmanageable. It was even necessary for Tojo, when he became Prime Minister in 1941, to seek legislation which would compel the various ministries to obey his orders. Such a diagnosis of the radical weaknesses in Japan's governmental structure at a juncture when her national existence was about to be staked upon its efficiency may seem too sweeping, but it could be supported by further evidence. It is sufficient to say here that the subsequent course of events, in both the economic and military spheres, shows that part of the failure of the

Japanese economy to meet the demands made upon it in time of war can be traced back to faulty arrangements in time of peace. That governments or individuals should contract bad habits is not surprising, but it is surprising that the rulers of Japan should not have realized how inadequate, even by their own standards, was their country's organization for a war of their own choosing against powerful enemies.

The degree of their economic miscalculations is easy to measure by results. More difficult is an assessment of their political judgement. There can be no doubt that the coalition which began to rule Japan in July 1940 was determined to make use of the European war to further an expansionist policy in Asia and, if possible, to settle the conflict with China on favorable terms. When France was defeated and England appeared to the Japanese to be about to follow her in disaster, the Konoye Government began to feel confident enough to probe the weaknesses of possible antagonists by such measures as flouting British and American interests in China, blackmailing the United Kingdom into closing the Burma Road, pressing the Netherland Indies for economic concessions and moving troops into northern Indo-China. In the summer of 1940 it even looked as if an attack upon British possessions in the Far East was imminent. But action was postponed, partly because the progress of the Battle of Britain raised doubts about the expected collapse of the United Kingdom, but also because the Japanese army and navy wished to complete their armament and to collect further stocks of basic materials. They appear to have decided that, tempting as it was, an attack upon British and Dutch territories alone would be strategically unsound, because it would leave on their flank unimpaired American strength which might intervene at a moment chosen by the United States. They were, moreover, not yet satisfied that they had the whole country with them, for despite their vigorous domestic propaganda there were still dissidents in high places and doubtless also among the people. The distribution of political influence within Japan was traditionally such that any decisive move required much bargaining and persuasion. The firmly established system of checks and balances was customary rather than constitutional, but it had the effect of delaying political action. Even within the ruling coalition there were differences of opinion on the timing and the length of each step taken on the road to war, and there were cautious or conservative elements whose hesitations had to be overcome.

This was the condition reached by the summer of 1941. The extremists continued to strengthen their position step by step, by committing Japan to engagements from which it was difficult if not impossible to withdraw. Perhaps this period was the most crucial in Japanese history, since a vital decision on war or peace is not a simple choice of alternatives at a given moment, but is influenced by the cumulative effect of previous commitments, none of which is separately decisive. The extremists had in July 1941, by a series of gradual manoeuvres, gone far towards creating a situation in which their voice would be dominant. They then took a long step by establishing bases in Southern Indo-China. All available evidence goes to show that they did not expect this move to evoke strong reactions from the United States or the United Kingdom. It was represented as nothing but a strategical development in the war against China, but its implications were perfectly clear. It was the first phase of a projected southward movement. It is interesting to note, from the captured German documents published in January 1948 by the United States Government, that the draft secret protocol of November 1940 to the agreement between the U.S.S.R. and the Tripartite Powers states that "Japan declares that her territorial aspirations centre in the area of Eastern Asia to the south of the Island Empire of Japan."[1] The sharp counter-measures of the United States and the United Kingdom came as a surprise to the extremists and threw the moderates into confusion, though they must have had some warning from the Japanese Embassy in Washington. The situation is well described in the Summary Report of the United States Bombing Survey, as follows:

> Though the conservative wing of the ruling coalition had endorsed each move of its coalition partners, it hoped at each stage that the current step would not be the breaking-point leading to war. It arranged and concluded the Tripartite Pact (September 1940) and hoped that the Western Powers would be sufficiently impressed with the might and solidarity of the Axis to understand the futility of further resistance. It approved of the Indo-China adventure, assuming that Japan would get away with this act of aggression as easily as with previous ones.

But while the freezing of Japanese assets and the embargo upon the export of strategic materials to Japan imposed by the Western Powers shocked the conservatives and frightened the moderates, they had already gone too far in their acquiescence. They could not now suggest any course but negotiations with the United States, and over the terms of these negotiations they could exercise no control, since the power of final decision had already passed into the hands of the extremists. All they could now hope for was that the extremists would make enough concessions to satisfy the United States, and this was a vain hope, because to make any effective concessions would be to admit that the whole of Japanese policy since 1931 had been a blunder, for which the

---

[1] J. Sontag and J. S. Beddie, eds., Declaration 3, Draft Secret Protocol No. 1, *Nazi Soviet Relations,* 1939–40 (U.S.A. Department of State, 1948), p. 257.

military party and its civilian allies were responsible. The Army's prestige would never recover from such a blow. War was inevitable. The only question now was what kind of war.

Such in broad outline was the political background of the decision to go to war. It remains to consider on what grounds the military leaders of Japan based their judgement that Japan could successfully challenge the United States and the British Commonwealth. It cannot be assumed that they blindly led their country into war with no prospect of success. Theirs was a considered policy, attended by calculated risks. Examined in retrospect it proves to have been based upon mistaken assumptions, and executed with insufficient skill and foresight; but it was not, as conceived, irrational. It must also be remembered that the economic sanctions imposed upon Japan in 1941 were such as to make war appear a reasonable, if dangerous, alternative.

The planners who decided that the risk of war could be taken were not blind to the frightful disparity between their own strength and that of their enemies. They counted upon certain favourable circumstances to balance their own deficiencies. Late in the summer of 1941 they were convinced that Germany would be victorious and that within a few months, Russia having been defeated, the United States and the United Kingdom would be obliged to accept supremacy of Germany in Europe. This outlook, though it promised them membership of a successful alliance, was in one respect not entirely pleasing to them, since they felt some distrust of their Axis partners, which the Germans in Japan by their arrogant behavior did nothing to diminish. Some Japanese expansionists therefore felt that their plans might be upset by a premature settlement of the European conflict, which would leave them without any spoils of war in the Pacific; and this fear probably, though not certainly, was an additional motive for the rapid seizure of territories in Asia from which they could derive supplies of oil and rubber, and strategic bargaining power. As they saw the position, those objectives—stepping stones to further expansion—could be attained by a short and restricted campaign. They would engage in hostilities in the Pacific for a strictly limited purpose. First they would conquer an area enclosed within a perimeter including Burma, Malaya, Sumatra, Java, Northern New Guinea, the Bismarck Archipelago, the Gilbert and Marshall Islands, Wake and the Kuriles. This, they calculated, could be achieved in a few months if American sea and air power could be weakened by surprise attacks upon Pearl Harbor and the Philippines. The United States, preoccupied with the European situation, would be unable to take the offensive before Japan had accomplished the necessary strengthening of the perimeter and established forward air and sea bases. Once firmly entrenched on that perimeter they could obtain from the occupied areas what they required to sustain and expand their deficient economy—oil, rubber, bauxite, metals, food. Thus supplied, they could wage defensive warfare which, it was supposed, would within a year or two weaken the American purpose and so lead to a compromise peace. Negotiation would leave to Japan a substantial portion of her gains and a dominant position in Eastern Asia.

This was not at that time a strategy which could be condemned out of hand as unrealistic. It could be regarded, and presented to the Japanese people, as a reasonable and honourable alternative to submitting to sanctions. It aroused misgivings in some circles in Japan, and even its proponents knew that it would throw a great strain upon Japan's capacity; but they counted upon the shock of rapid conquests, and upon the fighting qualities of their soldiers and sailors. Certainly in the first few months of the war nothing happened to make them revise their opinions. Their successes were greater and easier than they had foreseen.

So encouraged were they by their achievement that they began to consider an extension of their perimeter. They planned an advance into the Solomons and Port Moresby, to be followed by a further advance into New Caledonia, Samoa, and the Fijis, the capture of Midway and the occupation of the Aleutians. It was here that they made their first cardinal blunder, for . . . "by stretching and overextending her line of advance, Japan was committed to an expensive and exacting supply problem. She delayed the fortification of the perimeter originally decided upon, jeopardised her economic program for exploiting the resources of the area already captured and laid herself open to early counter-attack in far advanced and, as yet, weak positions."[2]

This blunder in execution also laid bare certain weaknesses in the original conceptions of the Japanese planners. Perhaps the most important of these was their misjudgement of the temper of the United States, for the attack on Pearl Harbor had a stimulating psychological effect upon the American people which in military importance far outweighed the losses sustained at Pearl Harbor. The Japanese army had persuaded the Japanese people that the democratic states were materialistic, irresolute, incapable of matching the unique Japanese spirit. They had argued, not without some plausibility, that the United States had for a decade or more shown a strong aversion to protecting its interests in the Far East by war-like measures, despite repeated provocation. They inferred that those interests were not regarded as of vital importance and that consequently in the long run a spirit of compromise would prevail. They seem to have been deceived by their own

[2] United States Strategic Bombing Survey, Summary Report, *Pacific War* (Washington, United States Government Printing Office, 1946), p. 4.

propaganda, for even after their initial reverses in the first half of 1942 at Midway and towards the end of the year at Guadalcanal, they appear still to have supposed that they could fight the war on their own terms. They did not yet realize that their original plan of restricted warfare, which could be sustained for a limited period by their 1941 economy was no longer feasible.

It was not until 1943 that they had fully grasped the fact that they could no longer dictate the scale or location of hostilities, but were involved in total war in which the initiative had already passed to the American forces. That they made this mistake is indicated by their failure to carry out complete economic mobilization until 1943. An index of the gross national product (computed by the United States Bombing Survey with the assistance of Japanese experts) shows a rise from 100 in 1940 to only 101 in 1941 and 102 in 1942. It was not until 1943 that a substantial increase was gained by a production drive which raised the figure to 113 for 1943 and 124 for 1944. This was the peak of Japanese production, and it was reached by forcing an ever-growing proportion of the total economy into direct war purposes, while straining the civilian population almost to breaking point. It was a remarkable performance, but it was too little and too late. No effort was made to carry out a coherent plan of overall expansion of the Japanese economy, perhaps because a balanced development was impossible in view of its previous distortion. Even if the foregoing explanation of the delay in carrying out full economic mobilization errs in placing too much emphasis upon a tardy appreciation of the strategic position, it is clear that the Japanese tradition of government depending upon slow and cautious compromise was ill-adapted for times of emergency that demanded bold decision and quick performance.

The subsequent course of the Pacific war needs no detailed recital here. It is enough to say that although the Japanese made after 1942 immense military and economic efforts to meet conditions for which they had not originally planned, both were insufficient to stem the tide which began to flow against them. Nearly all their calculations had gone wrong. The British Isles were not invaded, the Soviet Union did not collapse, the United States showed not the least disposition to compromise, but began to plan the outright defeat of Japan. The prospect of a negotiated peace vanished. Plans to draw upon the occupied territories for essential materials could not be executed, because submarine and air attacks upon Japanese shipping prevented not only the carriage of needed supplies to Japan, but also the full support of Japanese forces in the field. Japanese commanders have testified that only 20 per cent of the supplies dispatched to Guadalcanal reached their destination, and that of 30,000 troops landed, 10,000 died of starvation or disease and 10,000 were evacuated early in 1943 in a debilitated condition. Though Japanese troops everywhere fought stubbornly and well, inflicting heavy losses upon their opponents, by the opening months of 1943 not only had the Japanese advance been stopped, but their overall strategic plan had been upset. This was the result of an overwhelming superiority of American power, and it revealed a basic error in the initial premises of that plan. It had been supposed that the perimeter could be held indefinitely, but American experience showed after the engagements of 1942 that it was not necessary to reduce the whole perimeter. The widely spread Japanese positions were dependent upon supply by sea, and it was necessary to destroy them only at points selected by the American command. So long as attacks upon Japanese shipping were maintained, other points could be by-passed as a general advance was begun towards bases within striking distance of Japan.

It was after the evacuation of Guadalcanal, in February 1943, that thoughtful Japanese began to suspect that their prospects of victory had disappeared, while those who knew all the facts saw that the situation was desperate. It is surprising that, to quote the words of Hoshino, Chief Secretary of the Tojo Cabinet, "the real Japanese war economy only began after Guadalcanal." Perhaps even more surprising is the confusion which is revealed in the direction both of the war economy and the national strategy after that date. Full credit must be given to the Japanese people for their efforts to restore and develop their war potential after 1942, but their leaders seem never to have reached a clear and comprehensive view of their country's situation. Some rough estimates of national strength were compiled before the war. They were tentative and incomplete, and perhaps this was in the circumstances unavoidable.

But it is strange that, so far as is known, a full re-appraisal in the light of the new conditions was not attempted until September 1943. This was made not by the Government for its own purposes, but by Takagi, an officer of the Naval General Staff, at the request of Admiral Yonai, who had been out of office since his Cabinet fell in 1940. This influential statesman, when asked in 1945 what he considered the turning point of the war replied: "To be very frank, I think the turning point was the start. I felt from the very beginning that there was no chance of success." Takagi's report strengthened Admiral Yonai's fears that the prosecution of the war by the Tojo Government was unsatisfactory. It confirmed his judgement that Japan should seek a compromise peace before she suffered a crushing defeat. Yonai was not alone in this feeling. It was shared by certain influential persons outside the Government and a number of naval officers. They had indeed good reason for their anxiety. The circumstances beyond Japan's control were grave enough—the growing shortages of materials, losses of aircraft, warships and merchant vessels, and the certainty of long-range air attacks upon the centres of production at home. And, added to these, was growing confusion within Japan.

Nominally, by 1943 the Japanese Government had achieved full control of all national organs and activities, but Japan had evidently not become a solid authoritarian state. Animosity between Army and Navy was such that the submarine service resented the diversion of its vessels from combatant functions to army transport duties, and towards the end of the war the Army began to build submarines for its own use and declined naval advice. Army and Navy details, it is said, would fight outside factories for supplies designated for one or the other service. Ginjiro Fujihara, an industrial magnate who at a critical juncture became director of aircraft production, even alleged (no doubt untruthfully) that army and navy rivalry was responsible for keeping down the total output by about 50 per cent. In addition to their inter-service quarrels, the armed forces displayed hostility towards civilian organs. The director of the General Mobilization Bureau testified on interrogation that they would never disclose their stocks or discuss their requirements with him, would not submit demands through the appropriate ministry and thus thwarted all attempts at co-ordination of supply. Control bodies set up by the Government for key materials tried to enforce a system of priorities, but the Army and Navy would help themselves to supplies without troubling to obtain priority-certificates. Civilian manufacturing firms were, it is reported, obliged to resort to black market transactions in order to secure material or machines. It is of course easy to exaggerate the extent and importance of such abuses, which are common enough in all countries at war; but it is clear that there was a serious lack of harmony between the two fighting services. Admiral Toyoda (Commander-in-Chief Combined Fleet, and later Chief of Naval General Staff) said upon interrogation: "There was not full understanding and agreement between Army and Navy prior to and during the war." This discord he ascribed to the great political power of the Army, which the Navy did not share. It showed itself, he thought, not so much in operational matters as in the division of supplies. But General Yamashita, the Japanese commander in the Philippines, was only apprised of the intended naval strike on Leyte Gulf in a *written* communication from Tokyo which was two weeks on the way and reached him on the day of the operation.

Uneasy relations between Army and Navy were paralleled by quarrels between civilian organs. It is remarkable that, despite their reputed gift for careful and strict organization, the Japanese authorities were not in practice able to exercise their unlimited powers of control. Under a surface appearance of national unity, old divisions of opinion, old patterns of influence, persisted with very little change. It is perhaps comforting to discover that what appears to be a solid monolithic state can hide grave structural weaknesses behind a forbidding exterior.

By July 1944, the invasion of Saipan had succeeded and Tojo's Cabinet had collapsed. The strenuous efforts made to raise production in Japan had led to a considerable increase in capacity, yet by late in the summer output had begun to decline because shipping losses had cut down essential imports. National morale was still high but by the autumn of 1944 Japan was on the verge of economic collapse, and that was before the heavy strategical bombing of the home islands. Tojo was succeeded as Prime Minister by Koiso, a retired general, whose Government set up a Supreme War Direction Council intended ostensibly to strengthen national defence, but in fact obliged to consider ways of terminating the war. The story of the steps by which most of its members at length reached a decision in favour of surrender is a long and complicated one. Not much progress was made at first, but certain members of the Cabinet were cautiously working for peace and carrying on discussions with senior statesmen who, though out of office, retained great personal influence. High naval officers were predominant among the service men who favoured attempts to secure a negotiated peace, while the Army command still thought in terms of prolonged resistance, hoping that they could inflict such losses upon an invading force that a compromise could be secured, which would leave to Japan something better than the prospect of unconditional surrender. The peace party was growing in confidence, but only slowly, and was hampered by the fear that, since the Japanese people were still ignorant of the true state of affairs, a premature move might bring about internal chaos.

Meanwhile, with the loss of the Philippines and the intensification of bombing, which affected both military targets and urban populations, the situation became more and more desperate in the eyes of the peace party, less and less hopeful in the eyes of the last-ditchers. But it seems that there was little prospect of obtaining the agreement of any substantial portion of the Army leaders so long as Germany continued to resist. It was not until April 8, 1945 that the Koiso Government fell and was succeeded by a Cabinet under Admiral Suzuki, whose mission was to bring the war to an end, though publicly both Government and people were still committed to a continued resistance. Progress towards peace was still slow, for nobody would come out with an open declaration that the war was lost. Early in May, however—shortly after the end of the European war—the balance began to turn in favour of peace. Appraisals of the economic situation showed that the country was utterly incapable of continuing effective resistance, and there were even some signs of a decline in public morale. Still no specific proposals for ending the war were made, though on June 6 the

Supreme War Council definitely stated to the Emperor that it was necessary to bring it to an end. On June 20, the Emperor summoned the Council, and showed himself in favour of positive steps, including an approach to the Soviet Union with a request for mediation. Discussions with Russia made no progress, the Soviet Government temporized and the Japanese ambassador in Moscow reported that in his opinion there was no alternative to unconditional surrender.

Time went by, and still no firm decision had been reached when the Potsdam Declaration was issued on July 26, 1945. The Prime Minister, the Foreign Minister and the Navy Minister (Yonai) were in favour of accepting its terms, the War Minister and the Chiefs of Staff were opposed. It is interesting to note, as illustrating the nature of the opposition, that Toyoda had not approved of the war from the beginning, yet was unable to agree to unconditional surrender, which he thought dishonourable. A strong military group still held out for resistance to invasion. Differences of opinion continued until August 9, 1945, by which time an atomic bomb had been dropped on Hiroshima (August 6) and the Soviet Union had declared war upon Japan (August 9). After repeated meetings on August 9, just before midnight the Inner Cabinet appealed to the Emperor for a final expression of his wish and the Emperor declared in favour of peace. There were further cabinet discussions as to the interpretation of the Potsdam terms, but they were finally accepted on August 14. This was more than twelve months after the fall of the Tojo Government, and four months after the formation of the Suzuki Cabinet, which was certainly intended to bring an end to hostilities. It may well be asked why, in the light of Japan's inability, so manifest after the end of 1944, to carry the war to a successful conclusion, the discussion was prolonged well into 1945, while her factories and her houses were being destroyed, her warships sunk and her armies cut off from their homes? The answer is not clear, but it seems as if the delay was something dictated by the nature of Japanese institutions. The slow process by which an apparently unanimous will to war was created before 1941 had to be repeated in reverse before a will to peace could be announced.

The fact that the decision to accept the Potsdam terms was reached soon after the explosion of the atomic bomb and the Russian declaration of war has been interpreted as showing that the bomb and the Russian action were what produced Japan's surrender. This is a view which it is difficult to accept. It might be correct to say that these two menacing events accelerated a decision which was being reached by slow and devious processes characteristic of Japanese political life. But it cannot be truthfully said that any one single cause brought about the surrender; at the same time there is good reason for thinking that, even had no atomic bombing attacks been delivered, the disintegration of Japan's economic life, under sustained blockade and continued aerial and naval bombardment, would within a few months—perhaps weeks—after June 1945 have brought about unconditional surrender, even without the need for invasion. But all this is in the realm of conjecture, and not even the participants themselves can say with certainty what course the debates in the War Council would have taken in hypothetical conditions. Even if we were today certain that it was not the atomic bomb which caused the surrender, it would not follow that the decision to use the bomb was wrong. That decision was necessarily taken in the light of such sure knowledge as was then at the disposal of our Governments; and although intelligence reports on conditions in Japan were remarkably good, that knowledge was not sufficient to justify abstaining from the use of a weapon which might end the war quickly, and save the lives of thousands of allied prisoners, possibly hundreds of thousands of allied soldiers, to say nothing of great numbers of enemy soldiers and civilians. Discussion of the rights and wrongs of the use of the atomic bomb at Hiroshima frequently confuses two separate issues. If the question is whether it was immoral to use such a destructive weapon, then one must bring into consideration incendiary raids, such as that of the night of March 9, 1945, which killed probably 100,000 people and destroyed over 250,000 homes, in circumstances of appalling terror. If the question is whether the use of the atomic bomb was strategically unnecessary or (in the light of subsequent history) politically mistaken, then moral considerations are irrelevant so long as the right of a belligerent to attack civilian targets is admitted. There cannot by any rational standard of morals be a valid distinction between methods of killing civilians in which one is right and the other is wrong because it is quicker and more effective.

The Decision to Use
the Atomic Bomb

LOUIS MORTON

It is now more than ten years since the atomic bomb exploded over Hiroshima and revealed to the world in one blinding flash of light the start of the atomic age. As the meaning of this explosion and the nature of the force unleashed became apparent, a chorus of voices rose in protest against the decision that had opened the Pandora's box of atomic warfare.

The justification for using the atomic bomb was that it had ended the war, or at least ended it sooner and thereby saved countless American—and Japanese—lives. But had it? Had not Japan already been defeated and was she not already on the verge of surrender? What circumstances, it was asked, justified the fateful decision that "blasted the web of history and, like the discovery of fire, severed past from present"?[1]

The first authoritative explanation of how and why it was decided to use the bomb came in February 1947 from Henry L. Stimson, wartime Secretary of War and the man who more than any other was responsible for advising the President.[2] This explanation did not answer all the questions or still the critics. During the years that have followed others have revealed their part in the decision and in the events shaping it. These explanations have not ended the controversy, but they have brought to light additional facts bearing on the decision to use the bomb. With this information and with the perspective of ten years, it may be profitable to look again at the decision that opened the age of atomic warfare.

Reprinted by special permission from *Foreign Affairs*, January 1957, pp. 334–353. Copyright © 1956 by the Council on Foreign Relations, Inc., New York. Some footnotes have been omitted.

[1] James Phinney Baxter, 3rd, *Scientists Against Time* (Boston: Little, Brown, 1946), p. 419.

[2] Henry L. Stimson, "The Decision to Use the Atomic Bomb," *Harper's*, February 1947. The article is reproduced with additional comments in Henry L. Stimson and McGeorge Bundy, *On Active Service in Peace and War* (New York: Harper, 1948), chapter 13, and in *Bulletin of the Atomic Scientists*, February 1947.

THE INTERIM COMMITTEE

The epic story of the development of the atomic bomb is by now well known. It began in 1939 when a small group of eminent scientists in this country called to the attention of the United States Government the vast potentialities of atomic energy for military purposes and warned that the Germans were already carrying on experiments in this field. The program initiated in October of that year with a very modest appropriation and later expanded into the two-billion-dollar Manhattan Project had only one purpose—to harness the energy of the atom in a chain reaction to produce a bomb that could be carried by aircraft if possible, and to produce it before the Germans could.[3] That such a bomb, if produced, would be used, no responsible official even questioned. "At no time from 1941 to 1945," declared Mr. Stimson, "did I ever hear it suggested by the President, or by another responsible member of the Government, that atomic energy should not be used in the war." And Dr. J. Robert Oppenheimer recalled in 1954 that "we always assumed if they [atomic bombs] were needed, they would be used."[4]

So long as the success of the project remained in doubt there seems to have been little or no discussion of the effects of an atomic weapon or the circumstances under which it would be used. "During the early days of the project," one scientist recalled, "we spent little time thinking about the possible effects of the bomb we were trying to make"[5] It was a "neck-and-neck race with the Germans," the outcome of which might well determine who would be the victor in World War II. But as Germany approached defeat and as the effort to produce an atomic bomb offered increasing promise of successs, those few men who knew what was being done and who appreciated the enormous implications of atomic energy became more and more concerned. Most of this concern came from the scientists in the Metallurgical Laboratory at Chicago, where by early 1945 small groups began to question the advisability of using the weapon they were trying so hard to build. It was almost as if they hoped the bomb would not work after it was completed.

On the military side, the realization that a bomb would probably be ready for testing in the summer of 1945 led to concrete planning for the use of the new weapon, on the assumption that the bomb when

---

[3] The one exception was the Navy's work in the field of atomic energy as a source of power for naval vessels. *Hearings Before the Special Committee on Atomic Energy*, Senate, 79th Cong., 1st Sess., S.R. 179, pt. 3, pp. 364–389, testimony of Dr. Ross Gunn.

[4] Stimson, *Harper's*, p. 98; U.S. Atomic Energy Commission, *Transcript of Hearings Before Personnel Security Board in the Matter of Dr. J. Robert Oppenheimer, 12 April–6 May 1954* (Washington: G.P.O., 1954), p. 33.

[5] *Senate Hearings*, pt. 2, p. 302, testimony of Dr. John A. Simpson.

completed would work. By the end of 1944 a list of possible targets in Japan had been selected and a B-29 squadron was trained for the specific job of delivering the bomb. It was also necessary to inform certain commanders in the Pacific about the project, and on December 30, 1944, Major-General Leslie R. Groves, head of the Manhattan District, recommended that this be done.[6]

Even at this stage of development no one could estimate accurately when the bomb would be ready or guarantee that, when ready, it would work. It is perhaps for this reason—and because of the complete secrecy surrounding the project—that the possibility of an atomic weapon never entered into the deliberations of the strategic planners. It was, said Admiral William Leahy, "the best kept secret of the entire war" and only a handful of the top civilian and military officials in Washington knew about the bomb.[7] As a matter of fact, one bright brigadier-general who innocently suggested that the Army might do well to look into the possibilities of atomic energy suddenly found himself the object of the most intensive investigation. So secret was the project, says John J. McCloy, that when he raised the subject at a White House meeting of the Joint Chiefs of Staff in June 1945 it "caused a sense of shock, even among that select group."[8]

It was not until March 1945 that it became possible to predict with certainty that the bomb would be completed in time for testing in July. On March 15, Mr. Stimson discussed the project for the last time with President Roosevelt, but their conversation dealt mainly with the effects of the use of the bomb, not with the question of whether it ought to be used. Even at this late date, there does not seem to have been any doubt at the highest levels that the bomb would be used against Japan if it would help bring the war to an early end. But on lower levels, and especially among the scientists at the Chicago laboratory, there was considerable reservation about the advisability of using the bomb.

After President Roosevelt's death, it fell to Stimson to brief the new President about the atomic weapon. At a White House meeting on April 25, he outlined the history and status of the program and predicted that "within four months we shall in all probability have completed the most terrible weapon ever known in human history."[9] This meeting, like Stimson's last meeting with Roosevelt, dealt largely

---

[6] "Memo, Groves for CofS, 30 Dec. 1944 sub: Atomic Fission Bombs," printed in *Foreign Relations of the United States: The Conferences at Malta-Yalta, 1945* (Washington: G.P.O., 1955). . . .

[7] Admiral William D. Leahy, *I Was There* (New York: Whittlesey House, 1950), p. 434.

[8] John J. McCloy, *The Challenge to American Foreign Policy* (Cambridge: Harvard University Press, 1953), p. 42. See also . . . James F. Byrnes, *Speaking Frankly* (New York: Harper, 1947), p. 257.

[9] Stimson's memorandum of this meeting is printed in *Harper's*, pp. 99–100.

with the political and diplomatic consequences of the use of such a weapon rather than with the timing and manner of employment, the circumstances under which it would be used, or whether it would be used at all. The answers to these questions depended on factors not yet known. But Stimson recommended, and the President approved, the appointment of a special committee to consider them.

This special committee, known as the Interim Committee, played a vital role in the decision to use the bomb. Secretary Stimson was chairman, and George L. Harrison, President of the New York Life Insurance Company and special consultant in the Secretary's office, took the chair when he was absent. James F. Byrnes, who held no official position at the time, was President Truman's personal representative. Other members were Ralph A. Bard, Under Secretary of the Navy, William L. Clayton, Assistant Secretary of State, and Drs. Vannevar Bush, Karl T. Compton and James B. Conant. Generals Marshall and Groves attended at least one and possibly more of the meetings of the committee.

The work of the Interim Committee, in Stimson's words, "ranged over the whole field of atomic energy, in its political, military, and scientific aspects."[10] During the first meeting the scientific members reviewed for their colleagues the development of the Manhattan Project and described vividly the destructive power of the atomic bomb. They made it clear also that there was no known defense against this kind of attack. Another day was spent with the engineers and industrialists who had designed and built the huge plants at Oak Ridge and Hanford. Of particular concern to the committee was the question of how long it would take another country, particularly the Soviet Union, to produce an atomic bomb. "Much of the discussion," recalled Dr. Oppenheimer, who attended the meeting of June 1 as a member of a scientific panel, "revolved around the question raised by Secretary Stimson as to whether there was any hope at all of using this development to get less barbarous [sic] relations with the Russians."[11]

The work of the Interim Committee was completed June 1, 1945, when it submitted its report to the President, recommending unanimously that:

1. The bomb should be used against Japan as soon as possible.

2. It should be used against a military target surrounded by other buildings.

[10] Stimson, *Harper's*, p. 100.
[11] *Oppenheimer Hearings*, pp. 34, 257, testimony of Dr. Oppenheimer and Dr. Compton; Byrnes, *op. cit.,* pp. 260–261; Stimson, *Harper's*, pp. 100–101.

3. It should be used without prior warning of the nature of the weapon.

(One member, Ralph A. Bard, later dissented from this portion of the committee's recommendation.)

"The conclusions of the Committee," wrote Stimson, "were similar to my own, although I reached mine independently. I felt that to extract a genuine surrender from the Emperor and his military advisers, they must be administered a tremendous shock which would carry convincing proof of our power to destroy the empire. Such an effective shock would save many times the number of lives, both American and Japanese, than it would cost."[12]

Among the scientists working on the Manhattan Project were many who did not agree. To them, the "wave of horror and repulsion" that might follow the sudden use of an atomic bomb would more than outweigh its military advantages. "It may be very difficult," they declared, "to persuade the world that a nation which was capable of secretly preparing and suddenly releasing a new weapon, as indiscriminate as the rocket bomb and a thousand times more destructive, is to be trusted in its proclaimed desire of having such weapons abolished by international agreement."[13] The procedure these scientists recommended was, first, to demonstrate the new weapon "before the eyes of representatives of all the United Nations on the desert or a barren island," and then to issue "a preliminary ultimatum" to Japan. If this ultimatum was rejected, and "if the sanction of the United Nations (and of public opinion at home) were obtained," then and only then, said the scientists, should the United States consider using the bomb. "This may sound fantastic," they said, "but in nuclear weapons we have something entirely new in order of magnitude of destructive power, and if we want to capitalize fully on the advantage their possession gives us, we must use new and imaginative methods."[14]

These views, which were forwarded to the Secretary of War on June 11, 1945, were strongly supported by 64 of the scientists in the Chicago Metallurgical Laboratory in a petition sent directly to the President. At about the same time, at the request of Dr. Arthur H. Compton, a poll was taken of the views of more than 150 scientists at the Chicago Laboratory. Five alternatives ranging from all-out use of

[12] Stimson, *Harper's*, p. 101. The same idea is expressed by Sir Winston Churchill, *Triumph and Tragedy* (Cambridge: Houghton, 1953), pp. 638–639.

[13] "Report of the Committee on Social and Political Implications," signed by Professor James Franck of the University of Chicago and submitted to the Secretary of War, June 11, 1945, *Bulletin of Atomic Scientists*, May 1, 1946, p. 3.

[14] *Ibid.*, pp. 3–4.

the bomb to "keeping the existence of the bomb a secret" were presented. Of those polled, about two-thirds voted for a preliminary demonstration, either on a military objective or an uninhabited locality; the rest were split on all-out use and no use at all.[15]

These views, and presumably others, were referred by Secretary Stimson to a distinguished Scientific Panel consisting of Drs. Arthur H. Compton, Enrico Fermi, E. O. Lawrence and J. Robert Oppenheimer, all nuclear physicists of the first rank. "We didn't know beans about the military situation," Oppenheimer later said. "We didn't know whether they [the Japanese] could be caused to surrender by other means or whether the invasion [of Japan] was really inevitable. . . . We thought the two overriding considerations were the saving of lives in the war and the effect of our actions on the stability of the postwar world."[16] On June 16 the panel reported that it had studied carefully the proposals made by the scientists but could see no practical way of ending the war by a technical demonstration. Almost regretfully, it seemed, the four members of the panel concluded that there was "no acceptable alternative to direct military use."[17] "Nothing would have been more damaging to our effort," wrote Stimson, ". . . than a warning or demonstration followed by a dud—and this was a real possibility." With this went the fear, expressed by Byrnes, that if the Japanese were warned that an atomic bomb would be exploded over a military target in Japan as a demonstration, "they might bring our boys who were prisoners of war to that area."[18] Furthermore, only two bombs would be available by August, the number General Groves estimated would be needed to end the war; these two would have to obtain the desired effect quickly. And no one yet knew, nor would the scheduled ground test in New Mexico prove, whether a bomb dropped from an airplane would explode.[19]

Nor, for that matter, were all those concerned certain that the bomb would work at all, on the ground or in the air. Of these doubters, the greatest was Admiral Leahy, who until the end remained unconvinced. "This is the biggest fool thing we have ever done," he told Truman after Vannevar Bush had explained to the President how the bomb worked. "The bomb will never go off, and I speak as an expert on explosives."[20]

[15] *Ibid.*, p. 1; Leo Szilard, "A Personal History of the Bomb," in *The Atlantic Community Faces the Bomb*, University of Chicago Roundtable, No. 601, Sept. 25, 1949, p. 15. See also P. M. S. Blackett, *Fear, War, and the Bomb* (New York: Whittlesey House, 1949), pp. 114–116.

[16] *Oppenheimer Hearings*, p. 34.

[17] Quoted in Stimson, *Harper's*, p. 101. The Scientific Panel was established to advise the Interim Committee and its report was made to that body.

[18] *Ibid.*, Byrnes, p. 261.

[19] *Ibid., Oppenheimer Hearings*, p. 163, testimony of General Groves.

[20] Harry S. Truman, *Year of Decisions* (Garden City: Doubleday, 1955), p. 11. Leahy in his memoirs frankly admits this error.

Thus, by mid-June 1945, there was virtual unanimity among the President's civilian advisers on the use of the bomb. The arguments of the opponents had been considered and rejected. So far as is known the President did not solicit the views of the military or naval staffs, nor were they offered.

MILITARY CONSIDERATIONS

The military situation on June 1, 1945, when the Interim Committee submitted its recommendations on the use of the atomic bomb, was distinctly favorable to the Allied cause. Germany had surrendered in May and troops from Europe would soon be available for redeployment in the Pacific. Manila had fallen in February; Iwo Jima was in American hands; and the success of the Okinawa invasion was assured. Air and submarine attacks had virtually cut off Japan from the resources of the Indies, and B-29s from the Marianas were pulverizing Japan's cities and factories. The Pacific Fleet had virtually driven the Imperial Navy from the ocean, and planes of the fast carrier forces were striking Japanese naval bases in the Inland Sea. Clearly, Japan was a defeated nation.

Though defeated in a military sense, Japan showed no disposition to surrender unconditionally. And Japanese troops had demonstrated time and again that they could fight hard and inflict heavy casualties even when the outlook was hopeless. Allied plans in the spring of 1945 took these facts into account and proceeded on the assumption that an invasion of the home islands would be required to achieve at the earliest possible date the unconditional surrender of Japan—the announced objective of the war and the basic assumption of all strategic planning.

Other means of achieving this objective had been considered and, in early June, had not yet been entirely discarded. One of these called for the occupation of a string of bases around Japan in order to increase the intensity of air bombardment. Combined with a tight naval blockade, such a course would, many believed, produce the same results as an invasion and at far less cost of lives. "I was unable to see any justification," Admiral Leahy later wrote, ". . . for an invasion of an already thoroughly defeated Japan. I feared the cost would be enormous in both lives and treasure." Admiral King and other senior naval officers agreed. To them it had always seemed, in King's words, "that the defeat of Japan could be accomplished by sea and air power alone, without the necessity of actual invasion of the Japanese home islands by ground troops."[21]

The main arguments for an invasion of Japan—the plans called for an assault against Kyushu (Olympic) on November 1, 1945, and

[21] Leahy, *op. cit.*, pp. 384–385. . . .

against Honshu (Coronet) five months later—are perhaps best summarized by General Douglas MacArthur. Writing to the Chief of Staff on April 20, 1945, he declared that this course was the only one that would permit application of the full power of our combined resources —ground, naval and air—on the decisive objective. Japan, he believed, would probably be more difficult to invade the following year. An invasion of Kyushu at an early date would, moreover, place United States forces in the most favorable position for the decisive assault against Honshu in 1946, and would "continue the offensive methods which have proved so successful in Pacific campaigns."[22] Reliance upon bombing alone, MacArthur asserted, was still an unproved formula for success, as was evidenced by the bomber offensive against Germany. The seizure of a ring of bases around Japan would disperse Allied forces even more than they already were, MacArthur pointed out, and (if an attempt was made to seize positions on the China coast) might very well lead to long drawn-out operations on the Asiatic mainland.

Though the Joint Chiefs had accepted the invasion concept as the basis for preparations, and had issued a directive for the Kyushu assault on May 25, it was well understood that the final decision was yet to be made. By mid-June the time had come for such a decision and during that period the Joint Chiefs reviewed the whole problem of Japanese strategy. Finally, on June 18, at a meeting in the White House, they presented the alternatives to President Truman. Also present (according to the minutes) were Secretaries Stimson and Forrestal and Assistant Secretary of War John J. McCloy.[23]

General Marshall presented the case for invasion and carried his colleagues with him, although both Admirals Leahy and King later declared they did not favor the plan. After considerable discussion of casualties and of the difficulties ahead, President Truman made his decision. Kyushu would be invaded as planned and preparations for the landing were to be pushed through to completion. Preparations for the Honshu assault would continue, but no final decision would be made until preparations had reached the point "beyond which there would not be opportunity for a free choice."[24] The program thus approved by Truman called for:

1. Air bombardment and blockade of Japan from bases in Okinawa, Iwo Jima, the Marianas and the Philippines.

---

[22] This message is reproduced in *The Entry of the Soviet Union Into the War Against Japan: Military Plans, 1941–1945* (Department of Defense Press Release, September 1955), pp. 55–57.

[23] Forrestal says in his *Diaries* that neither he nor Stimson was present, while McCloy's definite recollection is that Stimson was present but Forrestal was not. A summary of this meeting is contained in *The Entry of the Soviet Union . . .*, pp. 77–85. . . .

[24] McCloy, *op. cit.*, p. 41. . . .

2. Assault of Kyushu on November 1, 1945, and intensification of blockade and air bombardment.

3. Invasion of the industrial heart of Japan through the Tokyo Plain in central Honshu, tentative target date March 1, 1946.

During the White House meeting of June 18, there was dicussion of the possibility of ending the war by political means. The President displayed a deep interest in the subject and both Stimson and McCloy emphasized the importance of the "large submerged class in Japan who do not favor the present war and whose full opinion and influence had never yet been felt."[25] There was discussion also of the atomic bomb, since everyone present knew about the bomb and the recommendations of the Interim Committee. The suggestion was made that before the bomb was dropped, the Japanese should be warned that the United States had such a weapon. "Not one of the Chiefs nor the Secretary," recalled Mr. McCloy, "thought well of a bomb warning, an effective argument being that no one could be certain, in spite of the assurances of the scientists, that the 'thing would go off.'"[26]

Though the defeat of the enemy's armed forces in the Japanese homeland was considered a prerequisite to Japan's surrender, it did not follow that Japanese forces elsewhere, especially those on the Asiatic mainland, would surrender also. It was to provide for just this contingency, as well as to pin down those forces during the invasion of the home islands, that the Joint Chiefs had recommended Soviet entry into the war against Japan.

Soviet participation was a goal long pursued by the Americans. Both political and military authorities seem to have been convinced from the start that Soviet assistance, conceived in various ways, would shorten the war and lessen the cost. In October 1943, Marshal Stalin had told Cordell Hull, then in Moscow for a conference, that the Soviet Union would eventually declare war on Japan. At the Tehran Conference in November of that year, Stalin had given the Allies formal notice of this intention and reaffirmed it in October 1944. In February 1945, at the Yalta Conference, Roosevelt and Stalin had agreed on the terms of Soviet participation in the Far Eastern war. Thus, by June 1945, the Americans could look forward to Soviet intervention at a date estimated as three months after the defeat of Germany.

But by the summer of 1945 the Americans had undergone a change of heart. Though the official position of the War Department still held that "Russian entry will have a profound military effect in that almost

[25] *The Entry of the Soviet Union. . .*, p. 83. . . .
[26] McCloy, p. 43. . . .

certainly it will materially shorten the war and thus save American lives,"[27] few responsible American officials were eager for Soviet intervention or as willing to make concessions as they had been at an earlier period. What had once appeared extremely desirable appeared less so now that the war in Europe was over and Japan was virtually defeated. President Truman, one official recalled, stated during a meeting devoted to the question of Soviet policy that agreements with Stalin had up to that time been "a one-way street" and that "he intended thereafter to be firm in his dealings with the Russians."[28] And at the June 18 meeting of the Joint Chiefs of Staff with the President, Admiral King had declared that "regardless of the desirability of the Russians entering the war, they were not indispensable and he did not think we should go so far as to beg them to come in."[29] Though the cost would be greater he had no doubt "we could handle it alone."

The failure of the Soviets to abide by agreements at Yalta had also done much to discourage the American desire for further cooperation with them. But after urging Stalin for three years to declare war on Japan, the United States Government could hardly ask him now to remain neutral. Moreover, there was no way of keeping the Russians out even if there had been a will to do so. In Harriman's view, "Russia would come into the war regardless of what we might do."[30]

A further difficulty was that Allied intelligence still indicated that Soviet intervention would be desirable, if not necessary, for the success of the invasion strategy. In Allied intelligence, Japan was portrayed as a defeated nation whose military leaders were blind to defeat. Though her industries had been seriously crippled by air bombardment and naval blockade and her armed forces were critically deficient in many of the resources of war, Japan was still far from surrender. She had ample reserves of weapons and ammunition and an army of 5,000,000 troops, 2,000,000 of them in the home islands. The latter could be expected to put up a strong resistance to invasion. In the opinion of the intelligence experts, neither blockade nor bombing alone would produce unconditional surrender before the date set for invasion. And the invasion itself, they believed, would be costly and possibly prolonged.[31]

According to these intelligence reports, the Japanese leaders were fully aware of their desperate situation but would continue to fight in the hope of avoiding complete defeat by securing a better bargaining

[27] Letter, Stimson to Grew, May 21, 1945, reproduced . . . in *The Entry of the Soviet Union . . .*, pp. 70–71.

[28] Walter Millis, ed., *The Forrestal Diaries* (New York: Viking, 1951), p. 78.

[29] *The Entry of the Soviet Union . . .*, p. 85. . . .

[30] Statement to Leahy quoted in Leahy, p. 369. . . .

[31] *The Entry of the Soviet Union . . .*, pp. 85–88. . . .

position. Allied war-weariness and disunity, or some miracle, they
hoped, would offer them a way out. "The Japanese believe," declared
an intelligence estimate of June 30, ". . . that unconditional surrender would be the equivalent of national extinction, and there are as
yet no indications that they are ready to accept such terms."[32] It appeared also to the intelligence experts that Japan might surrender at
any time "depending upon the conditions of surrender" the Allies
might offer. Clearly these conditions, to have any chance of acceptance, would have to include retention of the imperial system.[33]

How accurate were these estimates? Judging from postwar accounts of Japan, they were very close to the truth. Since the defeat at
Saipan, when Tojo had been forced to resign, the strength of the
"peace party" had been increasing. In September 1944 the Swedish
Minister in Tokyo had been approached unofficially, presumably in
the name of Prince Konoye, to sound out the Allies on terms for
peace. This overture came to naught, as did another the following
March. But the Swedish Minister did learn that those who advocated
peace in Japan regarded the Allied demand for unconditional surrender as their greatest obstacle.[34]

The Suzuki Cabinet that came into power in April 1945 had an
unspoken mandate from the Emperor to end the war as quickly as
possible. But it was faced immediately with another problem when the
Soviet Government announced it would not renew the neutrality pact
after April 1946. The German surrender in May produced another
crisis in the Japanese Government and led, after considerable discussion, to a decision to seek Soviet mediation. But the first approach,
made on June 3 to Jacob Malik, the Soviet Ambassador, produced no
results. Malik was noncommittal and merely said the problem needed
further study. Another overture to Malik later in the month also came
to naught.

At the end of June, the Japanese finally approached the Soviet
Government directly through Ambassador Sato in Moscow, asking
that it mediate with the Allies to bring the Far Eastern war to an end.
In a series of messages between Tokyo and Moscow, which the
Americans intercepted and decoded, the Japanese Foreign Office

---

[32] G-2 memorandum prepared for ODP and quoted in Ray S. Cline, *United States
Army in World War II. The War Department. Washington Command Post: The
Operations Division* (Washington: Department of the Army, Office of Military
History, 1951), p. 347. . . .

[33] *Ibid.* . . .

[34] Robert J. C. Butow, *Japan's Decision to Surrender* (Stanford: Stanford Univer-
sity Press, 1954), pp. 40, 54–57. Other accounts of the situation in Japan are Toshikazu
Kase, *Journey to the Missouri* (New Haven: Yale University Press, 1950); U.S. Strategic
Bombing Survey, *Japan's Struggle to End the War* (Washington: G.P.O., 1946); Taku-
shiro Hattori, *Complete History of the Greater East Asia War* (Japan: Masu Shobo
Co., 1953), v. 4.

CASE STUDIES

outlined the position of the government and instructed Ambassador Sato to make arrangements for a special envoy from the Emperor who would be empowered to make terms for Soviet mediation. Unconditional surrender, he was told, was completely unacceptable, and time was of the essence. But the Russians, on one pretext and another, delayed their answer until mid-July when Stalin and Molotov left for Potsdam. Thus, the Japanese Government had by then accepted defeat and was seeking desperately for a way out; but it was not willing even at this late date to surrender unconditionally, and would accept no terms that did not include the preservation of the imperial system.

Allied intelligence thus had estimated the situation in Japan correctly. Allied invasion strategy had been reexamined and confirmed in mid-June, and the date for the invasion fixed. The desirability of Soviet assistance had been confirmed also and plans for her entry into the war during August could now be made. No decision had been reached on the use of the atomic bomb, but the President's advisers had recommended it. The decision was the President's and he faced it squarely. But before he could make it he would want to know whether the measures already concerted would produce unconditional surrender at the earliest moment and at the lowest cost. If they could not, then he would have to decide whether circumstances warranted employment of a bomb that Stimson had already labeled as "the most terrible weapon ever known in human history."

THE DECISION

Though responsibility for the decision to use the atomic bomb was the President's, he exercised it only after careful study of the recommendations of his senior advisers. Chief among these was the Secretary of War, under whose broad supervision the Manhattan Project had been placed. Already deeply concerned over the cost of the projected invasion, the political effects of Soviet intervention and the potential consequences of the use of the atomic bomb, Stimson sought a course that would avoid all these evils. The difficulty, as he saw it, lay in the requirement for unconditional surrender. It was a phrase that might make the Japanese desperate and lead to a long and unnecessary campaign of attrition that would be extremely costly to both sides. But there was no way of getting around the term; it was firmly rooted in Allied war aims and its renunciation was certain to lead to charges of appeasement.

But if this difficulty could be overcome, would the Japanese respond if terms were offered? The intelligence experts thought so, and the radio intercepts from Tokyo to Moscow bore them out. So far as the Army was concerned there was much to be gained by such a course. Not only might it reduce the enormous cost of the war, but it would also make possible a settlement in the Western Pacific "before too many of our allies are committed there and have made substantial contributions towards the defeat of Japan."[35] In the view of the War Department these aims justified "any concessions which might be attractive to the Japanese, so long as our realistic aims for peace in the Pacific are not adversely affected."[36]

The problem was to formulate terms that would meet these conditions. There was considerable discussion of this problem in Washington in the spring of 1945 by officials in the Department of State and in the War and Navy Departments. Joseph C. Grew, Acting Secretary of State, proposed to the President late in May that he issue a proclamation urging the Japanese to surrender and assuring them that they could keep the Emperor. Though Truman did not act on the suggestion, he thought it "a sound idea" and told Grew to discuss it with his cabinet colleagues and the Joint Chiefs. On June 18, Grew was back with the report that these groups favored the idea, but that there were differences on the timing.

Grew's ideas, as well as those of others concerned, were summarized by Stimson in a long and carefully considered memorandum to the President on July 2. Representing the most informed military and political estimate of the situation at this time, this memorandum constitutes a state paper of the first importance. If any one document can be said to provide the basis for the President's warning to Japan and his final decision to use the atomic bomb, this is it.

The gist of Stimson's argument was that the most promising alternative to the long and costly struggle certain to follow invasion was to warn the Japanese "of what is to come" and to give them an opportunity to surrender. There was, he thought, enough of a chance that such a course would work to make the effort worthwhile. Japan no longer had any allies, her navy was virtually destroyed and she was increasingly vulnerable to air attack and naval blockade. Against her were arrayed the increasingly powerful forces of the Allies, with their "inexhaustible and untouched industrial resources." In these circumstances, Stimson believed the Japanese people would be susceptible to reason if properly approached. "Japan," he pointed out, "is not a nation composed of mad fanatics of an entirely different mentality from ours. On the contrary, she has within the past century shown herself to possess extremely intelligent people. . . ." But any attempt, Stimson added, "to exterminate her armies and her population by gunfire or other means will tend to produce a fusion of race solidity and antipathy. . . ."

---

[35] OPD Compilation for the Potsdam Conference, quoted in Cline, *op. cit.*, p. 345.
[36] Ibid., pp. 345–346.

A warning to Japan, Stimson contended, should be carefully timed. It should come before the actual invasion, before destruction had reduced the Japanese "to fanatical despair" and, if the Soviet Union had already entered the war, before Russian attack had progressed so far.[37] It should also emphasize, Stimson believed, the inevitability and completeness of the destruction ahead and the determination of the Allies to strip Japan of her conquests and to destroy the influence of the military clique. It should be a strong warning and should leave no doubt in Japanese minds that they would have to surrender unconditionally and submit to Allied occupation.

The warning, as Stimson envisaged it, had a double character. While promising destruction and devastation, it was also to hold out hope to the Japanese if they heeded its message. In his memorandum, therefore, Stimson stressed the positive features of the warning and recommended that it include a disavowal of any intention to destroy the Japanese nation or to occupy the country permanently. Once Japan's military clique had been removed from power and her capacity to wage war destroyed, it was Stimson's belief that the Allies should withdraw and resume normal trade relations with the new and peaceful Japanese Government. "I personally think," he declared, "that if in saying this we should add that we do not exclude a constitutional monarchy under her present dynasty, it would substantially add to the chance of acceptance."

Not once in the course of this lengthy memorandum was mention made of the atomic bomb. There was no need to do so. Everyone concerned understood clearly that the bomb was the instrument that would destroy Japan and impress on the Japanese Government the hopelessness of any course but surrender. As Stimson expressed it, the atomic bomb was "the best possible sanction," the single weapon that would convince the Japanese "of our power to destroy the empire."[38]

Though Stimson considered a warning combined with an offer of terms and backed up by the sanction of the atomic bomb as the most promising means of inducing surrender at any early date, there were other courses that some thought might produce the same result. One was the continuation and intensification of air bombardment coupled with surface and underwater blockade. This course had already been considered and rejected as insufficient to produce surrender, though its advocates were by no means convinced that this decision was a wise one. And Stimson himself later justified the use of the bomb on the

[37] In his diary, under the date June 19, Stimson wrote: "The last-chance warning . . . must be given before an actual landing of the ground forces in Japan, and fortunately the plans provide for enough time to bring in the sanctions to our warning in the shape of heavy ordinary bombing attack and an attack of S-1 [the atomic bomb]." Stimson and Bundy, p. 624.

[38] Stimson, *Harper's*, pp. 101, 104.

ground that by November 1 conventional bombardment would have caused greater destruction than the bomb. This apparent contradiction is explained by the fact that the atomic bomb was considered to have a psychological effect entirely apart from the damage wrought.[39]

Nor did Stimson, in his memorandum, consider the effect of the Soviet Union's entry into the war. By itself, this action could not be counted on to force Japan to capitulate, but combined with bombardment and blockade it might do so. At least that was the view of Brigadier-General George A. Lincoln, one of the Army's top planners, who wrote in June that "probably it will take Russian entry into the war, coupled with a landing, or imminent threat of landing, on Japan proper by us, to convince them [the Japanese] of the hopelessness of their position."[40] Why, therefore, was it not possible to issue the warning prior to a Soviet declaration of war against Japan and rely on that event, together with an intensified air bombardment, to produce the desired result? If together they could not secure Japan's surrender, would there not still be time to use the bomb before the scheduled invasion of Kyushu in November?

No final answer to this question is possible with the evidence at hand. But one cannot ignore the fact that some responsible officials feared the political consequences of Soviet intervention and hoped that ultimately it would prove unnecessary. This feeling may unconsciously have made the atom bomb solution more attractive than it might otherwise have been. Some officials may have believed, too, that the bomb could be used as a powerful deterrent to Soviet expansion in Europe, where the Red tide had successfully engulfed Rumania, Bulgaria, Jugoslavia, Czechoslovakia and Hungary. In an interview with three of the top scientists in the Manhattan Project early in June, Mr. Byrnes did not, according to Leo Szilard, argue that the bomb was needed to defeat Japan, but rather that it should be dropped to "make Russia more manageable in Europe."[41]

It has been asserted also that the desire to justify the expenditure of the two billion dollars spent on the Manhattan Project may have disposed some favorably toward the use of the bomb. Already questions had been asked in Congress, and the end of the war would almost certainly bring on a full-scale investigation. What more striking justification of the Manhattan Project than a new weapon that had ended the war in one sudden blow and saved countless American lives? "It was my reaction," wrote Admiral Leahy, "that the scientists and others wanted to make this test because of the vast sums that

[39] *Ibid.*, p. 105.
[40] Quoted in Cline, p. 344.
[41] Szilard, *op. cit.,* pp. 14–15.

had been spent on the project. Truman knew that, and so did other people involved."[42]

This explanation hardly does credit to those involved in the Manhattan Project and not even P. M. S. Blackett, one of the severest critics of the decision to use the bomb, accepted it. "The wit of man," he declared, "could hardly devise a theory of the dropping of the bomb, both more insulting to the American people, or more likely to lead to an energetically pursued Soviet defense policy."[43]

But even if the need to justify these huge expenditures is discounted —and certainly by itself it could not have produced the decision—the question still remains whether those who held in their hands a weapon thought capable of ending the war in one stroke could justify withholding that weapon. Would they not be open to criticism for failing to use every means at their disposal to defeat the enemy as quickly as possible, thereby saving many American lives?

And even at that time there were some who believed that the new weapon would ultimately prove the most effective deterrent to war yet produced. How better to outlaw war forever than to demonstrate the tremendous destructive power of this weapon by using it against an actual target?

By early 1945 the stage had been set for the final decision. Stimson's memorandum had been approved in principle and on July 4 the British had given their consent to the use of the bomb against Japan. It remained only to decide on the terms and timing of the warning. This was the situation when the Potsdam Conference opened on July 17, one day after the bomb had been successfully exploded in a spectacular demonstration at Alamogordo, New Mexico. The atomic bomb was a reality and when the news reached Potsdam there was great excitement among those who were let in on the secret. Instead of the prospect of long and bitter months of fighting the Japanese, there was now a vision, "fair and bright indeed it seemed" to Churchill, "of the end of the whole war in one or two violent shocks."[44]

President Truman's first action was to call together his chief advisers—Byrnes, Stimson, Leahy, Marshall, King and Arnold. "I asked for their opinion whether the bomb should be used," he later wrote. The consensus was that it should.[45] Here at last was the miracle to end the war and solve all the perplexing problems posed by the necessity for invasion. But because no one could tell what effect the bomb might have "physically or psychologically," it was decided to

[42] Leahy, p. 441.
[43] Blackett, op. cit., p. 138.
[44] Churchill, op. cit., p. 638.
[45] . . . Truman, op. cit., p. 415. General Eisenhower was at Potsdam and his advice, Truman says, was asked. The various participants differ in their recollections of this meeting. . . .

proceed with the military plans for the invasion.

No one at this time, or later in the conference, raised the question of whether the Japanese should be informed of the existence of the bomb. That question, it will be recalled, had been discussed by the Scientific Panel on June 16 and at the White House meeting with the JCS, the service Secretaries and Mr. McCloy on June 18. For a variety of reasons, including uncertainty as to whether the bomb would work, it had then been decided that the Japanese should not be warned of the existence of the new weapon. The successful explosion of the first bomb on July 17 did not apparently outweigh the reasons advanced earlier for keeping the bomb a secret, and evidently none of the men involved thought the question needed to be reviewed. The Japanese would learn of the atomic bomb only when it was dropped on them.

The secrecy that had shrouded the development of the atomic bomb was torn aside briefly at Potsdam, but with no visible effect. On July 24, on the advice of his chief advisers, Truman informed Marshal Stalin "casually" that the Americans had "a new weapon of unusual destructive force." "The Russian Premier," he recalled, "showed no special interest. All he said was that he was glad to hear it and hoped we would make 'good use of it against the Japanese.'"[46] One cannot but wonder whether the Marshal was preoccupied at the moment or simulating a lack of interest.

On the military side, the Potsdam Conference developed nothing new. The plans already made were noted and approved. Even at this late stage the question of the bomb was divorced entirely from military plans and the final report of the conference accepted as the main effort the invasion of the Japanese home islands. November 15, 1946, was accepted as the planning date for the end of the war against Japan.

During the conference, Stalin told Truman about the Japanese overtures—information that the Americans already had. The Marshal spoke of the matter also to Churchill, who discussed it with Truman, suggesting cautiously that some offer be made to Japan. "Mr. Stimson, General Marshall, and the President," he later wrote, "were evidently searching their hearts, and we had no need to press them. We knew of course that the Japanese were ready to give up all conquests made in the war." That same night, after dining with Stalin and Truman, the Prime Minister wrote that the Russians intended to attack Japan soon after August 8—perhaps within two weeks after that date.[47] Truman presumably received the same information, confirming Harry Hopkin's report of his conversation with Stalin in Moscow in May.

[46] Truman, p. 416. . . .
[47] Truman, p. 396; Churchill, p. 642. See also Byrnes, p. 205; Leahy, p. 420.

All that remained now was to warn Japan and give her an opportunity to surrender. In this matter Stimson's and Grew's views, as outlined in the memorandum of July 2, were accepted, but apparently on the advice of the former Secretary of State Cordell Hull it was decided to omit any reference to the Emperor. Hull's view, solicited by Byrnes before his departure for Potsdam, was that the proposal smacked of appeasement and "seemed to guarantee continuance not only of the Emperor but also of the feudal privileges of a ruling caste." And should the Japanese reject the warning, the proposal to retain the imperial system might well encourage resistance and have "terrible political repercussions" in the United States. For these reasons he recommended that no statement about the Emperor be made until "the climax of Allied bombing and Russia's entry into the war."[48] Thus, the final terms offered to the Japanese in the Potsdam Declaration on July 26 made no mention of the Emperor or of the imperial system. Neither did the declaration contain any reference to the atom bomb but simply warned the Japanese of the consequences of continued resistance. Only those already familiar with the weapon could have read the references to inevitable and complete destruction as a warning of atomic warfare.

The receipt of the Potsdam Declaration in Japan led to frantic meetings to decide what should be done. It was finally decided not to reject the note but to await the results of the Soviet overture. At this point, the military insisted that the government make some statement to the people, and on July 28 Premier Suzuki declared to the press that Japan would ignore the declaration, a statement that was interpreted by the Allies as a rejection.

To the Americans the rejection of the Potsdam Declaration confirmed the view that the military was still in control of Japan and that only a decisive act of violence could remove them. The instrument for such action lay at hand in the atomic bomb; events now seemed to justify its use. But in the hope that the Japanese might still change their minds, Truman held off orders on the use of the bomb for a few days. Only silence came from Tokyo, for the Japanese were waiting for a reply from the Soviet Government, which would not come until the return of Stalin and Molotov from Potsdam on August 6. Prophetically, Foreign Minister Tojo wrote Sato on August 2, the day the Potsdam Conference ended, that he could not afford to lose a single day in his efforts to conclude arrangements with the Russians "if we were to end the war before the assault on our mainland."[49] By that time, President Truman had already decided on the use of the bomb.

---

[48] *Memoirs of Cordell Hull* (New York: Macmillan, 1948), v. 2, p. 1593.
[49] Kase, *op. cit.*, p. 222.

Preparations for dropping the two atomic bombs produced thus far had been under way for some time. The components of the bombs had been sent by cruiser to Tinian in May and the fissionable material was flown out in mid-July. The B-29s and crews were ready and trained, standing by for orders, which would come through the Commanding General, U. S. Army Strategic Air Forces in the Pacific, General Spaatz. Detailed arrangements and schedules were completed and all that was necessary was to issue orders.

At General Arnold's insistence, the responsibility for selecting the particular target and fixing the exact date and hour of the attack was assigned to the field commander, General Spaatz. In orders issued on July 25 and approved by Stimson and Marshall, Spaatz was ordered to drop the "first special bomb as soon as weather will permit visual bombing after about 3 August 1945 on one of the targets: Hiroshima, Kokura, Niigata, and Nagasaki." He was instructed also to deliver a copy of this order personally to MacArthur and Nimitz. Weather was the critical factor because the bomb had to be dropped by visual means, and Spaatz delegated to his chief of staff, Major-General Curtis E. LeMay, the job of deciding when the weather was right for this most important mission.

From the dating of the order to General Spaatz it has been argued that President Truman was certain the warning would be rejected and had fixed the date for the bombing of Hiroshima even before the issuance of the Potsdam Declaration. But such an argument ignores the military necessities. For operational reasons, the orders had to be issued in sufficient time "to set the military wheels in motion." In a sense, therefore, the decision was made on July 25. It would stand unless the President changed his mind. "I had made the decision," wrote Truman in 1955. "I also instructed Stimson that the order would stand unless I notified him that the Japanese reply to our ultimatum was acceptable."[50] The rejection by the Japanese of the Potsdam Declaration confirmed the orders Spaaz had already received.

THE JAPANESE SURRENDER

On Tinian and Guam, preparations for dropping the bomb had been completed by August 3. The original plan was to carry out the operation on August 4, but General LeMay deferred the attack because of bad weather over the target. On August 5 the forecasts were favorable and he gave the word to proceed with the mission the following day. At 0245 on August 6, the bomb-carrying plane was airborne. Six and a half hours later the bomb was released over Hiroshima, Japan's eighth largest city, to explode 50 seconds later at a height of about 2,000 feet. The age of atomic warfare had opened.

[50] Truman, pp. 420–421.

Aboard the cruiser *Augusta* on his way back to the United States, President Truman received the news by radio. That same day a previously prepared release from Washington announced to the world that an atomic bomb had been dropped on Hiroshima and warned the Japanese that if they did not surrender they could expect "a rain of ruin from the air, the like of which has never been seen on this earth."[51]

On August 7, Ambassador Sato in Moscow received word at last that Molotov would see him the next afternoon. At the appointed hour he arrived at the Kremlin, full of hope that he would receive a favorable reply to the Japanese proposal for Soviet mediation with the Allies to end the war. Instead, he was handed the Soviet declaration of war, effective on August 9, Thus, three months to the day after Germany's surrender, Marshal Stalin had lived up to his promise to the Allies.

Meanwhile, President Truman had authorized the use of the second bomb—the last then available. The objective was Kokura, the date August 9. But the plane carrying the bomb failed to make its run over the primary target and hit the secondary target, Nagasaki, instead. The next day Japan sued for peace.

The close sequence of events between August 6 and 10, combined with the fact that the bomb was dropped almost three months before the scheduled invasion of Kyushu and while the Japanese were trying desperately to get out of the war, has suggested to some that the bombing of Hiroshima had a deeper purpose than the desire to end the war quickly. This purpose, it is claimed, was nothing less than a desire to forestall Soviet intervention into the Far Eastern war. Else why this necessity for speed? Certainly nothing in the military situation seemed to call for such hasty action. But if the purpose was to forestall Soviet intervention, then there was every reason for speed. And even if the Russians could not be kept out of the war, at least they would be prevented from making more than a token contribution to victory over Japan. In this sense it may be argued that the bomb proved a success, for the war ended with the United States in full control of Japan.

This theory leaves several matters unexplained. In the first place, the Americans did not know the exact date on which the Soviet Union would declare war but believed it would be within a week or two of August 8. If they had wished to forestall a Soviet declaration of war, then they could reasonably have been expected to act sooner than they did. Such close timing left little if any margin for error. Secondly, had the United States desired above everything else to keep the Russians out, it could have responded to one of several unofficial Japanese overtures, or made the Potsdam Declaration more attractive to Japan. Certainly the failure to put a time limit on the declaration suggests

[51] The statement is published in *The New York Times*, August 7, 1945. . . .

that speed was not of the essence in American calculations. Finally, the date and time of the bombing were left to Generals Spaatz and LeMay, who certainly had no way of knowing Soviet intentions. Bad weather or any other untoward incident could have delayed the attack a week or more.

There is reason to believe that the Russians at the last moved more quickly than they had intended. In his conversations with Harry Hopkins in May 1945 and at Potsdam, Marshal Stalin had linked Soviet entry with negotiations then in progress with Chinese representatives in Moscow. When these were completed, he had said, he would act. On August 8 these negotiations were still in progress.

Did the atomic bomb accomplish its purpose? Was it, in fact, as Stimson said, "the best possible sanction" after Japan rejected the Potsdam Declaration? The sequence of events argues strongly that it was, for bombs were dropped on the 6th and 9th, and on the 10th Japan surrendered. But in the excitement over the announcement of the first use of an atomic bomb and then of Japan's surrender, many overlooked the significance of the Soviet Union's entry into the war on the 9th. The first bomb had produced consternation and confusion among the leaders of Japan, but no disposition to surrender. The Soviet declaration of war, though not entirely unexpected, was a devastating blow and, by removing all hope of Soviet mediation, gave the advocates of peace their first opportunity to come boldly out into the open. When Premier Suzuki arrived at the palace on the morning of the 9th, he was told that the Emperor believed Japan's only course now was to accept the Potsdam Declaration. The militarists could and did minimize the effects of the bomb, but they could not evade the obvious consequences of Soviet intervention, which ended all hope of dividing their enemies and securing softer peace terms.

In this atmosphere, the leaders of Japan held a series of meetings on August 9, but were unable to come to agreement. In the morning came word of the fate of Nagasaki. This additional disaster failed to resolve the issues between the military and those who advocated surrender. Finally the Emperor took the unprecedented step of calling an Imperial Conference, which lasted until 3 o'clock the next morning. When it, too, failed to produce agreement the Emperor told his ministers that he wished the war brought to an end. The constitutional significance of this action is difficult for Westerners to comprehend, but it resolved the crisis and produced in the cabinet a formal decision to accept the Potsdam Declaration, provided it did not prejudice the position of the Emperor.

What finally forced the Japanese to surrender? Was it air bombardment, naval power, the atomic bomb or Soviet entry? The United States Strategic Bombing Survey concluded that Japan would have surrendered by the end of the year, without invasion and without the atomic bomb. Other equally informed opinion maintained that it was the atomic bomb that forced Japan to surrender. "Without its use," Dr. Karl T. Compton asserted, "the war would have continued for many months."[52] Admiral Nimitz believed firmly that the decisive factor was "the complete impunity with which the Pacific Fleet pounded Japan," and General Arnold claimed it was air bombardment that had brought Japan to the verge of collapse.[53] But Major-General Claire Chennault, wartime air commander in China, maintained that Soviet entry into the Far Eastern war brought about the surrender of Japan and would have done so "even if no atomic bombs had been dropped."[54]

It would be a fruitless task to weigh accurately the relative importance of all the factors leading to the Japanese surrender. There is no doubt that Japan had been defeated by the summer of 1945, if not earlier. But defeat did not mean that the military clique had given up; the Army intended to fight on and had made elaborate preparations for the defense of the homeland. Whether air bombardment and naval blockade or the threat of invasion would have produced an early surrender and averted the heavy losses almost certain to accompany the actual landings in Japan is a moot question. Certainly they had a profound effect on the Japanese position. It is equally impossible to assert categorically that the atomic bomb alone or Soviet intervention alone was the decisive factor in bringing the war to an end. All that can be said on the available evidence is that Japan was defeated in the military sense by August 1945 and that the bombing of Hiroshima, followed by the Soviet Union's declaration of war and then the bombing of Nagasaki and the threat of still further bombing, acted as catalytic agents to produce the Japanese decision to surrender. Together they created so extreme a crisis that the Emperor himself, in an unprecedented move, took matters into his own hands and ordered his ministers to surrender. Whether any other set of circumstances would have resolved the crisis and produced the final decision to surrender is a question history cannot yet answer.

---

[52] Compton, "If the Atomic Bomb Had Not Been Dropped," *Atlantic Monthly*, December, 1946, p. 54.

[53] H. H. Arnold, *Global Mission* (New York: Harper, 1949), p. 598. . . .

[54] *The New York Times*, August 15, 1945. . . .

The Korean War

MORTON H. HALPERIN

Prior to the outbreak of the Korean War, the United States believed that a major objective of the Soviet Union was to expand the area under its control. Thus, in responding to the North Korean attack—which had not been anticipated—American objectives were developed in the framework of the belief that the attack was part of a general plan for expansion and perhaps a prelude to general war. The United States sought to prevent the success of this Communist attempt to expand by the use of force in the belief that allowing the Soviets to succeed in Korea would encourage aggression elsewhere. General Omar Bradley expressed this purpose at the MacArthur hearings in describing Korea as "a preventive limited war aimed at avoiding World War III."[1] President Harry Truman later described his objectives in intervening in the Korean War in similar terms:

> Communism was acting in Korea just as Hitler, Mussolini, and the Japanese had acted ten, fifteen, and twenty years earlier. I felt certain that if South Korea was allowed to fall Communist leaders would be emboldened to override nations closer to our own shores. If the Communists were permitted to force their way into the Republic of Korea without opposition from the free world, no small nation would have the courage to resist threats and aggression by stronger Communist neighbors. If this was allowed to go unchallenged it would mean a third world war, just as similar incidents had brought on the second world war.[2]

The defense of Korea was partly motivated by the feeling that the action was necessary to convince the West Europeans that the United States would come to their aid. The Administration was wary of committing its military power, thereby leaving itself exposed to Soviet

From *Limited War in the Nuclear Age* by Morton H. Halperin, pp. 39–58. Reprinted by permission of the author. Some footnotes have been omitted.

[1] Hearings before the Committee on Armed Services and the Committee on Foreign Relations, *Military Situation in the Far East*, U.S. Senate, 82nd Congress, 1st Session, 1951, five parts, p. 154.

[2] Harry S. Truman, *Memoirs,* Vol. II: *Years of Trial and Hope.* Garden City, N.Y.: Doubleday & Co., 1956, p. 333.

aggression in Europe. During the latter stages of the Korean War, in fact, the major American buildup occurred in Europe and not in the Far East. The Administration was also aware of the danger of splitting the NATO alliance in a dispute over Far Eastern policy. A major objective throughout the war was to prevent adverse repercussions in Europe while using the episode to strengthen NATO and build up its military capability. America's NATO allies, particularly the British, constantly applied pressure on the United States to prevent expansion of the war and to bring it swiftly to a conclusion. Following an almost inadvertent reference by President Truman at a press conference to the possibility of using atomic weapons, British Prime Minister Clement Attlee flew to the United States to confer with Truman and to propose the seeking of a cease fire in Korea to be followed by the admission of Communist China to the United Nations. Partly because the defense effort in Korea was carried on under UN auspices, the United States felt obliged constantly to consult its allies on policy and was influenced by their continuous efforts to halt the expansion of the war and to bring about its conclusion.

Soviet objectives were more closely related to the situation in the Far East. The Soviets were interested in the capture of South Korea for its own sake and probably expected a relatively quick and easy North Korean victory. In addition, the Soviets probably hoped to prevent Japan's alignment with the Western powers. Allen Whiting has suggested the nature of the Soviet Far Eastern objective:

> In view of the multiple pressures directed at Japanese foreign policy, the Communist leaders may have conceived the Korean War as serving ends beyond the immediate control of the peninsula. Military victories in Taiwan and Korea could be heralded as ushering in the Communist era in Asia, and as demonstrating the impotence of America's "puppets," Chiang Kai-shek and Syngman Rhee. The resultant effect upon Japan might swing opportunistic groups behind existing neutralist opposition to Yoshida and prevent his supporting American policy.[3]

This interpretation of Soviet strategy in the Korean War was offered by John Foster Dulles right after the North Korean attack. Dulles, who was at the time the State Department planner for the Japanese Peace Treaty, suggested that the Korean attack may have been motivated in part by a desire to block American efforts to make Japan a full member of the free world. He conjectured also that the attack may have been ordered because the Communists could not tolerate the "hopeful, attractive Asiatic experiment in democracy" that was under way in South Korea.[4]

[3] Allen S. Whiting, *China Crosses the Yalu: The Decision to Enter the Korean War.* (New York: Macmillan Co., 1960), p. 37.

[4] *New York Times,* July 2, 1950.

The Chinese objectives in entering the Korean War were also based on general political considerations, but of a defensive nature. According to Whiting the Chinese also hoped to influence the course of United States-Japanese relations. Moreover they were worried about the loss of prestige they would suffer if they allowed the Western "imperialists" to march unhindered to their borders. And they were perhaps most concerned with the beneficial effects of United Nations success in Korea on the many opponents of the Communist regime still active and on Taiwan. Whiting concluded:

> In sum, it was not the particular problems of safeguarding electric-power supplies in North Korea or the industrial base in Manchuria that aroused Peking to military action. Instead, the final step seems to have been prompted in part by general concern over the range of opportunities within China that might be exploited by a determined, powerful enemy on China's doorstep. At the least, a military response might deter the enemy from further adventures. At the most, it might succeed in inflicting sufficient damage to force the enemy to compromise his objectives and to accede to some of Peking's demands. Contrary to some belief, the Chinese Communist leadership did not enter the Korean War either full of self-assertive confidence or for primarily expansionist goals.[5]

The Chinese apparently entered the war with the aim of saving at least some of North Korea. Their minimal objective was to preserve the identity of Communist North Korea rather than its total territorial integrity.

In an effort to secure the political effects discussed, American battlefield objectives and war-termination conditions underwent considerable fluctuation during the course of the war. When the United States first intervened, its objective was simply to restore peace and the South Korean border. Very early in the war and after the Chinese intervention, the United States considered a total withdrawal from Korea.[6] Later its battlefield objective expanded to include the unification of Korea. But in the end, the United States accepted a truce line which closely approximated the *status quo ante*. As Richard Neustadt has pointed out, Truman's original decision to seek the unification of Korea failed to take into account the political-effects objectives that the United States was pursuing, and in the end the recognition of this forced the abandonment of the unification effort.

> Had the unification of Korea been Truman's dearest object, its announcement as a war aim would have been another matter. But it was among the least of the objectives on his mind. In July and August 1950, in

---

[5] Whiting, *op. cit.,* p. 159.
[6] Courtney Whitney, *MacArthur: His Rendezvous with History.* New York: Alfred A. Knopf, 1956, pp. 429–431, 438.

December after Chinese intervention, in his struggles with MacArthur, and thereafter through his last two years of office, his behavior leaves no doubt about the many things he wanted more than that. He wanted to affirm that the UN was not a League of Nations, that aggression would be met with counterforce, that "police actions" were well worth their cost, that the "lesson of the 1930's" had been learned. He wanted to avoid "the wrong war, in the wrong place, at the wrong time," as General Bradley put it— and any "War," if possible. He wanted NATO strengthened fast, both militarily and psychologically. He wanted the United States rearmed without inflation, and prepared, thereafter, to sustain a level of expenditure for military forces and for foreign aid far higher than had seemed achievable before Korea.[7]

Once the Soviets recognized that they could not easily secure their objective of demonstrating American weakness and unwillingness to use force, they seemed to have abandoned the battlefield objective of capturing all of Korea. They may have been willing to accept an end to the war with part or perhaps even all of North Korea in Western hands, and ultimately settled for a virtual restoration of the *status quo ante*.

RISK OF CENTRAL WAR

The Korean War was fought before the era of intercontinental ballistic missiles and fusion weapons. Thus, while both sides could have expanded the war quickly and decisively, there was not the danger that now exists of a sudden unleashing of nuclear missiles which within an hour could destroy a large part of both the United States and the Soviet Union.

Even without this threat of a mutually devastating strategic exchange, the danger of a world war was nevertheless present, and both sides seem to have been determined to prevent its occurrence. Truman has reported that the major American aim in Korea was to prevent a third world war. The Russian decision to remain out of the war seemed to be partly motivated by a fear of igniting a global war. In this situation where neither side could gain a decisive advantage by going first, both sides seemed to recognize that, no matter who started the global war, both would suffer major losses. Though the United States could have attacked the Soviet Union with its very limited stockpile of atomic weapons, it probably could not have presented a Soviet ground attack in Western Europe which might have resulted in Communist domination of the European continent. The Soviets had almost no capacity to attack the United States and could not have prevented an American attack on the Soviet Union. Though both sides avoided forcing the other into starting a global war, neither was

---

[7] Richard E. Neustadt, *Presidential Power: The Politics of Leadership.* New York: John Wiley and Sons, 1960, p. 126.

constantly concerned with the possibility of "preemption" by its adversary.

The United States, however, was concerned that the Korean War should not lead it to expend those military capabilities which were considered an important deterrent to general war. In Korea the United States was employing the troops and the matériel which it felt were necessary to deter general war. At the MacArthur hearings, Air Force General Vandenburg rejected a senator's suggestion that the United States should commit a major part of the American Air Force to the Korean War effort. He argued instead that the United States must get a cease fire

> without endangering that one potential that we have which has kept the peace so far, which the United States Air Force; which, if utilized in a manner to do what you are suggesting, would [sic], because of attrition and because the size of the Air Force is such and the size of the air force industry is such that we could not still be that deterrent to [general] war which we are today.[8]

Soviet action during the war, including the failure to commit combat forces, suggests that they shared with the United States the desire to avoid a global war.

IMAGES OF THE ROLE OF FORCE

The North Korean attack on South Korea suggested the willingness of the Communists to seek a limited objective by a limited use of force. The Soviets probably intended to seize South Korea with the use of North Korean forces and then to halt their military operations. When the United States intervened, they recognized their miscalculation of American intentions, but proceeded on the assumption that American intervention need not lead to world war. The attack into South Korea, moreover, seems to have been motivated by the Soviet compulsion to fill power vacuums. In view of the specific United States declaration that South Korea was outside its defense perimeter, the Soviets reasonably could have counted on a quick and easy victory by the North Koreans. But, while Communist conduct during the war reflected a doctrine that included the limited use of military force and limited objectives, neither the Chinese nor the Russians seemed to have any idea of the optimum methods of communicating intentions and capabilities to the other side in the course of such a war.

American images of the role of force, on the other hand, seem to have been much less hospitable to the limitation of warfare. It would appear that the United States had not foreseen the possibility of Soviet

---

[8] *Military Situation in the Far East, op. cit.,* p. 1385.

military action in South Korea or any other local area unconnected with a general Soviet military offensive. The result was the American decision not to prepare for the defense of South Korea in view of the low estimate of its value in a general war. Thus the decision of June 1950 to defend South Korea was not based on a reestimate of South Korea's military importance, but on recognition that something had occurred for which American military doctrine had not been prepared. In making its policy decisions throughout the war, the United States was operating without any general theoretical notions of the nature of local war in the atomic age, and its decisions were probably affected by the lack of such theory.

Each side's image of the other's intentions influenced its decisions. The Soviets clearly underestimated the likelihood of American intervention. In the Soviet view American action in withdrawing its troops from Korea and the American declarations that it would defend South Korea only as part of its United Nations obligations had meant that the United States would not in fact defend South Korea. The Soviets failed to anticipate the partly moral and partly political American reaction to aggression. They were insensitive to the importance that the United States would attach to repelling "illegal" aggression, as opposed to less clear-cut violations of international law.

The American decision to intervene in Korea and the subsequent decisions were also based on and influenced by estimates of Soviet intentions.[9] In assessing the motives of the North Korean attack, American policy makers gave consideration and, to some extent, credence to five different interpretations, as follows:

1. The "diversionary move" interpretation. In view of the number of other areas, particularly Western Europe, that appeared more militarily significant than South Korea, the North Korean attack was seen as a diversionary move, aimed to draw American resources away from the areas where they were most important. Truman reports that he shared this view in part and was determined not to leave Europe vulnerable to Soviet aggression.

2. The "soft-spot probing" interpretation. By this image of Soviet doctrine, the Soviet compulsion to fill power vacuums had led to the attack on South Korea which had been abandoned by the United States and which was clearly incapable of defending itself.

3. The "testing" interpretation. This was the view that seemed to influence most Truman's image of the North Korean attack. It recalled the progress of Hitler's aggressive moves and asserted that the

---

[9] This discussion of the American image of Soviet doctrine is based on Alexander L. George, "American Policy-Making and the North Korean Aggression," *World Politics,* VII (January 1955), pp. 209–232.

North Korean attack should be seen as a prelude to attacks in other areas if that aggression were allowed to succeed. This view differed from the "soft-spot probing" interpretation in its assumption that the Communists' success in Korea would encourage them to attempt aggression in the other areas where Western defense capabilities were far stronger. In short the purpose of the Korean attack was to probe the firmness of Western intentions, and not simply to fill a power vacuum.

4. The "demonstration" interpretation. By this interpretation, the Soviets were mainly concerned with demonstrating their own strength and American weakness in order to promote, on a long-term basis, important shifts in political allegiance throughout the world.

5. The "Soviet-Far-East-strategy" interpretation. This interpretation put emphasis on the idea, already discussed, that the Soviets hoped to prevent the entrance of Japan into the Western camp and to pave the way for further Communist expansion in the Far East.

. . . The inclination of American policy makers toward the "testing" interpretation of Soviet doctrine—in which the Korean attack was equated with Hitler's early expansionist moves—may have reinforced the likelihood that the United States would intervene in Korea. If the "soft-spot probing" interpretation of Soviet conduct had been accepted instead, the United States might have been more prone to cede South Korea while taking steps to prevent the existence of power vacuums elsewhere. The belief that successful aggression would embolden the Soviets made the defense of South Korea seem crucial.

DOMESTIC POLITICAL PRESSURES

During the Korean War the Truman administration continued to pursue its domestic political goals. Despite the war there was politics-as-usual on both sides of the political fence. The President was constantly concerned with promoting his Fair Deal program, consolidating the position of the Democratic Party, strengthening his northern and western liberal support in Congress, and calming the political crises raised by such men as Senator Joseph McCarthy. Nor was the Administration immune to criticism from the Republican Party, which felt that it was possible, necessary, and desirable to attack the Administration's conduct as well as to question the basic concept of limiting war.

After the MacArthur hearings, a Republican minority report declared:

> We believe that a policy of victory must be announced to the American people in order to restore unity and confidence. It is too much to expect

that our people will accept a limited war. Our policy must be to win. Our strategy must be devised to bring about decisive victory.[10]

These few sentences suggest a number of important assumptions about the nature of wartime politics. The first is the notion that the unity of the American people can be achieved only with a declaration that victory is the goal. A further implication is that, after such a declaration, the method of achieving a battlefield victory becomes a "military" problem that is beyond the realm of partisan domestic politics. On the other hand, once the government admits that there are other political considerations that affect and moderate the goal of a strictly military victory, then, according to this Republican statement, it is legitimate to criticize the particular policy adopted. Unity will come only when the country is asked to back an absolute goal. If there is no such goal, then the opposition has a duty to examine and critically appraise the war effort.

Congress, as a whole, also felt itself free to criticize. The hearings into the firing of General Douglas MacArthur were striking in that they required the Administration, *during the war,* to justify its conduct and to explain what it hoped to accomplish in the war and how the war was being conducted, as well as to explicate a host of particulars which must have been of as much interest to the Communists as they were to the senators across the table. Actually the Chinese and the Russians. However, the senators' questions at hearings provided a unique and invaluable opportunity for the Administration to communicate what it wanted to communicate to this hearing did not have that motivation. Congress forced the Administration to discuss its strategy and objectives during the war without any apparent consideration of the effect this would have on the American war effort.

The quotation from the report of the Republican senators also reflects the then still strong American opposition to fighting a local war. The Senators stated flatly that the American people would not accept a strategy of limiting war, and indicated their rejection of the strategy as well. The implication is that during a local war the American government will be subjected to attacks from the political opposition, from Congress, and from public citizens on two grounds: the legitimacy of fighting such a war and the particular strategy employed in the war.

The general public seems to have shared the Republican senators' dissatisfaction with the course of the Korean War, at least in its later stages. On the other hand, the public apparently approved the decision of the Eisenhower administration to end the war short of victory as it had approved the initial decision to intervene. The public's

---

[10] *Military Situation in the Far East, op. cit.,* p. 3590.

frustration with the continuing war probably added to the margin of Eisenhower's victory in 1952; his ending the war enhanced the Republican image as the party of peace and increased the Eisenhower plurality in 1956. The Korean War does not seem to have had a major or lasting impact on popular political attitudes.[11] In this respect, American political leaders seem to have overestimated the effect of the war on the voting public. Korea is taken as demonstrating—as to some extent it did—that extended local wars which cannot be decisively won are not popular with the American public. Leading the United States into a major local war or expanding the war without securing a clear victory is likely to be perceived as a political liability; ending a war on almost any terms may be a political asset.

All these domestic pressures undoubtedly influenced the manner in which the Truman administration conducted its Korean operations, both by hampering its freedom of action and by increasing the costs of various actions.

ATOMIC WEAPONS

The most dramatic limit on the Korean War was that neither side used its atomic weapons. According to Brodie there were four reasons why these weapons were not used by the United States:[12]

1. The Joint Chiefs of Staff and civilian policy makers continued to feel that the war in Korea was basically a Soviet feint. There was, therefore, a strong case for conserving the then relatively limited stockpile of atomic weapons for the principal war which, they thought, would come in Europe. Their fear was not that the employment of nuclear weapons would lead to an expansion of the war and a Soviet attack on Europe, but rather that Korea was deliberately designed as a decoy to get the United States to exhaust its nuclear stockpile and conventional military resources so that the Soviets could later attack with impunity in Europe. It was the desire, then, to save resources and not the fear of provoking the enemy that was one of the main causes of the American decision not to use nuclear weapons in Korea.

2. American policy was also affected by the reports of local Air Force commanders that there were no suitable targets for atomic weapons in Korea. While the impact of this view was considerable, it apparently reflected an uninformed attitude about the possible uses of atomic weapons. Commanders in the field came to think, for example, that atomic bombs were of little use against bridges, a belief which Brodie explained as follows:

---

[11] Angus Campbell et. al., *The American Voter*. New York: John Wiley and Sons, 1960, pp. 49, 50, 527, 546, 555.

[12] Bernard Brodie, *Strategy in the Missile Age*. Princeton, N.J.: Princeton University Press, 1959.

This odd idea probably resulted from a mis-reading of the results at Hiroshima and Nagasaki. Some bridges were indeed badly damaged at those places and some were not, but for the latter it was generally forgotten that a bridge only 270 feet from ground zero at Hiroshima was actually 2,100 feet from the point of explosion, and also that it received its blast effect from above rather than from the side.[13]

Nuclear weapons were still relatively new and had not been extensively tested, and it is probable that commanders in the field were too busy to search out potential targets for nuclear weapons.

3. American allies, particularly the British, were strongly and emotionally opposed to the use of atomic weapons in the Korean War. This pressure from allies strengthened America's own anxieties and moral doubts about again using these weapons.

4. A subsidiary reason for the failure to use atomic weapons in the Korean War was the fear of the retaliatory employment by the Soviets of the few atomic weapons in their possession against Pusan or Japan, despite the American near monopoly of these weapons. Brodie doubts, however, whether this fear played a conscious part in the relevant decisions.

The first two motives just discussed will not be important in the future. The American stockpile of tactical nuclear weapons is now so great that military commanders may urge their use precisely because they are a nonscarce military resource, and certainly no argument can be made that they should not be used because they are scarce. Military officers now have a much better understanding of the capabilities of nuclear weapons, which, moreover, now come in much smaller packages. Thus it will be clear to military commanders that there would be suitable targets for their use in any conceivable future major limited war. While we can expect continued pressure from our allies against the use of nuclear weapons, certain allies might advocate their use in some situations. There will, however, be other international political pressures—for example, from the uncommitted or neutral states—against nuclear weapons, and the possibility of a Soviet nuclear response will be a much more important determinant of the decision.

We know much less about the details of the Russian decision not to use atomic weapons in Korea. The Russians seemed determined not to supply any matériel to the forces fighting in Korea which could clearly be labeled as having been supplied by them after the war began. This would certainly be the case with atomic weapons.[14] In addition, the

---

[13] *Ibid.,* p. 319n.
[14] It was also true, however, of the MIGs which the Soviets supplied probably with Russian pilots.

Soviet stockpile of such weapons was so small that its use in a localized military encounter might have seemed wasteful.

The limit observed by both sides seems not to have resulted from an attempt—or even an awareness of the need—to bargain with the enemy. However the Soviets were probably more restrained than the United States by the fear that the initiation of nuclear attacks would be met by a response in kind.[15]

The Chinese Communists seem genuinely to have feared the possibility of the American use of atomic weapons when they intervened in the Korean War. According to Whiting the Chinese felt that a nuclear response was a real possibility; intervention was considered risky and every effort was made to delay it and to minimize its consequences. The extent of this Chinese concern was reflected both in its shelter-building program and in domestic Chinese Communist propaganda. But Peking was reassured by the three-week testing period of relatively small Chinese intervention which revealed that United States aircraft, though authorized to bomb the Korean ends of the Yalu bridges, were forbidden to venture into Chinese territory.

The background of the limit on the use of atomic weapons in the Korean War, then, suggests a failure of both sides to understand what the other side was likely to do and what the other side's fears and goals were. It also suggests that, to a large extent, the determination of limits is based on considerations other than those that result from the battlefield interaction. Some of the other limiting points established in the war reveal the same pattern.

CHINESE INTERVENTION

One of the major expansions of the Korean War was the decision of the United Nations Command to cross the thirty-eighth parallel. This decision was based partly on the military consideration that one could not stand by and allow the enemy forces to regroup for renewed attack just beyond the border, but also on political grounds—when the battlefield conditions changed in its favor, the United States decided to pursue the unification of Korea by military means. In crossing the parallel the United States was aware of the risk that it might trigger Chinese Communist intervention, and tried by reassuring statements to prevent it. But it apparently underestimated the Chinese reaction and, at the same time, failed to develop a concurrent strategy which, by retaliatory threats or other sanctions, could succeed in preventing Chinese intervention. As Whiting has suggested the threat to use atomic weapons on the Chinese mainland if the Chinese intervened

[15] However, if the use of atomic weapons had been confined to the Korean theater—that is, if the decision to use these weapons was not coupled with a decision to expand the war in some other way—it is not clear who would have gained from an atomic exchange.

might have been a much more effective deterrent than the attempt to reassure them that a march to the border did not presage an attack on mainland China.[16] The threat to use atomic weapons would have involved major political costs for the United States, and the American government might not have threatened to launch an atomic attack even if it had recognized that the threat might be effective. Had the Administration been aware of the fact that the fear of greater expansion might have deterred Chinese intervention, an alternative course might have been to threaten to expand the war to China with conventional weapons. But even this was not done. In fact, a decision was made before the intervention that Chinese intervention would not lead to conventional bombing beyond the Yalu. MacArthur reportedly believed that this decision had been leaked to the Chinese.[17]

In choosing, instead, to inform the Chinese of its limited objectives, the United States also considered it important to reassure the Chinese that their hydroelectric plants would not be jeopardized by a march up to the Yalu. But, as Whiting has pointed out:

> It was widely believed in Western circles that a determining factor in Chinese Communist concern over North Korea was the reliance of Manchurian industry upon power supplies across the border as well as along the Yalu River. This belief prompted explicit reassurances from Western spokesmen, both in Washington and at Lake Success, concerning "China's legitimate interests" near the frontier. Yet we have seen that Peking ignored this issue completely in its domestic as well as its foreign communications. The absence of propaganda about the protection of the hydroelectric installations, despite the need to maximize popular response to mobilization of "volunteers," suggests that this consideration played little if any role in motivating Chinese Communist intervention.[18]

In its advance through North Korea, then, the United Nations Command was attempting to communicate two points to the Chinese Communists: first, that it was prepared to go up to but not beyond the Yalu; and second, that it was prepared to respect China's legitimate interests in the northern regions of North Korea. The United States sought, therefore, to establish its limited objectives: that United Nations forces would take all North Korea, that the North Korean government would cease to exist, but China's legitimate industrial interests would be protected. An effort was made to assure the Chinese that the capture of North Korea would not be used as a springboard for an attack into China. The United States assumed that the limits

---

[16] Whiting, *op. cit.,* p. 162. Panikkar, the Indian ambassador in Peking, reported that the Chinese expected an atomic attack, but were nonetheless prepared to intervene.

[17] Whitney, *op. cit.,* pp. 455–456.

[18] Whiting, *op. cit.,* pp. 151–152.

were ones that the Chinese were interested in, and that these limits would serve to keep the Chinese out of the war. But Chinese interests were different and could only be satisfied by different boundary conditions to the war.

Neustadt argues that the Chinese were not in any way affected by the announcement of the United Nations' aim to destroy the North Korean government.

> To judge from what the Chinese said, and later did, Peking's concern was with MacArthur's military progress, never mind its foreign policy objective. Chinese concern was not confined to anything so simple as a buffer zone along the border; an entity called North Korea, not the border, was at stake (perhaps in roughly the same sense that South Korea, under reverse circumstances, was for Washington). Even had the UN promised restoration of an independent North once all resistance ceased—which, naturally, no one proposed—I know of nothing to suggest that Peking would have withheld intervention. The communist world does not take kindly, it appears, to the dismantling of a member state's facilities for governance: the party and the army. MacArthur's military progress threatened both, no matter what came after. In short, the military risks and diplomatic dangers usually associated with MacArthur's march across the parallel existed independent of the words used in the UN resolution. MacArthur's march was authorized before the words were seen, much less approved, at Lake Success.[19]

Washington was apparently convinced even in retrospect that its declarations did not influence the Chinese decision to enter the war and that no other declaratory policy could have altered the Chinese decision. American policy makers concluded that once the decision was made to cross the thirty-eighth parallel, nothing could be done to affect the Chinese decision. In fact, the State Department reportedly argued in December of 1950 that the Chinese decision to intervene was made prior to the crossing of the thirty-eighth parallel. In one sense, at least, this conclusion may be wrong: the Chinese position might have been altered by threats to expand the war with the use of atomic weapons against China. Moreover it is by no means certain that the Chinese were concerned with the preservation of the total territorial integrity of North Korea. As Whiting suggests an American commitment to advance only part way up the peninsula—that is, to permit the maintenance of the North Korean government in some part of its territory—might have been sufficient to deter the Chinese entrance into the war.

[19] Neustadt, *op. cit.,* p. 125.

Neither before nor during the first three months of war [Whiting wrote] did the degree of interest in Pyongyang evinced by Peking warrant acceptance at face value of its concern for a "just" peace, based upon the *status quo ante bellum*.

This is not to say that the Chinese Communist leadership was prepared to accept with equanimity the total defeat of North Korea. As a minimal goal, intervention must have been attempted to preserve an entity identifiable as the DPRK, and to prevent unification of all Korea under U.N. supervision. The late date of Chinese Communist entry into the war suggests that it was the political importance of the North Korean government, rather than its territorial integrity, that was at stake. Although intervention was officially predicated upon U.N. crossing of the thirty-eighth parallel, no Chinese People's Volunteers and Democratic People's Republic of Korea defense lines were established during the August-October period, not even to protect Pyongyang. To Peking, a "just" Korean peace was not an end in itself but rather a means towards fulfilling other related goals of policy.[20]

Thus, even after the crossing of the thirty-eighth parallel, Chinese intervention might have been prevented had the United States acted differently. Although trying to impose limits on expansion, the United States failed to grasp adequately either the reasons that the Chinese felt intervention was necessary or the threats that might have deterred their intervention. Both sides expanded the war, the United Nations by crossing the thirty-eighth parallel and the Chinese by entering the war. Each side failed to convey to the other the kind of counteraction to be expected which might have deterred expansion. China attempted to prevent the crossing of the thirty-eighth parallel by declaring her intention to intervene, but this intention, relayed by the Indian ambassador, was not taken seriously by the United Nations Command. The United Nations sought to prevent the Chinese entrance, not be threatening a further expansion but by attempting to satisfy the Chinese security interests that, it was assumed, might lead her to enter the war.

PORTS AND TROOPS

Despite the fact that United States planes, taking off from airfields in South Korea and Japan and from aircraft carriers, consistently bombed targets in North Korea, the Communists engaged in almost no bombing south of the thirty-eighth parallel. This was one of the major asymmetries of the war both from a legalistic point of view and in terms of interfering with the military operations of the enemy. Both sides apparently devoted considerable attention to the question of what targets to attack, and a variety of motives affected the relevant decisions.

[20] Whiting, *op. cit.,* pp. 155–156.

The American decision to bomb targets in North Korea was made prior to the commitment of American ground troops in June 1950. A month later permission was given to bomb industrial targets in North Korea, but the use of incendiary bombs was not allowed because of the civil damage that would have resulted. The Air Force was not authorized to bomb areas close to the Soviet and Chinese borders. Rashin was the single industrial center within the forbidden area and it was the only industrial target in North Korea which was not destroyed by mid-September when an end to strategic bombing was ordered by the Joint Chiefs. Not until June 1952 were attacks on the hydroelectric plants in North Korea authorized; within two weeks almost 90 percent of the North Korea power capacity was destroyed.[21]

American attacks on targets in North Korea steadily expanded. The attacks were aimed at affecting the immediate military situation. The restraints observed had several motives: (1) to avoid extensive civilian destruction considered undesirable on both humanitarian and propaganda grounds; (2) to avoid a spillover of the war into China or the Soviet Union (the spillover into China prior to her entry into the war probably did not have a major impact on Chinese policy, but the incursion did create propaganda and political difficulties); (3) to avoid damaging, in the case of the hydroelectric plants, targets considered vital to the Chinese so as to avoid their entrance into the war, presumably in retaliation.

The Communists exercised far greater restraint on their air forces. Except for a few night "heckling" attacks from small biplanes in the spring of 1951 no air attacks were made on any targets in South Korea. The Communist restraint was not the result of the absence of inviting military targets. The port of Pusan was an extremely inviting target for bombardment and mining. It was the key to the American logistic effort and frequently was lighted up all night. American logistic convoys and troops in the field also could have been hampered by air attacks. A number of factors seem to have influenced the Communist decision not to respond in kind to United Nations air attacks on North Korea:

1. The Communists might have believed that it would have been very difficult, if not impossible, for the United Nations to continue its operations in Korea if Pusan came under heavy attack, and that, once the United Nations committed itself to the defense of South Korea, it was no longer in a position to accept complete withdrawal. Therefore, if attacks on logistic lines made impossible the continued conduct of an effective ground war in Korea, the United States might have been forced to engage in strategic strikes against the Chinese, if not the

[21] Robert Frank Futrell, *The United States Air Force in Korea 1950-1953*. New York: Duell, Sloan and Pearce, 1961, pp. 449-452.

Russian, homeland.[22] If the Communists found this supposition credible, they may have concluded that, once their initial grab for South Korea failed, they could not afford to do anything that would lead to their complete control over South Korea.[23] They may have recognized that American confinement of the war to the Korean peninsula was dependent on her ability to fight there effectively.

2. In order to avoid attacks on Chinese air bases just north of the Yalu, Red airmen were not allowed to attack United Nations positions from these bases. Although the Communists were permitting the United States the sanctuary of bases in Japan and on aircraft carriers, they apparently were afraid that they would not be granted a similar sanctuary for bombing operations. United States planes managed to keep the North Korean airfields out of commission almost continuously throughout the war. Thus, given that the Chinese limited the use of their fields to staging operations and to fighter planes, the Communists were incapable of bombing operations.

3. There is some evidence to suggest that Soviet pilots constituted a significant part of the "Chinese" air force during the Korean War.[24] If this is true the explanation for target restraint may have been the desire to avoid the capture of Soviet airmen. This proof of direct Soviet involvement in the war would at the least have been politically damaging and, from a Soviet point of view, might have created an intolerable risk of American retaliation.

By the end of the war the United States was exercising almost no target restraint in North Korea and the Communists were doing no bombing in South Korea. Each side was guided by a complex series of motives and incentives. However, despite the asymmetry of the actions, there is nothing to suggest that either side treated its decisions on targeting as being closely related to, affected by, or likely to affect, the opponent's decisions on these questions.

EXPANSION AND LIMITATION

Decisions on expanding the United Nations operations resulted from the rejecting or approving of the field commanders' proposals by the Joint Chiefs of Staff or civilian officials. In some cases, particularly on the question of using atomic weapons, the military never

---

[22] The United States had secured British concurrence to bomb bases in China in the event of heavy air attacks from Chinese bases on United Nations troops (*H. C. Debs.,* 5th Series, CDXCVI, 970, Feb. 26, 1952) and this was probably communicated to the Chinese. However, Truman reported that he was convinced that Russia would come in if Manchurian bases were bombed.

[23] This thesis implies that the Chinese would not have driven the United Nations forces off the Korean peninsula by ground action even if they had the capability. There is no evidence to substantiate or invalidate this point.

[24] Futrell, *op. cit.,* pp. 370, 651–652.

made the request, and so, in some sense, no decision was made. On three occasions General MacArthur was refused his requests: to employ Chinese Nationalist troops, to impose a naval blockade on China, and to bomb bases and supply lines in China. But a number of MacArthur's requests for permission to expand the war were approved. These included the commitment of American ground forces, the Inchon offensive, and the crossing of the thirty-eighth parallel.

President Truman states that the National Security Council recommended the consideration of three factors relevant to the decision of whether to go on the offensive: action by the Soviet Union and the Chinese Communists, the views of friendly members of the United Nations, and the risk of general war.[25] These and other decisions were also influenced by American doctrine as well as by domestic political pressures. The balancing of the factors varied from decision to decision, but all played a role in the major decisions to limit or expand the war.

Much less is known about the Communist decision-making process or the factors which influenced their decisions to limit or expand the war. The initial decision to keep the Chinese out of the war seems to have been based largely on domestic conditions in China, particularly the desire of the Chinese to implement their program of economic growth and development, and their desire to avoid military entanglements at a time when they had not yet consolidated their hold over their own country.[26] The reasons for the Russians' abstention from open intervention in the war are less clear. The Soviets were determined not to do anything that directly labeled them as participants; they did not publicize the participation of any Russian "volunteers" in the war, nor provide any atomic capability, although they did supply large amounts of conventional military equipment. One likely explanation is the Russian fear that intervention would lead to general war. The United States had the capability of inflicting great destruction on the Soviet homeland with its stock of atomic weapons, while the Soviets had no capability of directly attacking the United States, although they might have been able to capture a large part of Western Europe with ground forces. Thus the Soviets, aware of their inferior strategic position, were probably determined to keep out of the war and to provide no excuse for a direct American attack on the Soviet Union.

Each side apparently made its decisions to limit the war for different reasons and with minimal attention to the battlefield interaction. In addition the two sides observed very different limits. What the United States did in North Korea was quite different from what the

---

[25] Truman, *op. cit.,* p. 359.
[26] It was probably based also on the belief that the United States would not intervene and that the North Korean army would capture all of South Korea. . . .

Communists did in South Korea, but the Chinese used a much greater percentage of their gross national product than the United States did. Nevertheless, while the United States used naval vessels and airplanes to bomb troops and airfields within Korea, the Communists did not. The United States engaged in logistical interdiction; the Communists did not. Each side, then, observed its own series of limits and restraints only in some very general way related to, and dependent on, the limits of the other side.

At least a few of the limits were symmetrical. Both sides restricted their military operations almost entirely to Korea, and neither used nuclear weapons. There was lack of symmetry in that all the military targets in North Korea were attacked but most in South Korea were not. The United States attacked the Chinese points of entry—the Yalu bridges; but the Chinese did not attack the United States' points of entry—the ports. Both sides observed a number of what Schelling has called "legalistic" limitations.[27] The United Nations carefully observed both the Chinese and Russian borders and tried to avoid crossing them inadvertently. There was symmetry in the absence of official declaration of war. The United Nations troops participated in the war in a "police action" capacity, and none of the countries involved, including the United States, declared war. The Chinese used "volunteers," and the Russians supplied equipment and presumably technicians, but little manpower for the battle.

In some cases the limits represented a recognition of the battlefield interaction. But the origin of many of the limits observed, and part of the explanation for others, lay not within the dynamics of the war itself, but within the domestic and international context in which the war was fought.

[27] Thomas C. Schelling, *Nuclear Weapons and Limited War.* RAND P-1620, Feb. 20, 1959, p. 1.

Controlling the Risks in Cuba

ALBERT AND ROBERTA WOHLSTETTER

The environment in which smaller powers face large ones, has, it is clear, changed drastically. The intensive development of nuclear and other modern weapons, the vast expansion of communications linking remote parts of the world have on the one hand increased the level of violence possible in a world conflict, and on the other seem to have made minor and local violence a world-wide public concern. It is not easy, however, to trace the implications of this changed environment. Public light on local violence does not pass with equal speed in both directions through the Iron and Bamboo Curtains. Though one striking movement of our time has been the multiplication of realigned, non-aligend and partly aligned nations and their use of many international forums, shifting modes of rivalry and co-operation continue to be dominated by the two principal centres of force: a many-centered East against a not-very-completely allied West. Overwhelming nuclear capabilities, in spite of the many hopeful or ominous predictions of rapid diffusion during the last twenty years, and in spite of the search for independence by the United Kingdom, France, China, and possibly others, still are concentrated in the United States and the Soviet Union.

How does the threat of great power violence increase the risks for the smaller powers? And how might the smaller powers affect the nuclear risks? In a contest between the great powers does the very size of their weapons of destruction inhibit, as it is said, any use of force? What is the role of non-nuclear force? And what are the uses of great power bases on foreign soil?

It is much easier to ask these questions than to answer them; and too much to hope that an analysis of the crisis over the Russian bases in Cuba can provide the answers. However a look at this crisis may illuminate a little the issues and so at least help make the questions more precise. All of the questions at any rate were raised in Cuba. There the two big powers and a small one were engaged in a three-cornered partial conflict (and partial co-operation); and nuclear weapons and their

From *Controlling the Risks in Cuba* (Adelphi Paper No. 7, April 1965), pp. 3–24. Reprinted by permission of the authors. Some footnotes have been omitted.

future, if not immediate, launching from these Russian bases outside the Soviet Union were at the very heart of the matter. It is frequently said that we were very close to nuclear war, that Russia and the United States played a desperate game of "Chicken," with the risks nearly out of control. Threats and warnings were signalled, and not always understood. And we now hear that the resolution of the crisis will affect all future risk-taking, that the crisis was a "turning point."

It is perhaps worth one more look then at this much inspected event, to see how some of the standard sayings about constraints and risks in the use of force apply. What were the interests and what were the dangers in the various policy alternatives open to each of the three powers directly engaged? And how did they affect allies less directly engaged?

THE VIEW FROM CUBA

From the standpoint of Cuba the basing of nuclear weapons there had some clear values. Mr. Theodore Draper,[1] an acute analyst of the development of Castro's Cuba, suggested rather early that Cuba may have invited the Russians to put their bombardment missiles there. Castro himself has fluctuated between attributing the idea to the Cubans and to the Russians. On our count, out of some half a dozen major mentions, the score is about even.[2] Whoever got the idea first, strategic bases in Cuba would have had their uses for Castro as well as for Khrushchev. For one thing there was the prestige; modern weapons impress neighbours and can raise the political status of the country which harbours them, especially if the neighbours are misinformed or uninformed. The prestige, to be sure, is precarious, as the United Kingdom, in spite of its great scientific competence, has found, first with *Blue Streak*, then with *Skybolt*, and now with the recently aired difficulties in the *Valiant* and TSR-2 programmes. However, in the less developed countries and even in secondary industrial powers, arms may be valued more for their flourish than their actual power. It seems that the sheer magnitude of the capabilities of the United States and the Soviet Union has outclassed the nuclear potential of others in ways that were quite unexpected by those who predicted nuclear weapons would be equalizers on the world scene. Yet France and China would scarcely agree, and a less developed country like Cuba might place a sizeable symbolic value on being only the host to nuclear installations.

[1] Interview, 6 December, 1962.

[2] Claude Julien, *Le Monde,* 22 and 23 March, 1963; followed by Castro's denial to *Prensa Latina,* 23 March, 1963; Jean Daniel, "Unofficial Envoy: An Historic Report from Two Capitals," *The New Republic,* 14 December, 1963, pp. 15–20; Herbert Matthews, "Return to Cuba," *Hispanic American Report,* Special Issue, January, 1964, p. 16; Juanita Castro, Speech to the World Affairs Council, Los Angeles, 8 February, 1965.

For another thing, the symbol had its important domestic uses. Within Cuba the presence of these bases, while essentially alien and forbidden to Cuban citizens, reinforced and confirmed Castro's defiance of the Northern colossus, made more persuasive his warnings of an American invasion, and distracted attention from gathering difficulties at home. These difficulties had been political as well as economic. 1962 had witnessed an open break in March between Castro and the old guard Communists, followed by a purging and reorganization of Cuba's single political party.[3] A severe drop (the first of several) in the sugar harvest from the preceding year (from 6.8 to 4.8 million tons) was among the early results of an ill-conceived attempt to diversify agriculture quickly at the expense of Cuban comparative advantage. Troubles had also begun to plague the industrial programme. The Cuban planners had left out of their plans the provision of raw materials for the factories they ordered, and were discovering to their dismay that in many cases it cost as much to import the raw materials as to buy the finished products abroad. An extraordinarily rapid collectivizing and statification of farms and even small commercial and manufacturing enterprises, at a pace unequalled in Russia, Asia, or middle Europe, had begun to affect production incentives and to require a large increase in managerial skills; meanwhile Cuba had been losing professionals through emigration. As these internal threats to the Revolution appeared, distraction may have been welcome.

In any case the move had international relevance for the future of Castro's variety of Communism, particularly in Latin America. The missile installation was seen by the Cubans as a great and unprecedented gesture of protection and solidarity by the most powerful country in the Communist world. Inevitably some of this power might be expected to rub off on Castro. By increasing his prestige, it could be expected to serve as an aid in his programme for spreading insurgency throughout Latin America. And it suggested that, like Castro's own communism, successful coups on the same model might be protected against counter-revolution and external attack. One of Castro's explanations for accepting Moscow's offer of long-range missiles could also support this interpretation. It was, he said, "not in order to assure our own defence, but foremost in order to reinforce Socialism on the international plane."[4]

---

[3] The ORI (Integrated Revolutionary Organization), now PURS, a fusion of the Cuban Communist Party and Castro's own 26 July Organization.

[4] Claude Julien, *Le Monde,* 22 March, 1963, reporting an interview which took place in January of that year. Castro repudiated some statements of this interview, but in view of Julien's reputation as an accurate journalist and some of the confirmable details of the setting and circumstances, there is much to suggest this account is authentic. The role of long-range missiles in his insurgency programme has been confirmed by his sister, Juanita Castro, in a talk 8 February, 1965, to the World Affairs Council, Los Angeles.

Speeches in September and early October, 1962, by Cuban communist leaders hammered at the theme, "Cuba is not alone," and Castro's public expressions of thanks to the Soviet Union were emotional to an extreme. Read today, with our present knowledge of the timing of arrangements to install the rockets, these pre-crisis speeches seem to contain implied threats of rocket fire against the United States in case of an invasion, and an identification of Cuba's fate with the final catastrophe. *Goetterdaemmerung.* Castro explained on 20 April, 1963, the second anniversay of Playa Giron, "When the missiles were installed here, it was no longer a problem of six or seven divisions, it was . . . a problem (for the United States) of having to confront the risk of a thermonuclear war." In a recent interview with Barnard L. Collier he made this more explicit. "The missiles were very logical to us. We were running the danger of conventional war . . . The conventional war would be most dangerous to us. We would be destroyed alone."[5]

Cuba was not alone in another sense, because the missile bases supplied hostages. They were a visible symbol that Russia was "contracting in," just as their withdrawal, Castro feared, might make it easier for the United States to underestimate the Soviet Union's solidarity with Cuba. Castro's statement to Collier suggests that the rationalization he had given earlier to the French reporter, Jean Daniel, for accepting missiles hardly represented his actual motives and estimates. To Daniel he had implied that if Russia extended only conventional military aid, the United States would not be deterred from invading, even though Russia would, in spite of American doubts, actually retaliate with thermonuclear weapons and so touch off world war;[6] Russian nuclear missiles in Cuba, however, would deter a US invasion and therefore prevent nuclear war altogether. To Collier, on the other hand, Castro made clear that he himself did not believe the Soviet Union would retaliate with nuclear weapons in the event of US conventional attack, and that if Cuba were to go down he would prefer that it be destroyed not alone, but on a grand scale along with a good deal of the rest of the world. As he said, "For us the danger of a conventional war and a world war were the same, the destruction of Cuba."[7]

---

[5] *New York Herald Tribune,* 17 August, 1964.

[6] According to Daniel's account of Castro's beliefs (*The New Republic,* 14 December, 1963, p. 18), Russia "recognized that if conventional military aid was the extent of their assistance, the United States might not hesitate to instigate an invasion, in which case Russia would retaliate and this would eventually touch off a world war." Russia therefore decided to install the missiles, and Castro accepted them as a matter of "honour." The passage just quoted was omitted from the *New York Times* version of the interview, but appears in the original in *L'Express,* 6 December, 1963.

[7] *New York Herald Tribune,* 17 August, 1964.

The presence of the missiles meant that the Soviet Union was more obviously engaged—in Castro's phrase, "highly compromised"—in the fate of Cuba. Though not, as it turned out, irretrievably; not at any rate when Russia was caught in the process of installation. If a substantial number of missiles had been installed and made operational before discovery, forcing withdrawal might have been somewhat harder. The quarantine of missiles and ground support equipment on their way to Cuba would, of course, no longer have been open to the United States. Something less focussed on the actual process of installing missiles would therefore have been necessary; perhaps a more general blockade or a still broader and more violent measure. Moreover, though this is arguable, it might have been somewhat more difficult psychologically for the Russians to withdraw immediately after the installation of the missiles than during the process. Perhaps this difficulty would have faded rapidly with time; after some years, surely withdrawal would again be easier. In any case, Chairman Khrushchev was caught *in flagrante*, in a difficult position to maintain.

In the event of conflict between the United States and Cuba, a considerable number of Russian missiles and bombers, at least twenty odd thousand Russian troops[8] and, still more, Russian prestige would have been put in jeopardy. To avoid Russian casualties in some of the attacks that might have been made at the end of October (for example, the non-nuclear bombing of Cuban bases manned by Russian forces) there would have had to be extreme selectivity in the American attack, or evacuation by the Russians on receipt of explicit warning; or some combination of the two. Russian forces in Cuba then, like American forces in Europe, though to a very much lesser extent, would have been hostage to the Cubans in the event of an attack by the United States. This point should not be pushed too far or regarded simply in formal terms. The United States forces which are hostage in Europe number now perhaps 350,000 men and many of their dependents. By comparison, a Russian force of 20 odd thousand, is a token. Nonetheless, a distinctly visible token. As Castro puts it today, "The Soviet Union is seriously compromised in the world with Cuba. That is important. It is like the US in Berlin."[9] But he observes that the "compromising" was even more serious with the surface-to-surface missiles in Cuba.

It was not simply the presence of Soviet troops in Cuba, but their manning and guarding of the long-range rockets that seems to have

---

[8] The estimate by President Kennedy in January, 1963, was 16,000 to 17,000 in Cuba, after a withdrawal of 4,500. 25 January, 1963, Press Conference, as reported in the *New York Times,* 26 January, 1963. The official American figure for the crisis period has stayed around 22,000. Castro now claims the number was much larger.

[9] Interview with Barnard Collier, *New York Herald Tribune,* 19 August, 1964.

faced the United States with a dilemma in October 1962. If the United States undertook some hostile action against Cuba, would it dare leave these lethal weapons alone? Would it not have to destroy them? And would this not bring Russia's intercontinental missiles down on the United States?

The line of argument suggested by these questions without a doubt is plausible. However, it persuades mainly by its vagueness. The precise circumstances and nature of the United States action and the risks to the Russians of their own alternative responses need to be specified, and these are only some of the things which would require examination. We shall not assess how the risks would have looked in connection with the various actions open to the United States, if the installations had been completed. We shall ask: What were the risks involved in the actions taken by the United States and in alternatives it considered during the process of the missile installation by the Russians? Much has been said about this, but how close *were* we to the brink?

Whether or not the Russians might have used their medium and intermediate range missiles located in Cuba or their intercontinental missiles based at home in retaliation against an attack on Cuba, desperate action by the Cubans themselves was another matter. Could the Cubans have used the Russian's missiles based in Cuba? If the surface-to-surface missiles had been in their charge, they may well have been more tempted than the Russians to use them. At least the threat to use these missiles against the United States in any of a number of circumstances might from the standpoint of the Cubans have had a considerable appeal. For one thing, the Cubans know less about the consequences of nuclear exchange: these are sobering, as Chairman Khrushchev used to keep telling Chairman Mao; and there is no reason to suspect that Khrushchev's successors—or ultimately Mao's—would be less sober. (Familiarity breeds respect.) For another, we are told, the Cuban Communists and the Russian ones are rather different. We even had some hints from Chairman Khrushchev on this subject. The Cubans are Southerners, impulsive, romantic revolutionaries; and they would put their own fate (or at least that of the current Cuban government) at stake in an American attack or an American-supported resistance. The Russians are Northern and more controlled (though there are those embarrassing nineteenth century Dostoievskian Russians); they are disciplined Bolsheviks (whose character was formed in conscious contrast to such Dostoievskian Russians); and for all of their twenty odd thousand, clearly much less intimately engaged in Cuba.

Whatever faith we attach to these contrasting characterizations, we have some actual observations on the contrasting behaviour of Chairman Khrushchev and the Cuban Communists. Or more exactly, we can at the very least contrast how the Russians behaved in the crisis and how the Cubans say they would have behaved. In the clutch the Chairman was eminently cautious and controlled about the triggering of Russian missiles in Cuba. The Cubans on the other hand suggested considerably more abandon. Che Guevara apparently had a beady eye on New York, and said later that he would have pulled New York down with Cuba. "If the rockets had remained, we would have used them all and directed them against the very heart of the United States, including New York, in our defence against aggression. But we haven't got them, so we shall fight with what we've got. In the face of an aggressor like the United States, there can be no solution other than to fight to the death, inflicting the maximum damage on the enemy."[10]

This sort of threat might be compared with that posed by a small nuclear power, according to General Pierre Gallois and other enthusiasts for the spread of nuclear weapons. In the writings of these theorists the precise service performed by nuclear weapons for the small powers is seldom very clear. If one of the two major powers planned a nuclear first strike against a small nuclear power, such as Cuba might have become, or for that matter, a secondary industrial power like France, the small power's arsenal might not offer much of a deterrent. To deter a first strike, a nuclear force must be able to survive it. And a second strike capability is a more complicated matter than enthusiasts for diffusion have understood.

However, sometimes the use of nuclear weapons by a small power is contemplated as response to lesser attacks by the great power: a massive retaliation theory, in short, with the smaller power appearing in the role of miniature massive retaliationist. Such nuclear retaliation against a non-nuclear move by a great power would of course be suicidal. The small power is not likely to have a genuine second strike capability against Russia or the United States; if these countries are careful, it is still less likely to have a "preclusive" first strike capability, that is, an ability to prevent the great nuclear power from retaliating. From a responsible leader of a smaller power, then, the threat of a miniature massive retaliation might not be very convincing. It is not clear that Guevara, for example, who has a reputation for disciplined intelligence, would be as abandoned in fact as he claims in retrospect. After all, Chairman Khrushchev tried to sound rather reckless in advance of the crisis. In mid-September of 1962 he called the attention of the governments of the world and world opinion to "the provocations which might plunge the world into the disaster of a universal world war with the use of thermonuclear weapons. . . ." "Bellicose reactionary elements of the United States have long since been conducting in the United States Congress and in the American press an unbridled

---

[10] Interview, 28 November, 1962, with a Longon *Daily Worker* correspondent, reported in the *Los Angeles Times,* 11 December, 1962.

propaganda campaign against the Cuban Republic, calling for an attack on Cuba, an attack on Soviet ships carrying the necessary commodities and food to the Cuban people, in one word, calling for war."
". . . One cannot now attack Cuba and expect that the aggressor will be free from punishment for this attack. If this attack is made, this will be the beginning of war."[11] In short, interception of Russian ships carrying arms to Cuba would mean the start of World War III.

On the other hand, some leaders in small countries have earned a reputation for recklessness. Guevara's uncompromising speed in nationalizing industry, and immediate full implementation of what he regards as communist principles, have an element of ruthlessness and lack of realism which is not the same as recklessness but which should make us thoughtful. And it may be that Castro himself could convince us with a suicidal threat. The *Venceremos* ("We shall win") with which all Cuban letters now are signed might be hollow, but Castro might just mean the *Patria o Muerte* ("Fatherland or Death") which precedes it.[12] He has had a long personal history of near suicidal defiance of big forces; his casual and disastrous assault on the Moncada barracks on 26 July, 1953; his landing on the *Gramma* in Oriente in 1956, announced in advance to Batista, calamitous not only to most of his companions but to the inhabitants who expected him two days earlier; to say nothing of some hair-raising student escapades. *Frente a Todos* ("Against Everybody") has been his slogan.[13] One can understand that more than the traditional guerrilla doctrine of protecting the leader might have influenced Fidel's subordinates to keep him home in the headquarters of the Sierra Maestra when they went out on a raid. When he was in charge, casualties were prohibitive. His own life has been charmed, but not that of his followers. It should give any prospective father figure—or even a brother figure, Russian or otherwise—considerable pause.[14]

[11] *New York Times,* 12 September, 1962. (Soviet Government Statement released by *Tass.*)

[12] He describes the Cubans manning the surface-to-air missiles today in precisely these terms. They are "disciplined and fatherland-or-death types" (Speech, 21 January, 1965). If he had surface-to-surface missiles, he might very well man them with the same "types" and, at the least, almost certainly so describe them.

[13] *Frente a Todos* is the title Fidel gave to his reply in Mexico in 1955 to charges against him of corruption and usurpation of power by the Ortodoxo Party and other groups fighting Batista in Cuba.

[14] Fidel's actual father had trouble. When Fidel was 13 years old he organized a strike of sugar workers against his father, and later when he was 18, his mother reports in a biography written with one of Castro's sisters, that she permitted him to call his father an exploiter and a landlord, one of "those who abuse the powers they wrench from the people with deceitful promises." While the father reacted in rage, Fidel apparently still expected (and received) his financial support even after his marriage, demanded $1,000 to buy weapons for the Moncada attack, left the house finally with $100. Castro's vilification and attack of big forces may have aimed at a continued dependence rather than an absolute break in relations. The United States turned out to be a less tolerant father, withdrawing economic support, intending damage, and even inflicting some, when Castro carried on too long, too noisily, too roughly.

Castro in charge of nuclear rockets might be convincingly reckless.[15] It is precisely this case which would appear to be intolerable to both of the two opposing great powers. It is clear that a persisting threat by Cuba to use nuclear weapons in response to unspecified or vaguely specified non-nuclear moves by the United States would be very hard for the US to bear. But it would also raise grave problems for the Soviet Union. Russia would have every motive to preclude or stop such a threat or, if this were not possible, to separate herself as clearly as could be from the threatener.

From the standpoint of the Cuban people a miniature massive-retaliation policy would place them in double jeopardy. It would raise the stakes and conjure up the possibility of nuclear destruction either before or after a Cuban move. However, the hazards to Cubans were increased considerably by the presence even of Russian-controlled missiles.

The issue of Russian control is raised very acutely by the nightmare vision of Cuba pulling Russia down along with New York. No doubt with exactly this in mind Mr. Khrushchev made every attempt to assure Mr. Kennedy that there was nothing whatsoever to worry about from those romantic Cubans. Good, solid, stolid, sensible Russians were guarding the safety catches on the missiles in Cuba: "The means which are located on Cuba now, about which you are talking and which as you say concern you, are in the hands of the Soviet officers. That is why any possibility of accidental usage of those means, which might cause harm to the United States, is excluded."[16] During the crisis as well as earlier, Chairman Khrushchev indicated that he subscribed to the analysis of the Cubans as temperamental Southerners. "The Cubans are very volatile people, Mr. Khrushchev said, and all of the sophisticated hardware provided for their defence was entirely under the control of Soviet officers . . . and it would never be fired except on his orders as Commander in Chief of all of the armed forces of the Soviet Union."[17]

Of course this raises some interesting questions. How sure could Khrushchev be? What about the use of force by Castro to jump Big Brother *(Frente a Todos)*? Mightn't he try to get hold of Russian nuclear weapons for use against the United States and so ultimately to ensure the engagement of Russia? (To say nothing of the rather grandiose plans he has expressed for spreading his revolution beyond the

[15] Some European analyses of the crisis suggest that Castro and the Cubans differed from Khrushchev in that the Cubans do not believe in nuclear threats in response to less than nuclear attack. The claim cannot survive an examination of Castro's and Guevara's speeches. Such suicidal nuclear threats were not only contemplated by Castro, but might be more persuasive issuing from him than from Khrushchev.

[16] 27 October, 1962, message to President Kennedy, published 28 October, 1962, *New York Times.*

[17] Interview with W. E. Knox, American industrialist, *New York Times* Magazine, 18 November, 1962, "Close Up of Khrushchev During a Crisis," described as taking place "a little more than three weeks ago."

Andes.) That, we may surmise, was what a good many of those 22,000 Russian troops were there to prevent: they were there to see that the weapons and in particular the war heads, if they were on the island, would be totally inoperable when seized. Newspaper reports have made clear that the Russian bases were heavily guarded and the Cubans, with the possible exception of a few of the elite, never got near the weapons.

But could these Russian forces be relied on? We know that the Russian troops in the satellites wavered during the revolts in Eastern Europe in the 1950s. The Russians have since rotated their security forces more frequently. However, seeing to it that nuclear weapons would not fall into the hands of irresponsible Cuban users is a much simpler job than preventing sympathetic collusion between rebels and an occupying force. It requires only a very small elite force whose loyalty could be relied on. And the loyalty of even a random sample of Russians might be trusted here: letting Cubans get hold of these weapons would mean placing all of Russia and a good deal else in jeopardy. In any case, there are more sophisticated methods of assurance available. The United States, on 5 July, 1962, announced that it was initiating a programme to install electronic locks (the Permissive Action Link) on its weapons to protect them against unauthorized use. These locks would require release from a central source, possibly very distant. Analogous remote keys conceivably could be held in Moscow itself. And while there is no public evidence whatsoever of mechanical or electronic devices so used in the Soviet Union, a tight political control seems most probable, given the structure of Soviet society; physical possession of these potent weapons would be dangerous in the hands of a dissident internal faction. The interests of the larger powers clearly coincide in preventing unauthorized firings by their own citizens. And both want to keep the keys out of the desperate hands of a smaller power. In the event it was the interests of the major powers that dominated.

So far we have treated the crisis mainly from the viewpoint of the small power. How did these missile bases figure in the calculations of the big powers?

THE VIEW FROM THE SOVIET UNION

Much ink has been spilled over whether the Soviet move into Cuba had a purely political significance for the Russians, or whether Soviet bases in Cuba had also a military worth to them. But Soviet objectives can be both political and military; these purposes are not separate, and neither the political nor military is very simple or pure. If the "purely political" is somewhat nebulous, the "purely military," a kind of art-for-art's sake, has no meaning at all.

The leaders of the Soviet Union in any case, when they address the communist world, have never made the separation. In fact, the shift in the balance of forces, which according to Mr. Khrushchev had come drastically to favour the Socialist countries, was clearly linked in his pronouncements to the development of Soviet military power, and was accompanied by a drum fire of rocket threats against the United States, and all of the countries in which the United States bases its military forces. And this supposed shift in military power is not unrelated to a vision of a future, totally communist world, whether this be single or many-centred. Many American and British writers recently have assured us that the Soviet Union is a *status quo* power, a "have" or satisfied power. This is all very well, but Chairman Khrushchev did not seem to know it. The *status quo* he was looking for seemed to be, as he had told it to Walter Lippmann, the *status quo post* rather than *ante* a major transformation. And there is no evidence that Khrushchev's successors look on the matter more comfortably for the West. To say that they would prefer this to be a peaceful transformation and indeed believe that it may well be, does not exclude latent military power as a major element in the expected transformation. Otherwise one would have to count every acquiescence to a threat of force as a peaceful change. Latent or actual communist military force monitored the early take-overs in Eastern Europe at the end of the war and prevented a reversal of the revolutions in 1953 and 1956. The possibility of its use defined the rules of behaviour both for internal opposition and outside aid. The possible use or threat to use military force is an operative element in many political transformations. In any case, it is apparent that the military build-up in Cuba had a considerable number of entwined political-military functions.

First it should be recalled that the introduction of strategic bombardment vehicles, MRBMs, IRBMs, and IL 28s capped a vast piling up, started considerably earlier, of active defences and ground forces which could be used to defend Cuba against internal as well as external attack, and the building of a base in Cuba which could serve as a centre of weapons transfer and material aid to insurgency in Latin America. From the standpoint of the Soviet Union the purposes of such a build-up partially coincide with some of the Cuban interests we have sketched. The important split between the Russians and the Red Chinese is not accurately represented as an ideological contrast between the foreswearing of any use of revolutionary violence by the Russians and its reckless advocacy by the Chinese. There are of course important differences in national interests. But the Chinese are considerably less reckless and the Russians more flexible and opportunistic than the conventional picture suggests.

Specifically for the Russians, the military build-up was in part a reaffirmation of the relationship between Russia and Cuba, a healing of wounds after the rift in March, 1962, that had resulted in the flight of Escalante, the old line Communist Party bureaucrat. It was a visible demonstration to those who were unaligned or falling out of line that for a small power to line up with the Soviet Union even near the centre of American power was safe, that a changeover to communism would not be reversed and that the power of the Soviet Union was committed as safeguard against any threat of reversal. More than this, by successfully defying the United States, forcing it to accept this major move into Cuba, the Soviet Union could powerfully influence the expectations of the rest of the world, most obviously those of the Latin Americans, but also those expectations and hopes that affect the outcome in Berlin and in more remote regions of Southeast and Southern Asia. And the expectations affected were specifically about relative strength and the will to use that strength. The large-scale Russian introduction of nuclear bombardment vehicles would have appeared also directly to answer the persuasive official American analyses of US superiority published in 1961 and 1962. The tendencies toward division within the communist world only reinforced some of these purposes. For the move was a Soviet blow in competition with the Chinese for leadership of the Socialist countries, and for leading the way in transforming the uncommitted world—and eventually that part of the world now committed to what they regard as the wrong side.

We have been discussing functions objectively served rather than Soviet conscious motivation, which must necessarily remain obscure. If, for example, the move had been successful, if the Soviet Union had gone before the United Nations to defend it, and the United States had acquiesced in the accomplished fact, it might have served any or all of the preceding military-political functions. On the other hand, if the success had been less complete, if the United States had not acquiesced, Soviet withdrawal might then have exacted as a price American withdrawal from some of its military bases on the territory of allies. The tentative skirmishing in the Khrushchev-Kennedy correspondence on the Turkish-Cuban base swap indicated one line of Soviet interest. But elimination of military bases is a directly military as well as political fact. This has been somewhat obscured, because the significance of overseas bases themselves for the 1960s has been understood only in a rather cloudy and sometimes quite erroneous fashion in the current Western discussions. How about the Cuban bombardment bases themselves? Some commentators have stated in rather unqualified fashion that they had essentially no military worth.[18]

[18] See, for example, *The New Republic,* 3 November, 1962, pp. 3ff; *The Reporter,* 22 November, 1962, pp. 21ff; *The Bulletin of the Atomic Scientists,* Vol. 19 (February, 1963), pp. 8ff.

Perhaps the first thing to be said is that it is not very sensible to talk with great confidence on these subjects. Responsible judgement here is difficult even with complete access to privileged information. The classified data are uncertain, the public data still more so, and few of the commentators have looked carefully at the quantitative implications of even the public data. Many who doubted the Russians would install bombardment vehicles in Cuba simply took at face value Chairman Khrushchev's statement that such weapons would add nothing to the capabilities provided by their intercontinental rockets. And then when it was clear that Khrushchev had gambled a great deal on precisely such installations, they persisted in dismissing their military significance. As we have already suggested, such bases have a variety of functions, but Khrushchev's gamble should at least have raised some doubts in the minds of those who dismiss their strategic value out of hand.

Part of the confusion comes from the fact that the military value of these Russian installations was not likely to consist in their efficiency as an addition to the Russian deterrent to American nuclear attack. Because of their proximity, their known position, and their lack of shelter, warning, or protected reliable communications, they would not have been hard to eliminate in an opening blow, nor would they have severely complicated an attack by a large reliable missile force;[19] and so they were not likely to be an economic way to increase a Russian second strike capability. The more likely strategic value concerned their significance for a possible Russian preclusive first-strike, as weapons that, in case of need during a grave crisis of escalation, would help to blunt an American retaliation. Resolution of such an issue would involve a detailed analysis of the entire complex mechanism of American retaliation, as it existed in 1962, including not merely the vehicles (that is, the missiles and aircraft), their physical disposition, their protection and degree of readiness, but also the system for commanding and controlling their response and penetrating enemy defences. For good reason, data on this subject are not publicly available. And overall statements on capability by public officials necessarily must be designed not simply to convey information to the public, important though that is, but also to limit information to the enemy and to affect his estimates favourably to ourselves. A resolution of this complex issue cannot therefore be made one way or the other. Even the much simpler partial question, the comparative vulnerability of our bombardment vehicles to distant as distinct from close, land-based attack, is necessarily shrouded with secrecy.

---

[19] During the 1950s the belief was widespread that even very vulnerable unprotected bases, if widely separated, would present insuperable co-ordination problems for a missile attack. . . .

Recognition of these limitations on analysis is the beginning of wisdom.

Take the partial problem of protecting the vehicles against the initial blow, from far-off or near-by. This is a quantitative matter demanding more than the standard caution. The probability that a vehicle will survive depends among other things on the number of attacking vehicles, their reliability, their average aiming accuracy, the kiloton yield of their nuclear warheads, and the degree of resistance of the vehicles under attack. This dependence moreover is not simply linear. The number of weapons, for example, required to destroy a vehicle sheltered to a sufficient degree will within relevant limits vary as the square of the average aiming accuracy. That is, double the inaccuracy and four times the number of attacking vehicles are required; triple the inaccuracy and nearly ten times the number of attackers are needed. Requirements are sensitive also to yield and degree of resistance, though less so. Changes in requirement are something less than proportionate to changes in yield or resistance: they vary as the two-thirds power: if a shelter is 8 or 27 times harder, the number of attackers required for a given probability of destruction would increase by factors of 4 or 9 respectively. But the average inaccuracy, for example, of even our own weapons can only be uncertainly estimated with complete access to classified tests. Our estimates of the performance of Russian weapons must be still more uncertain. Estimates are in any case not public and are frequently misrepresented with great confidence in the press. Moreover they change rather rapidly. A careful reading of the public press will confirm that the publicly stated average inaccuracies of bombardment missiles have decreased in the last few years by very large amounts; public estimates have been divided by at least five. Yet a factor of 3 reduction in inaccuracy can lower requirements to destroy hard targets by a factor of 9; a factor of 5 reduction, by 25. Even estimates of the number of vehicles of various types in the Russian force, we know from experience, have been in error. And the errors have not always been in one direction. The Cuban example illustrates some of the uncertainties. Here in a small area close by, under the most intense and continuous air reconnaissance, we counted some 30 missiles; and the Russians removed 42.[20] These comments suggest the limits of our own discussion.

The point to be made then is that some of these sensitive performance characteristics for the offensive vary with distance and improve significantly with close proximity: the important parameter of guidance accuracy, for example. Reliability is another performance

---

[20] ". . . we never knew how many missiles were brought into Cuba. The Soviets said there were 42. We have counted 42 going out. We saw fewer than 42." Roswell L. Gilpatric, 11 November, 1962. ABC's Issues and Answers, telecast.

characteristic which can improve with the simplified missiles possible at close range. A typically blithe argument assessing the military worth of Cuban bases states that while accuracy is improved in the shorter ranges, on the other hand bomb yields are necessarily smaller. Unfortunately, as we have indicated, changes in accuracy affect requirements much more sensitively than changes in yield. And, what is more, there is no law of nature suggesting that a missile payload declines at shorter ranges. For a given thrust, other things being equal, the opposite is true. It is possible to throw larger payloads at shorter distances. All of this is relevant for an exclusive choice between distant and close-in attack.

However, the second point to be noted is that *in the short run* this was not the choice open to the Russians. In the long run they could choose to build intercontinental missiles and base them in Russia, say, or spend an equal amount of resources for missiles based in Cuba. But in the years 1962 and 1963 the Russian bombardment force capable of reaching the United States was sharply limited. The missiles they sent to Cuba were a net addition to this force, since, based in Russia or in one of the European satellites, they could not reach the United States. Moreover the number of MRBMs—48—and the IRBMs—apparently between 24 and 32—which were already installed or on the way[21] was quite sizeable in relation to the public Western and American government estimates of the Russian intercontinental missile force and approximately equalled the Institute of Strategic Studies' estimate of 75 Soviet ICBMs.[22]

Third, our short run need not be so short as to stop in mid-December, 1962—the time the Department of Defence indicated as the operational date for the IRBMs of 2200 nautical mile range. In fact, it appears that the Russians had in addition to the roughly 75 medium and intermediate range missiles shipped to Cuba in 1962 hundreds more that could acquire by location in Cuba the ability to bomb American targets. The ISS estimate suggests a force of MRBMs alone ten times as large as the total number of MRBMs and IRBMs emplaced in Cuba, and beyond this, a growing total force of IRBMs. Further shipments of medium and intermediate range missiles could have been installed in Cuba, if the United States offered no interference, with the same impressive speed that characterized the installation of the first 75. The MRBMs were activated "with the

[21] On the CIA and DOD public accounts, there were 48 MRBMs for which launch positions had been prepared (there were 24 launchers). For the IRBMs, 17 erectors were counted on the way out, with the 17th reckoned by the Americans as a spare. Briefing, 6 February, 1963, by Mr. John Hughes, Special Assistant to General Carroll, reprinted in *Department of Defence Appropriations for* 1964. US Congress, House of Representatives 88th Session, Part I, Washington, DC, 1963.
[22] "The Military Balance," 1962–1963.

passage of hours.'' (For example, two sets of photographs separated by less than 24 hours, displayed an increase of perhaps 50 per cent in the amount of equipment.[23] There has been almost universal agreement on the logistic efficiency of the Soviet operation.) Such a change in location might have corrected at a stroke what appears to be a great imbalance in the composition of the Russian strategic force: it is heavily weighted towards attacking European theatre targets and by comparison neglects American forces based outside Europe, though these make up the principal retaliatory strength of the alliance.

Fourth, the axis of attack from Cuba outflanked the Ballistic Missile Early Warning System. Unlike submarine launched missiles, of the range estimated to be available to the Soviet Union, these Cuban based missiles would have covered essentially all of the United States, with little or no warning.[24] The co-ordination problems for the Russians are less severe than were suggested by some writers at the time of the crisis, and in fact on the whole before attacking it is easier to communicate at a great distance with land based missiles than with distant submerged submarines.

All of the above is in the short or fairly short run. For a long run in which the Russians were free to spend resources, to build new ICBMs based in Russia or new medium or intermediate range ballistic missiles based in Cuba, the choice this opens up to them cannot be dismissed out of hand. As some of the commentators suggested, the shorter range missiles are cheaper. If they are drastically cheaper for a desired level and type of performance, they would offer the Russians a significantly larger destruction capability for a given budget. Some long run mixture of close and distant basing then might be optimal for a Russian force, providing their decision makers with an improved option in a crisis to strike first.

In sum, Cuba offered to the Russians the means for a very large and immediate expansion of the forces capable of hitting elements of the American retaliatory force based in the United States. Moreover further large increments were readily available. The effect of such a rapid increase in power on the actual military balance could not be lightly dismissed; and the political uses of even an apparent change seemed evident.

[23] According to a Defence Department spokesman, 22 October, 1962.

[24] Doubts about this coverage persist in some European and American analyses. They appear to be based on a poorly reasoned uncritically sceptical commentary by Roger Hagan and Bart Bernstein, ''The Military Value of Missiles in Cuba,'' *Council for Correspondence Newsletter,* 22 November, 1962. Hagan and Bernstein relied on newspaper and magazine accounts of intelligence data that themselves confused the MRBMs and IRBMs installed in Cuba with the shorter range T-1 and T-2 and they misread the public statements about the expected operational-date and number of IRBMs.

THE VIEW FROM THE UNITED STATES

The sudden installation of a sizeable number of nuclear bombardment vehicles in Cuba, and the long-term prospects of such a base very near American shores, offered much foundation for sober thought about significant alterations in the military balance. This balance is not a simple one-dimensional matter and neither were the effects of such an installation. However, as we have already indicated, the Russian military build-up touched many problems of defence other than the preservation of a United States second-strike capability in the event of a thermonuclear war. It affected the political and military stability of Cuba and Latin America. And President Kennedy was acutely conscious of the political effects of even the *appearance* of a vast Soviet increase in military power. "The Cuban effort," he commented after the crisis, with Russian deception in mind, "has made it more difficult for us to carry out any successful negotiations, because this was an effort to materially change the balance of power . . . not that [the Soviets] were intending to fire [the missiles] . . . But it would have politically changed the balance of power. It would have appeared to, and appearances contribute to reality."[25]

One of the least understood aspects of the crisis from the standpoint of American as well as Russian interests concerned the role of overseas bases. It was the building of a Russian overseas base of course that prompted the crisis. Our discovery of the installation was preceded by Khrushchev's public deprecation of its utility, his statement that it would add nothing to his long-range rockets based in the Soviet Union. In Western discussion, during the crisis and since, of concessions or disengagements, the possibility of giving up American bases overseas was prominent. The issue was somewhat blurred by the focus on the Turkish-based *Jupiters* whose removal had been planned before the crisis and ironically was delayed by Soviet demand for their removal during the crisis itself. For good reason. Whether or not the *Jupiter* installations were useful, it was apparent that their removal under pressure would be a very different thing from the dismantling of the *Thors* in England, initiated sometime before because they were not worth their keep. (In fact one of the writers of this essay had written a series of critical analyses of the *Thors* and *Jupiters* beginning in 1957; but was clear that October 1962 would have been a poor date for a change.) In any case, the deficiencies of the *Thor* and *Jupiter* bases should not be taken as an example of the general worthlessness or for that matter of the lessening value of overseas bases.

In the West, liberal and conservative opinion sometimes meet on common ground in the depreciation of the role of overseas bases in the

---

[25] *Washington Post,* 18 December, 1962. The right contrast with mere appearance is not a steady intent to fire, but a contingent choice in future crises.

1960s. Suggestions that modern developments in missilery make them unnecessary might be quoted from the surviving massive retaliationists, but also from *The Liberal Papers*.[26]

Such suggestions are a vast over-simplification of the military implications of current and future states of the art of war. It is true that the deterrent function of some American weapons in a big thermonuclear war was much more dependent on overseas bases when the predominant part of the US force was the short-legged B-47. However, thermonuclear war is not the only problem of national and alliance defence or of the defence of non-aligned powers. US defence programmes have stressed more and more the threat of non-nuclear, conventional and unconventional warfare—moreover, thermonuclear war itself is a lot more complicated than this deprecation of overseas bases suggests.

In brief, overseas bases have vital roles in a possible central war in the 1960s and 1970s—both for deterrence and for limiting damage in case deterrence fails. They do dilute and can dilute even more Soviet offensive preparations by posing the need to set up a *variety* of defensive barriers. They are an important source of continuing information on the enemy. They can be made to complicate the design of his attack —for example, with the extension of the present bomb alarm system. Under several plausible contingencies of outbreak they can help spoil his attack. All this for a thermonuclear war.

But even more obviously today overseas bases have a dominant role in non-nuclear wars. They affect the speed with which the West can react and the cost and size of reaction to aggressions in remote parts of the world. The role of Japan in fighting the Korean war, the movements in May 1962 from various stations to Thailand, and later movements of weapons from Thailand in support of the Indians in their battle with the Chinese all illustrate the continuing importance of overseas bases.

For the Russians also overseas bases in the 1960s and 1970s might conceivably come to have an important role. And this role would have principally to do with non-nuclear internal and external wars. Dr. Guy Pauker suggested a while ago that the massive Russian military aid to Indonesian or other overseas base areas might be the only way Russia has of influencing events in Southeast Asia directly rather than

---

[26] "The United States may find that it will no longer need bases around the periphery of the USSR and Communist China, and that instead, pending effective arms reduction, it should place its chief reliance on long-range missiles to be delivered from its own territory," p. 268, *The Liberal Papers*, ed. James Roosevelt, Anchor Books, Doubleday and Co., Garden City, New York, 1962.

And "The question would then arise whether the security of Japan would be more effectively safeguarded by the use of United States long-range missiles in case of an emergency than by the presence of American troops and/or weapons on Japanese territory." p. 269, *ibid.*

through the agency of its quarrelsome Chinese sometime partner and rival. Whatever the case for the Soviet Union, recent American policy unambiguously requires distant logistic support. The explicit shift in the last four years to stress conventional and unconventional non-nuclear war makes it more necessary than ever, and yet the importance of overseas bases seems to be less and less understood. Perhaps the recent troubles in India and Malaysia, with the demands they may place on British bases east of Suez as well as some American ones, will make their worth more generally appreciated. Less than nuclear contests remote from one or both of the great powers may nevertheless engage their interests in conflict, but such contests are hard to influence without overseas bases.

Our discussion of Cuba suggests that not all the interests of the United States conflict with those of the Soviet Union. Mr. Khrushchev and Mr. Kennedy were both clear about their mutual interest in keeping Castro's finger off a nuclear trigger. On the other hand, the view from the Soviet Union indicates that, in spite of talk about "overriding" interests of both sides in avoiding nuclear war, there are many fundamental points at issue between the great powers. And while there is hardly a doubt that both sides would be worse off in the event of a nuclear war, and that they do and should spend considerable energies and resources in avoiding it, the dubious note in the phrase "overriding interests . . ." is struck by the adjective "overriding." It suggests that the opposing interests are negligible, well understood, and easily resolved or likely to be resolved in the near-term future, if only, we are told, the politicians are sincere.

President Kennedy did not take the Soviet build-up in Cuba as an act unrelated to the future of the world. He related it to Chairman Khrushchev's desire to see the world transformed, to sponsor struggles of liberation, and to revise what the Russians regard as "abnormal" situations, such as West Berlin. In his October 22 speech announcing the Amerian blockade of arms shipments to Cuba, President Kennedy warned that any hostile acts at other points on the globe (he mentioned West Berlin specifically) would meet with equal American determination, and he called upon Mr. Khrushchev to "abandon this course of world domination."

The encounter over this small island, then, on the American view, had to do with the future of the world. However, in this encounter, not only Cuba, but the rest of the aligned and non-aligned world—the OAS, NATO, China, the United Nations—were subordinated to a passive role. The chief actors were the opposing nuclear powers. Castro could obstruct, delay and complicate the resolution of the issue, but in the end he was hardly able to affect it centrally. Members of the OAS and NATO were apprised of the President's decision to institute a quarantine a few hours before it was announced to the public, and the actual signing of the Presidential proclamation of quarantine, was delayed to obtain the formal approval of the OAS members. These friends of the United States without exception rallied to its support and in the week of unrelenting pressure to get the missiles out, their consensus played a part. To assess its importance one should contemplate what might have been the effect of dissent. Can we be sure that a welter of doubts and alternative proposals might not have altered Khrushchev's estimate of the singleness of American resolve? If it had, the crisis might not have ended where it did.

Mr. Khrushchev had worse luck in his dealings with some of his allies. But in the end it was President Kennedy's and Chairman Khrushchev's decisions that determined events. The difficulty in sharing such momentous decisions raises important domestic issues in a democracy, but it has even more obvious problems for allies whose fate may be affected by those decisions.

Nonetheless what transpired was by no means a game of nuclear "Chicken," as the advocates of unilateral disarmament suggest; both President Kennedy and Mr. Khrushchev showed acute consciousness and care about the risks. (Some sober and excellent analysts accept the analogy of "Chicken," but the differences seem to us more significant than the identities. Bertrand Russell, who introduced the parallel in the 1950s as a paradigm of international behaviour today, meant precisely to suggest the recklessness of the statesmen, and the triviality and childishness of what was at issue—a kind of loss of face with the other children in the neighbourhood.) Nor was Cuba a case in which there was no danger of military action. There were possibilities of escalation, of the spread and intensification of violence. The risks of nuclear war are never zero. But the President was aware also of the risks of escalation in *inaction*. Inaction in Cuba would have invited, for example, a spiralling series of actions over Berlin.

From the timing of Mr. Khrushchev's move in Cuba it seems likely that he was conscious of the relation between Cuba and a climax to East-West disagreements over Berlin. President Kennedy at any rate was explicit about the connection. Retreat from a prominent public and formal stand that the United States had taken as recently as mid-September would have invited Mr. Khrushchev to believe that the United States would retreat also in Berlin. (This might also have come to be the belief of the allies of the United States.) However, the risks that Mr. Khrushchev would have undertaken in Berlin are, for a variety of reasons, considerably larger than the risks he undertook in Cuba. The government of the United States had tried to make it clear that if the Soviet Union moved on Berlin or on the Central European front, then NATO in spite of local communist superiority, would throw into the breach a very large conventional force, including perhaps a half dozen American divisions. If these were destroyed or in danger of destruction, it is evident that the risks of an American nuclear response would be raised enormously.

One cliche and over-simple view that seems to have a special appeal in crisis has it that the threat of force or the use of a low level of violence, including even a partial blockade, leads naturally to higher levels of violence. But in Cuba a very rudimentary and limited use of force, reversed the direction, started it down. There was in fact at no time during the crisis any suggestion on the part of President Kennedy and his immediate staff that this was a careless game of bluff, in which they incautiously might let a war get started by chance or unauthorized acts. On the contrary there was every attempt to resist the act of desperation proposed from both the left and the right. "We have been determined," President Kennedy said on 22 October, "not to be diverted from our central concerns by mere irritants, and fanatics." Newspaper accounts during the crisis and a Senate Report published at the end of January, 1963, stressed the extreme concern of the President and his executive committee with even the minute details of actions taken at the lowest levels of government.[27] There was no dearth of management of the crisis.

Some of the statements of President Kennedy and even more those of Chairman Khrushchev may be a little misleading in this respect. In the case of Mr. Khrushchev, up to a certain point he may have wanted to convey an impression of recklessness. When confronted with the threat of having a Russian freighter boarded and searched, he asserted that this "would make talks useless" and bring into action the "forces and laws . . . of war";[28] it would have "irretrievably fatal consequences."[29]

In other words he was indicating to President Kennedy that interception of a freighter would involve thermonuclear massive retaliation, either as a deliberate act of the Russians or because he would not be able to restrain and control his own forces. Not he, but the laws of war would be in charge. After the crisis had receded, moreover, Chairman Khrushchev was anxious to represent his retreat as a statesman's action to save the world from the imminent peril, "the direct threat of world thermonuclear war which arose in the Caribbean area."[30] "If one or the other side had not shown restraint, not done everything needed to avert the outbreak of war, an explosion of irreparable consequences would have followed."[31] He made more than a suggestion

---

[27] Senator Henry M. Jackson (Democrat, State of Washington), *Los Angeles Times*, 29 January, 1963, and "The Administration of National Security: Basic Issues" for the Committee on Government Operations, 1963.

[28] Message to President Kennedy on 27 October, 1962: "you, in your statement, said that the main aim is not only to come to an agreement [but also to] undertake measures to prevent a confrontation of our ships and thus aggravate the crisis and thus [ignite the fires] of a military conflict in such a confrontation, after which any talks would be already useless as other forces and laws would go into action, the laws of war." *New York Times*, 28 October, 1962.

[29] *Ibid.*

[30] Speech of 12 December, 1962, to the Supreme Soviet, *New York Times*, 13 December, 1962.

[31] *Ibid.*

after the event that the danger of recklessness arose from "the ruling circle of the United States who are rightly called 'madmen.' The madmen insisted and insist now on starting a war as soon as possible against the Soviet Union."[32] Mr. Khrushchev's open and bitter contest with the Chinese and Albanian Communists also required pointed reference to the imminent dangers of thermonuclear war. However, at the peak of the crisis and in fact in the same letter in which he tried for the last time to suggest an inevitable and uncontrollable thermonuclear response to the interception of a Soviet freighter, Chairman Khrushchev made it very plain that he was in careful, thorough and self-conscious charge of the decision on whether or not to respond with nuclear weapons. It was here in fact that he in particular stressed that the Cuban missiles were under his control. And in the following day he emphasized again that "the Soviet government will not allow itself to be provoked."[33] Finally in his *post-mortem* speech to the Supreme Soviet on 12 December, 1962, he indicated that both the Russian and American "sides displayed a sober approach, and took into account that unless such steps were taken that could help overcome the dangerous development of events, a third World War might break out." The madmen in the ruling circle of the United States then were very sober lunatics; and the sober Russians understood that.

Some of President Kennedy's statements in the crisis and after may also have overstated the likelihood of a nuclear exchange. He was appropriately anxious to express the gravity of his concern about such a catastrophe. Theodore Sorensen makes clear that President Kennedy was aware of the pitfalls of public utterance at this time. "His warnings on the presence of Soviet missiles in Cuba had to be sufficiently sombre to enlist support around the world without creating panic here at home."[34] And so on 22 October, 1962, he talked of the world "at the abyss of destruction." In his acceptance of Mr. Khrushchev's retreat on 28 October, 1962, he seemed also to accept the validity of Mr. Khrushchev's earlier threat of uncontrollability. "Developments were approaching a point where events could have become unmanageable." Though control was evident in every one of his moves, President Kennedy's statements did not stress in words that he was in control. It has therefore been possible to misconstrue just what were the risks in the crisis.

The matter is of great importance. The fact that Cuba could be isolated makes a great contrast with the problem in Central Europe. But even on the Central European front American policy differs

[32] *Ibid.*
[33] Message to President Kennedy of 28 October, 1962.
[34] *Decision-Making in the White House,* Columbia University Press, New York, 1963, p. 47.

markedly from that of a dictator who uses a reputation for irresponsibility and apparent willingness to usher in *Goetterdaemmerung* for even minor gains. Threats of uncontrollability should be administered by prescription, against special dangers, and in small doses. Its use except *in extremis* is not compatible with a reputation for being both sane and meaning what one says.

In fact the main risks were of a local, non-nuclear action involving the United States and Russian forces. The possibilities of isolating a limited conflict have seldom been clearer. The situation is very different from Berlin. Remote islands are better than enclaves in satellite territory in this respect. Cuba, surrounded by water rather than East Germans, very distant from the centre of Russian conventional power, did not represent, nor was it contiguous to, any interests that the Soviet Union had dominated for many years. How likely was Chairman Khrushchev to launch missiles at the United States to retrieve a gamble for a quick expansion of this communist foothold in the Western Hemisphere, itself a windfall? Retreat in fact has not even meant the loss of the foothold.

What was threatened was a local non-nuclear action, a measure of very limited violence, only the boarding of ships. On the staircase of ascending steps in the use of force there would have been many landings, many decision points, at which either side could choose between climbing higher or moving down. The United States' nuclear retaliatory force would have made a Soviet missile strike against the United States catastrophic for Russia. But the United States also had an immense local superiority in conventional forces. The Soviet Union clearly would have lost the non-nuclear exchange. Chairman Khrushchev stepped down to avoid a clash of conventional forces in which he would have lost. To avoid this level of loss he would have had irresponsibly to risk very much higher levels.

Some distinguished American analysts tell us that our local superiority in conventional force was an inessential convenience affecting our self-confidence, but not Khrushchev's. Without a deep psychoanalysis of the former Chairman, this would be rather hard to prove or disprove. However, so bald a separation of the determinants of decision on the two sides seems most implausible. Each side strained to affect the anticipations of the other by act as well as word, and its own expectations depended in part on how it read the other's. The American leadership knew that Khrushchev had no basis for confidence in the outcome of any clash with conventional arms in the Caribbean; and a world to lose if he resorted to nuclear weapons.

Inevitably, the question of how nuclear and how conventional arms figured in forcing Khrushchev's withdrawal was much disputed once the crisis had passed, although it is doubtful whether many of the disputants changed their views as a result either of the crisis or the post-crisis debate. Witnesses at the Congressional hearings in the following spring at any rate interpreted events according to their predispositions.[35] Those who had held before the crisis that a strategic nuclear threat can credibly and safely deter all but rather minor border incursions testified that "strategic superiority" was the major factor forcing Khrushchev's withdrawal. Those who had believed that nuclear force—in particular a clear-cut second-strike nuclear capability—is vital, but inadequate as a response to an important range of provocations, took the withdrawal as illustrating "the cutting edge" of the conventional sword. This single encounter where the United States had both the capability to dominate in a conventional conflict and also to inflict overwhelming nuclear damage could not demonstrate once and for all that conventional superiority will always have a major utility; still less could it show that it might easily be dispensed with. Witnesses such as Secretary McNamara who valued and had greatly increased useable conventional capability in the preceding two years, were in charge of controlling the risks during the crisis. They deployed and prepared to use a vast conventional force, including several hundred thousand men poised for invasion. While continuing to deter nuclear action by the Russians, they prepared a mounting sequence of threats short of nuclear war. The dispensability of these moves can only be conjectured. Relying on more desperate threats might have worked, but would clearly have been a greater gamble.

The relevance to Berlin of the Cuban crisis was, as we have said, immediately recognized by the President and the other members of the EXCOM, for a retreat in Cuba would have been evidence of a likely retreat in Berlin. But our firmness in Cuba cannot conclusively show the opposite. Some Americans are concerned to play down our conventional superiority in Cuba lest it suggest, illogically to be sure, that we would be firm *only* where we have conventional superiority. But for us as for the Russians the stakes as well as the risks are larger in Berlin.

Not that the risks were small in Cuba. The menace of actual conflict between American and Russian forces even in battle with conventional weapons was emphasized by the long history of debate on the massive retaliation theory. As General Maxwell Taylor's account makes clear, much of the doctrinal dispute among the Joint Chiefs had taken the form of a seemingly scholastic argument over the definition of "general war."[36] "General war" had been defined as a conflict between the forces of the United States and those of the Soviet Union, and the definition assumed and made explicit that nuclear weapons

[35] *Military Procurement Authorization, Fiscal Year 1964*, Committee on Armed Services, US Senate, 88th Congress, First Session, 1963, pp. 507, 896 and *passim*, Cf. also *Hearings on Military Posture*, House Armed Services Committee, 1963.

[36] *The Uncertain Trumpet*, Harper Brothers, New York (1959), 1960, pp. 7ff, 39, 117.

would be used from the outset. The definition was an attempt to enforce by semantics, so to speak, a belief that any hostile contact between American and Russian troops would bring immediate nuclear devastation, and so to discourage such a contact. But in Cuba it was apparent that conventional attack on the Russian missile bases was one of the alternatives contemplated and that therefore the United States was separating the decision to do battle with the Russians from the decision to initiate a nuclear war. Decisions to board Russian ships were even more obviously kept distinct from a nuclear decision.

Chairman Khrushchev was right in his later assertion that the United States and the Soviet Union were both in full control of their nuclear forces.

CONTROL AND AUTOMATIC STAIRS

We stress the point only because, in this respect, some of the American official statements made at the height of the crisis did less than justice to American policy. Any suggestion that the United States could not control its responses even in boarding a Russian freighter, would be bound to raise disturbing questions at home. And under some circumstances it would be self-defeating. If Chairman Khrushchev had thought that American decision makers themselves believed their next move would push events out of control, that they had, in the legal phrase, the last clear chance to avoid nuclear war, he might very well have doubted the desperate move and so have been rather less deterred and less alarmed than the American public and America's allies. He might have found it inconceivable that the American President would deliberately let matters get unmanageable. In fact well before the Cuban crisis the President and Secretary McNamara and Secretary Rusk had declared, and their subordinates had elaborated, a thoughtful doctrine of controlled response, up to and including the conduct of a nuclear war. Yet, as we have mentioned, President Kennedy's statement of 22 October, excellent as it was on the whole, focussed, for understandable reasons, on "the abyss of destruction." And in attempting to get across the essential message of the American nuclear guarantee for neighbours in Latin America, it indicated that "any nuclear missile launched from Cuba against any nation in the Western Hemisphere" would evoke "a *full* retaliatory response upon the Soviet Union" (our italics). This does not sound like a controlled response. The attempt, it appears, was to say that the United States would respond to a missile against its neighbours as it would respond to one against itself. This latter policy would leave open the possibility of controlled reaction. The United States has made clear that a single nuclear missile launched against the United States need not trip an uncontrolled "full" response.

However, it was even more important to make clear, and in American behaviour it was evident, that the United States did not exclude the possibility of control in the non-nuclear spectrum. In fact it insisted upon it. It responded in a carefully limited way to an aggression which involved the installation, but not the firing, of a nuclear weapon. Against such a move the Cuban crisis demonstrated the relevance and the adequacy of the lowest non-nuclear moves in an ascending series of non-nuclear threats and actions: the threat to board and search freighters for military equipment, a single actual boarding of a chartered Lebanese ship, the imposition of a selective economic blockade, a general blockade, the threat or the actual use of bombing with high explosives against strategic missile bases, the threat or actual use of paratroops, and so forth. The later steps in the sequence never had to be more than latent. But one of the reasons the limited American threat worked was that the United States was willing to take the next steps, if necessary, and had the power to do so—to make each next step less profitable for the Soviet Union.

Before the crisis, the alternatives for policy were discussed in terms of a few bare possibilities: a pure American military invasion, a total blockade, or doing nothing. In the crisis it appeared the world was richer in alternatives than had been conceived by extremists of the left or right. There is a good deal between doing nothing and all-out nuclear war, and an appropriate intermediate response could make a nuclear war less rather than more likely. President Kennedy observed that these alternatives became apparent in the course of five days of discussion, that without this time for hammering out alternatives, he might have chosen less wisely and more extremely.[37] The history of this crisis should be an important corrective for the loose assumption that the only time available for decision in the nuclear age is 15 minutes—a magic number supposed to represent the time from radar intercept to impact of an ICBM following a least energy path.

Professor Richard Neustadt, who has written most perceptively about the use, the limits, and the risks of using American presidential power, has taken the Cuban missile confrontation to illustrate the President's extreme awareness of the new dimensions of these risks, of the fact that somewhere in a succession of decisions he may make one that can neither be reversed nor repaired.[38] It has probably always been true that at some time in a sequence of diplomatic acts, warnings of possible military actions, and military acts themselves, statesmen have felt "things in the saddle," events taking over. It then becomes extremely unlikely that adversaries will back away from the contest or its intensification. Even though the new level of violence is likely to leave both of them worse off than *before* the sequence of threats and

[37] *Washington Post*, 18 December, 1962.
[38] *Administration of National Security. Hearings Before the Sub-Committee on National Security Staffing and Operations of the Committee on Government Operations*, United States Senate, 88th Congress, 1st Session. Part I, 1963. p. 76ff.

pre-war manoeuvres had started, nonetheless, there may be some point of no return in the sequence. At that point the outcome may appear to be better than the risk of stopping. The fact that today decisions taken in crisis might precipitate a disaster on a scale without precedent in history is sobering.

There is a sense of course in which any large scale war does enormous, irreparable harm. Population growth and economic recovery after the war replace the lives lost, the wealth annihilated and the suffering, only in a statistical sense that ignores precisely who died and what treasures were destroyed. Some nuclear conflicts might start by miscalculation and end by being quickly brought under control, and conceivably could do less material damage than World War II and I. Nonetheless such a standard is terrible enough and a nuclear war could be enormously worse. This new sense of the possibility of irreparable harm says a good deal about the psychological burden of the Presidency. And not only the Presidency. The Chairman of the CPSU explicitly referred to the ''irreparable'' consequences of a failure in restraint by either side. It makes clear why neither Nikita Khrushchev nor John Kennedy behaved like the irrational juvenile delinquents who are sometimes presumed to occupy the seats of power today, strapped by their seatbelts in a carefree game of Chicken.

Where the alternative is to be ruled by events with such enormous consequences, the head of a great state is likely to examine his acts of choice in crisis and during it to subdivide these possible acts in ways that make it feasible to continue exercising choice. This sort of behaviour does not fit an increasingly popular and professional picture which has it that political leaders may be thoughtful, responsible and close to reality in between crises, but overreact passionately during the crises themselves. However, there is a good deal of professional evidence as well as common sense opinion to indicate that, as Dewey put it, when any thinking is going on, it is likely to be because there has been some trouble. Routine experience may lead us imperceptibly to ignore a slowly changing or suddenly new reality, but we do sometimes rise to a challenge with heightened alertness and an increased sense of responsibility, especially on matters of great moment. The behaviour of the decision makers in the Cuban crisis at any rate provides a counter example to a good many pessimistic predictions derived from studies by behavioural scientists concerned with reducing international tension.[39]

---

[39] Generalising from 1914, some studies predict that as tensions rise in a crisis, decision makers will tend to decide emotionally rather than by calculation. The range of alternatives they see will narrow and they will be less able to assess the likely consequences of each possible choice. They will see less time before the enemy strikes and this will lead to still greater tension, to a tendency to value early action and dislike delay, to depreciate the dangers of violent action and the rewards of non-violent action, and to

A process of escalation is usually thought of simply as an increase in violence growing out of a limited conflict in which an adversary may act to stave off his loss or an opponent's prospective success. The aspect of "escalators" that inspired its use in this connection, we suspect, is the fact that moving stairways carry a passenger on automatically without any effort of his will. However, as we have suggested there are down-escalators as well as up-escalators, and there are landings between escalators where one can decide to get off or to get on, to go up or down, or to stay there; or take the stairs. Just where automaticity or irreversibility takes over is an uncertain but vital matter, and that is one of the reasons a decision maker may want to take a breath at a landing to consider next steps. It is apparent from President Kennedy's own descriptions of the Cuban crisis as well as Mr. Sorensen's that he gave enormous value to the cautious weighing of alternatives made possible by the interval of almost a week; to the five or six days mentioned for hammering out the first decision. And the decision made was precisely one that left open a variety of choices. Finally the availability of less desperate choices than acquiescence or holocaust had been prepared before the crisis by the deliberate policy of preserving options, developing a force capable of flexible response.

One way in which the overhanging possibility of an irreversible disastrous decision might operate today is to bring on an immobility that, paradoxically, reduces the alternatives to a few extremes. The irreversible sequence might be started then by a desperate act to avoid the loss that looms in the extreme of retreat. But there is more than one way to arrive at a paralysis and gross reduction of choice. The opposite path, proceeding on the perception that commitment is inevitable, can advance commitment to a much earlier stage than necessary in the process of coercion and resisting coercion. This is the danger inherent in threats of massive retaliation. That war can be so massive a disaster tempts us to use the threat of this disaster to paralyse an adversary bent on aggression; but it may end in our own paralysis. The Cuban missile crisis at any rate illustrated an intensive search among alternatives to find a threat that could be executed with a minimal risk, and a slowly ascending sequence of threats which could not be challenged by the Soviet Union without making its position still worse.

accept suspicions and fears as facts. There predictions are necessarily somewhat vague. None of them, however, appears to have been borne out by the behavior of decision makers in the missile crisis. See *Content Analysis, a Handbook with Applications for the Study of International Crisis* by Robert C. North, Ole R. Holsti, M. George Zaninovich, and Dina A. Zinnes, Northwestern University Press, 1963, Appendix B, for the hypotheses derived from 1914 and contrast with materials derived from the Cuban crisis and presented by Holsti, North and Brody in *Peace Research Society (International) Papers*, Vol. 2, Oslo, 1965.

There is an important class of situations in which a crisis may be precipitated as the result of an unfounded or exaggerated mutual distrust. These are cases where, in the words of the most brilliant analyst of such reciprocal fears, "people may vaguely think they perceive that the situation is inherently explosive, and respond by exploding."[40] But some of the time guns go off because we do not know they are loaded; grenades explode because we think they are duds; or enemies attack because we are so sure they will not attack that we are unprepared for it. The Cuban missile crisis should remind us of these equally important situations in which an excess of trust or self-confidence causes the trouble, and a sharp awakening to the possibilities of explosion helps bring the trouble under responsible control. Tactics of deception typically attempt to induce trust where it is not warranted. Khruschev and Gromyko during the prelude to the crisis simply lied. And the traditional confidence man feeds on the gullibility and wishfulness of his target. "Never give a sucker an even break" evokes a long history of cases where it is not mutual distrust that is explosive, but fond belief on the one side, a willingness to exploit it on the other, and a violent sense of outrage by the victim at having his innocence exploited. But the victim need not explode. He can carefully signal the danger to his adversary.

The resolution of the missile crisis may be regarded as in the main a brilliant example of a successful communication of a precise and firm intention. However, in some of its aspects, and especially in its generation, the crisis illustrates the possibilities of miscommunication. Under other circumstances, such miscommunication might not have had so fortunate an ending. Moreover, the misunderstandings do not fit one current wishful stereotype: that our troubles stem only from our failure to realize how like us our adversaries really are. Our estimates and those of the Russians, just before the missile confrontation, resembled each other mainly in that they each too easily assumed an identity in modes of thought and valuation. They illustrate rather the difficulty one always has in breaking out of the circle of one's own notion of what is normal in national behaviour.

The missile crisis was precipitated by some poor Russian and American estimates of each other's willingness to take risks. The American leaders did not believe the Russians would be foolhardy enough, in the face of President Kennedy's explicit warning against it, to put into Cuba missiles which were capable of hitting the United States. The Russians on the other hand did not think the Americans would risk a direct confrontation.

The false estimates on both sides did not concern whether the United States had clearly warned the Russians not to put in place in

[40] T. C. Schelling, *The Strategy of Conflict*, p. 208.

Cuba surface-to-surface missiles with a significant capability to hit the United States. They had to do with Russian disbelief that the President would act in case they ignored his warning, and an American judgement that the Russians would recognize that the President meant what he said. Yet one curious aftermath of the crisis is a rewriting of history, especially in Europe, that questions not merely whether it was obvious that President Kennedy meant what he explicitly stated in September, but doubts even that he had said it.

The situation is somewhat confused by the interminable wrangle over the distinction between "offensive" and "defensive" weapons. There is of course no sharp distinction between the two and there are many interconnections. An aggressor can defend himself, limit the destruction wreaked against his own territory, among other subtler ways, by using surface-to-surface missiles or bombers to reduce his victim's retaliatory forces before they take off; and once his victim's retaliatory forces are launched on their way, he can use active and passive defences, such as surface-to-air missiles, jet fighters and civil defence to reduce his victim's retaliation further. Moreover, the Cuban surface-to-air missiles and fighters themselves illustrate that active defences can be used to prevent or to impede surveillance and so help to cover the build-up of a force of surface-to-surface missiles and manned bombers. Even the direct use of fighter aircraft or short-range missiles with the help of torpedo boats would provide some minimal capability to hit American coastal targets. All of this ignores still subtler interconnections between the threats or the use of "offensive" or "defensive" weapons.

However, the distinction the President made between offensive and defensive weapons served the purpose of warning well enough, because he made very clear what weapons he had in mind as "offensive." On 4 September he said, ". . . the Soviets have provided the Cuban government with a number of anti-aircraft defence missiles with a slant range of 25 miles which are similar to early models of our Nike. . . . There is no evidence . . . of the presence of offensive ground-to-ground missiles; or of other significant offensive capability either in Cuban hands or under Soviet direction and guidance. Were it to be otherwise, the gravest issues would arise."

In other words the President drew a line with a broad and hairy brush between offensive and defensive weapons in general, but he clearly classed Russian medium and intermediate range surface-to-surface missiles in the offensive category. Emplacing them in Cuba would be strategic trespass. Moreover, the Russians understood him. Their government authorized *Tass* to state on 11 September ". . . there is no need for the Soviet Union to shift its weapons . . . to any other country, for instance Cuba . . . the Soviet Union has rockets so powerful to carry . . . nuclear warheads that there is no need to search for sites for them beyond the boundaries of the Soviet Union . . . the Soviet Union has the capability from its own territory to render assistance to any peace-loving state and not only to Cuba."

The President knew that the message had been understood. He believed it would be respected. It was this last conviction, supported by Soviet reassurances, "both public and private, in September, that proved illusory in the following month. In President Kennedy's words,

> I don't think that we expected that he (Khrushchev) would put the missiles in Cuba, because it would have seemed such an imprudent action for him to take, as it was later proved. Now, he obviously must have thought that he could do it in secret and that the United States would accept it. So that he did not judge our intentions accurately.

The Americans assumed in short that the Russians understood that Americans are tolerant but cannot be pushed beyond a certain point, especially when that point has been clearly and publicly announced. But just how imprudent is was for the Russians to put missiles in Cuba depended on whether the Americans were willing to force a showdown. So the American estimate that the Russians would not emplace the missiles depended on an American judgement about how the Russians thought Americans would act. Moreover, there is no doubt that President Kennedy's judgement of the American character was right. His own behaviour, with its brief explosion of anger at Gromyko's continuing deception, and the bitter repetition in the 22 October speech "That statement was false" was in a long tradition of sharp moral reactions at confidence betrayed. In more controlled form, it repeated the indignation of acting Secretary Polk and President Wilson at the decoded German message showing that while the German foreign minister had been talking peace he had plotted to encourage a Mexican attack on the United States. Or the fury of Secretary Hull and President Roosevelt at the Japanese representatives Kurusu and Nomura at the time of Pearl Harbour.

On the other hand, to the Russians surely President Kennedy's response was an extraordinary over-reaction. Chairman Khrushchev had enunciated and withdrawn a succession of ultimata on Berlin beginning in 1958, and done so with distinct disappointment, but with comparative equanimity. He could hardly have understood either the enormous importance conferred by domestic party debate (with the Bay of Pigs disaster in the background) on the specific line the President had drawn between offensive and defensive weapons, or the great to-do over the deception. (Khrushchev's experience with cases in which Americans themselves had used deception might have suggested the accompanying sense of guilt and half-heartedness with which this is done. The American response to the shooting down of the U2 piloted by Powers in 1960 forms an interesting cultural contrast with the indignant denial by the Soviet government in the United Nations of actions revealed by the detailed reconnaissance photos of the missiles in Cuba.) Each side in short tended to project its own psychology or certain stereotypes about the behaviour of the other. The Russians acted on the assumption that the Americans were so driven by domestic politics as to be unlikely to react in any decisive way; or that they would act like Russians.

In the period of withdrawing the missiles, once again, Americans tended to project American behaviour on to the Russians. Just as they had exaggerated the Russian estimate of risks and underestimated Russian daring, they now overestimated Russian reluctance to withdraw after a nice try. But here too Russian behaviour is very different from American. The prospect of humiliation was of enormous importance to President Kennedy. It did not have quite the same importance for Khrushchev. Serious students of Russian behaviour with such different approaches as George Kennan and Nathan Leites have long observed that "the Kremlin has no compunction about retreating in the face of superior force."[41] After the withdrawal, many journalists recalled Brest-Litovsk and Lenin's phrase about the good revolutionary being willing to crawl in the mud. But that recollection was much rarer in the actual week of quarantine and crisis. By December, 1962, Khrushchev himself was referring to Lenin's "sensible" and "temporary" concession. The Albanian dogmatists who criticized the withdrawal of missiles, he claimed, were sliding down Trotsky's path of unyielding infantilism at Brest. But the missile withdrawal was not even a temporary retreat, much less a capitulation. The concessions, Khrushchev said, were "mutual."[42]

Such cultural contrasts are of course a matter of degree; but nonetheless real. Ruth Benedict's *The Chrysanthemum and the Sword* offers a brilliant analysis of Japanese feelings toward retreat and humiliation—as far exceeding in depth and range American emotions on the subject. And there are limits to Bolshevik tolerance in withdrawal.

INTERESTS AND INFLUENCE OF THE
TWO PRINCIPALS AND THEIR ALLIES

This retrospect of the interests and policy alternatives open to the three powers in the crisis indicates the need for refining some of the

[41] George Kennan, *American Diplomacy*, 1900–1950, p. 112. See also Nathan Leites, *Study of Bolshevism*, Chapter 19, and his recent "Kremlin Thoughts: Yielding, Provoking, Rebuffing, Retreating." RM 3618-ISA, the RAND Corporation, May, 1963, pp. 24ff.
[42] Speech, 12 December, 1962.

questions with which we started. When we say that in the nuclear age force is no longer an instrument of policy, it is not clear whether this is description or exhortation. In fact a blockade, it was generally agreed in September, 1962, was an act of war. Attitudes and definitions changed in October. This is a delicate matter of semantics. The American interdiction of ships carrying arms to Cuba was called a "quarantine." Nonetheless it was an act of force. And threats of higher levels of violence were implicit at every stage in the developing crisis. The questions at issue directly affected Soviet, Cuban, and United States military power.

The availability of nuclear weapons to the great powers had a double aspect. The weapons imposed the need for great responsibility and careful, very conscious control over the limited encounters that took place. On the other hand the use of lower levels of violence in such encounters is in a certain sense encouraged by the knowledge that a decision to escalate to nuclear weapons would be irrational and inappropriate for either of the participants and, for the prudent men in control, uncharacteristically irrational. And prudent antagonists can co-operate to insulate nuclear weapons from less prudent third parties. These encounters were rather clearly isolable from a decision to use nuclear weapons. Each of the nuclear powers took the time and had the information to see that the initiation of nuclear weapons would badly worsen its own position.

American nuclear power immobilized Russian nuclear power. And American local superiority in non-nuclear force together with a demonstrated willingness to use it discouraged further destabilizing moves. The familiar saying that overwhelming nuclear force simply disables its possessor from using any force at all is a rather shallow paradox. Nevertheless thermonuclear weapons clearly suit only the gravest purposes. And while small nations are less able to affect events than big ones, they do have an effect. There are serious limits to the control even a great nuclear power has over its non-nuclear allies. This applies more obviously to relations between the United States and its allies than it does to Russia's relations with its friends. Even allies whose defence and economy depend almost wholly on the United States are, as the headlines continually remind us, far from being its puppets. A variety of South Korean and South Vietnamese regimes in the last few years has made this point vivid. And the point is much more obvious for allies that are themselves great nations.

But in this crisis at any rate a small communist power was the object of contention between its protector and its adversary and could not decisively affect the outcome. It had some capability for mischief, but even this was limited. Close and receding allies of the Soviet Union and the United States as well as the non-aligned countries could do little more than endorse or criticize after the fact. In the climactic encounter it was the United States and the Soviet Union who determined events.

The loneliness of the President's decision in such a crisis raises essential problems for allies, whose fates might be affected by it. They have an interest in sharing and influencing the decision. But also in seeing to it that the decision can be made—in avoiding paralysis. This is an essential dilemma of nuclear control. In some sense the problem is quite as acute from the standpoint of American citizen as it is from that of a Briton, or an Italian, or a Frenchman, or a citizen of any of the NATO or OAS countries. In the five or six days in which the course of quarantine was selected, only an extremely small number of people (the President himself suggested a maximum of 15) had any share in the choice.

In spite of the very just allied as well as domestic concern, this is not the sort of problem that can be neatly "solved." It can be softened somewhat, and essentially the same methods can widen both allied and domestic participation. The crises themselves and the time for decision in crises are, we have suggested, likely to occupy a good deal longer interval than the magic 15 minutes frequently referred to when nuclear dangers are in mind. The small group concerned with the actual management of the crisis conceivably could then include a few high level allied political figures. It is notable that in the missile crisis, while allies were not notified of the American quarantine until the day before its public announcement, the decision itself undertook a very minimal use of force, leaving many decision points still open in the future conduct of the affair.

More important, one can prepare for a variety of contingencies in advance of crises; one can determine what might be done, if they occur. In fact, the quadripartite planning for Berlin at the very least strongly influenced President Kennedy and his immediate associates, predisposed them to the consideration of firm but carefully measured responses to any local action, and also made them more highly conscious of the world-wide repercussions inherent in many such "local" crises.

Unfortunately, however, acute perception of the importance of far off points in space tends to be highly localized in time—to be mostly limited, in fact to times of crisis.[43] The problem of sharing contingency

[43] There was a strand of European opinion that seized on the Americans' firm response to Cuba as somehow a verification of the thesis that United States interests are also highly localized; it would act strongly in its own interests, when threatened close to home, but not in Europe, not, for example, in Berlin. We may leave aside the rather curious inference from the fact of positive reaction to a strong provocation close to home—to the conclusion that there would be no reaction to a more distant challenge. However, a careful scrutiny of the American response to Cuba would suggest that far from showing that the United States would not defend Berlin, the defence of Cuba from the very first revelation of the Soviet move was recognized to be a vital part of the defence of Berlin, and the fate of Berlin was prominent in the contingency planning.

planning is complicated by the fact that allies are notoriously ambivalent about distant troubles. Before the crisis itself, they are likely to feel that the remote problem is not very important from their point of view; they may believe either that the chances of disaster are small; or that the disaster will be local. They are almost sure to feel their resources are limited and they have troubles "of their own." Indeed America's troubles with Cuba tended to be deprecated by its allies as something of an American obsession. The United States on the other hand naturally often felt that its allies underestimated the depth and complexity of the threat of communism in Latin America, and its possible ultimate worldwide importance.

NATO collaboration in shaping policy for future crises is not easy for crises in the NATO treaty area. It is a good deal harder for any of the multiplicity of crises that, arising outside the NATO periphery, may ultimately be of concern to NATO. Nonetheless it seems that, for those allies that feel a concern, rather more contingency planning in common, formal or informal, bilateral or multilateral, could be done.

The interests of Latin American governments and people in the outcome of the missile crisis was most obvious. It was the first time that these countries had come directly in the shadow of a nuclear war. And the discovery of the missiles and their forced withdrawal in a dangerous crisis had a large emotional impact. While some of the concern was directed against the United States, on the whole Castro lost ground. By pulling Latin America into the centre of a confrontation between the two principal nuclear powers, he appeared to an increased number of Latin Americans to be dangerously irresponsible. Even Goulart's Brazil and Mexico, which had opposed OAS concert against Castro, backed the President's blockade; and there is no doubt that such effects lasted long beyond the crisis. The losses Castro suffered contrast with his exalted hopes before the crisis that Russian missiles in Cuba would fortify his prestige and influence in Latin America. But they do not show that his hopes were unfounded; just that he had gambled. Smaller countries may feel a great deal of ambivalence about the acquisition of nuclear weapons by their neighbors. So the mingled fear, pride, respect, and distrust inspired in Asia today by the first Chinese nuclear test. The main trouble with Castro's gamble from his standpoint was that it failed; at least for the time.

Finally a note of caution: it is easy to read too much into events, even those of outstanding importance. Once the crisis had passed, perhaps inevitably it was greeted as the herald of a new era—a testing and final stabilization of "the balance" of nuclear power between the Soviet Union and the United States, an essential elimination of the danger of nuclear war for the foreseeable future. Especially in Europe the notion seems widespread that the Cuban missile crisis represented a "turning point." But such an interpretation should be suspect in particular when advanced by those who before the missile crisis had felt the era of effortless stability and already arrived, and then during the crisis swung to the opposite extreme of panic in exaggerating the likelihood of war. In fact the "balance" is too vaguely defined, too complex and too changeable for any such assurance. The hazards of change are political as well as technical and military. It would be a mistake to regard the Soviet's emplacement of missiles in Cuba as something like a crucial experiment deliberately conducted by the Russians and establishing for them definitely once and for all that the West is determined to resist any changes in the balance—however the "balance" is defined. Khrushchev himself quickly rejected Lord Home's hopeful declaration that the Russians, sobered by their recent experience in Cuba, might from that time revise their international role.

The Western show of determination in the missile crisis had its effects. Perhaps, as has been said, it made easier the conclusion of the test ban. Perhaps it contributed to the ultimate fall of Khrushchev. At least it provided both Khrushchev's foreign and domestic rivals with a sequence of two misdeeds to cite—"adventurism" followed by "capitulationism."[44] In spite of the ready vocabulary of abuse available to describe the sequence, such an apparently opportune advance followed by a prudent withdrawal in the face of superior force is entirely consistent with a marxist canon of behaviour, which fixes no time-table for communist expansion. The effects of the Western determination, however, in the long run are uncertain and are hardly likely to be definitive. It is most implausible to suppose that this one major Communist failure will foreclose all future significant attempts, should opportunities arise, to make further advance.

The world has changed then; but not completely. It is surely no simpler now than it was before. There are many possible dangers to the West other than a precisely timed world conspiracy of a perfectly unified, permanently hostile communist camp. Some have to do with intense communist rivalries and the great variety of "communisms" today. Even an abating hostility impels caution, so long as the change is uncertain, intermittent and slow. The transformation of the whole world need hardly be at stake, only substantial parts of it. Castro is no Tito, nor a satellite, nor an immediate military threat, nor simply a minor nuisance, but a persistent source and model for insurgency and terror in the hemisphere.

Inevitably, one extreme reading of the missile crisis took it as proving that Communists in a showdown will always retreat, that we need only face them in the future with the alternative of nuclear disaster for them to abandon any use of force to transform the world. This simple view fortunately is not very influential. Yet, if it is dangerously

---

[44] Statement by the People's Government of China of 1 September, 1963.

implausible to suppose that a few future military confrontations are capable of having this happy result, it is at least equally implausible to hold that a single encounter has already had it.

Implementing Flexible Response: Vietnam as a Test Case

JOHN LEWIS GADDIS

In order to discuss the implementation of "flexible response," it is necessary to make a choice. One can examine in overview a series of events in which that strategy manifested itself: the Bay of Pigs, Laos, Berlin, the Cuban missile crisis, the Dominican Republic. Or, one can focus in detail on the event that because of its duration, divisiveness, and cost, overshadowed them all: the war in Vietnam. There are two good reasons for choosing the second approach. First, American policy in Southeast Asia reflected in microcosm virtually all of the elements of "flexible response" as applied in practice. Second, Kennedy, Johnson, and their advisers regarded Vietnam as a fair test of that strategy: it had been Eisenhower's inability to deal with that and comparable problems that had produced the "flexible response" critique in the first place; if the strategy could not be made to work in Vietnam, then there would be serious grounds upon which to question its applicability elsewhere. American leaders took on this test fully aware of the potential difficulties, but at the same time fully confident of their ability to surmount them through a strategy designed to meet just that kind of situation.

To say that their confidence was misplaced is to understate: rarely have accomplishments turned out so totally at variance with intended objectives. The war did not save South Vietnam, it did not deter future

From *Strategies of Containment: A Critical Appraisal of Postwar American National Security Policy* by John Lewis Gaddis. Copyright © 1982 by Oxford University Press, Inc. Reprinted by permission.

aggression, it did not enhance the credibility of United States commitments elsewhere in the world, it did not prevent recriminations at home. It is too easy to blame these disparities on deficiencies in the postwar national security decision-making structure, substantial though those may have been. There has been, as we have seen, no single or consistent approach to containment; to indict all manifestations of that strategy is only to be vague. Nor is it helpful to ascribe the failure in Vietnam to the shift in leadership at the White House after November 22, 1963, however strikingly the personalities of Kennedy and Johnson may have differed. For the fact is that Johnson followed the stategy of "flexible response" faithfully in Vietnam, perhaps more so than Kennedy himself would have done.

The American defeat there rather grew out of assumptions derived quite logically from that strategy: that the defense of Southeast Asia was crucial to the maintenance of world order; that force could be applied in Vietnam with precision and discrimination; that means existed accurately to evaluate performance; and that the effects would be to enhance American power, prestige, and credibility in the world. These assumptions in turn reflected a curiously myopic preoccupation with process—a disproportionate fascination with means at the expense of ends—with the result that a strategy designed to produce a precise correspondence between intentions and accomplishments in fact produced just the opposite.

I

Officials of the Kennedy and Johnson administrations liked to insist that their policies in Vietnam were consistent with the overall direction of American foreign policy since 1947: that conflict, they maintained, was but another in a long series of steps taken to demonstrate that aggression did not pay. "The challenge that we face today in Southeast Asia," Johnson argued, "is the same challenge that we have faced with courage and that we have met with strength in Greece and Turkey, in Berlin and Korea, in Lebanon and in Cuba." The "great lesson of this generation" was that "wherever we have stood firm, aggression has ultimately been halted."[1] To question the need for a similar commitment to South Vietnam, these statements implied, was to dispute the very assumptions that had sustained the strategy of containment from its beginnings.

[1] Johnson remarks at Syracuse University, August 5, 1964, *JPP:1963-4*, p. 930; Johnson remarks to members of Congressional committees, May 4, 1965, *JPP: 1965*, p. 487. See also Rostow to Kennedy, August 17, 1961, Kennedy Papers, NSC File, Box 231, "Southeast Asia—General"; McNamara statement, "United States Policy in Vietnam," March 26, 1964, *DSB*, (April 13, 1964), p. 566; Johnson address at Johns Hopkins University, April 7, 1965, *JPP: 1965*, p. 395; Johnson remarks to National Rural Electric Cooperative Association, July 14, 1965, *ibid.*, p. 751; Johnson press conference statement, July 28, 1965, *ibid.*, pp. 794-95.

In fact, though, a gradual shift had taken place in those assumptions over the years. Kennan, it will be recalled, had stressed distinctions between vital and peripheral interests, between varieties of threats to them, and between levels of feasible response given available means; the Kennedy and Johnson administrations made no such distinctions. Kennan had sought to maintain the global balance of power by applying a combination of political, economic, military, and psychological leverage in carefully selected pivotal areas; Johnson by 1965 was relying almost exclusively on the use of military force in a theater chosen by adversaries. Kennan had hoped to harness forces of nationalism, even where communist, to contain the expanding power and influence of the Soviet Union; Johnson sought to oppose communism, even where nationalist, for the purpose of preserving American credibility in the world. And, in a final ironic twist, Johnson and later Nixon came to rely with plaintive consistency on the assistance of the Soviet Union; the original target of containment, to extricate the United States from the tangle in which its own strategy had ensnared it.

One might explain these remarkable mutations as the result of obtuseness, short-sightedness, or even absent-mindedness, but there is no evidence these qualities played any more prominent role during the Kennedy-Johnson years than is normally the case. What was distinctive about those administrations, though, was their commitment to symmetrical response, and it is here that one must look to account for an evolution of strategic thinking all the more striking for the fact that those carrying it off seemed unaware that it had occurred.

It had been, of course, NSC-68 that had shifted perceptions of threat from the Soviet Union to the international communist movement; that document had also provided a rationale for expanding means and, as a consequence, interests. Eisenhower had rejected the analysis of means set forward in NSC-68, but not its assessment of threats or interests; for this reason he had been willing to extend an ambiguous commitment to the defense of South Vietnam through the SEATO treaty,* an initiative consistent with his administration's concern to achieve maximum deterrence at minimum cost. Expense was

---

*The SEATO treaty, signed September 8, 1954, provided that in case of "armed attack" against any of the signatories or against states or territories which the signatories "by unanimous agreement may hereafter designate," they would "in that event act to meet the common danger in accordance with [their] constitutional processes." In the event of a threat "other than by armed attack" or "by any fact or situation which might endanger the peace of the area," the signatories would "consult immediately in order to agree on the measures which should be taken for the common defense." South Vietnam was not a signatory to the treaty, but a protocol attached to it did extend its provisions to cover "the States of Cambodia and Laos and the free territory under the jurisdiction of the State of Vietnam," (*American Foreign Policy, 1950–1955: Basic Documents* [Washington: 1957], pp. 913–14, 916.)

of less concern to Kennedy who, confronted with an upsurge of Viet Cong insurgency, reverted to NSC-68's concept of expandable means but coupled it with a determination to honor Eisenhower's commitment, even though it had been extended largely as a substitute for means. At the same time, Kennedy was determined to lower the risks of escalation or humiliation that earlier strategy had run; this resolve led, in time, to the deployment of American ground forces, first as "advisers" to the South Vietnamese, then, under Johnson, as full-fledged combatants.[2]

But what, precisely, was the United States interest in Vietnam? Why was the balance of power at stake there? Walt Rostow had warned in his 1962 "BSNP" draft that "major losses of territory or of resources would make it harder for the U.S. to create the kind of world environment it desires, . . . generate defeatism among governments and peoples in the non-Communist world, or give rise to frustrations at home." But when pressed to explain why the "loss" of such a small and distant country would produce these drastic consequences, Washington officials generally cited the SEATO treaty obligation, which, if not honored, would raise doubts about American commitments elsewhere in the world. "The integrity of the U.S. commitment is the principal pillar of peace throughout the world," Rusk wrote in 1965. "If that commitment becomes unreliable, the communist world would draw conclusions that would lead to our ruin and almost certainly to a catastrophic war."

This was curious reasoning. It required justifying the American commitment to South Vietnam as essential to the maintenance of global stability, but then portraying that stability as endangered by the very vulnerability of Washington's commitment. It involved both deterring aggression and being held hostage to it. The confusion, it would appear, stemmed from the failure of both the Kennedy and Johnson administrations to articulate independently derived conceptions of interest in Southeast Asis; instead, they tended to view the American stake there as determined exclusively by threats and obligations. The security of the United States, indeed of the entire non-communist world, was thought to be imperiled wherever communist challenges came up against American guarantees. Vietnam might be insignificant in itself, but as a point of intersection between threat and commitment, it was everything.

Nothing in this argument required the threat to be centrally directed, or even coordinated with communist activities elsewhere. There were, to be sure, frequent references early in the war to the

[2] Rostow draft, "Basic National Security Policy," March 26, 1962, p. 9; Rusk memorandum, July 1, 1965, *Pentagon Papers*, IV, 23. See also Rusk and McNamara to Kennedy, November 11, 1961, *ibid.,* II, 111; Johnson remarks to members of Congressional committees, May 4, 1965, *JPP: 1965,* p. 486; and Rostow to McNamara, May 2, 1966, Johnson Papers, NSF Agency File, Boxes 11–12, "Defense Department Vol. III."

Sino-Soviet plan for "world domination,"[3] but these became less common as evidence of the Moscow-Peking split became irrefutable. Rationales then shifted to the containment of China, but only briefly; by early 1965 the predominant concern, as Under-Secretary of Defense John McNaughton put it, was simply "to avoid a humiliating US defeat (to our reputation as a guarantor)."[4] Communism need not pose a coordinated threat to the world balance of power, then, but because victories for communism at the expense of the United States, even if uncoordinated, could result in humiliation, the challenge to global stability was no less real. The only difference was that it was now Washington's fear of retreat that linked these threats together, not the internal discipline and control of international communism itself.

Nor did the American commitment in question need to have been prudent. There was a definite sense within the Kennedy administration that Eisenhower had overextended the United States in Southeast Asia: Rostow, as has been seen would have preferred a less formal alliance structure based on offshore strongpoints;[5] Robert Komer, one of his assistants, privately described SEATO in 1961 as a "millstone" directed against non-existent dangers of overt aggression. Nonetheless, Rostow wrote Kennedy later that year: "Surely we are hooked in Viet-Nam; surely we shall honor our . . . SEATO commitment." The problem, simply, was that the dangers of disengagement seemed at each stage to outweigh the costs of pressing on. "The reasons why we went into Vietnam . . . are now largely academic," McNaughton wrote in 1966. "At each decision point we have gambled; at each point, to avoid the damage to our effectiveness of defaulting on our commitment, we have upped the ante. We have not defaulted, and the ante (and commitment) is now very high."[6]

[3] See, for example, the Joint Chiefs of Staff to McNamara, January 13, 1962, *Pentagon Papers*, II, 664; Roger Hilsman address, Tampa, Florida, June 14, 1963, *DSB*, XIX (July 8, 1963), 44; Johnson remarks at the National Cathedral School, Washington, June 1, 1965, *JPP: 1965*, p. 600.

[4] McNaughton memorandum, "Proposed Course, of Action re Vietnam," March 24, 1965, *Pentagon Papers*, III, 695. See also Michael Forrestal to William P. Bundy, November 4, 1964, *ibid.*, p. 592. For further official perceptions of lack of coordination in the international communist movement, see Thomas L. Hughes to Hilsman, April 20, 1963, Kennedy Papers NSC Files, Box 314, Folder 6; Hilsman to Rusk, July 31, 1963, *ibid.*, Folder 10; Johnson to Lodge, March 20, 1964, *Pentagon Papers*, III, 511; Bundy to Johnson, October 21, 1964, Johnson Papers, National Security Files—NSC Staff, Box 2, "Memos for the President, vol. 7; Rostow to Rusk, December 16, 1964, *ibid.*, NSF Country Files—Vietnam, Box 11, "Memos, Vol. XXIII."

[5] See above, p. 223.

[6] Komer memorandum, "A Doctrine of Deterrence for SEA—The Conceptual Framework," May 9, 1961, Kennedy Papers, NSC Files, Box 231, "Southeast Asia—General"; Rostow to Kennedy, August 17, 1961, *ibid.;* McNaughton memorandum, January 18, 1966, *Pentagon Papers*, IV, 47. See also Rostow's draft, "Basic National Security Policy," March 26, 1962, pp. 141-44, and Arthur Schlesinger's account of Kennedy's conversation with Khrushchev at Vienna in June 1961, in *A Thousand Days*, p. 368.

There was a distinct self-reinforcing tendency in all of this. The more the administration defended its Vietnam policies in terms of safeguarding credibility, the more American credibility seemed to depend upon the success of those policies. "To leave Viet-Nam to its fate would shake . . . confidence . . . in the value of an American commitment and in the value of America's word," Johnson proclaimed in April 1965. And again, in May: "There are a hundred other little nations . . . watching what happens. . . . If South Viet-Nam can be gobbled up, the same thing can happen to them." And still again, in July: "If we are driven from the field in Viet-Nam, then no nation can ever again have the same confidence in . . . American protection."[7] Perceptions in international relations are only in part the product of what people believe; they arise as well from what nations claim. Given the frequency and intensity of these and other comparable pronouncements, it is hardly surprising that they were taken seriously, both at home and abroad. And yet the irony is that the administration made them to stave off pressures for withdrawal that could lead to humiliation; their effect, though, was to widen the very gap between promise and performance from which humiliation springs.

But why this extreme fear of humiliation in the first place? Partly, one suspects, because it might suggest weakness to adversaries: "lessons" of Munich, after all, were still very much alive. Vietnam had also become something of a matter of personal pride: "we have not lost a single nation to communism since 1959," Johnson liked to boast.[8] But a deeper concern, oddly enough, may have been not so much what the world might think as what the United States might do. There was, within both the Kennedy and Johnson administrations, a strange dread of American irrationality—of the unpredictable and uncontrollable reactions that might ensue if the United States was perceived to have "lost" Vietnam. Rusk and McNamara had warned as early as 1961 that such a development "would stimulate bitter domestic controversies in the United States and would be seized upon by extreme elements to divide the country and harass the Administration." Rostow's "BSNP" draft even raised the possibility that "the U.S. might rashly initiate war" if confronted by a major defeat.[9] Johnson may well have entertained the strongest fears of all: "I knew that if we let Communist aggression succeed in taking over South Vietnam," he later recalled,

[7] Johnson Johns Hopkins address, April 7, 1965, *JPP: 1965,* p. 395; Johnson remarks to members of Congressional committees, May 4, 1965, *ibid.,* p. 491; Johnson press conference statement, July 28, 1965, *ibid.,* p. 794.

[8] Johnson remarks in Hartford, Connecticut, September 28, 1964, *JPP: 1964.* See also Johnson's remarks in Detroit, Michigan, September 7, 1964, *ibid.,* p. 1050; and May, *"Lessons" of the Past,* especially pp. 112–14.

[9] Rusk and McNamara to Kennedy, November 11, 1961, *Pentagon Papers,* II, 111; Rostow draft, "Basic National Security Policy," March 26, 1962, p. 9. See also William P. Bundy to McNaughton, November 26, 1964, *Pentagon Papers,* III, 658.

there would follow in this country an endless national debate—a mean and destructive debate—that would shatter my Presidency, kill my administration, and damage our democracy. I knew that Harry Truman and Dean Acheson had lost their effectiveness from the day that the Communists took over in China. I believed that the loss of China had played a large role in the rise of Joe McCarthy. And I knew that all these problems, taken together, were chickenshit compared with what might happen if we lost Vietnam.[10]

The ultimate danger, then, was what the United States might do to itself if it failed to meet obligations it itself had established.

Shortly after the Johnson administration left office, William Whitworth, a writer for the *New Yorker,* sought to interview several of the former President's advisers on the underlying geopolitical rationale for the Vietnam War. The only one who would see him was Eugene V. Rostow, Walt Rostow's older brother, who had served as Under-Secretary of State for Political Affairs from 1966 to 1969. The ensuing discussion took on a revealing circularity. Asked why American security depended upon the defense of Southeast Asia, Rostow emphasized the need to maintain a "balance of power" in the world. But when queried as to why it had been necessary to do that, Rostow fell back upon a classic "flexible response" argument: the need to be able to handle, without resort to nuclear weapons, problems such as Vietnam. Whitworth found this puzzling: "We have the balance in order to deal with the problem, and we have to deal with the problem in order to preserve the balance. The theory is eating its own tail." "Well, in a sense, you're right," Rostow replied. "All I can say is that it has always been very dangerous for people when a potentially hostile power establishes hegemony. I can't particularize how that potential hegemony would be exercised, but I would prefer, even at considerable cost, to prevent the risk."[11]

This spectacle of theories eating tails was no rare thing in Vietnam: the expansion of means to honor a commitment made as a substitute for means; the justification of that commitment in terms of a balance of power made shaky by its very existence; the defense, in the interests of credibility, of policies destructive of credibility; the search, ultimately, for domestic consensus by means that destroyed that consensus—all of these reflect the failure of "flexible response" strategy to proceed in an orderly manner through the stages of identifying interests, perceiving threats, and selecting appropriate responses. Instead, both threats and responses became interests in themselves, with

---

[10] Quoted in Doris Kearns, *Lyndon Johnson and the American Dream* (New York: 1976), pp. 252–53. See also Lyndon B. Johnson, *The Vantage Point: Perspectives of the Presidency, 1963–1969* (New York: 1971), pp. 151–52.

[11] William Whitworth, *Naive Questions About War and Peace* (New York; 1970), pp. 105–6, 124.

the result that the United States either ignored or forgot what it had set out to do in Vietnam at just the moment it was resolving, with unprecedented determination, to do it.

II

A second prominent feature of "flexible response" as applied in Vietnam was the belief in "calibration," or "fine tuning"—that by being able to move up or down a range of precisely calculated actions, the United States could deter limited aggression without either extreme escalation or humiliation. "Our military forces must be . . . used in a measured, limited, controlled and deliberate way, as an instrument to carry out our foreign policy," one of McNamara's assistants wrote in late 1964. "Never must military operations become an end in themselves." Johnson made the same point some months later: he would not heed, he insisted, "those who urge us to use our great power in a reckless or casual manner. . . . We will do what must be done. And we will do only what must be done."[12] And yet, since this strategy in the end produced *both* escalation *and* humiliation, it would appear to have contained, as did official thinking on the balance of power, certain deficiencies.

Deterrence, ideally, should involve expressing determination without actually having to exhibit it. John Foster Dulles had attempted this delicate maneuver by threatening to use nuclear weapons to discourage aggression at all levels—an approach that at least had the merit of separating the projection of resolve from its actual demonstration, so long as skill, or luck, held out. Lacking the previous administration's self-confidence in such matters, convinced as well of the ineffectiveness of that strategy in limited war situations, Kennedy and his advisers had ruled out nuclear threats in areas like Southeast Asia, but not the need to manifest American firmness there. "We must produce quickly a course of action which convinces the other side we are dead serious," Rostow had warned Kennedy in August 1961. "What the U.S. does or fails to do," Maxwell Taylor added a few months later, "will be decisive to the end result."[13] The difficulty was that, short of embracing Dulles's strategy, all conceivable projections of resolve seemed to require, in one form or another, actual demonstrations of it.

[12] Joseph Califano draft presidential statement, December 2, 1964, enclosed in Califano to Bundy, December 3, 1964, Johnson Papers, NSF—Agency Files, Box 11-12, "Defense Department, Volume I"; Johnson message to Congress on Vietnam appropriations, May 4, 1965, *JPP: 1965*, p. 497. See also *JPP: 1963–64*, pp. 372, 1174; *JPP: 1965*, p. 489.

[13] Rostow to Kennedy, August 17, 1961, Kennedy Papers, NCS Files, Box 231, "Southeast Asia—General"; Taylor to Kennedy, October 24, 1961, *Pentagon Papers*, II, 88.

This did not bother the Joint Chiefs of Staff, who, as early as May 1961, had recommended the dispatch of United States troops to South Vietnam "to provide a visible deterrent to potential North Vietnamese and/or Chinese Communist action," and to "indicate the firmness of our intent to all Asian nations." An old Vietnam hand, Brigadier General Edward Lansdale, explained the rationale as follows:

US *combat* forces, even in relatively small units, are the symbol of our national power. If an enemy engages one of our combat units, he is fully aware that he automatically has engaged the entire power of the US. This symbol of real national strength, employed wisely in Germany, Greece, and the Formosa Straits in a manner not unlike that contemplated for Thailand and Vietnam, has "kept the peace." When the mission of such US force is properly announced and followed immediately by a firm action, recent history teaches that the effect is just the reverse of "escalation" and that our action obtains world support outside the [Sino-Soviet] Bloc.

"[T]he point of installing token U.S. forces before the event," Robert Komer added, "is to signal our intentions to the other fellow, and thus hopefully avoid having to face up to the commitment of substantial US forces after a fracas has developed." It was true that the United States might "end up with something approaching another Korea, but I think the best way of avoiding this is to move fast now before the war spreads to the extent that a Korean type commitment is required.[14]* This theory that immediate small-scale involvement could make massive long-term involvement unnecessary formed the basis of recommendations by Maxwell Taylor and Walt Rostow for the introduction of some 8,000 U.S. combat troops into South Vietnam in November 1961. "In our view," Taylor wrote the President, nothing is more calculated to sober the enemy and to discourage escalation . . . than the knowledge that the United States has prepared itself soundly to deal with aggression at any level."[15]

[14] Joint Chiefs of Staff to Gilpatric, May 10, 1961, *Pentagon Papers,* II, 49; Lansdale to Gilpatric, May 10, 1961, Kennedy Papers, NSC Files, Box 231, "Southeast Asia—General"; Komer to Rostow, August 2, 1961, *ibid.;* Komer to Bundy, October 31, 1961, *ibid.* See also Komer memorandum, "A Doctrine of Deterrence for SEA—The Conceptual Framework," May 9, 1961, *ibid.*

*"I'm no happier than anyone about getting involved in another squalid, secondary theatre in Asia. But we'll end up doing so sooner or later anyway because we won't be willing to accept another defeat. If so, the real question is not whether but how soon and how much!" (Komer to Bundy, October 31, 1961, Kennedy Papers, NSC Files, Box 231, "Southeast Asia—General.")

[15] Taylor to Kennedy, November 3, 1961, *Pentagon Papers,* II, 654. See also, on the Taylor-Rostow report, *ibid.,* II, 73–120; Rostow, *The Diffusion of Power,* pp. 270–71, 274–79; and Maxwell Taylor, *Swords and Ploughshares* (New York: 1972), pp. 225–48.

352   CASE STUDIES

But Kennedy had long been skeptical about the wisdom of sending
American forces to fight in Southeast Asia: he had reminded his advisers the previous July of "the reluctance of the American people and
of many distinguished military leaders to see any direct involvement of
U.S. troops in that part of the world. . . . [N]othing would be worse
than an unsuccessful intervention in this area." State Department
assessments reinforced this view:

> We do not think the presence of US troops would serve to deter infiltrations
> short of overt armed intervention. There is not much reason for supposing
> the Communists would think our troops would be much more successful
> against guerrilla operations in South Viet-Nam than French troops were in
> North Viet-Nam. Counter-guerrilla operations require highly selective ap-
> plication of force; selection requires discrimination; and alien troops simply
> lack the bases for discriminating between friend and foe, except by the
> direction in which they shoot.

If the South Vietnamese themselves were not willing to make a
"serious national effort," Dean Rusk warned in November, then it
was "difficult to see how [a] handful [of] American troops can have
[a] decisive influence." Persuaded by these arguments, concerned as
well about priorities elsewhere (notably Berlin) and the risk of upset-
ting negotiations then in progress on Laos, Kennedy deferred implementing the Taylor-Rostow recommendation for combat troops. It
would have been "like taking a drink," he explained to Arthur Schlesinger. "The effect wears off, and you have to take another."[16]
It is important to note, though, that Kennedy's decision against
sending combat troops to Vietnam was not a rejection of "calibration"
—just the opposite. The full Taylor-Rostow recommendations, he
thought, would have constituted too abrupt an escalation of pressure;
he preferred, instead, a more gradual approach, involving an increase
of American economic and military aid to Saigon, together with the
introduction of U.S. "advisers." Nothing in this procedure precluded
the dispatch of ground troops at a later date if that should become
necessary. Nor were there illusions as to the impact of these decisions
on American credibility: "We are fully cognizant," the State Department cabled Saigon, "of [the] extent to which [these] decisions if implemented . . . will sharply increase the commitment of our prestige
struggle to save SVN."[17] Kennedy's actions reflected doubts only

[16] Bundy memorandum, Kennedy meeting with advisers, July 28, 1961, Kennedy
Papers, NSC Files, Box 231, "Southeast Asia—General"; Policy Planning Council
memorandum, "Security in Southeast Asia," July 27, 1961, enclosed in McGhee to
Rostow, July 28, 1961, *ibid.;* Rusk to State Department, November 1, 1961, *Pentagon
Papers,* II, 105; Schlesinger, A *Thousand Days,* p. 547.
[17] Rusk to Nolting, November 14, 1961, *Pentagon Papers,* II, 119.

about the appropriate level of response necessary to demonstrate American resolve, not about the importance of making that demonstration in the first place.

"Calibration" during the next two years took the form primarily of efforts to transform South Vietnam into a sufficiently self-reliant anti-communist bastion so that no direct commitment of United States forces would be necessary. The goal, according to Roger Hilsman, was to devise "an integrated and systematic military-political-economic strategic counterinsurgency concept," to orient Saigon's military and security forces "increasingly toward counter-guerrilla or unconventional warfare tactics," to "broaden the effective participation of Vietnamese Government officials in the formulation and execution of government policy," and to "identify the populace with the Vietnamese Government's struggle against the Viet Cong."[18] All of this required several delicate balancing acts: moderating President Ngo Dinh Diem's autocratic control enough to win popular support for his government without at the same time weakening it to the point that it could not resist Viet Cong pressures; providing the assistance necessary for Diem to survive without discrediting him as an American puppet; taking care, simultaneously, to see that Washington's interest in Diem's survival did not allow him to make a puppet out of the United States. In the end, the line proved too fine to walk: frustrated by Diem's repression of Buddhist critics, fearful of a secret deal between his government and North Vietnam, Kennedy in August 1963 authorized a carefully orchestrated effort—in itself an example of "calibration"—to overthrow him.[19] As it happened, though, Washington was able to control neither the timing nor the manner of Diem's removal, nor had it given much thought to what would replace him; the effect was that the very instability Kennedy had feared dominated politics in Saigon for the next three years.

The resulting Viet Cong gains led the Johnson administration by the end of 1964 to approve what Kennedy had rejected—a combat role for the United States in Vietnam. Even so, though, the principle of "calibration" would still apply; there would be no sharp, all-out application of force. Rather, the plan, in Johnson's words, was for military pressures against North Vietnam "progressively mounting in scope and intensity for the purpose of convincing the leaders of the DRV that it is to their interest to cease to aid the Viet Cong and to respect the independence and security of South Vietnam." This "slow squeeze" strategy contemplated action strong enough to end the existing deteriorating situation, but not so violent as to knit the North

[18] Hilsman to Harriman, June 18, 1962, *Pentagon Papers,* II, 673.
[19] See, for example, Hilsman's elaborate "Action Plan" for South Vietnam, undated, Kennedy Papers, NSC File, Box 317, "Meetings on Vietnam"; also, the *Pentagon Papers,* II, 201–76.

Vietnamese people more closely together, provoke Chinese Communist intervention, arouse world opinion, or preclude opportunities for an eventual negotiated settlement. The objective, Bundy noted on the eve of the first air strikes against the North in February 1965, was "to keep before Hanoi the carrot of our desisting as well as the stick of continued pressure. . . . Once such a policy is put into force, we shall be able to speak in Vietnam on many topics and in many ways, with growing force and effectiveness."[20]*

The bombing campaign against North Vietnam was intended to be the most carefully calibrated military operation in recent history. Great significance was attached to not crossing certain geographic "thresholds" for fear of bringing in the Chinese, as had happened in Korea, to avoiding civilian casualties that might intensify opposition to the war within the United States and elsewhere, and to combining the bombing with various inducements, especially periodic bombing pauses and offers of economic aid, to bring Hanoi to the conference table. Target selection was done in Washington, often in the White House itself, with the President at times personally monitoring the outcome of particular missions. Extraordinary precision was demanded of pilots—one 1966 order specified that piers at Haiphong could be hit only if no tankers were berthed at them, that vessels firing on American planes could be struck only if they were "clearly North Vietnamese," and that no attacks were to be launched on Sunday.[21] Even with such restrictions, though, the scale and intensity of the bombing progressively mounted, from 25,000 sorties** and 63,000 tons of bombs dropped in 1965 to 108,000 sorties and 226,000 tons in 1967, from missions directed initially at military bases in the southern "panhandle" of North Vietnam to infiltration routes, transportation facilities, and petroleum storage areas throughout the country, ultimately to factories and power plants in the Hanoi-Haiphong complex itself.[22] And none of it produced discernible progress toward

[20] Johnson to Taylor, December 3, 1964, Johnson Papers, NSC Staff Files, Box 2, "Memos for the President, Vol. 7"; Bundy memorandum, "A Policy of Sustained Reprisal," February 7, 1965, *Pentagon Papers,* III, 690; Bundy to Johnson, February 7, 1965, *ibid.,* p. 311. See also Kearns, *Johnson and the American Dream,* pp. 264–65. For the evolution of the "slow squeeze" option, see the *Pentagon Papers,* III, 206–51, 587–683.

*Eugene Rostow argued that Johnson's "bold but prudent action in Vietnam had posed two things: that we would risk bombs over New York in order to protect Saigon, and that Moscow would not bomb New York to protect Hanoi. This was an event and a demonstration of capital importance, which should greatly fortify our system of alliances, and weaken that of our enemies." (Rostow memorandum, April 10, 1965, enclosed in Bill Moyers to Bundy, April 13, 1965, Johnson Papers, NSF Country Files: Vietnam, Box 16, "Memos—Vol. XXXII.")

[21] JSC to CINCPAC, June 22, 1966, *Pentagon Papers,* IV, 105–6.

**A sortie is one flight by one plane.

[22] George C. Herring, *America's Longest War: The United States and Vietnam,* 1950–1975 (New York: 1979), p. 147.

what it was supposed to accomplish: a tapering off of infiltration into South Vietnam, and movement toward negotiations.

Meanwhile, pressures had been building for the introduction of ground troops. Bundy had recommended this option as early as May 1964: the idea, he wrote Johnson, would be one of "marrying Americans to Vietnamese at every level, both civilian and military . . . to provide what [Saigon] has repeatedly asked for: the tall American at every point of stress and strain." "I do not at all think it is a repetition of Korea," he added in August. "It seems to me at least possible that a couple of brigade-size units put in to do specific jobs . . . might be good medicine everywhere." Rostow agreed, pointing out that such troops could usefully serve as bargaining chips in any future negotiations, and by February 1965 Rusk too had endorsed the idea, along with the bombing, as a way to send "a signal to Hanoi and Peiping that they themselves cannot hope to succeed without a substantial escalation on their part, with all the risks they would have to face."[23] The decisive argument in the end, though, proved to be General William Westmoreland's assertion that troops were needed to guard the air base at Da Nang from which some of the strikes against the north were being launched, a claim almost certainly advanced with a view to securing presidential authorization of a combat mission whose scope could then be widened far beyond the limited purposes for which it was made.[24] This "entering wedge" worked, and by early April 1965 Johnson had approved a combat role for United States forces in Vietnam. The pattern of escalation quickly went beyond Bundy's two brigades: from an initial deployment of 3,500 Marines at Da Nang, U.S. troop strength rose to 184,000 by the end of 1965, 385,000 by the end of 1966, and 486,000 by the end of 1967.[25] Nor, as the Tet offensive of early 1968 seemed to show, was there convincing evidence that those troops had come any closer to accomplishing their mission than had the bombing campaign.

What strikes one in retrospect about the strategy of calibrated escalation is the extent to which, as so often happened in Vietnam, the effects produced were precisely opposite from those intended. The objective of applying incremental pressures beginning in 1961 had been

[23] Bundy to Johnson, May 22 and August 31, 1965, Johnson Papers, NSF-NSC Staff Files, Box 1, "Memos for the President, Vol. 4," and Box 2, "Memos for the President, Vol. 6"; Rostow to McNamara, November 16, 1964, *Pentagon Papers,* III, 632; Rusk memorandum, "Viet-Nam," February 23, 1965, Johnson Papers, NSF Country File: Vietnam, Box 14, "Memos, Vol. XXIX."

[24] See, on this point, Guenter Lewy, *America in Vietnam* (New York: 1978), pp. 42–46; Robert L. Gallucci, *Neither Peace Nor Honor: The Politics of the American Military in Viet-Nam* (Baltimore: 1976), pp. 111–12; and the analysis in the *Pentagon Papers,* III, 429–33.

[25] Figures on troop strength are from Herbert Y. Schandler, *The Unmaking of a President: Lyndon Johnson and Vietnam* (Princeton, 1977), p. 352.

to avoid a massive American military involvement: token commitments, it was thought, would demonstrate resolve, thereby obviating the necessity for larger commitments later. The theory was not unlike that of vaccination, in that exposure to minimum risk was expected to provide immunities against more serious dangers. Another analogy, used at the time, was that of a plate-glass window, insufficiently strong in itself to keep out a thief, but capable of producing such conspicuous consequences if shattered as to discourage attempts from being made in the first place. Getting involved, in short, was the best way to avoid getting involved: "I deeply believe," Rostow had written in August of that year, "that the way to save Southeast Asia and to minimize the chance of deep U.S. military involvement there is for the President to make a bold decision very soon."[26]

Bold decisions were made (admittedly not in as bold a manner as Rostow had wanted), but the effect was hardly to minimize American involvement. United States manpower, resources, and prestige were far more deeply committed by 1968 than even "worst case" scenarios seven years earlier had indicated. McNamara had estimated in November 1961 that in the unlikely event that *both* North Vietnam and Communist China overtly intervened in the war, Washington might have to send six divisions, or 205,000 men. Peking did not intervene, Hanoi kept its own participation below the level of overt acknowledgment, but still the United States had more than doubled McNamara's prediction as to "the ultimate possible extent of our military commitment."[27] Calibrated pressures as a deterrent obviously had not worked.

One reason for this was a persistent lack of clarity as to who, or what, was being deterred. Impressed by Khrushchev's "wars of national liberation" speech, the Kennedy administration had at first located the roots of Viet Cong insurgency in Moscow: Rostow in 1961 had even advocated an early form of "linkage," making it clear to the Kremlin that no progress toward détente could take place while guerilla activity continued in Southeast Asia.[28]* By 1964, though,

---

[26] Rostow to Robert F. Kennedy, August 18, 1961, Kennedy Papers, NSC Files, Box 231, "Southeast Asia—General." See also Robert Komer, "A Doctrine of Deterrence for SEA—The Conceptual Framework," May 9, 1961, *ibid.*

[27] McNamara to Kennedy, November 8, 1961, *Pentagon Papers,* II, 108.

[28] Rostow to Kennedy, May 11, 1961, Kennedy Papers, NSC Files, Box 231, "Southeast Asia—General."

*Rostow wanted Kennedy to warn Khrushchev at Vienna that if the United States were "drawn deeper and more directly on to the Southeast Asian mainland," this would require a major increase in military spending and difficulties in relations with Moscow because "it is difficult for a democracy simultaneously to gear itself for possible military conflict and also to take the steps necessary to ease tensions and to expand the areas of U.S.-Soviet collaboration." (Rostow to Kennedy, May 11, 1961, Kennedy Papers, NSC Files, Box 231, "Southeast Asia—General.") There is no evidence that Kennedy actually raised this point with Khrushchev at Vienna—perhaps he realized that the Soviet leader might welcome rather than regret an American distraction in Southeast Asia.

Peking, not Moscow, had come to be seen as the culprit: the objective of American policy, National Security Council staff member Michael Forrestal argued late that year, should be to "delay China's swallowing up Southeast Asia until (a) she develops better table manners and (b) the food is somewhat more indigestible." The absence of official relations precluded opportunities for diplomatic "linkage" with Peking, however, and Johnson's advisers, remembering miscalculations during the Korean War, were extremely cautious about applying military pressure in any form. "China is there on the border with 700 million men," Johnson noted; "we could get tied down in a land war in Asia very quickly if we sought to throw our weight around."[29]

The alternative, it would appear, was direct pressure against Hanoi, but things were not quite that simple. John McNaughton in September 1964 identified at least four separate "audiences" aside from Moscow and Peking that the United States would have to influence: "the Communists (who must feel strong pressures), the South Vietnamese (whose morale must be buoyed), our allies (who must trust us as 'underwriters'), and the US public (which must support our risk-taking with US lives and prestige)." The difficulty, of course, was that actions directed at one "audience" might affect others in undesirable ways. Too sharp an escalation aimed at Hanoi risked alienating public opinion in the United States (especially during an election year), and elsewhere in the world, not to mention the danger of Chinese intervention. Moreover, such action would accomplish little as long as instability continued to reign in Saigon, as it had since the overthrow of Diem late in 1963. On the other hand, though, further restraint could only accelerate deterioration of the military situation in the South; it also conveyed the appearance of weakness and indecisiveness, not only in Hanoi and among American allies in Asia, but in Saigon itself, where the resulting low morale produced still more instability. The need, McNaughton argued, was for action taken "with special care—signaling to the DRV that initiatives are being taken, to the GVN that we are behaving energetically . . . , and to the US public that we are behaving with good purpose and restraint."[30]

---

[29] Forrestal to William P. Bundy, Novermber 23, 1964, *Pentagon Papers,* III, 644; Johnson remarks at the University of Akron, October 21, 1964, *JPP: 1964,* p. 1391. See also *ibid.,* pp. 1164–65.

[30] McNaughton draft, "Plan of Action for South Vietnam," September 3, 1964, *Pentagon Papers,* III, 559. See also Taylor to Rusk, August 18, 1964, *ibid.,* pp. 545–48; Bundy memorandum, meeting with Johnson, September 9, 1964, Johnson Papers, NSF-NSC Staff Files, Box 2, "Memos for the President, Vol. 6"; William H. Sullivan to William P. Bundy, November 6, 1964, *Pentagon Papers,* III, 594; Rostow to Rusk, November 23, 1964, *ibid.,* pp. 645–46; Taylor briefing of November 27, 1964, *ibid.,* pp. 671–72; William P. Bundy memorandum, November 28, 1964, *ibid.,* p. 676; Bundy memorandum, December 28, 1964, Johnson Papers, NSF—NSC Staff Files, Box 2, "Memos for the President, Vol. 7"; Bundy to Johnson, January 27, 1965, *ibid.* See also Leslie H. Gelb and Richard Betts, *The Irony of Vietnam: The System Worked* (Washington, D.C.: 1979), pp. 12–13.

But "calibration" implies a single target: where several exist, in a constantly shifting but interrelated pattern, the attainment of a precise correspondence between intentions and consequences becomes no easy matter.*

A second problem flowed directly from the first. By eschewing anything other than gradual escalation, matched carefully to the level of enemy provocation, the Johnson administration was in effect relinquishing the initiative to the other side. This was, of course, a standard military criticism of White House policy: the argument was that if only restraints on air and ground action could be lifted, the war could be ended rapidly.[31]† Given the subsequently demonstrated ability of the North Vietnamese and Viet Cong to hold out for years under much heavier pressures, the claim, in retrospect, seems unconvincing. Still, there was one valid element in the military's argument. Theorists of international relations have suggested that deterrence is more likely to work when a potential aggressor is unsure of his ability to control the risks involved in the action he is contemplating. If that confidence exists, deterrence will probably be ineffective.[32] This idea of cultivating uncertainty in the minds of adversaries had been central to Dulles's strategy of "retaliation"—with what effects it is impossible to say, given the difficulty of trying to prove what deterrence deterred. But uncertainty did not carry over into the strategy of "calibration." To proclaim that one intends to do only what is necessary to counter aggression and no more is, after all, to yield control over one's actions to those undertaking the aggression. Washington officials may have had the illusion that they were making decisions on Vietnam force deployments during the Johnson years, but in fact those choices were

---

*McNamara succinctly summarized the problem of impressing multiple "audiences" in a July 1965 memorandum to Johnson: "Our object in Vietnam is to create conditions for a favorable outcome by demonstrating to the VC/DRV that the odds are against their winning. We want to create these conditions, if possible, without causing the war to expand into one with China or the Soviet Union and in a way which preserves support of the American people and, hopefully, of our allies and friends." (McNamara to Johnson, July 20, 1965, Johnson Papers, NSF Country File: Vietnam, Box 74, "1965 Troop Decision.")

[31] See, for example, the Joint Chiefs of Staff to McNamara, January 22, 1964, *Pentagon Papers*, III, 497-98; also Gallucci, *Neighter Peace Nor Honor*, pp. 38-39

†Perhaps the most pungent expression of this idea came from General Thomas S. Power, Strategic Air Force Commander, who told a Pentagon audience in 1964 that "the task of the military in war was to kill human beings and destroy man-made objects," and to do it "in the quickest way possible." It had been "the moralists who don't want to kill" that had given "Hitler his start and got us into the mess in Cuba and Viet-Nam." The "computer types who were making defense policy don't know their ass from a hole in the ground." (Summary, Power briefing, April 28, 1964, Johnson Papers, NSF Agency File, Box 11-12, "Defense Dept. Vol. I")

[32] George and Smoke, *Deterrence in American Foreign Policy*, p. 529.

being made, as a consequence of the administration's own strategy, in Hanoi.[33]

The alternative, of course, was some kind of negotiated settlement with North Vietnam, an option the administration was careful never to rule out. "[We] should strike to hurt but not to destroy," Bundy noted in May 1964, "for the purpose of changing the North Vietnamese decision on intervention in the South." Taylor seconded the point some months later: "it is well to remind ourselves that 'too much' in this matter of coercing Hanoi may be as bad as 'too little.' At some point, we will need a relatively cooperative leadership in Hanoi willing to wind up the VC insurgency on terms satisfactory to us and our SVN allies."[34] But Johnson and his advisers were wary of a "neutralist" solution for South Vietnam along the lines of the shaky 1962 truce in Laos—perhaps with good reason, given the speed with which Hanoi violated the agreements eventually reached at Paris in 1973. The preferred option was to achieve successes on the battlefield, and then approach North Vietnam: "After, *but only after*, we have established [a] clear pattern [of] pressure hurting DRV and leaving no doubts in South Vietnam of our own resolve, we could . . . accept [a] conference broadened to include [the] Vietnam issue," the State Department cabled Saigon in August 1964; such negotiations, if they did occur, would have to bring "Hanoi (and Peiping) eventually [to] accept idea of getting out."[35] This familiar but elusive position of "negotiation from strength" had two difficulties: it contained no safeguards against attempts by Hanoi to bolster its own negotiating position, or against the progressively deeper American involvement the strategy of "calibration" was supposed to prevent.

Finally, the strategy of "calibration" broke down because it failed to ensure that force, once applied, would be used as a precise and discriminating instrument of policy. It provided no safeguards against the subordination of strategic interests to those of the organizations implementing the strategy. Large bureaucracies all too often develop their own institutional momentum: "standard operating procedures" can make an organization impervious either to instructions from above or feedback from below.[36] One strength of McNamara's

[33] See, on this point, Alain Enthoven to Clark Clifford, March 20, 1968, in Enthoven and Smith, *How Much Is Enough,* pp. 298-99; and Schandler, *The Unmaking of a President,* pp. 31-42, 46.

[34] Bundy to Johnson, May 22, 1964, Johnson Papers, NSF-NSC Staff File, Box 1, "Memos for the President, Vol. I"; Taylor to State Department, November 3, 1964, *Pentagon Papers,* III, 591. See also Taylor to State Department, August 18, 1964, *ibid.,* pp. 546-47.

[35] Rusk to Lodge, August 14, 1964, *ibid.,* II, 330. See also William P. Bundy's first draft of this cable, *ibid.,* III, 526.

[36] See, on this point, Graham T. Allison, *Essence of Decision: Explaining the Cuban Missile Crisis* (Boston: 1971), pp. 83, 89.

reforms in the Pentagon had been the extent to which he had overcome this problem in dealing with the military on nuclear and
budgetary matters. No such successes, however, occurred in Vietnam.
Instead, once American forces were committed, Washington seemed
to lose control, leaving the military with a degree of autonomy surprising in an administration that had prided itself on having reduced
military authority over the conduct of national security affairs.[37]

The generalization may seem out of place applied to a war whose
soldiers complained regularly about civilian-imposed constraints, but
the military's grievances in this regard should be treated with skepticism. It is true that during the early period of American involvement,
there were significant restrictions on the nature and scope of U.S.
military activity, but as time went on without the desired enemy
response, these gradually dropped away. By August of 1967, for example, the White House had authorized for bombing some 95 percent
of the North Vietnamese targets requested by the Joint Chiefs of Staff.
Moreover, the Air Force's perceived institutional interests were
allowed to influence the conduct of the air war in important ways.
Despite its obvious (and widely appreciated) inapplicability to guerilla
warfare, the Air Force insisted successfully on a campaign of strategic
bombing in North Vietnam, and even on the use of B-52's, designed
originally to deliver nuclear weapons against Soviet targets, to hit
suspected Viet Cong emplacements in the south. Similarly, it relied
heavily on high-performance jet aircraft for other bombing missions
in the south, despite studies indicating that slower propeller-driven
models would have been three times as accurate, from five to thirteen
times less costly, but with roughly the same loss ratio.[38] It was, in
retrospect, an adaptation of ends to fit preferred means, rather than
the other way around.

The tendency was even more obvious with regard to the ground
war. Like most of his army colleagues, General Westmoreland had little sympathy for or understanding of the irregular warfare concepts
that had been popular during the early Kennedy administration: the
function of infantry, he insisted, was to seek out, pursue, and destroy
enemy forces. As a consequence, he never seriously considered the
strategy of holding and securing territory recommended by most
counterinsurgency theorists, and implemented with considerable success by the Marines in the area around Da Nang in 1965 and 1966.[39]
Instead he chose to emphasize largescale "search and destroy" operations, designed to wear the enemy down through sheer attrition. These

[37] Gelb and Betts, *The Irony of Vietnam,* pp. 239–40; Lewy, *America in Vietnam,*
pp. 114–16

[38] Gallucci, *Neither Peace Nor Honor,* pp. 73–80; Lewy, *America in Vietnam,* p. 98.

[39] Gallucci, *Neither Peace Nor Honor,* pp. 114–15, 119–20; Lewy, *America in Vietnam,* pp. 43, 51, 117.

not only disrupted efforts at pacification and provided the enemy with sufficient advance warning to escape; they also frequently forced the Americans to destroy villages in order to reach Viet Cong troops and arms caches located deliberately within those villages. Random "harassment and interdiction" fire against "suspected" but unobserved enemy targets did little to convince inhabitants of the regions affected that their security would be enhanced by supporting Saigon. The Westmoreland strategy even involved, in some instances, the deliberate creation of refugees as a means of securing the countryside, as complete a reversal as can be imagined from the original objectives the American commitment in South Vietnam had been intended to serve.[40]

It was left to the Navy, though, to come up with the most striking example of weapons ill-suited to tasks by retrieving from mothballs the U.S.S. *New Jersey*, the world's last functioning battleship, for the purpose of shelling the jungle in a manner reminiscent of nothing so much as an incident in Joseph Conrad's "Heart of Darkness":

> Once, I remember, we came upon a man-of-war anchored off the coast. There wasn't even a shed there, and she was shelling the bush. It appears the French had one of their wars going on thereabouts. . . . In the empty immensity of earth, sky, and water, there she was, incomprehensible, firing into a continent. Pop, would go one of the six-inch guns; a small flame would dart and vanish, a little white smoke would disappear, a tiny projectile would give a feeble screech—and nothing happened. Nothing could happen. There was a touch of insanity in the proceeding, a sense of lugubrious drollery in the sight; and it was not dissipated by somebody on board assuring me earnestly there was a camp of natives—he called them enemies—hidden out of sight somewhere.[41]

It was all a remarkable departure from the injunctions to do just enough, but no more than was necessary, with which the United States had entered the conflict in Vietnam.

"[T]he central object of U.S. military policy is to create an environment of stability in a nuclear age," Rostow wrote in 1966; "this requires as never before that military policy be the servant of political purposes and be woven intimately into civil policy." To be sure, this had been the objective all along of the "calibration" strategy: it reflected the immense confidence in the ability to "manage" crises and control bureaucracies that was characteristic of "flexible response," the concern to integrate force and rationality, to find some

---

[40] *Ibid.*, pp. 52, 65, 99–101, 106, 108–14; 118–19; Frances FitzGerald, *Fire in the Lake: The Vietnamese and the Americans in Vietnam* (Boston: 1972), pp. 344–45.

[41] Joseph Conrad, *Heart of Darkness,* edited by Robert Kimbrough (New York: 1971), p. 14.

middle ground between the insanity of nuclear war and the humiliation of appeasement. But it was also a curiously self-centered strategy, vague as to the objects to be deterred, heedless of the extent to which adversaries determined its nature and pace, parochial in its assumption that those adversaries shared its own preoccupations and priorities, blind to the extent to which the indiscriminate use of force had come to replace the measured precision of the original concept. "Despite its violence and difficulties, our commitment to see it through in Vietnam is essentially a stabilizing factor in the world," Rostow had insisted, no doubt with complete sincerity and the best of intentions.[42] But when sincerity and good intentions come to depend upon myopic self-absorption, then the price can be high indeed.

III

One of the curious things about the breakdown of "calibration" was official Washington's chronic inability to detect the fact that it had failed. Gaps between objectives sought and results produced widened with only infrequent attempts to call attention to what was happening; those warnings that were advanced produced few discernible responses. This pattern suggests yet another deficiency in "flexible response" theory as applied in Vietnam: a persistent inability to monitor performance, an absence of mechanisms for ensuring that correspondence between the intent of one's actions and their actual consequences that is essential for an effective strategy.

That such lapses should have occurred is puzzling, given the great emphasis both Kennedy and Johnson placed on management techniques designed to achieve precise adaptations of resources to objectives. Exponents of "systems analysis" have explained that their ideas were not applied in Vietnam until it was too late to avoid involvement, but that, once put to use, they quickly revealed the futility of the existing strategy.[43] This view is correct, but narrow. It is true that the Systems Analysis Office in the Pentagon did not begin making independent evaluations of the war until 1966. But, in a larger sense, the Kennedy-Johnson management techniques had been present all along, in the form of both administrations' confidence that they could control bureaucracies with precision, use force with discrimination, weigh costs against benefits, and relate short-term tactics to long-term objectives. The inability to monitor performance, demonstrated so vividly in the failure of "calibration," suggests difficulties in applying these methods, but not their absence.

One reason these methods broke down in Vietnam was their heavy reliance on easily manipulated statistical indices as measurements of

---

[42] Rostow to McNamara, May 2, 1966, Johnson Papers, NSF Agency File, Boxes 11–12, "Defense Department Vol. III." See also Rostow's 1962 draft "Basic National Security Policy," p. 38.

[43] Enthoven and Smith, *How Much Is Enough,* pp. 270–71.

"progress" in the war. Here the primary responsibility rests with McNamara, who insisted on applying to that complex situation the same emphasis on quantification that had served him so well in the more familiar worlds of big business and the Pentagon.[44]* The difficulty, of course, was that the voluminous calculations McNamara insisted on were no better than the accuracy of the statistics that went into them in the first place: there were few if any safeguards against distortion. *"Ah, les statistiques!"* Roger Hilsman reports one South Vietnamese general as having exclaimed. "Your Secretary of Defense loves statistics. We Vietnamese can give him all he wants. If you want them to go up, they will go up. If you want them to go down, they will go down."[45] Or, in the succinct parlance of a later generation of computer specialists, "garbage in, garbage out."

The problem manifested itself first with regard to South Vietnamese performance following the introduction of United States advisers in 1961. The very presence of the Americans, it had been thought, would make possible more accurate monitoring of the situation,[46] but in fact the opposite occurred. The advisers depended on information furnished them by Diem's officers, many of whom combined a desire to please their powerful ally with a reluctance to risk their own necks in battle. The result was a deliberate inflation of statistical indices, the extent of which became clear only after the fall of Diem in November 1963. Of some 8,600 "strategic hamlets" Diem claimed to have constructed, it turned out that only about 20 percent existed in completed form. A high percentage of military operations initiated by Saigon—possibly as many as one third—were launched in areas where the Viet Cong were known *not* to be. One district chief had listed all twenty-four hamlets in his district as secure when in fact he controlled only three. "[T]he situation has been deteriorating . . . to a far greater extent than we had realized," McNamara acknowledged ruefully, "because of our undue dependence on distorted Vietnamese reporting."[47]**

[44] See David Halberstam's evocative portrait of McNamara in *The Best and the Brightest*, pp. 215–50.

*McNamara "has been trying to think of ways of dealing with this problem [Vietnam] for so long that he has gone a little stale," Bundy wrote to Johnson in June 1964. "Also, in a curious way, he has rather mechanized the problem so that he misses some of its real political flavor." (Bundy to Johnson, June 6, 1964, Johnson Papers, NSF—NSC Staff File, Box 2, "Memos for the President, Vol. 5.")

[45] Hilsman, *To Move a Nation*, p.523.

[46] See, on this point, the *Pentagon Papers*, II, 410–11.

[47] McNamara to Johnson, December 21, 1963, *ibid.*, III, 494. See also John McCone to McNamara, December 21, 1963, *ibid.*, p. 32; and Johnson, *The Vantage Point*, p. 63. The examples of distorted South Vietnamese reporting are from Hilsman, *To Move a Nation*, pp. 522–23.

**The difficulties, of course, did not end in 1963. The number of "Viet Cong" turned in under the Third Party Inducement Program, which provided monetary rewards for indentifying "defectors" willing to rally to Saigon's cause, rose from 17,836 in 1968 to

Not all such misrepresentations came from the South Vietnamese, though. Anxious to meet Washington's expectations of success, General Paul D. Harkins, commander of U.S. advisers in Vietnam, systematically ignored or suppressed reports from his own subordinates questioning Saigon's optimistic assessments of the war. As a result, Taylor and McNamara could report with conviction as late as October 1963 that "the tactics and techniques employed by the Vietnamese under U.S. monitorship are sound and give promise of ultimate victory."[48] Evidence that the situation was not in fact that rosy did occasionally surface, whether from the rare official visitor who managed to evade Harkins's packaged briefings and carefully guided tours, or from the more fequent published reporting of skeptical American correspondents in Saigon, among them Neil Sheehan and David Halberstam. But although Kennedy worried about these discrepancies, he at no point gave up primary reliance on official channels as a means of monitoring progress in the war; Johnson, if anything, depended on them more heavily.[49] It has been suggested that the accuracy of information tends to decline as the level of its classification rises, if for no other reason than that opportunities for independent verification are diminished thereby.[50] The proposition may not be universally applicable, but that the White House would have been better off reading Halberstam than Harkins seems beyond dispute.

These problems did not disappear with the onset of active American military involvement in Vietnam. The most notorious example, of course, was the use of enemy "body counts" as the chief indicator of "progress" in the ground war. The argument has been made that in such a conflict, where conventional indices—territory taken, distances covered, cities occupied—meant little, emphasis on these kinds of macabre statistics was unavoidable.[51]* That may be,

47,088 in 1969, at which point it was discovered that many of the alleged "defectors" were not Viet Cong at all, but South Vietnamese who had made a deal with friends to report them, and then split the reward. (Lewy, *America in Vietnam,* pp. 91-92.)

[48] Taylor and McNamara to Kennedy, October 2, 1963, *Pentagon Papers,* II, 187. See also Halberstam, *The Best and the Brightest,* pp. 200-205.

[49] Bundy memorandum, Kennedy meeting with Taylor and McNamara, September 23, 1963, Kennedy Papers, NSC Files, Box 200. "Vietnam Memos & Misc." See also Hilsman, *To Move a Nation* pp. 446-47, 502-4.

[50] Gallucci, *Neither Peace Nor Honor,* pp. 132-35; Gelb and Betts, *The Irony of Vietnam,* pp. 304-5. See also Roberta Wohlstetter, *Pearl Harbor: Warning and Decision* (Stanford: 1962), pp. 122-24.

[51] Dave Richard Palmer, *Summons of the Trumpet: U.S.-Vietnam in Perspective* (San Rafael, Cal.: 1978), pp. 119-20.

*The body count phenomenon even extended, at times, to digging up bodies for counting from freshly dug graves. (Lewy, *America in Vietnam,* p. 80.)

but what seems odd is the importance accorded them, given their widely acknowledged inaccuracy. Contemporary evaluations identified a margin of error of from 30 to 100 percent in these statistics, partly as the result of double or triple counting, partly because of the difficulty of distinguishing combatants from non-combatants, partly because of pressure from field commanders for higher and higher levels of "performance."[52] A more reliable index of success in the war was available—the number of North Vietnamese-Viet Cong weapons captured—but this was never given the significance of the body counts, probably because the figures were much less impressive. "It is possible that our attrition estimates substantially overstate actual VC/NVA losses," McNamara admitted in 1966. "For example, the VC/NVA apparently lose only about one-sixth as many weapons as people, suggesting the possibility that many of the killed are unarmed porters or bystanders."[53]

Similar statistical inflation occurred in the air war as well. Despite its acknowledged unreliability in an age of high-performance jet aircraft, pilot instead of photographic reconnaissance was generally used to measure the effectiveness of bombing in the North, presumably because damage claims tended to be higher. Photographic confirmation, when requested, was often not for the purpose of verifying pilot reports but to boost "sortie rates." Allocations of fuel and ordnance depended on these rates; they inevitably became an object of competition between the Air Force and the Navy, both of which shared the task of bombing North Vietnam. The results were predictable: a preference for aircraft with small bomb-load capacities which necessitated more frequent missions; the expenditure of bombs on marginal or already destroyed targets; even, during periods of munitions shortages, the flying of sorties without bombs. As one Air Force colonel put it: "bombs or no bombs, you've got to have more Air Force over the target than Navy."[54]

A second reason for the failure to monitor performance was a persistent tendency to disregard discouraging intelligence. It is a myth that the United States stumbled blindly into the Vietnam War. At every stage in the long process of escalation informed estimates were available which accurately (and pessimistically) predicted the outcome.* As early as November 1961, for example, the CIA was

[52] Lewy, *America in Vietnam*, pp. 78–82; Enthoven and Smith, *How Much Is Enough*, pp. 295–96.

[53] McNamara to Johnson, November 17, 1966, *Pentagon Papers*, IV, 371.

[54] Quoted in Gallucci, *Neither Peace Nor Honor*, p. 84; see also *ibid.*, pp. 80–85; Gelb and Betts, *The Irony of Vietnam*, pp. 309–10.

*"The information I received [on Vietnam] was more complete and balanced than anyone outside the mainstream of official reporting could possibly realize." (Johnson, *The Vantage Point*, p. 64.)

forecasting that North Vietnam would be able to match, through increased infiltration, any U.S. troop commitment to South Vietnam,
and that bombing the North would not significantly impede that
process. Two-and-a-half years later, a series of war games in which
several key officials of the Johnson administration took part produced precisely the same conclusion.[55] Despite his own enthusiasm for
this alternative in 1961 and 1964, Maxwell Taylor by 1965 was strongly
opposing the introduction of ground combat forces on the grounds
that a "white-faced soldier armed, equipped and trained as he is [is]
not [a] suitable guerrilla fighter for Asian forests and jungles." Clark
Clifford, Johnson's long-time personal friend and future Defense
Secretary, was warning in May 1965 that Vietnam "could be a
quagmire. It could turn into an open end commitment on our part that
would take more and more ground troops, without a realistic hope of
ultimate victory." George Ball, in a series of eloquent dissents from
official policy, stressed that "a deep commitment of United States
forces in a land war in South Viet-Nam would be a catastrophic error.
If there ever was an occasion for a tactical withdrawal, this is it."
Even William P. Bundy, one of the original architects of
"calibration," had concluded by June of 1965 that any level of commitment beyond 70,000 to 100,000 troops would pass "a point of
sharply diminishing returns and adverse consequences."[56]

"There are no signs that we have throttled the inflow of supplies
for the VC," McNamara acknowledged after five months of bombing. "Nor have our air attacks on North Vietnam produced tangible
evidence of willingness on the part of Hanoi to come to the conference
table in a reasonable mood." And even if military successes on the
ground could be achieved, there was no guarantee that these would
not simply "drive the VC back into the trees" from which they could
launch attacks at some future date. "[I]t is not obvious," the
Secretary of Defense admitted, "how we will be able to disengage our
forces from Vietnam." And yet, despite this gloomy appraisal,
McNamara recommended a continuation of the bombing and an increase in troop strength from 75,000 to 175,000–200,000 men. Early
in 1966, on the basis of no more encouraging signs of progress in
ground or air operations, he endorsed a new troop ceiling of 400,000

[55] Special National Intelligence Estimate 10-4-61. November 5, 1961, *Pentagon
Papers*, II, 107; Robert H. Johnson to William P. Bundy, March 31, 1965, Johnson
Papers, NSF Country Files: Vietnam, Box 16, "Memos Vol. XXXII." See also Gelb
and Betts, *The Irony of Vietnam*, pp. 25–26; Halberstam, *The Best and the Brightest*,
pp. 460–62; and Johnson, *The Vantage Point*, pp. 147–49.
[56] Taylor to State Department, February 22, 1965, *Pentagon Papers*, III, 419;
Clifford to Johnson, May 17, 1965, Johnson Papers, NSF Country Files: Vietnam, Box
74, "1965 Troop Decision"; Ball memorandum, "Cutting Our Losses in South Viet-
Nam," June 28, 1965, *ibid.*, Box 18, "Memos (B) Vol. XXV"; William P. Bundy
memorandum, "Holding On in South Vietnam," June 30, 1965, *ibid.*

men, acknowledging at the same time that the North Vietnamese and Viet Cong could probably match those increases. It might be possible, he thought, eventually to contain the enemy with 600,000 men, but that would risk bringing in the Chinese Communists. "It follows, therefore, that the odds are about even that, even with the recommended deployments, we will be faced in early 1967 with a military stand-off at a much higher level, with pacification hardly underway and with the requirement for the deployment of still more U.S. forces."[57]

McNamara's perserverance in the face of pessimism was not atypical—indeed, the Defense Secretary allowed the second sentiment to overwhelm the first sooner than most officials did. Westmoreland, in December 1965, for example, admitted that "notwithstanding the heavy pressures on their transportaion system in the past 9 months, they [the North Vietnamese] have demonstrated an ability to deploy forces into South Vietnam at a greater rate than we are deploying U.S. forces." Nevertheless, "our only hope of a major impact on the ability of the DRV to support the war in Vietnam is continuous air attack . . . from the Chinese border to South Vietnam." The CIA, whose assessments of the consequences of escalation had been especially discouraging, acknowledged in March 1966 that the bombing so far had been ineffective, but then recommended more of it, with fewer restraints. Later that year, in a comment characteristic of the resolute optimism of Johnson administration officials, Robert Komer argued that "by themselves, none of our Vietnam programs offer high confidence of a successful outcome. . . . Cumulatively, however, they *can* produce enough of a *bandwagon psychology* among the southerners to lead to such results by end-1967 or sometime in 1968. At any rate, do we have a better alternative?"[58]

The problem, as Komer suggested, was that however unpromising the prospects of continued escalation, the alternatives seemed even worse. Withdrawal would constitute humiliation, with all that implied for the maintenance of world order. Negotiations prior to establishing a "position of strength" could only lead to appeasement. Continuation of the status quo would not work because the status quo was too delicate. Public opinion remained solidly behind escalation until 1968; indeed, Johnson saw himself as applying the brake, not the accelerator.[59] As a result, there developed a curious mixture of gloom

[57] McNamara to Johnson, July 20, 1965, Johnson Papers, NSF Country File: Vietnam, Box 74, "1965 Troop Decision"; McNamara to Johnson, January 24, 1966, *Pentagon Papers,* IV, 49–51.

[58] Westmoreland cable, December 27, 1965, *Pentagon Papers,* IV, 39. The CIA and Komer reports are discussed in *ibid.,* pp. 71–71, 389–91. (Emphases in orginal.)

[59] Gelb and Betts, *The Irony of Vietnam,* pp. 159–60. See also Johnson, *The Vantage Point,* p. 147; and Kearns, *Lyndon Johnson and the American Dream,* p. 282.

and optimism: things were bad, they were likely to get worse before they got better, but since the alternatives to the existing strategy appeared even more forbidding, there seemed to be little choice but to "press on."

What has not been satisfactorily explained, though, is how the Johnson administration came to define its options so narrowly. In retrospect, quite a lot—negotiations on Hanoi's terms, a gradual relinquishment of responsibility for the war to the South Vietnamese, even a phased withdrawal in the anticipation of an eventual North Vietnamese-Viet Cong victory—would have been preferable to the strategy actually followed, which produced those same results but at vastly greater costs than if they had been sought in the mid-1960's. As George Kennan told the Senate Foreign Relations Committee in 1966, "there is more respect to be won in the opinion of this world by a resolute and courageous liquidation of unsound positions than by the most stubborn pursuit of extravagant and unpromising objectives."[60] But Johnson and his advisers could never bring themselves to consider "heretical" options, despite abundant evidence that their strategy was not working. Their hesitancy suggests still another reason for the failure to monitor performance in Vietnam: an absence of mechanisms for forcing the consideration of unpalatable but necessary alternatives.

Several explanations have been advanced to account for this lapse. It has been argued that there was a premium on "toughness" during the Kennedy-Johnson years; that advocates of a compromise settlement bore a far heavier burden of proof than did supporters of escalation.[61] But this view fails to explain Johnson's tenacious search for a negotiated settlement with Hanoi, carried on not just for the purpose of defusing opposition to the war at home but also in the genuine hope of finding a way out consistent with American credibility.[62] It has been pointed out that Johnson's circle of close advisers narrowed as critics of the war proliferated, and that this limited the Chief Executive's exposure to dissenting points of view.[63] But the President did keep on and listen to "house heretics" like George Ball; more significantly, he paid close attention to McNamara's growing doubts about the war in 1966 and 1967, but still refused to change the strategy.[64] It has recently been suggested that the whole national security decision-making system was at fault: the system "worked" in that it produced the results it had been "programmed" to produce, given prevailing assumptions about containment and the balance of

[60] Senate Committee on Foreign Relations, Hearings, *Supplemental Foreign Assistance Fiscal Year 1966—Vietnam* (Washington: 1966), pp. 335-36.

[61] Richard. J. Barnet, *Roots of War* (Baltimore: 1972), pp. 109-15.

[62] See the list of American peace initiatives and Hanoi's responses in Appendix A to Johnson, *The Vantage Point,* pp. 579-89.

[63] Gallucci, *Neither Peace Nor Honor,* pp. 132-34.

[64] See Johnson's personally drafted memorandum on McNamara's recommendations, December 18, 1967, in Johnson, *The Vantage Point,* pp. 600-601.

power since 1945; the error was in the "programming."[65] But this argument oversimplifies variations in perceptions of interests and threats over the years: while it is true that all postwar administrations have committed themselves to the general objective of containment, they have differed significantly over what was to be contained, and over the means available to do it.

It is this problem of perceived means that best explains the Johnson administration's inability to come up with alternatives in Vietnam. The mechanism that has most often forced the consideration of unpalatable options in the postwar years has been budgetary: when one knows one has only limited resources to work with, then distinctions between what is vital and peripheral, between the feasible and unfeasible, come more easily, if not less painfully. The Eisenhower administration found this out in 1954, when it decided that the "unacceptable" prospect of a communist North Vietnam was in fact preferable to the more costly alternative of direct U.S. military involvement. But, as has been seen, budgetary concerns carried little weight during the Kennedy and Johnson administrations. The theory of "flexible response" implied unlimited means and, hence, little incentive to make hard choices among distasteful alternatives.

Kennedy did from time to time emphasize the existence of limits beyond which Washington could not go in aiding other countries. "[T]he United States is neither omnipotent or omniscient," he pointed out in 1961: "we are only 6 percent of the world's population . . . we cannot right every wrong or reverse each adversary." It has been argued that the abortive 1963 plan for a phased withdrawal of American advisers from South Vietnam reflected Kennedy's sense that the limits of feasible involvement in that country were approaching.[66] But there is no conclusive evidence that Kennedy, on fiscal grounds, was considering a diminished American role there; certainly Johnson did not do so. The new President dutifully stressed the need for economy during his first months in office, but more for the purpose of enhancing his reputation with the business community than from any great concern about the limits of American power in the world scene.[67] And, as the Vietnam crisis intensified, so too did the conviction of Johnson and his advisers that the United States could afford whatever it would take to prevail there.

"[L]et no one doubt for a moment," Johnson proclaimed in August 1964, "that we have the resources and we have the will to

[65] Gelb and Betts, *The Irony of Vietnam,* pp. 2–3.

[66] Kennedy address at the University of Washington, November 16, 1961, *KPP: 1961,* p. 726. See also *ibid.,* pp. 340–41, 359; *KPP: 1963,* pp. 659–60, 735; and the *Pentagon Papers,* II, 161.

[67] *JPP: 1963–64,* pp. 44, 89, 122, 150.

follow this course as long as it may take." In a White House meeting the following month, Rusk pointed out that it had cost $50,000 per guerilla to suppress the insurgency in Greece in the late 1940's; in Vietnam "it would be worth any amount to win." Johnson agreed, emphasizing the need for all to understand "that it was not necessary to spare the horses." "Our assets, as I see them, are sufficient to see this thing through if we enter the exercise with adequate determination to succeed," Rostow wrote in November 1964; "at this stage in history we are the greatest power in the world—if we behave like it." Five months later, as direct American military involvement in Vietnam was beginning, McNamara informed the Joint Chiefs of Staff and the service secretaries that "there is an unlimited appropriation available for the financing of aid to Vietnam. Under no circumstances is a lack of money to stand in the way of aid to that nation." There were always costs in meeting "commitments of honor," Rusk commented in August of that year. "But I would suggest, if we look at the history of the last 30 or 40 years, that the costs of *not* meeting your obligations are far greater than those of meeting your obligations."[68]

"The world's most affluent society can surely afford to spend whatever must be spent for its freedom and security," Johnson told the Congress early in 1965. This assumption of virtually unlimited resources goes far toward explaining the persistence of what was acknowledged to be a costly and inefficient strategy: the idea was that if the United States could simply stay the course, regardless of the expense, it would prevail. "I see no choice," the President added, later that year, "but to continue the course we are on, filled as it is with peril and uncertainty and cost in both money and lives." It might take "months or years or decades," but whatever troops General Westmoreland required would be sent "as requested." "Wastefully, expensively, but nonetheless indisputably, we are winning the war in the South," Robert Komer concluded late in 1966. "Few of our programs—civil or military—are very efficient, but we are grinding the enemy down by sheer weight and mass." Westmoreland agreed. "We'll just go on bleeding them until Hanoi wakes up to the fact that they have bled their country to the point of national disaster for generations. Then they will have to reassess their position."[69]

        [68] Johnson remarks to American Bar Association meeting, New York, August 12, 1964, *ibid.*, p. 953; Bundy memorandum, Johnson conference with advisers, September 9, 1964, Johnson Papers, NSF—NSC Files, Box 2, "Memos for the President, Vol. 6"; Rostow to Rusk, November 23, 1964, *Pentagon Papers,* III, 647; McNamara to the Joint Chiefs of Staff and service secretaries, March 1, 1965, *ibid.,* p. 94; Rusk CBS-TV interview, August 9, 1965, *DSB,* LIII (August 30, 1965), 344. (Emphasis in original.)
        [69] Johnson report to Congress on national defense, January 18, 1965, *JPP: 1965,* p. 69; Johnson remarks to members of Congressional delegations, May 4, 1965, *ibid.,* p. 487; Johnson press conference, July 28, 1965, *ibid.,* pp. 795, 799; Komer memorandum, date not given, *Pentagon Papers,* II, 575; Westmoreland statement to press, April 14, 1967, quoted in Lewy, *America in Vietnam,* p. 73.

But McNamara's "systems analysis" specialists had reached the conclusion, by 1966, that it might take generations to bring the North Vietnamese to that point. Their studies showed, for example, that although enemy attacks tended to produce significant enemy casualties, operations launched by U.S. and South Vietnamese forces produced few if any. This suggested that despite the massive American military presence in the south, the North Vietnamese and Viet Cong still retained the initiative, and hence could control their losses. Other studies indicated that while bombing raids against North Vietnam had increased four times between 1965 and 1968, they had not significantly impaired Hanoi's ability to supply its forces in the south: enemy attacks there had increased on the average five times, and in places eight times, during the same period. The bombing was estimated to have done some $600 million worth of damage in the north, but at a cost in lost aircraft alone of $6 billion. Sixty-five percent of the bombs and artillery rounds expended in Vietnam were being used against unobserved targets, at a cost of around $2 billion a year. Such strikes, the analysts concluded, probably killed about 100 North Vietnamese or Viet Cong in 1966, but in the process provided 27,000 tons of dud bombs and shells which the enemy could use to make booby traps, which that same year accounted for 1,000 American deaths. But most devastating of all, the systems analysts demonstrated in 1968 that despite the presence of 500,000 American troops, despite the expenditure of more bomb tonnage than the United States had dropped in all of World War II, despite estimated enemy casualties of up to 140,000 men in 1967, the North Vietnamese could continue to funnel at least 200,000 men a year into South Vietnam indefinitely. As one analyst wrote, "the notion that we can 'win' this war by driving the VC/NVA from the country or by inflicting an unacceptable rate of casualties on them is false."[70]

Only the last of these studies had any noticeable impact outside the Office of the Secretary of Defense, though: persuasive though they were, there was little incentive, in an administration confident that it could sustain the costs of the war indefinitely, to pay any attention to them.[71] It was not until Johnson personally became convinced that the costs of further escalation would outweigh conceivable benefits that the discipline of stringency could begin to take hold. That did not happen until after the Tet offensive of February 1968, when the President received Westmoreland's request for an additional 206,000 troops, a figure that could not have been met without calling up Reserves and without major domestic and international economic dislocations.*

[70] Enthoven and Smith, *How Much Is Enough,* pp. 290–306.
[71] *Ibid.,* pp. 292–93.
*Curiously, Westmoreland's request was apparently prompted by the Chairman of the Joint Chiefs of Staff, General Earle G. Wheeler, as a means of forcing the reluctant Johnson to call up the Reserves. (Schandler, *The Unmaking of a President,* pp. 116, 138.)

Johnson had always regarded these as limits beyond which he would not go, not on the basis of rigorous statistical analysis, but rather from the gut political instinct that if he passed those points, public support for the war would quickly deteriorate.[72] In the end, then, the Johnson administration based its ultimate calculation of costs and benefits on criteria no more sophisticated than those employed by Eisenhower prior to 1961, or by Truman prior to 1950. The techniques of systems analysis, which had been designed to avoid the need for such arbitrary judgments, in fact only deferred but did not eliminate them.

Several circumstances discouraged the objective evaluation of performance in Vietnam. The military's relative autonomy gave it a large degree of control over the statistical indices used to measure "progress" in the war; this, combined with the organizationally driven compulsion to demonstrate success and the traditional reluctance of civilians in wartime to challenge military authority, made it difficult to verify charges of ineffectiveness.[73] Such accurate intelligence as did get through tended to be disregarded because the alternative courses of action thereby indicated seemed worse than the option of "pressing on." And the perception of unlimited means made perseverance even in the face of unpromising signals seem feasible: far from widening alternatives, the abundance of means, and the consequent lack of incentives to make hard decisions, actually narrowed them. As a result, the postwar administration most sensitive to the need to monitor its own performance found itself ensnared inextricably in a war it did not understand, could not win, but would not leave.

IV

But effectiveness in strategy requires not only the ability to identify interests and threats, calibrate responses, and monitor implementation; it also demands a sense of proportion, an awareness of how commitments in one sphere compare with, and can distract attention and resources away from, obligations elsewhere. Johnson and his subordinates thought they had this larger perspective: Vietnam, they repeatedly insisted, was important not just in itself, but as a symbol of American resolve throughout the world.* The line between a symbol and a fixation is a fine one, though; once it is crossed, perspectives

[72] Schandler, *The Unmaking of a President,* pp. 39, 56, 100–102, 228–29, 290–92. See also Johnson, *The Vantage Point,* pp. 149, 317–19, 406–7.
[73] See, on this point, Gallucci, *Neither Peace Nor War,* pp. 128–30.

*"The idea that we are here simply because the Vietnamese want us to be here . . . ; that we have no national interest in being here ourselves; and that if some of them don't

narrow, often unconsciously, with the result that means employed can become inappropriate to, even destructive of, ends envisaged. This narrowing of perspective, this loss of proportion, this failure to detect the extent to which short-term means can corrupt long-term ends, was the fourth and perhaps most lasting deficiency of "flexible response" as applied in Vietnam.

The tendency appeared vividly in South Vietnam itself, where the administration failed to anticipate the sheer strain several hundred thousand U.S. troops would place on the social and economic structure of that country. Despite American efforts to keep it down, the cost of living in the cities rose by at least 170 percent between 1965 and 1967, just as Westmoreland's "search and destroy" operations were swelling their populations with refugees. Corruption, of course, had always been present in Vietnam, but the proliferation of television sets, motorcycles, watches, refrigerators, and loose cash that accompanied the Americans greatly intensified it. "[T]he vast influx of American dollars," one observer recalls, "had almost as much influence . . . as the bombing had on the countryside":

> It turned the society of Saigon inside out. . . . In the new economy a prostitute earned more than a GVN minister, a secretary working for USAID more than a full colonel, a taxi owner who spoke a few words of English more than a university professor. . . . The old rich of Saigon had opposed the Communists as a threat to their position in society; they found that the Americans took away that position in a much quicker and more decisive fashion—and with it, what was left of the underpinning of Vietnamese values.

A similar phenomenon spread to rural areas as well: "Around the American bases from An Khe to Nha Trang, Cu Chi, and Chu Lai, there had grown up entire towns made of packing cases and waste tin . . . entire towns advertising Schlitz, Coca-Cola, or Pepsi Cola . . . towns with exactly three kinds of industry—the taking in of American laundry, the selling of American cold drinks to American soldiers, and prostitution for the benefit of the Americans."[74]

---

want us to stay, we ought to get out is to me fallacious," Ambassador Henry Cabot Lodge cabled from Saigon in 1966. "In fact, I doubt whether we would have the moral right to make the commitment we have made here solely as a matter of charity towards the Vietnamese and without the existence of a strong United States interest. . . . Some day we may have to decide how much it is worth to us to deny Viet-Nam to Hanoi and Peking—regardless of what the Vietnamese may think." (Lodge to State Department, May 23, 1966, *Pentagon Papers,* IV, 99–100.)

[74] FitzGerald, *Fire in the Lake,* pp. 315–16, 349, 352–53.

The effect of this overbearing presence was to erode South Vietnam's capacity for self-reliance, the very quality the Americans had sought to strengthen in the first place. To be sure, Washington never succeeded in controlling its clients in all respects: the very profligacy of the U.S. investment in South Vietnam made occasional threats to cut it off less than credible. "The harsh truth is," one report noted early in 1968, "that given a showdown situation or an intolerable divergence between GVN and US methods, the US advisor will lose." But recalcitrance is not the same thing as independence. The same report noted that "[t]he Vietnamese in the street is firmly convinced that the US totally dominates the GVN and dictates exactly what course shall be followed."[75] And Vietnamese at the military or governmental level, while certainly not puppets, while clearly resentful at the extent to which the Americans had come to dominate their culture, were at the same time terrified at the prospect that the Americans might one day leave.[76] The result was an ambiguous but deep dependency, the extent of which became clear only after the United States did at last withdraw from the war, in 1973.

It is hard to say, in retrospect, what the cross-over point would have been between the level of outside aid necessary to sustain South Vietnam against its enemies and the amount beyond which self-reliance would have been impaired. Perhaps there was no such point; perhaps South Vietnam never had the capacity to stand on its own. What is clear, though, is that Washington made few efforts to find out. The American buildup took place almost totally without regard to the destructive impact it was having on the society it was supposed to defend. "It became necessary to destroy the town, to save it," an Air Force major explained, following the bombing of a Mekong delta village occupied by Viet Cong after the Tet offensive in 1968.[77] The comment could be applied to the whole American experience in Vietnam, and to the dilemma of disproportionate means which the strategy of "flexible response," despite its original emphasis on matching response to offense, never seemed able to resolve.

Securing South Vietnam's independence had not been the only reason for the American presence in that country, though: there had also been a determination to show potential aggressors elsewhere that aggression would not pay. "To withdraw from one battlefield means only to prepare for the next," Johnson argued. "We must say in southeast Asia—as we did in Europe—. . . . 'Hitherto shalt thou

[75] MACCORDS report on Bien Hoa province for period ending December 31, 1967, *Pentagon Papers,* II, 406.

[76] FitzGerald, *Fire in the Lake,* p. 357.

[77] Quoted in Alexander Kendrick, *The Wound Within: America in the Vietnam Years, 1945-1974* (Boston: 1974), p. 251.

come, but no further.' "[78] Interestingly, administration officials did not consider success in South Vietnam as necessarily a requirement in communicating that message. However things turned out there, John McNaughton reflected in 1964, it was "essential . . . that [the] US emerge as a 'good doctor.' We must have kept promises, been tough, taken risks, gotten bloodied, and hurt the enemy very badly." Sustained reprisals against the north might not work, McGeorge Bundy acknowledged early in 1965—the chances of success, he thought, were between 25 and 75 percent. But "even if it fails, the policy will be worth it. At a minimum it will damp down the charge that we did not do all we could. . . . Beyond that, a reprisal policy . . . will set a higher price for the future upon all adventures of guerrilla warfare."[79] The important thing, in projecting resolve, was to make a commitment; failure, while both possible and undesirable, would not be as bad as not having acted in the first place.

And yet, the signal actually communicated was very different. The inability of the steadily growing American commitment to halt North Vietnamese infiltration or Viet Cong attacks—a pattern made painfully evident by the 1968 Tet offensive—seemed only to demonstrate the irrelevancy of the kind of power the United States could bring to bear in such situations: technology, in this respect, may well have been more of a hindrance than a help in Vietnam.[80] The war also confirmed Mao Tse-tung's theory that relatively primitive forces could prevail against more sophisticated adversaries if they had both patience and will, qualities Ho Chi Minh perceived more accurately than Johnson to be lacking in the American attitude toward Vietnam.[81] Finally, Washington's commitment in that country had grown to the point, by 1968, that the United States would have been hard-pressed to respond anywhere else in the world had a comparable crisis developed.[82] What was demonstrated in Vietnam, then, was not so much the costs of committing aggression as of resisting it. . . .

[78] Johnson address at Johns Hopkins University, April 7, 1965, *JPP: 1965*, p. 395.

[79] McNaughton draft memorandum, "Aims and Options in Southeast Asia," October 13, 1964, *Pentagon Papers*, III, 582; Bundy memorandum, "A Policy of Sustained Reprisal," February 7, 1965, *ibid.*, p. 314.

[80] See, on this point, Lewy, *America in Vietnam*, pp. 60, 96, 175, 181–82, 207, 306, 437–38.

[81] See especially "On Protracted War," in the *Selected Military Writings of Mao Tse-tung* (Peking: 1967), pp. 210–19.

[82] Johnson, *The Vantage Point*, p. 389. See also Schandler, *The Unmaking of a President*, pp. 109, 171.

"The Domestic Politics
of Cruise Missile
Development, 1970-1980"

ROBERT J. ART *and*
STEPHEN E. OCKENDEN

For the last ten years, cruise missiles have played a bewildering variety
of roles in the United States.* To the arms control community, they
have come to represent the most recent example of the inexorable
technological imperative that drives the arms race. To the proponents
of greater military spending, who fear that the United States is becoming second best, they have epitomized the American technological
edge that barely enables compensation for the Soviet Union's quantitative superiority. To the military services, they have been unwanted
competitors in the perennial Pentagonal fights for scarce funds. To
the technology community, they have been another gadget with which
to demonstrate its engineering wizardry. And to those heavily involved in the hautes politiques of American foreign policy, they have
been alternately a bargaining chip, an unwanted complication, and a
godsend for tough political problems.

From *Cruise Missiles: Technology, Strategy, Politics,* edited by Richard K. Betts.
Copyright © 1981 by the Brookings Institution, Washington, D.C., pp. 359-415.
Reprinted by permission.
    Due to the length of this article, we have omitted all footnotes to preserve the text in-
tact. For the full documentation, see original.

*The authors are indebted to Michael McGwire, Glenn Snyder, and Kenneth Waltz
for their perceptive comments on an earlier draft of this article. The bulk of the material
in this chapter is based on two hundred interviews with government officials who have
been directly involved with one or more aspects of the cruise missile. Stephen Ockenden
conducted one hundred of these interviews in 1977 and 1978, concentrating primarily on
the Air Force and the Navy. Robert Art conducted one hundred in 1980, concentrating
primarily on SALT, NATO, and the ground-launched cruise missile. Nevertheless, the
chapter is truly a collaborative effort. Most of the material, especially the political
nuances, cannot be found in the written public record; therefore intensive interviewing
(with confidentiality guaranteed) was necessary to reconstruct and analyze what had
happened. Because participants differ in their perceptions, the authors stipulated that
all information received from their interviews be confirmed by at least two persons,
each in a different bureau or office, before considering the information reliable. They
have also tried to reconfirm interview data with citations from the public record when
possible.

Cruise missiles have played these many roles in the varied arenas of American politics because they appear to be relatively cheap, promise great performance, and, most important, are adaptable to a broad range of military uses. Perhaps unique among the major weapon systems developed by the United States since World War II, cruise missiles have been an important factor in a large number of political arenas. Table 12-1 shows the six types of cruise missiles that were under development from 1970 through 1980 and the six political arenas in which each version figured. The variety of arenas and multiple versions of the missile in each one make a complicated story. Although it is the political intricacies—and the conclusions drawn from an analysis of them—with which we are concerned, this chapter will focus initially on the three modes of launch—air, land, and sea.

The following four propositions summarize the politics of cruise missile development in the United States from 1970 through 1980:

1. Without exception, the military services did not want cruise missiles if they threatened their respective dominant missions or ate into their scarce funds, both of which were in general the case. The long-range air-launched cruise missile (ALCM) was rammed down the throat of the Air Force. The Army refused to accept development responsibility for the ground-launched cruise missile (GLCM). The Air Force consequently got stuck with it and viewed it as a "national mission"—one it performed for the country, but that had little value for its own missions. The Navy—specifically, the carrier admirals—did not want the Tomahawk antiship missile (TASM) because it represented a clear and present danger to the mission of the carrier-based aircarft.

Table 12-1. *Cruise Missile Types and Political Arenas*

	Cruise missile types				
Political arenas	*ALCM[a] (A and B) (Air Force)*	*GLCM[b] (Air Force)*	*TASM[c] (Navy)*	*TLAM-N[d] (SLCM) (Navy)*	*TLAM-C[e] (Navy)*
SALT II politics	X	X	. . .	X	. . .
NATO politics	. . .	X	. . .	X	. . .
Office of the Secretary of Defense versus service politics	X	X	. . .	X	. . .
Intraservice politics	X	. . .	X	X	. . .
Executive-congressional politics	X	. . .	. . .	X	X
Intraexecutive politics	X	X	. . .	X	X

a. Short-range air-launched cruise missile (ALCM-A); long-range air-launched cruise missile (ALCM-B).
b. Ground-launched cruise missile.
c. Tomahawk antiship missile.
d. Tomahawk land-attack missile, nuclear armed (TLAM-N); sea-launched cruise missile (SLCM).
e. Tomahawk land-attack cruise missile, conventionally armed.

2. The cruise missile would not have proceeded as fast and as far, if indeed at all, had it not been for the intervention and support of high-level political figures in the Pentagon, the White House, and even the U.S. Department of State. For individuals operating at this level in the American government, the driving factors were negotiations with the Soviet Union on SALT I and II, the concern expressed by NATO's European members about the reliability of America's foreign policy and the credibility of the U.S. nuclear umbrella over them in the era of strategic parity between the superpowers, and White House anticipation of adverse congressional action on SALT II if this new technology were not developed to its fullest.

3. Technological innovation therefore did not create an irresistible force. It may be, as Samuel P. Huntington once said, "what is technically possible tends to become politically necessary." Technological innovation, however, only creates the necessary, not the sufficient, condition. At every crucial stage in the development of each type of cruise missile, high-level political intervention was necessary either to start it or to sustain it. As a consequence of this dichotomy between service resistance and high-level political pressure, the American government during the SALT II negotiations from roughly 1973 until 1977 was bargaining hard for systems that the services did not want.

4. Finally, Congress was the arena in which intraservice and Office of the Secretary of Defense (OSD)—service disputes were resolved on the surface, but it is by no means clear that members of Congress always knew what was going on in the Pentagon or that Congress prevailed. The role of Congress in the politics of cruise missile development during the 1970s remains the most difficult about which to generalize. Congress intervened at three crucial points during this decade and played the role of ally, lobbyist, judge, and gadfly, but an overall assessment of congressional influence in this case remains elusive. The decade of the 1970s was supposedly the era of congressional activism in defense matters, based on a quality and depth of staff that Congress theretofore had not possessed. That decade has been heralded as the decade of micromanagement, an intimate and continuous congressional involvement in the details of Pentagon policy. Congressional actions on the cruise missile during this period by no means fully support this view. Congress was heavily involved in the details of cruise missile development, but such involvement did not radically affect, deflect, or alter the course of the cruise missile. The more traditional view of Congress is the most sensible here: Congress exerted influence less by mastery of detail than by executive anticipation of likely congressional reactions to its proposed actions. And what the executive spent the most time anticipating were the general political contours on Capitol Hill.

THE AIR FORCE AND THE AIR-LAUNCHED CRUISE MISSILE

Since its inception, the United States Air Force has identified itself intimately with the manned strategic bombardment mission. It is this mission that provided the rationale for the separation of the Air Corps from the Army, that sustained Air Force identity and budgetary levels throughout much of the post–World War II era, that has driven the Air Force to press periodically for the modernization of the manned strategic bomber, and that was threatened by the long-range air-launched cruise missile in the early 1970s. In order to understand why the ALCM came about, the manner in which the Air Force reacted to it, and how the matter was finally resolved, it is first necessary to begin with the Air Force's plans in the 1960s to replace its aging B-52 fleet.

THE PENETRATING BOMBER AND THE AIR FORCE IN THE 1960s

Manned strategic bombers can attack the enemy either by penetrating hostile airspace and flying directly to their targets, or by standing off at great distances and releasing weapons that fly to the targets. The penetration mode provides flexibility because each bomber can fly alternate routes, conduct postattack reconnaissance, and recommit its weapons load as necessary. The price of flexibility comes quite high because penetrating bombers are expensive to build and operate. Their susceptibility to detection and destruction imposes stringent and hence costly requirements on designers. Although range and defensive armament requirements are less stringent for the stand-off mode, such bombers sacrifice flexibility, and their net weapons yield is diminished because a large portion of each weapon's weight is dedicated to the propulsion and guidance systems. Air Force doctrine has consistently favored the penetrating bomber, preferring the advantages of flexibility. Moreover, for many years the guidance and propulsion problems of long-range standoff weapons were considered too complex for solution. Consequently, since 1945 the Air Force has devoted a great deal of effort to improving the penetration capability of the manned bomber.

Events of the 1960s began to conspire against this traditional preference. Hoping to replace the B-52, the Air Force devoted its research efforts in the late 1950s to a follow-on aircraft that could fly higher and faster than any previous bomber. The result was the B-70, a bomber that could fly in excess of Mach 3 and at an altitude of 70,000 feet. In 1960, however, just as the Air Force was ready to commit funds to full-scale production of the B-70, the Russians dramatically demonstrated that the basic concept of the high penetrating bomber was obsolete. By shooting down the high-flying U-2 piloted by Francis Gary Powers, they showed that the B-70 too would be vulnerable to air defenses and thereby forced the Air Force to rethink its commitment to the penetrating bomber.

The Air Force responded to the U-2 incident in two ways: it began to develop a series of short-term modifications to the existing B-52 fleet, and it instituted a long-term study designed to produce a more effective manned penetrator. Most of the effort initially went into refurbishing the B-52 for low-altitude penetration by modifying the avionics and wings and by adding two types of defensive weapons—an air-to-surface missile (Hound Dog) and a decoy missile (Quail). Although both missiles were developed before the U-2 incident and hence were not optimized for low-level penetration, they added significantly to the life of the B-52. With a range of 600 miles, the Hound Dog gave the B-52 an ability to suppress enemy defenses; with a range of 250 miles, the Quail drew some defenses away from the mother aircraft. Each missile extended the range at which the bomber's weapons could be released and, moreover, augmented the low-level penetration capability of the B-52. Neither, however, yielded a long-range standoff capability: only two Hound Dogs were carried aboard a B-52, and the ranges of both missiles were too short to reach most targets within the Soviet Union from beyond its borders. Thus, although the Air Force modified the B-52 for low-level flight, the service remained committed to the penetration mode.

While work progressed on a short-term response to the U-2 incident, the Air Force began a series of conceptual studies for another manned bomber. After several years, the Air Force recommitted itself to the penetrating bomber in the guise of the advanced manned strategic aircraft (AMSA). It was this action that subsequently shaped how the Air Force viewed the cruise missile. The AMSA was to be a modern, small, versatile, supersonic bomber optimized for low-level dash, but flexible enough to fly at high altitudes. Early criteria established that the AMSA would have twice the range and five times the payload of the FB-111 and more than twice the speed of the B-52. The AMSA was to outperform any previous bomber and was to have the costly, if not potentially contradictory, characteristics of short takeoff, high speed, and a low-level terminal dash. As early as 1968, therefore, systems analysts within the Department of Defense began to express concern over the costs of the AMSA. Nonetheless, the Air Force obtained approval for the award of a development contract to Rockwell Aviation in June 1970, and the AMSA was renamed the B-1.

THE B-1 AND THE SUBSONIC CRUISE ARMED DECOY

Even with formal approval, the Air Force could not deploy the B-1 for several years. In the interim the B-52 had to be maintained and modernized by upgrading its defensive weaponry; the Hound Dog and Quail had been designed in the 1950s. Modernization, however, entailed two key constraints. First, the follow-on defensive weaponry to be put on the B-52 also had to be compatible with the B-1. Second, such weaponry could not challenge the penetration mission. For the B-1, in short, the new defensive weaponry would be a predictable techno-logical advance, not a radical reorientation in concept, to facilitate, not obviate, the role of the strategic penetrator.

For the Hound Dog, innovation proceeded quickly and with little difficulty, largely due to the political skill of the development team. Not without reason, the Hound Dog's replacement was named the short-range attack missile (SRAM), a small supersonic weapon designed to be carried within the bomber's weapons bay. These characteristics sacrificed range (30 to 100 miles for the SRAM, compared with 600 for the Hound Dog) for a substantial gain in high-speed performance and in the bomber's weapons load. This trade-off was by no means irrational (it clearly resulted in a superior offensive capability), but it was also not coincidental. The SRAM was designed specifically as a defense suppression weapon to assist bombers in the penetration mission. Its short range would have made it useful for little else. The SRAM project team was careful to moderate any claims and to downplay any characteristics that might threaten existing Air Force doctrine. As one of the team noted:

> The trick in any innovation is to balance the demands of the innovators with the political reality. We always took care to list modifications as "refurbishments" rather than as "upgrades." We kept everything as incremental as possible. It's a lot less threatening that way.

Due both to the technological superiority of the SRAM over the Hound Dog and to the political skill of the SRAM design team, the new weapon won ready acceptance within the Air Force and entered full production in 1972. By contrast, from the outset the project to replace the Quail decoy became mired in controversy, which shaped the Air Force attitude toward long-range cruise missiles throughout the 1970s. The Quail replacement became wrapped up in intraservice and Defense Department politics that struck at the heart of the ra-tionale for the penetrating bomber.

The controversy began with the fact that the Quail was not an optimal decoy for a low-level penetrating bomber. Having been designed in the 1950s, when penetrating bombers flew at high altitudes, the Quail could be a decoy for a bomber only in high-altitude flight and therefore could be used for only a portion of the B-52's flight profile. Because of its size, moreover, the Quail could be carried only in limited numbers aboard each aircraft. By the mid-1960s, the Air Force clearly recognized that it needed an advanced decoy to augment the low-level penetrating bomber of the future. As a result, the Air Force, the Strategic Air Command (SAC), and corollary agencies within the Department of Defense undertook a series of studies between 1967 and 1969 to establish the criteria for a decoy that would be capable of operating in the projected environment of Russian defenses. Of the many criteria arrived at, one was critical: the new decoy had to be compatible with the rotary launching rack developed for the SRAM. Bomber operations, it was concluded, would best be served if the new decoy, like the SRAM, were carried within the weapons bay of a penetrating bomber and were made interchangeable with the bomber's armaments. It was this interchangeability criterion that created the controversy over the new decoy and later over the long-range cruise missile.

Requiring that the new decoy fit the SRAM launcher imposed severe constraints on its size, volume, and weight, and hence on its range. Yet it was clear that the decoy had to travel much farther than the SRAM: a decoy limited to a one-hundred-mile range would provide only a few minutes' protection against Russian defenses. Therefore, Colonel Archie L. Wood, a member of the study group formed to examine decoys in 1967, proposed that the decoy be propelled by one of the small turbofan engines then under development by Williams Research Corporation and by other contractors. If it lived up to its promise, this engine would give a range of at least 500 miles. Concurrently, however, a private research organization suggested adding a nuclear warhead to the decoy in order to ensure that the Russians would be forced to expend resources on destroying those missiles even if they were recognized by radar as decoys.

To senior Air Force officers, of course, a decoy with a long range and armed with a nuclear warhead sounded very much like a standoff weapon. Moreover, there were serious questions about the technological feasibility of propelling and guiding a cruise missile over such long distances. Then skeptics of the penetrating bomber within the Department of Defense Office of Program Analysis and Evaluation (PA&E) quickly seized upon Wood's concepts as an alternative to the costly B-1. In short, the decoy quickly became transformed from a straightforward augmentation of the B-52's penetration capability into a potential competitor to the penetrating mission itself and hence to the B-1 aircraft.

The Air Force responded by monitoring and managing the program's development as closely as possible in order to ensure that the decoy did not become a full-fledged standoff weapon. The Air Force Systems Command took the unprecedented step of acting as subsystems integrator, a role normally reserved for the prime contractor. It placed the decoy project within the Systems Program Office designated for Reconnaissance, Strike and Electronic Warfare. Such close monitoring ensured that the decoy—now named the subsonic cruise armed decoy, or SCAD—would remain an augmentation of, rather than a replacement for, the penetrating bomber. The missile that ultimately emerged from this process was a scant 168 inches long and 21 inches in diameter. With a nuclear warhead, it would have a range of roughly 1,000 miles.

Within this context the SCAD entered its final and fatal controversy. In June 1972, Secretary of Defense Melvin R. Laird asked for and received supplemental appropriations to begin work on weapons that would provide assurances against any failure in the newly signed SALT I treaty. Among such programs was a vaguely defined strategic cruise missile for the Navy. Laird had first heard of cruise missile technology while serving on the House Appropriations Committee. His enthusiasm was fed both by Navy aides and by analysts in PA&E. He also felt that the Air Force was resisting the concept in order to protect the B-1. Laird therefore hoped that high-level OSD support for a new Navy cruise missile program would force the Air Force to develop its own long-range cruise missile.

For the moment, his hopes came to naught. Throughout 1972 and 1973, the debate grew more intense between those who wished to see the new Air Force decoys unarmed (subsonic cruise unarmed decoy—SCUD) and those who wished to see them armed (SCAD). At issue, of course, was the role of the penetrating bomber. A decoy with a 1,000-mile range and a nuclear warhead could grow into a standoff weapon. The advocates of such a development were explicit in their quest for a standoff replacement for the B-1. The issue, therefore, had fully crystallized. Both sides in the SCAD-SCUD debate wanted to force a resolution. Thus, on April 13, 1973, at a meeting of the Defense Systems Acquisition Review Council (DSARC), analysts from PA&E confronted analysts from the Air Force and urged that the decoys either be fully armed or canceled outright; PA&E saw unarmed decoys as a waste of money. Ironically, rather than trying to control the SCAD program any longer, the Air Force proposed that because the costs of the decoy had grown so prohibitive, it should be canceled and, even more, that the missile was no longer needed by the B-1. The result was foreordained: on July 6, 1973, Deputy Secretary of Defense William Clements notified Congress that the SCAD would be terminated.

THE B-1 AND THE ALCM-A

If the Air Force had, for the moment, killed a standoff missile, it had by no means generated public enthusiasm for the B-1. The bomber was running into an increasingly heavy opposition that was less concerned with doctrinal subtleties than with the B-1's ever-growing costs and decreasing performance. Over several years the B-1 had fallen behind schedule, below requirements, and over its original cost ceilings. Moreover, at the specific urging of Secretary Laird, Congress in late 1973 directed the Air Force, first, to coordinate its cruise missile research programs left over from the SCAD project with those of the Navy and, second, to investigate a standoff application for such missiles. The cost to the Air Force of these two actions was clear: it had begun to lose control over the development of bomber-launched weapons. The culmination of this trend came in a directive from Deputy Secretary of Defense Clements to the Air Force on December 19, 1973, that required it to begin the development of a formal ALCM program using SCAD propulsion technology and the terrain-contour-matching navigation under exploration by the Navy.

What had largely been implicit in the SCAD-SCUD debate was thus now explicit. The Air Force was being challenged to defend its B-1 bomber against a shift in doctrine. Opponents of the B-1 could now focus their efforts on the standoff solution to bomber modernization rather than merely express their concern over cost and performance figures. The Air Force's answer to the challenge, however, was ingeniously simple: they brought the SCAD back to life. The weapon the Air Force offered as an ALCM was structurally identical to the SCAD, which it had earlier claimed would be insufficient for a standoff missile because of its small size and its design as a decoy. There was no search for a new design to meet the congressional and Defense Department directives because the ALCM-SCAD hybrid had the advantage of limited range. Within the Air Force, high-level opposition was directed, not at cruise missiles per se, but rather at *long-range* cruise missiles that could threaten the development of a penetrating bomber. Use of the SCAD airframe for a cruise missile thus served both to answer demands from outside actors and to keep the B-1 alive in the face of mounting opposition.

Ironically, however, it was Air Force efforts to save the B-1 that ultimately contributed to its demise. In an attempt to put the challenge of the ALCM to rest once and for all, the Air Force, at OSD direction, initiated a comprehensive study of bomber alternatives in August 1973. For the ensuing sixteen months, the Air Force, in conjunction with representatives from the OSD and the Joint Chiefs of Staff, worked on the widely heralded Joint Strategic Bomber Study (JSBS). The study looked at seven possible mixes of existing and potential aircraft, each armed with a varying number of gravity bombs, SRAMs, and ALCMs. Not surprisingly, the study concluded that the best possible force consisted of penetrating B-1 bombers rather than a force of standoff cruise missile carriers.

The critical assumption of the JSBS was that the United States would spend a sum of money equal to that dedicated for B-1 construction. In other words, the study concluded that once cost was fixed at that level, a B-1 fleet put twice as many warheads on target as the next best fleet of bombers. This assumption necessarily gave the expensive B-1 bomber an advantage in marginal rates of return because the study failed to address the question of how many warheads on target should be factored into the computer model. In addition, the study made a number of questionable assumptions about American-Russian offensive-defensive interchanges and remained unduly optimistic in its assessment of American defensive electronic warfare capabilities. The results of the JSBS were so controversial that what the Air Force had hoped would be the definitive case in favor of the B-1 instead quickly became a rallying point for its opponents. Gleeful critics in Congress found it difficult to refrain from referring to the study as the "Joint Strategic B.S."

In the meantime, the Navy's cruise missile program began to show great promise. Because the Navy did not constrain its missile to the dimensions of the SRAM launcher, it had greater range and could be a clear alternative to the Air Force cruise missile for the air-launched mission. As a result, the DSARC in late 1974 ordered that the Air Force ALCM project be phased back and closely coordinated with the Navy project. Thus the Air Force was steadily losing control over the ALCM program. It was caught in an impossible bind. If the Air Force did nothing to improve the range of its own missile, Defense Department officials could always turn to the Navy. If instead the Air Force began to increase the range of its ALCM, it would shoot itself in the foot. Either way, the B-1 would be undercut.

Although the B-1 was subject to cost overruns and performance failures, it was a superlative aircraft. The real question was whether it was sensible to purchase 244 of these planes at $80 million to $100 million apiece when equally effective alternatives might be available for substantially less money. Matters came to a head in mid-1976 when Congress adopted a measure designed to appease both critics and supporters. After several attempts to kill the B-1 outright, House and Senate conferees directed that procurement funds for the first eight B-1s be allocated at the rate of only $87 million per month through January 31, 1977. Although this would not terminate expenditures on the troubled program, it would ensure that the next administration would have the chance to evaluate the aircraft before buying it in bulk.

In the interim, the Air Force tried to solve the challenge of a long-range Navy cruise missile by extending the range of its own missile, but not to the point that the rationale for the B-1 would be threatened. At a meeting of the DSARC on January 9, 1977, however, shortly before the Carter administration assumed office, the OSD directed the Air Force to develop an extended-range ALCM by stretching the fuselage of its prototype missile and to give the extended-range missile (ALCM-B) priority over the shorter-range ALCM-A. Finally, the OSD ordered that the Air Force project merge with the Navy cruise missile program in a Joint Cruise Missile Project Office, but with the

Navy in control. The Air Force had thus been ordered to build a true standoff missile, with Navy supervision to ensure compliance.

The stretched fuselage of the ACLM-B made the missile incompatible with the doctrine of penetration because it extended the ALCM's range to 1,300 miles or more. It also made the missile incompatible with the design of the B-1 because the aircraft had been built with three separate weapons bays, each just large enough to carry a SRAM launcher. The extension of the ALCM's length by five feet meant that it could no longer be carried internally. External mounting on wing pylons, however, would give the B-1 a substantially larger radar cross section, cut its speed and range, and thereby make it unsuitable for low-level penetration. With the B-1, therefore, the Air Force faced two choices: either not carry the ALCM-B at all or undermine the principal design features of the aircraft. Consequently, in order to save the B-1, the Air Force fell back on the B-52, the plane it had hoped to retire from service, proposing a mixed force of penetrating B-1s armed with SRAMs and ALCM-As and standoff B-52s armed with the long-range ALCM-B. The mixed force would mean a smaller purchase of B-1s than the 244 originally envisioned, but it would still keep the penetrating mission alive under the rationale of diversifying the bomber force. By early 1977, therefore, the stage was set for the final confrontation.

BOMBER POLITICS AND THE ALCM-B

Immediately upon assuming office, President Jimmy Carter reduced the planned 1977 purchase of B-1s from eight to five and ordered Secretary of Defense Harold Brown to undertake still another analysis of the B-1 in order to investigate other alternatives to the bomber modernization question. In turn, Secretary Brown directed his assistant secretary for program, analysis, and evaluation, E. C. Aldridge, to chair the Modernization of the Strategic Bomber Force Study, with inputs from the Air Force, the Joint Chiefs of Staff, the Office of International Security Affairs, and the Office of Defense Research and Engineering. The study was transmitted to Brown on May 11, 1977.

Brown asked the group to focus on two critical factors. First, he wanted a reassessment of the intelligence estimates about Russian air defenses and therefore directed that the analysis examine the likelihood that the Russians might soon deploy look-down-shoot-down radars capable of countering low-flying penetrating bombers. Second, he asked the group to determine whether the low radar cross section of the cruise missile would be an effective counter to such defenses. The study then analyzed two main alternative approaches to modernizing the bomber force: B-52s armed with cruise missiles and deferral of B-1 production, or B-52s with cruise missiles and continuance of B-1 production. This made it possible to analyze three types of forces: a pure penetrating bomber force, a pure cruise missile force, and a mixed force of penetrators and standoff bombers armed with cruise missiles.

In his memorandum transmitting the study to Secretary Brown, Aldridge stressed the overall conclusion of the group's efforts: "cost-effectiveness analysis does not provide a clear choice among the three types of forces; therefore, factors other than cost-effectiveness must be relied upon to make the decision." Three additional conclusions were offered: (1) for the next ten years, penetrating bombers were likely to be able to penetrate Russian air defenses; (2) for this period, the B-1 and the B-52Gs and Hs would be equally cost-effective as penetrators, but after that, the B-52 would be closed out by improvements in the Soviet Union's air defenses, but the B-1 would not; and (3) "a mixed force hedges against defense improvements that could be uniquely effective against either penetrating bombers or cruise missiles."

The difficulty in reaching a firm recommendation on which of the three options to take stemmed from the inability to determine how much Russian air defenses would improve after the ten-year period that the group took as its focal point, which carried the analysis through 1990. The study did conclude that the B-1 would be able to penetrate Russian air defenses longer than the B-52, but ultimately that it too would no longer be effective. It could not, however, say with certainty how much longer and therefore could not specify the time when the B-1 would be closed out. Thus, although the study could not choose one option as clearly superior, it did recommend continued production of the B-1 at a reduced rate to preserve the mixed bomber force as the best hedge against the uncertainties about Russian defenses. On the basis of this analysis Secretary Brown recommended to the president that he continue production of the B-1, but not at the rate requested by the Air Force.

Brown's recommendation was reviewed during May and June at the White House by staff from the National Security Council and the Office of Management and Budget. Three factors clearly affected the general perspective with which the staff viewed the entire issue. First, of course, was President Carter's stated opposition to the B-1 during his campaign. Any analytical case for continued production of the plane would have to be compelling if the president were to reverse himself on what had become the political symbol of his attitude toward defense spending. Second was the relation between what would be decided on the B-1 and the ALCM on the one hand and the SALT II treaty negotiations with the Soviet Union on the other. After the Russian's summary rejection of the March comprehensive proposal, the United States had proposed to the Soviet Union in late April a "three-tier" approach in which ALCMs with a maximum range of 2,500 kilometers would be permitted. It would be unfair to conclude that the administration was preserving the long-range ALCM option because it had already decided to cancel the B-1. But it would not be unfair to conclude that the administration was trying to preserve this option should it decide to cancel the B-1 penetrator and opt for the standoff force of B-52s armed with long-range cruise missiles. Third, and directly related to the second, were concerns over the political and strategic implications of the increasing vulnerability of the Minutemen. Key White House officials were unanimous that the United States could not put all its eggs into one strategic basket, the sea-based deterrent force. No decision had yet been made on the MX program. Carter's closest advisers wanted to make certain that, whatever the president decided about the B-1, the bomber leg of the triad would be kept effective. If the B-1 were to be canceled, therefore, a major program to keep the air-breathing component of the strategic forces viable was essential. The political ramifications, both at home and abroad, of failure to modernize both the bomber and the land-based force would be unacceptable. Thus, the first factor inclined Carter toward cancellation of the B-1. The second enabled him to do so without undue SALT II complications with the Soviet Union. And the third mandated that he had better have a defensible "big-league" program to preserve the bomber force if he did.

Carter's advisers presented the president with four options: (1) the Air Force case, argued eloquently by Chief of Staff General David C. Jones, for a force of 244 B-1 bombers at a cost of at least $30 billion; (2) the standoff or pure cruise missile force, with cancellation of the B-1 and any other plans to build a penetrating bomber, with the B-52s serving as the platforms for long-range ALCMs in the near term, and with an undefined follow-on platform when the B-52s wore out; (3) the arms control option of doing nothing for the bomber force, which meant canceling the B-1, living with aging B-52s, and ultimately accepting a two-legged triad; and (4) the curtailed B-1 force, which entailed a slowing of the development of the B-1, a careful look at its costs and capability, an imposing of less stringent requirements on it for penetration, speed, and range, and a production purchase of seventy to seventy-five.

On substantive grounds, none of the president's advisers recommended the first option. Each was highly skeptical of the Air Force's cost estimates and did not trust its assurances about the long-term ability of the B-1 to penetrate the likely improvements in Russian air defenses. Although the B-1 had a lower radar cross section than the B-52, nevertheless it was still large enough that it would have to rely on electronic countermeasures (ECM) that threw out a great deal of electromagnetic energy. The fear was that in time the Russians would improve their high-speed computer ability enough to be able to triangulate the electromagnetic energy generated by the B-1's ECM and thereby pinpoint its location. Secretary Brown was asked point-blank by the president "whether ECM will cut the mustard over the next twenty to thirty years." Brown could not guarantee that it would. White House analysis, in short, had reconfirmed the conclusion of the OSD's modernization study: the technical case for the B-1 was marginal. Jones, speaking for the Air Force, said nothing to alter that view. He knew that the Air Force case had two large soft spots—underestimation of costs and overestimation of penetration capability. He therefore chose not "to get into an analytic tennis match" with Brown, but rather to stress the perceptual dimension—that the United States had to be number one militarily in the world, that it could and therefore should build the world's best bomber, that it had already started to modernize the sea-based deterrent and was thinking about how to do so for the land-based force, and that now was the time to begin modernization of the bomber force. But the analytical and technical case against full-scale production of the B-1 was too strong, and the president could, with good conscience, reject it. As one adviser close to this decision stated: "I'm sure the president remembered his campaign promise, but the technical case against the Air Force proposal was compelling."

The third option was the preferred choice of those who were concerned about the arms control implications of cruise missiles. But because of concern about the increasing vulnerability of the Minuteman force and because the administration was not yet in a position to make a decision about the proposed MX (technical experts had just told the generals that the covered-trench deployment for the MX was highly vulnerable to attack), that option was summarily rejected by Carter and his advisers. At home and abroad, the political costs of allowing the strategic deterrent to become two-legged, or to appear to be slowly going entirely to sea, were intolerable.

The decision, therefore, came down to a choice between the second and fourth options. Brown, Zbigniew Brzezinski, and ultimately Bert Lance privately and strongly urged Carter to select the fourth option. Political and substantive factors lay behind their recommendation. Politically, some sort of B-1 program would strengthen the president's hand in selling a SALT II accord to the hard-liners in Congress, keep up the pressure on the Russians to negotiate, and lessen the pressure from the Air Force for the MX. (The B-1, moreover, was more clearly suited for retaliation, while the MX had first-strike overtones.) Substantively, reservations about how well a long-range cruise missile would perform, when one had not yet been dropped out of a B-52 and when the guidance problems were still formidable, made total reliance on an unproved weapon look too risky. A curtailed production of the B-1, moreover, would preserve the option of a mixed force that still remained the best hedge against future uncertainties. A more modest B-1 than that proposed by the Air Force, produced at a more modest rate, would enable the president to give the Air Force a new bomber, but also to say that he had kept his campaign promise because he had changed the program with respect to both cost and capability. Carter's advisers had fashioned the fourth option in order to give the president the ability to have his political cake and eat it too.

The president, however, had built up too strong a political investment in opposing production of the B-1 and perhaps also an ingrained dislike of it. He was impressed with the promised performance of the long-range ALCM. And perversely enough, as one participant put it: "The existence of the B-1 made the cruise missile option feasible." If the promise of the long-range ALCM were not fulfilled, the administration could resurrect the B-1. Thus, on June 30, the president canceled production of the B-1 and ordered development of the long-range ALCM to be accelerated. But concomitantly the B-1 was to be kept in development and flying, avionics were to be put in and tested, and the progress of the program was to be monitored closely. Whether politics per se decided the fate of the B-1 remains unclear. What is clear is that the case between the long-range ALCM and the B-1 was so close that politics *could* have decided it.

Once the final decision was made, development of the ALCM-B proceeded apace. The Air Force had no choice but to proceed with the only remaining development project that could keep the bomber viable. Ironically, the Air Force itself eventually cooled on the B-1, though not on a penetrating bomber. A reevaluation of bomber needs by the OSD in 1978 once again raised the choices among a pure force of penetrators, a pure force of standoff bombers, and a mixed force. Although the Air Force continued to believe in the merits of the penetrating bomber and the B-1 program had been kept alive as a technology base, Air Force officials had begun to switch their preferences to a high-altitude penetrator for the 1990s. Indeed, 1980 saw the unusual situation of such congressional critics of the B-1 as Senators John C. Culver and George S. McGovern demanding the development of a new manned penetrator based on the B-1 airframe. Some in the Air Force preferred to develop an interim penetrator based on the FB-111 for use in the 1980s. These differing viewpoints reflected either ignorance or knowledge of the Stealth technology program, which was designed to reduce the radar detectability of penetrating aircraft. By late 1980, the United States had committed itself to a standoff cruise missile bomber, but was once again exploring a penetrating bomber because of the belief that a mixed force was the best hedge against Russian air defense improvements.

In retrospect, the ALCM-B was so long delayed because of the threat it presented to the Air Force's preferred mission of penetrating strategic bombardment. Indeed, so highly did the Air Force value its doctrine and new penetrator that it took the combined efforts of many in Congress, the Department of Defense, and the White House to force adoption of a long-range standoff cruise missile. The ALCM-B might have been built with far less difficulty and delay had its original proponents recognized and adapted to the dominant thinking within the Air Force. But these proponents had conspicuously forced crucial trade-offs into the open and in the process had deliberately challenged the central doctrine of the Air Force. Such zealotry delayed rather than promoted the service's acceptance of the inevitable. This story contrasts significantly with the behavior of the Navy cruise missile innovators.

THE NAVY AND THE SEA-LAUNCHED CRUISE MISSILE

While the Air Force has a relatively tight hierarchical structure, the Navy has long been more decentralized and organized around three autonomous factions or "unions"—the surface fleet, the carrier fleet, and the underwater fleet. This decentralized structure shaped much of the politics of cruise missile development within the Navy because it gave cruise missile proponents there more freedom to maneuver than their Air Force counterparts had.

For most of the post-World War II era, admirals with an aviation background have dominated the Navy. Because aircraft carriers had proved their worth in World War II, the Navy subsequently organized itself around carrier attack groups, with the main function of the surface fleet being the support of the aviation arm. The bulk of the forward striking power of the Navy was concentrated in aircraft, and consequently the lion's portion of the Navy's budget was consumed by the carrier fleet. The Russian Navy, by contrast, was unable to match the American Navy in aircraft carriers. Instead, Soviet naval planners opted for relatively primitive and inexpensive surface-to-surface missiles as the principal means by which to exert long-range striking power. Even small patrol craft, when armed with long-range antiship missiles, could pose a significant threat to enemy fleets, a fact quickly recognized by Soviet naval officers who were forced to counter the American naval threat with limited resources. The surface-to-surface missile fulfilled the role for the Soviet Navy that the kamikaze had fulfilled for the Japanese: inexpensive air-breathing surface-to-surface weapons were designed to shatter a vastly superior enemy.

For much of the postwar era, the American Navy tended to downplay the threat posed by Soviet antiship missiles because the aviators claimed that their aircraft could destroy Russian missile platforms before the missiles could be launched, or, failing that, could shoot down incoming missiles with such weapons as the F-14/Phoenix system and its predecessors. Dominant doctrine held that U.S. surface vessels did not need long-range surface-to-surface capabilities of their own. At stake was both a roles-and-missions assignment and a claim to a substantial portion of the Navy's budget. So long as the aviation arm continued to dominate the Navy, the chances of adopting a long-range surface-to-surface missile (SSM) remained slim.

THE MISSILE CHALLENGE TO THE SURFACE FLEET IN THE 1960s

By the early 1960s, however, the continued emphasis on carrier forces provoked increasing dissatisfaction within the surface fleet. Several officers began to argue that the Russian antiship missile had to be taken seriously. Others argued that the surface Navy had for too long been subordinated to carriers. Dissent became vocal, and any incidents that dramatized the vulnerability of the surface fleet were likely to serve as rallying points to challenge the dominant doctrine.

The Cuban missile crisis provided the first rallying point. During the course of preparing contingency plans for a possible invasion of Cuba, the Navy had to confront the fact that small *Komar-* and *Osa-*class patrol boats, armed only with Styx missiles, could hide out in the lengthy Cuban shoreline and threaten devastation of an invasion fleet. The Navy was forced to acknowledge the capabilities of antiship cruise missiles. This crisis spawned a series of study projects designed to augment terminal defenses against incoming missiles and to upgrade the air-to-surface capabilities of the aviation arm. The most significant development was the agreement by Secretary of the Navy Paul H. Nitze to undertake a major research program on surface-to-surface missiles. The formal idea behind this initiative had originated with Captain Worth Bagley, then an assistant to Nitze, and Captain Elmo R. Zumwalt, Jr., then director of the Navy's Division of Systems Analysis. Nitze agreed in principle to the Bagley-Zumwalt proposal in 1966, which laid the groundwork for the Navy's eventual adoption of the sea-launched cruise missile (SLCM).

A second major rallying point occurred on October 22, 1967. On this date, the Israeli destroyer *Eilat,* while patrolling off Port Said, was sunk in a matter of minutes by four Styx missiles launched from an Egyptian *Komar-*class patrol boat riding at anchor behind the Port Said breakwater. Here was dramatic evidence of the value of the Russian investment in surface-to-surface missiles. Because the sinking of the *Eilat* was so shocking, it prompted immediate research by the Navy. Efforts focused both on short-term upgrading of the terminal defense capability of Navy vessels to shoot down incoming missiles and on longer-term efforts to procure an improved air-to-surface missile to attack enemy missile platforms. Admiral Thomas H. Moorer, the chief of naval operations (CNO), had long been concerned that Russian missile ships threatened the fleet; but he was convinced that the best response was a superior air-to-surface missile, not a new extended-range surface-to-surface missile for the surface fleet. Since 1966 he had therefore sponsored several study programs and had drafted a standing operational requirement (O.R.) for a new air-to-surface missile.

The surface sailors wanted an extended-range SSM as quickly as possible. They had Nitze's 1966 agreement for support, but they recognized that in the immediate future the chances of developing an SSM were not good. Admiral Moorer had chosen to respond to the *Eilat* incident by enhancing the capabilities of the carrier fleet, not those of the surface fleet. The 1966 Nitze directive, moreover, was not specific. It would take time to translate this document into a full-fledged program. Therefore, if the surface fleet were to press hard at the outset for its own SSM program, it would certainly face a funding conflict and probably provoke a more serious and debilitating roles-and-missions dispute with the aviators.

The advocates of a new SSM quickly perceived that the best strategy was to "satisfice," not maximize—to adapt an air-to-surface missile to SSM applications rather than press for a completely new weapon. This would both minimize conflict and create the opening wedge for a genuine surface-to-surface missile. Consequently, the decision was made to treat Nitze's directive as an addendum to the standing operational requirement for a new air-to-surface missile, which was then revised in 1967 to include both a surface- and an air-launch capability. The surface sailors had gotten their foot in the door. But the aviators had extracted a significant concession, for as Admiral Zumwalt recalls:

> The most significant string attached to this order was the verbal message relayed to me through the aide system that the missile was to have a range of no more than fifty miles if it was to be acceptable to the CNO. Evidently, the aviators' union was still nervous about its prerogatives.

The range limitation constrained the surface fleet more than the aviators. An air-launched missile could be carried to the general vicinity of its target and released from a distance of fifty miles without unduly endangering the aviator. The aviators had little reason to press for a longer missile range and indeed every incentive to press for a shorter range. They were justifiably skeptical about releasing missiles from over-the-horizon distances because the guidance problems at such distances were still unsolved. Only the surface fleet wanted the longer ranges, the only means by which the surface fleet on its own could fire at Soviet missile ships before they fired their missiles at American ships. Yet so long as the aviators were developing the new tactical missile, a dramatic increase in range was not likely to come about.

It therefore became clear to the surface fleet proponents that their only hope lay in ensuring that the new air-to-surface missile would have as much growth potential as possible; thus it was crucial to make certain that the new missile was fitted with an air-breathing, not a rocket, engine. (A rocket engine was constrained in range because of the weight added by the need to carry its own oxidizers.) Yet the quest for an air-breathing engine had to be conducted in such a way as to avoid alarming the aviators. This, in turn, required a tacit alliance with the aviators against the ordnance division of the Naval Material Command. As one participant made clear:

> We recognized that if we were going to get cruise missiles, we would have to maximize the chance that there would be an air-launched cruise missile. The fundamental obstacle would be the carrier Navy. The major bureaucratic challenge would therefore be tasking the O.R.
>
> If the O.R. were sent to NAVORD [Naval Ordnance Systems Command], it would have failed because of carrier opposition and because NAVORD couldn't do anything right anyway. If it were sent out as an advanced weapon, it would go to R&D, where it would have languished forever. So it was drafted as an O.R. to the advanced group of Air-05 [the Material Acquisition Division of the Air Systems Command].

This manipulation set in train the program that ultimately produced the Harpoon cruise missile. The Naval Air Systems Command (NAVAIR) took the lead in exploring design concepts for the new air-to-surface missile ordered by Admiral Moorer, accepting the proviso that the new missile would also be capable of surface launching. By 1971, competitive airframe contracts had been awarded to two companies; by 1974, a development contract had been awarded for an air-breathing turbojet engine. Thus by the early 1970s the surface fleet proponents of an extended range ship-to-ship missile had allied themselves with the aviators to push for a new air-to-surface missile. While the Harpoon missile was not a true extended-range SSM, it represented a victory for the surface fleet dissidents, but what they ultimately sought was the longer-range Tomahawk, not the Harpoon.

INTRASERVICE POLITICS AND THE TOMAHAWK MISSILE

After assuming the duties of chief of naval operations, Elmo Zumwalt tried to interest the service in a submarine-launched antiship cruise missile. At nearly the same time, Melvin Laird wanted to develop a strategic cruise missile for insurance if the SALT I treaty failed. It was the confluence of these two stimuli that produced the program for the Tomahawk missile—one that did not readily fulfill the expectations of either Zumwalt or Laird, but aptly fulfilled the needs of the surface fleet.

Shortly after becoming CNO, Zumwalt appointed Admiral Robert Kaufman to chair an ad hoc panel on a submarine-launched antisurface ship interim missile. The Kaufman panel's charge was to investigate both a new antiship missile and for later development a new submarine to carry it. The panel was formed in September 1970 and ordered to report by November. The Kaufman panel wanted to propose cost-effective alternatives for an attack submarine that would succeed the recently completed SSN-668 class. But in order to accommodate both antisubmarine torpedoes and antiship missiles, the panel deemed it necessary to increase the hull size of the new submarine. Moreover, because the antisubmarine mission was valued most, the submarine commander would have to keep his torpedo tubes fully loaded with antisubmarine weapons at all times. This, in turn, pushed the Kaufman panel to recommend that the new antiship cruise missile be launched from vertical tubes. This would have the added advantage of extending the range of the missile because vertical tubes could be made larger in diameter than torpedo tubes, thereby allowing a larger missile engine. In its final report the Kaufman panel called for a new tactical antiship missile that would be launched from a new submarine, called the submarine tactical antiship weapons system (STAWS).

After the panel returned its recommendations, the Naval Air Systems Command, then overseeing development of the Harpoon, was asked to investigate the design of the proposed tactical antiship missile. In April 1971, a NAVAIR study group returned a report recommending that the new missile take one of three general configurations: an encapsulated Harpoon for Vertical Launch; a follow-on to the Harpoon with twice the payload and a range of 120–140 miles; or a strategic land-attack cruise missile with a 1,600-mile range. The submariners were not interested in the last proposal. They were well satisfied with the Polaris and Poseidon missiles, and moreover they were skeptical that any air-breathing missile could obtain the ranges mentioned by NAVAIR. Nonetheless, the NAVAIR studies convinced Admiral Zumwalt that a long-range cruise missile could be built with relatively little difficulty. He therefore ordered studies to be conducted on developing an advanced cruise missile (ACM).

At this point, Admiral Hyman G. Rickover, the "father of the nuclear Navy," entered the picture. He had begun development of a new 60,000-horsepower reactor in 1968 and wanted to mate this engine with the STAWS proposal. He had become convinced, moreover, that the Navy needed to enhance cruise missile capability. He began to lobby within the Navy and before several congressional committees for a fully dedicated cruise missile submarine based on his reactor, the STAWS design concept, and the advanced cruise missile proposals coming out of NAVAIR. Rickover thus sought to redefine the STAWS from an inexpensive attack submarine into a dedicated or single-purpose expensive submarine, and, in doing so, to sell his newest reactor to the Navy. Rickover's interest served to sustain the advanced cruise missile project in the face of possible opposition because the divergence in design between the advanced cruise missile and the ongoing Harpoon program had led to a decision to create another entirely separate advanced cruise missile project office. This was set up under Captain Walter M. Locke, the guidance project officer in the old Harpoon office, and placed administratively under NAVAIR. The Naval Ordnance Systems Command (NAVORD), however, wanted to obtain control of the ACM program under the rationale that it was the appropriate parent organization for developing surface-to-surface missiles. This argument was sound in terms of the formal organization charts, but weak in terms of practical bureaucratic politics, for NAVORD faced two determined opponents in Admirals Zumwalt and Rickover.

Zumwalt insisted on developing a cruise missile for use aboard surface vessels. He recognized that, because of the power within the Navy of the carrier admirals, his best chance lay in letting the innovators in NAVAIR develop a missile such as the Harpoon, which could later be adapted to other applications. Rickover believed that NAVAIR was more imaginative and efficient than NAVORD. The result of this high-level sponsorship and interest was that the ACM program office remained under NAVAIR, where work proceeded rapidly. Although Rickover's sponsorship served to keep the ACM project alive, ironically it proved the kiss of death for the STAWS program. STAWS had grown under Rickover's prompting into an expensive proposal that contradicted Zumwalt's commitment to purchasing a larger number of less costly ships, not fewer more costly ones. The STAWS program was quietly dropped in 1972.

Although the original impetus had disappeared with the STAWS concept, the research on cruise missiles was pushed forward at Zumwalt's personal insistence. At this point, Secretary of Defense Melvin Laird sought from Congress an authorization for a vaguely defined strategic cruise missile (SCM) for possible use aboard those polaris submarines retired from the fleet under the terms of SALT I. The ACM office had itself explored a strategic variant of cruise missiles. Because the two programs—the ACM and the SCM—shared a common technological orientation, it made great sense to consolidate them into one program. Politics, however, was of even greater importance than shared technology. Zumwalt and the advocates of a long-range antiship missile knew they could better protect their program politically if they consolidated it with Laird's missile. On its own the tactical antiship variant of the ACM faced an uncertain future. Although as yet it was only an internal study concept, its critics within the Navy were powerful and numerous. The strategic cruise missile, however, was directly sponsored by the secretary of defense, even though Laird was as much interested in inducing the Air Force to explore ALCM technology as he was in finding a good use for retired Polaris submarines.

Therefore, if the ACM could be integrally linked to Laird's missile and treated simply as a technological derivative rather than a wholly separate program, its future would be better assured. It was thus only sensible to arrange a marriage of convenience. And in the process Zumwalt had created a tacit alliance with Laird. Combined with Zumwalt's manipulation, Laird's intervention thus set the Navy on a nearly irreversible course. By November 6, 1972—the date of the consolidation order—the surface fleet proponents of a new surface-to-surface missile had effectively won their battle, even if they did not realize it at the time. There were many bureaucratic obstacles and technological uncertainties still to overcome, but the consolidation tied a weak proposal to a strong one and vastly increased the likelihood that the Navy would produce a long-range surface-launched antiship missile.

Ironically, it was the strategic variant that proved the most troublesome aspect of the entire project. Although Congress fully endorsed the antiship missile, the justification for the strategic variant appeared unclear, and the weapon came under severe criticism. Defense Department officials had been initially interested in the SCM-ACM project in order to keep up research on turbofan propulsion after the demise of the SCAD project, but this rationale disappeared with the revival of the ALCM-A project. Thus, the technological justification for the strategic missile that the Defense Department could present to Congress was quite tenuous, and the strategic rationale appeared weak. Congressional critics feared that a nuclear-armed cruise missile aboard attack submarines would jeopardize the antisubmarine warfare mission and add nothing to the sea-based strategic deterrent. The 2,000-mile range of the missile would require the submarine that carried it to operate closer to Russia's shorelines than the Poseidon-armed strategic ballistic missile submarines in order to hit the same targets. Yet the Navy had sought for years to extend, not decrease, the range of its strategic missiles in order to increase the operating ocean space of its strategic submarines and reduce their vulnerability to detection. Moreover, if the attack submarine was to be used in the strategic deterrent mode, then it would become a platform dedicated to retaliating against Russian cities, not to killing enemy submarines. It was no surprise, therefore, that in July 1973 Congress froze funding for the strategic SLCM; and the Senate later eliminated the entire project. House and Senate conferees agreed in late 1973 to restore funding for the strategic program, but only with the proviso that the Navy develop a clear rationale for it and simultaneously explore tactical antiship cruise missiles.

The fuzziness in the Navy's official mission for the SLCM,

however, was not mindless. What was strategic nonsense to Congress made effective politics within the Navy. The conceptual flexibility of the Navy cruise missile program offered innovators the means to overcome significant obstacles within the Navy in their quest for a long-range surface-to-surface missile. It offered Defense Department officials an opportunity to spur Air Force work on the ALCM. It did not unduly raise the hackles of the carrier lobby because of its very fuzziness. It later permitted the Navy to compete for the ALCM mission, made a ground-launched version readily available, and resulted in an antiship missile. Had not such flexibility existed from the outset, the technologists might well have prematurely closed their designs; and the opponents of a surface-to-surface missile might very well have killed it. So long as the strategic cruise missile, however vaguely defined, was perceived as the lead program within the Navy, the tactical antiship version could be treated as a fortuitous spin-off. Although the Navy drafted a requirement for a tactical version of the cruise missile in November 1974, it distinctly paced this program behind the one for the strategic cruise missile. Before late 1974, therefore, the Navy repeatedly emphasized that it had no requirement for a tactical antiship missile. After late 1974, when it had developed such a requirement, the Navy repeatedly stressed that it was merely investigating an inexpensive derivative of the strategic program initiated by Secretary Laird.

Such moderation in pursuit of an antiship missile extended to the design features of the SLCM as well. Until late 1976, development plans called for mounting a Harpoon turbojet engine rather than the more capable turbofan engine on the antiship version of the cruise missile. As later testimony was to indicate, the turbofan engine was the superior choice for an antiship missile. By adhering to the turbojet engine during the early stages of development, however, the proponents of the antiship missile minimized the visibility of their program and hence their challenge to the carrier fleet.

Finally, the carrier fleet was not the only source of potential opposition to an antiship missile. The missile was also downplayed before Congress, where the early stages of development posed two problems. First, although Congress itself had urged in 1973 that a tactical antiship missile be built, the costs of such a program alone would have been prohibitively high. But if the missile was treated as merely one of a generic set of missiles, including the strategic version, development costs could be amortized over several programs and thereby kept low. Second, it was crucial to make the SLCM and the shorter-range Harpoon look as dissimilar as possible. If Congress had felt so inclined, it could have canceled the Harpoon, which had suffered cost overruns, in favor of the more capable SLCM. But this would deny the Navy a surface-to-surface missile capability in the near term and also threaten to open fully the roles-and-missions dispute between the carrier and surface fleets. Proponents of the antiship version of the SLCM could always downplay their ultimate goal of obtaining a truly long-range antiship missile out of the SLCM program by pointing to the fact that they had the Harpoon. If the Harpoon was killed, they would be forced into the open. Thus, from both a cost and a bureaucratic perspective, it was better to downplay the antiship missile and press for the strategic missile. As one observer noted:

> It's not unfair to say that at first the strategic missile was forced down the Navy's throat. It had to be pushed, but you can say that it provided the impetus for Tomahawk. It got us the bucks. We couldn't have carried the tactical SLCM on our own.

THE STRATEGIC SLCM IN SEARCH OF A MISSION

For a variety of reasons, therefore, the Navy chose to emphasize the ill-defined strategic cruise missile rather than any specific derivatives. The missile played a role within the Navy, not as Melvin Laird had intended, but rather as the vehicle by which intraservice disputes could be deferred until the antiship missile became a fait accompli. So as not to raise the hackles of the carrier admirals, the surface fleet made the submariners the spear carriers in this campaign. They were forced to go before Congress each year to defend a program for themselves that they did not want. Aside from their skepticism about the promised performance of the SLCM, the submariners were downright hostile to the operational implications of a strategic SLCM for their boats. The principal rationale offered for the weapon was that it would provide a strategic nuclear reserve aboard attack submarines for use in controlled responses in limited nuclear wars or in a third strike. The submariners also found themselves citing such dubious merits as the weapon's leverage in arms control negotiations.

To have built a submarine-launched strategic nuclear missile could have meant forcing attack submarines to offload valuable antisubmarine weapons in order to prepare for a mission that had little, if any, justification. To fire the SLCM at a target deep in the Soviet Union, moreover, would entail moving the attack submarines in toward enemy coastlines, thereby increasing the risk of detection. The firing of a SLCM would generate bubbles and acoustic signals that could reveal the submarine's location. In addition, because guidance alignment required at least twenty minutes after the missile was loaded into a torpedo tube, a submarine could fire only infrequent salvos while assuming high risks of detection. Finally, if the strategic SLCMs were to be integrated into the single integrated operational plan, attack submarines, like strategic ones, would be forced to keep in more frequent contact with SAC headquarters, thereby risking detection and sacrificing considerable operational flexibility. Simply put, submarines could not be simultaneously attack and strategic.

Members of Congress were quick to notice such difficulties, but curiously enough there was little risk to the Navy that the SLCM program would be canceled, precisely because it was flexible and vague enough to gain wide support. It could serve as a technology program for advocates of increased research and development in Congress or the Defense Department. It could serve as a SALT bargaining chip for persons concerned with American-Russian arms control talks. It could serve as another addition to the strategic nuclear forces for those who were pressing for nuclear superiority. It could serve as the baseline technology for those who wished to see modernization of NATO's long-range theater nuclear forces. And it could serve as a prod to the Air Force for those who wished to accelerate the ALCM. The Navy's strategic cruise missile was a weapon system for all seasons precisely because it had no clearly defined mission. Few people in the Navy, particularly among the submarine forces, ever wanted the strategic SLCM. But few in the Navy were motivated strongly enough to work for its cancellation, and many outside the Navy, especially in the OSD, pushed strongly for it.

By 1976, however, after the tactical antiship missile had gained considerable momentum, the environment was safe enough for the proponents of the antiship missile to come out in the open. Thus, in a highly significant shift in testimony, Admiral James L. Holloway III, the CNO, repeatedly argued in 1976 that the Navy had to pursue a tactical missile, even if the strategic variant were banned by Congress or by arms control negotiations. This testimony opened the door for a major realignment in the Navy's cruise missile programs. The conference committee of the Armed Services Committees steered money toward the tactical SLCM and provided funds for a turbofan rather than a turbojet engine, thereby considerably extending the range of the antiship missile. Simultaneously, of course, the Navy moved quietly to drop the turbojet engine from its tactical variant. Thereafter, in response to congressional criticism about the utility of a strategic cruise missile, the Navy changed its tack. It gave the program a new name—the Tomahawk—and presented two variants—a conventionally armed Tomahawk antiship missile (TASM) and a nuclear-armed land-attack missile (TLAM). The latter was indistinguishable in design and capability from the earlier strategic cruise missile that had drawn such congressional criticism, but in order to preserve the variant, the Navy changed its mission. Rather than being targeted only against strategic targets within Russia, the TLAM would be a worldwide theater nuclear weapon. Later on, the Navy, under pressure from Secretary of Defense Brown, further refined the TLAM into the TLAM-N (the nuclear variant) and the TLAM-C (the conventional variant).

In short, the decisions taken in 1976 formalized a chain of actions and decisions that had been carefully orchestrated over the preceding three years in the quest for a new extended-range antiship missile. Full recognition was given to the TASM by the Department of Defense in January 1977, at the DSARC stage II meeting, when Deputy Secretary Clements ordered the development of the TASM, the GLCM, and the ALCM, and a slowdown on the TLAM. Although Secretary of Defense Brown subsequently slowed the development of the antiship missile pending progress in over-the-horizon target-acquisition technology, the fundamental point remained unchanged. The surface fleet dissidents had won a major victory by 1976 and had successfully challenged the carrier admirals, the dominant group within the Navy.

Ironically, since 1976 the successor to the strategic cruise missile has remained a weapon largely in search of a mission. The TLAM has been viewed as a possible weapon for use in non-NATO theater nuclear contingencies (the worldwide mission), as a possible candidate for nuclear warfare at sea in defense of the fleet (the global sea control mission), and, to this day, as a strategic reserve. In order to develop the TLAM without signaling to NATO that the United States might develop the capability to put NATO's long-range theater nuclear forces (LRTNF) out to sea,* the Department of Defense, under the specific urgings of Congress, has promoted the TLAM-C, which was to serve as the airframe technology base for the TLAM during the sensitive negotiations over NATO's LRTNF modernization. The TLAM-C is now offered as a candidate for precision attacks against high-value shoreline targets, a mission equally dubious in view of the extraordinarily high costs of each missile. Although both versions of the TLAM remain vaguely defined and subject to continuing controversy, the Navy and the Congress have fully accepted the TASM. In short, the case of the Navy sea-launched cruise missile demonstrates that skill at bureaucratic politics can often overcome immense obstacles to weapons innovation.

SALT II AND NATO'S THEATER NUCLEAR FORCES

Until 1977, the Air Force and the Navy were resistant, if not hostile, to the development of long-range air- and sea-launched cruise missiles. The former threatened the mission of the penetrating bomber; the latter, the missions of both fleet aircraft and attack submarines. And yet, at the same time, because of the dynamics of SALT II negotiations, it was the long-range versions that most interested the Defense Department, the White House, and the State Department. By late 1976, the same pattern of developments began to happen to the ground-launched version. The White House, the OSD, and ultimately

---

* This point will be fully explained in the last section of this chapter.

the State Department began to worry about both the Europeans' reactions to SALT II and their increasing concerns about the emerging imbalance in theater nuclear forces. Especially the latter factor pushed high-level civilians toward development of the ground-launched cruise missile, a system that neither the Army nor the Air Force wanted. In order to understand the dichotomy between service attitudes toward these three systems on the one hand and those of civilians at the pinnacles of executive power on the other, it is necessary to look at the SALT II negotiations and their effects on the NATO alliance.

CRUISE MISSILES IN SALT II POLITICS

From 1973, when negotiations on a SALT II accord began in earnest, until June 1979, when the Treaty on the Limitation of Strategic Offensive Arms was signed between the United States and the Soviet Union, the cruise missile figured centrally in the packages put together by the executive and offered to the Russians. Initially, the ALCM was the most prominent, but by 1976 the SLCM and GLCM had developed equal visibility. All three versions played roles: first, as bargaining chips by which to wrest concessions from the Russians; second, as political lubricants with which to gain the acceptance by Congress and the NATO allies of a SALT II accord; and, third, as significant military options to be protected in their own right because of their presumed enhancement of America's strategic retaliatory forces.

Over this seven-year period, the executive branch developed a seemingly endless number of SALT II packages to offer the Soviet Union. Many never saw the light of day. Three proposals, however, stand out because they were presented formally to the Russians, they affected Russian attitudes toward subsequent American proposals, and they highlight the larger political considerations that motivated high-level civilians and shaped their attitudes toward cruise missiles. The first is Henry Kissinger's offer of January 1976 and subsequent offers to count American bombers armed with cruise missiles as part of the 1,320 launchers mounted with multiple independently targetable reentry vehicles (MIRVs) permitted each party by the 1974 Vladivostok accord in exchange for constraints on the Russians' Backfire bomber. The second is the Carter administration's March 1977 comprehensive proposal, in which all cruise missiles were to be limited in range to 2,500 kilometers in exchange for deep cuts in both sides' overall strategic launchers and in Russia's heavy missiles. Third is the three-tier proposal made in April 1977 by the United States, in which ALCMs were limited in range to 2,500 kilometers, and SLCMs and GLCMs to 600 kilometers if they were deployed during a three-year period.

In seeking to produce a SALT II accord, Gerald Ford and Henry Kissinger confronted three central problems: first, how to produce an agreement that would satisfy the equal overall aggregates proviso attached by the Senate to the SALT I treaty; second, what to do with the newly emerging cruise missile technology that had not been covered by SALT I, was being pushed by the Pentagon, and was increasingly worrying the Russians; and third, how to treat the Backfire bomber that appeared to some as an intermediate-range plane not capable of hitting the United States, to others as capable of being upgraded to reach the United States, and to the Russians as a system that should not be counted in the SALT II aggregates because it fell into the same category as America's theater nuclear forward-based systems (FBS) deployed in Europe. The Russians were particularly vehement about the Backfire issue, since in SALT I they had agreed to exclude FBS even though those systems could target the western military districts of the Soviet Union. The Backfire, they maintained, could not target the continental United States. The Americans were now asking them to count in the overall aggregates weapons that could not hit the United States while simultaneously insisting that weapons that could hit Russia should not be counted. It was the asymmetry in the American position that piqued the Russians.

The questions of overall aggregates, Backfires, and cruise missiles came to a head at Vladivostok in 1974. Kissinger's attitude toward the cruise missile remains unclear. Some say he viewed it only as a chip to be bargained away, but because of Pentagon resistance and Russian interest it instead became a chip that refused to go away. Others maintain that he never intended to trade away the cruise missile, particularly the ALCM, but only to use it to extract concessions from the Soviet Union because he accepted the then prevailing view that it would assist in preserving a mixed force of penetrators and standoff bombers. The Russians, however, wanted to ban all cruise missiles with ranges over 600 kilometers, whether they were ground-, sea-, or air-launched. The United States countered (orally, according to some at Vladivostok, but certainly immediately afterward in an exchange of letters) that the air-launched ban applied only to ballistic, not cruise, missiles. To sweeten the pot, Kissinger agreed to count heavy bombers in the overall ceiling of 2,400 strategic launchers. The Soviet Union agreed to exclude FBS from the overall aggregates in return for the United States' dropping its insistence on a cut in Russia's heavy intercontinental ballistic missiles.

From January through September 1976, the Ford administration made three proposals to the Soviet Union in order to reach an accord on these two issues. In January 1976 Kissinger flew to Moscow and proposed to limit the Russians to a total of 250 Backfires for five years, in return for which the United States would agree to count heavy bombers armed with cruise missiles in the subceiling agreed to at Vladivostok. ALCMs with ranges over 2,500 kilometers and SLCMs and GLCMs with ranges over 2,000 kilometers would not be deployed. The Russians countered with a 600-kilometer limit for the SLCM and GLCM and apparently did not oppose the 2,500-kilometer range limit for the ALCM. Based on an initiative by the director of the Arms Control and Disarmament Agency, Fred C. Iklé, and Secretary of Defense Donald H. Rumsfeld, the United States offered another proposal in February to break the January deadlock on the cruise missile issue. ALCMs would be treated as in the January offer. In a separate protocol, tied to an agreement about the Backfire, was the offer to limit *deployed* SLCMs and GLCMs to 600 kilometers, but to permit flight testing on both up to ranges of 2,500 kilometers. That offer was repeated again in September. The Ford administration, in short, had "invented" the protocol that was to figure so prominently in the Carter administration's April 1977 three-tier approach, which in turn ultimately became the basis of the 1979 SALT II executive agreement. The NATO allies were informed about the January proposal, but were not aware of the details of the February and September initiatives.

Thus through 1976 the U.S. government was clearly protecting the standoff bomber option and preserving its flexibility on SLCMs and GLCMs. It had developed a consensus on the military value of the long-range ALCM, at least among high-level civilians, but had given little thought to the military utility of the sea and ground versions.

The September 1976 proposal was the last made by the outgoing Ford administration. From a variety of motives, newly elected President Jimmy Carter decided at the outset not to take the Vladivostok agreement with the September additions as the basis for resuming negotiations with the Soviet Union. Instead, he put forth what came to be called the comprehensive proposal. It called for deep cuts in the overall strategic launchers permitted both sides (from 2,400 to somewhere between 1,800 and 2,000); a reduction in launchers mounted with MIRVs (from 1,320 to somewhere between 1,100 and 1,200); an entirely new subceiling on ICBM launchers equipped with MIRVs (550); a reduction in Russia's heavy missiles (from 300 to 150); exclusion of Backfire from the overall strategic launcher ceiling as long as Russia adhered to restrictions on its range; and a 2,500-kilometer range limit on all types of cruise missiles deployed during the time the treaty would be in force.

Carter's motives in offering such a radical proposal were complex. In his election campaign he had called for reductions in the superpowers' nuclear arsenals and had attacked the style and substance of Kissinger's diplomacy. He had, moreover, to deal with the relentless buildup in Russia's heavy missiles that many thought posed a threat to America's Minuteman force, a problem that neither the SALT I treaty nor the Vladivostok agreement with the September additions had solved. He had, finally, to respond to the pressures from Senate hard-liners, led by Henry M. Jackson, to obtain an agreement that was more beneficial to the United States than either SALT I or Vladivostok. Secretary of Defense Brown took the lead in pushing for an approach that would meet these goals through deep cuts. Brown's proposal gave Carter what he needed: an approach that had his own political stamp on it, not Kissinger's, and that responded to both his own arms control instincts and his political needs of the moment. The proposal also gave Brown what he wanted: a reduction in the vulnerability of Minutemen that would be achieved by deep cuts in Russia's heavy missiles and limits on testing rather than by increases in U.S. forces. Strategic logic nicely dovetailed with political needs. It was a beautifully crafted compromise.

The only problem, of course, was that the Russians summarily rejected it, not even bothering to offer any counterproposals. They insisted on returning to Vladivostok as the basis for negotiations. Because the Carter administration thought it had no choice, it returned to matters as they had been left by Ford and Kissinger. It offered a "new" proposal in April 1977 that combined a three-tier approach: a treaty, a protocol, and a statement of common understandings. ALCMs would appear in the treaty, limited in range to 2,500 kilometers. SLCMs and GLCMs would appear in the protocol, limited in range to 600 kilometers if they were deployed, but to be tested at ranges up to 2,500 kilometers. The treaty would last through 1985; the protocol through the end of 1981. Any reductions on overall strategic launchers would be modest.

The similarity between Carter's April proposal and Ford's September offer is not accidental: having failed in its radical approach, Carter simply resurrected the final Ford package. This account makes clear what many have claimed: the Carter administration might very well have reached early agreement with the Soviet Union (although not with the U.S. Senate) on a SALT II accord had it accepted the Vladivostok agreement with the September additions as the starting point for negotiations. Carter was initially pushed by political needs and strategic concerns not to do so. He picked up the pieces by taking his predecessor's approach when forced to do so. The final SALT II accord of June 1979 largely resembled the April proposal, except that the ALCM range limits were dropped. More than most have realized, the final accord reflected the handiwork of Henry Kissinger.

EUROPEAN CONCERNS ABOUT AMERICA'S NUCLEAR UMBRELLA

In its early negotiations with the Soviet Union, the Carter administration had preserved the 2,500-kilometer limit for the ALCM because it did not know what it would decide about the B-1. Once the administration decided to cancel production, the long-range ALCM became essential for the preservation of an effective strategic bomber force in the 1980s. The case for the SLCM and GLCM was more complex because it involved political considerations vis-à-vis not only the Russians but also the Europeans.

The Russians appeared to fear the SLCM and GLCM even more than the ALCM and took a much tougher negotiating posture on them. In the case of the ALCM, the Soviet Union could at least detect standoff bombers through its reconnaissance satellites and surmise that cruise missiles had been fired from them, even if it could not track the missiles once they were launched. Cruise missiles fired from mobile ground launchers or submerged submarines, however, would be practically impossible to see, even with the most sophisticated satellite and other capabilities. The eventuality that hundreds, if not thousands, of SLCMs and GLCMs could be fired at long ranges from either Western Europe or at sea against the Soviet Union appeared to offer the Americans the chance to upset the strategic nuclear balance in a dramatic fashion. The Soviet Union therefore insisted that both the SLCM and GLCM, if they were deployed before 1982, be limited to a range that would reduce, if not eliminate, their strategic threat to Russia. In order to reach an agreement with the Soviet Union on an overall SALT II treaty, the United States conceded on deployment ranges, but preserved its right to flight test SLCMs and GLCMs at much longer ranges.

In agreeing to the 600-kilometer deployment limit and preserving the 2,500-kilometer testing limit, the Carter administration felt that it had pulled off a great negotiating coup. In the middle of 1977, SLCMs and GLCMs had not even completed development. They would not be ready to deploy until 1982 at the earliest, about the time when the protocol provisions limiting their deployment ranges would self-destruct. In fact, the protocol had been carefully designed to end precisely when the administration thought the GLCM and SLCM would be ready for full-scale production and deployment. The United States, therefore, had not given anything away to the Russians. Not only had it preserved a military option for the future, but it also had retained its ability to develop that option fully during a period of supposed restraint.

What seemed a great negotiating coup to the Americans, however, appeared to the Europeans to be a great potential giveaway. They worried that the United States had set a dangerous precedent: they feared that upon expiration of the protocol the United States would cave into Russian pressure and extend it. To the Europeans, matters were made worse by the other provisions and lapses of the April three-tier proposal. The United States had preserved the long-range ALCM option for its central strategic systems. It had done nothing to constrain Russia's deployment of two weapons—the SS-20 and the Backfire—that most threatened Western Europe. Although the issue of the Backfire was not yet settled, the Europeans knew that the

United States was working quite hard to ensure that its range would not be intercontinental. Hence, the United States appeared to be magnifying the long-range theater nuclear force threat to the Europeans in order to reduce the long-range strategic threat to its own territory. The fact that the Europeans had not been consulted about the protocol before it was presented to the Russians only made them more suspicious.

Throughout the spring, summer, and fall of 1977, the Carter administration went to great lengths to deal with these suspicions by sending to Europe a series of joint State-Defense Department briefing teams. The problem with these trips, however, was that the United States was too honest in its views about the sea and ground versions of the cruise missile. Under the lead of the State Department, the Carter administration was trying to educate the Europeans about the cruise missile, to explain the state of American thinking about the GLCM and SLCM (which was not very advanced at the time), and to show that the cruise missile was not the answer to all of NATO's problems. The attempt to be honest, however, only made the problem worse. The Europeans, particularly the Germans, thought that the Americans were trying to talk them out of cruise missiles for NATO, not educate them about their merits and demerits. The problem in part was that the Europeans had become accustomed to the United States taking the lead in nuclear matters. They were not used to "participatory consultation" at the formative stages of an administration's thinking. But because the administration had not informed the Europeans about the protocol before presenting it to the Russians, it had no choice but to engage in some type of consultation to repair the political damage that had been done. The difficulty was that the administration did not yet know what it wanted to do with cruise missiles, and it knew that the Europeans did not know what they wanted to do with them. The Europeans only knew that they did not want to be forced to do *without* them before they had a chance to look closely at them.

The differences in views on these matters were rooted in the difference in national perspectives and military circumstances that have characterized the NATO alliance since its inception. The Europeans' military dependence on the United States has always made them acutely sensitive to the slightest shifts in America's military policy. At the outset, President Carter set a tone in military matters that did little to assuage this sensitivity. First, in his campaign and after, he expressed a desire to banish nuclear weapons from the face of the earth. Second, three months into office, he offered a SALT II package to the Russians that seemed designed to provoke their rejection. Third, from the beginning, he put heavy pressure on the British, the French, and especially the Germans to restrict their sales of nuclear power-generating equipment so as to minimize the likelihood that nuclear weapons could be made from it. The first unsettled the Europeans because their security rested centrally on nuclear deterrence. The second threatened the viability of a détente in which they had a great economic stake. And the third appeared to be a not so subtle attempt by the United States to prevent the Europeans from commercially exploiting a technology in which they were developing an edge over the Americans.

Finally, American-European and especially American-German relations were strained to the hilt by Carter's handling of the enhanced radiation weapon, or what became known as the neutron bomb, in mid-1977. The sensitivities of European governments to their publics' growing unhappiness with all things nuclear required crafting an elaborate scenario for NATO acceptance of the neutron bomb. By changing his mind at the last minute, President Carter undercut Chancellor Helmut Schmidt, who had worked hard and spent much political capital with his fellow European Social Democrats to line them up behind deployment of these weapons. Carter also undercut his own State Department, which had worked for months to devise an acceptable means for the European governments to accept these weapons. Carter's reversal reinforced the Europeans' perception of him as vacillating and his government as uncoordinated and, worse, called into great doubt the ability of the United States to lead NATO. The neutron bomb fiasco largely determined both the resolve and manner with which the Carter administration approached the LRTNF case, making clear three important requirements: first, to be absolutely clear about what the Europeans really wanted; second, to regain American leadership within NATO; and, third, to prove that NATO could collectively make clear-cut decisions.

These events may have enhanced Europe's unease about the reliability of the United States, but the unease was there to begin with. A deeper concern was at work—the credibility of the American nuclear umbrella—for which the cruise missile had become the tangible political symbol. Would the United States risk New York for Hamburg now that the two superpowers had reached strategic parity? This was the underlying issue that Carter's actions during his first fourteen months had further aggravated. But strategic parity was enshrined in the SALT I treaty of 1972 and thus predated Carter. By 1975 the Europeans had begun seriously to ponder the strategic consequences for them of superpower parity. The substance of the 1977 protocol and the manner in which it had been revealed crystallized these fears. Just as the SS-20 had come to symbolize the growing Russian threat to Western Europe that America's central strategic systems were not counteracting, so did American actions on the GLCM and SLCM come to symbolize America's unwillingness to counter that threat *within* Europe. Carter had made a difficult problem worse, but he had not created it.

After Schmidt made a speech before the International Institute for Strategic Studies in London in October 1977 proclaiming the SS-20 to be a great threat to Western Europe, the Carter administration knew that it had to take Europe's concerns about the SS-20, the Backfire, and the protocol's limitations on the GLCM and SLCM seriously. Taken together, these symbolized to the Europeans the disadvantageous position in which they would find themselves if a SALT II accord were concluded along the April three-tier approach. Strategic parity would be enshrined, but nothing would be done to redress a perceived imbalance in the LRTNF balance in Europe that threatened to open up a "gap in the spectrum of deterrence" in favor of the Soviet Union. If deterrence rested upon the ability to match the enemy's moves with similar ones at every step of the escalation ladder, then NATO would shortly be missing a rung. Even though the Carter administration assured the Europeans that a response by the Soviet Union with its LRTNF could and would be met with an American strategic counterresponse, the Europeans were not assured.

The Carter administration found itself in a bind. It could not push cruise missiles on the Europeans because, by doing so, it would be admitting that America's strategic systems were not sufficient to protect them. Besides, the administration was not certain whether the Europeans really wanted cruise missiles. State Department officials in particular were wary of repeating the multilateral nuclear force (MLF) debacle of the early 1960s. After the neutron bomb fiasco, the MLF precedent heightened this sense of caution throughout the American government. The administration did not want to force on the Europeans nuclear forces that they initially appeared to want but ultimately might reject. At the same time, however, the United States could not tell the Europeans that they could not have cruise missiles because that would further inflame their fears about a superpower condominium at their expense. The logic of the situation dictated that the administration could neither force upon, nor deny to, the Europeans the cruise missiles constrained in the protocol.

Parallel to this bind on cruise missiles was the ambiguity over the coupling-decoupling argument. Strategically, one could argue that an American deployment of new LRTNF would fill in the gap in the deterrent spectrum because at every step in the deterrent or escalation ladder every Soviet action could be met in kind. Strategically, however, one could also argue that the deployment of long-range systems in Europe would decouple events on the European battlefield from America's nuclear umbrella. Such systems would enable the United States to hit Russia from Europe, thereby avoiding use of its strategic forces and allowing the United States to wage a nuclear war with Russia but confining the devastation to Europe and Russia. By deployment of LRTNF in Europe, the United States could conduct a limited nuclear war confined to the central front. On military grounds, both arguments made sense. But because the issue at heart was a political one, it was political attitudes that determined which view would prevail. And, as one participant in this decision remarked, because of the central role in the alliance played by the Germans, "coupling was whatever the Germans said it was."

Given the political difficulties associated with taking one line or the other, the administration invented the High Level Group (HLG) to plumb the depth of European concern about decoupling and interest in cruise missiles. It met from December 1977 through March 1979 and was chaired by Assistant Secretary of Defense for International Security Affairs David E. McGiffert, who initially maintained American neutrality on the cruise missile. However, at the second meeting of the HLG in February 1978 at Los Alamos, a consensus developed among the middle-level politico-military representatives that some type of hardware response to the SS-20 and the Backfire was necessary. Once this consensus had emerged, the United States took the lead in the staff work necessary to determine the available options. In the Pentagon, PA&E conducted a cost-effectiveness study on the alternatives of deploying GLCMs, SLCMs, and ALCMs on tactical aircraft, a new medium-range ballistic missile, and an extended-range follow-on to the Army's Pershing I, the Pershing II.

The study did not conclude that any one option was clearly superior on both cost and military grounds. The ultimate decision to deploy both GLCMs and the Pershing II came as a consequence of considering both military and political factors. On military grounds, it was decided that a mix of both ballistic and cruise missiles was advantageous because of the hedge against improvements in Soviet air defenses that such a mixed force would provide. The Pershing II was preferred because its cost estimates looked more reliable than those for the MRBM and it had an earlier initial operational capability. The ALCM on tactical aircraft suffered from all the vulnerability problems that tactical aircraft stationed in Europe had. The GLCM was not cheaper than the SLCM if dedicated platforms were built for the latter, but the GLCM had the political advantage of being highly visible when deployed on land. SLCMs looked to the Europeans much as did the Polaris submarines that had been assigned since the early 1970s to the supreme allied commander of NATO's forces: they were available but they were invisible. Military factors called for a mixed force; political factors called for a visible and early-deployed land-based force.

True to form, once the decision had been made to deploy the GLCM, the secretary of defense had trouble finding a service to give it to. The Army had earlier rejected interest in taking on development of the GLCM. It feared a roles-and-missions fight with the Air Force over whether the GLCM was akin to an artillery shell for interdiction, in which case it fell into the Army's province, or whether it was akin to a strategic projectile (the Air Force's province). The Army in the mid-1970s was also more concerned with building up its conventional capability in Europe. The opportunity costs of having to pay for another system dedicated solely to the nuclear mission (besides the Pershing II) were too great. Finally, the Army feared that it might be put in the position of developing a system that would never be deployed: along with the decision to deploy LRTNF was a decision to pursue arms control negotiations with the Soviet Union in order to limit both side's deployment of these forces. In the late 1970s, it was not completely clear whether GLCMs were a chip to be bargained away or a system to be deployed.

For its part, the Air Force wanted nothing to do with the GLCM. It, too, was worried about paying for the costs of developing what might turn out to be a bargaining chip. It wanted to continue with the modernization of its tactical fighter forces, to which it had committed a large fraction of its budget in the 1970s. It had no taste for a mission that involved pushing around in the mud a cumbersome weapon that moreover required no pilot to fly it. Largely because the Army already had the Pershing II and because the GLCM could not be given to the Navy, the Air Force got stuck with it. Air Force enthusiasm for the GLCM has been reflected in the spending priority attached to it: the Air Force has consistently put the GLCM near the bottom of its budget priorities, only to have PA&E allocate more dollars to it. Just like the ALCM and the SLCM, the GLCM was a weapon that none of the services wanted. It was pushed upon the Air Force because of the larger political decisions taken by the Carter administration.

CONCLUSIONS

The overriding conclusion from the above analysis is inescapable: not one of the present versions of the cruise missile was readily embraced by any service. The Air Force accepted the long-range ALCM only because the president ordered it to do so. It reluctantly accepted the GLCM, but viewed it as a national, not an Air Force, mission and consistently gave it low priority during the annual budget negotiations with the secretary of defense. The Army successfully fought having to accept the GLCM, not only because it already had the Pershing II, but also because Secretary of Defense Brown and his predecessors agreed with Army leaders, especially Chief of Staff Creighton Abrams, that the highest priority had to be put on rebuilding the Army after Vietnam and on refurbishing America's ground forces in Europe. The Navy fought the SLCM if dedicated platforms were required to carry it and, if not, had to grasp for rationales to justify its existence. The TLAM-C came into being only because Secretary Brown unilaterally put money into the Navy's budget to develop it. The TASM was the

only version that one powerful subgroup within any of the services enthusiastically desired, but the Navy surface fleet had to proceed
cautiously and indirectly to get it. Thus, all of the present five versions
of the cruise missile owe their existence largely to the political incentives—born of SALT II politics, NATO alliance considerations, and
the political needs of presidents—that caused high-level political ap-
pointees within the executive branch to push for their development. It
was these factors that converted the technologically possible into the
politically necessary.

In terms of *intraservice* politics it is clear why no service readily embraced cruise missiles. The dominant group within each service—the
strategic bombers in the Air Force, the carrier admirals in the Navy,
and the NATO-conventional arms lobby in the Army—opposed any
cruise missile variant that threatened what it conceived to be the service's central mission. Within the area of intraservice politics, the
dominant group must always negotiate the allocation of resources
with the other subgroups and parcel out a reasonable amount to them.
The dominant group, however, will firmly resist those innovations
that threaten its claim over the bulk of service resources, question the
relevance of its wisdom and experience, and, ultimately, menace it
with obsolescence. In this respect, military organizations differ little
from other bureaucracies. They are highly resistant to radical change.
And, for that reason, political intervention from the outside is
necessary if radical change is to occur. This overall conclusion, central
though it is, does not exhaust the lessons to be derived from a decade
of development of the cruise missile. There are three more.

First, intraservice politics does not take place in a void. Changes in
both the external balance of military forces and the perceived nature
of the military threat vitally affect the political balance among the
service subgroups contending for their share of resources. Clearly, the
military climate of the seventies differed from that of the fifties and
sixties. Nuclear weapons were where the money was in the fifties, and
each service and all its major subgroups got into the nuclear business.
With the flexible response doctrine of the sixties, the services obtained
more nuclear weapons and large increases in their conventional forces.
In the early sixties, both interservice and intraservice competition was
dampened by real budget increases that made the nuclear and conventional buildup simultaneously possible. In the late sixties, the Vietnam
War created a consensus for the allocation of resources to the conventional effort.

For the services in the seventies, the overriding factors were the
tremendous growth of Russia's strategic nuclear forces and buildup in
conventional forces, the depletion of America's conventional capability
(especially in Europe) due to Vietnam, the failure to invest in the

modernization of conventional forces, and, finally, a severe budgetary stringency exacerbated by high and continuous inflation. For a time, the political elite was able to enforce restraint in the amount of resources allocated to the strategic nuclear forces and thereby emphasize their modernization rather than expansion. But because Russia's vastly expanded strategic forces gave it a security shield behind which it could exert conventional forces on a global scale, the United States began to pay greater attention to the effects of strategic equivalence on the conventional balance. As had been the case in the early sixties, concern was expressed that greater stability at the strategic level (a low probability of general nuclear war between the superpowers) increased the likelihood of tactical instability (conventional wars on the peripheries). Particularly in the Air Force and the Navy, this development enhanced the political position of those who argued for an improved conventional war-fighting capability.

However, there were concerns about nuclear forces as well. The SALT II accord of 1972 was not universally accepted as desirable; nor was there agreement that strategic nuclear parity obtained, in good part because no political consensus existed on what was meant by parity. Furthermore, concern about the size and continuing modernization of Russia's strategic nuclear forces spawned changes in beliefs about the uses and levels of the U.S. strategic forces. It also produced much analysis on what the change in the strategic nuclear balance meant for the theater nuclear force balance. These concerns about nuclear forces did not diminish the position of those who argued for more attention to conventional forces. However, the severe budgetary stringency that prevailed in the seventies intensified interservice competition for the defense pie and intraservice competition over the nuclear versus the conventional missions. The latter was especially the case within the Air Force and the Navy.

In this complex military environment, the balance of political forces within each service began to shift. The balance shifted least within the Army largely because of widespread acceptance within it of the primacy of the conventional mission. GLCMs devoted to a long-range theater nuclear mission ranked low in Army needs. A significant segment even wanted to give up the Pershing I and certainly not develop the Pershing II, because such labor-intensive systems would magnify the Army's manpower problems. The Navy began to shift its emphasis away from nuclear power projection against the Soviet homeland to protection of the surface fleet and control of the seas. As a consequence, the surface and submarine fleets gained political power at the expense of the carrier admirals. The Air Force witnessed the political coming of age of the Tactical Air Command, which assumed a position of near equality with the Strategic Air Command.

Tactical interdiction and air superiority have always been valued in the Force, but they took a prominence in peacetime (compared to the strategic bombing mission) not previously characteristic of the Air Force. The changes in the political balance of forces within each service should not be overstated, but neither should they be underestimated.

These changes in the military environment and in the politics of intraservice competition unambiguously favored only one version of the cruise missile: the TASM. A conventional weapon dedicated to the protection of the surface fleet, it was in tune with the greater emphasis placed on control of the seas. The ultimate fate of the TLAM-C is not clear. Although it is conventionally armed, its high unit cost makes its military worth still debatable. The ALCM-B was so much caught up in the vortex of SALT II and presidential-congressional bomber politics in the seventies that it was lifted out of the arena of intraservice politics. The TLAM-N and the GLCM are single-purpose, theater-based, nuclear systems. In general, but especially in periods of fiscal stringency, the services have consistently preferred to deploy dual-purpose systems capable of both a nuclear and a conventional mission. With the greater concern for the conventional balance in the seventies, the services considered theater-based nuclear systems as a necessary evil. Theater nuclear weapons must be bought in order to be able to fight what the services see as the most likely war—a conventional one. Theater nuclear systems must be deployed for deterrent, not for war-fighting purposes.

Because of the crosscurrents in the military environment of the seventies, the only easily discernible trend within all of the services is a greater emphasis on conventional war-fighting capabilities. It is precisely this trend that largely explains Army resistance to the GLCM and lack of enthusiasm for the Pershing II, Navy ambivalence about the TLAM-N and significant support for the TASM, Air Force unhappiness with the GLCM, and, presumably in the eighties, Tactical Command ecstasy over a conventionally armed medium-range air-to-surface missile. The dynamics of intraservice politics explains the central conclusion of this chapter, that civilian intervention was required for the development of the cruise missile.

A second conclusion concerns the relevance of bureaucratic politics. As commonly understood, this phenomenon refers to the pulling, hauling, and tugging that goes on in the executive branch over a given issue, with the resultant policy often one that none of the participants initially or even eventually desired. The outcomes of cruise missile development in the seventies, however, occurred in spite of, not because of, bureaucratic politics. Within the services there was a great deal of bureaucratic politicking, most of it ultimately to little avail. The Air Force did not want the ALCM-B. It was forced to take it. The Air Force did not want the GLCM. It was forced to take it. The

Navy had little enthusiasm for the TLAM. It was forced to take it. Only in the case of the TASM does bureaucratic politics explain a great deal about the final outcome. Even here, as in other cases, outside political intervention was necessary to produce the outcome that politicians wanted.

In terms of the scope of bureaucratic politics within the executive branch, the GLCM case is the most interesting because it fully involved all the main national security participants: the Defense Department, the State Department, the Arms Control and Disarmament Agency, and the White House. Yet all the major participants, with the possible exception of the Joint Chiefs of Staff and NATO's supreme allied command, were initially dubious about the need for more nuclear weapons in Europe. The State Department and the Arms Control Agency may have been more skeptical than their counterparts in the Pentagon—PA&E and International Security Affairs—but only in degree. All came to support the deployment of more theater nuclear weapons in Europe largely because the Germans pushed hard for them. Faced with pressure from without, the United States government acted more like a unitary actor on this issue than a house divided. The divisions that did occur revolved more around the issues of how many weapons to deploy and under what rationale than on the decision of whether to deploy them. As with most pivotal issues in American foreign policy since 1945, there was more unity at the top than commonly thought.

Finally, the third conclusion to be drawn from this case concerns its implications for the congressonal role in weapon systems decisions. Formally, the power of the purse has always given Congress the authority and the capability to play major roles in American foreign and defense policy. Yet in the past Congress has not always availed itself of this opportunity. In recent years, it has become a virtual cliché to assert that Congress has assumed a prominent, if not dominant, role in national security policy. To support this view, analysts have typically pointed to such events as the 1969 antiballistic missile debate, the Cooper-Church amendment limiting American involvement in Indochina, the passage of the War Powers Resolution in 1973, the refusal to provide promised assistance to the government of South Vietnam, and the Turkish arms embargo. Coupled with the growth of micromanagement in defense programs, these events are taken as signs of a new activism in Congress.

It is clear that in the 1970s Congress significantly expanded its oversight ability in defense matters. Hearings before the Armed Services Committees were carried on by numerous subcommittees, each of which had authority over defense programs in a specific area. Such subcommittee specialization not only yielded extensive and intensive information, but also constrained the ability of the Department of

Defense to reprogram money from function to function because each subcommittee authorized programs and established budgetary ceilings in a highly detailed fashion. In the past decade, moreover, there was a major growth in the quantity and quality of professional staff. Over 18,000 staffers, many with advanced professional training and considerable executive experience, were employed in the standing committees, the offices of individual legislators, and such investigative arms as the Congressional Research Service, the Office of Technology Assessment, the Congressional Budget Office, and the General Accounting Office. Finally, passage of the Congressional Budget and Impoundment Control Act of 1974 gave Congress a significant institutional advantage. It was now possible for Congress as a whole to set budgetary priorities in advance of appropriations rather than build budgets from the bottom up in disaggregated committee fashion. In short, Congress in the seventies acquired the capability to constrain, manage, or even initiate highly detailed programs and policies.

Because the cruise missile program began in the late 1960s and early 1970s, when congressional activism in defense first came to the fore and congressional analytical capability was beginning to expand, it is useful to use this case in order to draw tentative conclusions about the effectiveness of congressional micromanagement in defense matters. Our analysis casts doubt on the view that Congress's influence, if not its role, somehow changed radically in the seventies. An assessment of three specific congressional interventions in the cruise missile program illustrates the point.

First, in 1972 and 1973, Congress acted as an ally of the secretary of defense by authorizing research on long-range cruise missiles. The program was pushed by Secretary of Defense Laird for reasons related to SALT II. It was necessarily vaguely defined, given Laird's ulterior motives. Latitude for congressional micromanagement was extremely limited because the program was in early development. The connections between the SCAD, SCM, and ACM programs were ill defined. In this instance, congressional funding was vital to the success of the cruise missile program. The congressional role, however, was one of a supporter, not a meddlesome backseat driver. The second significant intervention occurred in 1976 when Congress ordered the Pentagon to accelerate the tactical antiship missile and demanded that it clarify the rationale for the land-attack version. In this instance, the congressional actors thought they had acted as a judge of the worth of several programs. As our analysis made clear, however, the Navy had little interest in a land-attack program that had served largely to camouflage the activities of the surface fleet. Few Navy officials were disheartened by Congress's displeasure over the land-attack version. Although Congress had made it harder for those high-level Defense Department officials who wanted to build the land-attack missile, this action did not kill that version. Unknowingly, it had acted as an ally of the surface fleet proponents of the antiship missile and, therefore, had done little to alter the preferences of the Navy activists.

The third intervention occurred in 1979 when Congress forced the Pentagon to initiate development of the TLAM-C program. In this instance, Congress acted as a successful lobbyist because it started a program that very few in the OSD or the Navy wanted. The background for this action began in earlier years. In 1976, as in 1972, the Senate Armed Services Subcommittee on Research and Development had taken the lead in criticizing the TLAM-N and reducing its funding. In 1976, as in 1972, the House Armed Services Committee, always more enthusiastic about new technologies than its Senate counterpart, had restored some funding for it. The program had limped along in the Pentagon, however, because no one quite knew what to do with it.

Some incentives were present, however, to keep it going. Until mid-1976, the Navy surface fleet used the TLAM-N to protect the TASM. After these proponents no longer needed it to protect the TASM, the OSD kept it alive because by then America's NATO allies were expressing interest in SLCMs and GLCMs. The OSD kept the TLAM-N going during 1977 and 1978, but had lost enthusiasm by 1979 once it knew the NATO High Level Group had chosen the GLCM over the SLCM. In anticipation of the December 1979 NATO ministerial meeting, where NATO was formally to approve the GLCM's deployment, the OSD downplayed the SLCM and accelerated the GLCM. During the summer and fall of 1979, the Carter administration was highly sensitive to any actions that might threaten an affirmative decision in December. Specifically, the administration worried about what was called the "SLCM escape-hatch scenario"—the fear that, because deployment of land-based cruise missiles was proving to be politically difficult within Europe, the governments there might seize upon any pretext to back away from the consensus they had reached within the HLG on the GLCM. The administration thought that if it funded the TLAM-N, then its NATO allies might use this to "go to sea" with the cruise missile in order to defuse the political opposition that was building on the GLCM. The House Armed Services Committee, however, wanted the TLAM-N built. The compromise reached between Secretary Brown and the committee was to accelerate development of the TLAM but in the conventional version. Once again, it was high-level politics—this time a mixture of congressional-executive and American-European politics—not service interest, that forced development of a cruise missile.

The meaning of these three specific congressional interventions is difficult to assess. In its first intervention, Congress clearly allied with the executive to fund a program even though one of its houses was highly skeptical of its stated mission. In its second intervention, Congress slowed development of a program that most in the Pentagon were happy to see slowed. Only in its third intervention did Congress force the hand of a reluctant Pentagon. Clearly Congress was attuned to both technological details and the fine points of larger military purposes. Congress also gave the administration what it wanted more often than not. Only once was micromanagement employed, in the sense of intervening to run a program in a fashion the executive opposed. The three key congressional programmatic interventions on the cruise missile during the 1970s do not impressively support the conclusion that Congress has become the defense micromanager. But that does not mean that Congress had little influence. It affected the program in its specifics more through support of than opposition to executive preferences. Continuity with the past thus appears stronger than a sharp break with it. Congress functioned more in the traditional roles of lobbyist, gadfly, supporter, and arbitrator than as detailed manager of ongoing programs.

Why, then, did the United States develop cruise missiles when none of the services wanted them? The answer, quite simply, is that the politicians did, and their preferences prevailed. The final word on the broad politics of cruise missile development in the seventies is this: had it not been for politics, the cruise missile in all its present versions might never have existed.

Part III
Arms Races and
Arms Control

In deciding where, when, and how to use military power, national leaders must ask themselves how much force they need in order to do what they wish. The calculation of how much is needed depends partly on the goals being pursued. Coercion or conquest will usually require more force than would be needed to dissuade a foe from attacking one's country. The calculation of how much is needed also depends on the reactions of other states to the types and amounts of forces one procures. State A may have increased its forces only to find that any possible gains are soon negated by similar increases made by State B. State A may then decide that the prize is worth the payment of an extra price and may add still more to its forces. State B may decide likewise. State A may decide to up the ante again and so forth. Situations in which this action-reaction phenomenon occurs—where B's actions depend on A's and A's on B's—can be called arms races.

Under what circumstances do such interactions occur? Are some types of weapons more likely to produce arms races than others? How can arms races be controlled? These are the questions that the four authors explore. Bernard Brodie asks what the sensible political, military, and economic objectives of arms control are. Samuel P. Huntington undertakes a historical comparison of arms races to determine whether quantitative or qualitative races are the more unstable. Charles H. Fairbanks, Jr., examines the unintended and unwanted consequences of the Washington Naval Treaty of 1922. Warner R. Schilling explains why the United States did not contest the efforts of the Soviet Union in the 1960s and '70s to achieve strategic parity and questions the stability of the strategic balance of the early 1980s.

On the Objectives
of Arms Control

BERNARD BRODIE

The volume of literature on arms control contrasts sharply with the dearth of results in actual armaments limitation or control. Thus huge disparity between fullness of advice and leanness of practical results suggests a good deal about both the character of that advice and the magnitude of the practical difficulties—and especially about the failure of the former to adjust to the latter.

The ample quantity of the writing on arms control in the face of what would seem to be such poor prospects of realization reflects also an aspiration, amounting often to religiosity, in much of the motivation for that writing. Although we must be grateful for whatever propels motivation in what we feel intuitively to be a good cause, we must also be suspicious of that kind of motivation which corrupts the endeavor.[1]

All but a minute proportion of the works that I have seen on the general subject of arms control fail to be of any utility for the policymaker, and thus also for the student of policy making, except insofar as some of those writings conveniently provide for the interested layman some technical knowledge about weaponry. That failure is naturally due to various characteristics, but one common characteristic that I should put at the top of the list is *persistent failure to clarify and analyze objectives,* which of course precludes any rigorous and consistent adherence to the soundest objectives. Naturally, this clarification should not have to be done over and over again, but it would be useful to have it be done occasionally.

ARMS CONTROL OBJECTIVES AND PERCEPTIONS

An appropriate analysis of objectives would inevitably entail a pragmatic approach—we want our objectives to be mutually consistent, to be worth achieving, and to be in some degree achievable—and

From *International Security,* Summer, 1976, p. 17-36. Reprinted by permission of The MIT Press Journals.

[1] I can only hope that what I have seen is a fair and representative sampling. A manuscript for a bibliography of items related to and about arms control, prepared by Professor Richard Dean Burns, comes to some 900 pages of double-spaced typing. It will be published in 1976 or 1977 by the Clio Press of Santa Barbara, California.

that in turn entails a properly empirical utilization of our experience. We have had much relevant experience with arms control negotiations, with the armaments competitions that have stimulated efforts at control, and above all with war, the prospect of which ultimately dominates everything having to do with arms competitions and the efforts to control them.

Inasmuch as arms control efforts seek to affect future events, we have to be conscious of the degree of our uncertainty about the future, in which we are instructed by our experience with surprise in the past. Perhaps an appreciation for this uncertainty will inhibit our choice of arms control objectives, but if so, that is simply the way the ball bounces.

I am using the term "arms control" in a sense which accords with the popular conception but which some would regard as unduly restrictive. It was right once to make the point that the kind of arms control that may be most important in the long run is that which depends on tacit rather than explicit agreement—also that arms control for the purpose of enhancing security does not usually imply reducing the overall costs of our armaments but may in particular respects mean raising them.[2] Though of some perennial application, those points were more pertinent to the Eisenhower years than to the present. Anyway, the more common and narrower conception, which I accept, identifies the term "arms control" with some degree of limitation or reduction of particular armaments, and it implies also explicit rather than merely tacit international agreement. There is indeed substantial extra value in the relevant agreements being explicit.

The objectives of arms control are usually not stated, but when they are stated, they are only rarely if ever reflectively considered. Apparently this is because most writers feel that the merit of their implied or declared objectives is too obvious to need consideration.[3] Not only are some two, three, or four objectives usually held to be obviously desirable, but even the order of their priority seems to be a matter for declaration rather than examination. Among the numerous statements that might be quoted to illustrate this point, I choose one which I find specially provocative but which reflects fairly the view most commonly held by the vast majority of those who write on arms control. Herman Kahn and Anthony Weiner say that the purpose of arms control is:

[2] These ideas were prominent in the work of Thomas C. Schelling. See especially the book by him and Morton H. Halperin, *Strategy and Arms Control* (New York: Twentieth Century Fund, 1961).

[3] Hedley Bull's *The Control of the Arms Race* (New York: Praeger, 1961) does indeed devote the first chapter to "The Objectives of Arms Control," but I find it exploratory rather than analytical. This and the above-mentioned book by Schelling and Halperin, both published in the same year, both short, remain to this date the landmark books in the field.

. . . to improve the inherent stability of the situation, decrease the occasions or the approximate causes of war within the system, and decrease the destructiveness and other disutilities of any wars that actually occur. One may also add to this last, 'decrease the cost of defense preparation,' but we would argue that this would take a rather low priority to the first three objectives.[4]

This statement puts the aim of saving money not only last but in a separate sub-category of lesser worthiness than the other three. Those three in turn really boil down to only two, because the first two mentioned refer to the common aim of reducing the probability of war, and the third, which thus becomes the second, has to do with reducing the destructiveness of war if it should occur.

One notices in passing that giving priority to the twin aims of reducing the probability of war and of reducing its destructiveness if it occurs—the reference is almost always to war between the two superpowers—reflects an implicit appraisal of the existing probability of war. Some would protest that if war breaks out the penalties are so vast that *any* possibility of its occurring warrants whatever efforts we can make to counteract that possibility. Still, we know that few would greatly bestir themselves to cope with an evil that they regard as having only a miniscule probability of occurring. Individual views on armaments and arms control cover a wide range, and it is important to establish that one prime factor accounting for the differences is the individual's appraisal of the probability of war—an appraisal that is usually vaguely felt and nearly always implicit rather than explicit.

I find the Kahn-Weiner statement provocative because of their view of priorities. My own contrary view is that in a pragmatic approach to arms control the object of saving money really deserves a superior rating to that of saving the world. This conclusion must imply, among other things, either a high confidence that the probability of war between the two superpowers will continue to be extremely low, or the conviction that in any case we cannot do much about that probability through arms control. To make explicit and thus also to clarify what is otherwise ambiguous, let me record that I subscribe to both propositions.

Although one can defend a low expectation of superpower conflict by citing only objective factors, one must admit that the *weighting* of those factors depends upon a substantial increment of subjective and thus intuitive judgement.[5] Besides obliging one to be tolerant of differing opinions, this fact throws the main burden of the argument on the

---

[4] Herman Kahn and Anthony Weiner, "Technological Innovation and the Future of Strategic Warfare," *Astronautics and Aeronautics* (December, 1967), p. 28.

[5] I have dealt at greater length with the question of the probability of war between the United States and the Soviet Union in my *War and Politics* (New York: Macmillan, 1973), especially in chapters 6 and 9.

latter of the two above propositions—that arms control negotiations and the resulting agreements, if any, will rarely make important contributions to reducing either the probability of war or its destructiveness. There are several reasons for this, of which two stand out particularly: (1) each party is extremely suspicious of the adversary's efforts to disarm him in weaponry regarded as truly important, and (2) apart from a few simple and obvious devices like the "hot line" between Washington and Moscow, experience assures us that it is not at all a simple matter to determine objectively, let alone get international agreement upon, those arms limitation measures that will really advance the ends of greater stability and lesser destructiveness.

That leaves us with the mere matter of saving money, on which governments, unlike amateur observers, never look askance. Governments are at all times coping intensively with a number of recalcitrant economic problems, which in recent years have included marked inflationary pressures and also growing alternative demands for the monies raised from public restive about taxes. Competitive pressures from the chief foreign rival will at times force a commitment to expenditures which government leaders may feel to be of doubtful utility from the military point of view, or changed conditions will make less necessary or desirable what was previously considered essential. Yet political reasons may militate against cutting back unilaterally. Each government also finds itself pressed by its own military in a conflict where the rival government, which has similar problems, may occasionally be a useful ally.

We have already noticed that every participant in the national debate on arms control carries with him as part of his intellectual and emotional baggage some kind of appraisal of war-probability which inevitably affects his relevant attitudes. Obviously it will affect his feelings on how much one should try to accommodate to the views of the bargaining partner. It is an old story that one important reason why arms limitation conferences have so often failed or yielded only the most meager results is that both sides bring with them to the conference a contingent of experts, whether in uniform or not, whose whole professional predisposition is to look upon that bargaining partner as the prospective military adversary. They also feel a pronounced distaste for giving up any of those armaments with which they individually identify themselves and which they may have fought for on the domestic scene. There are also those left at home who can be counted upon to influence the debate that will precede any ratification. Depending on the moods of the time these experts may feel obliged to give lip service to arms limitation, but they will bring to the process a tight and often arbitrary measure of proportionality.

All that is of course familiar, but there is another less observed facet of the problem. Those who entertain a low estimate of superpower war probability will incline towards the idea that for deterrence purposes the fact of being powerful is much more important than the exact character or structure of that power. This attitude makes for more flexibility in the critical negotiations, and also for acceptance as a matter of course of the important distinction between deterrence capabilities and war-fighting capabilities. The former capabilities are those which are menacing enough, under expected conditions of low mutual motivation for war, to preclude the adversary's giving serious consideration to exploiting the means and paying the price of defeating them.

Those persons, on the other hand, who regard the danger of super-power war as appreciable are consistent in arguing that the best deterrence force is the optimum fighting force. They will run into difficulties with their insistence on this point when they contemplate the ultimate in strategic nuclear deterrence, where war-fighting capabilities seem to dissolve into irrelevance. Herman Kahn's well-known parable of the doomsday machine (designed by Americans to blow up the world if it should detect some five nuclear weapons exploding anywhere over the United States) demonstrated hypothetically that deterrence and war-fighting capabilities are *not* the same thing, at least at the maximum levels of warfare.[6] At theater levels of warfare, however, war-fighting capabilities are much more relevant to deterrence, and anyway, one wants the monies allocated to fighting forces to be spent efficiently, which means efficiently for fighting purposes. Even so, it is likely that an effort concentrated on deterrence will be less costly by wide margins than one concentrated on matching or out-doing the opponent in war-fighting capabilities.

All sorts of slogans get in the way of a reasonable handling of this problem, such as the common assertion that our efforts should be guided exclusively by the opponent's capabilities, not by our estimate of his intentions. This slogan is not likely to be fully followed in practice, because our sense of threat is inevitably qualified by our operating image of the opponent, which may be of one who wants to be strong but also wants desperately to avoid war. Nevertheless, the slogan does act to exacerbate competitive pressures.[7] These pressures certainly increase the disposition to match the rival's military efforts in degree, and they also to some extent dispose us to imitate him in kind. Obviously our military have their own ideas in some matters, but they and we will be uneasy with too radical a departure from the major pattern the rival is following. Thus both sides build up huge conventional forces in an age of nuclear weapons.

[6] See Herman Kahn, *On Thermonuclear War* (Princeton: Princeton University Press, 1960), pp. 145–151.
[7] I discuss the issue of "capabilities versus intentions" at greater length in my *Escalation and the Nuclear Option* (Princeton: Princeton University Press, 1966), ch. 7.

AGREEING UPON ARMS CONTROL OBJECTIVES

We turn now to some examples which will illustrate and perhaps also elaborate the various points made above. On the general issue of the difficulty of winning acceptance even of agreements that would seem to be obviously in the security interests of the participants, a recent and conspicuous example is the history of the effort to avoid proliferation of nuclear weapons. There is little overt dissension anywhere to the belief, which is almost universal within the United States, that the general proliferation of nuclear weapons among non-possessing nations would be a threat to world peace. This view seems to be held even by some governments that have refused to sign the Non- Proliferation Treaty of 1968, including the French government—which has, however, not hesitated to attempt to sell to governments like that of South Korea not only nuclear power plants but also plutonium reprocessing plants to go with them. In this case we do have a treaty, the achievement of which was one of the leading aims of American foreign policy for several years before its accomplishment. Still, the considerable resistances to the adoption of that treaty are well known. At this writing 98 nations are parties to it and 12 that have signed have not yet ratified. Both figures leave out some quite important states.[8] What is more, the treaty itself has more than its share of legal escape hatches, quite apart from the fact that it is more than usually subject to evasion or violation.

Ah, one protests, but is not this too blatant an example of inequality, where nations are being asked to sign a self-denying ordinance not subscribed to by some nations including our own, and where the compensation is all too abstract? No doubt, but when are the benefits of an arms limitation treaty not abstract—except insofar as they directly result in the saving of money? The fact remains that a proposition that commends itself overwhelmingly to virtually all interested citizens in the United States—and most arms limitation proposals do not meet that criterion—quite clearly does not commend itself universally. The treaty we do have is not worthless but neither is it worth very much. The actual plans of signatory nations concerning their own military nuclear programs have probably been little if at all affected by that treaty. The objective of the treaty is still worth pursuing, certainly in the direction of curbing the almost wanton distribution of nuclear power reactors and especially of plutonium reprocessing plants, but we have reason to be aware of the limited prospects of its success. In other examples we shall be considering, it is much less clear whether the objective is worth pursuing.

---

[8] Japan became the 98th party to the treaty with the deposit of its instrument of ratification on June 8, 1976.

DETERMINING WHAT IS NEGOTIABLE:
THE CASE OF TACTICAL NUCLEAR WEAPONS

One critical example of an arms limitation objective that we are in danger of pursuing too hastily involves tactical nuclear weapons (TNWs). These are commonly believed to be the most ill-begotten of a noisome race of weapons, particularly objectionable because they are unnecessary. In this view they should not be used even in the event of a major attack by the Soviet Union upon our own and allied forces in Europe and at sea. To use them, the argument goes, is to wipe out the only meaningful stop (or "firebreak") between theater warfare and the suicidal strategic kind. Why the slide from one to the other should be so steep and slippery is not explained, no doubt because the reasons are considered too obvious to require explanation.

The notion that TNWs are on the whole more dangerous than useful to their possessor derives from an idea developed and advocated in the early 1960s, mostly by a group of analysts then at the RAND Corporation.[9] If the United States and its NATO allies built up their conventional ground and air forces to something like parity with those of the Warsaw Pact, these men argued, the "nuclear threshold" would be raised to so high a level as virtually to eliminate the chances of its being breached even in an outbreak of major military action in Europe—which, everyone agreed, could be initiated only by a Soviet attack. They further insisted that inasmuch as everyone would understand that our European allies would be much more willing to resist Soviet aggression if they were highly confident that the resulting battle would remain non-nuclear, the proposed posture would greatly enhance real deterrence.

Thus, the 7,000 American TNWs reported to be stationed in Europe are held to be exceptionally available tokens to be offered in any arms reduction proposals to the Soviet Union. Secretary of State Henry A. Kissinger has already offered to reduce them by 1,000 if the Soviet Union will make an offsetting—though not similar—reduction in its armed forces in Europe. Whatever Kissinger's own beliefs on the subject may be—and he is on record as being dubious of the views of the conventional-war enthusiasts—he is aware that an offer of this kind meets the minimum of objections from the Pentagon, the Congress, and other relevant agencies. Alain Enthoven, however, would go much further than Kissinger. He would reduce their number unilaterally without offsetting concessions, and not *by* 1,000 but *to* 1,000.[10]

[9] Leadership of this group within RAND must be credited to Albert Wohlstetter, though Alain C. Enthoven has been the most frequent spokesman in print for their position. Others among them known for their publications include Malcolm Hoag, W. W. Kaufmann, and Henry Rowen.

[10] See Alain C. Enthoven, "U. S. Forces in Europe: How Many? Doing What?" *Foreign Affairs,* (April 1975), pp. 512–532.

To the layman 1,000 nuclear weapons will seem like an adequate number for any purpose, but if those retained are ever really adapted to tactical uses, which would mean among other things greatly reducing the yields on most of them, 1,000 would certainly not be adequate. Enthoven would reduce the number of TNWs in Europe primarily to free for conventional war purposes the men now assigned to guarding them, which he numbers at 30,000. And he would retain the 1,000 strictly to deter the Soviet Union from using TNWs in its attack.

Whether the Europeans could ever have high confidence that a major war in Europe would remain non-nuclear, or whether such confidence ought under any circumstances to be entertained, are among the vital questions which have not been scrutinized. The group that originated this mode of thought believed the logic of the new idea to be so compelling that it would be quickly accepted by the Soviet military leaders as well as allied ones, not to mention our own. To be sure, involved Americans were determined not to lose a war in Europe. There would be no first use by us *unless we found ourselves losing.* The Russians were apparently expected to accommodate to this rigidity on our part, which they would no doubt consider somewhat peculiar, and to do so without using nuclear weapons.

One notes a complete absence of empirical inquiry about various of the radical assumptions that went into this doctrine. *What* Europeans were meant by *the* Europeans who would supposedly resist under one set of circumstances but not under another? Did anyone try to find out whether that was really the opinion of those few Europeans who would make the critical decisions? Would the Russians launch a large-scale attack without the determination to win, swiftly, and would they expose themselves to the hazards of such a duel while leaving entirely to us the choice of weapons? What did their overt doctrine tell us on these matters? These and comparable questions which were subject to fruitful investigation were not in fact investigated. One notices also that the original protagonists of this view harbored a sufficiently high expectation of a Soviet attack in Europe to advocate with some urgency a considerable and costly improvement of NATO forces, though they seemed to find it forensically necessary to insist that in military manpower the NATO forces were already very nearly equal to those of the Warsaw Pact.[11]

The theory was attractive enough to win ready converts in the

[11] Dr. Enthoven has been consistently arguing this point in several publications, the most recent being his aforementioned *Foreign Affairs* article. On page 516 Enthoven holds that Warsaw Pact forces on M-Day plus 60 would be only 1,241,000 (as compared with NATO's 1,105,000). One wonders what happened to that Soviet Union which, without allies, suffered the loss of five to six million troops in the first 5½ months of war in 1941, and then went on to win. The estimate is Albert Seaton's in his *The Russo-German War, 1941-1945* (New York: Praeger, 1971), p. 208n.

428 ARMS RACES AND ARMS CONTROL

highest reaches of the Kennedy Administration, including the President himself and his vigorous Secretary of Defense, Robert S. McNamara. And what was a novel and radical doctrine 15 years ago has now in the mid-1970s become the conventional wisdom of the interested public and of most of the defense community. Professional military officers tend today to be ambivalent on the use of TNWs, being ready in principle to use them if the other side uses them first, or, as something of an afterthought, in the event we find ourselves losing without them. But whether their forces are organized, equipped, and trained to make so swift a shift from one form of warfare to another is a pertinent question—to which the answer almost certainly is "no". The military did, after all, like that part of the theory which justified their requesting a good deal more of the kind of equipment they were accustomed to, albeit modernized. And, as some of them have frankly admitted, they have simply stopped thinking much about the problem. The most extraordinary example of how one service has adjusted to the idea that TNWs would surely not be used in a war with the Soviet Union is the manner in which our surface combat fleet has developed around huge attack carriers, any one of which could be volatilized by one small nuclear weapon, deliverable by aircraft, surface vessel, submarine, or even shore-based missile launcher.

Thus, a theory has been accepted almost without challenge simply because it is a seductive one. One wants to believe it, especially if one can be persuaded that forces organized for the non-use of nuclear weapons make for more rather than less deterrence. Some theories are of course self-fulfilling, and this one might be so if we were not talking about war—which always presupposes an adversary with intentions and drives of his own. Under the circumstances, however, it is a dangerous theory as well as a costly one. The conventional forces it calls for in NATO have not been provided, and would be of dubious utility if they were. Our NATO allies were never impressed with the American idea, and besides they felt the threat from the Soviet Union to be diminishing. That situation was not conducive to spending more on defense. Anyway, European policymakers have a long-standing fondness for nuclear *deterrence,* and if the strategic variety seems less dependable to them than formerly, as it clearly (and perhaps fortunately) does, they are that much less willing to relinquish the theater kind. Since 1967 they have found it expedient to give lip service within NATO to the concept of "graduated response," but they are far from fleshing our their purely conventional capabilities. They have indeed been tending in the opposite direction.

One of the primary ideas upon which the whole conventional war construct is based is that large-scale conflict between the superpowers can be the result of accident. By "accidental war" is presumably meant that which comes despite neither side wanting it, and with neither side realizing until war is actually upon it that the policy it is pursuing makes that war unavoidable. This notion has given rise to the concept of the "pause," intended to permit the enemy to reconsider his behavior before one introduces nuclear weapons against him.

Presumably this kind of accident is made possible by the very existence of nuclear weapons, for within the definition of the term given above, no such thing as accidental war has happened within the last three hundred years, if ever. And it really is bizarre to think that the presence of nuclear weapons can make nations more reckless and disportive in bearding their opponents than ever before, in a word more ready to risk war in the conviction that it will not come. Thus we pay heavy extra premiums in our defenses simply because most of those who currently philosophize about strategy have made no effort to acquaint themselves with the history of war.

In the context of TNWs, what about the aim of diminishing the destructiveness of war? The answers, in diminishing order of importance, are about as follows: First, the surest way of reducing the destructiveness of war is to deter it, and insofar as theater forces are required for deterrence they should be as effective in that role as possible. For *any* given sum of expenditures the best theater deterrence force is the most efficient fighting force, and that means a force organized, trained, and equipped for using the most modern weapons, certainly including nuclear ones. The prevailing assumption is, of course, that an attack upon it will *not* be an accident. Second, the decision to use nuclear weapons would in any case not be primarily ours to make, especially with the basic premise in all our war plans being that the opponent is the aggressor; defense plans have to consider not the most desired but the most likely mode of enemy attack. Third, there is no *prima facie* evidence that a battle fought with TNWs would be more destructive to the terrain over which it is fought or to noncombatants in the theater than the conventional battles we have known in the two world wars. It might well be the other way round. The critical factor in destructiveness to the terrain is usually the rate of movement of the contending armies, the destructiveness tending to be inversely proportional to the swiftness with which one side pushes back or destroys the other. Also, with nuclear weapons it is very much a matter of the types most used and the manner in which they are employed—something that should be studied intensively in advance, largely for the sake of minimizing undesired collateral damage.

DECIDING ON WEAPON NUMBERS

Leaving now the matter of TNWs, but pursuing the important objective of "limiting the destructiveness of war if it comes," we might briefly consider the views of Herbert York, who has been active in efforts to get agreements to reduce the size of nuclear stockpiles, especially of strategic nuclear weapons.[12] There can be little question that American and Soviet strategic nuclear weapons already deployed or otherwise available for use have grown in numbers far beyond any reasonable conception of military need and certainly of deterrence. This has been a result mainly of competitive pressures and of such technological advances as MIRV. The requirement to escape the threat of having one's retaliatory force obliterated by surprise attack is solved far better by the manner of its deployment than by multiplying its weapons. Though the long-term viability of our silo-protected ICBMs may be in doubt, alternative means of deployment, such as submarine-launched missiles, make it absurd to sound alarms about the imminent danger of the Russians developing a "first-strike capability"—a complaint frequently voiced by former Secretary of Defense Melvin Laird. Equally dubious were the public expressions of another recent Secretary of Defense, James R. Schlesinger, who argued that with the kind of accuracy that promises to become available in the cruise missile we should develop what was formerly called a "damage-limiting" capability, that is, limiting damage to ourselves by destroying enemy missiles in their silos.

Why then, has it been so difficult for York to get a sympathetic hearing for his views, even in such milieus as the Arms Control and Disarmament Agency (ACDA)? One of the reasons, no doubt, is that nuclear weapons already produced and deployed are so much sunk capital, not especially costly to maintain in their land-based missile configurations and certainly not when stockpiled. The budget for all American strategic nuclear forces, which includes bombers and missile submarines and all monies spent on related research and development, was in FY 1976 about 18 percent of our entire defense budget. Those costs would not be substantially reduced simply by phasing out warheads. Also, with the passing of the years the possibility of a strategic nuclear exchange seems to have become in most people's minds more and more remote, and one reason for that is precisely the horrendous number of weapons. It is one thing to say that we have far more than enough weapons for deterrence, but who is to say—and to persuade others—how far that number can reasonably drop before deterrence is in fact diminished? Who wants to rock the boat, especially since large numbers are also a protection against the alleged "destabilization" that tends to result from various kinds of technological innovation? Many people show a deep concern about "superiority," about relative "throw-weights" and all the rest, and although these fears do point to the importance of fruitful negotiation

---

[12] Of his many writings on the subject, one of the most comprehensive is *Race to Oblivion* (New York: Simon and Schuster, 1970).

to find mutual limits, they also reflect an abiding confidence in numbers which has to be, if not honored, at least humored.

Most important of all, however, in accounting for the lack of receptiveness to York's ideas is the fact that, precisely because the number of weapons is so huge, the realization of his ideas would require a *drastic* reduction in those numbers—not just 10 or 20 percent but something well over 90 percent! If the object is to retain the kind of deterrence which strategic nuclear weapons provide against any kind of war with the rival superpower, but to decrease materially the grimness that would follow a failure of deterrence—we should have to know how to draw the curve for the marginal utility of weapons. We should than have to hunt for something like an optimum balance between deterrence on the one hand, and on the other hand reasonable (?) limits to destructiveness if deterrence fails. We should then have to develop a consensus within the country, at least among relevant bureaucracies and the Congress, that we had found the optimum zone of figures, following which we should have to embark upon appropriate negotiations abroad. And because the figure to be aimed at is now so much lower than before, negotiations would have to include not only the Soviet Union but also China, France, and Britain. No one should presume to say that the day will never arrive when such a chain of events is possible, but it is certainly not on the horizon.

ASSESSING THE ARMS RACE

The competitive pressures mentioned above bring us to another of the alleged major causes of war which arms control is supposed to curb—the arms race. It is an article of faith among most of those who write on arms control that curbing the arms race in order to keep the peace of the world is what arms control is all about, or at least mostly about. Among these writers arms competitions or "races" are alleged to be by themselves the most potent—the word "inevitable" is frequently in evidence—of the causes of war.

The idea is on the face of it somewhat illogical. Why the pressures of an arms competition, however costly, irritating, or even alarming they may become, should move one of the competitors to try to resolve it all by resorting to the immeasurably more costly and hazardous arbitrament of war is not easy to see, unless he happens to be greatly superior, in which case the competition should not bother him. If the competition is downgraded to being only a potent contributing cause, then we should focus on what comes first and consider how much the arms competition really contributes. It may in fact derive from the prime cause, which we must assume to be political, in which case it is simply part of the working out of the animosity, that is, it is more an effect than a cause.

The arms competition we have been witnessing in the Middle East is clearly of the latter kind. We see both sides frantically attempting between wars to rearm themselves against another outbreak that both sides believe highly likely if not inevitable. In such situations, however, the major provocations to violence clearly lie outside the arms competition itself and almost totally account for that competition. Conditions of the moment which the aggressor finds favorable to himself *may* help to trigger a war, but that does not alter the basic quality we see in the competition, which is that it is entirely derivative from the hostility and not the other way round.

What may be called the "classical" arms race, on the other hand, follows a model where the rivals measure their arms progress against each other, out of considerations of status and of ultimate security against *conceivable* warlike situations, but where the focus is more on competition itself than on any high or imminent expectation of war. The latter situation fairly describes the competition between the United States and the Soviet Union during at least the last decade—which is in some contrast to the situation of the 1950s when the expectation of war was considerably higher.[13]

Arms races of this latter type are fairly recent phenomena. In older times the size of the military forces of the prince depended on his wealth, pride, and territorial ambitions, but a number of factors were missing then that seem to be essential in the modern type of competition. Among them are rapid technological progress and also a level of productivity of the national economy which makes for a good deal of "fat"—as contrasted with the subsistence-level economy that characterized most nations before the 19th century. There are in modern times vast resources free for competitive military buildups that were not comparably free at an earlier time.

Probably the most celebrated arms race in history is the Anglo-German naval race that began with the German naval laws of 1898 and 1900. It stands out as the stereotype of the modern arms race, and it was indeed hard and furious. It has for that reason often been charged with being a primary cause of Britain's entry into World War I. There is much instruction in studying that race, particularly in seeing how the Germans rationalized a vain and improvident policy and how badly they misjudged the British. There can be no doubt that

---

[13] We should note here Albert Wohlstetter's denial that there is an arms race between the two superpowers, though he concedes there is an arms competition which raises costs on both sides. I have assumed above that the two terms were sufficiently imprecise to be virtually interchangeable. See Wohlstetter's "Is There a Strategic Arms Race?," *Foreign Policy*, No. 15 (Summer, 1974), pp. 3–20 and No. 16 (Fall, 1974), pp. 48–81. See also Michael L. Nacht's critique of Wohlstetter's view in the same journal, No. 19 (Summer, 1975), pp. 163–177, and Wohlstetter's reply to Nacht and others in No. 20 (Fall, 1975), pp. 170–198.

it caused much irritation and even some alarm in Britain. But we know now a good deal about the motivations of Britain's pre-war diplomacy and also about that week of groping in the Cabinet that finally brought Britain's declaration of war in August 1914. The evidence is overwhelming that the German naval competition was of far less than prime significance in provoking the British decision. It had had virtually nothing to do with Britain's departing "splendid isolation" to conclude its alliance with Japan in 1902 and its *entente* with France in 1904. In subsequent events, including the *entente* with Russia in 1907, it had loomed somewhat larger, but it was still only part of the whole image of Germany that the several pre-war crises and the posturing of a vainglorious kaiser helped to produce. Finally there was the clear and blatant violation of the Belgium Neutralization Treaty of 1839.[14]

No doubt the British tolerance for the German competition derived from their confidence that they could maintain the naval fighting superiority that was so important to them. To outbuild the Germans was costly but feasible, and far less costly than fighting them. That fact, too, points to something instructive about that race and especially to how it differed from any kind of armaments race that could possibly exist today between the United States and the Soviet Union.

The unit of account for fleet fighting power at the time of that race was the battleship—after 1906 the Dreadnought-type battleship—designed and built primarily for fighting its like on the high seas. Once built it might also be used for other purposes, like shore bombardment, but it was never put in hazard for such purposes if there was a chance that it might be needed for contending with enemy battleships. Because the British succeeded in building more battleships than the Germans and because they also built ships with bigger guns, they maintained a battle superiority which both sides knew to be overwhelming. When it came to the contest of battle fleets in World War I, the British Grand Fleet simply contained the German High Seas Fleet for four years of war and made the latter quite useless. It did so while being mostly silent and at anchor. On the one occasion that the two fleets met, off Jutland, the entire preoccupation of the German commander was with escape.

Thus, with surface fleets even more than with armies, the fact that the military units of each side fought comparable military units of the

---

[14] On official British attitudes towards Germany, a number of fascinating once-secret memoranda are reprinted in Kenneth Bourne's *The Foreign Policy of Victorian England,* 1830-1902 (London: Oxford University Press, 1970). Despite the terminal date in the book's title, the memoranda which are especially interesting cover the period from 1901 to 1914 (pp. 462-504). See especially the long extract from the major policy memorandum of 1 January 1907 by Eyre Crowe, who bore the misleading title of Senior Clerk in the Foreign Office, pp. 481-493.

other gave real meaning to a margin of superiority. Such meaning is lost in the present armaments rivalry with the Soviet Union, in which it is basic that we are dealing with weaponry where the units are *not* primarily intended to fight each other. Certainly that is characteristic of the whole family of nuclear weapons which, despite frequent allegations to the contrary, are the weapons most effective in keeping the two nations firmly on course—that is, on the course of avoiding war with each other. Also, there is between the superpowers nothing comparable now to the peculiar and one-sided vulnerability of Britain to the interruption of her sea-borne communications, a vulnerability which absolutely obliged her to insist on clear superiority on the seas.

That nuclear weapons are not intended primarily to fight each other may be denied by proponents of counterforce targeting. Until the conclusion of the SALT I agreements, some were excited also by the qualified capability of ABMs to destroy incoming nuclear warheads high above the ground—a possibility that seemed to promise to make warfare once more a duel, to be fought this time in space. However, few students of the problem can deny that success for a counterforce strategy must depend on some quite unpredictable variables and, especially because of the several alternative means of retaliatory attack, *is bound always to be critically limited.*

In the present situation there is even less reason than before to worry about the alleged provocatory nature of arms races. We may even allow ourselves some astonishment at how little such provocations seem to matter, either in diplomacy or in everyday life. Both superpowers have weapons aimed at each other that could spell for each something approaching obliteration. Neither side has anything remotely resembling a defense except its power of retaliation. It is a circumstance that, at the dawn of the nuclear age, people predicted would be quite intolerable. But the feared condition arrived gradually, and as people came to live with it, proved not only tolerable but also not without its own peculiar comforts. There developed a sense that no issue existed to induce the superpowers to go to war with each other when such a penalty for doing so hung over them mutually—a condition quite new in the world's history.

There are now, as there always have been, the habitual sounders of alarm about losing some margin of superiority, either in ships at sea, in throw-weight of missiles, or whatnot. But despite the jingoism on the far right evoked by the 1976 primaries, the national audience seems to be lacking something in responsiveness. When before has a secretary of state, who incidentally enjoyed a considerable and unusual reputation for understanding strategic issues, replied to some fulminations from the Defense Department, as Kissinger did in 1974, with the exclamation: "What in the name of God is strategic superiority? What is the significance of it politically, militarily, operationally, at this level of numbers?"

For our purposes we are not obliged to determine whether Kissinger is right or wrong in the sentiment reflected in his exclamation. What it does tell us incontrovertibly is that whatever arms race is going on currently, and however costly it may be, it is not in itself adding very much to the irritations and provocations that arise from time to time between the two major rivals. An arms race may indeed cause them to treat each other with more respect than they otherwise would, but that too has its net utilities.

We have learned over the three decades that nuclear weapons have been with us that the balance of terror is *not* delicate. For either superpower to attack the other because of an optimistic guess of the latter's vulnerabilities is obviously to take a risk of cataclysmic proportions. Neither can be seduced into such an error by some apparent shift in the relationship of forces—usually more apparent to technicians than to politicians. Nor will either superpower be seduced by the appearance of some new mechanical contrivance which at best affects only a part of the whole scheme of things, usually a small part.

The terms "destabilizing" and "stabilizing" have become fashionable in referring to various technological developments. Their use commonly reflects a limited perception of how each development alters or fits into the entire technological *and* political universe in which we live. No doubt a prolonged somnolescence by the United States concerning qualitative and quantitative changes in the arms balance would in time prove dangerous, especially if it were not accompanied by a drastic downward reassessment of our foreign policy interests. But the fate of ourselves and of the world is not going to hang on what we do or fail to do about some object like the cruise missile. Not long ago the alleged fate-determining object was the ABM. It sometimes helps to remember the several invasion panics in England in the mid-19th century, when the adoption of steam propulsion by warships was supposed to have created "a steam bridge across the Channel."

BUDGETING FOR DEFENSE

If arms competitions are not in themselves dangerous, which is to say significantly provocative of an inclination to war, they are certainly costly. An international agreement which succeeds in limiting that competition is an important and welcome way of limiting those costs. Naturally one does not wish to save money at the cost of a significant impairment of security, but the role for intelligent arms control is precisely to find and exploit instances where there is no such conflict.

There are some, to be sure, who argue that the arms race, if there is one, is not too costly. Many, including President Ford, have pointed to our current defense budget as being "only" 6 percent of our GNP, which they call an historically low proportion that should be considered a floor on our military expenditures. Some, like former Secretary of Defense Schlesinger, make statements arguing a positive value for their own sake in high military expenditures, claiming that any attempt to reduce them sends the "wrong signals" to the Soviet leaders. Reasoning from the 6 percent figure Schlesinger was looking forward with no apparent pain to annual defense budgets of $150 billion by 1980.

One might point out that 6 percent of GNP is historically a low peacetime figure for the United States only since the Korean War. One could suggest also that national and indeed worldwide trends make governments more responsible for social welfare than formerly, and these trends, which appear politically irreversible at least for the United States, make 6 percent of GNP for military expenditures considerably more burden than it used to be. This percentage currently represents approximately $100 billion. We are also becoming increasingly aware that percentage of GNP is a much less meaningful figure than percentage of the national budget, for the latter represents monies being raised by taxation and by deficit financing, and we are becoming acutely aware of the limits, disutilities, and special pains associated with both. The defense budget is still by far the largest single category in the national budget, and it accounts for roughly 35 percent of it.

But is all this relevant? The notion that it pays to spend extra billions just to send the "right" signals abroad ought to be rejected as most unlikely to be "cost-effective" compared with other means of signaling. What are the "right signals" supposed to be anyway? What signals are in fact sent by simply boosting military expenditures? If these and related questions are not in the narrow sense researchable, they are certainly worth more thought than they usually get by those who urge the Schlesinger view. That view, while not necessarily in conflict with efficient military expenditure, is not likely to be conducive to it either.

The merit of explicit, mutual agreements on arms control is that both sides are committed to the same course of action, usually for the same or at least similar reasons. That makes the signals mutual. Just as cost-effectiveness analysis was devised and pursued for the sake of avoiding sheer waste in military expenditures (it is usually expressed in other ways, but they amount to the same thing), so arms control should be conceived as an important and fruitful means of avoiding waste. For that we should not have to make apologies.

Two examples should suffice to illustrate the practical application of our argument. The first is the Washington Naval Limitation Treaty of 1922, later supplemented by the London Naval Treaty of 1930. These treaties are among the very few in history—if there are indeed others of comparable weight—in which the several great powers succeeded by free mutual agreement not only in limiting future building in a primary military category but actually in reducing significantly levels already reached. The motivation on all sides was entirely economic, though naturally in the speeches applauding the signing ceremonies the benign consequences for world peace were duly rung in.[15]

The other, more recent example was the effective demolition of the ABM programs of the United States and the Soviet Union as a result of the SALT 1 agreements of 1972. To anyone who had followed the ABM debate in the United States, this result was astonishing. Few historical debates on armaments had aroused the passions that this one did, with experts in the related technologies arrayed on both sides. The substance of the debate was mostly over the efficacy of the Sentinel system, a name changed to "Safeguard" by President Nixon, who showed himself to be one of its most ardent champions. In pushing the necessary supporting acts through a once-reluctant Senate, Nixon did indeed use the "bargaining chip" argument along with several others, but his obvious ardor for the system itself made it difficult to give credence to this explanation.

The fact that it ultimately did prove to be a bargining chip does not quite dispel one's doubts as to whether it was so conceived all along. It appears likely that President Nixon underwent a real change of heart about ABM, the rapidly growing problem with inflation no doubt having much to do with his change. Inflation clearly made him look harder at the data that brought into question the efficacy and utility of the system, including new developments like MIRVs, the cruise missile, and alternatives to fixed silos for ICBMs, especially land-mobile systems.

In any case, the motivation and justification for doing away mutually with the ABM (actually, in the first instance, limiting it) were almost entirely economic. It cannot plausibly be argued that it enhanced our security to accomplish this result; neither does it make much sense to say that it diminished it.[16] The ABM lent itself ideally to the action taken for the following basic reasons: (1) it was not yet acquired and deployed; (2) its efficacy was always questionable and becoming more so; (3) it would be an extraordinarily expensive system to build,

[15] The standard monograph on the first and most important of these treaties, that of Washington in 1922, is still Harold and Margaret Sprout, *Toward a New Order of Sea Power* (Princeton: Princeton University Press, 2nd ed., 1943.)

[16] One of the few hold-outs on the latter view is Dr. Donald G. Brennan, in his "When the SALT Hit the Fan," *National Review,* vol. 24, (June 23, 1972) pp. 685–692. See also his testimony in the ratification hearings of the SALT 1 agreements. It is important to notice that Dr. Brennan never thought that the ABM would be effective in protecting cities unless offensive forces were suitably limited. In his current view, the massive buildup of offensive forces since the late 1960s has diminished the feasibility (though not the desirability) of such a posture, at least based on current technology, to near the vanishing point.

deploy, and maintain; and (4) it would be difficult domestically to win a consensus on dropping it except through an instrument that obliged the Soviet Union to do likewise.

The original SALT agreement limited each side to two sites, one being the capital or "national command authority," the other being a single field site containing no more than 100 interceptor missiles of all types (in the United States the Spartan and the Sprint missiles). It quickly became obvious that the Congress would never support a system for the single city of Washington. An amendment in 1974 to the SALT agreement limited each side to one site only. The United States by then had built such a site, at Grand Forks, North Dakota, but in 1975 the Congress, facing the choice of appropriating $60 million to continuing it for another year or $40 million for liquidating it, chose the latter course. It is difficult to tell what the total expenditure had been at that time—it had cost about $4 billion to develop just the Spartan missile with its special nuclear warhead, of which some 30 were built—but there is no doubt that many times that sum was saved by abandoning it.

It retrospect the ABM may look like a system that virtually cried out for mutual abrogation, but it certainly did not look so at the time. The support for it within the defense community was intense. Now the ABM appears to have been a target of opportunity, torpedoed at just the right time and by the right means.

It should be the prime function of an intelligently directed arms control program always to be looking out for more such targets. They will be found especially among emerging systems, but also among those existing ones which are costly to maintain and of dubious marginal utility. One might, for example, nominate for consideration our aircraft bombing force, including both the proposed B-1 and the existing 400 B-52s. What is the marginal utility of this force *along with* our submarine-launched and our land-based missiles? If some bombers are desirable, do we need all those proposed? It would indeed take some stout-hearted men to explore this issue together with, or perhaps in the face of, the Air Force, but such a course is not unprecedented. The naval treaties of 1922 and 1930 were bitterly opposed by the chief naval officers and the navy leagues of virtually all the countries involved, which makes their achievement all the more remarkable. Perhaps the required stout-heartedness *is* what arms control is all about.

Arms Races:
Prerequisites and Results

SAMUEL P. HUNTINGTON

INTRODUCTION

Si vis pacem, para bellum, is an ancient and authoritative adage of
military policy. Of no less acceptance, however, is the other, more
modern, proposition: "Armaments races inevitably lead to war."
Juxtaposed, these two advices suggest that the maxims of social
science, like the proverbs of folklore, reflect a many-sided truth. The
social scientist, however, cannot escape with so easy an observation.
He has the scholar's responsibility to determine as fully as possible to
what extent and under what conditions his conflicting truths are true.
The principal aim of this essay is to attempt some resolution of the
issue: When are arms races a prelude to war and when are they a
substitute for war?

Throughout history states have sought to maintain their peace and
security by means of military strength. The arms race in which the
military preparations of two states are intimately and directly interrelated is, however, a relatively modern phenomenon. The conflict
between the apparent feasibility of preserving peace by arming for war
and the apparent inevitability of competitive arms increases resulting
in war is, therefore, a comparatively new one. The second purpose of
this essay is to explore some of the circumstances which have brought
about this uncertainty as to the relationship between war, peace and
arms increases. The problem here is: What were the prerequisites to
the emergence of the arms race as a significant form of international
rivalry in the nineteenth and twentieth centuries?

For the purposes of this essay, an arms race is defined as a progressive, competitive peacetime increase in armaments by two states or
coalition of states resulting from conflicting purposes or mutual fears.
An arms race is thus a form of reciprocal interaction between two
states or coalitions. A race cannot exist without an increase in arms,
quantitatively or qualitatively, but every peacetime increase in arms is
not necessarily the result of an arms race. A nation may expand its
armmaments for the domestic purposes of aiding industry or curbing

From *Public Policy,* 1958, pp. 41–83. Copyright © 1958 by John Wiley & Sons, Inc.
Reprinted with permission of John Wiley & Sons, Inc.

unemployment, or because it believes an absolute need exists for such an increase regardless of the actions of other states. In the 1880s and 1890s, for instance, the expansion of the United States Navy was apparently unrelated to the actions of any other power, and hence not part of an arms race. An arms race reflects disagreement between two states as to the proper balance of power between them. The concept of a "general" arms race in which a number of powers increase their armaments simultaneously is, consequently, a fallacious one. Such general increases either are not the result of self-conscious reciprocal interaction or are simply the sum of a number of two-state antagonisms. In so far as the arms policy of any one state is related to the armaments of other states, it is a function of concrete, specific goals, needs, or threats arising out of the political relations among the states. Even Britain's vaunted two-power naval standard will be found, on close analysis, to be rooted in specific threats rather than in abstract considerations of general policy.

PREREQUISITES FOR AN ARMS RACE

. . . Certain conditions peculiarly present in the nineteenth and twentieth centuries would appear to be responsible for the emergence of the arms race as a frequent and distinct form of international rivalry. Among the more significant of these conditions are: a state system which facilitates the balancing of power by internal rather than external means; the preeminence of military force-in-being over territory or other factors as an element of national power; the capacity within each state to increase its military strength through quantitative or qualitative means; and the conscious awareness by each state of the dependence of its own arms policy upon that of another state.[1]

---

[1] Since an arms race is necessarily a matter of degree, differences of opinion will exist as to whether any given relationship constitutes an arms race and as to what are the precise opening and closing dates of any given arms race. At the risk of seeming arbitrary, the following relationships are assumed to be arms races for the purposes of this essay:

1. France v. England	naval	1840–1866
2. France v. Germany	land	1874–1894
3. England v. France & Russia	naval	1884–1904
4. Argentina v. Chile	naval	1890–1902
5. England v. Germany	naval	1898–1912
6. France v. Germany	land	1911–1914
7. England v. United States	naval	1916–1930
8. Japan v. United States	naval	1916–1922
9. France v. Germany	land	1934–1939
10. Soviet Union v. Germany	land	1934–1941
11. Germany v. England	air	1934–1939
12. United States v. Japan	naval	1934–1941
13. Soviet Union v. United States	nuclear	1946–

Balancing power: external and internal means. Arms races are an integral part of the international balance of power. From the viewpoint of a participant, an arms race is an effort to achieve a favorable international distribution of power. Viewed as a whole, a sustained arms race is a means of achieving a dynamic equilibrium of power between two states or coalitions of states. Arms races only take place between states in the same balance of power system. The more isolated a nation is from any balance of power system the less likely it is to become involved in an arms race. Within any such system, power may in general be balanced in two ways: externally through a realignment of the units participating in the system (diplomacy), or internally by changes in the inherent power of the units. The extent to which the balancing process operates through external or internal means usually depends upon the number of states participating in the system, the opportunity for new states to join the system, and the relative distribution of power among the participating states.

The relations among the states in a balance of power system may tend toward any one of three patterns, each of which assigns somewhat different roles to the external and internal means of balancing power. A situation of *bellum omnium contra omnes* exists when there are a large number of states approximately equal in power and when there is an approximately equal distribution of grievances and antagonisms among the states. In such a system, which was perhaps most closely approximated by the city-states of the Italian Renaissance, primary reliance is placed upon wily diplomacy, treachery and surprise attack. Since no bilateral antagonisms continue for any length of time, a sustained arms race is very unlikely. A second balance of power pattern involves an all-against-one relationship: the coalition of a number of weaker states against a single *grande nation*. The fears and grievances of the weaker states are concentrated against the stronger, and here again primary reliance is placed upon diplomatic means of maintaining or restoring the balance. European politics assumed this pattern in the successive coalitions to restrain the Hapsburgs, Louis XIV, Frederick II, Napoleon and Hitler. At times, efforts may be made to bring in other states normally outside the system to aid in restoring the balance.

A third pattern of balance of power politics involves bilateral antagonisms between states or coalitions of states roughly equal in strength. Such bilateral antagonisms have been a continuing phenomenon in the western balance of power system: France vs. England, Austria vs. France and then Prussia (Germany) vs. France, Austria-Hungary vs. Russia, the Triple Alliance vs. the Triple Entente, and now, the United States vs. the Soviet Union. In these relationships the principal grievances and antagonisms of any two states become concentrated upon each other, and as a result, this antagonism becomes the primary focus of their respective foreign policies. In this situation, diplomacy and alliances may play a significant role if a "balancer" exists who can shift his weight to whichever side appears to be weaker. But no balancing state can exist if all the major powers are involved in bilateral antagonisms or if a single overriding antagonism forces virtually all the states in the system to choose one side or the other (bipolarization). In these circumstances, the balancing of power by rearranging the units of power becomes difficult. Diplomatic maneuvering gives way to the massing of military force. Each state relies more on armaments and less on alliances. Other factors being equal, the pressures toward an arms race are greatest when international relations assume this form.

In the past century the relative importance of the internal means of balancing power has tended to increase. A single worldwide balance of power system has tended to develop, thereby eliminating the possibility of bringing in outside powers to restore the balance. At the same time, however, the number of great powers has fairly constantly decreased, and bilateral antagonisms have consequently become of greater importance. Small powers have tended to seek security either through neutrality (Switzerland, Sweden) or through reliance upon broadly organized efforts at collective security. The growth of the latter idea has tended to make military alliances aimed at a specific common foe less reputable and justifiable. . . . Alliances were perhaps the primary means of balancing power in Europe before 1870. Between 1870 and 1914, both alliances and armaments played important roles. Since 1918 the relative importance of armaments has probably increased. The primary purpose of the military pacts of the post-World War II period, with the possible exception of NATO, generally has been the extension of the protection of a great power to a series of minor powers, rather than the uniting of a number of more or less equal powers in pursuit of a common objective. In addition, the development of democractic control over foreign policy has made alliances more difficult. Alignments dictated by balance of power considerations may be impossible to carry out due to public opinion. Rapid shifts in alliances from friends to enemies also are difficult to execute in a democratic society. Perhaps, too, a decline in the arts of diplomacy has contributed to the desire to rest one's security upon resources which are "owned" rather than "pledged."

Elements of power: money, territory, armaments. Arms races only take place when military forces-in-being are of direct and prime importance to the power of a state. During the age of mercantilism, for instance, monetary resources were highly valued as an index of power, and, consequently, governmental policy was directed toward the accumulation of economic wealth which could then be transformed into military and political power. These actions, which might take a variety of forms, were in some respects the seventeenth century equivalents of the nineteenth and twentieth century arms races. In the eighteenth century, territory was of key importance as a measure of power. The size of the armies which a state could maintain was roughly proportional to its population, and, in an agrarian age, its population was roughly proportional to its territory. Consequently, an increase in military power required an increase in territory. Within Europe, territory could be acquired either by conquest, in which case a surprise attack was probably desirable in order to forestall intervention by other states, or by agreement among the great powers to partition a smaller power. Outside of Europe, colonial territories might contribute wealth if not manpower to the mother country, and these could be acquired either by discovery and settlement or by conquest. Consequently, territorial compensations were a primary means of balancing power, and through the acquisition of colonies, states jealous of their relative power could strive to improve their position without directly challenging another major state and thereby provoking a war.

During the nineteenth century territory bacame less important as an index of power, and industry and armaments more important. By the end of the century all the available colonial lands had been occupied by the major powers. In addition, the rise of nationalism and of self-determination made it increasingly difficult to settle differences by the division and bartering of provinces, small powers and colonies. By expanding its armaments, however, a state could still increase its relative power without decreasing the absolute power of another state. Reciprocal increases in armaments made possible an unstable and dynamic, but none the less real equilibrium among the major powers. The race for armaments tended to replace the race for colonies as the "escape hatch" through which major states could enhance their power without directly challenging each other.

The increased importance of armaments as a measure of national power was reflected in the new emphasis upon disarmament in the efforts to resolve antagonisms among nations. The early peace writers, prior to the eighteenth century, placed primary stress upon a federation of European states rather than upon disarmament measures. It was not until Kant's essay on "Eternal Peace" that the dangers inherent in an arms race were emphasized, and the reduction of armaments made a primary goal. In 1766 Austria made the first proposal for a bilateral reduction in forces to Frederick the Great, who rejected it. In 1787 France and England agreed not to increase their naval establishments. In 1816 the Czar made the first proposal for a general reduction in armaments. Thenceforth, throughout the nineteenth century problems of armament and disarmament played an increasingly significant role in diplomatic negotiations.[2]

[2] Merze Tate, *The Disarmament Illusion* (New York, 1942), p. 7.

Capacity for qualitative and quantitative increases in military power. An arms race requires the progressive increase from domestic sources of the absolute military power of a state. This may be done quantitatively, by expanding the numerical strength of its existing forms of military force, or qualitatively, by replacing its existing forms of military force (usually weapons systems) with new and more effective forms of force. The latter requires a dynamic technology, and the former the social, political and economic capacity to reallocate resources from civilian to military purposes. Before the nineteenth century the European states possessed only a limited capacity for either quantitative or qualitative increases in military strength. Naval technology, for instance, had been virtually static for almost three centuries: the sailing ship of 1850 was not fundamentally different from that of 1650, the naval gun of 1860 not very much removed from that of 1560.[3] As a result, the ratio of construction time to use time was extremely low: a ship built in a few months could be used for the better part of a century. Similarly, with land armaments, progress was slow, and only rarely could a power hope to achieve a decisive edge by a "technological breakthrough". Beginning with the Industrial Revolution, however, the pace of innovation in military technology constantly quickened, and the new weapons systems inevitably stimulated arms races. The introduction, first, of the steam warship and then of the ironclad, for instance, directly intensified the naval competition between England and France in the 1850s and 1860s. Throughout the nineteenth century, the importance of the weapons technician constantly increased relative to the importance of the strategist.

Broad changes in economic and political structure were at the same time making quantitative arms races feasible. The social system of the *ancien régime* did not permit a full mobilization of the economic and manpower resources of a nation. So long as participation in war was limited to a small class, competitive increases in the size of armies could not proceed very far. The destruction of the old system, the spread of democracy and liberalism, the increasing popularity among all groups of the "nation in arms" concept, all permitted a much more complete mobilization of resources for military purposes than had been possible previously. In particular, the introduction of universal military service raised the ceiling on the size of the army to the point where the limiting factor was the civilian manpower necessary to support the army. In addition, the development of industry permitted the mass production and mass accumulation of the new weapons which the new technology had invented. The countries which lagged behind

---

[3] Bernard Brodie, *Sea Power in the Machine Age* (Princeton, 2nd ed., 1944), p. 181; Arthur J. Marder, *The Anatomy of British Sea Power* (New York, 1940), pp. 3-4.

in the twin processes of democratization and industrialization were severely handicapped in the race for armaments.

In the age of limited wars little difference existed between a nation's military strength in peace and its military strength in war. During the nineteenth century, however, the impact of democracy and industrialism made wars more total, victory or defeat in them became more significant (and final), military superiority became more critically important, and consequently a government had to be more fully assured of the prospect of victory before embarking upon war. In addition, the professional officer corps which developed during the nineteenth century felt a direct responsibility for the military security of the state and emphasized the desirability of obtaining a safe superiority in armaments As a result, unless one of the participants possessed extensive staying power due to geography or resources, the outcome of a war depended almost as much upon what happened before the declarations of war as after. By achieving superiority in armaments it might be possible for a state to achieve the fruits of war without suffering the risks and liabilities of war. Governments piled up armaments in peacetime with the hope either of averting war or of insuring success in it should it come.

Absolute and relative armaments goals. A state may define its armaments goals in one of two ways. It can specify a certain *absolute* level or type of armaments which it believes necessary for it to possess irrespective of the level or type possessed by other states. Or, it can define its goal in *relative* terms as a function of the armaments of other states. Undoubtedly, in any specific case, a state's armaments reflect a combination of both absolute and relative considerations. Normally, however, one or the other will be dominant and embodied in offical statements of the state's armaments goals in the form of an "absolute need" or a ratio-goal. Thus, historically Great Britain followed a relative policy with respect to the capital ships in its navy but an absolute policy with respect to its cruisers, the need for which, it was held, stemmed from the unique nature of the British Empire.

If every state had absolute goals, arms races would be impossible: each state would go its separate way uninfluenced by the actions of its neighbors. Nor would a full scale arms race develop if an absolute goal were pursued consistently by only one power in an antagonistic realtionship: whatever relative advantage the second power demanded would be simply a function of the constant absolute figure demanded by the first power. An arms race only arises when two or more powers consciously determine the quantitative or qualitative aspects of their armaments as functions of the armaments of the other power. Absolute goals, however, are only really feasible when a state is not a member of or only on the periphery of a balance of power system. Except in these rare cases, the formulation by a state of its armaments goal in absolute terms is more likely to reflect the desire to obscure from its rivals the true relative superiority which it wishes to achieve or to obscure from itself the need to participate actively in the balancing process. Thus, its Army Law of 1893 was thought to give Germany a force which in quantity and quality would be unsurpassable by any other power. Hence Germany

> was, in the eyes of her rulers, too powerful to be affected by a balancing movement restricted only to the continent. . . . From this time on Germany considered herself militarily invulnerable, as if in a state of splendid isolation, owing to the excellence of her amalgam army.[4]

As a result, Germany let her army rest, turned her energies to the construction of a navy, and then suddenly in 1911 became aware of her landpower inferiority to the Dual Alliance and had to make strenuous last minute efforts to increase the size of her forces. Somewhat similarly, states may define absolute qualitative goals, such as the erection of an impenetrable system of defenses (Maginot Line) or the possession of an "ultimate" or "absolute" weapon, which will render superfluous further military effort regardless of what other states may do. In 1956 American airpower policy was consciously shaped not to the achievement of any particular level of air strength relative to that of the Soviet Union, but rather to obtaining an absolute "sufficiency of airpower" which would permit the United States to wreak havoc in the Soviet Union in the event of an all-out war.[5] The danger involved in an absolute policy is that, if carried to an extreme, it may lead to a complacent isolationism blind to the relative nature of power.

The armaments of two states can be functionally interrelated only if they are also similar or complementary. An arms race is impossible between a power which possesses only a navy and one which possesses only an army: no one can match divisions against battleships. A functional realtionship between armaments is complementary when two

---

[4] Arpad Kovacs, "Nation in Arms and Balance of Power: The Interaction of German Military Legislation and European Politics, 1866–1914" (Ph.D. Thesis, University of Chicago, 1934), p. 159.

[5] For the most complete statement of the sufficiency theory, see Donald A. Quarles, Secretary of the Air Force, "How Much is 'Enough'?" *Air Force,* XLIX (September, 1956), pp. 51–52: ". . . there comes a time in the course of increasing our airpower when we must make a determination of sufficiency. . . .

"Sufficiency of airpower, to my mind, must be determined period by period on the basis of the force required to accomplish the mission assigned. . . . Neither side can hope by a mere margin of superiority in airplanes or other means of delivery of atomic weapons to escape the catastrophe of such a [total] war. Beyond a certain point, this prospect is not the result of *relative* strength of the two opposed forces. It is the *absolute* power in the hands of each, and in the substantial invulnerability of this power to interdiction."

See also H. Rept. 2104, 84th Cong., 2d Sess., p. 40 (1956).

military forces possessing different weapons systems are designed for combat with each other. In this sense, an air defense fighter command complements an opposing strategic bombing force or one side's submarine force complements the other's antisubmarine destroyers and hunter-killer groups. A functional relationship is similar when two military forces are not only designed for combat with each other but also possess similar weapons systems, as has been very largely the case with land armies and with battle fleets of capital ships. In most instances in history, arms races have involved similar forces rather than complementary forces, but no reason exists why there should not be an arms race in the latter. The only special problem posed by a complementary arms race is that of measuring the relative strengths of the opposing forces. In a race involving similar forces, a purely quantitative measurement usually suffices; in one of complementary forces, qualitative judgments are necessary as to the effectiveness of one type of weapons system against another.

Even if both parties to an arms race possess similar land, sea and air forces, normally the race itself is focused on only one of these components or even on only one weapons system within one component, usually that type of military force with which they are best able to harm each other.[6] This component or weapons system is viewed by the states as the decisive form of military force in their mutual relationship, and competition in other forces or components is subordinated to the race in this decisive force. The simple principles of concentration and economy of force require states to put their major efforts where they will count most. The arms race between Germany and England before World War I was in capital ships. The arms race between the same two countries before World War II was in bombers and fighters. The current race between the Soviet Union and the United States has largely focused upon nuclear weapons and their means of delivery, and has not extended to the massing of conventional weapons and manpower. In general, economic considerations also preclude a state from becoming involved at the same time in two separate arms races with two different powers in two different forms of military force. When her race in land forces with France slackened in the middle 1890s, Germany embarked upon her naval race with Great Britain, and for the first decade of the twentieth century the requirements of this enterprise prevented any substantial increase in the size of the army. When the naval race in turn slackened in 1912, Germany returned to the rebuilding of her ground forces and to her military manpower race with France.

---

[6] Other things being equal, this will probably be the "dominant weapon" in Fuller's sense, that is, the weapon with the longest effective range. See J. F. C. Fuller, *Armament and History* (New York, 1945), pp. 7–8.

Two governments can consciously follow relative arms policies only if they are well informed of their respective military capabilities. The general availability of information concerning armaments is thus a precondition for an arms race. Prior to the nineteenth century when communication and transportation were slow and haphazard, a state would frequently have only the vaguest notions of the military programs of its potential rivals. Often it was possible for one state to make extensive secret preparations for war. In the modern world, information with respect to military capabilities has become much more widespread and has been one of the factors increasing the likelihood of arms races. Even now, however, many difficulties exist in getting information concerning the arms of a rival which is sufficiently accurate to serve as the basis for one's own policy. At times misconceptions as to the military strengths and policies of other states become deeply ingrained, and at other times governments simply choose to be blind to significant changes in armaments. Any modern government involved in an arms race, moreover, is confronted with conflicting estimates of its opponent's strength. Politicians, governmental agencies and private groups all tend to give primary credit to intelligence estimates which confirm military policies which they have already espoused for other reasons. The armed services inevitably overstate the military capabilities of the opponent: in 1914, for instance, the Germans estimated the French army to have 121,000 more men than the German army, the French estimated the German army to have 134,000 more men than the French army, but both countries agreed in their estimates of the military forces of third powers.[7] Governments anxious to reduce expenditures and taxes pooh-pooh warnings as to enemy strength: the reluctance of the Baldwin government to credit reports of the German air build-up seriously delayed British rearmament in the 1930s. At other times, exaggerated reports as to enemy forces may lead a government to take extraordinary measures which are subsequently revealed to have been unnecessary. Suspicions that the Germans were exceeding their announced program of naval construction led the English government in 1909 to authorize and construct four "contingency" Dreadnoughts. Subsequently revelations proved British fears to be groundless. Similarly, in 1956 reports of Soviet aircraft production, later asserted to be considerably exaggerated, influenced Congress to appropriate an extra $900 million for the Air Force. At times, the sudden revelation of a considerable increase in an enemy's capabilities may produce a panic, such as the invasion panics of England in 1847–48, 1951–53, and 1959–61. The tense atmosphere of an arms race also tends to encourage reports of

[7] Bernadotte E. Schmitt, *The Coming of the War: 1914* (New York, 2 vols., 1930), I, 54n.

mysterious forces possessed by the opponent and of his development of secret new weapons of unprecedented power. Nonetheless, fragmentary and uncertain though information may be, its availability in one form or another is what makes the arms race possible.

ABORTIVE AND SUSTAINED ARMS RACES

An arms race may end in war, formal or informal agreement between the two states to call off the race, or victory for one state which achieves and maintains the distribution of power which it desires and ultimately causes its rival to give up the struggle. The likelihood of war arising from an arms race depends in the first instance upon the relation between the power and grievances of one state to the power and grievances of the other. War is least likely when grievances are low, or, if grievances are high, the sum of the grievances and power of one state approximates the sum of the grievances and power of the other. An equality of power and an equality of grievances will thus reduce the chances of war, as will a situation in which one state has a marked superiority in power and the other in grievances. Assuming a fairly equal distribution of grievances, the likelihood of an arms race ending in war tends to vary inversely with the length of the arms race and directly with the extent to which it is quantitative rather than qualitative in character. This section deals with the first of these relationships and the next section with the second.

An arms race is a series of interrelated increases in armaments which if continued over a period of time produces a dynamic equilibrium of power between two states. A race in which this dynamic equilibrium fails to develop may be termed an abortive arms race. In these instances, the previously existing static equilibrium between the two states is disrupted without being replaced by a new equilibrium reflecting their relative competitive efforts in the race. Instead, rapid shifts take place or appear about to take place in the distribution of power which enhance the willingness of one state or the other to precipitate a conflict. At least one and sometimes two danger points occur at the beginning of every arms race. The first point arises with the response of the challenged state to the initial increases in armaments by the challenging state. The second danger point is the reaction of the challenger who has been successful in initially achieving his goal to the frantic belated efforts of the challenged state to retrieve its former position.

The formal beginning of an arms race is the first increase in armaments by one state—the challenger—caused by a desire to alter the existing balance of power between it and another state. Prior to this initial action, a pre-arms race static equilibrium may be said to exist. This equilibrium does not necessarily mean an equality of power. It simply reflects the satisfaction of each state with the existing distribution of power in the light of its grievances and antagonisms with the other state. Some of the most stable equilibriums in history have also been ones which embodied an unbalance of power. From the middle of the eighteenth century down to the 1840s, a static equilibrium existed between the French and British navies in which the former was kept roughly two-thirds as strong as the latter. After the naval race of 1841–1865 when this ratio was challenged, the two powers returned to it for another twenty year period. From 1865 to 1884 both British and French naval expenditures were amazingly constant, England's expenditures varying between 9.5 and 10.5 million pounds (with the exception of the crisis years of 1876–77 when they reached 11 and 12 million pounds) and France's expenditures varying from 6.5 to 7.5 million pounds.[8] In some instances the equilibrium may receive the formal sanction of a treaty such as the Washington arms agreement of 1922 or the treaty of Versailles. In each of these cases, the equilibrium lasted until 1934 when the two powers—Germany and Japan—who had been relegated to a lower level of armaments decided that continued inferiority was incompatible with their national goals and ambitions. In both cases, however, it was not the disparity of power in itself which caused the destruction of the equilibrium, but rather the fact that this disparity was unacceptable to the particular groups which assumed control of those countries in the early 1930s. In other instances, the static equilibrium may last for only a passing moment, as when France began reconstructing its army almost immediately after its defeat by Germany in 1871.

For the purposes of analysis it is necessary to specify a particular increase in armaments by one state as marking the formal beginning of the arms race. This is done not to pass judgment on the desirability or wisdom of the increase, but simply to identify the start of the action and reaction which constitute the race. In most instances, this initial challenge is not hard to locate. It normally involves a major change in the policy of the challenging state, and more likely than not it is formally announced to the world. The reasons for the challenging state's discontent with the status quo may stem from a variety of causes. It may feel that the growth of its economy, commerce, and population should be reflected in changes in the military balance of power (Germany, 1898; United States, 1916; Soviet Union, 1946). Nationalistic, bellicose, or militaristic individuals or parties may come to power who are unwilling to accept an equilibrium which other groups in their society had been willing to live with or negotiate about (Germany and Japan, 1934). New political issues may arise which cause a deterioration in the relationships of the state with another power and which

---

[8] See Richard Cobden, "Three Panics: An Historical Episode," *Political Writings* (London, 2 vols., 1867), II, p. 308; The Cobden Club, *The Burden of Armaments* (London, 1905), pp. 66–68.

consequently lead it to change its estimate of the arms balance necessary for its security (France, 1841, 1875; England, 1884).

Normally the challenging state sets a goal for itself which derives from the relation between the military strengths of the two countries prior to the race. If the relation was one of disparity, the initial challenge usually comes from the weaker power which aspires to parity or better. Conceivably a stronger power could initiate an arms race by deciding that it required an even higher ratio of superiority over the weaker power. But in actual practice this is seldom the case: the gain in security achieved in upping a 2:1 ratio to 3:1, for instance, rarely is worth the increased economic costs and political tensions. If parity of military power existed between the two countries, the arms race begins when one state determines that it requires military force superior to that of the other country.

In nine out of ten races the slogan of the challenging state is either "parity" or superiority." Only in rare cases does the challenger aim for less than this, for unless equality or superiority is achieved, the arms race is hardly likely to be worthwhile. The most prominent exception to the "parity or superiority" rule is the Anglo-German naval race of 1898-1912. In its initial phase, German policy was directed not to the construction of a navy equal to England's but rather to something between that and the very minor navy which she possessed prior to the race. The rationale for building such a force was provided by Tirpitz's "risk theory": Germany should have a navy large enough so that Britain could not fight her without risking damage to the British navy to such an extent that it would fall prey to the naval forces of third powers (i.e., France and Russia). The fallacies in this policy became obvious in the following decade. On the one hand, for technical reasons it was unlikely that an inferior German navy could do serious damage to a superior British fleet, and, on the other hand, instead of making Britain wary of France and Russia the expansion of the German navy tended to drive her into their arms and consequently to remove the hostile third powers who were supposed to pounce upon a Britain weakened by Germany.[9] One can only conclude that it is seldom worthwhile either for a superior power to attempt significantly to increase its superiority or for a weaker power to attempt only to reduce its degree of inferiority. The rational goals in an arms race are parity or superiority.

In many respects the most critical aspect of a race is the initial response which the challenged state makes to the new goals posited by the challenger. In general, these responses can be divided into four

---

[9] For the risk theory, see Alfred von Tirpitz, *My Memoirs* (New York, 2 vols., 1919), I, pp. 79, 84, 121, 159-160, and for a trenchant criticism, E. L. Woodward, *Great Britain and the German Navy* (Oxford, 1935), pp. 31-39.

categories, two of which preserve the possibility of peace, two of which make war virtually inevitable. The challenged state may, first, attempt to counterbalance the increased armaments of its rival through diplomatic means or it may, secondly, immediately increase its own armaments in an effort to maintain or directly to restore the previously existing balance of military power. While neither of these responses guarantees the maintenance of peace, they at least do not precipitate war. The diplomatic avenue of action, if it exists, is generally the preferred one. It may be necessary, however, for the state to enhance its own armaments as well as attempting to secure reliable allies. Or, if alliances are impossible or undesirable for reasons of state policy, the challenged state must rely upon its own increases in armaments as the way of achieving its goal. In this case a sustained arms race is likely to result. During her period of splendid isolation, for instance, England met the French naval challenge of the 1840s by increasing the size and effectiveness of her own navy. At the end of the century when confronted by the Russo-French challenge, she both increased her navy and made tentative unsuccessful efforts to form an alliance with Germany. In response to the German challenge a decade later, she again increased her navy and also arrived at a rapprochement with France and Russia.

If new alliances or increased armaments appear impossible or undesirable, a state which sees its superiority or equality in military power menaced by the actions of another state may initiate preventive action while still strong enough to forestall the change in the balance of power. The factors which enter into the decision to wage preventive war are complex and intangible, but, conceivably, if the state had no diplomatic opportunities and if it was dubious of its ability to hold its own in an arms race, this might well be a rational course of behavior.[10] Tirpitz explicitly recognized this in his concept of a "danger zone" through which the German navy would pass and during which a strong likelihood would exist that the British would take preventive action to destroy the German fleet. Such an attack might be avoided, he felt, by a German diplomatic "peace offensive" designed to calm British fears and to assure them of the harmless character of German intentions. Throughout the decade after 1898 the Germans suffered periodic scares of an imminent British attack. Although preventive action was never seriously considered by the British government, enough talk went on in high British circles of "Copenhagening" the German fleet to give the Germans some cause for alarm. In the "war in sight"

[10] On the considerations going into the waging of preventive war, see my "To Choose Peace or War," *United States Naval Institute Proceedings*, LXXXIII (April, 1957), pp. 360–62.

crisis of 1875, the initial success of French rearmament efforts aimed at restoring an equality of military power with Germany stimulated German statesmen and military leaders carefully to consider the desirability of preventive war. Similarly, the actions of the Nazis in overthrowing the restrictions of the Treaty of Versailles in the early 1930s and starting the European arms build-up produced arguments in Poland and France favoring preventive war. After World War II at the beginning of the arms race between the United States and the Soviet Union a small but articulate segment of opinion urged the United States to take preventive action before the Soviet Union developed nuclear weapons.[11] To a certain extent, the Japanese attack on the United States in 1941 can be considered a preventive action designed to forestall the inevitable loss of Japanese naval superiority in the western Pacific which would have resulted from the two-ocean navy program begun by the United States in 1939. In 1956 the Egyptians began to rebuild their armaments from Soviet sources and thus to disturb the equilibrium which had existed with Israel since 1949. This development was undoubtedly one factor leading Israel to attack Egypt and thereby attempt to resolve at least some of the outstanding issues between them before the increase in Egyptian military power.

At the other extreme from preventive action, a challenged state simply may not make any immediate response to the upset of the existing balance of power. The challenger may then actually achieve or come close to achieving the new balance of military force which it considers necessary. In this event, roles are reversed, the challenged suddenly awakens to its weakened position and becomes the challenger, engaging in frantic and strenuous last-ditch efforts to restore the previously existing military ratio. In general, the likelihood of war increases just prior to a change in military superiority from one side to the other. If the challenged state averts this change by alliances or increased armaments, war is avoidable. On the other hand, the challenged state may precipitate war in order to prevent the change, or it may provoke war by allowing the change to take place and then attempting to undo it. In the latter case, the original challenger, having achieved parity or superiority, is in no mood or position to back down; the anxious efforts of its opponent to regain its military strength appear to be obvious war preparation; and consequently the original challenger normally will not hesitate to risk or provoke a war while it may still benefit from its recent gains.

Belated responses resulting in last-gasp arms races are most clearly seen in the French and British reactions to German rearmament in the

[11] *Ibid.,* pp. 363–66.

1930s. The coming-to-power of the Nazis and their subsequent rearmament efforts initially provoked little military response in France. In part, this reflected confidence in the qualitative superiority of the French army and the defensive strength of the Maginot Line. In part, too, it reflected the French political situation in which these groups most fearful of Nazi Germany were generally those most opposed to large armies and militarism, while the usual right-wing supporters of the French army were those to whom Hitler appeared least dangerous. As a result, the French army and the War Ministry budget remained fairly constant between 1933 and 1936. Significant increases in French armaments were not made until 1937 and 1938, and the real French rearmament effort got under way in 1939. France proposed to spend more on armaments in that single year than the total of her expenditures during the preceding five years. By then, however, the five-to-one superiority in military effectives which she had possessed over Germany in 1933 had turned into a four-to-three inferiority.[12]

Roughly the same process was going on with respect to the ratio between the British and German air forces. At the beginning of the 1930s the Royal Air Force, although a relatively small force, was undoubtedly much stronger than anything which the Germans had managed to create surreptitiously. During the period from 1934 to 1938, however, the strength of the RAF in comparison to the Luftwaffe steadily declined. In July 1934, Churchill warned Parliament that the German air force had then reached two-thirds the strength of the British Home Defense Air Force, and that if present and proposed programs were continued, the Germans would achieve parity by December 1935. Baldwin assured the Commons that Britain would maintain a fifty per cent superiority over Germany. Subsequently, however, Churchill's estimates proved to be more correct than those of the Government, and the air program had to be drastically increased in 1936 and 1937. By then, however, two years had been lost. In 1936 Germany achieved parity with Britain. In the spring of 1937 the Luftwaffe exceeded the RAF in first-line strength and reserves. By September 1938 it was almost twice as large as the RAF, and the production of aircraft in Germany was double that in England. The British vigorously pushed their efforts to make up for lost time: British aviation expenditures which had amounted to 16.8 million pounds in 1934–35 rose to 131.4 millions in 1937–38, and were budgeted at 242.7 millions for 1939–40. The Germans were now on top and the British the challengers moving to close the gap. The

---

[12] N. M. Sloutzski, *World Armaments Race, 1919–1939* (Geneva Studies, Vol. XII, No.1, July 1941), pp. 45–46, 99–101. In 1933 the French army numbered approximately 508,000 men, the German army roughly 100,000. In 1939 the French army numbered 629,000 men, the German army 800–900,000.

readiness of the Germans to go to war consequently was not unnatural. As far back as 1936, the British Joint Planning Staff had picked September 1939 as the most likely date for the beginning of a war because in the fall of 1939 Germany's armed strength would reach its peak in comparison with that of the allies. This forecast proved true on both points, and it was not until after the start of the war that the British began seriously to catch up with the head start of the Luftwaffe. British aircraft production first equalled that of the Germans in the spring of 1940.

A slightly different example of a belated, last minute arms race is found in the German-French and German-Russian competitions of 1911–1914. In this instance, deteriorating relations between the two countries led both to make strenuous efforts to increase their forces in a short time and enhanced the willingness of each to go to war. For a decade or more prior to 1911, German and French armaments had been relatively stable, and during the years 1908–1911 relations between the two countries had generally improved. The Agadir crisis of 1911 and the Balkan War of the following year stimulated the Germans to reconsider their armaments position. Fear of a Franco-Russian surprise attack and concern over the quantitative superiority of the French army led the Germans to make a moderate increase in their forces in 1912. In the spring of 1913 a much larger increase of 117,000 men was voted. Simultaneously, the French extended their term of military service from two to three years, thereby increasing their peacetime army by some 200,000 men. The Russians also had an extensive program of military reorganization under way. During the three year period 1911–14 the French army increased from 638,500 men to 846,000, and the German army from 626,732 to 806,026 men. If war had not broken out in 1914, the French would have been faced with an acute problem in maintaining a military balance with Germany. The population of France was about 39,000,000, that of Germany 65,000,000. During the twenty years prior to 1914 the French trained 82 per cent of their men liable for military service, the Germans 55 per cent of theirs. As a result, the two armies were approximately equal in size. If the Germans had continued to expand their army, the French inevitably would have fallen behind in the race: the extension of service in 1913 was a sign that they were reaching the limit of their manpower resources. Their alternatives would have been either to have provoked a war before Germany gained a decisive superiority, to have surrendered their goal of parity with Germany and with it any hope of retrieving Alsace-Lorraine, or to have stimulated further improvement of the military forces of their Russian ally and further expansion of the military forces of their British ally— perhaps putting pressure on Great Britain to institute universal military service. The Germans, on the other hand, felt themselves menaced by the reorganization of the Russian army. Already significantly outnumbered by the combined Franco-Russian armies, the Germans could hardly view with equanimity a significant increase in the efficiency of the Tsarist forces. Thus each side tended to see itself losing out in the arms race in the future and hence each side was more willing to risk a test of arms when the opportunity presented itself in 1914.

The danger of war is highest in the opening phases of an arms race, at which time the greatest elements of instability and uncertainty are present. If the challenged state neither resorts to preventive war nor fails to make an immediate response to the challenger's activities, a sustained arms race is likely to result with the probability of war decreasing as the initial action and counteraction fade into the past. Once the initial disturbances to the pre-arms race static equilibrium are surmounted, the reciprocal increases of the two states tend to produce a new, dynamic equilibrium reflecting their relative strength and participation in the race. In all probability, the relative military power of the two states in this dynamic equilibrium will fall somewhere between the previous status quo and the ratio-goal of the challenger. The sustained regularity of the increases in itself becomes an accepted and anticipated stabilizing factor in the relations between the two countries. A sustained quantitative race still may produce a war, but a greater likelihood exists that either the two states will arrive at a mutual accommodation reducing the political tensions which started the race or that one state over the long haul will gradually but substantially achieve its objective while the other will accept defeat in the race if this does not damage its vital interests. Thus, a twenty-five year sporadic naval race between France and England ended in the middle 1860s when France gave up any serious effort to challenge the 3 : 2 ratio which England had demonstrated the will and the capacity to maintain. Similarly, the Anglo-German naval race slackened after 1912 when, despite failure to reach formal agreement, relations improved between the two countries and even Tirpitz acquiesced in the British 16 : 10 ratio in capital ships.[13] Britain also successfully maintained her two-power standard against France and Russia for twenty years until changes in the international scene ended her arms competition with those two powers. Germany and France successively

---

[13] Some question might be raised as to whether the Anglo-German naval race ended before World War I or in World War I. It would appear, however, that the race was substantially over before the war began. The race went through two phases. During the first phase, 1898–1905, German policy was directed toward the construction of a "risk" navy. During the second phase, 1906–1912, the Anglo-French entente had removed the basis for a risk navy, and the introduction of the Dreadnought opened to the Germans the possibility of naval parity with Britain. By 1912, however, it was apparent to all that Britain had the will and the determination to maintain the 60 percent superiority which she desired over Germany, and to lay "two keels for one" if this should be necessary. In

increased their armies from the middle 1870s to the middle 1890s when tensions eased and the arms build-up in each country slackened. The incipient naval races among the United States, Britain, and Japan growing out of World War I were restricted by the Washington naval agreement; the ten-year cruiser competition between the United States and England ended in the London Treaty of 1930; and eventually the rise of more dangerous threats in the mid-1930s removed any remaining vestiges of Anglo-American naval rivalry. The twelve-year arms race between Chile and Argentina ended in 1902 with a comprehensive agreement between the two countries settling their boundary disputes and restricting their armaments. While generalizations are both difficult and dangerous, it would appear that a sustained arms race is much more likely to have a peaceful ending than a bloody one.

QUANTITATIVE AND QUALITATIVE ARMS RACES

A state may increase its military power quantitatively, by expanding the numerical strength of its existing military forces, or qualitatively, by replacing its existing forms of military force (normally weapons systems) with new and more effective forms of force. Expansion and innovation are thus possible characteristics of any arms race, and to some extent both are present in most races. Initially and fundamentally every arms race is quantitative in nature. The race begins when two states develop conflicting goals as to what should be the distribution of military power between them and give these goals explicit statement in quantitative ratios of the relative strenghts which each hopes to achieve in the decisive form of military force. The formal start of the race is the decision of the challenger to upset the existing balance and to expand its forces quantitatively. If at some point in the race a qualitative change produces a new decisive form of military force, the quantitative goals of the two states still remain roughly the same. The relative balance of power which each state desires to achieve is independent of the specific weapons and forces which enter into the balance. Despite the underlying adherence of both states to their original ratio-goals, however, a complex qualitative race

---

addition, increased tension with France and Russia over Morocco and the Balkans turned German attention to her army. In 1912 Bethmann-Hollweg accepted as the basis for negotiation a British memorandum the first point of which was: "Fundamental. Naval superiority recognized as essential to Great Britain." Relations between the two countries generally improved between 1912 and 1914: they cooperated in their efforts to limit the Balkan wars of 1912-13 and in the spring of 1914 arrived an agreement concerning the Baghdad railway and the Portuguese colonies. By June 1914 rivalry had abated to such an extent that the visit of a squadron of British battleships to Kiel became the occasion for warm expressions of friendship. "In a sense," as Bernadotte Schmitt says, "potential foes had become potential friends." *The Coming of the War: 1914*, I, pp. 72-73; Sidney B. Fay, *The Origins of the World War* (New York, 2 vols., 1928), I, pp. 299ff.; Tirpitz, *Memoirs*, I, pp. 271-72.

produced by rapid technological innovation is a very different phenomenon from a race which remains simply quantitative.

Probably the best examples of races which were primarily quantitative in nature are those between Germany and France between 1871 and 1914. The decisive element was the number of effectives each power maintained in its peacetime army and the number of reserves it could call to the colors in an emergency. Quantitative increases by one state invariably produced comparable increases by the other. The German army bill of 1880, for instance, added 25,000 men to the army and declared in its preamble that "far-reaching military reforms had been carried out outside of Germany which cannot remain without influence upon the military power of the neighboring countries." These increases it was alleged would produce "too considerable a numerical superiority of the enemy's forces."[14] Again in 1887 Bismarck used Boulanger's agitation for an increase in the French army as a means of putting through an expansion of the German one. After the French reorganized their army in 1889 and drastically increased the proportion of young men liable to military service, the Germans added 20,000 men to their force in 1890. Three years later a still larger increase was made in the German army and justified by reference to recent French and Russian expansions. Similarly, the naval race of 1884–1905 between England, on the one hand, and France and Russia, on the other, was primarily quantitative in nature. Naval budgets and numerical strengths of the two sides tended to fluctuate in direct relation with each other.

A qualitative arms race is more complex than a quantitative one because at some point it involves the decision by one side to introduce a new weapons system or form of military force. Where the capacity for technological innovation exists, the natural tendency is for the arms race to become qualitative. The introduction of a new weapons system obviously is normally desirable from the viewpoint of the state which is behind in the quantitative race. The English-French naval rivalry of 1841–1865 grew out of the deteriorating relations between the two countries over Syria, Tahiti and Spain. Its first manifestation was quantitative: in 1841 the number of seamen in the French navy which for nearly a century had been about two-thirds the number in the British navy was suddenly increased so as to almost equal the British strength. Subsequently the large expansions which the French proposed to make in their dockyards, especially at Toulon, caused even Cobden to observe that " a serious effort seemed really to be made to rival us at sea."[15] The Anglo-French quantitative rivalry subsided with the departure of Louis Philippe in 1848, but shortly

[14] Kovacs, "Nation in Arms," p. 36.
[15] Cobden, "Three Panics," p. 224.

thereafter it resumed on a new qualitative level with the determination of Napoleon III to push the construction of steam warships. The *Napoléon*, a screw propelled ship of the line of 92 guns, launched by the French in 1850 was significantly superior to anything the British could bring against it, until the *Agamemnon* was launched two years later. The alliance of the two countries in the Crimean War only temporarily suspended the naval race, and by 1858 the French had achieved parity with the British in fast screw ships of the line. In that year the French had 114 fewer sailing vessels in their navy than they had in 1852, while the number of British sailing ships had declined only from 299 to 296. On the other hand, the British in 1852 had a superiority of 73 sailing ships of the line to 45 for the French. By 1858, however, both England and France had 29 steam ships of the line while England had an enhanced superiority of 35 to 10 in sailing ships. A head start in steam construction and conversion plus the concentration of effort on this program had enabled the French, who had been hopelessly outnumbered in the previously decisive form of naval power, to establish a rough parity in the new form. In view of the British determination to restore their quantitative superiority and the superior industrial resources at their disposal, however, parity could only be temporary. In 1861 the British had 53 screw battleships afloat and 14 building while the French had only 35 afloat and two building.[16]

By the time that the British had reestablished their superiority in steam warships, their opponents had brought forward another innovation which again threatened British control of the seas. The French laid down four ironclads in 1858 and two in 1859. The first was launched in November 1859 and the next in March 1860. The British launched their first ironclad in December 1860. The British program, however, was hampered by the Admiralty's insistence upon continuing to build wooden warships. The French stopped laying down wooden line of battleships in 1856, yet the British, despite warnings that wooden walls were obsolete, continued building wooden ships down through 1860, and in 1861 the Admiralty brought in the largest request in its history for the purchase of timber.[17] Meanwhile, in the fall of 1860 the French started a new construction program for ten more ironclads to supplement the six they already had underway. The British learned of these projects in February 1861 and responded with a program to add nine new ironclads to their fleet. In May 1861, the French had a total of fifteen ironclads built or building, the British only seven. From 1860 until 1865 the French possessed superiority or parity with the British in

[16] *Ibid.,* pp. 304–308, 392–93.
[17] *Ibid.,* pp. 343, 403; Robert G. Albion, *Forests and Sea Power* (Cambridge, 1926), p. 408.

ironclad warships. In February 1863, for instance, the French had four ironclads mounting 146 guns ready for action, the British four ironclads mounting 116 guns. Thanks to the genius and initiative of the director of French naval construction, Dupuy de Lôme, and the support of Napoleon III, there had occurred, as one British military historian put it,

> an astonishing change in the balance of power which might have been epoch-making had it not been so brief, or if France and Britain had gone to war, a reversal which finds no place in any but technical histories and which is almost entirely unknown in either country today. In a word, supremacy at sea passed from Britain to France.[18]

This was not a supremacy, however, which France could long maintain. By 1866, Britannia had retrieved the trident. In that year England possessed nineteen ironclads, France thirteen, and the English superiority was enhanced by heavier guns. Thereafter the naval strengths of the two powers resumed the 3:2 ratio which had existed prior to 1841.

In general, as this sequence of events indicates, technological innovation favors, at least temporarily, the numerically weaker power. Its long-run effects, however, depend upon factors other than the currently prevailing balance of military strength. It was indeed paradoxical that France should make the innovations which she did make in her naval race with England. In the 1850s and 1860s France normally had twice as much timber on hand in her dockyards as had the British, and she was, of course, inferior to England in her coal and iron resources. Nonetheless she led the way in the introduction of steam and iron, while the Royal Navy, which was acutely hampered by a timber shortage clung to the wooden ships.[19] In this instance, on both sides, immediate needs and the prospects of immediate success prevailed over a careful consideration of long-term benefits.

The problem which technological innovation presents to the quantitatively superior power is somewhat more complex. The natural tendencies for such a state are toward conservatism: any significant innovation will undermine the usefulness of the current type of weapons system in which it possesses a superiority. What, however, should be the policy of a superior power with respect to making a technological change which its inferior rivals are likely to make in the near future? The British navy had a traditional answer to this problem: never introduce any development which will render existing ships obsolete but be prepared if any other state does make an innovation to push ahead

---

[18] Cyril Falls, *A Hundred Years of War* (London, 1953), p. 102.
[19] Albion, *Forests and Sea Power*, pp. 406-07; Brodie, *Sea Power in the Machine Age*, p. 441.

an emergency construction program which will restore the previously existing ratio. While this policy resulted, as we have seen above, in some close shaves, by the beginning of the twentieth century it had become a fundamental maxim of British naval doctrine. Consequently, Sir John Fisher's proposal in 1904 to revolutionize naval construction by introducing the "all big gun ship" which would render existing capital ships obsolete was also a revolution in British policy. In terms of its impact upon the Anglo-German naval balance, Fisher's decision was welcomed by many Germans and condemned by many British. Although the construction of Dreadnoughts would force Germany to enlarge the Kiel Canal, the Germans seized the opportunity to start the naval race afresh in a class of vessels in which the British did not have an overwhelming numerical superiority. For the first few years the British by virtue of their headstart would have a larger number of Dreadnoughts, but then the German yards would start producing and the gap which had to be closed would be much smaller in the Dreadnoughts than in the pre-Dreadnought battleships. The introduction of the Dreadnought permitted the Germans to raise their sight from a "risk" navy (which had become meaningless since the Anglo-French entente in any event) to the possibility of parity with Britain. To many Britishers, on the other hand, construction of the Dreadnought seemed to be tantamount to sinking voluntarily a large portion of the British navy. The tremendous number of pre-Dreadnought capital ships which the Royal Navy possessed suddenly decreased in value. Great Britain, one British naval expert subsequently argued, had to write off seventy-five warships, the Germans only twenty-eight. British naval superiority fell by 40 or 50 per cent: in 1908 England had authorized twelve Dreadnoughts and the Germans nine; in pre-Dreadnought battleships the British had 63 and the Germans 26.[20]

Fisher's policy, however, was undoubtedly the correct one. Plans for an all-big-gun ship had been under consideration by various navies since 1903. The Russo-Japanese War underwrote the desirability of heavy armaments. The United States authorized the construction of two comparable vessels in March, 1905, and the Germans themselves were moving in that direction. The all-big-gun ship was inevitable, and this consideration led Fisher to insist that Britain must take the lead. While the superiority of the Royal Navy over the German fleet was significantly reduced, nonetheless at no time in the eight years after 1905 did the Germans approach the British in terms of numerical equality. Their highest point was in 1911 when their Dreadnought battleship and battle-cruiser strength amounted to 64 per cent of the

[20] Hector C. Bywater, *Navies and Nations* (London, 1927), pp. 27–28; Fay, *Origins of the World War,* I, p. 236.

British strength.[21] Thus, by reversing the nineteenth century policy of the British navy, Fisher avoided the British experience of the 1850s and 1860s when technological innovations by an inferior power temporarily suspended Britain's supremacy on the seas.

The very incentive which an inferior power has to make a technological innovation is reason for the superior power to take the lead, if it can, in bringing in the innovation itself. The British-Dreadnought debate of 1904–1905 had its parallels in the problem confronting the American government in 1949–1950 concerning the construction of a hydrogen bomb. Like the British, the Americans possessed a superiority in the existing decisive type of weapons system. As in the British government, opinion was divided, and the arguments pro and con of the technicians and military experts had to be weighed against budgetary considerations. As with the Dreadnought, the new weapons system was pushed by a small group of zealots convinced of the inevitability and necessity of its development. In both cases, humanitarian statesmen and conservative experts wished to go slow. In each case, the government eventually decided to proceed with the innovation, and, in each case, the wisdom of its policy was demonstrated by the subsequent actions of its rival. In an arms race, what is technically possible tends to become politically necessary.

Whether an arms race is primarily quantitative or primarily qualitative in nature has a determining influence upon its outcome. This influence is manifested in the different impacts which the two types of races have on the balance of military power between the two states and on the relative demands which they make on state resources.

Qualitative and quantitative races and the balance of power. In a simple quantitative race one state is very likely to develop a definite superiority in the long run. The issue is simply who has the greater determination and the greater resources. Once a state falls significantly behind, it is most unlikely that it will ever be able to overcome the lead of its rival. A qualitative race, on the other hand, in which there is a series of major technological innovations in reality consists of a number of distinct races. Each time a new weapons system is introduced a new race takes place in the development and accumulation of that weapon. As the rate of technological innovation increases each separate component race decreases in time and extent. The simple quantitative race is like a marathon of undetermined distance which can only end with the exhaustion of one state or both, or with the state which is about to fall behind in the race pulling out its

---

[21] I am indebted to a paper by Mr. Peter E. Weil on "The Dreadnought and the Anglo-German Naval Race, 1905–1909" for statistics on British and German naval strengths.

firearms and attempting to despatch its rival. The qualitative race, on the other hand, resembles a series of hundred yard dashes, each beginning from a fresh starting line. Consequently, in a qualitative race hope springs anew with each phase. Quantitative superiority is the product of effort, energy, resources, and time. Once achieved it is rarely lost. Qualitative superiority is the product of discovery, luck, and circumstance. Once achieved it is always lost. Safety exists only in numbers. While a quantitative race tends to produce inequality between the two competing powers, a qualitative race tends toward equality irrespective of what may be the ratio-goals of the two rival states. Each new weapon instead of increasing the distance between the two states reduces it. The more rapid the rate of innovation the more pronounced is the tendency toward equality. Prior to 1905, for instance, Great Britain possessed a superiority in pre-Dreadnought battleships. By 1912 she had also established a clear and unassailable superiority in Dreadnoughts over Germany. But if Germany had introduced a super-Dreadnought in 1909, Great Britain could never have established its clear superiority in Dreadnoughts. She would have had to start over again in the new race. A rapid rate of innovation means that arms races are always beginning, never ending. In so far as the likelihood of war is decreased by the existence of an equality of power between rival states, a qualitative arms race tends to have this result. A quantitative arms race, on the other hand, tends to have the opposite effect. If in a qualitative race one power stopped technological innovation and instead shifted its resources to the multiplication of existing weapons systems, this would be a fairly clear sign that it was intending to go to war in the immediate future.

Undoubtedly many will question the proposition that rapid technological innovation tends to produce an equality of power. In an arms race each state lives in constant fear that its opponent will score a "technological breakthrough" and achieve a decisive qualitative superiority. This anxiety is a continuing feature of arms races but it is one which has virtually no basis in recent experience. The tendency toward simultaneity of innovation is overwhelming. Prior to World War I simultaneity was primarily the result of the common pool of knowledge among the advanced nations with respect to weapons technology. The development of weapons was largely the province of private firms who made their wares available to any state which was interested. As a result at any given time the armaments of the major powers all strikingly resembled one another.[22] During and after World

[22] See Victor Lefebure, "The Decisive Aggressive Value of the New Agencies of War," in The Inter-Parliamentary Union, *What Would Be the Character of a New War?* (New York, 1933), pp. 97–101. See also Marion W. Boggs, *Attempts to Define and Limit "Aggressive" Armament in Diplomacy and Strategy* (Columbia, Mo., 1941),

War I military research and development became more and more a governmental activity, and, as a result, more and more enshrouded in secrecy. Nonetheless relative equality in technological innovation continued among the major powers. The reason for this was now not so much access to common knowledge as an equal ability and opportunity to develop that knowledge. The logic of scientific development is such that separate groups of men working in separate laboratories on the same problem are likely to arrive at the same answer to the problem at about the same time. Even if this were not the case, the greatly increased ratio of production time to use time in recent years has tended to diminish the opportunity of the power which has pioneered an innovation to produce it in sufficient quantity in sufficient time to be militarily decisive. When it takes several years to move a weapons system from original design to quantity operation, knowledge of it is bound to leak out, and the second power in the arms race will be able to get its own program under way before the first state can capitalize on its lead. The *Merrimac* reigned supreme for a day, but it was only for a day and it could be only for a day.

The fact that for four years from 1945 to 1949 the United States possessed a marked qualitative superiority over the Soviet Union has tended to obscure how rare this event normally is. American superiority, however, was fundamentally the result of carrying over into a new competitive rivalry a weapons system which had been developed in a previous conflict. In the latter rivalry the tendency toward simultaneity of development soon manifested itself. The Soviet Union developed an atomic bomb four years after the United States had done so. Soviet explosion of a hydrogen weapon lagged only ten months behind that of the United States. At a still later date in the arms race, both powers in 1957 were neck and neck in their efforts to develop long-range ballistic missiles.

The ending of an arms race in a distinct quantitative victory for one side is perhaps best exemplified in the success of the British in maintaining their supremacy on the seas. Three times within the course of a hundred years the British were challenged by continental rivals, and three times the British outbuilt their competitors. In each case, also, implicitly or explicitly, the bested rivals recognized their defeat and abandoned their efforts to challenge the resources, skill and determination of the British. At this point in a quantitative race when it appears that one power is establishing its superiority over the other, proposals

---

p. 76: ". . . the history of war inventions tends to emphasize the slowness and distinctively international character of peacetime improvements; no weapon has been perfected with secrecy and rapidity as the exclusive national property of any one state. At an early stage all nations secure access to the information, and develop not only the armament, but measures against it."

are frequently brought forward for some sort of "disarmament" agreement. These are as likely to come from the superior side as from the inferior one. The stronger power desires to clothe its *de facto* supremacy in *de jure* acceptance and legitimacy so that it may slacken its own arms efforts. From 1905 to 1912, for instance, virtually all the initiatives for Anglo-German naval agreement came from the British. Quite properly, the Germans regarded those advances as British efforts to compel "naval competition to cease at the moment of its own greatest preponderance." Such proposals only heightened German suspicion and bitterness. Similarly, after World War II the Soviet Union naturally described the American nuclear disarmament proposal as a device to prevent the Soviet Union from developing its own nuclear capability. A decade later a greater common interest existed between the Soviet Union and the United States in reaching an arms agreement which would permanently exclude "fourth powers" from the exclusive nuclear club. In disarmament discussions the superior power commonly attempts to persuade the inferior one to accept as permanent the existing ratio of strength, or, failing in this effort, the superior power proposes a temporary suspension of the race, a "holiday" during which period neither power will increase its armaments. In 1899 the Russians, with the largest army in Europe, proposed that for five years no increases be made in military budgets. In 1912–14 Churchill repeatedly suggested the desirability of a naval building holiday to the Germans who were quite unable to perceive its advantages. In 1936 the United States could easily agree to a six year holiday in 10,000 ton cruisers since it had already underway all the cruisers it was permitted by the London Treaty of 1930. Similarly, in its 1957 negotiations with the Soviet Union the United States could also safely propose an end to the production of nuclear weapons. The inferior participant in disarmament negotiations, on the other hand, inevitably supports measures based not upon the existing situation but either upon the abstract principle of "parity" or upon the inherent evil of large armaments as such and the desirability of reducing all arms down to a common low level. Thus, in most instances, a disarmament proposal is simply a maneuver in the arms race: the attempt by a state to achieve the ratio-goal it desires by means other than an increase in its armaments.

The domestic burden of quantitative and qualitative races. Quantitative and qualitative arms races have markedly different effects upon the countries participating in them. In a quantitative race the decisive ratio is between the resources which a nation devotes to military purposes and those which it devotes to civilian ones. A quantitative race of any intensity requires a steady shift of resources from the latter to the former. As the forms of military force are multiplied a larger and larger proportion of the national product is devoted to the purposes of the race, and, if it is a race in military manpower, an increasing proportion of the population serves a longer and longer time in the armed forces. A quantitative race of any duration thus imposes ever increasing burdens upon the countries involved in it. As a result, it becomes necessary for governments to resort to various means of stimulating popular support and eliciting a willingness to sacrifice other goods and values. Enthusiasm is mobilized, hostility aroused and directed against the potential enemy. Suspicion and fear multiply with the armaments. Such was the result of the quantitative races between the Triple Alliance and the Triple Entente between 1907 and 1914:

> In both groups of powers there was a rapid increase of military and naval armaments. This caused increasing suspicions, fears, and newspaper recriminations in the opposite camp. This in turn led to more armaments and so to the vicious circle of ever growing war preparations and mutual fears and suspicions.[23]

Eventually a time is reached when the increasing costs and tensions of a continued arms race seem worse than the costs and the risks of war. Public opinion once aroused cannot be quieted. The economic, military and psychological pressures previously generated permit only further expansion or conflict. The extent to which an arms race is likely to lead to war thus varies with the burdens it imposes on the peoples and the extent to which it involves them psychologically and emotionally in the race. Prolonged sufficiently, a quantitative race must necessarily reach a point where opinion in one country or the other will demand that it be ended, if not by negotiation, then by war. The logical result of a quantitative arms race is a "nation in arms," and a nation in arms for any length of time must be a nation at war.

A qualitative arms race, however, does not have this effect. In such a race the essential relationship is not between the military and the civilian, but rather between the old and the new forms of military force. In a quantitative race the principal policy issue is the extent to which resources and manpower should be diverted from civilian to military use. In a qualitative race, the principal issue is the extent to which the new weapons systems should replace the old "conventional" ones. In a quantitative race the key question is "How much?" In a qualitative race, it is "How soon?" A quantitative race requires continuous expansion of military resources, a qualitative race continuous redeployment of them. A qualitative race does not normally increase arms budgets, even when, as usually happens, the new forms of military force are more expensive than the old ones. The costs of a qualitative race only increase significantly when an effort is made to maintain both old and new forms of military force: steam and sail;

---

[23] Fay, *Origins of the World War*, I, p. 226.

ironclads and wooden walls; nuclear and nonnuclear weapons. Transitions from old to new weapons systems have not normally been accompanied by marked increases in military expenditures. During the decade in which the ironclad replaced the wooden ship of the line British naval expenditures declined from £12,779,000 in 1859 to less than eleven million pounds in 1867.[24] Similarly, the five years after the introduction of the Dreadnought saw British naval expenditures drop from £35,476,000 in 1903-04 to £32,188,000 in 1908-09. During the same period estimates for shipbuilding and repairs dropped from £17,350,000 to £14,313,900. The years 1953-1956 saw the progressive adoption of nuclear weapons in the American armed forces, yet military budgets during this period at first dropped considerably and then recovered only slightly, as the increased expenditures for the new weapons were more than compensated for by reductions in expenditures for nonnuclear forces.

Quantitative and qualitative arms races differ also in the interests they mobilize and the leadership they stimulate. In the long run, a quantitative race makes extensive demands on a broad segment of the population. A qualitative race, however, tends to be a competition of elites rather than masses. No need exists for the bulk of the population to become directly involved. In a quantitative arms race, the users of the weapons—the military leaders—assume the key role. In a qualitative race, the creators of the weapons—the scientists—rival them for preeminence. Similarly, the most important private interests in a quantitative race are the large mass production industrial corporations, while in a qualitative race they tend to be the smaller firms specializing in the innovation and development of weapons systems rather than in their mass output.

While the rising costs of a quantitative race may increase the likelihood of war, they may also enhance efforts to end the race by means of an arms agreement. Undoubtedly the most powerful motive (prior to the feasiblity of utter annihilation) leading states to arms limitations has been the economic one. The desire for economy was an important factor leading Louis Philippe to propose a general reduction in European armaments in 1831. In the 1860s similar motives stimulated Napoleon III to push disarmament plans. They also prompted various British governments to be receptive to arms limitation proposals, provided, of course, that they did not endanger Britain's supremacy on the seas: the advent of the Liberal government in 1905, for instance, resulted in renewed efforts to reach accommodation with the Germans. In 1898 the troubled state of Russian finances was largely responsible

---

[24] James Phinney Baxter, 3rd, *The Introduction of the Ironclad Warship* (Cambridge, 1933), p. 321.

for the Tsar's surprise move in sponsoring the first Hague Conference. Eight years later it was the British who, for economic reasons, wished to include the question of arms limitation on the agenda of the second Hague Conference.

The success of rising economic costs in bringing about the negotiated end of an arms race depends upon their incidence being relatively equal on each participant. A state which is well able to bear the economic burden normally spurns the efforts of weaker powers to call off the race. Thus, the Kaiser was scornful of the Russian economic debility which led to the proposal for the first Hague Conference, and a German delegate to that conference, in explaining German opposition to limitation, took pains to assure the participants that:

> The German people are not crushed beneath the weight of expenditures and taxes; they are not hanging on the edge of the precipice; they are not hastening towards exhaustion and ruin. Quite the contrary; public and private wealth is increasing, the general welfare, and standard of life, are rising from year to year.[25]

On the other hand, the relatively equal burdens of their arms race in the last decade of the nineteenth century eventually forced Argentina and Chile to call the race off in 1902. The victory of Chile in the War of the Pacific had brought her into conflict with an "expanding and prosperous Argentina" in the 1880s, and a whole series of boundary disputes exacerbated the rivalry which developed between the two powers for hegemony on the South American continent. As a result, after 1892 both countries consistently expanded their military and naval forces, and relations between them staggered from one war crisis to another. Despite efforts made to arbitrate the boundary disputes,

> an uneasy feeling still prevailed that hostilities might break out, and neither State made any pretence of stopping military and naval preparations. Orders for arms, ammunition, and warships were not countermanded, and men on both sides of the Andes began to declaim strongly against the heavy expenditure thus entailed. The reply to such remonstrances invariably was that until the question of the boundary was settled, it was necessary to maintain both powers on a war footing. Thus the resources of Argentina and Chile were strained to the utmost, and public works neglected in order that funds might be forthcoming to pay for guns and ships bought in Europe.[26]

These economic burdens led the presidents of the two countries to arrive at an agreement in 1899 restricting additional expenditures on armaments. Two years later, however, the boundary issue again flared

---

[25] Quoted in Tate, *Disarmament Illusion*, p. 281. See also pp. 193–94, 251–52.
[26] Charles E. Akers, *A History of South America* (New York, new ed., 1930), p. 112.

up, and both sides recommenced preparations for war. But again the resources of the countries were taxed beyond their limit. In August 1901
the Chilean president declared to the United States minister "that the
burden which Chile is carrying . . . is abnormal and beyond her
capacity and that the hour has come to either make use of her armaments or reduce them to the lowest level compatible with the dignity and
safety of the country."[27] Argentina was also suffering from severe
economic strain, and as a result, the two countries concluded their
famous *Pactos de Mayo* in 1902 which limited their naval armaments
and provided for the arbitration of the remaining boundary issues.

In summary, two general conclusions emerge as to the relations between arms races and war:

(1) War is more likely to develop in the early phases of an arms race
than in its later phases.
(2) A quantitative race is more likely than a qualitative one to come
to a definite end in war, arms agreement, or victory for one side.

ARMS RACES, DISARMAMENT, AND PEACE

In discussions of disarmament, a distinction has frequently been
drawn between the presumably technical problem of arms limitation,
on the one hand, and political problems, on the other. Considerable
energy has been devoted to arguments as to whether it is necessary to
settle political issues before disarming or whether disarmament is a
prerequisite to the settlement of political issues. The distinction between arms limitation and politics, however, is a fallacious one. The
achievement of an arms agreement cannot be made an end in itself.
Arms limitation is the essence of politics and inseparable from other
political issues. What, indeed, is more political than the relative
balance of power between two distinct entities? Whether they be
political parties competing for votes, lobbyists lining up legislative
blocs, or states piling up armaments, the power ratio between the units
is a decisive factor in their relationship. Virtually every effort (such as
the Hague Conferences and the League of Nations) to reach agreement on arms apart from the resolution of other diplomatic and
political issues has failed. Inevitably attempts to arrive at arms
agreements have tended to broaden into discussions of all the significant political issues between the competing powers. On the other
hand, it cannot be assumed that arms negotiations are hopeless, and
that they only add another issue to those already disrupting the relations between the two countries and stimulating passion and suspicion. Just as the problem of armaments cannot be settled without

[27] Quoted in Robert N. Burr, "The Balance of Power in Nineteenth-Century South
America: An Exploratory Essay," *Hispanic American Historical Review,* XXXV
(February, 1955), 58n.

reference to other political issues, so is it also impossible to resolve these issues without facing up to the relative balance of military power. The most notable successes in arms limitation agreements have been combined, implicitly or explicitly, with a resolution of other controversies. The Rush-Bagot Agreement, for instance, simply confirmed the settlement which had been reached in the Treaty of Paris. The *Pactos de Mayo* dealt with both armaments and boundaries and implicitly recognized that Argentina would not intervene in west coast politics and that Chile would not become involved in the disputes of the Plata region. The Washington naval agreements necessarily were part and parcel of a general Far Eastern settlement involving the end of the Anglo-Japanese alliance and at least a temporary resolution of the diplomatic issues concerning China. As has been suggested previously, in one sense armaments are to the twentieth century what territory was to the eighteenth. Just as divisions of territory were then the essence of general diplomatic agreements, so today are arrangements on armaments. If both sides are to give up their conflicting ratio-goals and compromise the difference, this arrangement must coincide with a settlement of the other issues which stimulated them to develop the conflicting ratio-goals in the first place. If one state is to retreat further from its ratio-goal than the other, it will have to receive compensations with respect to other points in dispute.

While arms limitation is seldom possible except as part of a broader political settlement, it is also seldom possible if the scope of the arms limitation is itself too broad. One of the corollaries of the belief that arms races produce wars is the assumption that disarmament agreements are necessary to peace. Too frequently it has been made to appear that failure to reach a disarmament agreement leaves war as the only recourse between the powers. In particular, it is false and dangerous to assume that any disarmament to be effective must be total disarmament. The latter is an impossible goal. Military force is inherent in national power and national power is inherent in the existence of independent states. In one way or another all the resources of a state contribute to its military strength. The discussions in the 1920s under the auspices of the League conclusively demonstrated that what are armaments for one state are the pacific instruments of domestic well-being and tranquility for another. The history of general disarmament conferences persuasively suggests the difficulties involved in deciding what elements of power should be weighed in the balance even before the issue is faced as to what the relative weight of the two sides should be. At the first Hague Conference, for instance, the Germans were quick to point out that the Russian proposal for a five year holiday in military budget increases was fine for Russia who had all the men in her army that she needed, but that such a restriction would not prevent Russia from building strategic railways to her western border which would constitute a greater menace to Germany than additional Russian soldiers. The demand for total disarmament frequently reflects an unwillingness to live with the problems of power. A feasible arms limitation must be part of the process of politics, not of the abolition of politics.

The narrower the scope of a proposed arms limitation agreement, the more likely it is to be successful. Disarmament agreements seldom actually disarm states. What they do is to exclude certain specified areas from the competition and thereby direct that competion into other channels. The likelihood of reaching such an agreement is greater if the states can have a clear vision of the impact of the agreement on the balance of power. The more restricted the range of armaments covered by the agreement, the easier it is for them to foresee its likely effects. In general, also, the less important the area in the balance of power between the two states, the easier it is to secure agreement on that area. Part of the success of the Washington agreements was that they were limited to capital ships, and, at that time, particularly in the United States the feeling existed that existing battleships were obsolete and that in any event the battleship had passed its peak as the supreme weapon of naval power. Similarly, in 1935 Germany and England were able to arrive at an agreement (which lasted until April 1939) fixing the relative size of their navies—something which had been beyond the capability of sincere and well-meaning diplomats of both powers before World War I— because air power had replaced sea power as the decisive factor in the arms balance between Germany and England. Restrictions on land armaments have generally been harder to arrive at than naval agreements because the continental European nations usually felt that their large armies were directly essential to their national existence and might have to be used at a moment's notice.

Successful disarmament agreements (and a disarmament agreement is sucessful if it remains in force for a half decade or more) generally establish quantitative restrictions on armaments. The quantitative ratio is the crucial one between the powers, and the quantitative element is much more subject to the control of governments than is the course of scientific development. Furthermore, a quantitative agreement tends to channel competition into qualitative areas, while an agreement on innovation tends to do just the reverse. Consequently, quantitative agreement tends to reduce the likelihood of war, qualitative agreement to enhance it. In the current arms race, for instance, some sort of quantitative agreement might be both feasible, since the race is primarily qualitative in nature, and desirable, since such an agreement would formally prohibit the more dangerous type of arms race. On the other hand, a qualitative agreement between the two countries prohibiting, say, the construction and testing of intercontinental ballistic missiles, might well be disastrous if it should stimulate a quantitative race in aircraft production, the construction of bases, and the multiplication of other forms of military force. In addition, the next phase in the arms race, for instance, may well be the development of defenses against ballistic missiles. A qualitative answer to this problem, such as an effective anti-missile missile, would, in the long run, be much less expensive and much less disturbing to peace than a quantitative answer, such as a mammoth shelter construction program, which would tax public resources, infringe on many established interests, and arouse popular concern and fear. Continued technological innovation could well be essential to the avoidance of war. Peace, in short, may depend less upon the ingenuity of the rival statesmen than upon the ingenuity of the rival scientists.

The balancing of power in any bipolar situation is inherently difficult due to the absence of a "balancer." In such a situation, however, a qualitative arms race may be the most effective means of achieving and maintaining parity of power over a long period of time. The inherent tendency toward parity of such a race may to some extent provide a substitute for the missing balancer. In particular, a qualitative race tends to equalize the differences which might otherwise exist between the ability and willingness of a democracy to compete with a totalitarian dictatorship. The great problem of international politics now is to develop forms of international competition to replace the total wars of the first half of the twentieth century. One such alternative is limited war. Another is the qualitative arms race. The emerging pattern of rivalry between the West and the Soviet bloc suggests that these may well be the primary forms of military activity which the two coalitions will employ. As wars become more frightening and less frequent, arms races may become longer and less disastrous. The substitution of the one for the other is certainly no mean step forward in the restriction of violence. In this respect the arms race may serve the same function which war served: "the intensely sharp competitive *preparation* for war by the nations," could become, as William James suggested, *"the real war,* permanent, unceasing. . . ."[28] A qualitative race regularizes this preparation and introduces an element of stability into the relations between the two powers. Even if it were true, as Sir Edward Grey argued, that arms races inevitably foster suspicion and insecurity, these would be small prices to pay for the avoidance of destruction. Until fundamental changes take place in the structure of world politics, a qualitative arms race may well be a most desirable form of competition between the Soviet Union and the United States.

---

[28] *Memories and Studies* (New York, 1912), p. 273.

*"The Washington Naval Treaty,
1922-1936"*

CHARLES H. FAIRBANKS JR.

As America debates whether to ratify the new SALT agreement, it is useful to recall what happened in the first great period of arms limitation agreements, 1921-1936. A brief look at the details of the Washington Naval Treaty of 1922, the most successful of the interwar negotiations, sheds some light on current questions.

Unlike SALT I and II, the Washington treaty involved serious arms *reduction:* Each of the three main naval powers scrapped roughly half their existing battleships and almost all of the enormous tonnage under construction. It was agreed that for a decade no new battleships would be built. The core of the treaty was a ratio freezing approximately the strength in battleships then existing, and extending it to aircraft carriers: The ratio among the United States, Britain and Japan was 5:5:3.

Qualitative limits were imposed as well, limiting battleships to 35,000 tons and cruisers to 10,000 tons (with 8-inch guns). In the London Treaty of 1930 limits were placed on the numbers of other types of ships.

The Washington treaty had real accomplishments. It saved all the countries involved a vast amount of money and stopped for nearly 20 years the increase in battleship size, just then swelling monstrously. The treaty also showed that in circumstances like these, where there was no deep opposition of political interests, stopping an arms race could indeed decrease international tension. Finally, the treaty provided a universal and principled covering which psychologically eased acceptance of shifts in power relationships—Britain's loss of naval superiority for the first time in 200 years and the abandonment of the Anglo-Japanese alliance—that could have been far more disturbing if baldly presented.

At the same time, the treaty turned out not to be, as Lord Balfour, the head of the British delegation, proclaimed, an "absolute unmixed benefit to mankind, which carried no seeds of future misfortune."

To begin with, it soon became apparent that the treaty had actually spurred the arms race in important ways. Stephen Roskill, the naval historian, writes that "all in all, the first effect of the limitation treaty on Britain . . . was to produce greater activity in naval building than at any time since the armistice [of 1918]." No one foresaw this outcome, but it is hardly surprising. To negotiate, a nation needs to carefully compare its forces with those of other countries, highlighting areas of relative weakness. Then, in order to reassure doubters about the treaty, these missing forces must be supplied, as President Carter proposes to do with the MX. It is thus all too easy for the arms limitation process to wind up in incessant arms accumulation to remedy security weaknesses created or brought to light by the original agreements: the equivalent of pouring water into a perforated bucket.

A NEW WEAPON

As soon as the battleship race was halted in the early twenties, a race began in cruisers, which had been relatively neglected. The United States had only three modern cruisers, the British Empire 60. The cruisers constructed after the treaty displaced 10,000 tons, the treaty limit, while almost all existing cruisers were half this size and armed with 6-inch or 4-inch guns rather than 8-inch. The arms limitation treaty had quickly brought into existence a new and much more powerful weapon, the "Treaty Cruiser."

It is easy to see why this was likely to take place. The pace of technological innovation in weapons is normally limited by the fact that military staffs, like all bureaucracies, are embedded in a mass of routine administrative duties. From these ordinary duties there are most likely to emerge conservative, incremental decisions on weapons: Adding a few, or improving the type slightly, with each budget cycle.

A treaty negotiation, on the other hand, forces far-reaching reassessment of weapons policy. To develop their negotiating positions, the American, British and Japanese governments needed to know from their naval staffs what was the most useful type of cruiser. It is scarcely surprising that the answer turned out to be that the optimum cruiser is a cruiser twice as big as existing cruisers.

By a somewhat similar process the Washington treaty encouraged the emergence of the aircraft carrier, a new weapon neglected by the battleship admirals then dominating every major navy. In ordinary circumstances those admirals would never have chosen to invest in aircraft carriers rather than battleships. Once their cherished battleship force had been cut to the bone in negotiations, however, they developed a sudden but natural awareness of the need for aircraft carriers, and discovered that the unfinished hulls of four battleships just stricken under the treaty terms could be converted quite nicely into giant aircraft carriers for the U.S. and Japan.

In two crucial areas, then, the Washington treaty's effort to reduce weapons actually resulted in more weapons and in faster technological development of weapons. The general problem posed by these cases is whether there is any way of preventing such unintended consequences, tied to the negotiating process, from countering the intended arms control results of an agreement. If not, we may be forced to ask whether the arms control *treaty* is a bad means of arms control.

There appeared a second problem as well. As Pearl Harbor made clear, the aircraft carrier was a weapon that, as compared with the battleship, encouraged striking first in a crisis, and therefore somewhat increased the chances of war. The aircraft carrier was far better adapted to carry out swift attack from a distance than the lumbering battleship, while at the same time its thin, gasoline-laden hull could not withstand attack like the battleship's thick carapace.

At Midway and other carrier battles there was a strong tendency for the side that struck first to win. If one wants to do everything that would make war less likely—the primary object of all arms limitation agreements—one will not want to encourage the shifting of the weapons mix towards weapons, like the aircraft carrier, that may encourage a first strike. But the Washington treaty had precisely this effect.

Fortifications—a "weapon" that impedes successful war—were prohibited by the treaty in the Western Pacific. This destabilizing concession had to be made to get Japan to accept the politically disagreeable 5:5:3 ratio. The general spirit that dominated arms limitation efforts in the twenties as in SALT II—the opposition to greater quantities of weapons in the abstract—completely blinded negotiators and planners to the particular effects of specific weapons on the preservation of peace.

Looking back at the twenties, it is not clear whether it was the quantity of weapons in the abstract or the character of specific weapons that held out greater danger of war. In the nuclear age, it seems increasingly clear that any danger of the former kind is outweighed by the destabilizing effect of particular weapons, such as big land-based ballistic missiles like the Soviet SS-18, that can annihilate enemy forces when striking first but are vulnerable themselves to attack.

While the treaty worked in some ways to decrease the chances of war and in other ways to increase it, some of its indirect effects weakened U.S. and British security if war did come.

Public opinion in the United States and Britain tended to be lulled by the treaty into ignoring defense. In ten of the 18 years between the treaty and World War II the U.S. Congress did not authorize the building of a single warship, while Japan laid down several ships every year. The result was that by the late thirties Japan, entitled by the 1922 and 1930 treaties to 60% of U.S. strength, had actually been allowed to build to 80% of parity. It proved impossible to restore the treaty ratio by December 7, 1941. As with any commodity where there was zero demand for ten years, the armor plate and heavy gun industries withered, factories were abandoned and workers were retrained in other trades.

When freed of the treaty limits by Japanese abrogation (as of 1936) the U.S. and Britain continued to build 35,000-ton battleships with 14-inch or 16-inch guns, while Japan went immediately to 64,000 tons and 18-inch guns.

As this suggests, the signatories had different conceptions of what the treaty meant. The United States and Britain tended to see their commitment to the treaty as commitment to the spirit of the treaty, which might call for more than its formal provisions. Japan quite honorably interpreted the treaty to mean the letter of the treaty. To get around treaty limits, Japan laid down submarine tenders that could be quickly converted into aircraft carriers and cruisers whose 6-inch guns could be quickly exchanged for the 8-inch guns of heavy cruisers.

The United States also exploited the treaty provisions in less startling ways. By a somewhat sophistic interpretation of an apparently unrelated clause in the Washington treaty American officials squeezed out another 3,000 tons displacement for their new aircraft carriers, but then nervously did not list it in official tables.

NEW UNCERTAINTY

These cases bring us to a further unintended consequence which the Washington and London treaties share with other arms limitation agreements: They encourage attempts to extract from the treaty unforeseen advantage for one side, and at the extreme, cheating. Deception is always an attractive possibility in arms races, but the need to work within the definite limits imposed by a formal agreement vastly increases the incentives for deception or for testing the limits of the treaty as the U.S. did. This sort of behavior creates in turn new uncertainty, which it is precisely one of the greatest aims of arms limitation agreements to avoid.

The end of the Washington-London treaty system was clear in 1934 when Japan gave the required two years' warning to abrogate the treaty. It is little reproach to an arms limitation treaty that it could not dam up the volcanic forces that had begun to stir and crackle in the Japan of the thirties. But this case does point out a final problem that all arms limitation agreements must face. Arms limitation agreements, which by their very nature involve precise ratios and numbers of arms permitted to each side, are far more specific and detailed than most treaties.

They thus lack the flexibility that enables most international agreements to bend with change and be infused with a new political content—as the meaning of NATO, for example, has shifted substantially over the years. When the rigid structure of an arms limitation agreement can no longer contain changed political forces, it will snap apart. The cost may be heavy: After an arms limitation treaty not renewed, as after a divorce, one cannot return to the starting point.

In the case of the Washington-London treaty system, by the middle thirties Japan had experienced a vast economic and technological growth relative to Britain and the United States; Japan was on the march, while the United States and Britain had become more passive in foreign policy. The naval ratio 5:5:3 inevitably presented itself to many Japanese as the symbol of an inferior position in the international community that no longer corresponded to realities. At the same time the United States and Britain were understandably unwilling to change a ratio that they felt had been definitely nailed down in 1922. The outcome was the 1936 abrogation of a treaty that had already for several years bred in Japan resentment rather than harmony.

Arms control agreements are a means to bring about one of the loftiest human aims, the preservation of peace. By a natural process we have seen the tool as a thing as noble as its purpose. But over the last 58 years of arms limitations agreements it has appeared that this tool has some inherent tendencies to defeat the purpose for which we are using it. From such treaties there have repeatedly emerged major unintended side effects that did not help or, at worst, directly opposed the preservation of peace.

Some specific arms limitation agreements are good on balance, as the Washington treaty may have been. But the architects of an arms limitation treaty in the 1970s have a duty to explain how they have fashioned its specific provisions to deal with the kinds of unintended consequences that have come to light since the twenties.

Concepts in the 1970s:
The Search for Sufficiently Equivalent
Countervailing Parity

WARNER R. SCHILLING

The attainment by the Soviet Union of numerical equality with the United States in strategic delivery vehicles was an event of major military and political significance. Starting in 1964, when the Soviet Union had 389 strategic delivery vehicles and the United States had 1,880, the Soviet Union had surpassed the United States in the number of ICBMs by 1970, in the number of SLBMs by 1975, and in the total number of ICMBs, SLBMs, and long-range bombers by 1973. In June 1979, when the two powers formally agreed to the common ceiling of 2,400 vehicles, the Soviet Union actually had 2,504 deployed delivery vehicles and the United States 2,058.

The major military effect of the Soviet build-up to date has been to increase greatly the amount of death and destruction the Soviet Union could produce in the United States, by either a first or a second strike, without significantly affecting the amount of death and destruction the United States could produce in the Soviet Union. Indeed, measured in terms of warheads surviving a Soviet first strike, the second-strike capability of the United States was larger in 1980 than it was in 1964, when the Soviet build-up began.

A nuclear exchange in the early 1960s probably would have cost the Soviet Union some three to four times as many fatalities as those suffered by the United States, even if the Soviet Union had struck first, whereas by the late 1970s, the Soviets were in a position, at least in a first strike, to inflict more fatalities on the United States than the United States, in its second strike, could inflict on the Soviet Union. Most would agree that, in a meaningful sense of the term, the Soviets have moved from a position of strategic inferiority to one of strategic parity, and that this event has complicated, not eased, the American task of coping with Soviet purposes and power.

The purpose of this article is to review the reasons why the United States did not contest the Soviet build-up; to describe how the United States has defined its strategic objectives in light of this build-up; to

From *International Security,* Fall, 1981, pp. 17–36. Reprinted by permission of the MIT Press Journals.

analyze some of the problems the United States has met in trying to implement those objectives; and to present some summary comments on the current state of Soviet-American parity and the prospects for the near future.

THE UNITED STATES ACCEPTS PARITY

Why did the United States fail to contest the Soviet build-up? The answer must start with some conception of what the United States would have had to have done in order to have "matched" the increase in Soviet offensive forces. Would this have required the United States to have maintained its 1964 *ratio* of superiority over the Soviet Union in delivery vehicles or warheads? Certainly the United States did not do this. Given the 1980 Soviet force of some 2,500 delivery vehicles and 6,000 warheads, the United States would now need about 12,000 delivery vehicles and 50,400 warheads, instead of its present force of some 2,058 vehicles and 9,200 warheads. Would the United States have matched the Soviet build-up if it had maintained its 1964 *margin* of superiority in numbers of delivery vehicles or warheads? Actually, in the case of warheads, the United States did do this; it had about 3,400 more warheads than the Soviet Union in 1964 and about 3,200 more warheads in 1980. Or, since delivery vehicles are potential targets for warheads, is the most appropriate measure the ratio between the warheads of the United States and the delivery vehicles of the Soviet Union? In 1964, this ratio was 8.7, and it was 3.7 in 1980. Does this mean that the Soviet Union has yet to achieve parity?

These numbers are cited to illustrate an obvious but important point: the differences in these or any other numbers used to measure the state of the Soviet-American strategic balance have to be related to differences in the actual results or outcomes of a nuclear war before they can be said to have any military meaning. Dropping nuclear weapons on a country is an act subject to diminishing returns. Accordingly, maintaining a constant ratio or margin of superiority over an opponent in some index of nuclear power (delivery vehicles, warheads, megatons) is not an act of constant military consequence. The military consequence, for example, of the United States' being able to deliver eight times as many warheads on Soviet cities as the Soviet Union could deliver on American cities will be significantly affected by whether the Soviet capability is 100, 1,000, or 10,000 warheads.

Expressed in terms of war outcomes—i.e., the actual amount of death and destruction a nuclear war would produce on any given set of targets—a successful American effort to match or offset the Soviet build-up would have prevented the increase in Soviet offensive forces from a) increasing the amount of death and destruction the Soviet Union could cause in the United States, and b) decreasing the amount of death and destruction the United States could cause in the Soviet

Union. Seen in these terms, it is clear that the United States did match or offset the Soviet build-up in the second respect. Since 1964, as best can be judged from the public record, there has been no real change in the amount of death and destruction the United States could cause in the Soviet Union in the event of a major nuclear war.

The failure of the United States to match or offset the Soviet build-up was, then, the failure to prevent that build-up from increasing the amount of death and destruction the Soviet Union could cause in the United States. How might the United States have prevented this increase? To have kept the amount of death and destruction the Soviet Union could cause constant (i.e., to 1964 levels), the United States would have needed to add to its capabilities for damage limitation: to its ability to destroy through counterforce strikes (using its own offensive forces) Soviet ICBMs, SLBMs, and strategic bombers before they could be launched against the United States; to its ability to destroy through active defenses (air and ballistic missile defense systems and antisubmarine warfare [ASW] systems) the Soviet forces which would survive the counterforce attack; and to its ability to protect through passive defenses (shelters and other means for offsetting the effects of nuclear explosions) the American population, industry, and other targets of value from the explosions of the Soviet warheads that would penetrate American defenses.

In the late 1960s, the ability of the United States to add significantly to its damage-limiting capabilities by adding only to its offensive forces was limited. There seemed no certain way to destroy Soviet SLBMs, at least once they were deployed on an increasing number of submarines. And while the deployment of MIRVs would give the United States the potential for a counterforce capability against Soviet ICBMs and bomber bases, this potential could be exercised effectively only through a preemptive first strike, one which would catch the Soviet forces before the Soviets had actually launched their attack. This was not a strategy, however, for which there was much political support in the United States, and it was, in any event, a strategy which the Soviet Union might offset by launching its land-based forces on warning, i.e., in the interval between the time the Soviets detected that the Americans had launched their missiles and the time their warheads exploded on target.

The key to keeping the increase in Soviet offensive forces from increasing the amount of death and destruction the Soviets could cause in the United States lay in additional American programs for defense: civil defense, air defense, and ballistic missile defense. But these were precisely the programs the United States decided not to pursue, and it was through its failure to deploy these defensive systems, rather than by failing to maintain some ratio or margin in offensive forces, that the United States lost its opportunity to maintain nuclear superiority.

The decision not to deploy a major ABM system to protect American cities was the critical choice in what was, in effect, an American decision not to try to prevent, by adding to America's damage-limiting capabilities, the Soviet build-up from increasing the amount of death and destruction the Soviet Union could produce in the United States. . . . Why did the United States decide not to deploy a major ABM system for city defense? This decision was influenced by technical reservations about the efficacy of the system then available and by the belief, on the part of some, that since peace had to rest on the Soviet-American balance of terror, it would be best for each state to remain naked before its enemy. But the primary argument against the deployment of an ABM system for city defense was that it would only lead to a Soviet-American arms race without any resulting military gain.

Secretary of Defense McNamara was an articulate advocate of the thesis that, if the Americans deployed an ABM system for the purpose of reducing the death and destruction the Soviets could cause in the United States, the Soviets would respond by building whatever additional offensive forces would be required to offset the effects of the ABM system. Since the United States would do the same if the Soviets deployed an ABM system, McNamara concluded that it would be in the interest of both powers to ban the deployment of ABMs. Otherwise, the superpowers would be forced into an expensive and potentially dangerous arms race which would, at best, leave them in the end exactly where they had started in terms of the death and destruction each could cause the other.

This argument had a counter. As the Joint Chiefs of Staff pointed out, since the United States had by far the larger gross national product, the United States could outspend and outbuild the Soviets in the deployment of both defensive and offensive forces. Thus, if the United States was willing to persist in the armaments competition and spend whatever it took, the United States would, in the end, regain and retain the ability to inflict much more destruction on the Soviet Union than the Soviet Union could cause in the United States.

Given this argument, it is clear why President Johnson decided in 1967 to seek an agreement with the Soviet Union to ban the deployment of ABMs. He was in no political position to spend whatever it took in a major new strategic arms competition with the Soviet Union. He had the Vietnam War and the Great Society to finance. . . . Essentially the same considerations led President Nixon in 1969 to continue Johnson's policy. Nixon, too, had the Vietnam War on his hands, and he came to office intent on reducing, not increasing, the federal budget. Moreover, both presidents confronted an American public not disposed to support programs for nuclear defense. . . . The acquisition of offensive forces can be supported, however reluctantly, in the belief that they are necessary to prevent a nuclear war. The rationale for defensive programs, however, necessarily entails the belief that a nuclear war might actually occur, and this the attentive public and most elites find a very uncomfortable and therefore unpopular suggestion.

Why did the United States agree to the other form of parity the Soviet Union has achieved: equality in the number of strategic nuclear delivery vehicles (as SALT–counted)? The American decision not to offset the destructive effect of the Soviet build-up by increasing the damage-limiting forces of the United States was not accompanied by a decision to accept equality with the Soviet Union in the number of delivery vehicles. American intelligence underestimated the rate and duration of the Soviet build-up, and in the mid- and late-1960s, American officials continued to talk about the need for and the prospect of continued American numerical superiority over the Soviet Union. Thus, the SALT proposal designed by the Johnson Administration for offensive forces called for a freeze in the number of ICBMs and SLBMs in the expectation that such a freeze would leave the United States with the larger number of missiles.

The United States never decided to seek equality with the Soviet Union in the total number of delivery vehicles; it was driven to that position by the course of the Soviet build-up. The Nixon Administration developed a proposal providing for equality in the number of ballistic missiles (but excluding bombers, of which the United States had the larger number) when it became clear that the total number of Soviet missiles would equal that of the United States. The administration changed to a proposal for equality in the total number of missiles and bombers when it became clear that this Soviet total would equal that of the United States. Then, as the Soviet build-up continued, the administration was driven to proposals designed simply to bring a halt to that build-up. This was finally done in May 1972, in an agreement which limited the superpowers to the number of ballistic missile launchers they each then had built or building. The resulting numbers were hardly equal: 2,358 for the Soviet Union, and 1,710 for the United States.

By the early 1970s, then, the Soviet Union had achieved parity (or better) with the United States in the total number of strategic nuclear delivery vehicles, as well as in the ability to inflict death and destruction, and this new numerical relationship was codified in the SALT II Treaty. Of the two forms of parity, the numerical relationship has received by far the most attention, because of the publicity and debate associated with the SALT agreements. But the SALT numbers, whether the 2,400 total or the others specified in the 1979 treaty (e.g., those relating to the numerical limits on launchers for MIRVed delivery vehicles, the maximum number of re-entry vehicles permitted on various missiles, or the provisions relating to launch-weight and throw-weight) fix so few of the variables that would affect the actual outcome of a nuclear war (whether all-out or limited, long or short), that they cannot be taken as a meaningful guide to either the absolute or the relative military capability of either superpower.

PARITY AND U.S. STRATEGIC CONCEPTS

How has parity affected the strategic objectives and concepts of the United States? The decision not to offset the increase in Soviet offensive forces by major additions to the capabilities of the United States for damage limitation still left open the question of what the United States would do in response to the Soviet build-up. At the most general and important level of policy, the United States decided to do nothing. It decided not to change any of the three major purposes for which it maintained strategic forces: to deter a nuclear attack on the United States and its forces overseas; to deter a nuclear attack on its allies; and to help to deter a conventional attack on its allies.

The question of just what strategic concepts would guide American policy in the effort to maintain these major objectives in an age of parity was formally addressed by the Nixon Administration in 1969 through the means of a National Security Council study memorandum and a subsequent NSC decision memorandum. In January 1970, President Nixon christened the results of this study the strategy of "sufficiency," and the specific concepts involved were later revealed by Secretary of Defense Laird in his annual posture statements.

In the decade since, there have been major changes in American acquisition policy (the number and kind of strategic forces bought, or not bought); in deployment policy (where and how those forces are based and on what kind of alert); and in employment policy (the plans for actually using strategic forces). But there have been relatively few changes in American strategic concepts, that is, in the terms and propositions with which acquisition, deployment, and employment policy have been debated and justified (although not always decided), at least as those concepts have been revealed publicly by U.S. declaratory policy. . . . In essence, all [subsequent] secretaries have embroidered on the requirements first listed by Laird—that the United States should maintain strategic forces capable of 1) assured destruction and 2) flexible options; forces that are 3) equal to those of the Soviet Union and 4) perceived as equal; and forces that 5) contribute to crisis stability.

ASSURED DESTRUCTION

In 1965, McNamara identified assured destruction with the ability to destroy about 33 percent of the population and 66 percent of the industry of the Soviet Union. These figures owed more to his appreciation for the diminishing returns that would follow from the allocation of additional forces to produce higher levels of destruction than to any analysis of how Soviet leaders might actually weigh urban-industrial damage against the possible gains from hypothetical wars. It is for this reason that the figures have remained relatively constant ever since.

It would be a mistake, however, to conclude that American policy has defined its requirements for second-strike targets solely or even mainly in terms of blowing up people and plant in the Soviet Union. . . . American employment policy has always aimed at the destruction of military as well as nonmilitary targets in the Soviet Union, and since 1974, at least, the United States has not even targeted people or industry *per se* but rather Soviet "recovery resources," with a reported requirement to destroy 70 percent of such resources. . . . It is also clear, as Secretary Brown stated in his report for FY 1981, that the United States designs its strategic forces to destroy the military and political power of the Soviet state, as well as its cities and citizens. Less clear is why the United States is not more explicit in its declaratory policy about its plans and capabilities for producing destruction in the Soviet Union. The purpose of the U.S. strategic force is, after all, to deter the Soviets, not to surprise them with more or different destruction than they had expected.

Parity, in sum, has not substantially affected American plans and capabilities for assured destruction. The recent emphasis in declaratory policy on the American ability to destroy Soviet political and military targets (as compared to industrial-urban targets) probably reflects some changes in U.S. acquisition and employment policy, but if so, they are developments which are evolutionary in character (rather than the result of major changes in priorities), and they owe more to changes in American judgments about the kinds of costs that will deter Soviet leaders than they do to changes in the level of Soviet forces.

FLEXIBLE OPTIONS

The United States has long had an interest in a strategy which provided it with more choices than doing nothing or launching immediate, all-out strikes against the full range of targets in the Soviet Union, and the SIOP (Single Integrated Operations Plan) has contained a number of such options (e.g., strikes against only Soviet strategic forces or other military targets) since the early 1960s. Thus, in his Ann Arbor speech in 1962, Secretary McNamara stated that the United States was prepared, even after a Soviet attack, to withhold strikes against Soviet cities provided the Soviet Union exercised a similar restraint.

The advent of parity has increased the interest of the United States in adding to the range of these choices. . . . The United States has sought to maintain not only a secure second-strike capability for assured destruction but a capability that does not have to be used in a hurry: hence the U.S. interest in acquiring strategic forces and associated C^3I

systems that can endure if withheld from use. Given a Soviet capability to match the United States in the amount of death and destruction it can produce, the United States has nothing to gain from rushing to all-out war. If nuclear weapons are to be used at all, it makes more sense to use them selectively against non-urban targets, keeping the bulk of U.S. forces in reserve to hold Soviet cities at risk and, thereby, hopefully, deterring the Soviets from attacking American cities.

The policy of planning to initiate the use of nuclear weapons to respond to what otherwise might be a successful Soviet conventional attack on Western Europe continues to be most controversial. Flexible options involving theater as well as strategic nuclear weapons presumably have been designed for three different purposes: to make the Soviets think about the risks they are running (but what if they decide to keep on fighting?); to make the Soviets sorry by destroying targets of value, e.g., their political control structure (but how does this save Western Europe?); and to make the Soviets lose by destroying their military forces (but if the Soviets respond in kind, what keeps Western Europe from becoming a radioactive Ben Tre?)

Specialists have argued over the desirability and feasibility of such policies for more than twenty years, as well as over the desirability and feasibility of alternative policies (e.g., NATO conventional forces strong enough to defend Western Europe without relying on the first use of nuclear weapons, or the development of European nuclear forces strong enough to make a European first use credible). . . . Parity has not led the United States to back away from plans and preparations for the first use of nuclear weapons in defense of Western Europe.

The probability that the United States would actually carry out its nuclear threat, in the judgment of the present writer, has been little affected by the advent of parity, and the credibility of the threat ought, therefore, to be about as good as it ever was, which is a carefully chosen phrase. On the face of it, if the costs of an all-out nuclear war have risen from 30 million to 140 million dead Americans, the United States ought to be significantly less willing to risk such a war in defense of Western Europe. But this argument begs the question of how willing, on a scale of 1 to 10, the United States was to risk 30 million fatalities. More to the point, the argument assumes that statesmen have some calculus through which they can rationally weigh their objects against such variations in their risks and costs, which, of course, they do not.

In the event, an American use of nuclear weapons in defense of Western Europe will occur when and if American leaders conclude that, if they do not fire a limited number of nuclear weapons now (to try to stop the Soviets from overrunning Western Europe), they will face a major nuclear exchange later (with a Soviet Union bloated from conquest and disdainful of American will). For a choice of this order, the fact that the costs of a major exchange have increased will be at best irrelevant. As for the credibility of the American nuclear threat, there is certainly little political logic in the argument of those who find it hard to believe that the United States would be willing to initiate a limited use of nuclear weapons in order to keep from losing Western Europe, but easy to believe that once those weapons had been used, the Soviet Union would be quite willing to engage in a continuing and escalating exchange in order to gain Western Europe. Parity has not, after all, decreased the costs of all-out war for the Soviet Union.

STRATEGIC EQUALITY

The American decision not to hold to 1964 levels the amount of death and destruction that the Soviets could produce in the United States did not answer the question of whether there was any limit at all, relative or absolute, that the United States would try to place on the military consequences of the Soviet build-up.

One obvious answer was to maintain a balance in which the United States and the Soviet Union could produce equal amounts of death and destruction, and this was the decision reached by the Nixon Administration in the fall of 1969 in its decision memorandum on strategic forces. As explained later by Secretary Laird, the United States would maintain forces capable of preventing the Soviet Union from "gaining the ability to cause considerably greater urban/industrial destruction than the United States could inflict on the Soviets.". . . Thus, the review of strategic policy conducted by the Carter Administration in 1977 reportedly concluded that a major nuclear exchange would probably result in a minimum of 140 million American fatalities, as compared to about 113 million Soviet fatalities.

The disparity in these expected fatalities (which represent about 65 percent of the American and 44 percent of the Soviet population) owes more to differences in the target structure of the two countries—the United States has a higher percentage of its population in cities—than it does to differences in their strategic forces, although if the yields of American warheads were as large as those of the Soviets, the disparity would be less marked. In the case of industry, destruction still would be approximately equal, for in this case the target structure is more nearly identical, in the sense that the percentage of industrial installations that can be destroyed by any given number of 100-kiloton weapons is about the same in both countries.

Whether the difference between 65 percent and 44 percent fatalities is a case of a "considerably greater" difference (e.g., one that would lead the Soviets to believe that they had the superior bargaining position in time of crisis: "my unmitigated horrible catastrophe would be better than your horrible unmitigated catastrophe") is, of course, a matter on which judgments can differ. But the issue does raise the question of what disparity the United States would consider significant: 70–35? 66–22? 80–20?

PERCEIVED EQUALITY

Throughout the 1970s, the United States has been concerned with the appearance of the strategic balance, as well as with its reality, and has been intent on maintaining forces that are not only equal to those of the Soviet Union but are perceived as equal. . . . The Soviet build-up has enabled the Soviet Union, over time, to surpass the United States in such measures as the total number of missiles, the total number of delivery vehicles, and the total amount of megatonnage. Moreover, while the United States has retained a lead in the total number of warheads (as a result of its earlier deployment of MIRVs), the larger throw-weight of the Soviet missiles gives the Soviet Union the potential (unless its deployment of MIRVs is constrained by the terms of SALT II or some comparable agreement) to overtake the United States in the total number of warheads as well.

These Soviet numerical advantages have led many Americans to fear that the Soviet Union might be tempted to use the threat of nuclear war to intimidate or blackmail the United States, its allies, or other states. Equally disturbing to the United States is the possibility that its allies or other states, believing that the Soviet Union has the superior nuclear force, might be led to yield or accommodate to Soviet interests, and the Soviets could gain the political results of nuclear superiority without even having to threaten, much less fight, a nuclear war.

In theory, of course, the United States—in designing its own forces for assured destruction, flexible options, and strategic equality—has already built the forces it needs to deter attacks or threats by the Soviet Union and to deny the Soviet Union the ability to achieve any meaningful advantage, political or military, from a nuclear exchange, whether limited or all-out, short or long. But Washington is nonetheless seized with the worry that the Soviet Union or other states might be led to contrary judgments by examining the charts and graphs (all supplied by the United States) that compare the forces of the super-powers in terms of various static and dynamic measures: numbers of warheads, delivery vehicles, equivalent megatons, countermilitary potential, or the ratio of post-exchange warheads, or megatons, etc. And it has been, therefore, U.S. policy that all of these measures cannot be permitted to favor the Soviet Union and that a Soviet lead in some must be offset by an American lead in others.

It is at least plausible that most foreign elites are poorly informed about the various numerical measures that preoccupy Washington (if not indifferent to those measures); that they confuse trends with balances (the Soviets are gaining; the Soviets are ahead), and weapon developments with weapon deployments (the Americans have tested cruise missiles; the Americans have cruise missiles); and that their judgments about the state of the Soviet-American nuclear balance are significantly influenced by their perceptions of the conventional weapons balance and by their judgments about other aspects of state power (e.g., the state of the American economy), as well as by their reactions to major foreign-policy and military events (e.g., Vietnam, Iran, Afghanistan).

For all this, the American concern for how the strategic balance is perceived by friends, foes, and allies is not unwise. It is simply misplaced. What is questionable is the present American policy of focussing that concern on the numerical differences between Soviet and American forces as expressed in various static and dynamic indices. These numerical differences are of consequence only to the extent that they can affect the amount of destruction that would occur to targets of value in the event of a nuclear exchange. Accordingly, the numerical differences need to be translated into war outcomes before their military consequence, if any, can be judged.

A Soviet "lead" that could result in an adverse war outcome should, of course, be corrected. But numerical differences that cannot be related to adverse war outcomes should be addressed by American declaratory policy, not redressed by American acquisition policy. The appropriate American response in this case is not to add to some component of its strategic forces in order to change the direction of a curve on a chart, but to explain to its allies and friends (and to the Soviet Union, if need be) that the numerical differences in question would have no significant bearing on the outcome of a nuclear exchange, either in terms of the kind and number of targets the United States is intent on destroying or in terms of the ability of the United States to prevent the Soviet Union from achieving its own objectives.

CRISIS STABILITY

One of the most important American strategic objectives has been the maintenance of a strategic balance that provides for crisis stability: a balance in which neither side has any incentive to strike first in time of crisis. Ideally, this entails a balance in which neither side can see any difference between striking first or striking second, either in terms of the destruction it could cause the enemy or in terms of the destruction it would receive itself. In reality, of course, there will always be some gain from striking the first blow, if only for the disruption it would bring to the other side's capabilities for C^3I. Nonetheless, in an age of parity, the United States has everything to gain from a balance which permits the Soviets to believe that, however probable war may seem in time of crisis, they have nothing to lose by waiting, that time (and further negotiation, even at the risk of an American first strike) will not work against them.

Throughout the 1970s, the concern of the United States for crisis stability has been focussed on the issue of the prelaunch survivability of its fixed-site ICBMs. . . . The Soviets will shortly have the theoretical ability to destroy about 90 percent of the U.S. ICBM force (1,054 missiles presently containing about 24 percent of the U.S. warheads), and the Soviets could do this by firing as few as 210 of their 1,400 ICBMs. This, it is alleged, would give them an incentive to fire first in time of crisis. The United States has, therefore, decided to reduce the vulnerability of its ICBMs by deploying a new missile (the MX) in a mobile mode. But the MX will have the capability (either in conjunction with part of the Minuteman force or alone, given a reprogramming capability) of destroying more than 90 percent of the Soviet ICBM force, which presently contains about 75 percent of the Soviet warheads. This, it is alleged, will also give the Soviets an incentive to fire first in time of crisis.

The United States has rejected one answer to this apparent dilemma: the deployment of a mobile missile with a less effective countersilo capability than the MX, which would insure the prelaunch survivability of the U.S. ICBM force without jeopardizing the survivability of the Soviet ICBM force. The reason, as stated by Secretary Brown, is that strategic equality (both real and perceived) requires that the United States have as effective a prompt countersilo capability as the Soviet Union and that both powers be required to cope with the costs of off-setting the MIRV threat to the fixed-site ICBM.

This position illustrates the relative priority of crisis stability among the strategic objectives of the United States. The position also appears to assume that the Soviets will respond to the deployment of MX by adding to their submarine-launched missiles and/or expending the large resources necessary to provide themselves with a mobile ICBM, rather than choosing potentially more destabilizing responses, such as doing nothing or placing their ICMBs in a launch-on-warning posture.

How might the countersilo capabilities involved actually affect crisis stability? A demonstration that the Soviets could destroy 90 percent of the American ICBM force is a demonstration only that the Soviets could destroy 90 percent of the ICBM force. It says nothing about the kind of gains the Soviets could achieve in terms of damage limitation from such a strike. Obviously, if all the United States had were fixed-site ICBMs, the Soviets would gain a great deal. On the other hand, if the United States had 100,000 survivable warheads in its submarine and bomber forces, the Soviets would gain nothing by eliminating some 1,900 ICBM warheads. Where, between these limiting cases, is the present strategic balance? Would a Soviet first strike serve only to reduce their fatalities from 45 percent to 40 percent of their population, or the destruction of their industrial installations from 75 percent to 71 percent? What incentive would differences of this order give Soviet statesmen to strike first in time of crisis, given that the best way to avoid destruction is to avert war?

Clearly, without information about what the destruction of this or that percentage of the ICBM force would mean in terms of war outcomes, it is difficult to reach a judgment about the extent to which the vulnerability of the Minuteman force will or will not present the Soviets with an incentive to strike first is a crisis. There is, of course, no way in which that vulnerability can be seen as a gain for crisis stability, but even after the deployment of the MX, the United States would still retain some 80 percent of its ICBMs, 66 percent of its ICBM megatonnage, and 41 percent of its ICBM warheads in the fixed-site mode. Why, then, would not the deployment of the MX still leave the Soviets with an incentive to strike first in time of crisis?

Would the deployment of the MX undermine crisis stability by threatening the Soviet ICBM force? If numbers tell the story, the United States can pose a greater threat to Soviet ICBMs than the Soviets can pose to American ICBMs, even without the MX. By 1982, given the information publicly available about the capabilities each side is expected to have by that date if they continue to adhere to the terms of SALT II, the Soviets could, by firing some 210 SS-18s (using some 2,100 warheads) destroy about 91 percent of the American ICBMs and thereby destroy some 1,960 warheads, about 18 percent of the expected U.S. total by that date. But the United States, by firing 550 Minuteman IIIs (using 1,650 warheads with the presently programmed improvements in their yield and accuracy) and by concentrating its fire on the 820 MIRVed Soviet ICBMs, could destroy some 4,300 Soviet warheads, about 39 percent of the expected 1982 Soviet total.

What difference would this make for the amount of destruction the Soviet Union could cause in the United States? Why would this not give the Soviet Union an incentive to strike first in time of crisis? Why would the deployment of the MX give the Soviets any greater incentive for such a first strike, especially since they can be expected to have added greatly to their sea-based warheads by the time the MX is deployed? The strategic debate has focussed on numbers of missiles and warheads as if they were living creatures whose survival was of value in their own right, to the near exclusion of any effort to relate these military means to potential differences in the war outcomes among which statesmen might actually be able to discriminate in terms of values about which they do care.

American strategy is much clearer on how it proposes to prevent nuclear war than it is on its objectives should deterrence fail and war actually start. The present strategy of countervailing power, most recently expressed in Carter's Presidential Directive 59 of August 1980, a strategy for denying the Soviets any prospect of victory on whatever political or military terms they might care to define it, has a fine Old Testament ring to it: an eye for an eye, a tooth for a tooth, and, if need be, city for city. But if war should start, how is it to be ended? Are the superpowers doomed to engage in a Kwakiutl Indian potlatch ceremony, tossing troops, missiles, and finally cities into the nuclear fire to show how much they value Western Europe or whatever else may be at stake in the conflict?

Clearly, more thought needs to be given to strategies for war termination, and the proper beginning is to consider how a nuclear war might begin. Given parity and the mutual destruction it presently permits, sane statesmen will have to be driven, cornered, and boxed into firing nuclear weapons. They will resort to nuclear war only in the belief that they cannot avoid it. It follows that if the war is to be stopped, statesmen will need to be persuaded that the perceptions that led them to war were wrong or that things have now changed and there is more room for political negotiation than they had earlier thought.

To this end, military policy can contribute by providing forces and strategies that permit at least the possibility of limiting the war, forces and strategies that can buy time, not consume it. The American interest in planning flexible options and in the acquisition of forces that can be withheld from use without cost to their later effectiveness is, therefore, an important step in the right direction. But it is only the first step, for, in the age of parity, once a nuclear war starts, the United States and the Soviet Union will limit damage, if at all, by the exercise of political, not nuclear initiatives.

THE PROSPECTS FOR PARITY

What are the prospects for strategic parity in the 1980s? Many Americans . . . now have serious reservations about the concept of parity and the SALT agreements associated with it. These American critics can be grouped into three schools of thought. There are those who believe that the United States does not have parity (that the strategic balance as codified in SALT II actually favors the Soviet Union). There are those who believe that the United States cannot get parity (that the Soviets are intent on strategic superiority, an objective which makes the effort to negotiate parity through SALT at best infeasible and at worst an exercise leading to a false sense of security). And there are those who believe that the United States should not want parity (that its own military objectives, particularly the credibility of its nuclear guarantees to its allies, are better served by superiority).

The issues associated with these three arguments are complex, and only a few general comments can be made here. With regard to the question of whether SALT II provides for parity, it is important to distinguish between numerical and military parity. The primary purpose of the treaty was to provide a means for codifying parity in the number of deployed strategic delivery vehicles, and this was done by counting silos, submarine launch tubes, and certain kinds of bombers. The terms of the treaty also permit, if the parties exercise all the options permitted, each side to have an equal number of warheads. Given the need to count weapon characteristics that could be unilaterally verified and the ambiguous character of the Soviet Backfire bomber, the treaty probably provides about as feasibly as one could for numerical equality in deployed strategic delivery vehicles.

Does this mean that the treaty provides for military parity, for equality in the ability to produce death and destruction? The answer is obvious: SALT II does not insure military parity. There is too much left out. There are, for example, no limits on defensive systems (air defense, civil defense, and ASW systems), and there are no provisions governing the reliability of delivery vehicles or the yields and accuracies of the warheads they can carry, not to mention the absence of any terms affecting the strategy and tactics with which each side can employ its strategic forces.

The best that SALT agreements can do is to bound a few of the characteristics of each side's strategic forces. Within these limits, a number of war outcomes might be possible. Thus, to lay the burden of insuring military equality on any SALT agreement dealing with offensive weapons is to mistake the potentiality of the instrument.

The only appropriate question to ask of SALT II, or of any comparable treaty, is whether its provisions prevent the United States from achieving military parity. In this connection, the most telling criticism of the SALT II Treaty relates to the inability of the United States to persuade the Soviets to reduce the throw-weight of their strategic forces by eliminating some or all of their SS-18 missiles. The Soviet advantage in throw-weight gives them the greater megatonnage which, *ceteris paribus,* gives them a greater capability for destruction. But in comparing Soviet and American strategic forces, very little is *paribus.* Thus, if the Soviets were to substitute their "lighter" SS-19 missiles for their SS-18s, or even if they were to dismantle their SS-18s in return for the dismantling of an equal number of American Minuteman III missiles, the Soviets would still retain a large advantage in megatonnage. Moreover, as previously noted, the disparity in fatalities that a nuclear war might bring owes more to the asymmetry in the distribution of the populations in the two countries than it does to the difference in their total megatonnage.

What of the argument that the Soviets are not interested in parity, in a balance providing for equal destruction, but are intent on superiority and victory? Soviet declaratory policy has . . . always placed a greater emphasis on strategies for preemption and launching-on-warning than does at least current American doctrine. These pronouncements have not been matched, however, by Soviet deployment policy. The Soviets keep relatively few of their ballistic missile-firing submarines at sea; their bombers are not on alert; and until recently neither were most of their ICBMs.

More consequential, in the judgment of most Americans, are the Soviet statements stressing the need for war-fighting, war-winning capabilities, in contrast to the American interest in stable deterrence through mutual assured destruction. In this case, Soviet declaratory policy is matched by a Soviet acquisition policy that is clearly intent on a damage-limiting capability. The Soviets have developed a counter-silo capability with their ICBMs; they allocate large resources to air defense; they are striving to improve their forces for ASW (as is also the United States); and the Soviet civil defense program is better funded, better organized, and potentially far more effective than that of the United States.

To date, none of these efforts have gained the Soviets a major damage-limiting capability, but that does not detract from the seriousness of their effort or their determination to gain as decisive a military advantage as they can. In this respect, Soviet policy probably owes less to insights from Lenin or Clausewitz than it does to the interest of the professional military in winning, not losing wars, although if the Soviet military have a clear operational definition of what would constitute a "victory" in a major nuclear exchange, it is well hidden. As for Soviet civilian leaders, they are probably more interested in neutralizing U.S. strategic power than in engaging it. If the fear of retaliation can ground SAC in the event of a European war, this is, for Soviet purposes, as good as destroying it.

Does soviet strategy, then make parity an infeasible American objective? Again, the distinction between numerical parity, as codified by SALT, and military parity is critical. The Soviets may well be genuine in their commitment to the numerical limitations reached in SALT and to the principle of equality in numbers of delivery vehicles or warheads. But they no doubt also see SALT, as they saw détente in general, as a framework for continued competition and are determined, within the constraints of SALT, to secure whatever military advantages they can.

American policy needs, therefore, to recognize that the case for SALT II (or any comparable agreement), as a means for placing equal numerical limits on certain characteristics of the offensive forces of the two sides, does not stand or fall on the extent of the Soviet commitment to equal military outcomes. The issue is whether the United States would find it easier to deny the Soviets any expectation of victory or advantage within the constraints of a SALT agreement or without them. Since SALT II does not prevent the United States from deploying any weapons it presently considers necessary to implement its strategy of countervailing power, and since the treaty does bound the Soviet threat in at least some important dimensions, the United States would probably find it cheaper to insure military parity within the constraints of the agreement than it would without them.

But is parity a desirable goal? Parity, in both its numerical and military sense, may be compatible with SALT II and capable of being maintained within its limits, but why should the United States settle for a strategy of denial, a strategy that commits it to an unending effort to offset Soviet initiatives, with the consequent risk that its reactions may not always be timely? Why not, instead, regain American superiority?

A return to American superiority (to a balance in which the death and destruction in the Soviet Union would be far greater than that in the United States) would be the clearest and most decisive way of insuring that the Soviets saw no prospect of victory in a nuclear war; would restore vitality to America's nuclear guarantees to its allies; and would help put an end to the worries (or hopes) of those who believe the long-run trends of global power are running in favor of the Soviet Union. Moreover, should deterrence ever fail, American superiority would provide a far more certain means for limiting damage than the exercise of frantic political initiatives to negotiate an end to the war before it terminated in an all-out exchange. Superiority would not, of course, insure the United States against extensive destruction in a nuclear war, but if the United States could develop the capability to reduce expected fatalities to even 20 percent of the population, this would be an act of immeasurable political and military consequence.

As pointed out in the second section of this article, a return to American superiority would require the United States to do far more than add to the quantity and quality of its offensive forces (the MX, Trident II, cruise missiles, and a new strategic bomber). To reduce significantly the destruction the Soviet Union could cause in the United States would require a massive deployment of effective defensive systems: for ballistic missile defense; for air defense; for ASW; and for civil defense.

Above all, the United States would require the determination to wage a long and costly armaments race with the Soviet Union. A Soviet Union presently intent on superiority can hardly be expected to acquiesce in a return to strategic inferiority. It will be necessary for the United States to offset the Soviet offsets that offset America's offsets to their offsets and to persist in this effort. But the United States has the larger and more efficient economy and the more sophisticated technology, and in the end, given the will (and given, especially, effective new technologies for ballistic missile defense), the United States could prevail until the Soviets were finally quantitatively and qualitatively outbuilt and outclassed.

Starting with Dwight Eisenhower, six presidents have looked at this prospect, blanched, and backed off. They must have seen something! And what they saw were inordinately high costs: war-level military budgets sustained over an indefinite number of years, with all that those budgets would entail for domestic programs and services, for the American standard of living, and for the control of the American economy. They also saw an American public and Congress, not to mention members of the Executive and other elites, who showed no real disposition for preparing to fight (as compared to preparing to prevent) a nuclear war, and who evidenced no faith in the arguments of those who contend that there can be significant differences in the degree of disaster that a nuclear war would bring.

Given time and advice, Reagan, too, is likely to back away from an effort to regain American superiority. All aside from his determination to reduce the federal budget and to address the problems of inflation and unemployment, if he is serious in his commitment to redress the deficiencies in American conventional forces, including the need to restore American naval superiority in the North Pacific while maintaining a major naval presence in the Indian Ocean, he will have problems enough in selling his budgets to a Congress which is already worried about the consequences of his policies for domestic welfare programs. In his program for strategic forces, then, Reagan is likely to settle for an increase in offensive weapons (including a new strategic bomber) and a new slogan (e.g., "strategic forces second to none") but to avoid a commitment to the acquisition of forces that would give the United States a real capability for damage limitation.

But time and advice may not be this president's lot. He has committed himself to the renegotiation of SALT II, but he has come to office with many advisers who question not only the existence of parity but its feasibility and desirability. He has also come to office when the 1972 ABM treaty is under increasing question, particularly from those who are attracted to the contribution that a missile defense system could make to the prelaunch survivability of the MX.

There is a fair prospect, then, that the Reagan Administration could lead the United States into a "little arms race." In this future, the superpowers would fail to renegotiate SALT II and cease to observe the terms of both that agreement and the interim agreement of SALT I and, perhaps, in time the terms of the ABM treaty as well. The resulting competition in strategic arms would lead to a more uncertain and changing strategic balance and to a relationship from which the superpowers would find it difficult to return to another effort to constrain their competition through SALT. But the "little arms race" would still leave the United States without the capabilities required to achieve a decisive superiority over the Soviet Union in terms of the death and destruction each could inflict upon the other—a superiority clear enough to be recognized by all concerned in Moscow and Washington, in London and Bonn, and in Tokyo and Peking.

There is only one event on the horizon that could change this last prospect. The next Soviet-American confrontation is going to be most dangerous. The Soviets, as a result of their build-up in conventional as well as strategic forces, believe that the balance of power has shifted significantly in their favor since the early 1960s, and it is reasonable to believe that they will expect the results of the next confrontation to reflect tht change in power. This time, in contrast to the Cuban missile crisis in 1962, they will expect the Americans to blink first. The United States, on the other hand, will be determined to stand fast and to demonstrate that, the Soviet build-up to the contrary, its commitments are as good as ever.

Should this confrontation result in anything that Americans might intepret as a defeat, as might conceivably happen in an area like the Middle East, where the United States is presently at some disadvantage, the American reaction will be strong and across the board, politically and militarily. Allies and alliances will be critically weighed and reexamined; the United States will want to see who was there when it needed them, and who was not. But whatever the outcome of that evaluation, Americans are most likely to associate their defeat with the change in the strategic balance and to pull out all stops in an effort to regain strategic superiority. And in this event, the "big arms race," rejected in the late 1950s and in the 1960s and the 1970s will start in earnest in the 1980s

Part IV
Issues for the Eighties

With the loss of numerical strategic superiority in the middle 1970s, Americans worried ever more about the credibility of strategic deterrence, about ballistic missile defense at home and conventional defense in Europe, about the stability of the world as gradually more countries acquire nuclear weapons, and about America's ability to project power abroad to uphold its interests. The selections in Part IV address these issues.

In the first section, Robert Jervis questions the meaning of nuclear superiority. Desmond Ball raises doubts about the ability of a country to command and control nuclear forces during a strategic nuclear war. Conversely, Paul Nitze argues that with nuclear superiority the Soviet Union might believe that after its first strike the United States would be self-deterred. Colin Gray makes the case for reexamining both ballistic missile defenses and our deterrent strategy. McGeorge Bundy and his three American associates argue against our long-standing policy of using nuclear weapons in Europe should NATO be unable to contain a conventional Soviet attack, a policy that Karl Kaiser and his three German associates strongly support.

In the next section, Kenneth N. Waltz questions the conventional wisdom by arguing that the measured spread of nuclear weapons may increase the chances of peace and promote international stability, a thesis that Louis Dunn strongly contests. In the final section, Huntington offers an expansive view of America's interests and corresponding military requirements. Josh Epstein criticizes the logic of the strategy of "horizontal escalation." Waltz presents a more modest estimate both of interests and of needs.

*Why Nuclear Superiority
Doesn't Matter*

ROBERT JERVIS

Recent debates on the role of nuclear weapons in American defense policy have not clarified the important issues or dealt with the underlying assumptions that are involved. While some of the specifics of the arguments are new, the basic questions are as old as the nuclear era and can be referred to as the dispute between those who advocate a policy of Assured Destruction (AD) and those who call for Flexible Response (FR). Proponents of AD believe that any nuclear war will be all-out war and therefore that the United States need only have an assured capacity to destroy an enemy's cities even if forced to absorb a first strike. Proponents of FR hold that there is a range of military contingencies for which the United States must be prepared and that nuclear weapons can be used in a variety of such contingencies in a more flexible, limited way. The main arguments against AD, now as in the past, are that it is not credible and would lead to disaster if deterrence failed; the central argument against FR is that it is costly, ineffective, and dangerous. This article generally defends the AD position and argues that FR misunderstands the nature of nuclear deterrence.

ASSURED DESTRUCTION AND FLEXIBLE RESPONSE

Proponents of AD argue that the vulnerability of population centers in both the United States and the Soviet Union that comes with mutual second-strike capability has transformed strategy. Because a military advantage no longer assures a decisive victory, old ways of thinking are no longer appropriate. The healthy fear of devastation, which cannot be exorcised short of the attainment of a first-strike capability, makes deterrence relatively easy. Futhermore, because cities cannot be taken out of hostage, the perceived danger of total destruction is crucial at all points in the threat, display, or use of force.

Four implications follow. First, because gaining the upper hand in purely military terms cannot protect one's country, various moves in a limited war—such as using large armies, employing tactical nuclear

From *Political Science Quarterly,* vol. 94, no. 4, Winter 1979–80, pp. 617–633. Reprinted by permission.

weapons, or even engaging in limited strategic strikes—are less important for influencing the course of the battle than for showing the other side that a continuation of the conflict raises an unacceptable danger that things will get out of hand. New weapons are introduced not to gain a few miles of territory, but to engage in what Schelling has called competition in risk taking.[1] Escalation dominance—the ability to prevail at every level of military conflict below that of all-out war—is thus neither necessary nor sufficient to reach one's goals, be they to preserve the status quo or to change it. Being able to win on the battlefield does not guarantee winning one's objectives, since the risk of escalation may be too great to justify the expected benefits.

Second, it does not matter which side has more nuclear weapons. In the past, having a larger army than one's neighbor allowed one to conquer it and protect one's own population. Having a larger nuclear stockpile yields no such gains. Deterrence comes from having enough weapons to destroy the other's cities; this capability is an absolute, not a relative one.[2]

Third, if national security is provided by one's capability to destroy the opponent, not by the possession of a more effective military machine than the other side, then the force that drives the security dilemma is sapped. The security dilemma is created by the fact that in the prenuclear era weapons and policies that made one country secure made others insecure. An army large enough to protect the state was usually large enough to threaten a neighbor with invasion, even if the state did not intend such a threat. But when security comes from the absolute capability to annihilate one's enemy, then each side can gain it simultaneously. Neither side need acquire more than a second-strike capability and, if either does, the other need not respond since its security is not threatened.[3]

A fourth aspect of the AD position is that nuclear war is very unlikely because to initiate it a statesman would have to be willing to run the risk that his country's population centers would be destroyed. Not only is "the balance of terror . . . decidedly not delicate,"[4] but, because statesmen know that imprudent action could lead to all-out war, the resulting deterrence covers a lot more than attacks on one's

[1] The phrase is attributed to Thomas Schelling in Herman Kahn, *On Escalation* (Baltimore, Md.: Penguin, 1968), p. 3. The topic is discussed in Schelling, *Arms and Influence* (New Haven, Conn.: Yale University Press, 1966), pp. 92–125.

[2] Thus there is a second meaning in the title of the book of brilliant essays written in 1946 by Bernard Brodie, Arnold Wolfers et al., *The Absolute Weapon* (New York: Harcourt, Brace, 1946).

[3] Many proponents of AD also argue that the Soviet Union would feel threatened by increases in American strategic forces, however, and this fear is in some tension with the brief described here.

[4] Bernard Brodie, *War and Politics* (New York: Macmillan, 1973), p. 380.

homeland. To take any major offensive action is to run an intolerably high risk of escalation. The United States and the Soviet Union may engage in fierce rhetorical battles and even use force in such peripheral areas as Africa and Asia, but there are sharp limits to how far they can push each other. The chance that such attempts would lead to total destruction is simply too great. (And it can be too great even though it is very low. That is, even a very small probability of escalation is sufficient to deter serious encroachments.)

The Flexible Response position is different on all counts. Its logic is best seen in terms of what Glenn Snyder has called the stability-instability paradox.[5] Because the balance is so stable at the level of all-out nuclear war, each side is relatively free to engage in provocations and military actions at lower levels of violence. The most obvious application of this argument is that if NATO lacks the ability to defend Europe with conventional weapons, it faces the danger of having to fight such a war: thus the Soviet second-strike capability would "deter our deterrent" (to paraphrase the title from an article by Paul Nitze).[6] The same argument can be applied to more bizarre situations. To secure some highly valued goal the Russians might destroy most of the American Minuteman force. Since its cities were still in hostage, the United States would be deterred from striking back at Soviet cities.

For the advocates of FR, the United States must be prepared to fight a war—or rather a variety of wars—in order to gain a better chance of deterring the Soviets from making any military moves, to deter them from escalating if they do move, and to secure as favorable an outcome as possible at any level of violence. In contrast to the AD view, FR argues that in the nuclear era, as in earlier times, the absolute amount of armaments on each side is less important than the relative amounts because each nation's military forces as well as its population centers are potential targets. As decision makers stop thinking that any war must be total and realize that the stability-instability paradox allows a wider range of contingencies of controlled and less self-defeating strikes, the importance of the details of the strategic balance becomes clear.[7]

Proponents of FR thus disagree with the AD position that the inherent riskiness of any major provocation in the nuclear era means that a second-strike capability protects against much more than an

---

[5] Glenn Snyder, "The Balance of Power and the Balance of Terror," in *The Balance of Power,* ed. Paul Seabury (San Francisco, Calif: Chandler, 1965). This paradox was seen by Snyder as explaining why mutual second-strike capability could lead to conventional wars; the proponents of FR take this one step further by arguing that the overall strategic stability also allows for limited nuclear wars.

[6] Paul Nitze, "Deterring Our Deterrent," *Foreign Policy* 25 (Winter 1976-77): 195-210.

[7] U.S., Congress, Senate, Committee on Armed Services, *Hearings on Fiscal Year 1975 Authorization,* 93rd Cong., 2d sess., 1974, p. 51.

unrestrained assault on the country's homeland. Secretary of Defense Brown argues that "we now recognize that the strategic nuclear forces can deter only a relatively narrow range of contingencies, much smaller in range than was foreseen only 20 or 30 years ago."[8] Similarly, Brown, like Schlesinger before him, claims that "only if we have the capability to respond realistically and effectively to an attack at a variety of levels can we . . . have the confidence necessary to a credible deterrent."[9] But the proponents of AD would reply, this argument advocating something approximating escalation misses the point. No state can respond "effectively" in the sense of being able to take its population centers out of hostage; thus, it is the willingness to run risks and the perceptions of this willingness that will determine whether a response is "realistic" and a threat is credible.

STABILITY, PREDICTABILITY, AND SOVIET INTENTIONS

Much of the difference between the two schools of thought turns on differing ideas about stability. Both groups agree on the overwhelming importance of preserving one's cities. But for the proponents of FR, the common interest in avoiding a mutually disastrous outcome can be used as a lever to extract competitive concessions. Either side can take provocative actions because the other cannot credibly threaten to respond by all-out war. Proponents of AD, on the other hand, see stability as broader, and deterrence as covering a wider set of interests, since it follows from the reasonable fear that any challenge to an opponent's vital interest could escalate. Paradoxically, stability is in part the product of the belief that the world is not entirely stable, that things could somehow get out of control.

There are two elements that influence beliefs about the extent to which the risks of escalations could be kept limited and controlled, and it is not surprising that advocates of AD and FR disagree about both. The first element is the American reaction and the Soviet anticipation of it. Advocates of FR fear that the Russians might be certain enough that the United States would not use nuclear weapons in response to a major provocation to make such a provocation worth taking. Those who support a policy of AD deny this, noting that the United States has behaved too unpredictably for any state to be sure what it will do. Part of the reason for the disagreement on this point is that proponents of both AD and FR project their views onto the governments of the United States and the Soviet Union. The latter believe, and the former deny, that a large Russian arms build-up would intimidate the United States.

---

[8] Department of Defense, *Annual Report, F.Y. 1980* (Washington, D.C.: Government Printing Office, 1979), p. 76. Brown's posture statement is a combination of FR and AD and so is more honest, but less coherent, than many of the previous statements.

[9] Department of Defense, *Annual Report, F.Y. 1979* (Washington, D.C.: Government Printing Office, 1978), p. 54.

The other element in the belief about whether the risks would seem controllable is a judgment about the inherent limits of manipulation and prediction in human affairs. While these factors are rarely discussed explicitly, the tone of much of the FR writings implies that men can make fine, complex, and accurate calculations. Friction, uncertainty, failures of implementation, and the fog of battle do not play a major role. Men see clearly, their subordinates are able to carry out intricate instructions, and the other side gets the desired message. Thus Secretary Brown recently argued that "if we try bluffing [the Russians with a threat of massive retaliation], ways can be found by others to test our bluffs without undue risk to them."[10] Such attempts would involve reasonable risks only if the situation were under complete control and seen by the Soviets as relatively safe, and then only if they believed this to be the case. (But many proponents of FR also believe that the United States cannot rely on tactical nuclear weapons to defend Europe because their use could too easily lead to all-out war. This fits oddly with the belief that the superpowers could fight a limited strategic war.)

For the advocates of AD, this is a dream world. War plans can be drawn up on this basis, but reality will not conform. Furthermore, decision makers having experienced the multiple ways in which predictions prove incorrect and situations get out of control, do not commit the fallacy of believing that escalation could be carefully manipulated and thus would not place any faith in the precise options of limited nuclear warfare. FR advocates see the need for a policy they consider to be prudential in the sense of being able to cope with unlikely but dangerous contingencies because they do not think decision makers can be counted on to avoid terrible risks; proponents of AD do not think American policy has to cover such remote possibilities because they are confident that statesmen are at least minimally prudent.

This difference in beliefs—or perhaps I should say in intuitions—goes far to explain why some of the proponents of FR see a much greater danger of a Russian first strike than do advocates of AD. One would not expect any difference of opinion here since the question seems entirely technical. But it is not. To launch a first strike in the belief that one could destroy most of an opponent's strategic forces is to accept a set of complex and uncertain calculations: the weapons have never been tested under fully operational conditions; accuracies are estimated from performances over test ranges, which may be different when the missiles are fired over different parts of the earth; the vulnerability of the other side's silos (and one's own) can never be known with certainty before the war; and the effects on the environment of huge

---

[10] Department of Defense, *Annual Report, F.Y. 1980*, p. 75.

nuclear explosions can only be guessed at. The same orientation that leads one to believe that statesmen could be sufficiently confident of their ability to prevent escalation to allow them to engage in major provocations also fits with the conclusion that statesmen might place sufficient confidence in their estimates to launch a disarming strike.

If differences in beliefs about the risks inherent in major provocations are one source of the dispute between AD and FR, another is a difference in perceptions of the risks that the Russians are willing to run. Most proponents of AD argue that while the desire to expand is not completely absent, the Russians are not so strongly motivated in this regard as to be willing to endanger what they have already gained. Proponents of FR argue not that the Russians want war, but that they care enough about increasing their influence to run significant risks to reach that goal. And by acquiring massive military might, the Russians could hope to be better able to expand without courting dangerous confrontations. The proponents of AD would reply that almost no decision maker in the world's history would embark on a course of expansion while his cities were held hostage. The sort of leaders the proponents of FR posit are very rare—even Hitler probably was not an example, since he knew that if he could militarily defeat the Allies he could protect his own country.

Because the advocates of AD believe the Russians to be less strongly motivated than do those who call for FR, they believe that much less deterrence, both in terms of the damage that the United States needs to inflict and the probability that it will be inflicted, will be sufficient. Thus there is a disagreement over "how much credibility is enough": two policy analysts therefore might agree on how likely the Russians thought it was that a limited war would escalate and disagree over whether they would be deterred.[11]

SITUATIONS CALLING FOR FLEXIBLE RESPONSE

The basic concern of the proponents of FR is that the threat to attack Soviet population centers is not credible when the Russians can respond in kind. In a crisis the United States must "have a wider choice than humiliation or all-out nuclear action," to use President Kennedy's terms.[12] The danger that the proponents of FR see was expressed well by Secretary of Defense Schlesinger in 1975: "If one side should remove the other's capability for flexible and controlled

[11] This also partially explains why many of the proponents of FR think that the threat to destroy Russian cities would be an insufficient deterrent and that the United States should develop a targeting policy aimed at convincing the Soviet leaders that their regime would not be able to maintain control of the country after a war.

[12] "Radio and Televison Report to the American People on the Berlin Crisis, July 25, 1961," in *Public Papers of the Presidents of the United States: John F. Kennedy, 1961* (Washington, D.C.: Government Printing Office, 1962), p. 535.

responses, he might find ways of exercising coercion and extracting concessions without triggering the final holocaust. . . . No opponent should think that he could fire at some of our Minuteman or SAC [Strategic Air Command] bases without being subjected to, at the very least, a response in kind. No opponent should believe that he could attack other U.S. targets of military or economic value without finding similar or other appropriate targets in his own homeland under attack. . . . Above all, no opponent should entertain the thought that we will permit him to remove our capability for flexible strategic responses."[13]

We can examine the problem more clearly by seeing that Schlesinger and other proponents of FR blur the distinction between two kinds of wars. The first involves demonstration attacks. Since they do not require large numbers of missiles, neither the size of each side's force nor its vulnerability is important. The second is a counterforce war of attrition in which the Russians would launch the first nuclear strike, trying to destroy as much of the American strategic force as possible, either in one blow or by moving more slowly and taking out the opposing forces in a series of strikes. Although the United States would still be able to attack the Soviet Union's cities, the only result of such a strike would be to have U.S. cities blown up thirty minutes later. If the U.S. strategic force is vulnerable, the Russians can destroy much of it without using a similar proportion of their force. But, and this is crucial, it is only in counterforce wars of attrition that the comparison of each side's counterforce capabilities matters.

Examining a number of contexts in which defense problems arise, one can see that the distinction between attacks that have an effect by demonstrating resolve and those that aim at reducing an opponent's capability recurs and is closely tied to the basic difference between the AD and FR positions. If the AD position is correct and counterforce wars of attrition are not a real possibility in the nuclear era, then the United States does not have to worry that its Minuteman force is vulnerable or that the Russians have a greater ability to destroy hard targets than the United States does. To evaluate the arguments, it is useful to examine the potentially critical situations.

PROTECTING EUROPE

One major fear is that the Soviets could launch a large-scale conventional attack that would conquer Europe unless the United States escalated. If the United States tried to stave off defeat by employing tactical nuclear weapons, the Soviets could reply in kind, nullifying any advantage the West may have gained. One FR remedy would be to

<hr />

[13] Department of Defense, *Annual Report, F.Y. 1976 and F.Y. 197T* (Washington, D.C.: Government Printing Office, 1975), pp. II-4—II-5.

develop the means to defend against an attack at any level of violence. Thus the West would deploy conventional forces to contain a conventional attack and tactical nuclear weapons to cope with a like attack. This alluring argument is not correct. An aggressor could attack in the face of escalation dominance if he believed that the defender would not pay the price of resisting, a price that includes a probability that the fighting will spread to each side's population centers. The other side of this coin is that a state that could be confident of winning a military victory in Europe could be deterred from attacking or deterred from defending against an attack by the fear that the war might spread to its homeland. Only if the risk of such escalation could be reduced to zero would this element disappear and purely military considerations be determinative. The advocates of FR thus overstate the efficacy of their policy.

Of course if the United States lacks escalation dominance it would have to take the initiative of increasing the level of violence and risk in the event of a Soviet attack on Europe. But the onus of undertaking the original move would still remain with the aggressor. And since the level of risk is shared equally by both sides, what is likely to be more important than the inhibition against having to take the initiative is the willingness or unwillingness to approach the brink rather than concede defeat, a factor not linked to escalation dominance. Furthermore, some practical considerations reinforce this conclusion. As Bernard Brodie argued, it is hard to imagine that the Soviets would launch a conventional attack in the face of NATO's tactical nuclear weapons. Such an attack would require massed troops that would be an inviting target for NATO's tactical nuclear weapons. The Soviets could not be sufficiently confident that their strategic or tactical nuclear forces would deter such a NATO response to leave their armies so vulnerable.[14] And for the Russians to initiate a tactical nuclear war would raise two difficulties. First, the uncertainties about how such a war would be fought are so great that it would be hard for any country to be confident that it would win. Second, a war of this level of violence would be especially likely to trigger the American strategic force.

An alternative FR policy is for the United States to develop large enough strategic forces to threaten, and carry out if need be, a counterforce strike with some of its forces, even though doing so would not leave the Soviet Union totally disarmed. While the Soviet Union could retaliate against American population centers, it would not do so because its own cities were still in hostage. Thus the United States could launch its strike "secure in the knowledge that the United

---

[14] Bernard Brodie, *Escalation and the Nuclear Option* (Princeton, N.J.: Princeton University Press, 1966).

States had a residual ICBM force that could deter attack upon itself."[15] This notion of security is an odd one, resting as it does on the confident prediction that the Russians would calmly absorb a counterforce first strike. This is especially odd because while the proponents of FR tell us that we should pay close attention to Soviet military doctrine, on this point they blithely disregard these texts which stress preemption and deny that limited nuclear wars are possible.

A similar error is embodied in Secretary of Defense Schlesinger's defense of limited nuclear options on the grounds that because the United States has commitments to allies, "we require a nuclear capability that has an implementable threat and which is perceived to have an implementable threat. Unless, in the event of certain hostile acts, we have a threat that we can implement, the existence of the American force structure does not contribute logically to deterrence." If, on the other hand, the United States has the ability to launch limited nuclear strikes, he continues, it "will not be self-deterred from responding to . . . an act of aggression."[16] But the concept of "self-deterrence" is not useful and the argument cannot be sustained. The United States is being deterred by the fear of Soviet retaliation. This danger is present as long as the Soviets have second-strike capability; thus, it is a consequence not of Soviet "superiority" but of parity. Even if the United States reached Schlesinger's goal of preserving "an essential strategic equilibrium with the USSR both in capabilities and in targeting options,"[17] the costs and risks of employing the options would remain.

The argument that the side that had better counterforce capability could safely launch such an attack even though the other side would not be disarmed pertains only in wars of attrition in which each side tries to reduce the other's strategic capability and spares the other's cities. The claim that the United States can employ this option to protect Europe is the opposite side of the coin of the claim that if the Soviet Union had a large margin of counterforce superiority, it could use it to coerce the West. The validity of this claim turns on whether a war of attrition is a serious possibility or whether the danger that such a conflict would escalate to attacks on population center would dominate decision makers' calculations.

PREEMPTION

Some proponents of FR think it most unlikely that the Russians would launch an attack on Europe, but fear that if the Soviet strategic

[15] Colin Gray, "The Scope and Limits of SALT," *Foreign Affairs* 56 (July 1978): 788.
[16] U.S., Congress, House, Committee on Armed Services, *Hearings on Military Posture and H.R. 12564, Department of Defense Authorization for Appropriations for Fiscal Year 1975*, 93rd Cong., 2d sess., 1974, part 1, pp. 47, 49.
[17] Ibid., p. 29.

force was much more effective than the American one and if a significant proportion of the American strategic force were vulnerable, the
Russians might make a preemptive strike in a grave crisis, perhaps one
they had not sought, if they thought that war was very likely. The
ability to hit missile silos and command and control facilities that the
proponents of FR call for, however, increases this danger, since it
enables the United States to destroy a large proportion of USSR's
land-based missiles (and most of the Soviet strategic force is land
based) if the United States were to strike first. It is a bit disingenuous
to argue that the United States needs a new type of missile to decrease
the chance that the Soviet Union would attack without also
acknowledging that some of the incentive the Russians would have to
attack those missiles comes from the very accuracy that is supposedly
needed in order to fight a counterforce war.[18]

More importantly, preemption makes sense only if being struck
first is much worse than getting the first blow in. A state whose leaders
believe that war will lead to total devastation will have no incentive to
preempt even if many of their missiles are vulnerable. Here, as at
other points, the proponents of FR make the crucial mistake of concentrating on purely military factors—the numbers and characteristics
of weapons on both sides—and ignoring the role of military moves as
generators of risk. The FR argument is that deterrence requires a sufficient number and kind of forces so that if the other side struck first,
it would be militarily worse off than if it had not. Thus it would be
dangerous if the Russians were able to use, for example, 200 missiles
with 2,000 warheads and knock out most of the American ICBMs. As
Secretary of Defense Brown has put it: "we must ensure that no
adversary could see himself better off after a limited exchange than
before it. We cannot permit an enemy to believe that he could create
any kind of military or psychological asymmetry that he could then
exploit to his advantage."[19] But the fact that the Russians would have
gained a more favorable ratio of missiles does not mean that they
would be closer to any meaningful goal or even that they would be
closer to it than they would have been if the United States struck first
and the ratio of missiles available was less favorable to them. The only
meaningful goals would be to preserve their cities and, if possible,
prevail in the dispute. But gains in purely military terms do not accomplish these objectives in wartime any more than they do in
peacetime. As long as each side retains the ability to destroy the
other's society, having more warheads than an opponent is an advantage only if it makes the opponent back down, and the proponents of

[18] The United States might get around this dilemma by building missiles that were invulnerable, but that lacked accurate MIRVs. It is interesting to note that the U.S. Air
Force has done a much better job of developing a powerful and accurate missile than it
has in making that missile able to survive a Russian attack.
[19] Department of Defense, *Annual Report, F.Y. 1979*, p. 56.

FR have not shown how it will make such a contribution. The military advantages of striking first can only be translated into political gains if the war remains counterforce and the state with the most missiles left after a series of exchanges prevails without losing its population centers.[20] The FR fallacy here is parallel to that involved in the claim that escalation dominance is necessary or sufficient for deterring or prevailing in a conflict in Europe. Competition in risk taking, rather than competition in military capability, dominates.

COUNTERFORCE WARS OF ATTRITION AND THE BALANCE OF RESOLVE

In a counterforce war of attrition the numbers and characteristics of the weapons would matter a great deal. As in the prenuclear era, what would be crucial would not be absolute capability, but the relative strengths of the opponents. The basic argument of the AD school is undercut because the primary targets of the warheads are not population centers but other weapons. Is the likelihood of counterforce wars of attrition sufficient to warrant the necessary preparations? Could there be a nuclear war in which population centers were spared and the outcome determined by which state is able to do the better job of reducing the other's military forces? Even if the Russians had the ability to win such a war, they would have to be desperate or willing to run terribly high risks to place sufficient faith in American self-restraint to order an attack. Even if the United States could win such a war, its threat to initiate it would not be credible (for example, in response to a Soviet attack on Europe) unless the Russians believed that the United States thought that control would be maintained throughout its course.

This control would have to be maintained, furthermore, although unprecedented numbers of civilians would be killed; a large Russian counterforce strike could not be limited to destroying only military targets. Although it would be obvious to the president that most American population centers were still held hostage, sufficient damage would have been done to raise sharply the danger of an all-out response. The chance of such a reaction—which would be present even if the United States said it would not react in this way—would have to weigh very heavily on the Soviet decision makers.

But the existence of tight control would not ensure the success of a strategy of attrition. If the Russians launched a counterforce strike and the United States did not retaliate against Soviet cities, it might nullify a Russian war-fighting strategy by not responding at all. This may seem as bizarre as a counterattack on population centers, but on closer examination it makes some sense. Why should the United States

---

[20] This point is overlooked by Paul Nitze in "Assuring Strategic Stability in an Era of Detente," *Foreign Affairs* 54 (January 1976): 226–30, and in "Deterring our Deterrent," p. 210.

retaliate? What would the Russians have gained by destroying a significant portion of the U.S. strategic force? Why would they be in a better position to work their will after a strike than before it? If the United States acts as though it is weakened, it will be in a worse bargaining position, but this is within American control. To withhold a response, while maintaining the ability to destroy Russian cities later, could as easily be taken as a sign of high resolve as of low. The United States would forego hitting many Russian military targets, but this would not sacrifice much of value since attacking them would not limit the Soviet ability to destroy the United States. Only if a war in Europe were being fought at the same time, and thus a failure to respond created or magnified an imbalance of land forces, would withholding a return counterforce strike give up something of value. But for the Soviets to attack American strategic forces (and NATO tactical nuclear forces) in conjunction with fighting a war in Europe would be to run a very high risk of an American counterattack on Soviet population centers.

The possibility of not responding to a Soviet counterforce strike points to the odd nature of a nuclear war of attrition. The benefit of the efforts to reduce an opponent's strategic forces comes only near the end, when the state is able to take its society out of hostage. Unless and until that point is reached, the side that is "losing" the counterforce war of attrition can do nearly as much damage to the side that is "winning" as it could before the war started. Military efforts can succeed only if the "loser" allows them to by sparing the "winner's" cities. Of course it will be costly for the "loser" to initiate counterstrikes against population centers, since the "winner" will presumably retaliate. But this is true regardless of the details of the strategic balance.

If the ultimate threat, even during a war of attrition, is that of destroying cities, it is clear that such wars are more competition in risk taking than they are attempts to gain an advantage on the battlefield. To concentrate on the military advantages that accrue to one side or the other by counterforce attacks is to ignore the fact that in any nuclear war the element of threat of escalation will loom very large.[21] This general point is missed by Secretary of Defense Brown when he says that the ability to hit a wide range of military targets "permits us to respond credibly to threats or actions by a nuclear opponent."[22] But what is crucial is less the capability than the willingness to use it. Even if the United States had the ability to match the Soviets round for round, target for target, it might not do so—and the Russians might move in the belief that the United States would not respond—because

---

[21] Indeed the incentives for the state that is behind in a counterforce war to escalate increase as its military situation worsens. If it fears it may soon lose its second-strike capability, the losing state may well feel greater pressure to up the ante while it still can.

[22] Department of Defense, *Annual Report, F.Y. 1980*, p. 78.

the costs and risks were felt to be too great. And even if the United States lacked such a capability, the Soviet fear of an all-out response could lead it to expect that any provocation would be prohibitively costly. Since what matters in limited strategic wars, even if they involve targets that are predominantly military, is each side's willingness to run high risks, it is the "balance of resolve" rather than the "balance of military power" that will most strongly influence their outcomes.[23] Extra ammunition cannot compensate for weakness in will or a refusal —perhaps a sensible refusal—to run the risk of destruction.

The importance of competition in risk taking implies that demonstration attacks would be more useful than attempts to reduce an opponent's military capabilities. Such attacks could be aimed at a military installation, an isolated element of an opponent's strategic forces, a command and control facility, or a city. The purpose of such an action would be to inflict pain, show resolve, and raise the risks of all-out war to a level that an opponent would find intolerable. Such risks, of course, weigh on both sides, but only by willingly accepting high risks can a state prevail. In addition to high resolve, in order to engage in nuclear demonstrations a state needs to be able to carry out a certain number of limited options. But the ammunition requirements are nowhere near as high as they are for a counterforce war of attrition (and both sides can simultaneously have the capability for demonstrations).

Demonstration strikes would exert pressure in three ways. First, they would exact some degree of punishment on the other side. But the immediate pain inflicted would probably be less important than the underlying motivation of these strikes—the implied threat to do more harm unless the opponent complies with the attacking state's demands. This threat gains its credibility because the attacking state has shown that it is willing to engage in very risky actions that have increased the chance that targets in its own country would be struck. When both sides have second-strike capability, one side prevails in a crisis, not by showing that it can inflict pain on the other (for this is obvious and true for the both sides), but by demonstrating that it feels so strongly about the issue at stake that it is willing to be hurt in return rather than suffer a defeat. Third, any nuclear attack increases the chance that uncontrolled escalation will occur. It is this specter that exerts so much pressure on statesmen not to use nuclear weapons in the first place or to make concessions in any conflict in which they are used. Even if one side launched a counterforce strike, the war would almost surely end before either had run out of ammunition. Resolve,

---

[23] For further discussion of this point see Robert Jervis, "Deterrence Theory Revisited," *World Politics* 31 (January 1979): 314–22. The Soviet stress on the importance of the "correlation of forces" is not inconsistent with this notion.

not capability, would be the limiting factor. When Secretary Brown claims that "fully effective deterrence requires forces of sufficient size and flexibility to attack selectively a range of military and other targets"[24] and argues that to do this the United States needs an invulnerable ICBM, he is either thinking in terms of a war of attrition or overstating the number of warheads the United States needs.

POSSIBLE OBJECTIONS

Before drawing the conclusions that are implicit in the previous analysis, I should note three obvious objections. First, it can be argued that if I am right, and the strategic balance is quite stable, an increase in American arms will not have dire consequences.[25] Since all the United States can lose by additional deployment is money, argue the critics, is is better to play it safe and buy the extra systems. Moreover, how can anyone be sure that a war of attrition will not occur? But surely there must be some judgments about plausibility, some concern for costs, and some consideration of the chance that the United States might teach others lessons that are both incorrect and dangerous. The new weapons cost a lot of money and avoiding waste is not a goal to be scorned lightly.[26] Furthermore, although there are no strong and direct links between the adversaries' defense budgets or between the budgets and the degree of superpower conflict, it is hard to keep the military and political tracks entirely separate. A final line of rebuttal is the most important: to develop a posture based on the assumption that limited nuclear wars are possible is to increase the chance that they will occur. If the Russians already believe in the possibility that such wars could be kept limited, U.S. acceptance of this position would increase the likelihood of their occurrence. On the other hand, if the Russians now find these kinds of war incomprehensible, they might learn to accept them if the United States talked about them long and persuasively enough. This could decrease the chance that a nuclear war would immediately involve the mass destruction of population centers, but at the cost of increasing the chance of more limited nuclear wars—which then could escalate. Such a trade-off is highly likely, and even Schlesinger acknowledged that adoption of his

[24] Speech before the Council on Foreign Relations and the Foreign Policy Association, New York, 5 April 1979, p. 3. Also see Department of Defense, *Annual Report, F.Y. 1980,* pp. 77–78.
[25] There is a similar contradiction in McGeorge Bundy's claim that although nuclear superiority is meaningless, we need arms control agreements "To Cap the Volcano" (*Foreign Affairs* 48 [October 1969]: 1–20).
[26] Bernard Brodie argues that the strategic balance is so stable that saving money should be the main goal of arms control ("On the Objectives of Nuclear Arms Control," *International Security* I [Summer 1976]: 17–36). His position is further developed in "The Development of Nuclear Strategy," ibid. 2 (Spring 1978): 65–83. I am greatly indebted to these articles.

doctrine might increase the chance of limited nuclear strikes.[27]

The second objection is that my analysis ignores the fact that the Russians do not accept the notion that mutual assured destruction creates stability. Soviet military doctrine is an arcane field that cannot be treated in detail here, although the bulk of the evidence indicates that the Soviet view of strategy is very different from the American.[28] They appear to take war more seriously. Indeed, much of Soviet military doctrine is pure military doctrine—that is, the ideas are not particularly Russian or particularly Marxist but simply those one would expect from people charged with protecting society and winning wars. Many statements by Soviet generals are similar to statements by American generals when the latter are not influenced by the ideas or constrained by the power of the civilian leadership; many American military officials seek the same program that the Russians are following. Thus one cannot draw from the fact that Russians probably buy more than is needed for deterrence the inference that they are willing to run high risks to try to expand. The American generals who call for higher spending are not necessarily more bellicose than those who disagree with them.[29] Both the Russian and the U.S. generals may want to prepare for the worst and get ready to fight if a war is forced on them. The Russians may be buying what they think is insurance, and we do not ordinarily think that someone who buys a lot of insurance for his car is planning to drive recklessly.

While there is considerable evidence that the Russians want military forces that would provide as good an outcome as possible should war be forced on them, there is very little evidence that they think that such forces could be used to coerce the West. It has yet to be shown that they think that a superior ability to destroy military targets provides a shield behind which they can make political advances or that Soviet military doctrine measures American deterrence in terms of the United States' ability to match their posture. The Russians may not accept the idea that mutual vulnerability is a desirable state of affairs, but they seem to understand very well the potency of the American threat to destroy their society. Indeed their outlook is uncongenial to a counterforce war of attrition. While the Russians probably would attack U.S. strategic forces in the event of war, they have not talked about sparing the opponent's cities. Instead, they seem to be planning to hit as many targets as they can if war breaks out.

[27] House Armed Services Committee, *Hearings on Military Posture*, p. 50.

[28] For a dissenting view, see Raymond Garthoff, "Mutual Deterrence and Strategic Arms Limitation in Soviet Policy," *International Security* 3 (Summer 1978): 112–47.

[29] A study of postwar situations reveals that the U.S. military often advised against foreign military adventures. See Richard Betts, *Soldiers, Statesmen, and Cold War Crises* (Cambridge: Harvard University Press, 1977).

Even if the Russians were to say that they believed a war of attrition was possible, the United States would not have to adopt such a view. While it takes the agreement of both sides to fight a counterforce war, this is not true for AD. If one side denies that counterforce wars could be kept limited and convinces the other side that it believes this, the other cannot safely act on its doctrine. The Russians understood this in the periods when McNamara and Schlesinger were enunciating their doctrines, and American statesmen took their professions of disbelief seriously. Even if the Russians were to reverse their position, they would have to take American denials seriously also.

A third objection is that although the Soviet superior ability to destroy strategic forces and the related existence of Minuteman vulnerability is not a strategic problem, it is a political problem. Accordingly, because other nations are influenced by indicators of nuclear superiority, the United States must engage in this competition. (This argument loses some credibility since most people who make it also claim that superiority is meaningful apart from these perceptions.) There are several lines of rebuttal. First, there is little evidence that European or Third World leaders pay much attention to the details of the strategic balance. Second, the United States provides most of the information and conceptual framework that underpins third-party discussions of the balance. The United States might be able to persuade others that it would behave differently because the Russians could wipe out much of the American capability to destroy Soviet missiles. But it would probably be easier to convince them that this was not true. Few world leaders expect the United States and the Soviet Union to fight a war of attrition. Moreover, if the Russians believe that superiority matters and thus may be somewhat emboldened, the bargaining advantages they will gain will be slight if the United States holds to the position that this is nonsense. If the United States convinces the Soviet Union that it does not see a meaningful difference in strength, the USSR cannot safely stand firm in crisis bargaining because it will not have any reason to think that the United States is more likely to retreat.

CONCLUSIONS

We can draw several conclusions. The question of which side has greater ability to destroy the other's strategic forces matters only in a war of attrition. Such a war seems unlikely enough so that it is not worth spending large sums and running considerable dangers to prepare for it. Because either side can use its nuclear weapons to destroy its opponent's population centers, the danger of escalation would play a very large role in any war and could not be controlled by having more missiles, more accurate missiles, and more invulnerable missiles than the other side. The nuclear revolution cannot be undone.

As we have seen, many of the arguments about the supposed dangers following from Soviet superiority in fact are consequences of parity. The American deterrent is deterred by the fact that its cities are vulnerable, not by the fact that the Russians have some supposed military advantage. Since neither the United States nor the Soviet Union can take its cities out of hostage, the state that is willing to run the greatest risks will prevail. Many of those who call for the United States to match or surpass the Soviet's nuclear arsenal are trying to have the United States compensate for what they feel is a weakness of resolve by an excess in weaponry. But such a deficiency, if it exists, cannot be compensated. A wider range of options will merely give the Russians more ways, and safer ways, of coercing the West.

If the balance of resolve is so important, is the United States at a disadvantage compared to the Soviet Union? Some would argue that the United States has shown in Vietnam that it will not fight to defend its interests and those of its allies. But few dominoes fell after April 1975; other states may have been less impressed by the final American withdrawal than they were by its willingness to spend so much blood and treasure on an unimportant country. Furthermore, resolve is not so much an overall characteristic of an actor as it is a factor that varies with the situation because it reflects the strength of the state's motivation to prevail on a given issue. The state defending the status quo has the advantage in most conflicts in which the balance of resolve is crucial because it usually values the issue or territory at stake more than its opponent does.[30] It is easier for a state to convince the other side that it will fight to hold what it has than it is to make a credible threat to fight rather than forego expansion. A world in which resolve matters so much may not be so bad for the United States.

Even if both sides recognize the greater determination of the side defending the status quo, accidents and miscalculations are still possible, especially in situations growing out of a crisis in a third area. To rely solely on AD may be too dangerous. Some degree of insurance can be purchased by a continuation of the present American posture, which includes the availability of limited nuclear options. But these should be demonstrations, keyed to competition in risk taking, not attempts to wage a war of attrition; thus, the United States would not have to match the Soviets on any of the standard measures of nuclear power. It does not take a superior or even an equal military force to show by limited use that one is willing to take extreme measures rather than suffer a defeat. Such costs and risks are the trading chips of bargaining in the nuclear era; even if the United States had the weapons and doctrine for an FR policy, it could not avoid relying on them.

[30] Jervis, "Deterrence Theory Revisited," p. 318.

Although the United States should be able to conduct limited nuclear demonstrations, it should not stress this part of its policy. At this point there is no reason to think that such fantastic measures will ever be necessary, and they should be looked on as something to be done only in the most dire emergency, not as a tool of statecraft. Too much discussion of the possibility of such strikes might lead either or both sides to believe that the risks of a limited exchange were manageable, that escalation would remain under tight control. At best, the United States would therefore create a world in which limited nuclear wars were more likely to occur. At worst, these beliefs would be tested and proven to be incorrect.

Of course a policy of AD supplemented by the ability to conduct demonstration attacks may not succeed. The specter of all-out war is probably compelling enough to make both sides so cautious as to render forcible changes of the status quo on important issues too dangerous to be attempted. But miscalculations are possible, even in situations that seem very clear in retrospect, and states are sometimes willing to take what others think are exorbitant risks to try to reach highly valued goals. Both a cautionary tale and reminder that superior military capability does not guarantee deterrence is provided by the Japanese decision to go to war in 1941. Japan struck because her leaders saw the alternative not as the foregoing of gains, but as losing "her very existence."[31] They were thus very highly motivated—much more so than American decision makers thought. Furthermore, they knew perfectly well that they could not win an all-out war. But they were not expecting to have to fight such a war; they thought that the war would be limited as the United States would prefer to concede dominance in East Asia rather than engage in a long and costly struggle. It is alway possible that the Russians might similarly believe that a nuclear war could be kept limited because the United States would rather concede than move closer to the abyss. The penalty for miscalculation would be much greater for Russia than it was for Japan, and so their caution should be much greater. The danger remains, however, and it cannot be met by building more weapons.*

[31] Robert Butow, *Tojo and the Coming of the War* (Princeton, N.J.: Princeton University Press, 1961), p. 203.

*I would like to thank Desmond Ball, Richard Betts, Thomas Brown, James Digby, James King, George Quester, Michael Mandelbaum, Stanley Sierkiewicz, Dennis Ross, and Glenn Snyder for comments, and the Solomon Guggenheim Fund for financial support.

Counterforce Targeting:
How New? How Viable?

DESMOND BALL

US strategic nuclear policy can usefully be divided into several different facets, of which the most important are declaratory policy and action policy. Declaratory policy is that set of public pronouncements made by the President, the Secretary of Defense or sometimes other senior Administration officials regarding the requirements of deterrence, targeting policy, and strategic doctrine. Action policy, on the other hand, comprises the actual war-fighting strategy that the United States would adopt in a nuclear exchange; the designation of the forces to be used and the targets to be hit, and the allocation of the forces to those targets; and the rate at which the exchange is to proceed. It is the policy laid down in various Presidential memoranda, spelt out in the *Nuclear Weapons Employment Policy* (NUWEP) issued by the Secretary of Defense, and given effect in the Single Integrated Operational Plan (SIOP). These documents are highly classified, and only very infrequently have responsible officials chosen to publicly discuss any details of this aspect of US strategic nuclear policy.

Most of the public discussion of action policy is therefore based on extrapolations from the declaratory level. In the mid- and late-1960s, for example, when the Department of Defense annual reports stressed the requirements for Assured Destruction, there was a widespread concomitant assumption that the US strategic nuclear forces were targeted principally on Soviet urban-industrial centres. However, extrapolations of this sort have invariably been quite wide of the actuality, since the periods when declaratory policy has coincided with the realities of targeting practice have been few and far between. Declaratory policy has generally moved in cycles, with the emphasis sometimes on counter-city targeting, massive retaliation, and assured destruction, on the one hand, and sometimes on counterforce, damage-limitation, limited and selective options, and escalation control on the other hand. By comparison, action policy has been remarkably resilient. US war plans have *always* contained a wide range of target categories, including Soviet military capabilities, political and military command, control and communication (C^3)

From *Arms Control Today,* February 1981, pp. 1–9. Reprinted by permission systems, and economic and industrial centres. The principal changes in the plans since the late 1940s and early 1950s have been, first, an enormous increase in the number of potential target installations, from about 70 in 1949 to about 40,000 some three decades later; and, second, the division of these targets into an increasingly large array of "packages" of varying sizes and characteristics, providing the National Command Authorities (NCA) with "customized" options for an extremely wide range of possible contingencies. These two developments have been due only very marginally to changes in US basic national security policy. Far more important determinants have been, first, the growth of the US strategic nuclear forces (from 50 atomic bombs in May 1948 when the Joint Chiefs of Staff approved the "Halfmoon" Joint Emergency War Plan to the more than 9,000 bombs and missile re-entry vehicles in the SIOP forces today); and, second, the increasingly detailed intelligence regarding potential target installations in the Soviet Union that was derived from overflights of U-2 spy aircraft in 1956–60 and then, since August 1960, from surveillance satellites. The designation of some 40,000 target installations in SIOP-5D not only allows great scope for choice but, given that there are less than 10,000 weapons available for SIOP employment, actually requires such choice.

From this perspective, there was little new in the Presidential Directive on strategic nuclear targeting policy (PD-59) that President Carter signed on 25 July 1980. Indeed, there is a direct historical lineage between PD-59 and a series of studies set in train soon after President Nixon took office in January 1969. These studies led directly (if rather fitfully) to National Security Study Memorandum (NSSM)-169, approved by President Nixon in late 1973, and then, in turn, to National Security Decision Memorandum (NSDM)-242, signed by the President in January 1974.

NSDM-242 contained three principal policy components. The one which engaged the most public debate was the re-emphasis on the targeting of a wide range of Soviet military forces and installations, from hardened command and control facilities and ICBM silos to airfields and Army camps. The second element of NSDM-242 was the requirement for 'escalation control', whereby the National Command Authorities (NCA) should be provided with the ability to execute their selected options in a deliberate and controlled fashion throughout the progress of a strategic nuclear exchange. And, third, NSDM-242 introduced the notion of 'withholds' or 'non-targets', i.e. things that would be preserved from destruction. Some of these, such as 'population per se', have now been exempted absolutely from targeting; others, such as the centres of political leadership and control are exempted only for the purposes of intra-war deterrence and intra-war bargaining, and strategic reserve forces are to be maintained to allow their eventual destruction if necessary.

NSDM-242 also authorised the Secretary of Defense to promulgate the *Policy Guidance for the Employment of Nuclear Weapons* and the associated *Nuclear Weapons Employment Policy* (NUWEP), signed by Secretary Schlesinger on 4 April 1974. The NUWEP was developed through close military and civilian cooperation, and sets out the planning assumptions, attack options, targeting objectives and the damage levels needed to satisfy the political guidance. (For example, the NUWEP contains the requirement that the US strategic nuclear forces must in all circumstances be able to destroy 70 per cent of the Soviet industry that would be needed to achieve economic recovery after a nuclear war). The concepts and objectives set out in NSDM-242 and NUWEP provided the framework for the development of new strategic nuclear war plans. The first Single Integrated Operational Plan (SIOP) prepared under the new guidance was SIOP-5, which was formally approved in December 1975 and took effect on 1 January 1976.

There was some apprehension within the Pentagon in early 1977 that the Administration of President Carter and Secretary Brown might move to reverse the developments of the previous several years, but it proved unfounded. On 24 August 1977, President Carter issued PD-18, entitled *US National Strategy,* which explicitly reaffirmed the continued use of NSDM-242 and NUWEP in "the absence of further guidance for structuring the US strategic posture". This further guidance was provided by a Nuclear Targeting Policy Review (NTPR), an inter-agency study directed by Leon Sloss in the Pentagon. Various supporting studies were undertaken throughout the Defense establishment during 1978, on such subjects as Soviet views on nuclear warfighting, the possibility of exploiting Soviet fears of China, and problems of termination of nuclear war. Phase One of the NTPR was completed in December 1978, and formed the basis of a new Presidential Directive drafted in early 1979. Although the NSC staff pressed for the formal acceptance of this draft there was opposition from the State Department and from some elements within the Pentagon, and it was shelved for more than 15 months—until it was retrieved just prior to the Democratic Convention, revised and up-dated, and formally signed by the President on 25 July as PD-59.

SIOP-5D includes some 40,000 potential target installations, as compared to about 25,000 in 1974 when NUWEP was promulgated and the development of SIOP-5 initiated. These targets are divided into four principal groups, each of which in turn contains a wide range of target types. The four principal groups are the Soviet nuclear forces, the general purpose forces, the Soviet military and political leadership centres, and the Soviet economic and industrial base. Examples of targets within each category were given by the Defense Department to the Senate Armed Services Committee in March 1980:

(i)   Soviet nuclear forces:
      ICBMs and IRBMs, together with their launch facilities
         (LF's) and launch command centres (LCCs).
      Nuclear weapons storage sites.
      Airfields supporting nuclear-capable aircraft.
      SSBN bases.

(ii) Conventional military forces:
      Kasernes.
      Supply depots.
      Marshalling points.
      Conventional air fields.
      Ammunition storage facilities.
      Tank and vehicle storage yards.

(iii) Military and political leadership:
      Command posts.
      Key communications facilities.

(iv) Economic and industrial targets:
      (a) War supporting industry
           Ammunition factories.
           Tank and armoured personnel carrier factories.
           Petroleum refineries.
           Railway yards and repair facilities.
      (b) Industry that contributes to economic recovery
           Coal.
           Basic steel.
           Basic aluminium.
           Cement.
           Electric power.

The SIOP is further divided into four general categories of options available for the employment of nuclear weapons: Major Attack Options (MAO), Selected Attack Options (SAO), Limited Nuclear Options (LNO, which are "designed to permit the selective destruction of fixed enemy military or industrial targets"), and Regional Nuclear Options (RNO, which are "intended, for example, to destroy the leading elements of an attacking enemy force"). Within each of these classes of options are a wide range of further options, including so-called "withholds", four general categories of which have been publicly identified: population centres; national command and control centres (exempted from attack at least in the initial phases of a nuclear exchange so as to enhance the prospects of escalation control); particular countries targeted in the SIOP (so that attacks on the Soviet Union would not necessarily involve simultaneous attacks on Eastern

Europe, China, Cuba, Vietnam or other countries included in the SIOP); and "allied and neutral territory". Special categories of targets have also been delineated for pre-emptive attacks against the Soviet Union and for launch-on-warning (LOW) or launch-under-attack (LUA) scenarios in the event of unequivocal warning of a Soviet attack.

While the general structure and contents of the SIOP will be essentially maintained, there are some five particularly noteworthy aspects of the recent developments in targeting policy which warrant consideration. The first, and the one which featured most prominently in journalistic discussion of PD-59, was the directive that relatively less emphasis be accorded the destruction of the Soviet economic and industrial base and that greater attention "be directed toward improving the effectiveness of our attacks against military targets." It should be noted, however, that military targets already account for more than half the 40,000 target installations in the SIOP (as compared to some 15,000 economic-industrial targets), and that the destruction of these has always been a prime objective. (For example, Attack Options I and II in the 1962 SIOP were aimed at "the destruction or neutralization of [Soviet] strategic nuclear delivery forces" and "[conventional] military forces and military resources in being" respectively; the successful execution of Attack Option II would have reduced the "Soviet-Satellite residual ground forces" to seven Soviet and 10 Satellite divisions and neutralized the Bloc air forces as effective combat elements).

A second noteworthy aspect of the recent developments, and one of greater novelty, is the appreciation that the choice of targets is as much an exercise in deterrence as the execution of the plans is in warfighting. As one White House official stated in late 1977, at the outset of NTPR:

> "In the past nuclear targetting has been done by military planners who have basically emphasized the efficient destruction of targets. But targetting should not be done in a political vacuum.
> Some targets are of greater psychological importance to Moscow than others, and we should begin thinking of how to use our strategic forces to play on these concerns."

Hence, there have been some changes to the targeting guidance so as to exploit potential Soviet fears, such as threatening the Soviet food supply and making a target of Soviet troops and military facilities in the Far East ("kicking the door in!") so that the Soviet Union would be more vulnerable to attack from China; and some consideration has been given to the adaptation of targeting to the dismemberment and regionalization of the USSR, enhancing the prospects for regional insurrection during and after a nuclear exchange.

The most important consequence of this notion of targeting what the Soviets fear most, however, is the attention now being devoted to the targeting of the Soviet assets for political control—the Soviet state and its instruments of domestic and external coercion. This includes key CPSU and governmental buildings, military headquarters, command centres, KGB offices and border posts, communications facilities, etc. Again, US war plans have always included some installations of this sort—for example, some 2,000 of the 40,000 potential targets designated in SIOP-5D are leadership and control targets; however, it would not be unreasonable to expect that by the time SIOP-6 is authorised these targets would account for as much as 20 per cent of the Soviet target base—perhaps some 10,000 out of a likely total of 50,000 designated target installations.

A third point, emphasized by Secretary Brown in a message to the defence ministers of the NATO countries on 10 August, is that greater attention has been accorded planning for the use of very limited and selective options in order to "improve the contribution of our strategic nuclear forces to deterrence across the full spectrum of threats with which we must all be concerned". Various packages of selected attack options (SAOs), limited nuclear options (LNCs) and regional nuclear options (RNOs) are being prepared for use in not just nuclear situations but also in what hitherto would have been purely conventional situations. According to testimony of the Commander of the Strategic Air Command (SAC), General R.H. Ellis, before the Senate Armed Services Committee in March 1980,

> Deterrence can no longer be neatly divided into subgroups, such as conventional and nuclear. It must be viewed as an interrelated, single entity. SAC is developing new options which provide the National Command Authorities with additional flexibility to respond to future conflicts in a timely and controlled manner.

As an example of the use of RNOs and LNOs, General Ellis suggested that "combat missions could be launched from Andersen [Air Force Base in Guam] to the Middle East" in response to Soviet conventional military activity in that region. As an example of an SAO, plans for nuclear strikes against Soviet military facilities near Iran, including military bases and airfields inside the Soviet Union, have been prepared so as to "significantly degrade Soviet capabilities to project military power in the Middle East-Persian Gulf region for a period of at least 30 days".

A fourth point is that PD-59 emphasizes that the pre-planned target packages in the SIOP must be supplemented by the ability to find new targets and destroy them during the course of a nuclear exchange. While Soviet strategic nuclear installations and economic and industrial facilities would remain essentially fixed during wartime, there would be much movement of Soviet conventional military forces (including second echelon formations) and much of the Soviet political and military leadership would presumably be relocated. PD-59 requires the development of new reconnaissance satellites and signals intelligence (SIGINT) systems to provide the real-time intelligence capabilities necessary to effect this rapid retargeting.

The fifth noteworthy aspect of the recent developments in targeting policy is the recognition that the current US command, control and communication (C^3) system is inadequate to support any policy of extended nuclear war-fighting.

In this respect, PD-59 should be considered together with Presidential Directives 53 and 58 and a wide range of other measures intended to improve the survivability and the endurance of the US C^3 system. PD-53. entitled *National Security Telecommunications Policy* and signed by President Carter on 15 November 1979, proclaimed that "it is essential to the security of the US to have telecommunications facilities adequate to satisfy the needs of the nation during and after any national emergency, . . . to provide continuity of essential functions of government, and to reconstitute the political, economic and social structure of the nation". Its principal goal is described as ensuring "connectivity between the National Command Authority and strategic and other appropriate forces to support flexible execution of retaliatory strikes during and after an enemy nuclear attack". PD-58, signed by the President on 30 June 1980, is concerned with the maintenance of "continuity of government". It directs the Department of Defense and other agencies to improve the capacity of selected parts of the government, from the President on down, to withstand a nuclear attack. The measures under consideration include plans for evacuating military and civilian leaders from Washington in time of crisis; the construction of new hardened shelters for key personnel, data processing equipment and communication systems; and the improvement of early-warning systems.

All of these various developments are intended not just to improve the US capability to actually fight a nuclear war, in a tightly controlled fashion, but in so doing to also enhance the US deterrent posture. But to be of value to deterrence these moves must be credible, and be perceived as such by both the Soviet and US national command authorities. However, is it really possible to conduct a strategic nuclear exchange, no matter how controlled, without significant civilian casualties? How realistic, both as a strategic policy and as a targeting objective, is the notion of targeting the Soviet political and military leaderships and their control apparatus? Is it really possible to design a C^3 system that can operate in a nuclear environment in such a way and for a sufficient length of time to support the current US strategic policy of *escalation control*? And, in any case, is the Soviet

Union likely to cooperate in US efforts to control a nuclear exchange?

With respect to the first question, there seems little doubt that even granted the precision with which intercontinental strategic nuclear delivery vehicles can now be targeted, the collateral casualties that would accompany any limited counterforce exchange would still be very high. A comprehensive counterforce attack against the United States would involve strikes against the 1054 ICBM silos, two FBM submarine support bases (Bremerton and Charleston) and 46 SAC bomber bases. Whereas the ICBM silos are generally located in relatively unpopulated areas, the two SSBN bases and many of the bomber bases are quite near major cities. Depending on the assumptions made about the scale and character of the Soviet strikes, US fatalities from such a comprehensive counterforce attack range from two to 20 million, with 14 million perhaps the most reasonable. In the case of a comprehensive US counterforce attack against the Soviet Union, the targets would include nearly 1400 ICBM silos, three SSBN bases (Severomorsk near Murmansk, Petropavlovsk on the Kamchatka Peninsula, and Vladivostok, the major Soviet city in the Far East), 32 major air bases, and perhaps also the 700 IRBMs and MRBMs. Many of these are located in some of the most densely populated areas in the Soviet Union. Twenty-two of the 32 major air bases, some three-quarters of the IRBM and MRBM sites, and more than half the 26 Soviet ICBM fields are located west of the Ural Mountains. Fatalities from a US counter-ICBM attack alone would range from 3.7 to 27.7 million, depending principally on the level of fallout protection assumed; a full counterforce attack against bomber bases and FBM submarine support facilities as well as ICBM silos would obviously kill many more than this. Four of the ICBM fields (Kozelsk, Teykovo, Kostroma and Yedrovo) are located sufficiently close to Moscow and spread around in such a way that the national capital would receive extensive fallout regardless of the prevailing wind direction. Given casualties of this magnitude, and the particular Soviet difficulty of distinguishing a comprehensive counterforce attack from a more general military cum urban-industrial attack, the notion of limiting a nuclear exchange to supposedly surgical counterforce operations appears rather incredible.

Second, there would seem to be many problems with the concept of counter-political control targeting. One is that political control assets comprise, potentially at least, an extemely large target set. Political control in the Soviet Union emanates from the Kremlin in Moscow outward though the capitals of each of the Republics and down through those of the Oblasts and the Krays. Targeting the CPSU headquarters and other governmental and administrative buildings in each of these, as well as military headquarters and command posts and KGB centres throughout the Soviet Union could require many thousands of weapons.

There is also the problem that the locations of many political control assets are not known. This is a tacit admission in the following statement by Secretary Brown in his F.Y. 1981 Posture Statement:

> "Hardened command posts have been constructed near Moscow and other cities. For the some 100,000 people we define as the Soviet leadership, there are hardened underground shelters near places of work, and at relocation sites outside the cities. The relatively few leadership shelters we have identified would be vulnerable to direct attack."

Even where facilities have been identified, it would be difficult (if not impossible) to know exactly which elements of the leadership had dispersed to which facilities.

Moreover, the destruction of the political control facilities does not necessarily mean the destruction of the political control personnel. KGB officers are less likely to be in KGB buildings than dispersed among the population they are tasked with monitoring and controlling.

Indeed, this points to a larger problem. Many of the political and military leadership centres are located in or near major urban areas—particularly Moscow and the Republic capitals. Attacks on these would be virtually indistinguishable from counter-city attacks. Escalation control would be difficult to pursue following such attacks.

In fact, such attacks would probably mean the end of escalation control. As Colin Gray has pointed out:

> "Once executed, a very large strike against the Soviet political and administrative leadership would mean that the US had 'done its worst.' If the Soviet Government, in the sense of a National Command Authority, were still able to function, it is likely that it would judge that it had little, if anything, left to fear."

Finally, a counter political control strike would make it impossible for the Soviets to negotiate war termination.

The third question pertains to the vulnerability of the strategic command, control and communication (C^3) infrastructure. Despite the fact that the US has spent some $25b. on stragetic C^3 over the past decade, much of it on means of enhancing the survivability of particularly critical C^3 systems, it remains the case that the C^3 infrastructure is more vulnerable and has less endurance than the strategic forces it is intended to support. Strategic C^3 systems are vulnerable to all the threats to which the forces could be subject plus a variety of additional ones. The strategic forces gain protection through hardening, proliferation, mobility and camouflage. Many C^3 systems, such as radar sites, VLF antennae and satellite sensor systems are necessarily relatively 'soft'; some C^3 elements, such as the National Command Authorities, cannot be proliferated; major command posts, satellite ground stations and communication nodes are generally fixed; and radar sites and communication stations are extremely difficult to camouflage because of their electronic emissions. C^3 systems are generally more vulnerable to the blast effects of nuclear weapons than are the strategic forces, and have various peculiar vulnerabilities as well—susceptibility to electromagnetic pulse, electronic jamming, deception, etc.

The vulnerabilities of such critical elements of the strategic C^3 architecture as the National Command Authorities (NCA) themselves; the airborne C^3 systems which are relied upon for continuity of command and control in a nuclear environment; the satellite systems used for communications, early-warning, photographic reconnaissance and signals intelligence; the 'hot line' which would be required for communication and negotiation between the adversary leaderships; and the communication systems for the FBM submarines, which at least in the US case carry half the warheads of the strategic nuclear forces—these impose quiet debilitating physical constraints on the situations in which escalation might be controlled, the time period over which control might be maintained, and the proportion of the SIOP forces that could be employed in a controlled fashion. The boundary of control in any militarily significant exchange (as compared to demonstration strikes) is unlikely to lie beyond either a few days or a few tens of detonations!

The fourth problem with respect to the practicality of the concepts embodied in PD-59 is that control and limitation require that all the participants in the conflict be willing and have the capability to exercise restraints—in weapons, in targets, and in political objectives. It is most problematical as to whether the Soviets would "play the game." Despite some improvements in the capabilities for control. Soviet doctrine still seems to be that in the event of a nuclear exchange the Soviet forces would be used massively and simultaneously against a range of targets—nuclear forces, other military forces, the military-industrial base and, almost certainly, the US and NATO military, political, and administrative control centres.

Finally, the recent developments in targeting policy have some important implications for arms control. So long as declaratory policy emphasized concepts such as Assured Destruction or Sufficiency, it was possible to develop firm criteria for determining the size and characteristics of the US strategic nuclear forces. War-fighting concepts, on the other hand, are essentially open-ended in terms of force requirements. To cover all the Soviet political control assets and the wider range of military targets as required by the new targeting guidance will in turn require a large increase in the SIOP forces, as will the requirement for strategic reserves to both cover Soviet second-echelon forces and provide intra-war deterrence against escalation to urban-industrial attacks. On 9 April 1979, General Ellis wrote to Secretary Brown to the effect that US strategic force levels were inadequate to support the policy of countervailing targeting—at least without the deployment of "sufficient numbers" of air-launched cruise missiles (ALCMs), Trident SLBMs, and MX ICBMs. Moreover, increased expenditures on strategic C^3 systems and real-time surveillance capabilities are also required. To be effective, then, the recent targeting developments are likely to come into conflict with arms control objectives.

The Carter Administration began with great enthusiasm for arms control. It was not to last. Much of the opposition to the original draft of PD-59 that was prepared in early 1979 was based on arms control arguments—in particular, Secretary of State Vance believed that formal approval of the "new" doctrine would endanger the prospects for SALT II. President Carter's endorsement of PD-50 on 14 August 1979, however, signalled the death knell of the arms control stance of his administration; according to that directive, arms control was to be pursued only insofar as it served broader US national security interests. In an environment of increasing Soviet military capabilities, and increasing Soviet willingness to use those capabilities, the technological momentum which produced greater counterforce potential and more sophisticated C^3 systems proved irresistible. Under the Reagan administration there will be no attempt at resistance; instead, the concepts that are embodied in NSDM-242, the NUWEP and PD-59 will be pursued to even further extremes. From this perspective the fact that many of these concepts have inherently insoluble problems is not merely unfortunate; given the propensity of many members of the new administration to accept the possibility of limited nuclear war it is also extremely dangerous.

REFERENCES

Ball, Desmond, "Developments in US Strategic Nuclear Policy Under the Carter Administration," ACIS Working Paper No. 21, Center for International and Strategic Affairs, University of California, Los Angeles, February 1980.

Ball, Desmond, "Soviet ICBM Deployment", *Survival,* (Vol. XXII, No. 4), July/August 1980, pp. 167–170.

Brown, Harold, "The Objective of U.S. Strategic Forces", Address to the Naval War College, Washington, 20 August 1980.

Gray, Colin S., "Targeting Problems for Central War", *The Naval War College Review,* January/February 1980.

House Armed Services Committee, *Hearings on Military Posture and H.R. 1872,* (USGPO, Washington, D.C., 1979), Book 1 of Part 3, pp. 6–26.

Richelson, Jeffrey T., "The Dilemmas of Counter power Targeting", *Comparative Strategy,* (Vol. 2, No. 3), pp. 223–237.
Senate Armed Services Committee, *Department of Defense Authorization for Fiscal Year 1981,* (USGPO, Washington, D.C., 1980), Part 5, pp. 2720–2722.

Deterring Our Deterrent

PAUL NITZE

During much of Henry Kissinger's dominance over U.S. foreign policy, détente with the Soviet Union was the centerpiece of that policy. U.S. military strength was viewed as necessary to make détente work, rather than to make possible actual defense of ourselves or our allies against Soviet military pressure; Kissinger said that war with the Soviet Union was unthinkable.

This view was supported by the proposition that any war between the Soviet Union and ourselves would be nuclear and would inevitably result in hundreds of millions of casualties on both sides. This, in turn, implied that it makes little difference, within limitations of the type contemplated by the Vladivostok accord, whether the Soviet side comes to have more or bigger offensive warheads, the degree to which they improve their weapons technology, the extent of the asymmetrically better Soviet defenses (both active and passive), or whether one side or the other strikes first, provided only that we maintain strategic offensive forces for retaliation approximately as numerous and powerful as those we now have and have programmed for the future.

No more serious question faces us than whether these propositions are true or false.

To assess their probable truth or falsity, three sets of considerations are pertinent: One has to do with the interaction of policy and military strategy; the second concerns the various methods of assessing relative capabilities; the third relates to the interaction between the perceived strategic balance and foreign policy, including détente.

POLICY AND MILITARY STRATEGY

Twenty years ago, I wrote the following:

> A strong case can be made that no rational body of men would initiate a general atomic war unless they believed that the power of their initial attack and its immediate effects on the enemy would be so great as to assure that the subsequent phases of the war would be substantially one-sided. In order to achieve such a one-sided result, the attacking side (either Russia in an initial attack, or the West in response to an aggression by Russia or China which could be met only by general war) would logically concentrate the full power of its initial atomic attack on the military—primarily the retaliatory—capabilities of the other side. The attacker's object would be to destroy, in the initial blow, a large proportion of the base structure from which the defender must launch his retaliatory action (including the planes or missiles on the bases and the submarines and carriers which might support the main retaliatory action). The attacker would attempt to destroy a sufficiently large proportion of this base structure to reduce the power of the defender's retaliatory action to a level which the attacker's own defense system could contain. If he should succeed in this attempt he will have assured that the remaining phases of the war will be substantially one-sided. . . . The side which has lost effective control of the intercontinental air spaces will face a truly agonizing decision. It may still have the capability of destroying a few of the enemy's cities. But the damage it could inflict would be indecisive and out of all proportion to the annihilation which its own cities could expect to receive in return.[1]

Today some of the phrases in that passage seem out of date, but I believe the central points remain valid, particularly those which emphasize that the objective of military strategy under the circumstance of actual conflict would be to bring the war to an end under conditions less disastrous than other possible outcomes.

A much more succinct and elliptical formulation appeared in the November 1975 issue of *Communist of the Armed Forces,* the leading Soviet military publication:

> The premise of Marxism-Leninism on war as a continuation of policy by military means remains true in an atmosphere of fundamental changes in military matters. The attempt of certain bourgeois ideologists to prove that nuclear missile weapons leave war outside the framework of policy and that

[1] Paul H. Nitze, "Atoms, Strategy and Policy," Foreign Affairs, January 1956.

nuclear war moves beyond the control of policy, ceases to be an instrument of policy and does not constitute its continuation is theoretically incorrect and politically reactionary.

Implicit in this statement is the view that a war involving nuclear missiles should and can be an extension of policy. A suicidal war would not be an extension of policy; therefore Soviet military forces should not be limited in capability to that sufficient to assure mutual destruction. The force requirements for meeting the criterion of making war an extension of policy for one's own side are reasonably obvious, and include the following:

1. A powerful counterforce capability—one sufficient to reduce the enemy's offensive and defensive capabilities significantly and progressively below one's own;

2. Forces sufficiently hardened, dispersed, mobile, or defended as to make a possible counterforce response by the other side disadvantageous—that is, such that a counterforce response would only serve to weaken the relative position of the responder by using up a far higher percentage of his surviving forces than the percentage of the attacker's reserve forces he could hope to destroy;

3. Sufficient survivable reserve forces, whether or not there were such a counterforce response, to hold the enemy's population and industry disproportionately at risk;

4. Active and passive defense measures, including civil defense and hardened and dispersed command and control facilities, sufficient to ensure survival and control even if the enemy response to the initial counterforce attack were an immediate retaliatory strike on one's population and industry;

5. The means and the determination not to let the other side get in the first blow—i.e., to pre-empt if necessary.

An examination of the Soviet strategic nuclear program and their military doctrinal literature indicates that they are indeed attempting to achieve capabilities consistent with fulfilling all five requirements. One cannot, of course, prove or disprove judgments as to Soviet reasoning. But the programs begun about 1962 and continued at a high level of effort since that time seem to reflect a fundamental state of mind on the Soviet side that contains no doubt as to the desirability of a force which can meet this set of criteria.

ASSESSING NUCLEAR CAPABILITIES

That the Soviets are making rapid and significant progress in their strategic force programs is clear. But to assess the degree of Soviet progress in achieving these goals, to determine the truth or falsity of the judgments implied by Kissinger's policy statements, and to decide whether and to what extent U.S. strategic programs should be augmented or modified, the U.S. and Soviet relative nuclear capabilities must be assessed in detail and in a pertinent manner. Furthermore, it is important to illuminate the questions, how much is enough for the Soviet side to believe that a nuclear war could, for them, be an extension of policy through military means, and how much is enough for us to deny them that possibility.

There are three distinctly different ways, increasing in depth and sophistication . . . to measure relative capabilities and crisis stability. These are:

1. That which each side has *before* a strike;

2. That surviving to the United States and that remaining to the Soviet side *after an initial counterforce strike* by the Soviets;

3. That remaining to each side *after an exchange* in which the Soviet side attacks U.S. forces and the United States responds by reducing Soviet reserved forces to the greatest useful extent.

The first method involves so-called "static" indicators. It does not assess how these capabilities might react upon each other in an actual exchange. It tends not to differentiate between those capabilities useful in a counterforce role and those useful in holding the other side's population and industry hostage.

The second method, being the first step in a dynamic analysis, is more sophisticated. It reflects the counterforce capabilities of those weapons used in the initial counterforce strike, but does not distinguish between the counterforce and the countervalue capabilities of the forces remaining to each side after that first step.

The third method, which carries the dynamic analysis a step further, most clearly brings out the stability or potential instability of the relationship by making it possible to assess the relative counterforce capabilities of each side and the countervalue capabilities remaining to each side after a two-sided counterforce exchange in which all useful counterforce targets have been addressed.

The following charts illustrate the results of one such set of analyses. A word about the indices shown in these charts. In comparing the two disparate strategic forces, different indices are more significant in the different methods of analysis. In Figure 1, the most useful static index is the index of equivalent weapons (EW) of a strategic force (perhaps the most sophisticated single index, a measure which accounts for the number and yield of the warheads, the accuracy of those warheads, and the characteristics of the targets against which they might be used). In Figure 3, since the counterforce targets which it was considered useful to address have been addressed, the primary indices of interest are the countervalue ones. These include throw-weight (TW), which is the best overall measure of the countervalue potential of a strategic force;[2] total megatons, which is the best index of aggregate fallout effects; equivalent megatons, which is the best index of aggregate blast damage effects; and numbers of weapons, which is the best index of target coverage.

The calculations reflected in these charts are based on the assumption that U.S. forces would be on a normal alert status when attacked. Strategic warning generated by Soviet implementation of civil defense preparations, or by an evolving crisis situation, would enable the United States to bring additional forces, primarily a portion of the non-alert bomber forces, up to an alert status. Based on optimistic assumptions as to the additional forces that could be brought up to alert, this could reduce the Soviet advantage after a counterforce exchange (as shown in Figure 3), by 20 per cent in number of warheads and 40 per cent in megatonnage. This result, however, is highly dependent upon the timely deployment of the B-1 force, which has not yet been finally approved. The effect of Soviet implementation of its evacuation program and other aspects of its civil defense program, which such strategic warning would permit, could be significantly more important in limiting its potential civilian casualties than the increase in numbers and megatonnage available to the United States as a result of having had such warning.

BALANCE OF DEPLOYED FORCES
(Static or preattack levels)

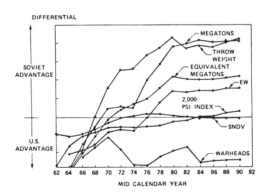

EW: equivalent weapons
SNDV: strategic nuclear delivery vehicles

FIGURE 1.

---

[2] "Throw-weight" is a measure of the useful weight of payload that can be propelled to intended distance.

CAPABILITIES AFTER SOVIET FIRST STRIKE

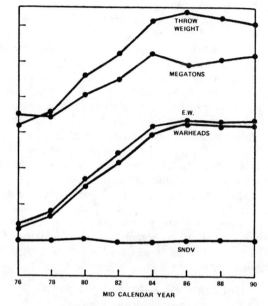

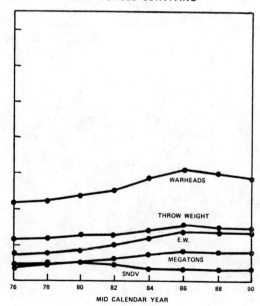

FIGURE 2.

COMPARISON OF ALTERNATIVE INDICES OF CAPABILITY
(After a counter force exchange)

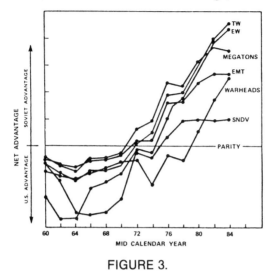

FIGURE 3.

SOVIET—U.S. THROW-WEIGHT RATIOS

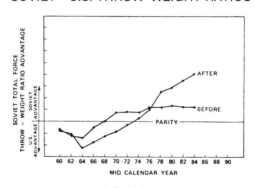

FIGURE 4.

Trends shown in these charts by all methods and in all indices move in a direction favorable to the Soviet Union from the mid-1960s through the mid-1980s. Today, after a strategic nuclear counterforce exchange under normal U.S. alert conditions, the Soviet Union would hold superiority in all indices of capability except numbers of warheads, and even that sole remaining U.S. advantage would be gone within two or three years. Neither SALT I nor the projected SALT II agreements (assumed for the analyses shown) have had—or promise

—any discernible effect in arresting the trend toward an increasingly large margin of Soviet superiority. Moreover, the relationship is becoming unstable; the Soviets in coming years will be able to increase their ratio of advantage by attacking U.S. forces (the obverse, however, is not true). This is shown in Figure 4, where methods one and three (before-any-strike, and after-a-counterforce-exchange) are compared for the ratios of throw-weight. The point at which the curves cross indicates that point at which the Soviets could, by initiating such an exchange as postulated here, increase the ratio of advantage they held before the exchange.

U.S. OPTIONS AND SOVIET CIVIL DEFENSE

Does any of this make any difference? Isn't it true that we could, in the event of a Soviet counterforce attack, forgo a counterforce response and devote all of our surviving forces to an attack on Soviet population and industry? Wouldn't such an attack satisfy Kissinger's estimate of hundreds of millions of casualties on both sides? Isn't deterrence thereby assured?

It is desirable that the Soviet leadership should think so. It is, moreover, possible that a president, in the absence of all other options other than surrender, would make the decison, in the limited time which might be available for him for decision, to launch such a countervalue retaliatory attack. But is it desirable for a future president to be in the position of having no other useful option? Is this the high quality deterrence to which the United States is entitled and strove mightily over post-World War II decades to maintain? And would the Soviet leadership think it must lose hundreds of millions of citizens if the president were to make that decision?

I believe the answer to all these questions is negative.

Let me begin with the last question. The Soviet Union has for many years put emphasis upon the planning, organization, and training of cadres to implement a civil defense program. That program calls for the substantial evacuation of its cities and industrial plants, the sheltering of those who must stay, and the rapid construction of expedient fallout shelters by those who are evacuated and cannot otherwise be protected. In some of their civil defense manuals, the Soviets have estimated that the effective implementation of this program should hold casualties to 3 per cent or 4 per cent of their population. This would be a large number of casualties, but not hundreds of millions, and not a number large enough to keep their society from being able to recover with reasonable speed. This goal may not be achievable; there are many uncertainties. However, it is possible to make some gross approximations of the possible effectiveness of Soviet civil defense.

The most difficult nuclear effect for a dispersed population to defend against is fallout. Fallout is proportional to the megatonnage and the fission fraction of the weapons which are ground burst. The United States has, over the last 15 years, substantially reduced the megatonnage of its weapons in favor of more numerous, smaller yield, more accurate warheads. Today our most survivable force is our Poseidon submarine force at sea; the aggregate megatonnage of its 2,000 or so normally alert reliable warheads is approximately 80 megatons. Because of their relatively low individual yield, it would be best to use them against point targets even in a countervalue attack, and they are most effective when fused for a height of burst optimum for blast damage effects; they would, however, then produce negligible fallout. Against such an attack the stated goal of the Soviet civil defense program might well be achieved.

Our alert bomber force is our next most survivable force. Its aggregate deliverable megatonnage could be 10 times as much as that of our alert SLBM force, but the alert bombers must be launched-on-warning and a prompt decision made as to the targets which they are to hit; otherwise their survivability would be little better than that of the non-alert bombers.

Of course, the Minuteman missiles with a megatonnage roughly equal to that of the alert bomber force could be launched from under attack, but to do so allows only minutes for the decision to be made. Rough computations indicate that if all these forces were used in an all-out and immediate countervalue response to a Soviet counterforce first strike, the estimates in the Soviet civil defense manuals are overoptimistic from the Soviet viewpoint. They are not, however, wholly out of the ball park. The usual assumption that the United States possesses vast population overkill is, in essence, without foundation.

The crucial question is whether a future U.S. president should be left with only the option of deciding within minutes, or at most within two or three hours, to retaliate after a counterforce attack in a manner certain to result not only in military defeat for the United States but in wholly disproportionate and truly irremediable destruction to the American people. I believe not. This would be to make certain that military strategy had completely escaped from the control of policy.

U.S. vs. SOVIET DEFENSE PROBLEMS

Does any of this make any difference short of a nuclear war? The defense problems of the United States and the Soviet Union are quite different. The United States must be able to project its power over many thousands of miles to support allied defense structures on lines close to the concentrations of Soviet power. The Soviet basic defensive task is much simpler; that is, to maintain military preponderance on the exterior lines of its relatively compact land mass. Its only difficult problem is its long and narrow lines of communication to eastern Siberia. There can be little doubt that the Soviet Union has more than adequate military power for this basic defensive task.

For many years, U.S. strategic nuclear preponderance has made it possible to offset Soviet military superiority at the periphery and to deter its offensive employment. It has also made it possible for the United States confidently to use the seas for projection of its supporting power despite the Soviet Union's always very real sea denial capabilities.

An imbalance in favor of the Soviet Union in the strategic nuclear relationship would reverse these factors.

There is a further problem, moreover, in that the Soviet Union has in recent years been paying increasing attention to projectible power, including air mobility, longer-range tactical air capabilities, intermediate-range missiles and projectible sea power. To counter such capabilities in the absence of confidence in the adequacy of our nuclear deterrent, could be difficult and imprudent. Not to counter them could leave us with wholly inadequate tools of policy.

COUNTERFORCE vs. COUNTERVALUE

What bearing does the foregoing analysis have upon the future design of our strategic forces? A clear distinction should be made between counterforce and countervalue aspects of nuclear strategy. Neither can be ignored; both are essential to meaningful deterrence; but the requirements for each are different, distinguishable, and important.

In the past we have failed to appreciate this distinction and have thus fallen between two stools. We have prided ourselves on our advanced technology which has given us superior accuracy, higher yield-to-weight ratios in smaller yield re-entry vehicles (RVs), and leadership in developing multiple independently targeted re-entry vehicles (MIRVs). For political reasons and because of the presumed destabilizing nature of a counterforce capability, we have, however, forgone the accuracy and yield combinations which would give us high single-shot kill capabilities against Soviet silos and other hardened targets. On the other hand, in part to reduce the widespread destruction of a nuclear war, if it were to occur, we have progressively reduced the megatonnage of our force. This megatonnage is now so low that it is possible for the Soviet Union to plan a civil defense program which would make a far smaller percentage of their population hostage to a U.S. countervalue attack, particularly after it has been reduced in capability by an initial Soviet counterforce attack, than our population is to a Soviet countervalue response.

The Soviet leadership appears to be fully conscious of the differing requirements for countervalue and counterforce capabilities. The question has been asked why the Soviets continue to test high megatonnage single RVs on their SS-18s and SS-19s. I believe the answer is that they see the importance of deterring the deterrent; in other words, they wish to be able, after a counterforce attack, to maintain sufficient reserve megatonnage to hold U.S. population and industry hostage in a wholly assymmetrical relationship. Concurrently, the accuracy and yield combinations and numbers of MIRVed RVs they are deploying promise to meet their full requirements for a highly effective counterforce capability and still permit the withholding of a substantial number of missiles carrying large single RVs.

The question at issue is whether we also would be well advised to make a distinction between forces dedicated to a counterforce role and forces reserved for a countervalue role, and, if so, how much is enough in survivable forces for each of these two roles? My view is that we would be well advised to do so and that it is not impossible to find reasonable criteria to determine, within rough limits, how much is enough for each role. I would suggest two sets of criteria.

The first criterion would be to assure that the relationship of the yield, accuracy, survivability, and reliability of the two sides' forces is such that the Soviet side could not hope by initiating a counterforce exchange to improve either the absolute excess in pounds of its throw-weight over ours, or the ratio of its throw-weight to ours. To achieve this, it is necessary that we deploy forces which result in bringing the throw-weight line in Figure 3 closer to the parity line. This requires an increase in Minuteman survivability, through development of a new multiple-aim-point basing mode, an increase in Minuteman throw-weight, through development of the MX missile, and a substantial improvement in the single-shot kill probability of the U.S. RVs against hard targets, through the development and deployment of missiles and RVs with the requisite combination of accuracy, yield, and reliability to give high probability of destroying some 1,500 to 2,000 hard targets.

The second criterion would be to assure that the forces remaining to the United States after a counterforce exchange would be fully adequate to keep the Soviet population hostage to a countervalue attack in the face of the most effective civil defense programs we judge it possible for the Soviet Union to mount. Something of the order of 3,000 deliverable megatons remaining in reserve after a counterforce exchange should satisfy the second criterion.

Rough computations indicate that we should be able to satisfy both criteria if we deploy 550 MX missiles in a multiple-aim-point mode, if we deploy the Trident II missile in an appropriate number of Trident submarines, if we develop their accuracy and reliability to the levels which now seem technologically feasible, and if we proceed with the planned B-1 deployments augmented with strategic cruise missiles. Such developments and deployments will, however, take time. In the meantime, in order to retain sufficient deterrence during the time required to restore a stable balance, urgent attention should be given to determining quick and possibly temporary fixes necessary to meet the problem as it is apt to emerge in the late 1970s and early 1980s. These include rapid development and deployment of a mobile transporter-erector-launcher and hardened capsule for Minuteman III, a variety of simplified point defenses of the class suggested by Richard Garwin[3] and others, provision for a potential rapid increase in bomber and SLBM alert rates and testing of reliable and appropriate methods to launch Minuteman from under verified large-scale attack against our silos.

The objective of such short- and long-range programs would not be to give the United States a war-fighting capability; it would be to deny to the Soviet Union the possibility of a successful war-fighting capability. We would thus be acting to maintain a situation in which each side is equally and securely deterred from initiating the use of nuclear weapons against the other or the allies of the other. It is only if, and when, we persuade the Soviet side that there is no reasonable prospect that they can successfully alter that situation that we can expect them seriously to negotiate for long-term agreements assuring stable mutual deterrence at lower and equal levels of strategic nuclear capabilities.

A New Debate
on Ballistic Missile Defence

COLIN S. GRAY

Ten years after the anti-ballistic missile debate of 1969–70, the strategic environment has changed enough to suggest to many commentators the need for ballistic missile defence (BMD) technologies. A

[3] U.S., Congress, Testimony prepared for the Joint Committee on Defense Production, April 28, 1976.
Colin S. Gray, "A New Debate on Ballistic Missile Defence," *Survival,* March/April 1981, The International Institute of Strategic Studies, pp. 60–71. Reprinted by permission.
To save space, we have omitted some footnotes. For full documentation, see original.

new debate over the merits of different kinds of BMD is coming, but the terms of that debate are largely unformed. As of 1981, there are more than sufficient grounds for reopening a policy debate not only about BMD'S possible merit for stabilizing the Soviet-American strategic balance according to the criteria of mutual assured (societal) vulnerability, but also about the fundamental wisdom of the offence-dominance which has characterized US strategic doctrine and posture for the better part of fifteen years. This latter issue bears directly upon philosophies of deterrence, as well as upon the relevance of US capabilities to possible foreign-policy needs and the compatibility of US nuclear strategy with American values.

This article does not argue that the anti-ABM coalition of ten years ago was wrong, that the 1972 ABM Treaty was a mistake, or that the United States should hasten to invest heavily in BMD systems for the 1980s and 1990s. All it argues is that the strategic world, and much of informed Western opinion about it, has changed so markedly since the very early 1970s that, given the inherent importance of the subject, the question of the policy relevance of BMD of different kinds should be raised anew.

Our knowledge of Soviet 'strategic culture', and of Soviet strategic 'style' in arms competition, has undermined the plausibility of a good many of the anti-ABM arguments popular ten years ago; and the disadvantageous evolution of the multi-level military balance in the 1970s, in an era characterized by intensive arms negotiations, has cast significant doubts upon the value of a Western concept of strategic stability born in an era of US strategic superiority. In short, BMD technology has changed, Western understanding of the Soviet Union has changed, and Western appreciation of what is, and is not, an adequate strategic concept, has changed. In these very general terms, at least, it may be claimed that it would be inappropriate to view the negative decision on BMD enshrined in the ABM Treaty of 1972 as constituting a historically definitive judgment. On 14 March 1969 President Nixon announced the reorientation of the US ABM programme, renamed *Safeguard* (from *Sentinel*), away from the provision of 'light' or 'thin' area coverage of urban-industrial America and towards the defence of *Minuteman* ICBM silos. Although the mix of system components was different in the new hard-point defence orientation, it did not escape technical critics that *Safeguard* was being charged with a mission for which its major components had not been designed. Above all else, critics argued that the ABM system, and in particular its few missile site radars, was far more vulnerable to attack or degradation than was the target set it was defending. The distinction between the BMD of hard-point targets (such as ICBM silos and launch-control centres) and urban-industrial targets is of fundamental importance, both for the scale of the technological challenge and possibly for the strategic consequences. Many, if not most, of the more doctrinaire anti-BMD arguments of 1969–70 related solely to city defences, not to the defence of hardened point targets.

Basically, there were five classes of anti-BMD argument advanced ten years ago: these were that BMD would not work; that, whether or not it would work, it was not needed; that it would destroy the stability of deterrence (a generic charge which embraced the accusations that it would promote arms-race instability and crisis instability, and would endanger the prospects for success of the then novel SALT enterprise); that it would mean a threat to particular localities ('bombs in the back yard'); and that it was a make-work project for an alleged military-industrial complex.

In 1969–70 it was argued that *Safeguard* would not work. It was claimed that the system's radars could be neutralized by the 'blackout' effects of well-timed precursor attacks, or by the effects produced by defensive missile warheads, and that the computer software, the directing brain of the defence, simply could not cope reliably with the volume of information, assessments and battle management orders required. In addition, it was argued that the radar identification and discrimination of real targets (re-entry vehicles as opposed to decoys, chaff, missile tank fragments and other debris) beyond the atmosphere was too imprecise to allow confidence in the exoatmospheric intercept ability of the *Spartan* ABM. Also, it was claimed that the Soviet Union could always adopt a 'brute-force' solution to US BMD deployment—that deployment would simply be saturated by more incoming re-entry vehicles than there were interceptors available. For a variety of 'strategic cultural' and bureaucratic-political reasons, the US defence community has long been friendly to the modern equivalent of the belief voiced by British Prime Minister Stanley Baldwin in 1932 that 'the bomber will always get through'. (Fortunately for Britain and the United States this dogma was challenged successfully by the Tizard Committee, with the consequence that the RAF of 1940 had a modern air defence system and an obsolete bomber force.)

The predicted technical incompetence of BMD in 1969–70 was buttressed by fairly casual reference to such offensive ploys as 'salvage-fusing', whereby an in-coming warhead would be detonated by an interceptor warhead detonation, and the deployment of manoeuvering re-entry vehicles (MARVS). Both methods are technically possible but, as of 1981, both are generally judged to be very difficult and costly to design and effect. A missile or capability that is very probably good enough to cope with even severe threats usually has to be defended against purely theoretical threats that are extremely unlikely to materialize.

The claim that BMD would not work frequently did not refer to an anticipated 'catastrophic' failure of the defence, but rather to the expectation that no BMD system would be 100% effective. This claim is of little importance for the active defence of ICBM silos or shelters, but it is often held to be a devastating critique of city defence. While granting that 'leakage' can be permitted, indeed even planned for, with ICBM silo or shelter defence (one might choose to 'give' an enemy a fraction of his hard targets, in order to concentrate defence assets to protect the rest), it is not true that an imperfect city defence is valueless. 'Leakage' can be controlled and even directed to an important degree. The heavy defence of a target may discourage its being targeted, while leakage can be controlled by deploying more interceptor missiles (this is not to deny that heavy defence may lead to heavy targeting allocation). For reasons of technological deficiency, treaty-constrained deployment or unilaterally detemined force size, the United States might well be in a position to deny Soviet ICBM and SLBM direct access to most of her urban-industrial assets, though possibly at the cost of denying protection to some. No matter how proficient the ballistic missile defences may be, there can be no guarantee that a few warheads could not penetrate. No defence system should be expected to 'work' with absolute and total success. A measure of 'hardening' for urban-industrial America through civil defence should be the principal policy response to the inevitable defence 'leakage' problem.

Next, it was believed widely, and by people of some strategic sophistication, that BMD was not needed. This claim was relevant to the 1969 *Safeguard* reorientation of the BMD programme. It was argued that there was no plausible threat on the horizon to the pre-launch survivability of the silo-housed *Minuteman* ICBM (Secretary of Defense Melvin Laird's claims for the counterforce first-strike potential of the SS-9 Mod 4, with 3×5 MT MIRVS, were generally discounted. And—should that claim be overtaken unexpectedly by events—it was argued that it was less than obvious that a theoretically vulnerable *Minuteman* should be defended: the United States could abandon her land-based missile force or seek survivability through some form of deceptive basing.

The complex deterrence stability argument against BMD referred, strictly, only to a BMD system deployed in an attempt to defend American society. Apart from its uncertain potential for expansion into a city defence scheme, the hard-point defence of ICBM silos was by definition innocent of this charge. In the late 1960s the bulk of the official US defence and arms-control community believed that strategic stability, 'a truly divine goal' as one commentator put it,[1] was logically inherent in the very character of modern weapon technology. Each super-power, it was thought, requires unrestricted

[1] John Newhouse, *Cold Dawn: The Story of SALT* (New York: Holt, Rinehart and Winston, 1973), p. 9.

military access to the societal assets of the other, while remaining un-
questionably confident in the ability of its strategic offensive forces to
survive a first strike by the super-power adversary. The 'stable deterrent' was the deterrent able to survive surprise attack and wreak unacceptable damage upon the adversary's society. It was believed—
though the belief was based on nothing more substantial than abstract
(and ethnocentric) strategic logic—that the Soviet Union would see any
area defence of the American homeland as a potentially fatal challenge
to her retaliatory capability, which she would have to overcome.

ABM AND STRATEGIC LOGIC

This strategic logic meant that BMD deployment for urban-
industrial coverage would stimulate an 'offsetting' Soviet offensive
response: hence, the arms-race instability. Similarly, BMD coverage
of societal assets would imply a greater US willingness to break out of
an acute political crisis by military means, since a President might
come to believe that his country actually could wage, survive and
recover from a nuclear war. By extension, it was argued that if BMD
coverage of US urban-industrial targets would necessarily stimulate a
Soviet offensive programme response (in order to preserve Soviet
assured destruction capability), it could not fail to undermine the basis
for a SALT accord. Such an accord would be negotiable only if the
two sides lacked major incentives to build up their strategic offensive
force arsenals.

On this thesis, if American ABM deployment were drastically curtailed the Soviet Union should lack any powerful incentive to deploy
strategic offensive forces beyond those needed to cover the US urban-
industrial target base (and some military targets). George Rathjens
reflected this opinion in his observation that 'with the right kind of
ABM agreement, incentive for either side to expand its offensive
missile forces or to put MIRVS on them would be much reduced since,
in the absence of concern about adversary ABM deployment, each
side could be confident that it had an adequate deterrent even if it
believed that a large fraction of its strategic force might be destroyed
by preemptive attack.'[2]

However reasonable such expectations were at the time, the plain
facts of the 1970s would appear to destroy the theory that informed
this claim. The Soviet Union, in the context of the ABM Treaty, proceeded to test and deploy the kind of strategic offensive missile force
that one would have expected if a serious US city BMD system had

    [2] 'A Break-Through in Arms Control', *Bulletin of the Atomic Scientists,* vol. 26,
no. 6 (June 1971), p. 5.

existed.[3] It might be suggested that Soviet ICBM and SLBM programmes in the 1970s would have been pursued even more energetically
had the United States proceeded with BMD—and particularly with a
BMD system which provided some urban-industrial coverage.
However, that argument is both inherently improbable and implausible. The Soviet Union, with a diminishing rate of economic growth,
has been modernizing in every category of military capability. The
development, testing and deployment of her MIRV-equipped fourth-
generation, ICBM (SS-16 to SS-19)[4], has constituted an investment of
awesome magnitude. On the available evidence it is not obvious that
the Soviet ICBM and SLBM programmes (with their nuclear warhead
production requirements) could have been on a very much greater
scale if the US had deployed BMD. Indeed, if the Soviet Union decided
that BMD deployment required a response in kind, they might even
have been smaller.

In retrospect, the last two classes of objection to BMD
deployment—popular resistance to 'bombs in the back yard', and the
quest for both a substantive and a symbolic victory over an alleged
sinister military-industrial complex—appear largely to have been
period-piece rallying cries. However, although it is true to claim that
American communities had lived in peace for many years with
nuclear-armed air defence missile sites, and that popular ground
swells against the munitions makers had been conspicuous by their
absence since the days of the Nye Committee (1934), the fact remains
that the popular suspicions generated in connection with ABM
(though really stemming from Vietnam) have had a lasting impact
upon the structure of the domestic politics of defence in the United
States. The ABM was the principal weapon-system victim of the new-
found lack of trust in official military wisdom which the American
public derived from its Vietnam experience. Politically fatal though
these objections could be, they were irrelevant to the strategic merits
of BMD deployment.

Arguments dating from 1970 to the effect that BMD will not work
simply do not apply to the BMD technologies of 1980–90. Yet, given
the sources of doctrinaire opposition to BMD deployment, the

---

[3] It may be argued that the United States also proceeded with deployments which
made sense primarily in terms of an active defence environment (i.e. *Minuteman* III and
Poseidon C-3). This is correct, but it should be remembered that US MIRV deployment
began in 1970, more than two years before the ratification of the ABM Treaty, and that
by the late summer of 1972 the US already had 200 *Minuteman* III, and 160 *Poseidon*
C-4, deployed. Moreover, US MIRV deployment may have played a significant role in
persuading Soviet leaders that their extant BMD capability had little strategic promise.
[4] The SS-16, unlike the other three, has not been deployed, though it may have been
stockpiled in modest numbers (say 100–200).

technical accomplishment of the US Army's BMD programme has
had very little impact on policy debate, because the government has
not had a strategic conceptual framework with a place for any BMD
deployment.

For ease and convenience of treatment, BMD is here assumed to be
one of two kinds: the defence of American society, or the defence of
American strategic forces (most particularly, of the ICBM force).
Notwithstanding the residual uncertainties as to the probable operational effectiveness of ICBM against silos, there is today no serious
argument about the prediction that within a year the US ICBM force,
as presently constituted, will be almost totally vulnerable to a Soviet
first strike. Several anti-ABM spokesmen in the *Safeguard* debate of
1969–70 granted that they would recommend active hard-point
defence, when and if 'the threat' materialized. If they meant what they
said, they should be pressing today for BMD for the US ICBM force.
There is a consensus within the American defence community that the
silo-housed *Minuteman* ICBM deployment is on the verge of being
changed from a secure second-strike retaliatory force into a lightning
conductor for pre-emptive first-strike destruction.

Unlike the situation ten years ago, when the US body politic was
debating the merits of the *Safeguard* ABM system, in 1980 the US has
a low-risk BMD technology that has been designed for a dedicated
hard-point defence. The US Army's Low Altitude Defense System
(LOADS), described below, is capable of intercepting *only* at an
altitude (about 4,000 ft) which would provide a 'keep out' zone so
restricted that unprotected humans or unhardened structures or communication facilities would be fatally vulnerable to offensive warheads exploded beyond that zone. Because of the ABM Treaty of 1972
(as amended in 1974), with its restriction to one site and its severe
radar and interceptor limits, plus the residue of negative doctrinal
feeling which has survived from early 1970s, LOADS has not been
considered on it cost-competitive merits with other alternatives for the
preservation of the US ICBM force. It is not at all obvious that
LOADS should be deployed in the near future in defence of US
ICBM—the deceptive basing route for *Minuteman*/MX appears to be
cost-effective *vis-à-vis* even substantial threat growth—but there can
be little doubt that the negative reactions which even today are caused
by the very mention of BMD preclude objective analysis of the competitive merits of hard-point BMD.

There may still be some good reason for believing that the BMD of
American cities and other high-value economic targets would be
undesirable, but the kind of 'deterrence instability' arguments advanced ten to fifteen years ago have lost much, though not all, of their
popularity. With very few exceptions, the US defence and arms-
control community has come to the conclusion that the Soviet Union

does not hold to a concept of strategic stability that is at all recognizable in Western terms. Soviet defence planners may well be pleased to note the totally undefended character of the American homeland, but there is no evidence that would suggest a Soviet force planning requirement, judged to be essential for deterrence, to 'cover' an identified fraction of US civilian-economic assets. The active and passive defence of the homeland, as Michael Howard has suggested, is surely simply a matter of common sense.[5] The BMD of urban-industrial America ('thick' or 'thin') is very unlikely to deprive the Soviet Union of her 'deterrent', because the evidence at hand suggests very strongly that, for her, deterrent effect is a function of anticipated war-fighting prowess. To the best of our knowledge, she has little interest in actually punishing American society, and urban-industrial America would be a likely target only insofar as it contributed to the material resources for the conduct of a war. However, the Soviet Union has to be presumed to have an interest in maintaining a high probability of American self-deterrence.

One cannot be certain—there is a severe shortage of evidence—but on the basis of Soviet words and deeds it would appear that there is *no* Soviet assured destruction requirement *vis-à-vis* the American homeland which could be endangered by US area BMD deployment. If this tentative claim is correct, then the deterrence stability (arms-race, crisis and arms control) charges against US area BMD deployment are almost entirely the result of American strategic-cultural preconceptions: plausible but, in Soviet terms, incorrect. In the context of US BMD deployment, Soviet BMD would not be a destabilizing development.

PRESENT BMD TECHNOLOGY

In LOADS the US Army has developed a system dedicated to the defence of hardened targets. LOADS comprises a well hardened radar of modest dimensions (since it has only to discriminate, identify and provide engagement data for targets that have re-entered the atmosphere, and are vectored very narrowly),[6] and an inertially guided interceptor roughly half the size of the *Sprint* missile of *Safeguard* vintage. Although LOADS could defend the existing *Minuteman* fields, it is ideally suited, and indeed has been designed, to defend a deceptively based ICBM system.

The MX basing scheme as currently envisaged—200 ICBM deployed one to each 'linear track' with 23 horizontal shelters (the

---

[5] 'The Forgotten Dimensions of Strategy', *Foreign Affairs,* vol. 57, no. 5 (Summer 1979), pp. 982-3, 985.

[6] The LOADS radar is only one-fortieth the size of the radar required by the *Site Defense* BMD system. *Site Defense* is a direct technological extrapolation from *Safeguard*.

ISSUES FOR THE EIGHTIES

'loading dock', rapid horizontal 'shuffle' system)—multiplies the prospective effectiveness of LOADS to what should seem to Soviet General Staff analysts to be a profoundly discouraging degree. Specifically, if a shelter-warhead kill ratio of unity is assumed (and also—unrealistically—no reliability problem) the Soviet Union can be certain of 'killing' one MX for every 23 warheads dispatched to saturate a particular 'linear track'. However, if a minimal LOADS deployment (one interceptor per 'linear track') is added (at an estimated FY 1980 cost of $11–12 billion), Soviet targeteers—not knowing which shelter contained the MX missile—would have to double their warhead allocation, since the interceptor missile *could* be defending any of the 23 shelters. This is known as a 'preferential defense' tactic—the LOADS interceptor(s) would 'prefer' to defend the shelter with the missile, but the Soviet target planning staff would not know which that was. In principle, the Soviet Union could design an attack which might defeat LOADS cheaply: specifically, an initial barrage attack would 'flush' the interceptor, permitting a follow-up re-entry vehicle to attack the shelter which it had preferred to defend. In practice this tactic would, at best, be extremely difficult to effect and, at worst, would be technically infeasible. It is a classic 'back of the envelope' threat—ingenious but probably impractical, and scarcely likely to appeal to responsible Soviet attack planners.

LOADS differs from *Safeguard* in a number of ways: the interceptor missile and radar would themselves be deceptively based, as would the ICBM (MX or deceptively-based *Minuteman*) they were protecting; the LOADS radar, since it would have to provide intercept data only on the threat to one 23-shelter linear track, is harder (*vis-à-vis* nuclear effects) and far smaller than was the *Safeguard* missile site radar; and the intercept would occur at truly minimum altitude, thereby depriving the offence of virtually all of the usually cited 'spoofing' tactics using decoys.[7] On the negative side it must be said that the relatively close spacing of the MX shelters (roughly 6,000 ft apart, or slightly less), could pose noteworthy problems for LOADS radars looking at a threat coming in from the north southwards. The radars might have to look through the nuclear effects of weapons exploded in, or very close to, the threat corridor. However, a Soviet saturation attack that was 'walking in' from north to south would, or could (depending on the timing), entail the risk of severe 'fratricide' as warheads sought to penetrate through, or very close to, the cloud stems of previous explosions.[8]

[7] The traffic-handling capability of the data-processing equipment to be used in LOADS also marks a dramatic improvement over *Safeguard* (even allowing for the greater size and sophistication of the threat).

[8] 'Fratricide' is the phenomenon whereby nuclear explosions create local conditions that damage or destroy incoming warheads or cause them to deviate from their intended trajectories.

LOADS technology is currently scheduled for initial operational readiness in 1988. However, that lead-time is tied to questionable assumptions about the MX lead-time. At present the MX ICBM has an initial operating capability date of July 1986, a date which almost certainly could, and in my view should, be brought forward to December 1984 or January 1985. Since LOADS comprises so-called 'state-of-the-art' technology, there is no persuasive reason why it could not be deployed *with* the MX missile if the government so wished.

At present some defence commentators are arguing that deceptively based MX will be viable in relation to the possible growth of the Soviet threat (i.e. the increase in warheads capable of killing hard targets) *only* if LOADS is deployed. This is simply not true. The US defence community currently assumes that by 1986 the Soviet Union could deploy some 6,000–7,000 such warheads on her ICBM force. But when one allows, realistically, for the Soviet ICBM warheads needed to target *Minuteman*, *Titan* and other high-priority hard targets, and then makes prudent allowance for a Soviet reserve force requirement, it appears that the USSR would need something like 8,250 ICBM warheads to neutralize the deceptively based MX system (and other hard targets)—on an imprudent one warhead to one shelter basis. More sensibly, allowing for the unreliability of their offensive systems, Soviet planners would need to allocate nearly 13,000 warheads to neutralize the basic MX shelter deployment (and other hard targets). This, however, is only the beginning of the Soviet counterforce planning nightmare. 'Baseline' MX sheltering, at 4,600 shelters (200 'linear tracks', each with 23 shelters) will be designed so that it could be expanded to accommodate 9,200 shelters through so-called 'back filling'. Needless to say, the defence leverage acquired by doubling the deceptive basing structure makes LOADS even more cost-effective.

Beyond LOADS, the US Army is developing what is called an exoatmospheric 'overlay' BMD system. If fully developed the 'overlay' system will have characteristics qualitatively different from those of the exoatmospheric defence envisaged for the *Spartan* AMB in the *Safeguard* system. Above all, it will utilize a true revolution in optical discrimination and could greatly strengthen a hard-point LOADS deployment or provide area coverage for urban-industrial America. As currently envisaged, the 'overlay' system would entail the launching into the threat corridors of 'probe' missiles (activated by launch threat signals from the early-warning satellites) which would identify likely target vectors and would distinguish real targets from decoys, chaff and debris (the long-wave infrared part of the electromagnetic spectrum). These missiles would then 'hand over' their threat data to the warhead 'buses' of long-range interceptors, which would in their turn 'hand over' threat data to non-nuclear homing vehicles which could neutralize the targets through impact or fragmentation.

Exoatmospheric non-nuclear-kill is, at present, a high-risk technology. Nevertheless, LOADS and the exoatmospheric 'homing overlay' could, given appropriate funding, achieve initial operating capabilities in about 1985 and the early 1990s respectively. Almost needless to say, a two-tiered BMD system (or better still a three-tiered one—adding interception in the ballistic missile boost, or very early mid-course phase) could offer dramatic reductions in offensive 'leakage' compared with a one-layer system. Also, multi-tiering, relying on different kinds of discrimination (say, radar *and* optical), provides a substantial hedge against 'clever' offensive decoy design or tactics, or the catastrophic failure of particular defence discrimination and engagement technologies.

The technologies outlined above are those which the American BMD community believes, with more confidence (LOADS) or less (exoatmospheric 'homing' overlay), that it knows how to bring to operational reality in the 1980s and early 1990s. Beyond these basically conventional technologies lies the 'exotic' realm of directed-energy BMD systems. In time some of these are virtually bound to be very attractive candidates for deployment—almost certainly on space platforms. Space-based high-energy laser systems, designed to destroy ICBM and SLBM in their boost phases, could easily mark a historical change in the relationship between the offence and the defence in favour of the latter. However, major practical problems remain to be solved, and the United States (and presumably the Soviet Union) have scarcely even embarked on a laser versus laser counter-measures competition. This is not to dismiss directed-energy BMD—simply to be cautious about when it will become feasible.

WHAT BMD CAN DO

LOADS could be relevant to the defence of any hardened facility, not only of ICBM shelters. However, LOADS derives its extraordinary leverage from the nature of the deceptively-based ICBM scheme which permits preferential defence. The low altitude of LOADS target engagement and interception is a virtue in the defence of hard targets, because it permits both very high-quality aim point prediction (so that interceptors are not wasted on warheads directed against empty shelters) and confident discrimination between real re-entry vehicles and decoys. However, the low altitude of engagement prevents the system, as currently planned, from being relevant to the defence of such soft targets as air bases or urban areas. It is also worth mentioning that, because of the synergism of deceptive ICBM basing married to preferential BMD, deploying LOADS with MX *from the outset* would permit a considerably less extensive and cheaper MX missile and shelter system. Indeed, it could be argued that the overall cost of deceptively-based MX with LOADS, as opposed to deceptively-based MX alone, might be up to 30% less for similar operational effectiveness measured in terms of surviving warheads. For the active defence of fixed targets of known location—such as current ICBM silos, air fields, command, control and communications (C^3) centres and the like—it would be almost essential to have a multi-level BMD system embracing an exoatmospheric 'overlay' scheme, such as the one outlined above, plus a BMD deployment capable of interception in the atmosphere (though, in many cases, at a higher altitude than is intended for LOADS).

The 'overlay' system could provide a very valuable thickening for the LOADS defence of hard targets, could provide a thin area coverage of much of the continental US, or could even offer the prospect (in conjunction with a lower-level BMD interception scheme—for much reduced 'leakage') of making truly dramatic inroads into the weight of large-scale attacks against urban-industrial America. Population fatalities are related fairly directly to the quantity of megatonnage delivered. An 'overlay', plus lower level atmospheric BMD, could massively reduce the deliverable megatonnage by means of both successful interception and the so-called 'virtual attrition' caused by the expenditure of scarce Soviet missile payloads upon technology intended to defeat the defence).

It is possible to invent threats which could defeat a BMD system. Both LOADS and the 'overlay' system described here have easily identifiable potential technical problems. LOADS would have to function in an extremely severe nuclear environment. Perhaps its components would prove to be insufficiently hardened against weapon effects, or the system might lose its 'leverage' potential if the USSR uncovered the deception code governing the movement of MX missiles. Similarly, the 'overlay' system might be defeated by cleverly designed decoys or by manoeuvring re-entry vehicles. However, Soviet defence planners cannot organize such vulnerabilities cheaply or reliably.

Probably the single most telling argument for BMD deployments of the kinds discussed here is that—almost regardless of their precise mission—they must reduce the operational confidence of the offence. Deterrent effect is in good measure the product of sensible uncertainty, and BMD adds major technical and operational uncertainties to offensive tasks that are not certainly achievable anyway. The more 'clever' and sophisticated an attacker has to be in his planning, the more there will be that could go wrong. Short of actual trial by battle, Soviet military technologists could not be *certain* that their BMD penetration technology and tactics would function well.

POLICY ISSUES

The range of active defence options for the 1980s and 1990s raise policy issues that cannot be ignored. The revolution in optical discrimination, when added to the progress made in rapid data processing and the hardening of radars, means that opposition to BMD on the grounds that it will not work has weakened very appreciably. Furthermore, in the context of defensive tactics involving preferential protection, the use of two different methods of target discrimination (long-wave infra-red optical sensors in outer space and by radar within the atmosphere) means that fairly casual references to the growth of the Soviet threat (in quantity and quality) can no longer suffice to forestall a serious policy debate on the merits of deploying ballistic missile defence.

Given the above assessment of the feasibility of different kinds of non-exotic BMD systems, five broad political-strategic questions should be prominent in the new BMD debate of the 1980s. First, is it reasonable to believe that area BMD could contribute very usefully to deterrence? If 'thinly' deployed, area BMD might function as a 'firebreak', denying the USSR a very low-level response to a US strategic nuclear initiative but sufficing to deny any other country ballistic missile access to the American homeland. The 'firebreak' theory may have some merit, but it is vulnerable to the arguments that 'thin' area BMD might mislead some officials into believing that the world had become much safer for small-scale central war, and in any case small-scale nuclear strikes are not much in keeping with what is known about Soviet military style.

A better case for area BMD rests upon the proposition that a 'thick', or truly serious, multi-level deployment would usefully reduce American self-deterrence and so enhance the credibility of the extended deterrent. The American (and Western) defence community continues to ignore the plain fact that, in the absence of substantial homeland protection, US strategic nuclear forces lack both credibility as an extended deterrent threat and ability in the event of need. The Soviet Union cannot be certain that this is so (even incredible threats deter to some extent) but the required quality of deterrence, its robustness in periods of very acute political stress, could well be lacking if the US homeland continues to be totally at nuclear risk.

Second, is it possible that BMD, of both hard targets and urban-industrial areas, might serve to encourage arms-race stability? The pace and quality of Soviet offensive force deployments over the past decade can probably be explained in terms of some combination of defence-industrial momentum and anticipated war-waging (and hence, in Soviet eyes, deterrent) benefit. The manifest arms-race instability that has characterized the SALT (and ABM Treaty) era flows from the fact that the Soviet Union genuinely believed she could derive prospective military-political gain from pressing ahead with new offensive systems. American deployment of BMD technologies like those discussed above might serve to discourage her from continuing the course she has followed in recent years. At the very least, Soviet defence planners would have to judge serious US BMD deployment as reducing, and perhaps drastically reducing, the anticipated military-political returns from (some) offensive weapon programmes.

The undeniable facts of the strategic arms competition in the 1970s demonstrate that the absence of BMD has been fully compatible with an increasingly unstable strategic balance. The long-familiar claims that US BMD deployment would be futile and would contribute to instability lack obvious credibility. BMD deployment need not be futile—a capable technology could actually defend what it was designed to defend with an acceptable failure rate. Even if the Soviet Union tried to respond to the BMD deployment so as to negate it, she might not be able to do so. Moreover, area BMD focused upon the defence of American society may be far less liable to stimulate the arms race than generally is believed. As noted above, it is generally acknowledged today that the Soviet Union does not adhere to any known concept that resembles assured (society) destruction. Indeed, her civil defence programme, albeit of uncertain effectiveness, attests her lack of interest in the concept of *mutual* assured destruction at least. The Soviet government may well prefer US society to be unprotected, but that need not, and should not, serve as guidance for American defence policy.

Third, is it not possible that US BMD, of hard-points or of society at large, would stimulate the USSR into opening an arms competition in defensive systems? This has to be judged a distinct possibility. However, it would not obviously be undesirable. The Soviet Union does not have infinite resources to invest in strategic forces. Roubles devoted to the active defence of Soviet cities (and other economic targets) would be roubles not expended upon offensive systems that could kill Americans, or upon general-purpose forces that could seize territory. The SALT process, of which the surviving monument is the ABM Treaty, has virtually licensed a massive build-up in offensive forces. A BMD competition, oriented towards the defence of those targets that neither side should have much interest in actually striking (cities and other economic assets), could herald a long-overdue trend towards a somewhat safer world. However, the United States would certainly wish to be able to penetrate Soviet BMD of some kinds of targets. An important element in a renewed BMD debate should be consideration of the net benefit, or possible net loss, to US security in the context of bilateral BMD deployments.

Fourth, how valuable might BMD be if deterrence either failed or was irrelevant? As Fred Ikle suggested in an important article in 1973, it is probably unreasonable to expect nuclear deterrence to work indefinitely. Even skilled high-wire artists believe in safety nets. The probability of deterrence failure cannot be estimated—it may be very small— but highly improbable events do occur. If deterrence failed (and BMD, by its modest enhancement of the credibility of nuclear threats, should help to prevent this), a US President would very quickly discover that he was really very interested in intelligent war plans and in the physical protection of the United States—and scarcely at all in the punishment of Soviet society.

Finally, what message would US BMD deployment be likely to convey to Soviet leaders? This kind of question touches on the area of US defence thinking that has long been the weakest: the understanding of the adversary. Many people still believe that area BMD deployment would be politically provocative and destabilizing, because it would allegedly be interpreted by the Soviet Union as a signal that the United States was planning and preparing to wage war. All that need be answered to this and similar points is that the USSR has always viewed defensive preparation as constituting little more than common sense, reflecting responsible precautionary official behaviour. Preparing for the possibility of war is different from planning and preparing for premeditated war. Withdrawal from the ABM Treaty, if followed closely by steps to begin deployment of LOADS, should not, of course, carry any implication of 'war-waging' intentions.

Moreover, the Soviet Union might actually be reassured to see the United States building active homeland defences. US area BMD deployment carries with it the clear implication that the United States anticipates the possibility, indeed probability, of having to withstand a major attack on her society in the event of war. In Soviet eyes a United States whose homeland is naked of civil defense, BMD or noteworthy air defence, could be a United States that is (foolishly?) confident of achieving near-total first strike offensive success. In addition, a United States seen to be investing in BMD protection of her society might well appear to Moscow as a United States resolute and responsible in her approach to her international and national security duties.

On balance there is a strong case for reassessing every important aspect of BMD. Ideally, that exercise, which already is beginning in a modest way, should be approached in the spirit of a *net* assessment. That is to say, not merely should the possible merits and perils of BMD for the United States be considered, but so also should the merits and perils of continuing down the now traditional path which is dominated by offensive weapons.

1981 is an unusually appropriate year for a new BMD debate. SALT II, which amounted to recognition of the offensive-forces arms competition much as before, is virtually defunct; the AMB Treaty is due to receive its second quinquennial review in 1982, and the new US Administration has time for careful reassessment of its attitude to the ABM Treaty before the 1982 deadline; competent-looking BMD technologies are maturing; and there has been an almost revolutionary sea-change in the quality of American understanding of Soviet defence philosophy. It is worth recalling the words Donald Brennan wrote in 1969: 'I do not believe that any of the critics of BMD have

even the beginnings of a plausible program for achieving major disarmament for the offensive forces by, say, 1980. Many of them seem
committed to support forever a strategic posture that appears to favor
dead Russians over live Americans. I believe that this choice is just as
bizarre as it appears; we should rather prefer live Americans to dead
Russians, and we should not choose deliberately to live forever under
a nuclear sword of Damocles.'

"No First Use"

McGEORGE BUNDY
GEORGE F. KENNAN
ROBERT S. McNAMARA
GERARD SMITH

II

. . . . The disarray that currently besets the nuclear policy and
practices of the Alliance is obvious. Governments and their representatives have maintained an appearance of unity as they persist in their
support of the two-track decision of December 1979, under which 572
new American missiles of intermediate range are to be placed in
Europe unless a satisfactory agreement on the limitation of such
weapons can be reached in the negotiations between the United States
and the Soviet Union that began last November. But behind this
united front there are divisive debates, especially in countries where
the new weapons are to be deployed.

The arguments put forward by advocates of these deployments
contain troubling variations. The simplest and intuitively the most
persuasive claim is that these new weapons are needed as a counter to
the Soviet SS-20 missiles; it may be a recognition of the surface

Reprinted by permission of *Foreign Affairs,* Spring 1982, pp. 753–768. Copyright ©
1982 by the Council on Foreign Relations, Inc.

attractiveness of this positon that underlies President Reagan's strik-ing—but probably not negotiable—proposal that if all the SS-20s are dismantled the planned deployments will be cancelled. Other officials have a quite different argument, that without new and survivable American weapons which can reach Russia from Western Europe there can be no confidence that the strategic forces of the United States will remain committed to the defense of Western Europe; on this argument the new missiles are needed to make it more likely that any war in Europe would bring nuclear warheads on the Soviet Union and thus deter the aggressor in the first place. This argument is logically distinct from any concern about the Soviet SS-20s, and it probably ex-plains the ill-concealed hope of some planners that the Reagan pro-posal will be rejected. Such varied justifications cast considerable doubt on the real purpose of the proposed deployment.

An equally disturbing phenomenon is the gradual shift in the balance of argument that has occurred since the need to address the problem was first asserted in 1977. Then the expression of need was European, and in the first instance German; the emerging parity of long-range strategic systems was asserted to create a need for a balance at less than intercontinental levels. The American interest developed relatively slowly, but because these were to be American missiles, American planners took the lead as the proposal was worked out. It has also served Soviet purposes to concentrate on the American role. A similar focus has been chosen by many leaders in the new movement for nuclear disarmament in Europe. And now there are American voices, some in the executive branch, talking as if European acceptance of these new missiles were some sort of test of European loyalty to the Alliance. Meanwhile some of those in Europe who re-main publicly committed to both tracks of the 1979 agreement are clearly hoping that the day of deployment will never arrive. When the very origins of a new proposal become the source of irritated argu-ment among allies—"You started it!"—something is badly wrong in our common understanding.

A still more severe instance of disarray, one which has occurred under both President Carter and President Reagan, relates to the so-called neutron bomb, a weapon designed to meet the threat of Soviet tanks. American military planners, authorized by doctrine to think in terms of early battlefield use of nuclear weapons, naturally want more "up-to-date" weapons than those they have now; it is known that thousands of the aging short-range nuclear weapons now in Europe are hard to use effectively. Yet to a great many Europeans the neutron bomb suggests, however unfairly, that the Americans are preparing to fight a "limited" nuclear war on their soil. Moreover neither weapons designers nor the Pentagon officials they have persuaded seem to have understood the intense and special revulsion that is associated with killing by "enhanced radiation."

All these recent distempers have a deeper cause. They are rooted in the fact that the evolution of essentially equivalent and enormously excessive nuclear weapons systems both in the Soviet Union and in the Atlantic Alliance has aroused new concern about the dangers of all forms of nuclear war. The profusion of these systems, on both sides, has made it more difficult than ever to construct rational plans for any first use of these weapons by anyone.

This problem is more acute than before, but it is not new. Even in the 1950s, a time that is often mistakenly perceived as one of effortless American superiority, the prospect of any actual use of tactical weapons was properly terrifying to Europeans and to more than a few Americans. Military plans for such use remained both deeply secret and highly hypothetical; the coherence of the Alliance was maintained by general neglect of such scenarios, not by sedulous public discussion. In the 1960s there was a prolonged and stressful effort to address the problem of theater-range weapons, but agreement on new forces and plans for their use proved elusive. Eventually the proposal for a multilateral force (MLF) was replaced by the assignment of American Polaris submarines to NATO, and by the creation in Brussels of an inter-allied Nuclear Planning Group. Little else was accomplished. In both decades the Alliance kept itself together more by mutual political confidence than by plausible nuclear war-fighting plans.

Although the first years of the 1970s produced a welcome if over-sold détente, complacency soon began to fade. The Nixon Administration, rather quietly, raised the question about the long-run credibility of the American nuclear deterrent that was to be elaborated by Henry Kissinger in 1979 at a meeting in Brussels. Further impetus to both new doctrine and new deployments came during the Ford and Carter Administrations, but each public statement, however careful and qualified, only increased European apprehensions. The purpose of both Administrations was to reinforce deterrence, but the result has been to increase fear of nuclear war, and even of Americans as its possible initiators. Intended as contributions to both rationality and credibility, these excursions into the theory of limited nuclear war have been counterproductive in Europe.

Yet it was not wrong to raise these matters. Questions that were answered largely by silence in the 1950s and 1960s cannot be so handled in the 1980s. The problem was not in the fact that the questions were raised, but in the way they seemed to be answered.

It is time to recognize that no one has ever succeeded in advancing any persuasive reason to believe that any use of nuclear weapons, even on the smallest scale, could reliably be expected to remain limited. Every serious analysis and every military exercise, for over 25 years, has demonstrated that even the most restrained battlefield use would be enormously destructive to civilian life and property. There is no way for anyone to have any confidence that such a nuclear action will not lead to further and more devastating exchanges. Any use of nuclear weapons in Europe, by the Alliance or against it, carries with it a high and inescapable risk of escalation into the general nuclear war which would bring ruin to all and victory to none.

The one clearly definable firebreak against the worldwide disaster of general nuclear war is the one that stands between all other kinds of conflict and any use whatsoever of nuclear weapons. To keep that firebreak wide and strong is in the deepest interest of all mankind. In retrospect, indeed, it is remarkable that this country has not responded to this reality more quickly. Given the appalling consequences of even the most limited use of nuclear weapons and the total impossibility for both sides of any guarantee against unlimited escalation, there must be the gravest doubt about the wisdom of a policy which asserts the effectiveness of any first use of nuclear weapons by either side. So it seems timely to consider the possibilities, the requirements, the difficulties, and the advantages of a policy of no-first-use.

III

The largest question presented by any proposal for an Allied policy of no-first-use is that of its impact on the effectiveness of NATO's deterrent posture on the central front. In spite of the doubts that are created by any honest look at the probable consequences of resort to a first nuclear strike of any kind, it should be remembered that there were strong reasons for the creation of the American nuclear umbrella over NATO. The original American pledge, expressed in Article 5 of the Treaty, was understood to be a nuclear guarantee. It was extended at a time when only a conventional Soviet threat existed, so a readiness for first use was plainly implied from the beginning. To modify that guarantee now, even in the light of all that has happened since, would be a major change in the assumptions of the Alliance, and no such change should be made without the most careful exploration of its implications.

In such an exploration the role of the Federal Republic of Germany must be central. Americans too easily forget what the people of the Federal Republic never can: that their position is triply exposed in a fashion unique among the large industrial democracies. They do not have nuclear weapons; they share a long common boundary with the Soviet empire; in any conflict on the central front their land would be the first battleground. None of these conditions can be changed, and together they present a formidable challenge.

Having decisively rejected a policy of neutrality, the Federal Republic has necessarily relied on the nuclear protection of the United States, and we Americans should recognize that this relationship is not a favor we are doing our German friends, but the best available solution of a common problem. Both nations believe that the Federal

Republic must not have nuclear weapons of its own; both believe that nuclear guarantees *of some sort* are essential; and both believe that only the United States can provide those guarantees in persuasively deterrent peacekeeping form.

The uniqueness of the West German position can be readily demonstrated by comparing it with those of France and the United Kingdom. These two nations have distance, and in one case water, between them and the armies of the Soviet Union; they also have nuclear weapons. While those weapons may contribute something to the common strength of the Alliance, their main role is to underpin a residual national self-reliance, expressed in different ways at different times by different governments, which sets both Britain and France apart from the Federal Republic. They are set apart from the United States too, in that no other nation depends on them to use their nuclear weapons otherwise than in their own ultimate self-defense.

The quite special character of the nuclear relationship between the Federal Republic and the United States is a most powerful reason for defining that relationship with great care. It is rare for one major nation to depend entirely on another for a form of strength that is vital to its survival. It is unprecedented for any nation, however powerful, to pledge itself to a course of action, in defense of another, that might entail its own nuclear devastation. A policy of no-first-use would not and should not imply an abandonment of this extraordinary guarantee—only its redefinition. It would still be necessary to be ready to reply with American nuclear weapons to any nuclear attack on the Federal Republic, and this commitment would in itself be sufficiently demanding to constitute a powerful demonstration that a policy of no-first-use would represent no abandonment of our German ally.

The German right to a voice in this question is not merely a matter of location, or even of dependence on an American nuclear guarantee. The people of the Federal Republic have demonstrated a steadfast dedication to peace, to collective defense, and to domestic political decency. The study here proposed should be responsive to their basic desires. It seems probable that they are like the rest of us in wishing most of all to have no war of any kind, but also to be able to defend the peace by forces that do not require the dreadful choice of nuclear escalation.

IV

While we believe that careful study will lead to a firm conclusion that it is time to move decisively toward a policy of no-first-use, it is obvious that any such policy would require a strengthened confidence in the adequacy of the conventional forces of the Alliance, above all the forces in place on the central front and those available for prompt reinforcement. It seems clear that the nations of the Alliance together can provide whatever forces are needed, and within realistic budgetary constraints, but it is a quite different question whether they can summon the necessary political will. Evidence from the history of the Alliance is mixed. There has been great progress in the conventional defenses of NATO in the 30 years since the 1952 Lisbon communiqué, but there have also been failures to meet force goals all along the way.

In each of the four nations which account for more than 90 percent of NATO's collective defense and a still higher proportion of its strength on the central front, there remain major unresolved political issues that critically affect contributions to conventional deterrence: for example, it can be asked what priority the United Kingdom gives to the British Army of the Rhine, what level of NATO-connected deployment can be accepted by France, what degree of German relative strength is acceptable to the Allies and fair to the Federal Republic itself, and whether we Americans have a durable and effective answer to our military manpower needs in the present all-volunteer active and reserve forces. These are the kinds of questions—and there are many more—that would require review and resolution in the course of reaching any final decision to move to a responsible policy of no-first-use.

There should also be an examination of the ways in which the concept of early use of nuclear weapons may have been built into existing forces, tactics, and general military expectations. To the degree that this has happened, there could be a dangerous gap right now between real capabilities and those which political leaders might wish to have in a time of crisis. Conversely there should be careful study of what a policy of no-first-use would require in those same terms. It seems more than likely that once the military leaders of the Alliance have learned to think and act steadily on this "conventional" assumption, their forces will be better instruments for stability in crises and for general deterrence, as well as for the maintenance of the nuclear firebreak so vital to us all.

No one should underestimate either the difficulty or the importance of the shift in military attitudes implied by a no-first-use policy. Although military commanders are well aware of the terrible dangers in any exchange of nuclear weapons, it is a strong military tradition to maintain that aggressive war, not the use of any one weapon, is the central evil. Many officers will be initially unenthusiastic about any formal policy that puts limits on their recourse to a weapon of apparently decisive power. Yet the basic argument for a no-first-use policy can be stated in strictly military terms: that any other course involves unacceptable risks to the national life that military forces exist to defend. The military officers of the Alliance can be expected to understand the force of this proposition, even if many of them do not initially agree with it. Moreover, there is every reason for confidence that they will loyally accept any policy that has the support of their governments and the peoples behind them, just as they have fully accepted the present arrangements under which the use of nuclear weapons, even in retaliation for a nuclear attack, requires advance and specific approval by the head of government.

An Allied posture of no-first-use would have one special effect that can be set forth in advance: it would draw new attention to the importance of maintaining and improving the specifically American conventional forces in Europe. The principal political difficulty in a policy of no-first-use is that it may be taken in Europe, and especially in the Federal Republic, as evidence of a reduced American interest in the Alliance and in effective overall deterrence. The argument here is exactly the opposite: that such a policy is the best one available for keeping the Alliance united and effective. Nonetheless the psychological realities of the relation between the Federal Republic and United States are such that the only way to prevent corrosive German suspicion of American intentions, under a no-first-use regime, will be for Americans to accept for themselves an appropriate share in any new level of conventional effort that the policy may require.

Yet it would be wrong to make any hasty judgment that those new levels of effort must be excessively high. The subject is complex, and the more so because both technology and politics are changing. Precision-guided munitions, in technology, and the visible weakening of the military solidity of the Warsaw Pact, in politics, are only two examples of changes working to the advantage of the Alliance. Moreover there has been some tendency, over many years, to exaggerate the relative conventional strength of the U.S.S.R. and to underestimate Soviet awareness of the enormous costs and risks of any form of aggression against NATO.

Today there is literally no one who really knows what would be needed. Most of the measures routinely used in both official and private analyses are static and fragmentary. An especially arbitrary, if obviously convenient, measure of progress is that of spending levels. But it is political will, not budgetary pressure, that will be decisive. The value of greater safety from both nuclear and conventional danger is so great that even if careful analysis showed that the necessary conventional posture would require funding larger than the three-percent real increase that has been the common target of recent years, it would be the best bargain ever offered to the members of the Alliance.

Yet there is no need for crash programs, which always bring extra costs. The direction of the Allied effort will be more important than its velocity. The final establishment of a firm policy of no-first-use, in any case, will obviously require time. What is important today is to begin to move in this direction.

V

The concept of renouncing any first use of nuclear weapons should also be tested by careful review of the value of existing NATO plans for selective and limited use of nuclear weapons. While many scenarios for nuclear war-fighting are nonsensical, it must be recognized that cautious and sober senior officers have found it prudent to ask themselves what alternatives to defeat they could propose to their civilian superiors if a massive conventional Soviet attack seemed about to make a decisive breakthrough. This question has generated contingency plans for battlefield uses of small numbers of nuclear weapons which might prevent that particular disaster. It is hard to see how any such action could be taken without the most enormous risk of rapid and catastrophic escalation, but it is a fair challenge to a policy of no-first-use that it should be accompanied by a level of conventional strength that would make such plans unnecessary.

In the light of this difficulty it would be prudent to consider whether there is any acceptable policy short of no-first-use. One possible example is what might be called "no-*early*-first-use;" such a policy might leave open the option of some limited nuclear action to fend off a final large-scale conventional defeat, and by renunciation of any immediate first use and increased emphasis on conventional capabilities it might be thought to help somewhat in reducing current fears.

But the value of a clear and simple position would be great, especially in its effect on ourselves and our Allies. One trouble with exceptions is that they easily become rules. It seems much better that even the most responsible choice of even the most limited nuclear actions to prevent even the most imminent conventional disaster should be left out of authorized policy. What the Alliance needs most today is not the refinement of its nuclear options, but a clear-cut decision to avoid them as long as others do. . . .

VI

The first possible advantage of a policy of no-first-use is in the management of the nuclear deterrent forces that would still be necessary. Once we escape from the need to plan for a first use that is credible, we can escape also from many of the complex arguments that have led to assertions that all sorts of new nuclear capabilities are necessary to create or restore a capability for something called "escalation dominance"—a capability to fight and "win" a nuclear war at any level. What would be needed, under no-first-use, is a set of capabilities we already have in overflowing measure—capabilities for appropriate retaliation to any kind of Soviet nuclear attack which would leave the Soviet Union in no doubt that it too should adhere to a policy of no-first-use. The Soviet government is already aware of the awful risk inherent in any use of these weapons, and there is no current or prospective Soviet "superiority" that would tempt anyone in Moscow toward nuclear adventurism. (All four of us are wholly unpersuaded by the argument advanced in recent years that the Soviet Union could ever rationally expect to gain from such a wild effort as a massive first strike on land-based American strategic missiles.)

Once it is clear that the only nuclear need of the Alliance is for adequately survivable and varied *second strike* forces, requirements for the modernization of major nuclear systems will become more modest than has been assumed. In particular we can escape from the notion that we must somehow match everything the rocket commanders in the Soviet Union extract from their government. It seems doubtful, also, that under such a policy it would be necessary or desirable to deploy neutron bombs. The savings permitted by more modest programs could go toward meeting the financial costs of our contribution to conventional forces.

It is important to avoid misunderstanding here. In the conditions of the 1980s, and in the absence of agreement on both sides to proceed to very large-scale reductions in nuclear forces, it is clear that large, varied, and survivable nuclear forces will still be necessary for nuclear deterrence. The point is not that we Americans should move unilaterally to some "minimum" force of a few tens or even hundreds of missiles, but rather that once we escape from the pressure to seem willing and able to use these weapons first, we shall find that our requirements are much less massive than is now widely supposed.

A posture of no-first-use should also go far to meet the understandable anxieties that underlie much of the new interest in nuclear disarmament, both in Europe and in our own country. Some of the proposals generated by this new interest may lack practicability for the present. For example, proposals to make "all" of Europe—from Portugal to Poland—a nuclear-free zone do not seem to take full account of the reality that thousands of long-range weapons deep in the Soviet Union will still be able to target Western Europe. But a policy of no-first-use, with its accompaniment of a reduced requirement for new Allied nuclear systems, should allow a considerable reduction in fears of all sorts. Certainly such a new policy would neutralize the highly disruptive argument currently put about in Europe: that plans for theater nuclear modernization reflect an American hope to fight a nuclear war limited to Europe. Such modernization might or might not be needed under a policy of no-first-use; that question, given the size and versatility of other existing and prospective American forces, would be a matter primarily for European decision (as it is today).

An effective policy of no-first-use will also reduce the risk of conventional aggression in Europe. That risk has never been as great as prophets of doom have claimed and has always lain primarily in the possibility that Soviet leaders might think they could achieve some quick and limited gain that would be accepted because no defense or reply could be concerted. That temptation has been much reduced by the Allied conventional deployments achieved in the last 20 years, and it would be reduced still further by the additional shift in the balance of Allied effort that a no-first-use policy would both permit and require. The risk that an adventurist Soviet leader might take the terrible gamble of conventional aggression was greater in the past than it is today, and is greater today than it would be under no-first-use, backed up by an effective conventional defense.

VII

We have been discussing a problem of military policy, but our interest is also political. The principal immediate danger in the current military posture of the Alliance is not that it will lead to large-scale war, conventional or nuclear. The balance of terror, and the caution of both sides, appear strong enough today to prevent such a catastrophe, at least in the absence of some deeply destabilizing political change which might lead to panic or adventurism on either side. But the present unbalanced reliance on nuclear weapons, if long continued, might produce exactly such political change. The events of the last year have shown that differing perceptions of the role of nuclear weapons can lead to destructive recriminations, and when these differences are compounded by understandable disagreements on other matters such as Poland and the Middle East, the possibilities for trouble among Allies are evident.

The political coherence of the Alliance, especially in times of stress, is at least as important as the military strength required to maintain credible deterrence. Indeed the political requirement has, if anything, an even higher priority. Soviet leaders would be most pleased to help the Alliance fall into total disarray, and would much prefer such a development to the inescapable uncertainties of open conflict. Conversely, if consensus is re-established on a military policy that the peoples and governments of the Alliance can believe in, both political will and deterrent credibility will be reinforced. Plenty of hard questions will remain, but both fear and mistrust will be reduced, and they are the most immediate enemies.

There remains one underlying reality which could not be removed by even the most explicit declaratory policy of no-first-use. Even if the nuclear powers of the Alliance should join, with the support of other Allies, in a policy of no-first-use, and even if that decision should lead to a common declaration of such policy by these powers and the Soviet Union, no one on either side could guarantee beyond all possible doubt that if conventional warfare broke out on a large scale there would in fact be no use of nuclear weapons. We could not make that assumption about the Soviet Union, and we must recognize that Soviet leaders could not make it about us. As long as the weapons themselves exist, the possibility of their use will remain.

But this inescapable reality does not undercut the value of a no-first-use policy. That value is first of all for the internal health of the Western Alliance itself. A posture of effective conventional balance and survivable second-strike nuclear strength is vastly better for our own peoples and governments, in a deep sense more civilized, than one that forces the serious contemplation of "limited" nuclear scenarios that are at once terrifying and implausible.

There is strong reason to believe that no-first-use can also help in our relations with the Soviet Union. The Soviet government has repeatedly offered to join the West in declaring such a policy, and while such declarations may have only limited reliability, it would be wrong to disregard the real value to both sides of a jointly declared adherence to this policy. To renounce the first use of nuclear weapons is to accept an enormous burden of responsibility for any later violation. The existence of such a clearly declared common pledge would increase the cost and risk of any sudden use of nuclear weapons by either side and correspondingly reduce the political force of spoken or unspoken threats of such use.

A posture and policy of no-first-use also could help to open the path toward serious reduction of nuclear armaments on both sides. The nuclear decades have shown how hard it is to get agreements that really do constrain these weapons, and no one can say with assurance that any one step can make a decisive difference. But just as a policy of no-first-use should reduce the pressures on our side for massive new nuclear forces, it should help to increase the international incentives for the Soviet Union to show some restraint of its own. It is important not to exaggerate here, and certainly Soviet policies on procurement are not merely delayed mirror-images of ours. Nonetheless there are connections between what is said and what is done even in the Soviet Union, and there are incentives for moderation, even there, that could be strengthened by a jointly declared policy of renouncing first use. At a minimum such a declaration would give both sides additional reason to seek for agreements that would prevent a vastly expensive and potentially destabilizing contest for some kind of strategic advantage in outer space.

Finally, and in sum, we think a policy of no-first-use, especially if shared with the Soviet Union, would bring new hope to everyone in every country whose life is shadowed by the hideous possibility of a third great twentieth-century conflict in Europe—conventional or nuclear. It seems timely and even urgent to begin the careful study of a policy that could help to sweep this threat clean off the board of international affairs. . . .

Nuclear Weapons And
The Preservation Of Peace

KARL KAISER, GEORG LEBER,
ALOIS MERTES
AND FRANZ-JOSEF SCHULZE

A RESPONSE TO AN AMERICAN PROPOSAL FOR RENOUNCING THE
FIRST USE OF NUCLEAR WEAPONS

The appropriate strategy for the use of nuclear weapons has been
the subject of discussion since the North Atlantic Alliance was founded.
Open debate on these problems is part of the natural foundations of
an Alliance consisting of democracies which relate to each other as
sovereign partners. It is not the first time in the history of the Alliance
that fears about the danger of nuclear war have caused concern and
anxieties in all member countries, although these are more pronounced
today than before. They must be taken seriously. The questions posed
demand convincing answers, for in a democracy, policy on questions of
peace and war requires constantly renewed legitimization.

When McGeorge Bundy, George F. Kennan, Robert S. McNamara
and Gerard Smith submit a proposal to renounce the first use of nuclear
weapons in Europe,[1] the mere fact that it comes from respected
American personalities with long years of experience in questions of
security policy and the Alliance gives it particular weight. Their reflec-
tions must be taken particularly seriously in a country like the Federal
Republic of Germany which has a special interest in preserving peace,
because in case of war nuclear weapons could first be used on its
territory.

All responsible people must face the issues of the discussion initiated
by the four authors. It is necessary to think through all questions posed
and not to select only those ideas which cater to widespread anxieties.
What matters most is to concentrate not only on the prevention of
nuclear war, but on how to prevent *any* war, conventional war as well.
The decisive criterion in evaluating this proposal—like any new

Reprinted by permission of *Foreign Affairs,* Summer 1982, pp. 1157–1171. Copyright ©
1982 by the Council on Foreign Relations, Inc.
[1] "Nuclear Weapons and the Atlantic Alliance," published simultaneously in
Europa-Archiv, No. 7, 1982, and *Foreign Affairs,* Spring 1982, pp. 753–768. Page citations in the body of this article are to *Foreign Affairs.*

proposal—must be: Will it contribute to preserving, into the future, the peace and freedom of the last three decades?

Unfortunately, the current discussion on both sides of the Atlantic about the four authors' proposal has been rendered more difficult by a confusion between the option of the "first use of nuclear weapons and the capability for a "first strike" with nuclear weapons. The authors themselves have unintentionally contributed to this confusion by using both terms. "First use" refers to the first use of a nuclear weapon regardless of its yield and place; even blowing up a bridge with a nuclear weapon in one's own territory would represent a first use. "First strike" refers to a preemptive disarming nuclear strike aimed at eliminating as completely as possible the entire strategic potential of the adversary. A first strike by the Alliance is not a relevant issue; such a strike must remain unthinkable in the future as it is now and has been in the past. The matter for debate should be exclusively the defensive first use of nuclear weapons by the Western Alliance.

II

The current NATO strategy of flexible response is intended to discourage an adversary from using or threatening the use of military force by confronting him with a full spectrum of deterrence and hence with an uncalculable risk. The strategy also aims at improving the tools of crisis management as a means of preventing conflict. The deterrent effect of the doctrine rests on three pillars:

—the political determination of all Alliance members to resist jointly any form of aggression or blackmail;

—the capability of the Alliance to react effectively at every level of aggression; and

—the flexibility to choose between different possible reactions—conventional or nuclear.

The primary goal of this strategy is the prevention of war. To this end it harnesses the revolutionary new and inescapable phenomenon of the nuclear age for its own purposes. Our era has brought humanity not only the curse of the unprecedented destructive power of nuclear weapons but also its twin, the dread of unleashing that power, grounded in the fear of self-destruction. Wherever nuclear weapons are present, war loses its earlier function as a continuation of politics by other means. Even more, the destructive power of these weapons has forced political leaders, especially those of nuclear weapons states, to weigh risks to a degree unknown in history.

The longest period of peace in European history is inconceivable without the war-preventing effect of nuclear weapons. During the same time span more than a hundred wars have taken place in Asia, Africa, and Latin America, where the numbers of dead, wounded and refugees run into the millions.

The continuous increase in the number of nuclear weapons—now comprising many thousands of warheads with ever more refined delivery systems—instills in many people, for understandable reasons, anxieties about the consequences of a war with a destructive power that exceeds the human imagination. But the only new factor here is that more people realize these consequences than in the past. Many political and military leaders were already aware of them when these weapons were developed and the first test results were presented. The fear of the consequences of such a war has to this day fortunately led to a policy which has made an essential contribution to preventing war in Europe—but which at the same time has regrettably stimulated the buildup of arsenals, since neither side wanted to lapse into a position of inferiority.

The strategy of flexible response attempts to counter any attack by the adversary—no matter what the level—in such a way that the aggressor can have no hope of advantage or success by triggering a military conflict, be it conventional or nuclear. The tight and indissoluble coupling of conventional forces and nuclear weapons on the European continent with the strategic potential of the United States confronts the Soviet Union with the incalculable risk that any military conflict between the two Alliances could escalate to a nuclear war. The primary function of nuclear weapons is deterrence in order to prevent aggression and blackmail.

The coupling of conventional and nuclear weapons has rendered war between East and West unwageable and unwinnable up to now. It is the inescapable paradox of this strategy of war prevention that the will to conduct nuclear war must be demonstrated in order to prevent war at all. Yet the ensuing indispensable presence of nuclear weapons and the constantly recalled visions of their possible destructive effect, should they ever be used in a war, make many people anxious.

The case is similar with regard to the limitation of nuclear war: the strategy of massive retaliation was revised because, given the growing potential of destruction, the threat of responding even to low levels of aggression with a massive use of nuclear weapons became increasingly incredible. A threat once rendered incredible would no longer have been able to prevent war in Europe. Thus, in the mid-1960s the Europeans supported the introduction of flexible response, which made the restricted use of nuclear weapons—but also the limitation of any such use—an indispensable part of deterrence aimed at preventing even "small" wars in Europe. Critics of nuclear deterrence today misinterpret this shift in strategy, drawing from it a suspicion of conspiracy between the superpowers to wage a limited nuclear war on European territory and at the expense of the Europeans.

A renunciation of the first use of nuclear weapons would certainly rob the present strategy of war prevention—which is supported by the government and the opposition in the Federal Republic of Germany, as well as by a great majority of the population—of a decisive characteristic. One cannot help concluding that the Soviet Union would thereby be put in a position where it could, once again, calculate its risk and thus be able to wage war in Europe. It would no longer have to fear that nuclear weapons would inflict unacceptable damage to its own territory. We therefore fear that a credible renunciation of the first use of nuclear weapons would, once again, make war more probable.

A decisive weakness of the proposal by the four authors lies in their assertion that a no-first-use policy would render wars less likely, without producing sufficient evidence. Even though the restoration of the conventional balance which they call for (and which will be examined below) increases the conventional risk for the Soviet assault formations, such a policy would liberate the Soviet Union from the decisive nuclear risk—and thereby from the constraint that has kept the Soviet Union, up to now, from using military force, even for limited purposes, against Western Europe. The liberation from nuclear risk would, of course, benefit the United States to the same degree. It must be questioned, therefore, whether renunciation of first use represents a contribution to the "internal health of the Western alliance itself" (p. 66) or whether, instead, a no-first-use policy increases insecurity and fear of ever more probable war.

The argumentation of the four American authors is considerably weakened by their tendency to think in worst-case scenarios. They assume almost fatalistically a total irrationality of state behavior and the impossibility of controlling a supposedly irreversible escalation. We share the authors' opinion that the kind of Soviet adventurism that would undertake a nuclear first strike against the United States can be excluded as a serious possibility. We are also familiar with the recent studies which assert that a limited nuclear war probably becomes more and more difficult to control with increasing escalation. Here we cannot disagree. However, one must at the same time ask under what circumstances a first use of Western nuclear weapons in Europe—should it happen at all—would be probable. This is only thinkable in a situation where a large-scale conventional attack by the Warsaw Pact could no longer be countered by conventional means alone, thus forcing NATO to a limited use of nuclear weapons: small weapons in small quantities, perhaps even only a warning shot. All indications suggest that both sides would be extremely cautious, in order to avoid precisely the dreaded, possibly uncontrollable escalation which some studies rightfully present as a danger, and which the advocates of a no-first-use policy present as a certainty.

III

The Western Alliance is an alliance of equals. Its cohesion is therefore based on the greatest possible realization of the principles of equal risks, equal burdens and equal security. The present NATO strategy reflects this principle. It guarantees that the American military potential with all its components, conventional and nuclear, is included in the defense of Europe. Not only the inhabitants of the Federal Republic of Germany but also American citizens help bear the risks, the conventional as well as the nuclear. The indivisibility of the security of the Alliance as a whole and of its terrritory creates the credibility of deterrence.

The conclusions that can be drawn from the four authors' recommendations with regard to the commitment of the United States to the defense of Europe are profoundly disturbing. To be sure, they assert that no-first-use does not represent an abandonment of the American protective guarantee for Western Europe, but "only its redefinition" (p. 759). Indeed, that would be the case, but in the form of a withdrawal from present commitments of the United States.

The opinion of the four American authors that "the one clearly definable firebreak against the worldwide disaster of general nuclear war is the one that stands between all other kinds of conflict and any use whatsoever of nuclear weapons" (p. 757), amounts to no less than limiting the existing nuclear guarantee of protection by the United States for their non-nuclear Alliance partners to the case of prior use of nuclear weapons by the Soviet Union. Even in the case of a large-scale conventional attack against the entire European NATO territory, the Soviet Union could be certain that its own land would remain a sanctuary as long as it did not itself resort to nuclear weapons. This would apply even more to surprise operations aimed at the quick occupation of parts of Western Europe which are hardly defensible by conventional means.

In such a case, those attacked would have to bear the destruction and devastation of war alone. It is only too understandable that for years the Soviet Union has, therefore, pressed for a joint American-Soviet renunciation of first use of nuclear weapons, on occasion in the guise of global proposals. If the ideas of the authors were to be followed, conventional conflicts in Europe would no longer involve any existential risk for the territory of the Soviet Union and—despite the increased American participation in the conventional defense of Europe suggested by the authors—would be without such risk for the territory of the United States as well.

The authors' suggestion that "even the most responsible choice of even the most limited nuclear actions to prevent even the most imminent conventional disaster should be left out of authorized policy" (p. 762) makes completely clear that a withdrawal of the United States from its previous guarantee is at stake. They thus advise Western

Europe to capitulate should defeat threaten, for example if the Federal Republic were in danger of being overrun conventionally. The American nuclear guarantee would be withdrawn.

The authors assert that the implementation of their astonishing proposal would not be taken in Europe, and especially in the Federal Republic, "as evidence of a reduced American interest in the Alliance and in effective overall deterrence" (p. 761), but that, on the contrary, it would be the best means "for keeping the Alliance united and effective" (p. 761). On this point we beg to differ: the proposed no-first-use policy would destroy the confidence of Europeans and especially of Germans in the European-American Alliance as a community of risk, and would endanger the strategic unity of the Alliance and the security of Western Europe.

IV

Given a renunciation of nuclear first use, the risks of a potential aggressor doubtlessly become more calculable. Moreover, the significance of Soviet conventional superiority would thereby increase dramatically. Conventional war in Europe would once again become possible. It could again become a continuation of politics by other means. Moreover, NATO would face a fundamentally different conventional threat. The elimination of the nuclear risk would free the Warsaw Pact from the necessity to disperse attack forces. As a result NATO would have to produce significantly higher numbers of combat forces than today.

The assertion of the four American authors that there is a tendency to overestimate the conventional strength of the Soviet Union does not correspond to the most recent East-West force comparison undertaken by NATO. They do admit, however, that a no-first-use policy requires stronger conventional forces; in their opinion the Alliance is capable of accomplishing such a buildup within realistic budgets. We believe the authors considerably underestimate the political and financial difficulties which stand in the way of establishing a conventional balance through increased armament by the West. The case would be different if through negotiations a conventional balance could be reached by reductions in Warsaw Pact forces. The authors do not explore this possibility, but the long years of as yet unsuccessful negotiations for mutual and balanced force reductions (MBFR) demonstrate the obstacles on this path.

The establishment of balance through the buildup of Western conventional forces would likewise be extremely difficult. The costs would be of a magnitude that would dramatically exceed the framework of present defense budgets. Suggestions by the authors about possible savings in the nuclear area in case of no-first-use are of little benefit for the non-nuclear weapons states of Europe. (Such savings, incidentally, imply a significant reduction of the Western nuclear arsenal.) In our judgment, the United States and Great Britain would have to introduce the draft, and the European countries would have to extend their period of military service. Because of the necessity for a significantly higher number of military forces, the Federal Republic of Germany would have to accept on its territory large contingents of additional troops, those of the allies and its own: the Federal Republic would be transformed into a large military camp for an indefinite period. Do the four American authors seriously believe that the preconditions for the buildup required by their proposal exist in Western Europe—and the United States?

Even if an approximate conventional balance could be achieved in Europe, two disadvantages to the detriment of Western Europe would remain: first, the Soviet Union has a geographic advantage, it can always quickly change the balance of forces from the relative proximity of its territory; second, there would always be the possibility, not even excluded by the American authors, that, despite no-first-use, conventional war could in an advanced phase degenerate into nuclear war.

Moreover, in commenting skeptically about the idea of a nuclear-free zone, the authors themselves point out that the Soviet Union can move nuclear weapons relatively quickly from deep within its territory into such a zone. If a no-first-use policy is linked with a complete or at least substantial withdrawal of tactical nuclear weapons—and that is apparently meant by the authors—it would, moreover, be easier for the Soviet Union to reach Central Europe with nuclear weapons from its own territory than for the United States.

For Germans and other Europeans whose memory of the catastrophe of conventional war is still alive and on whose densely populated territory both pacts would confront each other with the destructive power of modern armies, the thought of an ever more probable conventional war is terrifying.

To Germans and other Europeans, an ever more probable conventional war is, therefore, no alternative to war prevention through the current strategy, including the option of a first use of nuclear weapons. While the four authors link their proposal with the laudable intention of reducing European anxieties about nuclear war, its implementation could result in anxieties about a more probable conventional war soon replacing anxieties about the much less probable nuclear war. The anti-nuclear protest movement in Europe suspects the United States and the Soviet Union of intending to wage a limited nuclear war on the territory, and at the expense, of the Europeans. Were the movement to apply the logic of its argument to the case of no-first-use, it would naturally arrive at a new suspicion: that a conventional war could now also be waged on European territory and at European expense—particularly since a nuclear risk for the superpowers would no longer exist. All that would then be necessary would be to paint a vivid picture of the terrors of conventional war—once again thinkable—and the insecurity of the Europeans would receive new and dangerous reinforcement.

V

We are grateful for the manner in which the four American authors of a no-first-use proposal have evaluated the particularly exposed position of the Federal Republic of Germany and the special difficulties which ensue for its security policy. It is, however, striking that they do not deal at all with a problem which does not, to be sure, pose itself for a world power like the United States but which the Federal Republic of Germany and all European Alliance partners have to keep in mind: the problem of protecting themselves from political pressure and preserving their free society.

The protection of a free society based on the rule of law is just as important a part of a policy of preserving peace as the prevention of war. War can always be avoided at the price of submission. It is naturally more obvious to Europeans, and in particular to Germans—in their precarious position within a divided country—than to the population of the American superpower that an actual military superiority of the Soviet Union, or a feeling of inferiority in Western Europe, can be exploited to put political pressure on Western Europe.

The feeling of vulnerability to political blackmail, as a result of the constant demonstration of superior military might, would be bound to grow considerably if the nuclear protector of the Atlantic Alliance were to declare—as suggested by the four authors—that it would not use nuclear weapons in case of a conventional attack against Europe. This applies in particular to those exposed areas which even with considerable improvements of conventional forces can only with great difficulty be conventionally defended, or not at all: these include, for example, North Norway, Thrace, and in particular, West Berlin. The protection of these areas lies solely in the incalculability of the American reaction.

The advice of the authors to renounce the use of nuclear weapons even in the face of pending conventional defeat of Western Europe is tantamount to suggesting that "rather Red than dead" would be the only remaining option for those Europeans then still alive. Were such advice to become policy, it would destroy the psychological basis necessary for the will to self-defense. Such counsel would strengthen tendencies in Europe to seek gradual voluntary and timely salvation in preventive "good conduct" and growing subservience vis-à-vis the Soviet Union for fear of war and Soviet superiority. The result would be to restrict the very freedom that the Alliance was founded to protect. . . .

The four American authors hope that a policy of no-first-use could help to clear the way towards a serious reduction of nuclear weapons on both sides. Their further comments on this topic, however, suggest that they themselves do not entertain exaggerated hopes. Indeed, the experience of recent years in the field of tactical nuclear weapons gives little cause for hope that the Soviet side is ready for genuine reductions. Moreover, it is questionable whether the Soviets are ready to renounce their conventional superiority built up at great sacrifice, stubbornly defended during decades and energetically expanded in recent years, at the very moment when such a superiority would be given an increased and decisive importance by a NATO renunciation of first use of nuclear weapons.

We share many of the concerns about the risks of nuclear war. They lead us to conclude that an energetic attempt to reduce the *dependence on an early first use* of nuclear weapons must be undertaken. To be sure, the authors also mention a "no-early-first-use" policy (p. 762) as a possible alternative, but in the last analysis they discard it as a mere variation of nuclear options and therefore call for a clear decision in favor of a renunciation of "any first use of nuclear weapons" (p. 761).

A reduction of dependence on an early use of nuclear weapons should, in the first place, be attempted through mutual, balanced and verifiable reductions of conventional forces by means of East-West negotiations which result in an adequate conventional balance. We have pointed out how difficult it would be to restore such a balance by the buildup of Western conventional armament. In our opinion the essential precondition posed by the authors for their suggested renunciation of first use can, therefore, not be fulfilled.

In sum, we consider efforts to raise the nuclear threshold by a strengthening of conventional options to be urgently necessary. The reduction of the dependence on first use, in particular on early first use of nuclear weapons, should be a question of high political priority in our countries.

The Western Alliance has committed itself to a renunciation from the very beginning: the renunciation of the first use of *any* force. The entire military planning, structure and deployment of forces are geared exclusively toward defense. The presence of nuclear weapons has contributed essentially to the success of the Alliance in preventing war and preserving freedom for three decades. We are convinced that a reduction of the dependence on an early use of nuclear weapons would serve this purpose. Under the circumstances of the foreseeable future, however, a renunciation of the option of first use would be contrary to the security interests of Europe and the entire Alliance.

Toward Nuclear Peace*

KENNETH N. WALTZ

What will the spread of nuclear weapons do to the world? I say "spread" rather than "proliferation" because so far nuclear weapons have proliferated only vertically as the major nuclear powers have added to their arsenals. Horizontally, they have spread slowly across countries and the pace is not likely to change much. Sort-term candidates for the nuclear club are not very numerous, and they are not likely to rush into the nuclear business. One reason is that the United States works with some effect to keep countries from doing that. Nuclear weapons will nevertheless spread, with a new member occasionally joining the club. Counting India and Israel, membership grew to seven in the first 35 years of the nuclear age. A doubling of membership in the next decade would be surprising. Since rapid changes in international conditions can be unsettling, the slowness of the spread of the nuclear weapons is fortunate.

Someday the world will be populated by 10 or 12 or 18 nuclear-weapon states (hereafter referred to as nuclear states). What the further spread of nuclear weapons will do to the world is therefore a compelling question.

THE MILITARY LOGIC OF SELF-HELP SYSTEMS

The world has enjoyed more years of peace since 1945 than had been known in this century—if peace is defined as the absence of general war among the major states of the world. The Second World War followed the first one within twenty-one years. As of 1983, 38 years had elapsed since the Allies' victory over the Axis powers. Conflict marks all human affairs. In the past third of a century, conflict has generated hostility among states and has at times issued in violence among the weaker and smaller ones. Even though the more powerful states of the world have occasionally been direct participants, war has been confined geographically and limited militarily. Remarkably, general war has been avoided in a period of rapid and far-reaching changes—decolonization; the rapid economic growth of some states;

*A shortened and revised version of Waltz, *The Spread of Nuclear Weapons: More May Be Better,* Adelphi Papers, No. 171 (London: International Institute of Strategic Studies, 1981).

the formation, tightening, and eventual loosening of blocs; the development of new technologies, and the emergence of new strategies for fighting guerrilla wars and deterring nuclear ones. The prevalence of peace, together with the fighting of circumscribed wars, indicates a high ability of the postwar international system to absorb changes and to contain conflicts and hostility.

Presumably features found in the postwar system that were not present earlier account for the world's recent good fortune. The biggest changes in the postwar world are the shift from multipolarity to bipolarity and the introduction of nuclear weapons. In this paper I concentrate on the latter.

States coexist in a condition of anarchy. Self-help is the principle of action in an anarchic order, and the most important way in which states must help themselves is by providing for their own security. Therefore, in weighing the chances for peace, the first questions to ask are questions about the ends for which states use force and about the strategies and weapons they employ. The chances of peace rise if states can achieve their most important ends without actively using force. War becomes less likely as the costs of war rise in relation to possible gains. Strategies bring ends and means together. How nuclear weapons affect the chances for peace is seen by examining the different implications of defense and deterrence.

How can one state dissuade another state from attacking? In either or in some combination of two ways. One way to counter an intended attack is to build fortifications and to muster forces that look forbiddingly strong. To build defenses so patently strong that no one will try to destroy or overcome them would make international life perfectly tranquil. I call this the defensive ideal. The other way to inhibit a country's intended aggressive moves is to scare that country out of making them by threatening to visit unacceptable punishment upon it. "To deter" literally means to stop someone from doing something by frightening him. In contrast to dissuasion by defense, dissuasion by deterrence operates by frightening a state out of attacking, not because of the difficulty of launching an attack and carrying it home, but because the expected reaction of the opponent will result in one's own severe punishment. Defense and deterrence are often confused. One frequently hears statements like this: "A strong defense in Europe will deter a Russian attack." What is meant is that a strong defense will dissuade Russia from attacking. Deterrence is achieved not through the ability to defend but through the ability to punish. Purely deterrent forces provide no defense. The message of the strategy is this: "Although we are defenseless, if you attack we will punish you to an extent that more than cancels your gains." Second-strike nuclear forces serve that kind of strategy. Purely defensive forces provide no deterrence. They offer no means of punishment.

The message of the strategy is this: "Although we cannot strike back at you, you will find our defenses so difficult to overcome that you will dash yourself to pieces against them". The Maginot Line was to serve that kind of strategy.

Do nuclear weapons increase or decrease the chances of war? The answer depends on whether nuclear weapons permit and encourage states to deploy forces in ways that make the active use of force more or less likely and in ways that promise to be more or less destructive. If nuclear weapons make the offense more effective and the blackmailer's threat more compelling, then nuclear weapons are bad for the world— the more so the more widely diffused nuclear weapons become. If defense and deterrence are made easier and more reliable by the spread of nuclear weapons, we may expect the opposite result. To maintain their security states must rely on the means they can generate and the arrangements they can make for themselves. It follows that the quality of international life varies with the ease or the difficulty states experience in making themselves secure.

Weapons and strategies change the situation of states in ways that make them more or less secure, as Robert Jervis has brilliantly shown. (ref. Jervis article) If weapons are not well suited for conquest, neighbors have more peace of mind. We should expect war to become less likely when weaponry is such as to make conquest more difficult, to discourage preemptive and preventive war, and to make coercive threats less credible. Do nuclear weapons have those effects? Some answers can be found by considering how nuclear deterrence and nuclear defense improve the prospects for peace.

First, wars can be fought in the face of deterrent threats, but the higher the stakes and the closer a country moves toward winning them, the more surely that country invites retaliation and risks its own destruction. States are not likely to run major risks for minor gains. Wars between nuclear states may escalate as the loser uses larger and larger warheads. Fearing that, states will want to draw back. Not escalation but deescalation becomes likely. War remains possible, but victory in war is too dangerous to fight for. If states can score only small gains, because large ones risk retaliation, they have little incentive to fight.

Second, states act with less care if the expected costs of war are low and with more care if they are high. In 1853 and '54 Britain and France expected to win an easy victory if they went to war against Russia. Prestige abroad and political popularity at home would be gained, if not much else. The vagueness of their expectations was matched by the carelessness of their actions. In blundering into the Crimean War they acted hastily on scant information, pandered to their people's frenzy for war, showed more concern for an ally's whim than for the adversary's situation, failed to specify the changes in behavior that threats were supposed to bring, and inclined toward testing strength first and bargaining second. In sharp contrast, the presence of nuclear weapons makes states exceedingly cautious. Think of Kennedy and Khrushchev in the Cuban missile crisis. Why fight if you can't win much and might lose everything?

Third, the question demands a negative answer all the more insistently when the deterrent deployment of nuclear weapons contributes more to a country's security than does conquest of territory. A country with a deterrent strategy does not need the extent of territory required by a country relying on a conventional defense. A deterrent strategy makes it unnecessary for a country to fight for the sake of increasing its security, and this removes a major cause of war.

Fourth, deterrent effect depends both on one's capabilities and on the will one has to use them. The will of the attacked, striving to preserve its own territory, can ordinarily be presumed stronger than the will of the attacker, striving to annex someone else's territory. Knowing this, the would-be attacker is further inhibited.

Certainty about the relative strength of adversaries also makes war less likely. From the late nineteenth century onward the speed of technological innovation increased the difficulty of estimating relative strengths and predicting the course of campaigns. Since World War II, technology has advanced even faster, but short of a ballistic missile defense (BMD) breakthrough, this does not matter very much. It does not disturb the American-Russian military equilibrium, because one side's missiles are not made obsolete by improvements in the other side's missiles. In 1906 the British Dreadnought, with the greater range and fire power of its guns, made older battleships obsolete. This does not happen to missiles. As Bernard Brodie put it: "Weapons that do not have to fight their like do not become useless because of the advent of newer and superior types." They may have to survive their like, but that is a much simpler problem to solve.

Many wars might have been avoided had their outcomes been foreseen. "To be sure," Georg Simmel once said, "the most effective presupposition for preventing struggle, the exact knowledge of the comparative strength of the two parties, is very often only to be obtained by the actual fighting out of the conflict." Miscalculation causes wars. One side expects victory at an affordable price, while the other side hopes to avoid defeat. Here the differences between conventional and nuclear worlds are fundamental. In the former, states are too often tempted to act on advantages that are wishfully discerned and narrowly calculated. In 1914, neither Germany nor France tried very hard to avoid a general war. Both hoped for victory even though they believed their forces to be quite evenly matched. In 1941, Japan, in attacking the the United States, could hope for victory only if a series of events that were possible but not highly probable took place.

Japan would grab resources sufficient for continuing the conquest of China and then dig in to defend a limited perimeter. Meanwhile, the United States and Britain would have to deal with Germany, which, having defeated the Soviet Union, would be supreme in Europe. Japan could then hope to fight a defensive war for a year or two until America, her purpose weakened, became willing to make a compromise peace in Asia (ref. Sansom article).

Countries more readily run the risks of war when defeat, if it comes, is distant and is expected to bring only limited damage. Given such expectations, leaders do not have to be insane to sound the trumpet and urge their people to be bold and courageous in the pursuit of victory. The outcome of battles and the course of campaigns are hard to foresee because so many things affect them. Predicting the result of conventional wars has proved difficult.

Uncertainty about outcomes does not work decisively against the fighting of wars in conventional worlds. Countries armed with conventional weapons go to war knowing that even in defeat their suffering will be limited. Calculations about nuclear war are differently made. A nuclear world calls for and encourages a different kind of reasoning. If countries armed with nuclear weapons go to war, they do so knowing that their suffering may be unlimited. Of course, it also may not be. But that is not the kind of uncertainty that encourages anyone to use force. In a conventional world, one is uncertain about winning or losing. In a nuclear world, one is uncertain about surviving or being annihilated. If force is used, and not kept within limits, catastrophe will result. That prediction is easy to make because it does not require close estimates of opposing forces. The number of one's cities that can be severely damaged is at least equal to the number of strategic warheads an adversary can deliver. Variations of number mean little within wide ranges. The expected effect of the deterrent achieves an easy clarity because wide margins of error in estimates of the damage one may suffer do not matter. Do we expect to lose one city or two, two cities or ten? When these are the pertinent questions, we stop thinking about running risks and start worrying about how to avoid them. In a conventional world, deterrent threats are ineffective because the damage threatened is distant, limited, and problematic. Nuclear weapons make military miscalculation difficult and politically pertinent prediction easy.

Dissuading a would-be attacker by throwing up a good-looking defense may be as effective as dissuading him through deterrence. Beginning with President Kennedy and Secretary of Defense McNamara in the early 1960s, we have asked how we can avoid, or at least postpone, using nuclear weapons rather than how we can mount the most effective defense. NATO's attempts to keep a defensive war conventional in its initial stage may guarantee that nuclear weapons, if used, will be used in a losing cause and in ways that multiply destruction without promising victory. Early use of very small warheads may stop escalation. Defensive deployment, if it should fail to dissuade, would bring small nuclear weapons into use before the physical, political, and psychological environment had deteriorated. The chances of de-escalation are high if the use of nuclear weapons is carefully planned and their use is limited to the battlefield. We have rightly put strong emphasis on strategic deterrence, which makes large wars less likely, and wrongly slighted the question of whether nuclear weapons of low yield can effectively be used for defense, which would make any war at all less likely still.*

An unassailable defense is fully dissuasive. Dissuasion is what is wanted whether by defense or by deterrence. The likelihood of war decreases as deterrent and defensive capabilities increase. Nuclear weapons and an appropriate doctrine for their use may make it possible to approach the defensive-deterrent ideal, a condition that would cause the chances of war to dwindle. Concentrating attention on the destructive power of nuclear weapons has obscured the important benefits they promise to states trying to coexist in a self-help world.

WHAT WILL THE SPREAD OF NUCLEAR WEAPONS DO TO THE WORLD?

Contemplating the nuclear past gives grounds for hoping that the world will survive if further nuclear powers join today's six or seven. This tentative conclusion is called into question by the widespread belief that the infirmities of some new nuclear states and the delicacy of their nuclear forces will work against the preservation of peace and for the fighting of nuclear wars. The likelihood of avoiding destruction as more states become members of the nuclear club is often coupled with the question of *who* those states will be. What are the likely differences in situation and behavior of new as compared to old nuclear powers?

NUCLEAR WEAPONS AND DOMESTIC STABILITY

What are the principal worries? Because of the importance of controlling nuclear weapons—of keeping them firmly in the hands of reliable officials—rulers of nuclear states may become more authoritarian and ever more given to secrecy. Moreover, some potential nuclear states are not politically strong and stable enough to ensure control of the weapons and control of the decision to use them. If neighboring, hostile, unstable states are armed with nuclear weapons, each will fear attack by the other. Feelings of insecurity may lead to arms races that subordinate civil needs to military necessities. Fears are compounded by the danger of internal coups in which the control

---

* I shall concentrate on nuclear deterrence and slight nuclear defense.

of nuclear weapons may be the main object of struggle and the key to political power. Under these fearful circumstances, to maintain governmental authority and civil order may be impossible. The legitimacy of the state and the loyalty of its citizenry may dissolve because the state is no longer thought to be capable of maintaining external security and internal order. The first fear is that states become tyrannical; the second, that they lose control. Both fears may be realized either in different states or in the same state at different times (ref. Dunn article).

What can one say? Four things primarily. First, possession of nuclear weapons may slow arms races down, rather than speed them up, a possibility considered later. Second, for less developed countries to build nuclear arsenals requires a long lead time. Nuclear power and nuclear weapons programs, like population policies, require administrative and technical teams able to formulate and sustain programs of considerable cost that pay off only in the long run. The more unstable a government, the shorter becomes the attention span of its leaders. They have to deal with today's problems and hope for the best tomorrow. In countries where political control is most difficult to maintain, governments are least likely to initiate nuclear-weapons programs. In such states, soldiers help to maintain leaders in power or try to overthrow them. For those purposes nuclear weapons are not very useful. Soldiers who have political clout or want it are not interested in nuclear weapons. They are not scientists and technicians. They like to command troops and squadrons. Their vested interests are in the military's traditional trappings.

Third, although highly unstable states are unlikely to initiate nuclear projects, such projects, begun in stable times, may continue through periods of political turmoil and succeed in producing nuclear weapons. A nuclear state may be unstable or may become so. But what is hard to comprehend is why, in an internal struggle for power, the contenders should start using nuclear weapons. Who would they aim at? How would they use them as instruments for maintaining or gaining control? I see little more reason to fear that one faction or another in some less developed country will fire atomic weapons in a struggle for political power than that they will be used in a crisis of succession in the Soviet Union or China. One or another nuclear state will experience uncertainty of succession, fierce struggles for power, and instability of regime. Those who fear the worst have not very plausibly shown how those expected events may lead to the use of nuclear weapons. Fourth, the possibility of one side in a civil war firing a nuclear warhead at its opponent's stronghold nevertheless remains. Such an act would produce a national tragedy, not an international one. This question then arises: Once the weapon is fired, what happens next? The domestic use of nuclear weapons is, of all the uses imaginable, least likely to lead to escalation and to threaten the stability of the central balance.

NUCLEAR WEAPONS AND REGIONAL STABILITY

Nuclear weapons are not likely to be used at home. Are they likely to be used abroad? As nuclear weapons spread, what new causes may bring effects different from and worse than those known earlier in the nuclear age? This section considers five ways in which the new world is expected to differ from the old and then examines the prospects for, and the consequences of, new nuclear states using their weapons for blackmail or for fighting an offensive war.

In what ways may the actions and interactions of new nuclear states differ from those of old nuclear powers? First, new nuclear states may come in hostile pairs and share a common border. Where states are bitter enemies one may fear that they will be unable to resist using their nuclear weapons against each other. This is a worry about the future that the past does not disclose. The Soviet Union and the United States, and the Soviet Union and China, are hostile enough; and the latter pair share a long border. Nuclear weapons have caused China and the Soviet Union to deal cautiously with each other. But bitterness among some potential nuclear states, so it is said, exceeds that experienced by the old ones. Playing down the bitterness sometimes felt by the United States, the Soviet Union, and China requires a creative reading of history. Moreover, those who believe that bitterness causes wars assume a close association that is seldom found between bitterness among nations and their willingness to run high risks.

Second, some new nuclear states may have governments and societies that are not well rooted. If a country is a loose collection of hostile tribes, if its leaders form a thin veneer atop a people partly nomadic and with an authoritarian history, its rulers may be freer of constraints than, and have different values from, those who rule older and more fully developed polities. Idi Amin and Muammar el-Qaddafi fit these categories, and they are favorite examples of the kinds of rulers who supposedly cannot be trusted to manage nuclear weapons responsibly. Despite wild rhetoric aimed at foreigners, however, both of these "irrational" rulers became cautious and modest when punitive actions against them might have threatened their ability to rule. Even though Amin lustily slaughtered members of tribes he disliked, he quickly stopped goading Britain once the sending of her troops appeared to be a possibility. Qaddafi has shown similar restraint. He and Anwar Sadat were openly hostile. In July of 1977 both launched commando attacks and air raids, including two large air strikes by Egypt on Libya's el Adem airbase. Neither side let the attacks get out of hand. Qaddafi showed himself to be forbearing and amenable to mediation by other Arab leaders. Shai Feldman uses these and other examples to argue that Arab leaders are deterred from taking inordinate risks not because they engage in intricate rational calculations but simply because they, like other rulers, are "sensitive to costs."

Many Westerners who write fearfully about a future in which third-world countries have nuclear weapons seem to view their people in the once familiar imperial manner as "lesser breeds without the law." As is usual with ethnocentric views, speculation takes the place of evidence. How do we know, someone has asked, that a nuclear-armed and newly hostile Egypt or a nuclear-armed and still hostile Syria would not strike to destroy Israel at the risk of Israeli bombs falling on some of their cities? More than a quarter of Egypt's people live in four cities: Cairo, Alexandria, Giza, and Aswan. More than a quarter of Syria's live in three: Damascus, Aleppo, and Homs. What government would risk sudden losses of such proportion or indeed of much lesser proportion? Rulers want to have a country that they can continue to rule. Some Arab country might wish that some other Arab country would risk its own destruction for the sake of destroying Israel, but there is no reason to think that any Arab country would do so. One may be impressed that, despite ample bitterness, Israelis and Arabs have limited their wars and accepted constraints placed on them by others. Arabs did not marshal their resources and make an all-out effort to destroy Israel in the years before Israel could strike back with nuclear warheads. We cannot expect countries to risk more in the presence of nuclear weapons than they have in their absence.

Third, many fear that states that are radical at home will recklessly use their nuclear weapons in pursuit of revolutionary ends abroad. States that are radical at home, however, may not be radical abroad. Few states have been radical in the conduct of their foreign policy, and fewer have remained so for long. Think of the Soviet Union and the People's Republic of China. States coexist in a competitive arena. The pressures of competition cause them to behave in ways that make the threats they face manageable, in ways that enable them to get along. States can remain radical in foreign policy only if they are overwhelmingly strong—as none of the new nuclear states will be—or if their radical acts fall short of damaging vital interests of nuclear powers. States that acquire nuclear weapons will not be regarded with indifference. States that want to be freewheelers have to stay out of the nuclear business. A nuclear Libya, for example, would have to show caution, even in rhetoric, lest she suffer retaliation in response to someone else's anonymous attack on a third state. That state, ignorant of who attacked, might claim that its intelligence agents had identified Libya as the culprit and take the opportunity to silence her by striking a conventional blow. Nuclear weapons induce caution, especially in weak states.

Fourth, while some worry about nuclear states coming in hostile pairs, others worry that the bipolar pattern will not be reproduced regionally in a world populated by larger numbers of nuclear states. The simplicity of relations that obtains when one party has to concentrate its worry on only one other, and the ease of calculating forces and estimating the dangers they pose, may be lost. The structure of international politics, however, will remain bipolar so long as no third state is able to compete militarily with the great powers. Whatever the structure, the relations of states run in various directions. This applied to relations of deterrence as soon as Britain gained nuclear capabilities. It has not weakened deterrence at the center and need not do so regionally. The Soviet Union now has to worry lest a move made in Europe cause France and Britain to retaliate, thus possibly setting off American forces. Such worries at once complicate calculations and strengthen deterrence.

Fifth, in some of the new nuclear states civil control of the military may be shaky. Nuclear weapons may fall into the hands of military officers more inclined than civilians to put them to offensive use. This again is an old worry. I can see no reason to think that civil control of the military is secure in the Soviet Union, given the occasional presence of serving officers in the Politburo and some known and some surmised instances of military intervention in civil affairs at critical times. And in the People's Republic of China military and civil branches of government are not separated but fused. Although one may prefer civil control, preventing a highly destructive war does not require it. What is required is that decisions be made that keep destruction within bounds, whether decisions are made by civilians or soldiers. Soldiers may be more cautious than civilians. Generals and admirals do not like uncertainty, and they do not lack patriotism. They do not like to fight conventional wars under unfamiliar conditions. The offensive use of nuclear weapons multiplies uncertainties. Nobody knows what a nuclear battlefield would look like, and nobody knows what happens after the first city is hit. *Uncertainty* about the course that a nuclear war might follow, along with the *certainty* that destruction can be immense, strongly inhibits the first use of nuclear weapons.

Examining the supposedly unfortunate characteristics of new nuclear states removes some of one's worries. One wonders why their civil and military leaders should be less interested in avoiding their own destruction than leaders of other states have been. Nuclear weapons have never been used in a world in which two or more states possessed them. Still, one's feeling that something awful will emerge as new nuclear powers are added to the present group is not easily quieted. The fear remains that one state or another will fire its new nuclear weapons in a coolly calculated preemptive strike, or fire them in a moment of panic, or use them to launch a preventive war. These possibilities are examined in the next section. Nuclear weapons may also be set off anonymously, or back a policy of blackmail, or be used in a combined conventional-nuclear attack.

Some have feared that a radical Arab state might fire a nuclear warhead anonymously at an Israeli city in order to block a peace settlement. But the state exploding the warhead could not be certain of remaining unidentified. Even if a country's leaders persuade themselves that chances of retaliation are low, who would run the risk? Nor would blackmail be easy to accomplish, despite one instance of seeming success. In 1953 Russia and China may have been convinced by Eisenhower and Dulles that they would widen the Korean war and raise the level of violence by using nuclear weapons if a settlement were not reached. In Korea we had gone so far that the threat to go further was plausible. The blackmailer's threat is not a cheap way of working one's will. The threat is simply incredible unless a considerable investment has already been made. Dulles's speech of January 12, 1954, seemed to threaten massive retaliation in response to mildly bothersome actions by others. The successful siege of Dien Bien Phu in the spring of that year showed the limitations of such threats. Capabilities foster policies that employ them. But monstrous capabilities foster monstrous policies, which when contemplated are seen to be too horrible to carry through. Moreover, once two or more countries have nuclear weapons, the execution of nuclear threats risks retaliation. This compounds the problem of establishing credibility.

Although nuclear weapons are poor instruments for blackmail, would they not provide a cheap and decisive offensive force when used against a conventionally armed enemy? Some people think that South Korea wants, and that earlier the Shah's Iran had wanted, nuclear weapons for offensive use. Yet one cannot say why South Korea would use nuclear weapons against fellow Koreans while trying to reunite them nor how she could use nuclear weapons against the North, knowing that China and Russia might retaliate. And what goals might a conventionally strong Iran have entertained that would have tempted her to risk using nuclear weapons? A country that takes the nuclear offensive has to fear a punishing blow from someone. Far from lowering the expected cost of aggression, a nuclear offense even against a non-nuclear state raises the possible costs of aggression to uncalculable heights because the aggressor cannot be sure of the reaction of other nuclear powers.

Nuclear weapons do not make nuclear war a likely prospect, as history has so far shown. The point made when discussing the possible internal use of nuclear weapons, however, bears repeating. No one can say that nuclear weapons will never be used. Their use, although unlikely, is always possible. In asking what the spread of nuclear weapons will do to the world, we are asking about the effects to be expected as a larger number of relatively weak states get nuclear weapons. If such states use nuclear weapons, the world will not end. The use of nuclear weapons by lesser powers would hardly trigger them elsewhere, with the United States and the Soviet Union becoming involved in ways that might shake the central balance.

DETERRENCE WITH SMALL NUCLEAR FORCES

A number of problems are thought to attend the efforts of minor powers to use nuclear weapons for deterrence. In this section, I ask how hard these problems are for new nuclear states to solve.

The forces required for deterrence. In considering the physical requirements of deterrent forces, we should remark the difference between prevention and preemption. A preventive war is launched by a stronger state against a weaker one that is thought to be gaining in strength. Aside from the balance of forces, a preemptive strike is launched by one state when another state's offensive forces are seen to be vulnerable.

The first danger posed by the spread of nuclear weapons would seem to be that each new nuclear state may tempt an old one to strike preventively in order to destroy an embryonic nuclear capability before it can become militarily effective. Because of America's nuclear arsenal, the Soviet Union could hardly have destroyed the budding forces of Britain and France; but the United States could have struck the Soviet Union's early nuclear facilities, and the United States and the Soviet Union could have struck China's. Long before Israel struck Iraq's reactor, preventive strikes were treated as more than abstract possibilities. When Francis P. Matthews was President Truman's Secretary of the Navy, he made a speech that seemed to favor our waging a preventive war. The United States, he urged, should be willing to pay "even the price of instituting a war to compel cooperation for peace." Moreover, preventive strikes against nuclear installations can be made by non-nuclear states and have sometimes been threatened. Thus President Nasser warned Israel in 1960 that Egypt would attack if she were sure that Israel was building a bomb. "It is inevitable," he said, "that we should attack the base of aggression even if we have to mobilize four million to destroy it."

The uneven development of the forces of potential and of new nuclear states creates occasions that seem to permit preventive strikes and may seem to invite them. Two stages of nuclear development should be distinguished. First, a country may be in an early stage of nuclear development and be obviously unable to make nuclear weapons. Second, a country may be in an advanced stage of nuclear development, and whether or not it has some nuclear weapons may not be surely known. All of the present nuclear countries went through both stages, yet until Israel struck Iraq's nuclear facility in June of 1981 no one had launched a preventive strike. A number of reasons combined may account for the reluctance of states to strike in order to prevent adversaries from developing nuclear forces. A preventive strike would seem to be most promising during the first stage of nuclear development. A state could strike without fearing that the country it attacked would return a nuclear blow. But would one strike so hard as to destroy the very potential for future nuclear development? If not, the country struck could simply resume its nuclear career. If the blow struck is less than devastating, one must be prepared to repeat it or to occupy and control the country. To do either would be difficult and costly.

In striking Iraq, Israel showed that a preventive strike can be made, something that was not in doubt. Israel's act and its consequences, however, make clear that the likelihood of useful accomplishment is low. Israel's strike increased the determination of Arabs to produce nuclear weapons. Israel's strike, far from foreclosing Iraq's nuclear future, gained her the support of some other Arab states in pursuing it. And despite Prime Minister Begin's vow to strike as often as need be, the risks in doing so would rise with each occasion.

A preventive strike during the second stage of nuclear development is even less promising than a preventive strike during the first stage. As more countries acquire nuclear weapons, and as more countries gain nuclear competence through power projects, the difficulties and dangers of making preventive strikes increase. To know for sure that the country attacked has not already produced or otherwise acquired some deliverable warheads becomes increasingly difficult. If the country attacked has even a rudimentary nuclear capability, one's own severe punishment becomes possible. Fission bombs may work even though they have not been tested, as was the case with the bomb dropped on Hiroshima. Israel has apparently not tested weapons, yet Egypt cannot know whether Israel has zero, ten, or twenty warheads. And if the number is zero and Egypt can be sure of that, she would still not know how many days or hours are required for assembling components that may be on hand.

Preventive strikes against states that have, or may have, nuclear weapons are hard to imagine, but what about preemptive ones? The new worry in a world in which nuclear weapons have spread is that states of limited and roughly similar capabilities will use them against one another. They do not want to risk nuclear devastation anymore than we do. Preemptive strikes nevertheless seem likely because we assume that their forces will be "delicate." With delicate forces, states are tempted to launch disarming strikes before their own forces can be struck and destroyed.

To be effective a deterrent force must meet three requirements. First, a part of the force must appear to be able to survive an attack and launch one of its own. Second, survival of the force must not require early firing in response to what may be false alarms. Third, weapons must not be susceptible to accidental and unauthorized use.

Nobody wants vulnerable, hair-trigger, accident-prone forces. Will new nuclear states find ways to hide their weapons, to deliver them, and to control them? Will they be able to deploy and manage nuclear weapons in ways that meet the physical requirements of deterrent forces?

Deterrent forces are seldom delicate because no state wants delicate forces and nuclear forces can easily be made sturdy. Nuclear weapons are fairly small and light. They are easy to hide and to move. Early in the nuclear age, people worried about atomic bombs being concealed in packing boxes and placed in the hold of ships to be exploded when a signal was given. Now more than ever people worry about terrorists stealing nuclear warheads because various states have so many of them. Everybody seems to believe that terrorists are capable of hiding bombs. Why should states be unable to do what terrorist gangs are thought to be capable of?

It is sometimes claimed that the few bombs of a new nuclear state create a greater danger of nuclear war than additional thousands for the United States and the Soviet Union. Such statements assume that preemption of a small force is easy. It is so only if the would-be attacker knows that the intended victim's warheads are few in number, knows their exact number and locations, and knows that they will not be moved or fired before they are struck. To know all of these things, and to know that you know them for sure, is exceedingly difficult. How can military advisers promise the full success of a disarming first strike when the penalty for slight error may be so heavy? In 1962, Tactical Air Command promised that an American strike against Soviet missiles in Cuba would certainly destroy 90 percent of them but would not guarantee 100 percent. In the best case a first strike destroys all of a country's deliverable weapons. In the worst case, some survive and can be delivered.

If the survival of nuclear weapons requires their dispersal and concealment, do not problems of command and control become harder to solve? Americans think so because we think in terms of large nuclear arsenals. Small nuclear powers will neither have them nor need them. Lesser nuclear states might deploy, say, ten real weapons and ten dummies, while permitting other countries to infer that the numbers are larger. The adversary need only believe that some warheads may survive his attack and be visited on him. That belief should not be hard to create without making command and control unreliable. All nuclear countries must live through a time when their forces are crudely designed. All countries have so far been able to control them. Relations between the United States and the Soviet Union, and later among the United States, the Soviet Union, and China, were at their bitterest just when their nuclear forces were in early stages of development, were unbalanced, were crude and presumably hard to control. Why should we expect new nuclear states to experience greater difficulties than the old ones were able to cope with? Moreover, although some of the new nuclear states may be economically and technically backward, they will either have an expert and highly trained group of scientists and engineers or they will not produce nuclear weapons. Even if they buy the weapons, they will have to hire technicians to maintain and control them. We do not have to wonder whether they will take good care of their weapons. They have every incentive to do so. They will not want to risk retaliation because one or more of their warheads accidentally strikes another country.

Hiding nuclear weapons and keeping them under control are tasks for which the ingenuity of numerous states is adequate. Nor are means of delivery difficult to devise or procure. Bombs can be driven in by trucks from neighboring countries. Ports can be torpedoed by small boats lying offshore. Moreover, a thriving arms trade in ever more sophisticated military equipment provides ready access to what may be wanted, including planes and missiles suited to nuclear warhead delivery.

Lesser nuclear states can pursue deterrent strategies effectively. Deterrence requires the ability to inflict unacceptable damage on another country. "Unacceptable damage" to the Soviet Union was variously defined by Robert McNamara as requiring the ability to destroy a fifth to a fourth of her population and a half to two-thirds of her industrial capacity. American estimates of what is required for deterrence have been absurdly high. To deter, a country need not appear to be able to destroy a fourth or a half of another country, although in some cases that might be easily done. Would Libya try to destroy Israel's nuclear weapons at the risk of two bombs surviving to fall on Tripoli and Bengazi? And what would be left of Israel if Tel Aviv and Haifa were destroyed?

The weak can deter one another. But can the weak deter the strong? Raising the question of China's ability to deter the Soviet Union highlights the issue. The population and industry of most states concentrate in a relatively small number of centers. This is true of the Soviet Union. A major attack on the top ten cities of the Soviet Union would get 25 percent of its industrial capacity and 25 percent of its urban population. Geoffrey Kemp in 1974 concluded that China would probably be able to strike on that scale. And, I emphasize again, China need only appear to be able to do it. A low probability of carrying a highly destructive attack home is sufficient for deterrence. A force of an imprecisely specifiable minimum capacity is nevertheless needed.

In a 1979 study, Justin Galen (pseud.) wondered whether the Chinese had a force physically capable of deterring the Soviet Union. He estimated that China had 60 to 80 medium range and 60 to 80 intermediate range missiles of doubtful reliability and accuracy and 80 obsolete bombers. He rightly pointed out that the missiles may miss their targets even if fired at cities and that the bombers may not get through the Soviet Union's defenses. Moreover, the Russians may be able to preempt, having almost certainly "located virtually every Chinese missile, aircraft, weapons storage area and production facility." But surely Russian leaders put these things the other way around. To locate virtually all missiles and aircraft is not good enough. Despite inaccuracies, a few Chinese missiles *may* hit Russian cities, and some bombers *may* get through. Not much is required to deter. What political-military objective is worth risking Vladivostok, Novosibirsk, and Tomsk, with no way of being sure that Moscow will not go as well?

The credibility of small deterrent forces. The credibility of weaker countries' deterrent threats has two faces. The first is physical. Will such countries be able to construct and protect a deliverable force? We have found that they can quite readily do so. The second is psychological. Will deterrent threats that are physically feasible be psychologically plausible? Will an adversary believe that the retaliation that is threatened will be carried out?

Deterrent threats backed by second-strike nuclear forces raise the expected costs of war to such heights that war becomes unlikely. But deterrent threats may not be credible. In a world where two or more countries can make them, the prospect of *mutual* devastation makes it difficult, or irrational, to execute threats should the occasion for doing so arise. Would it not be senseless to risk suffering further destruction once a deterrent force had failed to deter? Believing that it would be, an adversary may attack counting on the attacked country's unwillingness to risk initiating a devastating exchange by its own retaliation. Why retaliate once a threat to do so has failed? If one's policy is to rely on forces designed to deter, then an attack that is nevertheless made shows that one's reliance was misplaced. The course of wisdom may be to pose a new question: What is the best policy now that deterrence has failed? One gains nothing by destroying an enemy's cities. Instead, in retaliating, one may prompt the enemy to unleash more warheads. A ruthless aggressor may strike believing that the leaders of the attacked country are capable of following such a "rational" line of thought. To carry out the threat that was "rationally" made may be "irrational." This old worry achieved new prominence as the strategic capabilities of the Soviet Union approached those of the United States in the middle 1970s. The Soviet Union, some feared, might believe that the United States would be self-deterred (ref. Nitze article).

Much of the literature on deterrence emphasizes the problem of achieving the credibility on which deterrence depends and the danger of relying on a deterrent of uncertain credibility. One earlier solution of the problem was found in Thomas Schelling's notion of "the threat that leaves something to chance." No state can know for sure that another state will refrain from retaliating even when retaliation would be irrational. No state can bet heavily on another state's rationality. Bernard Brodie put the thought more directly, while avoiding the slippery notion of rationality. Rather than ask what it may be rational or irrational for governments to do, the question he repeatedly asked was this: How do governments behave in the presence of awesome dangers? His answer was "very carefully."

To ask why a country should carry out its deterrent threat once deterrence has failed is to ask the wrong question. The question suggests that an aggressor may attack believing that the attacked country may not retaliate. This invokes the conventional logic that analysts find so hard to forsake. In a conventional world, a country can sensibly attack if it believes that success is probable. In a nuclear world, a country cannot sensibly attack unless it believes that success is assured. An attacker is deterred even if he believes only that the attacked *may* retaliate. Uncertainty of response, not certainty, is required for deterrence because, if retaliation occurs, one risks losing all. In a nuclear world, we should look less at the retaliator's conceivable inhibitions and more at the challenger's obvious risks.

One may nevertheless wonder, as Americans recently have, whether retaliatory threats remain credible if the strategic forces of the attacker are superior to those of the attacked. Will an unsuccessful defender in a conventional war have the courage to unleash its deterrent force, using nuclear weapons first against a country having superior strategic forces? Once more this asks the wrong question. The previous paragraph urged the importance of shifting attention from the defender's possible inhibitions to the aggressor's unwillingness to run extreme risks. This paragraph urges the importance of shifting attention from the defender's courage to the different valuations that defenders and attackers place on the stakes. An attacked country will ordinarily value keeping its own territory more highly than an attacker will value gaining some portion of it. Given second-strike capabilities, it is not the balance of forces but the courage to use them that counts. The balance or imbalance of strategic forces affects neither the calculation of danger nor the question of whose will is the stronger. Second-strike forces have to be seen in absolute terms. The question of whose interests are paramount will then determine whose will is perceived as being the stronger.

Emphasizing the importance of the "balance of resolve," to use Glenn Snyder's apt phrase, raises questions about what a deterrent force covers and what it does not. In answering these questions, we can learn something from the experience of the last three decades. The United States and the Soviet Union have limited and modulated their provocative acts, the more carefully so when major values for one side or the other were at issue. This can be seen both in what they have and in what they have not done. Whatever support the Soviet Union gave to North Korea's initial attack on the South was given after Secretary of State Acheson, the Joint Chiefs of Staff, General MacArthur, and the Chairman of the Senate Foreign Relations Committee all explicitly excluded both South Korea and Taiwan from America's defense perimeter. The United States, to take another example, could fight for years on a large scale in Southeast Asia because neither success nor failure mattered much internationally. Victory would not have made the world one of American hegemony. Defeat would not have made the world one of Russian hegemony. No vital interest of either super-power was at stake, as both Kissinger and Brezhnev made clear at the time (Stoessinger, 1976, ch. 8). One can fight without fearing escala-tion only where little is at stake. And that is where the deterrent does not deter.

Actions at the periphery can safely be bolder than actions at the center. In contrast, where much is at stake for one side, the other side moves with care. Trying to win where winning would bring the central balance into question threatens escalation and becomes too risky to contemplate. The United States is circumspect when East European crises impend. Thus Secretary of State Dulles assured the Soviet Union when Hungarians rebelled in October of 1956 that we would not interfere with efforts to suppress them. And the Soviet Union's moves in the center of Europe are carefully controlled. Thus her probes in Berlin have been tentative, reversible, and ineffective. Strikingly, the long border between East and West Europe—drawn where borders earlier proved unstable—has been free even of skirmishes in all of the years since the Second World War.

Contemplating American and Russian postwar behavior, and inter-preting it in terms of nuclear logic, suggests that deterrence extends to vital interests beyond the homeland more easily than many have thought. The United States cares more about Western Europe than the Soviet Union does. The Soviet Union cares more about Eastern Europe than the United States does. Communicating the weight of one side's concern as compared to the other side's has been easily enough done when the matters at hand affect the United States and the Soviet Union directly. For this reason, West European anxiety about the coverage it gets from our strategic forces, while understand-able, is exaggerated. The United States might well retaliate should the Soviet Union make a major military move against a NATO country, and that is enough to deter.

The problem of extended deterrence. How far from the homeland does deterrence extend? One answers that question by defining the conditions that must obtain if deterrent threats are to be credited. First, the would-be attacker must be made to see that the deterrer considers the interests at stake to be vital. One cannot assume that countries will instantly agree on the question of whose interests are vital. Nuclear weapons, however, strongly incline them to grope for *de facto* agreement on the answer rather than to fight over it.

Second, political stability must prevail in the area that the deterrent is intended to cover. If the threat to a regime is in good part from internal factions, then an outside power may risk supporting one of them even in the face of deterrent threats. The credibility of a deterrent force requires both that interests be seen to be vital and that it is the attack from outside that threatens them. Given these conditions, the would-be attacker provides both the reason to retaliate and the target for retaliation. Deterrence gains in credibility the more highly valued the interests covered appear to be.

The problem of stretching a deterrent, which has so agitated the western alliance, is not a problem for lesser nuclear states. Their problem is to protect not others but themselves. Many have feared that lesser nuclear states would be the first ones to break the nuclear taboo and that they would use their weapons irresponsibly. I expect just the opposite. Weak states find it easier than strong states to establish their credibility. Not only are they not trying to stretch their deterrent forces to cover others but also their vulnerability to conventional attack lends credence to their nuclear threats. Because in a conventional war they can lose so much so fast, it is easy to believe that they will unleash a deterrent force even at the risk of receiving a nuclear blow in return. With deterrent forces, the party that is absolutely threatened prevails (Feldman 1980, ch. 1). Use of nuclear weapons by lesser states will come only if survival is at stake. And this should be called not irresponsible but responsible use.

An opponent who attacks what is unambiguously mine risks suffering great distress if I have second-strike forces. This statement has important implications for both the deterrer and the deterred. Where territorial claims are shadowy and disputed, deterrent writs do not run. As Steven J. Rosen has said: "It is difficult to imagine Israel committing national suicide to hold on to Abu Rudeis or Hebron or Mount Hermon." Establishing the credibility of a deterrent force requires moderation of territorial claims on the part of the would-be deterred. For modest states, weapons whose very existence works strongly against their use are just what is wanted.

In a nuclear world, conservative would-be attackers will be prudent, but will would-be attackers be conservative? A new Hitler is not unimaginable. Would the presence of nuclear weapons have moderated Hitler's behavior? Hitler did not start World War II in order to destroy the Third Reich. Indeed, he was surprised and dismayed by British and French declarations of war on Poland's behalf. After all, the western democracies had not come to the aid of a geographically defensible and militarily strong Czechoslovakia. Why then should they have declared war on behalf of a less defensible Poland and against a Germany made stronger by the incorporation of Czechoslovakia's armor? From the occupation of the Rhineland in 1936 to the invasion of Poland in 1939, Hitler's calculations were realistically made. In those years, Hitler would probably have been deterred from acting in ways that immediately threatened massive death and widespread destruction in Germany. And, if Hitler had not been deterred, would his generals have obeyed his commands? In a nuclear world, to act in blatantly offensive ways is madness. Under the circumstances, how many generals would obey the commands of a madman? One man alone does not make war.

To believe that nuclear deterrence would have worked against Germany in 1939 is easy. It is also easy to believe that in 1945, given the ability to do so, Hitler and some few around him would have fired nuclear warheads at the United States, Great Britain, and the Soviet Union as their armies advanced, whatever the consequences for Germany. Two considerations, however, work against this possibility. When defeat is seen to be inevitable, a ruler's authority may vanish. Early in 1945 Hitler apparently ordered the initiation of gas warfare, but no one responded (ref. Brown article). The first consideration applies in a conventional world; the second in a nuclear world. In the latter, no country will press another to the point of decisive defeat. In the desperation of defeat desperate measures may be taken, but the last thing anyone wants to do is to make a nuclear nation desperate. The unconditional surrender of a nuclear nation cannot be demanded. Nuclear weapons affect the deterrer as well as the deterred. All of the parties involved are constrained to be moderate because one's immoderate behavior makes the nuclear threats of others credible.

Arms races among new nuclear states. One may easily believe that American and Russian military doctrines set the pattern that new nuclear states will follow. One may then also believe that they will suffer the fate of the United States and the Soviet Union, that they will compete in building larger and larger nuclear arsenals while continuing to accumulate conventional weapons. These are doubtful beliefs. One can infer the future from the past only insofar as future situations may be like present ones for the actors involved. For three main reasons, new nuclear states are likely to decrease rather than to increase their military spending.

First, nuclear weapons alter the dynamics of arms races. In a competition of two or more parties, it may be hard to say who is pushing and who is being pushed, who is leading and who is following. If one party seeks to increase its capabilities, it may seem that the other(s) must too. The dynamic may be built into the competition and may unfold despite a mutual wish to resist it. But need this be the case in a strategic competition between nuclear countries? It need not be if the conditions of competition make deterrent logic dominant. Deterrent logic dominates if the conditions of competition make it nearly impossible for any of the competing parties to achieve a first-strike capability. Early in the nuclear age, the implications of deterrent strategy were clearly seen. "When dealing with the absolute weapon," as William T. R. Fox put it, "arguments based on relative advantage lose their point." The United States has sometimes designed its forces according to that logic. Donald A. Quarles argued when he was Eisenhower's Secretary of the Air Force that "sufficiency of air power" is determined by "the force required to accomplish the mission assigned." Avoidance of total war then does not depend on the "*relative* strength of the two opposed forces." Instead, it depends on the "*absolute* power in the hands of each, and in the substantial invulnerability of this power to interdiction." To repeat: If no state can launch a disarming attack with high confidence, force comparisons are irrelevant. Strategic arms races are then pointless. Deterrent strategies offer this great advantage: Within wide ranges neither side need respond to increases in the other side's military capabilities.

Those who foresee nuclear arms racing among new nuclear states fail to make the distinction between war-fighting and war-deterring capabilities. War-fighting forces, because they threaten the forces of others, have to be compared. Superior forces may bring victory to one country; inferior forces may bring defeat to another. Force requirements vary with strategies and not just with the characteristics of weapons. With war-fighting strategies, arms races become difficult, if not impossible, to avoid. Forces designed for deterring war need not be compared. As Harold Brown said when he was Secretary of Defense, purely deterrent forces "can be relatively modest, and their size can perhaps be made substantially, though not completely, insensitive to changes in the posture of an opponent." With deterrent strategies, arms races make sense only if a first-strike capability is within reach. Because thwarting a first strike is easy, deterrent forces are quite cheap to build and maintain. With deterrent forces, the question is not whether one country has more than another but whether it has the capability of inflicting "unacceptable damage" on another, with unacceptable damage sensibly defined. Once that capability is assured, additional strategic weapons are useless. More is not better if less is enough.

Deterrent balances are inherently stable. If one can say how much is enough, then within wide limits one state can be insensitive to changes in its adversaries' forces. This is the way French leaders have thought. France, as President Giscard d'Estaing said, "fixes its security at the level required to maintain, regardless of the way the strategic situation develops in the world, the credibility—in other words, the

ISSUES FOR THE EIGHTIES

effectiveness—of its deterrent force." With deterrent forces securely established, no military need presses one side to try to surpass the other. Human error and folly may lead some parties involved in deterrent balances to spend more on armaments than is needed, but other parties need not increase their armaments in response, because such excess spending does not threaten them. The logic of deterrence eliminates incentives for strategic arms racing. This should be easier for lesser nuclear states to understand than it has been for the United States and the Soviet Union. Because most of them are economically hard pressed, they will not want to have more than enough.

Allowing for their particular circumstances, lesser nuclear states confirm these statements in their policies. Britain and France are relatively rich countries, and they tend to overspend. Their strategic forces are nevertheless modest enough when one considers that their purpose is to deter the Soviet Union rather than states with capabilities comparable to their own. China of course faces the same task. These three countries show no inclination to engage in nuclear arms races with anyone. India appears content to have a nuclear military, capability that may or may not have produced deliverable warheads, and Israel maintains her ambiguous status. New nuclear states are likely to conform to these patterns and aim for a modest sufficiency rather than vie with one another for a meaningless superiority.

Second, because strategic nuclear arms races among lesser powers are unlikely, the interesting question is not whether they will be run but whether countries having strategic nuclear weapons can avoid running conventional races. No more than the United States or the Soviet Union will new nuclear states want to rely on executing the deterrent threat that risks all. And will not their vulnerability to conventional attack induce them to continue their conventional efforts?

American policy as it has developed since the early 1960s again teaches lessons that mislead. For two decades, we have emphasized the importance of having a continuum of forces that would enable the United States and her allies to fight at any level from irregular to strategic nuclear warfare. A policy that decreases reliance on deterrence increases the chances that wars will be fought. This was well appreciated in Europe when we began to place less emphasis on deterrence and more on defense. The worries of many Europeans were well expressed by a senior British general, in the following words: "McNamara is practically telling the Soviets that the worst they need expect from an attack on West Germany is a conventional counterattack." Why risk one's own destruction if one is able to fight on the ground and forego the use of strategic weapons?

The policy of flexible response lessened reliance on strategic deterrence and increased the chances of fighting a war. New nuclear states are not likely to experience this problem. The expense of mounting conventional defenses, and the difficulties and dangers of fighting conventional wars, will keep most nuclear states from trying to combine large war-fighting forces with deterrent forces. Disjunction within their forces will enhance the value of deterrence.

Israeli policy seems to contradict these propositions. From 1971 through 1978, both Israel and Egypt spent from 20 to 40 percent of their GNPs on arms. Israel's spending on conventional arms remains high, although it has decreased since 1978. The decrease followed from the making of peace with Egypt and not from increased reliance on nuclear weapons. The seeming contradiction in fact bears out deterrent logic. So long as Israel holds the West Bank and the Gaza Strip she has to be prepared to fight for them. Since they are by no means unambiguously hers, deterrent threats, whether implicit or explicit, will not cover them. Moreover, while America's large subsidies continue, economic constraints will not drive Israel to the territorial settlement that would shrink her borders sufficiently to make a deterent policy credible.

From previous points it follows that nuclear weapons are likely to decrease arms racing and reduce military costs for lesser nuclear states in two ways. Conventional arms races will wither if countries shift emphasis from conventional defense to nuclear deterrence. For Pakistan, for example, acquiring nuclear weapons is an alternative to running a ruinous conventional race with India. And, of course, deterrent strategies make nuclear arms races pointless.

Finally, arms races in their ultimate form—the fighting of offensive wars designed to increase national security—also become pointless. The success of a deterrent strategy does not depend on the extent of territory a state holds, a point made earlier. It merits repeating because of its unusual importance for states whose geographic limits lead them to obsessive concern for their security in a world of ever more destructive conventional weapons.

The frequency and intensity of war. The presence of nuclear weapons makes war less likely. One may nevertheless oppose the spread of nuclear weapons on the ground that they would make war, however unlikely, unbearably intense should it occur. Nuclear weapons have not been fired in anger in a world in which more than one country has them. We have enjoyed over three decades of nuclear peace and may enjoy many more. But we can never have a guarantee. We may be grateful for decades of nuclear peace and for the discouragement of conventional war among those who have nuclear weapons. Yet the fear is widespread, and naturally so, that if they ever go off, we may all be dead. People as varied as the scholar Richard Smoke, the arms controller Paul Warnke, and former Defense Secretary Harold Brown all believe that if any nuclear weapons go off, many will. Although this seems the least likely of all the unlikely possibilities, unfortunately it is not impossible. What makes it so unlikely is that, even if deterrence should fail, the prospects for rapid deescalation are good.

McNamara asked himself what fractions of the Soviet Union's population and industry the United States should be able to destroy in order to deter her. For military, although not for budgetary, strategy this was the wrong question. States are not deterred because they expect to suffer a certain amount of damage but because they cannot know how much damage they will suffer. Near the dawn of the nuclear age Bernard Brodie put the matter simply: "The prediction is more important than the fact." The prediction, that is, that attacking the vital interests of a country having nuclear weapons may bring the attacker untold losses. As Patrick Morgan more recently put it: "To attempt to compute the cost of a nuclear war is to miss the point."

States are deterred by the prospect of suffering severe damage and by their physical inability to do much to limit it. Deterrence works because nuclear weapons enable one state to punish another state severely without first defeating it. "Victory" in Thomas Schelling's words, "is no longer a prerequisite for hurting the enemy." Countries armed with only conventional weapons can hope that their military forces will be able to limit the damage an attacker can do. Among countries armed with strategic nuclear forces, the hope of avoiding heavy damage depends mainly on the attacker's restraint and little on one's own efforts. Those who compare expected deaths through strategic exchanges of nuclear warheads with casualties suffered by the Soviet Union in World War II overlook this fundamental difference between conventional and nuclear worlds.

Deterrence rests on what countries *can* do to each other with strategic nuclear weapons. From this statement, one easily leaps to the wrong conclusion: that deterrent strategies, if they have to be carried through, will produce a catastrophe. That countries are able to annihilate each other means neither that deterrence depends on their threatening to do so nor that they will do so if deterrence fails. Because countries heavily armed with strategic nuclear weapons can carry war to its ultimate intensity, the control of force, in wartime as in peacetime, becomes the primary objective. If deterrence fails, leaders will have the strongest incentives to keep force under control and limit damage rather than launching genocidal attacks. If the Soviet Union should attack Western Europe, NATO's objectives would be to halt the attack and end the war. The United States has long had the ability to place hundreds of warheads precisely on targets in the Soviet Union. Surely we would strike military targets before striking industrial targets and industrial targets before striking cities. The intent to do so is sometimes confused with a war-fighting strategy, which it is not. It would not significantly reduce the Soviet

Union's ability to hurt us. It is a deterrent strategy, resting initially on the threat to punish. The threat, if it fails to deter, is appropriately followed not by spasms of violence but by punishment administered in ways that convey threats to make the punishment more severe.

A war between the United States and the Soviet Union that got out of control would be catastrophic. If they set out to destroy each other, they would greatly reduce the world's store of developed resources while killing millions outside of their own borders through fallout. Even while destroying themselves, states with few weapons would do less damage to others. As ever, the biggest international dangers come from the strongest states. Fearing the world's destruction, one may prefer a world of conventional great powers having a higher probability of fighting less destructive wars to a world of nuclear great powers having a lower probability of fighting more destructive wars. But that choice effectively disappeared with the production of atomic bombs by the United States during World War II. Since the great powers are unlikely to be drawn into the nuclear wars of others, the added global dangers posed by the spread of nuclear weapons are small.

The spread of nuclear weapons threatens to make wars more intense at the local and not at the global level, where wars of the highest intensity have been possible for a number of years. If their national existence should be threatened, weaker countries, unable to defend at lesser levels of violence, may destroy themselves through resorting to nuclear weapons. Lesser nuclear states will live in fear of this possibility. But this is not different from the fear under which the United States and the Soviet Union have lived for years. Small nuclear states may experience a keener sense of desperation because of extreme vulnerability to conventional as well as to nuclear attack, but, again, in desperate situations what all parties become most desperate to avoid is the use of strategic nuclear weapons. Still, however improbable the event, lesser states may one day fire some of their weapons. Are minor nuclear states more or less likely to do so than major ones? The answer to this question is vitally important because the existence of some states would be at stake even if the damage done were regionally confined.

For a number of reasons, then, deterrent strategies promise less damage than war-fighting strategies. First, deterrent strategies induce caution all around and thus reduce the incidence of war. Second, wars fought in the face of strategic nuclear weapons must be carefully limited because a country having them may retaliate if its vital interests are threatened. Third, prospective punishment need only be proportionate to an adversary's expected gains in war after those gains are discounted for the many uncertainties of war. Fourth, should deterrence fail, a few judiciously delivered warheads are likely to produce sobriety in the leaders of all of the countries involved and thus bring rapid deescalation. Finally, war-fighting strategies offer no clear place to stop short of victory for some and defeat for others. Deterrent strategies do, and that place is where one country threatens another's vital interests. Deterrent strategies lower the probability that wars will begin. If wars start nevertheless, deterrent strategies lower the probability that they will be carried very far.

Nuclear weapons may lessen the intensity as well as the frequency of wars among their possessors. For fear of escalation, nuclear states do not want to fight long or hard over important interests—indeed, they do not want to fight at all. Minor nuclear states have even better reasons than major ones to accommodate one another peacefully and to avoid any fighting. Worries about the intensity of war among nuclear states have to be viewed in this context and against a world in which conventional weapons become even costlier and more destructive.

CONCLUSION

The conclusion is in two parts. After saying what follows for American policy from my analysis, I briefly state the main reasons for believing that the slow spread of nuclear weapons will promote peace and reinforce international stability.

IMPLICATIONS FOR AMERICAN POLICY

I have argued that the gradual spread of nuclear weapons is better than either no spread or rapid spread. We do not face a set of happy choices. We may prefer that countries have conventional weapons only, do not run arms races, and do not fight. Yet the alternative to nuclear weapons for some countries may be ruinous arms races with high risk of their becoming engaged in debilitating conventional wars.

Countries have to care for their own security with or without the help of others. If a country feels highly insecure and believes that nuclear weapons would make it more secure, America's policy of opposing the spread of nuclear weapons will not easily prevail. Any slight chance of bringing the spread of nuclear weapons to a full stop exists only if the United States and the Soviet Union constantly and strenuously try to achieve that end. To do so carries costs measured in terms of their other interests. The strongest means by which the United States can persuade a country to forego nuclear weapons is a guarantee of its security, especially if the guarantee is made credible by the presence of American troops. But how many commitments do we want to make, and how many countries do we want to garrison? We are wisely reluctant to give guarantees, but we then should not expect to decide how other countries are to provide for their security. As a neighbor of China, India no doubt feels more secure, and can behave more reasonably, with a nuclear-weapons capability than without it. The thought applies as well to Pakistan as India's neighbor. We damage our relations with such countries by badgering them about nuclear weapons while being unwilling to guarantee their security. Under such circumstances they, not we, should decide what their national interests require.

Some have feared that weakening opposition to the spread of nuclear weapons will lead numerous states to make them because it may seem that "everyone is doing it." Why should we think that if we relax, numerous states will begin to make nuclear weapons? Both the United States and the Soviet Union were more relaxed in the past, and these effects did not follow. The Soviet Union initially supported China's nuclear program. The United States continues to help Britain maintain her deterrent forces. By 1968 the CIA had informed President Johnson of the existence of Israeli nuclear weapons, and in July of 1970 Richard Helms, Director of the CIA, gave this information to the Senate Foreign Relations Committee. These and later disclosures were not followed by censure of Israel or by reductions of assistance to her. And in September of 1980 the Executive Branch, against the will of the House of Representatives but with the approval of the Senate, continued to do nuclear business with India despite her explosion of a nuclear device and despite her unwillingness to sign the Nuclear Non-Proliferation Treaty.

Assisting some countries in the development of nuclear weapons and failing to oppose others has not caused a nuclear stampede. Is the more recent leniency toward India likely to? One reason to think so is that more countries now have the ability to make their own nuclear weapons, more than forty of them according to Joseph Nye.

Many more countries can than do. One can believe that American opposition to nuclear arming stays the deluge only by overlooking the complications of international life. Any state has to examine many conditions before deciding whether or not to develop nuclear weapons. Our opposition is only one factor and is not likely to be the decisive one. Many states feel fairly secure living with their neighbors. Why should they want nuclear weapons? Some countries, feeling threatened, have found security through their own strenuous efforts and through arrangements made with others. South Korea is an outstanding example. Many South Korean officials believe that South Korea would lose more in terms of American support if she acquired nuclear weapons than she would gain by having them. Further, on occasion we might slow the spread of nuclear weapons by *not* opposing the nuclear weapons program of some countries. When we oppose Pakistan's nuclear program, we are saying that we disapprove of countries developing nuclear weapons no matter what their neighbors do. Failing to oppose Pakistan's efforts also sends a signal to potential nuclear states, suggesting that if a country develops nuclear weapons, a regional rival may do so as well and may do so without opposition from us. This message may give pause to some of the countries that are tempted to acquire nuclear weapons. After all, Argentina is to Brazil as Pakistan is to India.

Neither the gradual spread of nuclear weapons nor American and Russian acquiescence in this has opened the nuclear floodgates. Nations attend to their security in ways they think best. The fact that so many more countries can make nuclear weapons than do make them says more about the hesitation of countries to enter the nuclear military business than about the effectiveness of American policy. We can sensibly suit our policy to individual cases, sometimes bringing pressure against a country moving toward nuclear-weapons capability and sometimes quietly acquiescing. No one policy is right for all countries. We should ask what our interests in regional stability require in particular instances. We should also ask what the interests of other countries require before putting pressure on them. Some countries are likely to suffer more in cost and pain if they remain conventional states than if they become nuclear ones. The measured and selective spread of nuclear weapons does not run against our interests and can increase the security of some states at a price they can afford to pay.

It is not likely that nuclear weapons will spread with a speed that exceeds the ability of their new owners to adjust to them. The spread of nuclear weapons is something that we have worried too much about and tried too hard to stop.

THE NUCLEAR FUTURE

What will a world populated by a larger number of nuclear states look like? I have drawn a picture of such a world that accords with experience throughout the nuclear age. Those who dread a world with more nuclear states do little more than assert that more is worse and claim without substantiation that new nuclear states will be less responsible and less capable of self control than the old ones have been. They feel fears that many felt when they imagined how a nuclear China would behave. Such fears have proved unfounded as nuclear weapons have slowly spread. I have found many reasons for believing that with more nuclear states the world will have a promising future. I have reached this unusual conclusion for five main reasons.

First, international politics is a self-help system, and in such systems the principal parties do most to determine their own fate, the fate of other parties, and the fate of the system. This will continue to be so, with the United States and the Soviet Union filling their customary roles. For the United States and the Soviet Union to achieve nuclear maturity and to show this by behaving sensibly is more important than preventing the spread of nuclear weapons.

Second, given the massive numbers of American and Russian warheads, and given the impossibility of one side destroying enough of the other side's missiles to make a retaliatory strike bearable, the balance of terror is indestructible. What can lesser states do to disrupt the nuclear equilibrium if even the mighty efforts of the United States and the Soviet Union cannot shake it? The international equilibrium will endure.

Third, nuclear weaponry makes miscalculation difficult because it is hard not to be aware of how much damage a small number of warheads can do. Early in this century Norman Angell argued that war could not occur because it would not pay (1914). But conventional wars have brought political gains to some countries at the expense of others. Among nuclear countries, possible losses in war overwhelm possible gains. In the nuclear age Angell's dictum, broadly interpreted, becomes persuasive. When the active use of force threatens to bring great losses, war becomes less likely. This proposition is widely accepted but insufficiently emphasized. Nuclear weapons have reduced the chances of war between the United States and the Soviet Union and between the Soviet Union and China. One may expect them to have similar effects elsewhere. Where nuclear weapons threaten to make the cost of wars immense, who will dare to start them? Nuclear weapons make it possible to approach the deterrent ideal.

Fourth, nuclear weapons can be used for defense as well as for deterrence. Some have argued that an apparently impregnable nuclear defense can be mounted. The Maginot Line has given defense a bad name. It nevertheless remains true that the incidence of wars decreases as the perceived difficulty of winning them increases. No one attacks a defense believed to be impregnable. Nuclear weapons may make it possible to approach the defensive ideal. If so, the spread of nuclear weapons will further help to maintain peace.

Fifth, new nuclear states will confront the possibilities and feel the constraints that present nuclear states have experienced. New nuclear states will be more concerned for their safety and more mindful of dangers than some of the old ones have been. Until recently, only the great and some of the major powers have had nuclear weapons. While nuclear weapons have spread, conventional weapons have proliferated. Under these circumstances, wars have been fought not at the center but at the periphery of international politics. The likelihood of war decreases as deterrent and defensive capabilities increase. Nuclear weapons, responsibly used, make wars hard to start. Nations that have nuclear weapons have strong incentives to use them responsibly. These statements hold for small as for big nuclear powers. Because they do, the measured spread of nuclear weapons is more to be welcomed than feared.

What Difference Will It Make?

LEWIS DUNN

THE BREAKDOWN OF NUCLEAR PEACE

A number of analysts and observers, noting that predictions at the dawn of the nuclear age of a nuclear apocalypse have proved exaggerated, argue that there is little reason to fear the consequences of the further spread of nuclear weapons. Frequently at the core of such optimistic assessments is the belief that the very destructiveness of those weapons will both instill prudence in their new owners, making them less willing to use even minimal conventional force out of fear that conflict will escalate to use of nuclear weapons, and lead to stable deterrent relationships between previously hostile countries. But such a fear of nuclear war was only one of the underpinnings of the first decades' nuclear peace. Other equally significant geopolitical and technical supports may be absent in the conflict-prone regions to which nuclear weapons are now likely to spread.

A SPIRALING THREAT TO PEACE

With the spread of nuclear weapons to conflict-prone regions, the chances that those weapons will be used again increase greatly. The heightened stakes and lessened room for maneuver in conflict-prone regions, the volatile leadership and political instability of many of the next nuclear powers, and the technical deficiencies of many new nuclear forces all threaten the first decades' nuclear peace.

Not least to be feared is nuclear war caused by accident or miscalculation. During an intense crisis or the first stages of a conventional military clash, for example, an accidental detonation of a nuclear weapon—even within the country of origin—or an accidental missile launch easily might be misinterpreted as the first shot of a surprise attack. Pressures to escalate in a last-ditch attempt to disarm the opponent before he completes that attack will be intense. Similarly, a technical malfunction of a radar warning system or a human error in interpreting an ambiguous warning might trigger a nuclear clash. Or fear that escalation to nuclear conflict no longer could be avoided

From *Controlling the Bomb* by Lewis A. Dunn. Copyright © 1982 by Yale University Press, pp. 69–95. Reprinted by permission of the publisher, Yale University Press. Portions of the text and some footnotes have been omitted.

might lead to a country to get in the first blow, so as partly to disarm the opponent and to minimize damage.

Unauthorized use of nuclear weapons by the military also is a possibility. For example, faced with imminent conventional military defeat and believing there is little left to lose anyway, a few members of Pakistan's military could launch a nuclear strike against India to damage that country as much as possible. Or a few hard-line, fanatic Iraqi, Libyan, or even Egyptian officers might use their countries' newly acquired nuclear weapons in an attempt to "solve" the Israeli problem once and for all. These officers' emotional commitment to a self-ordained higher mission would overwhelm any fear of the adverse personal or national consequences. Aside from the initial destruction, such unauthorized use could provoke a full-scale nuclear conflict between the hostile countries.

But the first use of nuclear weapons since Nagasaki may be a carefully calculated policy decision. The bomb might be used intentionally on the battlefield to defend against invasion. For example, faced with oncoming North Korean troops, a nuclear-armed South Korea would be under great pressure to use nuclear weapons as atomic demolition land mines to close critical invasion corridors running the thirty miles from the border to Seoul. Similar military logic could lead to Israeli use of enhanced radiation weapons—so-called neutron bombs—in the next Arab-Israeli war.

A calculated disarming nuclear surprise attack to seize the military advantage also is possible in these high-stakes, escalation-prone regional conflicts, particularly when one side has a decided strategic advantage. For example, in the 1980s, internal political instability in Pakistan and simmering unrest in Kashmir could erupt into a conventional military clash between India and Pakistan. A nuclear-armed India then would be under intense pressure to attack the more rudimentary Pakistani nuclear force to prevent its use—whether by accident or intention—against India. In a nuclear Middle East, as well, fear of events getting out of hand would fuel arguments in favor of an Israeli first strike once a conflict had begun.

Aside from the increased threat of actual use of nuclear weapons, the nuclearization of conflict-prone regions may have other costly or dangerous consequences. Given the stakes, some new nuclear powers will think seriously about a preventive strike with conventional weapons to preserve their regional nuclear monopoly. Israel already has taken such military action against Iraq's nuclear weapons program and has stated its readiness to take further action as needed. And notwithstanding the limited Iraqi reaction to Israel's preventive strike—in large part due to Iraq's being tied down in its war with Iran—it might not be possible to prevent escalation after similar or larger future attacks.

Possession of nuclear weapons also may be used as an instrument of blackmail or coercion. A country with nuclear edge may implicitly or explicitly threaten the use of nuclear weapons to enforce its demands in regional crises or low-level confrontations. Just as U.S. strategic superiority contributed to the Soviet Union's decision to back down in the 1962 Cuban Missile Crisis, so might possession of nuclear weapons by Iraq, Israel, India, or South Korea affect the resolution of crises with weaker opponents.

In addition, tensions among the countries of newly nuclearized regions are likely to be exacerbated. Pakistan's nuclear weapons activities, for example, already have heightened India's suspicion and have slowed efforts to improve relations between the two countries. Pakistani testing and deployment of nuclear weapons would further worsen relations between India and Pakistan, not least because such activity would affront India's claim to regional preeminence. Should India step up its nuclear weapons activities in response and achieve clear-cut nuclear superiority, Pakistan's fears of Indian nuclear blackmail would be increased as well. Even the anticipation of a country's "going nuclear" can have adverse political effects. For example, Iraq's efforts to acquire nuclear weapons have heightened Israel's siege mentality and stimulated efforts by Syria, Saudi Arabia, and even Kuwait at least to master basic nuclear theory and know-how.

The greater the scope, the quicker the pace, and the higher the level of proliferation, the more severe will be the threat of nuclear conflict. As more countries acquire the bomb, the number of situations in which a political miscalculation, leadership failure, geographical propinquity, or technical mishap could lead to a nuclear clash will increase. As the pace of proliferation accelerates, the time available for countries to adjust to living with nuclear weapons will grow shorter. As countries move to the more advanced levels of proliferation—from untested bombs to full-fledged military deployment, there is more chance that some of these new nuclear forces will be technically deficient. Further, nuclear weapons will cease to be isolated symbols and will become an integral part of international relations within these volatile regions.

The initial outcroppings of more widespread proliferation in and of themselves also will call forth efforts to reduce the resultant threat of nuclear conflict. But few of the possible measures for mitigating the consequences of proliferation offer a high promise of success, while domestic and international constraints may hinder implementation of even these more limited measures. And the greater the scope, pace, and level of proliferation, the more difficult and complex management efforts will become. Thus, the spiraling risk of regional nuclear conflict will not be entirely offset by these management efforts.

THE GLOBAL SPILLOVERS

While more widespread proliferation most likely will not overturn the existing structure of world politics, it will adversely affect the superpowers, and their relationship, as well as the great powers. The optimism among some analysts about the benign consequences of further proliferation again is likely to be proved wrong.

LIMITS TO STRUCTURAL CHANGE

The Soviet Union and the United States are involved in nearly all of the regions to which nuclear weapons may spread in the 1980s, frequently supporting opposite sides in long-standing disputes. Neither is likely to sever alliance ties, drop clients and allies, or phase out economic and military involvement after nuclear weapons spread to these regions. In all probability, the leaders of both countries will continue to believe that compelling national interests—whether, for example, Western access to Middle East oil, expansion of Soviet power toward the Persian Gulf or its containment, the protection of traditional allies, and maintenance of the military balance in East Asia—outweigh any new or enhanced risks of continuing involvement. Besides, because of the competitive nature of the superpower relationship, officials in each country may be reluctant to disengage from these regions in the absence of reciprocal action by the other country lest the opponent be given a "free hand." And an unwillingness to sacrifice past investments made in pursuit of regional influence and military-political advantage is likely to buttress these arguments against disengagement.

It is equally doubtful that more widespread proliferation will lead to a Soviet-U.S. condominium to prevent the further spread of nuclear weapons, ban their use by new nuclear powers, and restore the superpowers' absolute domination of world politics. The competing political, economic, and military interests of the Soviet Union and the United States in regions such as South Asia and the Middle East are likely to take precedence over joint efforts to reduce the risk of local nuclear conflict. The superpowers' reliance on the nuclear threat in their own defense postures also may constrain joint action, particularly since the threat of escalation to nuclear conflict is critical to NATO's defense posture. The international costs—political, military, and economic—of an attempt to restore superpower domination of regional politics also would be high, and quite possibly thought by U.S. and Soviet leaders to be excessive. For many countries, including U.S. allies in Western Europe, a superpower condominium for nuclear peace would be a grave threat to their current freedom of action. It is also doubtful that the military problems of reasserting control would be manageable at an acceptable cost in light of increased

local capabilities for resistance, as exemplified by the Soviet experience in Afghanistan. Moreover, in the Middle East, the economic
penalties of intervention at least for the United States, could be great.
And while the domestic political constraints on active interventionism
abroad may be less for the Soviet leadership than for U.S.
policymakers, in neither country can they be overlooked.

The restoration of a more multipolar global political structure is
even less likely to result from the further spread of nuclear weapons.
The net impact on superpower strategic dominance of the emergence
of a group of lesser nuclear powers will be quite limited. Even the
deployment of nuclear forces by Japan and West Germany need not
fundamentally upset the existing structure: should the nuclear forces
of Japan and West Germany be equivalent to those of France and the
United Kingdom, there still would be a considerable gap between the
threat they could pose to the superpowers and the threat the superpowers would pose in return. The United States and the Soviet Union
also could raise the threshold nuclear capability necessary for Japan
or West Germany to mount a serious threat to either of their
homelands by renegotiating the 1972 Treaty between the United States
of America and the Union of Soviet Socialist Republics on the Limitation of Anti-Ballistic Missile Systems (ABM) to permit Soviet and
U.S. deployment of defenses against Japanese or West German
ballistic missiles. Besides, it is quite unlikely in any case that these
countries will decide to acquire nuclear weapons.

This conclusion that widespread proliferation will not overturn the
existing structure of world politics rests most of all on the assumption
that even in that changed environment the leaders of the United States
and the Soviet Union will continue to pursue their distinct national interests and objectives, utilizing force or the threat of force and relying
on prudence, crisis management, and marginal adjustment to deal
with the new risks. However, it is possible that following the use of
nuclear weapons by a new nuclear power—especially if that use almost
produces a nuclear confrontation between them—the United States
and the Soviet Union may be far more ready to negotiate about joint
disengagement and other steps to isolate newly nuclear regions. Alternatively, leaders in the Soviet Union and the United States could seek
to reassert their countries' capability to dictate the rules of the
regional nuclear game. The likelihood of such major adjustments
clearly will depend on whether the superpowers' assessment of the
direct risks to themselves and of the adequacy of traditional crisis
management changes markedly. But particularly in light of the limited
success of recent U.S. and Soviet efforts to reach agreement on
reciprocal strategic restraints as well as their conflicting global interests, ideologies, and national styles, even after one or more small-
power nuclear exchanges, the two superpowers probably will continue

to pursue only prudent ameliorative measures to reduce the risks of competitive involvement in newly nuclearized regions.

REDUCED SUPERPOWER FREEDOM OF ACTION

Periodically during the past decades, the United States has intervened militarily in regional confrontations, disputes, and limited conflicts outside of the European arena. The decision in 1980 to create the Rapid Deployment Joint Task Force for Middle East and Persian Gulf contingencies reflects a continued willingness to project U.S. power into conflict-prone regions in order to protect U.S. interests, allies, and friends. But the presence of nuclear weapons in some future contingencies will increase the military and political risks of intervention, reducing U.S. freedom of action.

Notwithstanding the threat of U.S. retaliation, nuclear weapons might be used against U.S. intervention forces. A desperate leader, thinking there was nothing left to lose, might launch a nuclear strike against landing troops or close-in off-shore naval operations, both of which would be vulnerable to even a few rudimentary nuclear weapons. Or, in the heat of battle, a breakdown of communications could result in the use of nuclear weapons by a lesser nuclear power. Also possible is an unauthorized attack on U.S. forces by the military of a new nuclear power. If needed adaptations of the tactics, training, and structure of these U.S. intervention forces are not made, U.S. intervention could prove very costly, and U.S. forces might even suffer stunning reversals.

Admittedly, U.S. policymakers could launch a limited nuclear strike to disarm the hostile new nuclear power rather than seek to "work around" this regional nuclear threat and risk valuable military assets. But the regional and global political costs to the United States of such a strike are likely to be so high as to make policymakers very hesitant to authorize it.

These heightened risks also are likely to reinforce the lingering, although somewhat muted, national presumption against intervention derived from the Vietnam experience. Consequently, the stakes needed to justify involvement in a newly nuclearized region probably will be greater than in the past. U.S. policymakers may choose not to intervene militarily in some situations where they previously would have acted.

The risks and complexities of military intervention will increase for the Soviet Union as well. In the eyes of a Soviet leadership that has intervened militarily only when the balance of forces appeared clearly favorable, the possible use of nuclear weapons against Soviet troops in a newly nuclearized region could be an excessive risk. To illustrate, Yugoslav deployment of battlefield nuclear weapons might discourage Soviet military action in a future domestic political struggle in

Yugoslavia. Similarly, even a slight possibility that Israel or South Africa would use nuclear weapons against Soviet ground or naval forces might help deter Soviet military entanglement in those regions. And the political costs of a nuclear disarming attack on a new nuclear power are likely to appear nearly as excessive to the Soviet Union as to the United States.

The eventual development by a few new nuclear powers of even a limited last-resort capability to threaten the homeland of one or the other superpower with nuclear attack or retaliation also would reduce both Soviet and American freedom of action. For example, should Israel acquire the capability to strike Odessa, Kiev, and Baku, the Soviet leaders might not be as willing to risk direct military involvement in the Middle East to support their Arab clients. Such a capability in Yugoslav or South African hands might have a comparable restraining effect on the Soviets. Or, though less likely, a radical Arab government might threaten to destroy one or more American cities in an attempt to blackmail the United States into not resupplying Israel in the midst of the next Middle East war. Of course, the risk of carrying out such a threat to a superpower would be extraordinary. But neither superpower could ignore the possibility that a leader who thought he had nothing left to lose might do so.

However, this threat of direct attack by a new nuclear power is likely to be greater for the Soviet Union than for the United States. Hardly any of the next countries likely to acquire the bomb will seek to target the U.S. homeland. Moreover, the geographical remoteness of the United States from potentially hostile new nuclear powers in the Middle East and Persian Gulf, combined with the technological backwardness of these countries, makes American cities somewhat less vulnerable than Soviet cities to such a nuclear strike. At least in the 1980s, to attack a U.S. city, Iraq or Libya—the most plausible opponents—probably would either have to smuggle a weapon into the United States by plane or boat or use a converted Boeing 707 or 747 registered as a private or corporate jet to deliver a bomb, counting on subterfuge and the steady decline of U.S. air defenses to penetrate U.S. airspace. Though possibly feasible, such unconventional modes of attack would be less technically reliable, limited in magnitude, and subject to interception by intelligence agencies.

In contrast, Israel, Yugoslavia, and South Korea already possess long-range nuclear-capable aircraft that can reach the Soviet Union and may well be able to slip through Soviet air defenses. South Africa and Israel also are said to be developing a crude cruise missile that could increase their capability to hit Soviet cities. Should Japan or West Germany acquire nuclear weapons, they would have little trouble targeting Soviet cities. Barring unexpectedly rapid technological progress, the breakdown of current restraints on the sale of cruise missiles and advanced missile guidance systems, or widespread traffic in space-booster technology and boosters themselves, the United States will continue to be less vulnerable to nuclear attack by a new nuclear power than will the Soviet Union—at least into the 1990s.

The constraining effect of more widespread possession of nuclear weapons of the superpowers should not be exaggerated. The superpowers' readiness and capability to control events abroad have already been lessened by the decreased legitimacy of using force, rising nationalism, the difficulties of bringing applicable force to bear in limited disputes, the availability of advanced weapons systems to regional powers, and the strengthening of countervailing economic instruments of power. So viewed, the further spread of nuclear weapons only contributes to a continuing, longer-term relative decline of superpower freedom of action. Moreover, as long as the two superpowers are ready to pay the necessary price, they could preserve a significant gap between their military capabilities and those of any new medium and lesser nuclear powers, including even Japan and West Germany. Further, in those situations where U.S. or Soviet interests are seen to justify either the military costs of working around lesser nuclear forces or the political costs of suppressing them, the superpowers most probably will be impeded but not prevented from realizing their objectives.

INCREASED RISK OF SUPERPOWER CONFRONTATION

Continued U.S. and Soviet pursuit of their respective interests in these newly nuclear conflict-prone regions also will entail acceptance of a higher risk of a U.S.-Soviet political-military confrontation. With the acquisition of nuclear weapons by long-standing regional enemies, there will be many more flashpoints for such a superpower clash. For instance, a preventive attack with conventional weapons, a surprise disarming strike, use of nuclear weapons on the battlefield, nuclear blackmail, a conventional attack backed by the threat of recourse to nuclear weapons, in each case by one superpower's ally against an ally of the other, all could trigger superpower involvement and confrontation. Both the Soviet Union and the United States would be under great pressure to "do something" to help their allies. While aware of the risks, Soviet and U.S. leaders might nonetheless be drawn into the conflict for fear that otherwise their past political, military, and economic investments in the regions would be wasted, their interests sacrificed, and their "reputations for action" ruined. But by responding, the superpower could set in motion an upward spiral of response and counterresponse, of initial entanglement and increased commitment, that may result in a direct confrontation between them.

Though present already, the risk of miscalculation on the part of the two superpowers also may be higher in situations involving newly nuclearized regions—again enhancing the chances of unwanted confrontation. In this new environment, either superpower may modify in unexpected ways its traditional assessment of the stakes, its preferred responses, or its readiness to run risks. Thus, whatever lessons about the other superpower's thinking and responses have been learned from prior regional crises may no longer be fully applicable. And this uncertainty could be most pronounced and most dangerous in the uncharted territory after the next use of nuclear weapons.

But concern about even indirect entanglement in crises or confrontations that could involve the use of nuclear weapons may make policymakers in Western Europe more cautious in extending existing political, economic, or military ties. Domestic pressures against heightened involvement could grow as well. Moreover, because of this fear, these policymakers might be even more reluctant to support U.S. military initiatives and may not permit use of facilities and bases on their territories, or agree to reallocate or transship material and supplies, or provide military forces.

As well, these Western European countries might be the targets of nuclear blackmail intended to make them stand aside in such clashes or withdraw previously offered assistance. For example, in the midst of an Arab-Israeli conflict in the late 1980s, Egypt, Iraq, or Libya could anonymously threaten to detonate a nuclear weapon previously smuggled into Portugal unless that country rescinded landing rights at air bases in the Azores for U.S. planes on their way to Israel with needed military equipment. Or West Germany might be the target of such an anonymous nuclear threat in an indirect effort to prevent the United States from shipping military equipment from NATO stocks to the Middle East. Besides, once nuclear weapons are more widely available, it could be quite difficult to distinguish a hoax from a serious threat, and, thus, even a hoax might suffice to disrupt such U.S. operations for a time.

Under certain conditions further proliferation also would increase considerably the cost and difficulty for France and Britain of maintaining a credible nuclear deterrent against the Soviet Union. Confronted by a growing threat to their homelands from new nuclear powers, or believing that such a threat was likely to emerge by the 1990s, the superpowers might renegotiate the 1972 AMB Treaty and deploy ballistic missile defenses. But to counter that change, these medium nuclear powers would have to develop and deploy costly and technically demanding systems able to penetrate those more extensive Soviet missile defenses. Failure to do so would lead to the increasing obsolescence of the French and British nuclear forces.*

*China's nuclear force would be similarly threatened with obsolescence by a Soviet missile defense capability.

DOMESTIC POLITICAL REPERCUSSIONS
NUCLEAR-ARMED TERRORISTS, IRREDENTISTS, AND SEPARATISTS

A considerably greater risk that terrorist and dissident groups will gain access to nuclear weapons will be another adverse consequence of the further spread of nuclear weapons. As more countries seek to acquire a nuclear weapons option by initiating sensitive reprocessing or enrichment activities, or set up actual weapons programs, the number of sites from which these groups could steal nuclear weapons material for a bomb will increase. The ensuing transportation of such material between a growing number of sites will further increase the risk of theft. Once a group possesses nuclear weapons material, the technical hurdles of processing that material and fabricating a nuclear weapon still would have to be overcome, but at least for some groups these difficulties would not be insurmountable. More important, a subnational group might opt for stealing the bomb itself, taking advantage of the probably less-than-adequate physical security measures of some new nuclear forces.

Hit-and-run clandestine terrorist groups, such as the Japanese Red Army, extreme left-wing Palestinian factions, the Italian Red Brigade, the Irish Republican Army (IRA), or successors to the Baader-Meinhof gang, may well regard a nuclear weapon as a means of extorting money or political concessions from a government, much as taking hostages is now. The countries of Western Europe, Japan, and the United States will be especially vulnerable to terrorist threats or attack because of their open societies. A group such as the IRA, claiming to represent a legitimate alternative government and dependent on popular support, might stop short of carrying out a nuclear threat even if its demands were not met. But members of the more radical and nihilistic fringe movements, such as the successors to the Baader-Meinhof gang and the Japanese Red Army, might think otherwise. To them, carrying out the threat might appear justified as a means of bringing down corrupt bourgeois society in a spasm of violence. Or, in the eyes of the most extreme Palestinian groups, use of a nuclear weapon might be thought justified as a way of mortally wounding Israel. Yet again, with the police closing in on them, these more radical, isolated terrorists could conclude that, since all was lost, it would be preferable to fall in a nuclear *Götterdämmerung*. Such a decision would be consistent with the near-suicide mentality shown in some past terrorist actions.

In contrast, the theft and threatened use of nuclear weapons may not appear a worthwhile tactic to a group such as the Palestinian Liberation Organization (PLO). Even though the PLO's freedom of action has been reduced by the Lebanese civil war, it still controls territory, administers to its refugee population, has a military force, and has been recognized by international bodies and foreign governments.

Rather than enhancing the PLO's claim that it is a legitimate government in exile, possession of a few stolen nuclear weapons could have the opposite effect. Theft of nuclear weapons would reinforce the PLO's reputation for extremism and unwillingness to accept minimal norms of international behavior and would make it harder for those Western European governments moving closer to the PLO's position on the Middle East to sustain that shift. Besides, should Israeli intelligence manage to locate these nuclear weapons, pressures to carry out a preventive strike, disregarding the risk of Soviet counteraction, would be intense. If Israel could not locate the nuclear weapons but knew that the PLO had them, the result is not likely to be Israeli acceptance of the need for a Palestinian state but Israeli unwillingness to compromise on that PLO demand. On balance, therefore, the costs to the PLO of stealing nuclear weapons appear to outweigh the benefits. Still, that conclusion reflects a Western weighing of costs and gains, which may prove as unfounded in this instance of Middle East maneuverings as it has on earlier occasions.

Separatist movements such as the Kurds or Arabs in Iran, the Baluchis in Pakistan, the Bengalis in India, the Moslems in the Philippines, or even the Basques in Spain might be more inclined to steal and threaten to use a nuclear weapon. For example, a separatist Baluchi movement might threaten to use stolen Pakistani nuclear weapons if the Pakistani central government mounted a new military campaign to restore its authority. Though extreme, such a threat would not be out of line with the bitter fighting so characteristic of these struggles for greater autonomy. Fearful of the consequences of cracking down on the separatists and under international and domestic pressure to find a "reasonable" settlement, the central government might come to terms with that group. Conversely, the central government could conclude that the costs of yielding to the separatists' demands were so great that it had no choice but to strike back, even using its own nuclear weapons against those of the separatists. But with little to lose, the Baluchis—and other separatist groups in other countries—might be ready to take that chance.

THE NUCLEAR COUP d'ETAT

In the 1980s and early 1990s, politically unstable new nuclear powers—such as Argentina, Brazil, Chile, Egypt, Iran, Iraq, Libya, Nigeria, Pakistan, South Korea, and Syria—might be vulnerable to nuclear coups d'etat. Particularly if the balance of political and military power between the rebels and the government were unclear, control of nuclear weapons—as compelling a symbol and instrument of national power as control of the airport, capital city, or radio and television stations—could greatly enhance the rebels' bargaining position. Control of nuclear weapons would change the psycological climate and afford rebel groups a means not only of demoralizing opponents but also of rallying supporters. The specter of nuclear destruction—should the situation get out of hand—quite possibly might lead civilian and military fence-sitters to come out in favor of a coup and even change the minds of some anti-coup forces. Moreover, just a few nuclear weapons in rebel hands could suffice to deter attack against them, assuming that the government was both unwilling to overwhelm the rebels with conventional force lest they retaliate with nuclear weapons and reluctant to use nuclear weapons first on its own territory in a surprise disarming attack. Consequently, more so than in past coups, efforts to dislodge such rebels would remain a test of wills and bargaining strategy. Nevertheless, nuclear weapons might be employed, either intentionally, by accident, or out of contempt and hatred.

Already on at least one occasion during the first decades of the nuclear age, access to nuclear weapons has figured in a domestic political upheaval. In April 1961, French army forces stationed in Algiers rebelled, demanding that the government in Paris reverse its decision to grant independence to Algeria. At the time, French scientists were preparing to test a nuclear weapon at the French Saharan test site in Reganne, Algeria, not too far from Algiers. Noting the proximity of the rebellion, the scientists called on the general in charge at Reganne to authorize an immediate test and thus avoid the possibility that the nuclear device would be seized by the rebel troops and used for bargaining leverage. Three days after the outbreak of the revolt, the order to detonate the device came directly from French President de Gaulle; there was no attempt to undertake precise experiments, only to use up all the available fissionable material.

THE CORROSION OF LIBERAL DEMOCRACIES?

At least some of the measures required to deal with the threats of clandestine nuclear attack—whether from a terrorist group or a new nuclear power—and of nuclear black marketing will be in tension with or in outright violation of the civil liberties procedures and underlying values of Western liberal democracies. Because of the stakes, there will be strong pressures to circumvent or set aside—in the United States and elsewhere—various constitutional and legal restrictions on invasions of privacy or other traditional civil liberties. Unauthorized, warrantless emergency searches based on skimpy evidence or tips might be made. Or broad neighborhood—even city-wide—searches may become legitimate in these instances, although existing laws in many countries, particularly the Fourth and Fourteenth Amendments in the United States, prohibit searches without specific definition of the site and evidence sought. The use of informants, warrantless or illegal wiretaps, and the secret detention and questioning of suspects for days or even weeks might follow, all motivated by the need to acquire information as fast as possible.

However, it may prove possible to contain this challenge to liberal democratic procedures and values. Within the United States, both rigorous administrative supervision of any emergency measures and strict judical review after the fact would help prevent those measures from spilling over their boundaries and corrupting procedures in other areas of law enforcement. Authorizing legislation and official policy statements also could stress the extraordinary character of those restrictions as a response to an exceptional threat while reemphasizing the more basic American belief in the worth, dignity, and sanctity of the individual that underlies respect for particular civil liberties.

But if the frequency of proliferation-related threats grows, and if violations of traditional civil liberties cease to be isolated occurrences, it will become more difficult to check this corrosion of liberal democracy here and elsewhere. For that reason, as well, concern about the many adverse consequences of increasingly widespread nuclear weapons proliferation is well founded.

The Renewal of Strategy

SAMUEL P. HUNTINGTON

CONVENTIONAL DETERRENCE

Conventional forces can contribute to deterrence in three ways. First, by their presence in an area they can increase the uncertainties and the potential costs an aggressor must confront, even if—like the allied troops in Berlin—they could not conceivably mount a successful defense of the area. Second, conventional military forces can deter by raising the possiblity of a successful defense and hence forcing the aggressor to risk defeat in his effort or to pay additional costs for success.

Reprinted with permission from *Strategic Imperative: New Policies for American Security*, copyright © 1982, Ballinger Publishing Company.

This has been the traditional deterrent role of the NATO conventional forces in West Germany. Third, conventional military forces can deter by posing the threat of retaliation against the aggressor. This has, of course, been the classic deterrent role of strategic nuclear forces. In principle, there is no reason why conventional military forces cannot do likewise, provided there is something of value to the potential aggressor, like the Soviet empire in Eastern Europe, against which such forces can retaliate. A strategy of conventional retaliation in the form of a prompt offensive into Eastern Europe would help to deter Soviet military action against Western Europe and conceivably also in the second deterrent zone. Posing such a threat is central to a 1980s strategy that emphasizes conventional rather than nuclear deterrence.

A strategy of conventional retaliation would constitute a needed additional corrective to the decline in the credibility of the strategic nuclear deterrent with respect to Europe. It would round out the NATO deterrent posture in Europe, complementing the decisions on the build-up of NATO conventional strength in the Long Term Defense Program and on theater nuclear force modernization to counter Soviet Backfires and SS-20s. This strategy might require some modest changes in the character, deployment, and levels of NATO forces in Germany, but they would not necessarily be substantial. Implementing a conventional retaliation strategy requires more change in the NATO military mind-set than it does in NATO military forces. Since the beginning, NATO has thought about conventional war almost exclusively in defensive terms. NATO strategy, codified in its present form in MC-14/3, adopted in December 1967, stresses forward defense, flexible response, the NATO triad of conventional, theater nuclear, and strategic nuclear forces, and the eventual restoration of prewar boundaries. It posits, in short, a basically defensive strategy. There is, however, no reason why a defensive alliance should, once war breaks out, be limited to a defensive strategy. For thirty years U.S. nuclear strategy has served a defensive purpose by being offensively oriented. U.S. and NATO conventional strategy in Europe should also have a major offensive component.

Since the beginning of NATO Western planning has assumed that the major battles in a conflict on the central front would be fought in West Germany. As a result, West Germans decry the devastation to which their country would be subjected, even in a purely conventional war. They quite appropriately insist on a forward defense strategy, engaging the Soviets as far as possible from their population centers in Bavaria, the Rhine and Ruhr valleys, and the Hamburg area. Such a strategy, however, means that the allied forces have to be strung out more or less evenly along the entire eastern border of the Federal Republic. At any given point, therefore, they are vulnerable to an overpowering Soviet concentration of offensive forces. The logical extension of the forward defense concept is to move the locus of battle eastward into East Germany and Czechoslovakia. The result would be more effective deterrence and, if deterrence failed, less devastation in West Germany.

Current NATO strategy contemplates the possibility of eventually launching a counteroffensive. A major difference exists, however, between a conventional counteroffensive and a conventional retaliatory offensive. A counteroffensive occurs after the enemy's offensive has been brought to a halt and allied forces have been regrouped and prepared to drive the Warsaw Pact forces out of those portions of Western Europe they have occupied. A conventional retaliatory offensive, like a nuclear retaliatory offensive, would, on the other hand, be launched immediately whether or not the Soviet conventional offensive had been stopped. A counteroffensive, in short, sequentially follows the enemy's offensive; a retaliatory offensive occurs, as far as possible, simultaneously with the enemy's offensive.

This distinction is of fundamental importance in terms of the impact of these two strategies on Soviet military planning. To date the Soviets have been free to concentrate all their planning and forces on offensive moves into West Germany. A Western retaliatory strategy would compel them to reallocate forces and resources to the defense of their satellites and thus to weaken their offensive thrust. Most importantly, it is generally recognized that the extent of satellite participation in a war with NATO will depend upon the scope and speed of Soviet success in the conflict. As long as the Soviets are successful, they are likely to have complacent and cooperative allies. If, however, they are stalemated or turned back, disaffection is likely to appear within the Warsaw Pact. A prompt allied offensive into Eastern Europe would stimulate that disaffection at the very start of the conflict. Neither the Soviets nor, more importantly, the satellite governments could view with equanimity West German tanks on the road to Berlin and Leipzig and American divisions heading for Prague, Budapest, and Warsaw. From the viewpoint of deterrence, such a prospect would tremendously enhance the undesirability of war for the governments of the satellite countries. Those governments, which provide almost half of the Warsaw Pact ground forces on the central front, would lose more than anyone else in such a war and hence would become a puissant lobby urging their Soviet partner not to initiate war. The deterrent impact of a conventional retaliatory strategy on the Soviets could be further enhanced by allied assurances to Eastern European governments that their countries would not be invaded if they opted for neutrality and did not cooperate in the Soviet attack on the West.

Creating the conventional military forces that could, with a high degree of certainty, stop a substantial Soviet invasion of Western Europe appears to be beyond the political will of Western European statesmen and publics. Creating a conventional strategy and military force, however, for a prompt retaliatory invasion of Eastern Europe should not be beyond the ingenuity of Western military planners. For years Western deterrent strategy has assumed that a Soviet nuclear attack on the United States would produce a prompt retaliatory response in kind. Theater nuclear modernization in Europe assumes that Soviet use of theater nuclear weapons against Western Europe must also be met by a prompt retaliation in kind. Surely it is rather anomalous that plans do not exist to respond to a Soviet conventional attack on Western Europe with a prompt retaliatory attack in kind on Eastern Europe. Failure to have the plans and the capability for such action is a major—and potentially dangerous—gap in the overall structure of deterrence.

A strategy of conventional retaliation would help ease NATO's nuclear dilemma in at least two ways. First, as the demonstrations of 1981–82 against Theater Nuclear Force (TNF) modernization indicated, significant elements of public opinion in Western Europe and the United States are deeply concerned about a strategy that relies heavily on nuclear weapons. Shifting the emphasis in alliance strategy from the defensive use of nuclear weapons to the offensive use of conventional forces would moderate this source of opposition to NATO military planning. Second, if aggression does occur, the ability to implement a conventional retaliatory strategy would raise the NATO nuclear threshold and thereby make it more likely that NATO could avoid the "deepening trap" of an increasingly improbable "first nuclear use" that Iklé (1980) warned about. Surely it is politically more credible, militarily more desirable, and morally far more legitimate to have a strategy which, if war occurs, contemplates efforts to liberate Eastern Europe by conventional means rather than early recourse to weapons that make likely the slaughter of countless European, Russian, and, in all probability, American civilians.

Moreover, a conventional retaliatory strategy in Europe is relevant not only to the defense of Western Europe. By forcing the Soviets to face the possibility of a two-front war, it also contributes to second-zone deterrence. The Soviet Union is surrounded both by potentially hostile states and potentially tempting opportunities to exploit its military capabilities for political advantage. Western strategy should capitalize on the former in order to limit the latter; Soviet strategy, just the reverse. A Soviet strategist can only see his country as encircled, and his perception would not be wrong. The classic response for a country in this position is to attempt to use the advantages it offers in terms of interior lines and the opportunities to divorce one area of action from another and thus to concentrate diplomatic attention and military force, if necessary, on one opponent or set of opponents at a time. The Soviet Union has a clear interest in attempting to separate its relations with Japan, China, Southwest Asia, Eastern Europe, Western Europe, and the United States into discrete packages, isolated, insofar as possible, one from the other. The logical corollary and preliminary to Soviet military action in China or the Persian Gulf is the fervent pursuit of detente in Europe; some rapprochement with China is a highly desirable prerequisite to military confrontation in Europe. . . .

The ability to deter Soviet military action against China, Southwest Asia, or Eastern Europe cannot rest primarily on military forces in those areas. It will be many years, perhaps decades, before China is capable of repulsing a Soviet punitive incursion. All the efforts to develop readily deployable U.S. forces for the Persian Gulf cannot remove Soviet geographical advantages or Soviet superiority to any indigenous forces that might oppose them. Nor could any satellite army in Eastern Europe by itself hope to hold the Soviet Army at bay for long. If deterrence is to be reasonably well assured, consequently, it must rest on the high probability that Soviet military action in any one area will also involve the Soviet Union in military hostilities in other areas. This can only happen if there exists a system of interlocking, reinforcing deterrents and if there is the military capability and strategy to take the offensive against Soviet vital interests in an area other than the one which the Soviets are threatening. . . .

The Japanese are prevented by their constitution, capabilities, and psychology from offensive action, and U.S. air or naval offensive action against the Soviet Union from Japan would be incompatible with the U.S.-Japanese alliance unless it was directly related to an imminent military threat to Japan. China's military forces are and will be for several years capable of only the most limited offensive actions against Siberia or Mongolia. No capabilities, obviously, exist for offensive action from Southwest Asia or Eastern Europe. Only in Western Europe do military forces exist that could pose a significant and credible offensive threat to vital Soviet interests. A conventional retaliatory strategy in central Europe is thus desirable not only to compensate for the eroded credibility of the nuclear deterrent as far as Europe is concerned but also to help meet the new needs to deter Soviet aggression elsewhere.

A conventional retaliatory strategy in Europe would not be a substitute for the deployment of Western forces in the Persian Gulf and Indian Ocean areas or for the modernization of the Chinese armed forces. It would, however, supplement and reinforce these efforts and limit the resources that had to be devoted to them by providing an alternative means of securing an equal amount of deterrence. It is, for instance, in all likelihood politically impossible to deploy Western ground forces in the Persian Gulf area so as to provide deterrence-by-presence. Deterrence-by-defense will be possible under some circumstances, but it will be difficult and expensive; and if the Soviets were free to concentrate their forces on Southwest Asia, they clearly could overrun any force that the Western allies and Japan might deploy in a reasonable amount of time. It consequently makes great sense, as Secretary of Defense Weinberger put it (1981), for the United States, if forced into war, to "be prepared to launch counter-offensives in other regions and try to exploit the aggressor's weaknesses wherever they exist." In 1980 and 1981 the European allies of the United States expressed concern at times about the possible reorientation of American military planning, programs, and money from preparation for a European war to the development of the Rapid Deployment Force and other forces for the projection of American power into the Persian Gulf area (*New York Times* 1981:13). Clearly the United States needs to develop that capability rapidly. The extent of the resources reallocated to that purpose from European defense could be reduced, European worries assuaged, and the security of the Persian Gulf area equally well advanced if NATO adopted a retaliatory strategy in Europe. At present the Soviet Union is free to engage in military adventures in the Persian Gulf without concern about its security along the Elbe even as Hitler in the 1930s could move militarily into Eastern Europe without worrying about his security along the Rhine. A retaliatory strategy in Europe consequently should be particularly appealing to the European allies both because it would move at least some of the fighting eastward if deterrence failed and because it would limit the pressure to reallocate allied military resources from Europe to the Indian Ocean.

A somewhat parallel logic would apply to the deterrence of a Soviet attack on China. The provision of military equipment to China, including some forms of lethal equipment, is appropriate and desirable in terms of strengthening defensive deterrence along the Soviet border. At some point, however, the provision of weapons to China will run into problems of distinguishing between defensive weapons, which could only be used against the only power that might attack China (that is, the Soviet Union), and offensive weapons, which might give the Chinese some capacity for deterrence-by-retaliation against the Soviets but which might also give them the capability to attack Taiwan, to occupy portions of Vietnam, Cambodia, and Laos, and to threaten Thailand and other members of the Association of South East Asian Nations (ASEAN). China itself has recognized its interest in a strong NATO. A NATO strategy of conventional retaliation would reduce the importance of re-arming China beyond a certain point and would contribute to Chinese security by forcing the Soviets again to confront the possibility of a two-front war and potentially disastrous losses in the West if they launched an attack on their enemy in the East.

Finally, with respect to Eastern Europe itself, a NATO conventional retaliatory strategy can provide an additional deterrent to Soviet military action against a satellite government that is attempting to broaden its independence. It would, consequently, encourage satellite governments to see how far they could go in loosening Soviet controls. In 1950 the deployment of American troops to Europe significantly encouraged Tito in his resistance to the Soviets (Windsor 1978). An allied retaliatory strategy could well have a comparable effect in promoting the "Finlandization," if not the "Titoization," of Eastern Europe.

The central need in the containment of Soviet military aggression in the 1980s is thus to see the problem of deterrence as a whole and the ways in which the various geographical and functional components of strategy interlock with each other. It is erroneous to suggest, as some have (Aspin 1976), that the Soviet military build-up on the Chinese frontier does not increase the threat to the West or to believe, as the Chinese never would, that NATO strength and strategy have no relevance to the defense of China. In the 1980s geographical linkage is the essence of deterrence. If it is in the interest of world peace and Western security that the Soviets not go into Iran, China, or Poland, that certainty should be greatly reduced. A defensive posture does not require a purely defensive strategy and, indeed, may be undermined by such a strategy. Neither the United States, nor its major allies, nor China, nor regional powers can produce the conventional military forces to defeat those which the Soviets could mass at whatever place they might be tempted to invade. "It is impossible," as Secretary Dulles said in 1954 (Kaufman 1956:14–15), to match the "potential enemy at all points on a basis of man-for-man, gun-for-gun, and tank-for-tank." This is still the case. In 1954 deterrence could be provided by relying "primarily on our massive mobile retaliatory power which we could use in our discretion against the major sources of aggression at times and places that we chose." This is no longer the case. In the 1980s, allied capacity to launch a conventional retaliatory offensive into Eastern Europe is essential to narrowing the gap between foreign policy and strategy and to insuring against Soviet aggression into either the first or second deterrent zones.

The reasons for NATO putting much greater emphasis on deterrence-by-retaliation seem overwhelming. Yet in some circles there is an apparent reluctance to confront this need, and four arguments are often advanced against a NATO strategy of conventional retaliation.

First, it is argued that NATO military forces are too weak to support an offensive strategy. As we have seen, during the 1970s the conventional and theater nuclear force balances in Europe did shift significantly toward the Warsaw Pact. Every effort should be made to rectify this situation and to reestablish a balance of forces more comparable to that which existed in the mid-1960s. If NATO moves forward with its current plans, the military balance in Europe should be more satisfactory in the later 1980s than it was in the early 1980s. Even the 1982 balance, however, would not preclude NATO from adopting a conventional retaliatory strategy. In the first place, the Pact's advantage on the central front is significant but not necessarily decisive (Mearsheimer 1982). In 1981 the Pact had an advantage in divisional manpower of 1.2-1.36 to 1 and in overall manpower of 1.15-1.2 to 1. The Pact was greatly superior in numbers of tanks, but in terms of armored division equivalents, the Pact advantage was only 1.2 to 1, which could very likely be compensated for by NATO strength in airpower. Unlike the Pact, NATO's air strength is overwhelming in attack planes capable of carrying out the deep interdiction and ground-attack missions necessary to support a ground offensive. The introduction of the Leopard and M-1 tanks will also increase NATO's ground offensive capabilities. The crucial element in any offensive, moreover, is not the overall military balance between the two sides but rather the military balance at the point of attack. The great advantage of the offensive is that the attacker chooses that point and hence can concentrate his forces there. History is full of successful offensives by forces that lacked numerical superiority, including the German offensive in the West in 1940, the Japanese offensives in Southeast Asia in 1941–42, and the North Vietnamese offensive in 1975 (Stuart 1981). Nothing in the existing balance of forces in central Europe rules out a NATO offensive strategy, and that balance is more likely to become more favorable than less favorable during the course of the decade.

In addition, a NATO offensive strategy would pose serious military problems for the Soviet Union. It would, as we have pointed out, require a reallocation of some Pact forces from offensive to defensive purposes. It would also confront the Soviets with just exactly the situation their doctrine and strategy attempt to avoid: one in which they do not have control of developments and in which they face a high probability of uncertainty and surprise. It would put a premium on flexibility and adaptability, qualities in which the Soviets recognize themselves to be deficient. Furthermore, a prompt allied offensive into Eastern Europe would greatly increase the probability of a protracted war. Soviet planning, however, is in large part directed toward a short-war scenario in which the Soviets score a breakthrough, occupy a substantial portion of West Germany, and then negotiate a cease fire from a position of strength. With a retaliatory strategy, however, Soviet armies might be in West Germany but allied armies would also be in East Europe, and driving them out would require more time for mobilization and organization of a counteroffensive.

The basic point, moreover, is deterrence. The prospects for the sustained success of the allied offensive into Eastern Europe do not have to be 100 percent. They simply have to be sufficiently better than zero and to raise enough unpleasant uncertainties to increase significantly the potential costs and risks to the Soviets of starting a war.

Second, it is at times argued that an allied retaliatory strategy, duplicating in some sense Soviet offensive strategy, would create instability in crises, in which each side would be tempted to strike first. Once implemented, however, this strategy should reduce the probability of crises in which either side seriously considers going to war. At present, assuming a lag of four to seven days in NATO mobilization, it is generally argued that Warsaw Pact numerical superiority would peak seven to twenty-one days after the Pact started mobilizing (Carnegie Endowment 1981). In any crisis, consequently, the Soviets would have substantial incentives to attack during this period before the mobilization and deployment of U.S. and West European reinforcements reduced their advantage. These incentives would decrease if they knew that such an attack would be met by an immediate Eastern European offensive by the on-line NATO forces. Similarly, in the absence of a planned NATO offensive, NATO success would depend entirely on its ability to blunt the Soviet offensive; NATO commanders would, consequently, be under greater incentive to launch preemptive "defensive" tactical air strikes against Soviet troop concentrations than they would be if NATO were itself prepared to launch a prompt retaliatory offensive.

Third, it is argued that instead of capitalizing upon the political weakness of the Soviet empire, a conventional retaliatory strategy would help to solidify the empire by enabling the Soviets to rally Eastern European governments and peoples to the defense of their homelands against Western imperialist aggressors. The Soviets, however, already make every effort to do this and consistently portray NATO as an aggressive alliance. It is not clear that they could say much more than they have been saying if NATO adopted a strategy of conventional retaliation. Again, it must be emphasized that the entire purpose of the strategy is deterrence: to create uncertainty in the minds of Soviet leaders as to what would happen in Eastern Europe. As has been argued, the adoption of this strategy should be accompanied with a clear invitation to Eastern European governments to avoid invasion by opting out of a Soviet-initiated war. At the very least, such an invitation would create uneasiness, uncertainty, and divisiveness within satellite governments, and hence arouse concerns among the Soviets as to their reliability. In practice, the allied offensive would have to be accompanied with carefully composed political-psychological warfare appeals to the peoples of East Europe stressing that the allies were not fighting them but the Soviets, and urging them to cooperate with the advancing forces and to rally to the liberation of their countries from Soviet military occupation and political control.

A conventional retaliatory strategy is based on the assumption that the West German reserves, territorial army, and populace will put up a more unified, comprehensive, and determined resistance to Soviet armies than the East German, Czech, Polish, and Hungarian armies and peoples will to the advance of West German forces into East Germany and American forces into elsewhere in Eastern Europe. (If this assumption is unwarranted, the foundations of not only a conventional retaliatory strategy but also of NATO would be in question.)

Finally, the point is made that while a conventional retaliatory strategy may make military and even political sense in terms of the relations between NATO and the Warsaw Pact, opposition to it within NATO would be so great that any effort to adopt it would simply tear the alliance apart. Such is the usual reaction to any new idea, however, and the arguments and need for such a strategy are simply overwhelming. Its adoption would, moreover, reduce the intensity of debate over other NATO issues. Theater nuclear modernization would still be necessary, but adoption of conventional retaliation would clearly help to assuage some of the concerns that underlie the debate over NATO's use of nuclear weapons. As indicated earlier, such a strategy would also ease the tensions involved in allocating forces between the Persian Gulf and Western Europe. A coalition of sixteen democratic countries obviously cannot change its strategy without much soul-searching, discussion, and controversy. The need to strengthen deterrence, however, is compelling; debate on the recasting of NATO strategy to meet the conditions of the 1980s should be delayed no longer. . . .

COPING WITH THIRD WORLD THREATS

The Soviet Union is the principal focus of U.S. strategic planning, and Soviet-American military conflict is more likely in the 1980s than in previous decades. The Soviet Union is not, however, the only conceivable source of threats to American vital interests, and the probability that American forces will engage Soviet forces is still less than the probability of their engaging other forces. Other governments or groups can threaten U.S. vital interests in three ways.

First, they can directly attack particular U.S. interests. A guerrilla force shooting rockets at ships going through the Panama Canal would pose a threat whether or not it had any affiliation with or support from the Soviet Union. An attack by the Iranian government or Islamic fundamentalist insurgents on Saudi oil facilities would pose a comparable threat whether or not those attacks had Soviet backing. The seizure of American embassies, planes, or citizens represents similar, if lower level, action to which the United States has to be prepared to respond militarily. The acquisition of nuclear weapons by a guerrilla group or, in some cases, by a government might also pose a direct challenge to American vital interests.

Second, some governments in the world are partial to the Soviets; others are partial to the West. A significant change in power between these two groups would have implications for U.S. security, even if the Soviet Union itself had not played any significant role in bringing that shift about. Coups d'état in Saudi Arabia or in other Persian Gulf states or local wars in that area, Southeast Asia, the Middle East, or Africa could engage American interests if they threatened friendly governments.

Third, local conflicts and instability in the Third World can create opportunities for the direct expansion of Soviet or Soviet-proxy military influence and presence. American interests are clearly to minimize these opportunities. At times, however, they will exist; non-military and conventional efforts at deterrence may fail; and the United States may find itself confronted with the need to respond to Soviet-bloc military actions in the Third World.

More specifically, the types of Third World military conflict that might pose threats to U.S. interests in the 1980s include: (1) coups d'etat against friendly governments; (2) insurrections or guerrilla in-surgencies against friendly governments; (3) local conflicts in which a friendly government is invaded or in danger of being defeated by a less friendly one; (4) any of the above in which Soviet or Soviet-proxy forces play a significant role.

The United States needs a strategy and the capabilities to deal with threats to its interests that arise from these types of conflicts. Declarations of American interest and deployments of American forces can help deter Soviet intervention and local aggression by regional powers. In some circumstances, they may also be able to reduce the likelihood of coups d'état against friendly regimes. It is difficult, if not impossible, however, to deter those whom one cannot locate, identify, or be sure exist. The United States, as Steven David has persuasively argued (1982), undoubtedly should be prepared to help friendly governments suppress coups d'état. The existence of some such U.S. capability—and knowledge of its existence—might have some deterrent effect on coup plotting in friendly countries. But these deterrent effects would be of a highly generalized nature, and the participants in any particular con-spiracy or cabal might well have good reason for thinking that such an American capability would not be terribly relevant for their case. Hence a strategy for coping with Third World threats has to be directed to both deterring those challenges that are predictable and responding to those challenges that are not.

While there clearly may be some measure of overlap, the four types of contingencies just mentioned are listed in an order that generally reflects ascending levels of violence. From the 1950s into the 1970s, American strategic attention was largely focused upon the second and third types of contingencies. The Korean Was was a clear Contingency

Three case; the Vietnam War was a combination of Contingencies Two and Three. In connection with these involvements, American strategists developed theories of limited war and of counterinsurgency. Relatively little attention was paid to strategies for coping either with coups d'état, which are frequent but seldom serious, or with Soviet military intervention in the Third World which until the mid-1970s was relatively minimal.

Insurrections and local wars remain highly likely in the Third World in the 1980s. Many of these could directly affect major American interests. These could include insurgencies in the Gulf area, in Central America and the Caribbean, and conceivably in South Africa. Local wars that might raise the issue of direct American military intervention to support a friendly government could occur in Southeast Asia (Vietnam versus Thailand), the Persian Gulf (Iran, Iraq, or Yemen versus Saudi Arabia), North Africa (Libya versus Egypt, Tunisia, or the Sudan; Algeria versus Morocco), the Horn of Africa (Ethiopia versus Somalia, Kenya, or the Sudan), and quite possibly elsewhere.

The probability of direct participation by U.S. military forces in either prolonged insurgencies or local wars remains, however, relatively low, except in situations where such conflict might directly affect concrete American interests, such as Saudi oil production. The impact of Vietnam is strongest and most relevant with respect to U.S. military involvement in counterinsurgency situations. The reluctance of any U.S. administration, Congress, and the public to countenance such involvement will undoubtedly remain high for most of the 1980s. The United States may often find it in its interests, as in El Salvador, to provide advice, training, money, and equipment to a friendly government fighting guerrillas. In the absence of a direct threat to concrete American interests or direct and overt involvement of Soviet or Soviet-proxy forces, the United States is not likely to find it militarily necessary, diplomatically desirable, or politically feasible to intervene with U.S. combat forces in such conflicts.

Fewer constraints exist on U.S. military involvement in a local interstate war. Major segments of the American establishment tend automatically to attribute legitimacy to revolutionary movements against Third World governments. They also tend almost automatically to attribute illegitimacy to any direct attack by one state on another across a recognized frontier. Consequently, there is likely to be greater public willingness to help a friendly government respond to an external attack than to an internal attack. In the absence of a simultaneous domestic insurgency or outside great power support, however, local interstate wars in the Third World do not generally lead to quick and decisive outcomes. The limited military capabilities of the combatants are more likely, as in the Iran-Iraq war, to lead to inconclusive stalemates, in which neither party is able to deal a death blow to the other. In this situation, the need for direct U.S. military involvement is also reduced.

During the 1970s the Persian Gulf assumed new importance as far as U.S. security is concerned. During the 1980s the probability of political instability in Saudi Arabia, Kuwait, Bahrein, the United Arab Emirates, and Oman is very high. Conceivably, a prolonged insurgency, a local interstate war, or direct Soviet military intervention could endanger oil supplies from this region to the United States and its allies. The most likely form of instability, however, is coups d'état against one or more of these conservative Gulf regimes. The underlying causes of political instability are inherent in the rapid increases in wealth, rising expectations, social dislocation, conflicts between Western and Islamic values, and development of modern armed forces. In Saudi Arabia and the other Gulf states, there are at least four major possible sources of instability. First, conflicts within the established elite (for example, between the Sudairi and Jiluwi factions in Saudi Arabia) could get out of hand, leading to efforts by one group to exclude the other from power. Second, the military and other professional groups produced by modernization could be antagonized by the corruption of the existing regime and by their own failure to share adequately in the riches of oil and hence could attempt to overthrow the existing system through a coup d'état. Third, Islamic fundamentalist groups (*ulemmas,* traditional tribal and local elites) could react against social and economic change, attempting a coup in order to stop such change. Fourth, Palestinian radical groups, alone or in conjunction with radical modernist or Islamic fundamentalist groups, could promote political upheaval so that less conservative regimes who are actively willing to support their cause against Israel could come into power.

All in all, the likelihood of the existing political elites in the Persian Gulf states surviving this decade is small. Even less likely is the survival of the existing political systems. It is difficult to predict the extent to which coups would bring to power regimes seriously hostile to U.S. interests. It is virtually certain, however, that *any* post-coup regime in a conservative Persian Gulf state will be less sympathetic to U.S. interests concerning oil and the Arab-Israeli dispute and more open to Soviet influence than the current regime in that state. In addition, a successful coup in one Gulf state could well trigger coup attempts in adjoining states. Coping with internal instability in Persian Gulf regimes is, consequently, a top priority for U.S. security policy in the 1980s. An overall strategy for dealing with these contingencies involves four elements.

First and most basic are efforts to conserve energy, to stockpile reserves, and to diversify energy sources so that the dependence of the

United States and its allies on oil from this potentially unstable area will be reduced. While such efforts deserved top priority, they probably will not significantly reduce U.S. dependence on Persian Gulf oil before the end of the decade. The dependence of U.S. allies on this oil will continue even longer.

Second, the United States can encourage the existing Gulf regimes to take steps to postpone or reduce the likelihood of a coup. These would include measures to moderate but sustain the pace of economic development; to distribute the fruits of development broadly among key groups in the population; to keep its military happy with money, promotions, and weapons; to divide the military establishment into two or more competing institutions; to limit corruption and distribute it widely; to negotiate the stationing of politically acceptable foreign forces in that country (for instance, Pakistani troops in Saudi Arabia) that could protect the regime; and to develop institutional channels so that those elements of the population which are mobilized through modernization can legitimately participate in politics.

Third, the United States can take measures in tacit cooperation with existing regimes to help them defeat coups if they should occur. In several instances in the recent past, outside assistance has played a significant role in defeating coups. The United States itself has acted to head off or defeat coups in Ethiopia, Venezuela, and elsewhere (David 1982). In a coup, communications play a vital role: the leaders of the coup have to convince the populace and, most importantly, potential supporters in the military and elsewhere that they have successfully deposed the previous regime and established themselves in power. The leader of the regime, on the other hand, has to demonstrate that he is still alive and functioning and able to appeal for support. The United States is fortunate that the Persian Gulf oil states are, indeed, located on the Persian Gulf. To assist in the defeat of coups in these states, the United States should provide radio transmitters and other communications facilities on ships off-shore, which could be used by government leaders to relay messages to their supporters and to appeal to their people. In addition, it would be wise for the United States to maintain a small specially trained, countercoup military force on U.S. ships in the region, equipped with helicopters and VSTOL (vertical short take-off and landing) aircraft, that could in a matter of hours respond to the request of a threatened government for help.

Finally, the United States should position itself so that the damage to its interests is reduced if a coup succeeds. It is in the American interest, consequently, to expand and diversify its relations with the Persian Gulf countries—financially, developmentally, militarily, technologically—so that any successor regime will find it difficult and costly to attack American interests and sever connections with the

United States. In addition, while it is difficult to predict who will lead a successor government, it is not so difficult to identify a small number of potential leaders for that government. In contrast to its behavior in Iran, the United States should attempt to develop and maintain friendly contacts with those individuals and groups likely to play leading roles in a successor regime.

The most serious sort of military contingency for the United States in the Third World would be direct Soviet or Soviet-proxy military participation in a coup, insurrection, or local war. The appropriate measures of nonmilitary and conventional deterrence can reduce significantly the probability of such involvement. Nonetheless, it still could happen, particularly in the Persian Gulf area. The likelihood of such intervention would be reduced if the United States were able to deploy ground forces in a deterrence-by-presence posture in the region. Such a deployment, however, would no doubt increase the already high probability of political instability in the region. To counter possible Soviet intervention, the United States needs to strengthen the Rapid Deployment Force authorized by President Carter in 1977, greatly expand and modernize its air and naval transport capabilities, pre-position equipment in the area where possible, maintain a respectable naval presence in the Arabian Sea, and negotiate agreements for access to local bases in emergencies. Although the Soviets probably could, if they wished, overwhelm local or allied forces in the northern Gulf area, the combination of these measures, plus a revision of NATO strategy to make them worry about their Eastern Europen flank, could provide fairly persuasive deterrence and then war-fighting capability if deterrence failed.

In the 1980s the United States may still have to come to the help of friendly governments fighting local interstate wars or combatting prolonged insurgencies, as it did in Korea and Vietnam. More than before, however, the United States will likely become involved in the other two contingencies located at opposing ends of the spectrum of violence: countercoup intervention, on the one hand, and counter-intervention against Soviet or proxy military forces, on the other. These two contingencies share one characteristic: they are unlikely to last long. A coup is a matter of hours or days at most. A Soviet military intervention to which the United States responded is also likely to be terminated quickly either because one side or the other has won what it wanted or because both sides react to the dangers of escalation by negotiating a cease-fire or disengagement. Because of their probable short duration, countercoup and counter-Soviet U.S. military interventions in the Third World are also likely to be more politically feasible than U.S. involvement in more prolonged civil and interstate wars. The theorists of limited war in the 1950s and 1960s discussed at length the ways in which war could be limited in terms of goals, targets, geographical areas, and forces and weapons employed. As the experiences of Korea and Vietnam make clear, however, the most significant limit on U.S. military action in a small-scale conflict is the limit of *time* (Huntington 1977). The American public simply will not permit its government to engage in long, drawn-out military actions to defend distant interests and to achieve ambiguous goals. Fortunately, the contingencies the United States is most likely to face during the 1980s are ones which will probably be of short duration. Thus, for both political and military reasons, U.S. strategy in Third World conflicts should be directed toward reacting promptly and achieving a quick decision.

A Strategy for the Rapid Deployment Force

KENNETH N. WALTZ

Although it is widely believed that the United States needs a Rapid Deployment Force, no one has defined the purposes that an RDF can be expected to serve. Much has been written about the design of the Force: the speed with which it should be able to move, and the troops and equipment it should be able to deploy. Little has been written about the problem of devising a strategy for its use. Design will dictate strategy unless a promising strategy is first devised. If design dictates strategy, Americans may find themselves with a Rapid Deployment Force both over-built and ill-suited to its tasks. As a new Administration takes over the task of developing an RDF, it should ask itself two questions. What ends does the United States want an RDF to serve? What is the best strategy for its use?

From *International Security,* Spring 1981, pp. 49–73. Reprinted by permission of the MIT Press Journals.

WHAT ENDS SHOULD AN RDF SERVE?

The lesson of America's Vietnam venture is neither that we should intervene militarily abroad nor that we should not. Instead, it is that we should do so only when three conditions obtain: Vital interests are at risk; non-military measures cannot adequately serve them; the use of force can reasonably be expected to accomplish our purposes.

The ability to act militarily carries with it the temptation to take military action. The common quality of military advice is conservatism. Military weakness leads soldiers to advise politicians to be cautious, to avoid war, or to seek its postponement until strength can be gathered. Military strength leads soldiers either to counsel preventive war while the moment of military superiority lasts or to strike quickly to nip trouble in the bud. A sizeable RDF would provide the latter temptation. Former Secretary of Defense Harold Brown referred to the Force as one of the four pillars of our military power, along with the strategic deterrent, the forces contributed to NATO, and the Navy. Picking up the cue, General Edward C. Meyer, Army Chief of Staff, emphasized the importance of getting the right mix of forces for the RDF because, as he said, we are "not just thinking of the Middle East or the Persian Gulf. Contingencies might arise in other areas, too." Developing the theme, General Maxwell Taylor, a former Chairman of the Joint Chiefs of Staff, looked toward a Force designed to deal in the next decade with threats "arising from continued Soviet malevolence supported by growing military power, the dependence of the United States and allies on Mideast oil and the turbulence of the developing world, where most of the overseas sources of imported raw materials are found." But since World War II, the malevolent activities of the Soviet Union, Eastern Europe aside, have produced gains that for the most part have been illusory and evanescent and are exceeded by the "loss" of such countries as Yugoslavia, China, and Egypt, countries in which the influence of the Soviet Union once seemed to be well established. Some political groups may want the Soviet Union's support while struggling to gain control of their governments. Once in power, they want to be as independent of the Soviet Union as they can manage to be and to reach this end will turn to the United States and other non-communist states. No state wants to be controlled by another. Angola is a recent illustration of this truth, and Algeria was an earlier one. We should avoid defining the Soviet Union's political-military activity in various parts of the world as automatically threatening American vital interests. Demonstrably, that has seldom been the case.

We should also view General Taylor's third threat with skepticism. He believes that turbulence in developing countries imperils us because most of our imported raw materials are found there. This is a simple error, and one easily fallen into. Oil aside, the industrial democracies produce about 45 percent of the world's raw materials; the less developed countries and the communist countries about equally account for the rest. In 1977, for example, two-thirds of our imports of roughly 25 critical materials came from Canada, Australia, South Africa, and other more developed countries, and over one-half from Canada alone. In classifying the third threat as being among the most dangerous we shall face, General Taylor exaggerates American dependence on less developed countries.

Moreover, the United States is markedly less dependent on imports, whatever their source, than most of the industrial non-communist countries are. Exports plus imports in the year 1975, for example, ranged from 32 percent to 41 percent of GNP for France, Germany, Italy, and the United Kingdom. For the United States the comparable figure was 14 percent. These data do not show that we suffer from no dependencies other than oil. They do show that our dependencies are relatively easy to manage. States are the more independent if they have reliable access to important resources, if they have feasible alternatives, if they have the ability to do without, and if they have leverage to use against others. The extent of American dependency varies both with how much we need them and with how much they in turn need us. We are far and away the world's largest supplier of foodstuffs, of the technologically most advanced manufactures, and of capital. Those who have what others want or badly need are in favored positions.

Because the United States is so well endowed, and because in various economic and technological ways, we can protect ourselves from the disruption of supplies coming in from outside, we ordinarily need not think of using force to protect economic interests. We should guard against adopting expansive definitions of our vital interests, as great powers often do, and of then assuming that military force should be used to secure them. Most American interests are better served by means other than military force. By defining vital interests narrowly and by using force sparingly, we can avoid the unnecessary commitment of force that would risk our having force unavailable in those rare cases where it might be well to use it.

It is a vital interest of the United States, as of other countries, to have reliable supplies of all sorts of materials, from bauxite and chromium to nickel and oil. For most—indeed for all but one—of many important materials, the United States is able to take care of itself *without* using military force. Oil is the exception. For the foreseeable future, no technical means now known can reduce our dependence on oil to manageable proportions if the worst should happen. The "if" clause should be emphasized because even in the case of oil, the United States operates on fairly wide margins. We are not as dependent on imported oil as are countries closely associated with us.

Table 1 makes this clear.

We import proportionately less oil than most other non-communist industrial countries do and get relatively little from the Middle East. Much of the production of oil for export is concentrated there, as Table 1 shows. In August of 1979, Persian Gulf countries produced 35 percent of the world's, and 45 percent of the non-communist world's, oil. Most of the oil produced elsewhere is consumed by the countries that produce it. Exported oil comes from Gulf states and from seven others. Production of the latter is about half that of the former and, Mexico aside, significant increases in production for export are likely to come only from the Middle East.

Countries are the more imperiled economically the greater their dependence on imported oil and the more their dependence concentrates on countries of the Persian Gulf. The United States is thus doubly fortunate. Our dependence is relatively low, and our suppliers are more dispersed geographically than those of our industrial competitors. Gulf countries can expect to experience political instability, and instability may spread from one country to another. Moreover, their proximity to the Soviet Union makes them susceptible to the military pressure and presence of the Soviet Union. In contrast, other oil exporting countries—flung across the map from Indonesia to Libya and Algeria, from Nigeria to Venezuela and Mexico—are not similarly vulnerable to the spread of internal unrest from one country to another or to military pressure from outside.

Oil is the only economic interest for which the United States may have to fight, yet interruption of oil exports from one or more OPEC countries would hurt the United States less and later than it would hurt most others. Former Secretary of Defense Harold Brown emphasized the point. "If the industrial democracies are deprived of access to those resources," he said in February of 1980, "there would almost certainly be a worldwide economic collapse of the kind that hasn't been seen for almost 50 years, probably worse." The shutting off of oil would create havoc among America's allies, who can do nothing "in the coming decades that would save them from irreversible catastrophe if it were cut off." Because the United States is less dependent on oil, he added sarcastically, "we would just face economic disruption, international chaos, and looming Soviet power." A major and prolonged reduction of oil exports would be damaging to us, would be even more damaging to some others, and would push the world toward economic ruin. To say that we should be prepared to act to prevent such damage is a statement that conforms to a modest definition of our vital interests.

Leaving aside the role others may play, the United States should be prepared to meet threats of three sorts: embargoes, disruption of oil production and export resulting from regional turmoil, and military attacks on, or subversion of, OPEC countries that would seriously interfere with the production and export of oil.

Table 1.

1978	United States	European Community	Japan
Oil as percent of total energy consumed	47%	55%	71%
Percent of oil imported	44	87	100
Percent of oil imported from Persian Gulf	30	57	73
Persian Gulf oil as percent of total energy consumed	7	28	51

Source: John M. Collins and Clyde R. Mark, "Petroleum Imports from the Persian Gulf: Use of U.S. Armed Force to Ensure Supplies," Issue Brief Number IB79046 (Washington, D.C.: Library of Congress, Congressional Reference Service, May 5, 1980), p. 2.

If we look at the RDF as part of a larger national security policy, as surely we should, then our first concern must be to position ourselves so that we shall seldom have to use force suddenly. The passage of time reduces the chances of committing force needlessly. With the passage of time two questions can usually be answered. Is the threat severe enough to require the use of force? Will internal and external political developments moderate or contain the threat before we need to use force?

How can the United States afford itself the luxury of time? The answer is simple: by building a large stockpile of oil, as we are now too slowly doing. A billion-barrel stockpile would carry us for four to six months, depending on rates of consumption and on how strictly we rationed ourselves, without any imports at all. In the summer of 1980, the United States had 92 million barrels in the stockpile, barely equal to two weeks' imports, and had not added to its reserve since early 1979. To put high priority on building an RDF while having dallied for years in building an oil reserve is odd policy. If I had to choose between a billion-barrel stockpile and an RDF, I would choose the former. A large American stockpile would help to meet each of the three sorts of threats for which we need to prepare. In fact, it would enable us to foil the first one: namely, embargoes. Embargoes are hard to sustain, as the first oil embargo showed. OPEC countries are politically, culturally, and economically diverse. Diverse countries have trouble uniting to maintain costly policies. The economic and political interests of some of the states mounting an embargo will surely conflict. Thus, during the short term of the first embargo, Libya began to sell oil apparently because it thought OPEC countries too soft on Israel, and Iraq began to sell oil apparently because it wanted the money. Most OPEC countries, their oil riches aside, are weak economically as well as militarily and politically. All the more so because many of their interests diverge, one can safely bet on their inability to sustain punitive policies against the great and major powers of the world. A four- to six-month stockpile would provide a comfortable margin of safety. A large American stockpile would also tell our allies that we may not respond quickly to threats that endanger oil supplies and would thus give them strong incentive to build their own stockpiles. Once oil suppliers see that only long-sustained embargoes can be effective, they have little reason to mount them.

A large oil stockpile, although highly useful in dealing with the second sort of threat, would by no means eliminate it. The second threat is that oil exports be severely reduced for a prolonged period because of revolution or chaos in one or more of the major oil exporters or because of war among them. The one country that could cause international economic disaster by its inability to export is Saudi Arabia, producing 9.5 million barrels daily (MMBD) out of a world total of 63.1 MMBD in August of 1979. The one region that could bring this result is the Persian Gulf area, producing about 21 MMBD. The big producers there, in addition to Saudi Arabia, were Iraq (3.3 MMBD), Iran (3.0–3.6), Kuwait (2.2), and the United Arab Emirates (1.8). The comparable figures for big producers outside of the Gulf area were Venezuela (2.3), Nigeria (2.2), Libya (2.0), Indonesia (1.6), Mexico (1.4), and Algeria (0.9).

The threat of severe reduction of oil supplies concentrates in the Persian Gulf. This is unfortunate. The dispersion of numerous sources would lessen the likelihood that enough of them would dry up at any one time to cause serious problems. The concentration of sources does, however, mean that we can focus on the problem of increasing the security of our access to them in just one region. The expectation that one or another of the Gulf countries will experience political unrest and turmoil, whether or not in the style of Iran, is widely shared. Most observers believe the danger of major stoppages of oil exports lies within and among these states, rather than arising externally from the Soviet Union.

Radical regimes, whether of the left or of the right, want to continue to sell oil. We know this was true of Libya and Iraq. It has also been true of Khomeini's Iran, which lowered the price of its oil in July of 1980 to stimulate lagging sales. Although radical countries want to sell oil, they may not be very good at producing it. Should the exports of a country be internally disrupted, a large stockpile of oil would again prove its worth. It would give the luxury of time—the ability to wait to see whether the country in question can regain control of its affairs, the ability to wait to see whether a revolutionary movement in one country infects others. Abiding solutions to most of a country's political problems have to be found by its citizens; foreigners can seldom be of much help. Moreover, most problems find fairly good solutions without the use of force. If this were not so, the world would always be at war.

We should be slow to intervene militarily when countries are wracked by internal pain. We should also be slow to intervene militarily in others' wars. Intervention risks making a bad situation worse. Moreover, a certain amount of fighting may be prerequisite to a stable outcome, leaving both sides discontented yet satisfied that more fighting would be useless. Are we then to be at the mercy of crises that we cannot control, even of crises threatening to engulf a number of countries and to result in a prolonged denial of oil? We shall have to answer "yes" unless we can devise a strategy for using an RDF that promises a reasonable possibility that we can keep oil flowing. That is the problem to be solved in the next section of this essay.

Meanwhile, we have to consider the third sort of threat, the use of military force or pressure by a state outside of the Gulf area to appropriate oil or divert its shipment. The Soviet Union, so it is feared, might back one faction in a civil war and ride into control of somebody's government. Or needing oil for itself and Eastern Europe in some not-so-distant future, the Soviet Union might move over the mountains into Azerbaijan and bring pressure on Iran to ship its oil northward. Or the Soviet Union might drop airborne troops directly into someone's oil fields in order to control them.

Having gained control, the Soviet Union would presumably want to sell oil to the United States and to others outside of its bloc and might be a more reliable supplier than some of the OPEC countries have been. It would have good economic reason to be so; in recent years, more than one-third of its hard-currency earnings have come from the sale of oil and natural gas. We would nevertheless not want to become dependent, and see others become dependent, on the Soviet Union for major amounts of oil. More important than speculating on how the Soviet Union would behave after securing control of some oil fields, or after gaining influence over the disposal of their products, is weighing the chances that she would try to do so, whether by subversion or by force. In politically unstable regions, subversion of governments is a constant possibility. Nevertheless, the Soviet Union has not enjoyed much of a yield from the politically fertile soil around the Persian Gulf. The United States, on the other hand, has been able to maintain commercially satisfactory relations with unfriendly Moslem states even while strongly supporting Israel. (From 1977 to 1980, Algeria and Libya were our third, fourth, or fifth largest suppliers of imported oil.) The past, however, does not guarantee the future; and

I shall ask in the second part of this paper whether a strategy for dealing with military intervention can also deal with the subversion of governments.

Compared to subversion, military intervention by the Soviet Union in Persian Gulf states is a remote possibility, partly because of difficulties the Soviet Union would face. But then we have to prepare militarily to meet remote dangers if their realization would be deeply damaging. We should prepare to deal with internal disruption and with external subversion and military invasion if they would bring major stoppages of oil supplies and thereby produce catastrophe on a world scale.

WHAT IS THE BEST STRATEGY FOR AN RDF?

An RDF should serve vital interests only and in serving them should be guardedly used. Force is a blunt instrument, costly to apply and difficult to control. The United States has many political and economic means for the furtherance of its interests, and they should be marshalled and used before force is brought into play. Even in situations where non-military means do not suffice, we should act militarily only if a strategy promising success can be devised. We should avoid the temptation of resorting to force because nothing else will avail. We should use force only if we can see a way of doing so that will enable us to get our way.

Since the Mexican War, we have fought all of our international wars overseas. In the months following the Soviet Union's invasion of Afghanistan in December of 1979, World War III was talked about as though it would be fought by relatively small forces, mainly American and Russian, in the far-away Middle East. The problem is not to develop a strategy that will enable us to fight such a war. Instead, the problem is to develop a strategy that will help us to avoid having to do so. If military action in the Middle East nevertheless becomes necessary, our policy should seek to confine and limit it, while managing to keep enough oil flowing to meet the minimal needs of importing countries.

How can this be accomplished? Uncertainty about what kind of force we need arises from confusion about its tasks. Confusion about what we may need to do, and feelings of discomfort about our ability to do it, are evident in official and unofficial statements.

—For example, in his State of the Union Address on January 23, 1980, President Carter made a commitment to defend the Persian Gulf region. He later mentioned that we would need the help of allies, apparently without having consulted them. American officials believed that we would have to do most of the fighting, with some of them hoping that Australian, British, and French troops would join in if the going got rough. Grounds for the hope were not given.

—For example, officials of the Department of Defense talked loosely about using tactical nuclear weapons if we should be losing a conventional fight with the Soviet Union in the Gulf area, but just how that would be done and with what expected response was not made clear.

—For example, officials of the Department of Defense signalled that if the Soviet Union confronts us in the Middle East, we may spread the war to areas where we can fight better. The Republican Party's 1980 Platform spells this out. It calls for the limited and permanent presence of American troops in the Gulf area with provision for their rapid reinforcement. The strategy envisions "military action elsewhere at points of Soviet vulnerability—an expression of the classic doctrine of global maneuver." But we are not living in the classical military age. We are living in the nuclear age, and too many soldiers and politicians are still thinking conventional thoughts. Our appropriate aim is not to escalate force indiscriminately and spread wars widely but to de-escalate force and narrow the compass of military conflicts.

—For example, solutions are propounded that will work only if the Soviet Union forebears, at least for a time. The Department of Defense plans to have fourteen Maritime Prepositioning Ships, loaded with equipment for three Marine brigades, deployed in the Indian Ocean and wherever American troops may be needed. The first two ships were funded in FY 1981 and the last one will not be available for at least five years. Noticing this, Jeffrey Record proposed turning the Marines into a light armored, heavy fire-power force that could be moved to a theater quickly. The suggestion seems sensible, but such a force also lies some distance in the future.

Vague references to help from allies, loose talk about using tactical nuclear weapons, odd ideas about spreading wars from one part of the world to another, indulgence in solutions that can work only if the Soviet Union waits until we effect them: Such hesitations and false starts are the inevitable result of hazy notions about what an RDF can and should do.

An RDF should not aim to defeat the Soviet Union in the Middle East, or to fight the Soviet Union to a standstill unless doing so is necessary in order to keep oil flowing. Two quite different forces might accomplish the latter purpose.

One kind of force is a war-fighting, defensive force. Once equipped and ready to go, would a force small and light enough to be able to make a timely appearance on the battlefield be able to stand up to forces of the Soviet Union, say, in Iran? That appears to be the most difficult case and thus the most useful one to examine. I am slow to conclude that we cannot prepare a war-fighting force that would dissuade the Soviet Union from moving into Iran and that could put up a lively fight if dissuasion should fail. The balance of advantages and disadvantages is not as severely tilted in the Soviet Union's favor as is commonly thought.

Major advantages of the Soviet Union are the following:

DISTANCE. The Persian Gulf is about 7,100 miles from the United States and about 1,100 from the Soviet Union.

TROOPS AVAILABLE. The United States has designated 97,700 army and marine corps troops for the RDF, including support units for one airborne division and aviation and logistic support for three marine brigades. The Soviet Union has nine divisions of 80 to 90,000 men on Iran's northern border and a total of 23 mechanized divisions of about 200,000 troops in the Caucasas, Transcaucasas, and Turkmenistan military districts, with attendant air power. The United States has one airborne division and one air assault division of 33,200 troops. The Soviet Union has seven airborne divisions of 49,000 troops.

TIME. The Wolfowitz Report estimates that the United States could place 20,000 troops in Iran in 30 days and that the Soviet Union in the same period could get 100,000 or more there.

The United States, however, would enjoy some important advantages, and the Soviet Union would suffer some serious disadvantages, if they met militarily in Iran. The United States used the "Persian Gulf corridor" during World War II to ship supplies to the Soviet Union. The Soviet Union can reverse the directions of movement and use the same corridor to bring troops and supplies to the south of Iran. Still, the route is a difficult one. Air cover would be hard to maintain. Roads and railroads are poor with narrow passes and bridges and in all more than 300 choke points. Supply stations and maintenance shops barely exist, and water is scarce. Although the Soviet Union has seven airborne divisions, it has the capability to lift only one of them over the 1,100 miles to the Persian Gulf. The Gulf is beyond the reach of most of the Soviet Union's fighter/attack aircraft, if those aircraft are based within the borders of the Soviet Union. Air dropped troops could not be supported by sea, could not be adequately supported by air, and could not be quickly supported by land. Even in the absence of national resistance, Russian troops and supplies would not enjoy easy passage through the Persian Gulf corridor. Nor would the Soviet Union gain advantage from its military occupation of Afghanistan. The Persian Gulf is 700 miles by straight line from Afghanistan. The Soviet Union would have to go through an even longer stretch of hostile territory if it came through Afghanistan than if it came through Iran's northern mountains.

The appropriate RDF for defensive use would be a highly mobile, light-armored, heavy fire-power force. It would be designed to take advantage of the Zagros Mountain barrier, which is 125 miles wide at Iran's northern border. It would also be designed for desert maneuvers that would further delay and deplete Russian forces on their way to the oil fields. Such a force might dissuade the Soviet Union from attacking and put up a good fight if dissuasion should fail.

The United States can build a defensive RDF, but it would not be a force that would best serve its interests in the long run or serve them at all in the short run. Speedy transport of the sizeable forces needed to fight the Soviet Union in the Middle East will be beyond our means until the middle 1980s. And we shall not have light and mobile forces of reasonable size able to use mountains and deserts to defensive advantage for some years to come. Even if the United States had them, climbing mountains and chugging through deserts are not what we want to do. Our interests do not concentrate in those areas, but on the shores washed by the Persian Gulf. We do not want control of countries, but only, if necesary, of the Gulf littoral. The oil is there, and it is there that our superior sea power gives us an advantage over the Soviet Union. We can gain further advantage if a force designed to meet external threats to the oilfields can also deal with internal disruptions.

We should first ask what course of action we will want to take, should disruptions in the Gulf area threaten oil supplies, a much likelier event than invasion by the Soviet Union. Secretary of Defense Brown sometimes spoke as if the problem to be solved were a relatively simple one. Feeling threatened from outside, a country invites us to add some of our force to its own. We do not intend, he said, "to threaten the sovereignty of any country or to intervene where we are not wanted. Rather, mobile, well-equipped, and trained conventional forces are essential to assist allies and other friends should conditions so dictate, and should our assistance be needed." Memories of World Wars I and II linger. The United States joins hands with an ally, uses its ports and airfields, and together they form a united front against a common enemy—a situation sometimes described as "supportive intervention within a permissive environment." But if our vital interests lie in the Middle East, we have to be prepared to solve the difficult problems there. To be prepared to deal with just the easy ones may not be enough.

RDF: A RESPONSE TO INTERNAL DISORDER?

The more difficult problem an RDF may face is that of establishing political order in someone else's country by using American troops. Military forces are not good at solving that problem. They are not instruments of government, something the United States recognized in World War II by preparing military government units to take over from soldiers in the governing of Germany and Japan once the war had been won. In a future oil crisis, the United States may face similar problems. Rather than being invited by a friendly government to give military help, it may be difficult to *find* a government or to know which of several factions promises to become one.

How can we use force with profit where the problem is posed not by someone's army but by someone's government? The answer is to occupy not a country but its oilfields. This changes the problem from one of governance, which we cannot reasonably expect to solve, to one of territorial control. The solution is not perfect, but it is probably the best we can do. The solution is imperfect for two reasons: because military forces from outside cannot prevent saboteurs from disrupting oil production before the troops arrive, and because the prospect of a strong country moving into a weak country's territory is distasteful. Even if military intervention succeeds in ensuring oil supplies in the short term, in undertaking such a course of action, the United States might incur such wrath from so many people that long-term losses would be greater than short-term gains. To avoid this is the task of diplomats, a more important one than the soldiers' because it is a prerequisite to useful military accomplishment. Politically, we should reduce hostility by proclaiming our limited aims, by securing the acquiescence of neighboring countries, and by gaining the open approval of oil-importing countries. After all, to avoid damage to oil fields and facilities is not in the American interest alone. It is in the interest of much of the world. We should also seek to convince countries experiencing disorder that our efforts to keep oil flowing and to keep fields and facilities undamaged are in its own interest and in the interest of whichever of the struggling factions may eventually gain political power.

If the threat to oil exports originates internally, our response should be slow and measured: slow because we want to give a country time to work out its political problems, measured because we want to keep hostility aimed at America as low as possible. Our response should be slow and measured above all because we want everyone to see that we waited as long as we could without risking the collapse of the world's economy. In the end, we shall have to say that for countries to deny their oil to starving economies is no more conscionable than it would be for us to deny food to starving people.

How would American troops operate in their presumably hostile environment? The RDF has to be prepared to force its way into the oil fields, to police them, and to secure the perimeter that encloses them. The perimeter to be defended may be a long one. Saudi Arabia's five principal oil fields cover about 10,000 square miles, or twice the area of Connecticut. The most serious threat, however, may not come from anyone's army or air force but from small bands of saboteurs. The Wolfowitz Report estimates that 65 percent of exported Gulf oil is shipped through three facilities, with eight "critical" pump sites. Ras Tanura and Juaymah are in Saudi Arabia, and Kharg Island lies off Iran. If plans are made, if replacement parts are stocked, and if technicians are available, repairs could in some cases be made "in a

matter of weeks." Otherwise "repairs might take months or years."
When the Report was written, the United States had no such plans. A
properly equipped reserve corps of technicians is as essential to an
RDF as are properly equipped troops.

RDF: A RESPONSE TO EXTERNAL THREATS

A second problem that an RDF would face is that of getting enough
force into some part of the Middle East fast enough to stay the hand
of the Soviet Union. How can the United States hope that a force able
to defend a perimeter against the disorganized forces of a country in
chaos or against the forces of some other Middle East country will be
able to stand up to a determined attack by the Soviet Union? The
answer is by linking a minimal defense to America's strategic deterrent. What we should strive for is an asset-seizing, deterrent force that
can handle both internal and external threats. An asset-seizing, deterrent force is an alternative to a war-fighting, defensive force. The
RDF should be designed to defend against countries of the Middle
East and to deter the Soviet Union.

The deterrent solution has been alluded to by various officials.
Secretary Brown, for example, thought that the United States could
"deter the Soviets" if we kept our heads and supported "the tack the
President has taken." Such statements raise more questions than they
answer, beginning with the question of what is meant by deterrence.
Much recent writing about deterrence lacks precision and clarity. Thus
Brown defined the essence of "our countervailing strategy" as denying "an enemy any plausible goal, no matter how he might attempt to
reach it." For deterrence to work, he continued, "our potential adversaries must be convinced that we possess sufficient military force so
that if they were to start a course of action which could lead to war,
they would be frustrated in their effort to achieve their objective or
suffer so much damage that they would gain nothing by their action."
Brown's usage compounds defense and deterrence. Defense aims to
dissuade someone from doing something by placing obstacles in his
way, by preparing to resist him. Defensive strategies tell a potential
opponent that to overcome the resistance he will encounter will be forbiddingly difficult. Deterrence aims to dissuade someone from doing
something by frightening him. Deterrent strategies tell a potential opponent that although he can seize his objective he may well have to
pay a disproportionate price for it through the damage he can expect
to suffer. Military strategies combine defense and deterrence in
various proportions and ways (ref. introduction).

"Defense" is often confused with "deterrence." When the
Wolfowitz Report refers to deterrence, defense is apparently meant.
"In principle," the Report says, "a deterrent based on mountain
defense should be feasible—especially if the objective is to guarantee

delays and casualties for the attacker.'' Because defense is emphasized over deterrence, help from allies and the use of tactical nuclear weapons are contemplated, along with a mountain defense. Other defense officials have said that if American ground forces, even in small numbers, can get in position before Russian troops arrive, the Soviet Union would have to decide whether to risk confrontation with our troops. Such statements pull toward a strategy of using conventional force as a tripwire and of signalling to the Soviet Union that snapping the wire may activate some of our strategic missiles. These two examples illustrate the sharp practical difference between strategies that rely heavily on defense and strategies that rely heavily on deterrence, as well as the lack of consensus among political leaders and force planners on a strategy for the Rapid Deployment Force.

Either way, dissuasion of the Soviet Union is what is wanted. Can it be achieved in the Persian Gulf area more by deterrence than by defense? How can we hope that deterrence will prevail in a distant area populated by weak and unstable states when so many have come to doubt whether deterrence covers even our European allies? How can we hope that our deterrent will cover more areas and more of our interests in an era of strategic parity than it was thought to cover in an era of American superiority? Superiority in strategic weapons is comforting; parity makes people feel uneasy; and inferiority would be unsettling. Such reactions are psychologically understandable even though they have nothing to do with the logic of deterrence and do not affect the military conditions under which deterrence prevails: namely, the possession of second-strike forces that can do severe damage. The credibility of deterrent threats is insensitive to variations in the size of strategic forces across wide ranges. Why this is true was understood better in the earlier years of the nuclear age than it is now. The logic of deterrence was more clearly lodged in the minds of those who helped develop the strategy than it is in the minds of those who now casually recall it. Unless one country by striking first can reduce another's strategic forces to the point where retaliation can be tolerated, the relative size of opposing forces is irrelevant.

Some Americans are concerned about the vulnerability of our strategic system because its land-based component can be struck and perhaps largely destroyed by the Soviet Union in the middle 1980s. If the Soviet Union did that, the United States would still have thousands of warheads at sea and thousands of bombs in the air. The Soviet Union could not be sure that we would fail to launch on warning or fail to retaliate. Uncertainty deters, and there would be plenty of uncertainty about our response in the minds of the Soviet Union's leaders. If no state can launch a disarming attack with high confidence, force comparisons are irrelevant. That we have 9,200 strategic warheads to the Soviet Union's 6,000 makes us no worse and no better off than we were when the ratio was even more in our favor. That the throw-weight of the Soviet Union's missiles exceeds those of the United States by several times makes the Soviet Union no better and no worse off than it would be were the ratio reversed.

A second-strike force is a necessary, but not a sufficient, condition for deterrence. Given only the military condition, no one can say whether deterrent threats are credible. Whether or not they are depends on what the threats are intended to cover. With second-strike forces, not military but political conditions determine the credibility of deterrence. Credibility does not depend on the ability to retaliate, which cannot be denied. Credibility depends on the will to do so. Deterrence gains in credibility the more highly valued the interests covered appear to be. Major and prolonged reduction of oil exports from the Persian Gulf would pose an absolute threat to the noncommunist world's economy and thus to the United States. With deterrent forces, the country that is absolutely threatened prevails.

That attacks on vital interests will provoke retaliation is not certain. But that does not matter. Uncertainty suffices because if retaliation occurs no one can be sure that limits will hold. In striking at a nuclear power's vital interests, one risks losing all not because thousands of warheads will immediately be fired but because there is some chance, however small, that force will get out of control. Who will risk losing all by attacking a nuclear power's vital interests? Lately, analysts have put too much emphasis on the retaliator's possible inhibitions and too little on the attacker's obvious risks. Credibility is not much of a problem because with vital interests at stake not much credibility is needed. Given an imbalance of interests, the attacker has to believe that the attacked *may* retaliate. That is enough to deter.

Once the military conditions for deterrence are met, the credibility of deterrence becomes a political question. What are the political conditions that must obtain if deterrent threats are to be credited? First, the would-be attacker must be made to see that the deterrer believes that the interests at stake are vital ones. Thus, by the presence of American troops, the United States stretches its deterrent to cover Western Europe. The presence of our troops makes the extent of American interest manifest. In a conflict between two countries equipped with second-strike forces, the balance of interests determines how the "balance of resolve," to use Glenn Snyder's apt phrase, is measured. Second, political stability must prevail in the area the deterrent is intended to cover. If the threat to a regime is mainly from internal factions, then an outside power may risk supporting one of them even in the face of deterrent threats. The credibility of a deterrent requires both that interests be seen to be vital and that it is the attack from outside that threatens them. Given these conditions, the would-be attacker provides both the reason to retaliate and the target for retaliation.

The first of the political conditions for credible deterrence is that the interest of the deterrer be seen to be a vital one. From the American standpoint, Persian Gulf oil meets this condition. The Soviet Union's gaining control of the Gulf area would be comparable to its seizing territory in Western Europe or Japan. American vital interests lie in these three areas, a fact that is easily seen by the Soviet Union as well as by others. If in a crisis, we were to put troops in the oil fields, it would make the depth of our interest, the extent of our determination, and the strength of our will manifest.

The deterrer needs a reason to retaliate, and the United States has reason enough. The deterrer also needs a target for retaliation. That we would strike if the Soviet Union tried to turn the Persian Gulf oil faucet off is sufficiently credible. But if saboteurs were to do it, who would we strike? The answer to that question helps to define the extent of the force required to serve as a tripwire. To rely on a tripwire force makes people uneasy. A thicker wire may make us feel more secure, but the point to emphasize is that the wire must be thick enough so that not a loose band of irregulars but only a national military force can snap it. This then gives the United States the target for retaliation and establishes the conditions under which deterrence prevails.

An asset-seizing, deterrent force solves the puzzles and problems discussed above. With an RDF designed for deterrence, the United States can achieve the rapid deployment that will enable the Force to live up to its title. Getting there first is more important than enlarging the Force beyond the point where it can perform its internal police and its external tripwire functions. Thickening the Force for the sake of our psychological comfort is less important than keeping the Force lean to aid its speedy deployment. On October 1, 1980, General P. X. Kelley, the first Commander of the RDF, told the House Committee on the Budget that although "we have a significant airlift capability in the Military Airlift Command, it is not sufficient to put a capital 'R' in 'Rapid'." To do so, he wisely added, "is one of my primary goals." Some deprecate the RDF by saying that "it will get there first with the least." But only that is required in order to implement a deterrent strategy against the Soviet Union. The effectiveness of a deterrent strategy depends on the credibility of threats and not on the ability to defend a position by force. Thus the 4,500 American troops in West Berlin cannot defend the city; they are there for the sake of deterrence.

With an RDF designed for deterrence, the United States can gain and hold the initiative. President Carter said, and others agreed, that we "cannot afford to let the Soviets choose either the terrain or the tactics to be used by any other country—a nation that might be invaded, their neighbors, our allies, or ourselves." With a defensive, war-fighting strategy how can we avoid letting the Soviet Union do the choosing? The answer that Secretary Brown, unnamed Defense officials, and the Republican platform gave is that we should strike the Soviet Union at places of our own choosing. The northern flank of NATO has been mentioned as a place we might choose. Surely the prospect of attacking there, if the Soviet Union should attack in the Middle East, neither delights the Norwegians nor scares the Russians. A defensive force calls for tactics of maneuver and diversion, with attendant risks that small and local confrontations become enlarged and spread. A deterrent force enables the United States to choose the territory to be seized and the strategy for holding it without enlarging and spreading the conflict.

With an RDF designed for deterrence, we can define and limit the conditions that call for the use of nuclear weapons. When military officials discuss their options, they are said to use "words like *horrendous* and *scary* and raise the specter of World War III." Secretary Brown and others, when they talked vaguely about using tactical nuclear weapons, invoked visions of force spiralling out of control. But nuclear weapons demand that their use be carefully planned, limited, and controlled. With a defensive strategy, the use of nuclear weapons is decided upon according to the fortunes of battle. With a deterrent strategy, the conditions for the use of nuclear weapons are clearly defined and advertised. A deterrent strategy, properly implemented, puts the Soviet Union on notice that maintaining a substantial flow of oil from Persian Gulf states is a vital American interest. Both the Soviet Union and the United States have been wary of direct confrontations over vital interests in all of the years since the Second World War. If such interference should ever occur, we need not engage in a riot of violence. Americans tend to emphasize their national vulnerabilities—the vulnerability of tankers going through the Strait of Hormuz to submarine attacks and the vulnerability of critical pumping sites to air attacks. The Soviet Union also suffers vulnerabilities. We need not threaten to destroy a country in order to deter it. Nothing about a deterrent strategy works against letting the punishment fit the crime. A deterrent strategy entails no use of nuclear weapons, if it succeeds, and can entail a limited and selective use, if it fails.

CONCLUSION

How well will an asset-seizing, deterrent strategy be liked? Probably not very well, despite its many advantages. Two questions should be asked. Can we improve it? Is a war-fighting, defensive strategy preferable? I can reply to the first question by saying that I hope others can improve the strategy I have described. The problem of developing a deterrent strategy to cover vital interests is well worked over. The problem of applying the strategy in areas of political instability and, if necessary, without the cooperation of local states has hardly been touched. More thought should be given to the possibilities.

The answer to the second question requires reflecting on the two strategies. For nine major reasons, I think that an asset-seizing, deterrent strategy is the better one.

—First, a force for fighting the Soviet Union would not be suited to the likeliest case: namely, political instability in Persian Gulf countries. A force for deterring the Soviet Union should be able to accomplish its three major tasks—coping with political disruptions, defending against attacks from within the Middle East, and deterring the Soviet Union.

—Second, a force for fighting would have to be much larger than a force for deterring the Soviet Union. The difficulties of achieving speed of movement, of maintaining logistic support, and of furnishing battlefield replacements would mount.

—Third, with an RDF designed for deterrence, the United States can avoid calling for help from reluctant allies except for naval support, the use of facilities, and enough cooperation to show that the enterprise is a collective one. The United States is a global power, and the task of a global power, sensibly defined, is to take care of regions where its vital interests lie if the countries in those regions cannot take care of themselves. West European countries and Japan can well do more to take care of themselves, while the United States tends to its own interests as well as theirs in the Persian Gulf. For the credibility of deterrence, situations should be kept simple and clear. The participation of allies in military operations would work against this.

—Fourth, for the United States to force its way into oil fields would be a politically costly and risky move. The cost and risk cannot be avoided no matter what strategy is followed. An RDF designed for deterring rather than for fighting the Soviet Union would, however, eliminate one cost and reduce risks. It would eliminate the need for a permanent military base in the Gulf region, a base that would be needed to prepare to fight a regional war against the Soviet Union. An American base in the region would draw opposition from many states and be a continual source of irritation. Moreover, a permanent American military presence would easily trigger action by the RDF even if in the absence of a base such action might have been avoided.

—Fifth, a defensive force could involve the United States in major fighting against the Soviet Union under conditions likely to be more difficult for us than for them. A war-fighting, defensive force may be able to keep Russian troops away from the oil fields, but this is a task added to that of securing the oil fields. The design of the RDF follows from its purpose and its tasks. The tasks are demanding, and we cannot make them less so. To keep oil flowing is the essential objective. Any objective added to it unnecessarily increases the demands on the Force.

—Sixth, both a defensive and a deterrent force would be at least somewhat dissuasive. Dissuasion is what we want to achieve by whatever combination of deterrence and defense. As the probability that a country's military moves can be effectively countered increases, the likelihood of its making those moves decreases. That statement suggests a credibility question that is seldom asked. Would a defensive force look strong enough to dissuade the Soviet Union from challenging it? Would Russian leaders believe that we would be willing and able to fight the Soviet Union to a standstill in the mountains and deserts of Iran? The Soviet Union is likelier to test an American defensive force than to test a deterrent force. The Soviet Union's leaders, operating in their own backyard, are in a good position to control escalation. They can reduce the scale of the fighting or withdraw behind their borders if force threatens to get out of control. Deterring the Soviet Union is less risky than fighting defensively against it.

—Seventh, an American deterrent strategy would be highly credible for reasons that I have suggested. We would be protecting a prize of undoubted value. In protecting it, we would not be able to fight to a very high level. If Russian forces challenged us directly, and if their force were about to overcome ours and take control of the oil fields, leaders of the Soviet Union would have to believe that in response, we might do something highly damaging to them. They do not have to believe that we will, but they do have to believe that we might—all the more so because if we pass, we lessen the credibility of American deterrence worldwide.

—Eighth, a defensive strategy cannot serve the United States while the forces for its implementation are being built. This, it is commonly agreed, will take fire or more years. In the meantime, we will have to rely on deterrence. Even those less fond of deterrence than I am may be persuaded that deterrence, if not as reassuring as defense, is better than defeat. If we can rely on deterrence for five years, why not rely on it longer?

—Ninth, an RDF designed for deterrence would be an oil force, useful mainly for the protection of our vital economic interest. It would not be useful where a great deal of force is needed and less than vital interests are threatened. Deterrent threats would then not be credible. The best policy uses the least force that will achieve its objective. A single-purpose force is better than a multi-purpose one. The former is likelier to remain uncommitted until the moment of its intended use arrives and thus to be available when needed most.

Military planners will prefer a larger defensive force over a smaller deterrent force designed mainly for one purpose. Fighting for one's ends seems, misleadingly I have argued, less risky than relying on deterrence. And military planners believe they should give the President more rather than fewer options. Because the strategy I advocate does not give the military a traditional and congenial role, its adoption depends on civilians taking the lead. This is as it should be. Soldiers and sailors, like civil servants, follow their own interests and habits unless they are told what to do.

Where vital interests are at issue, an RDF should be used to create a situation in which deterrence applies. I have sought to show how this can be done even in situations customarily thought to be at least amenable to deterrent strategies—that is, where internal chaos makes it unclear how to retaliate and against whom. The strategy does this by physically staking out our claim to the vital resource, by establishing a perimeter, and by saying that if the Soviet Union attacks so hard that we cannot hold, we shall retaliate against appropriate targets. Our troops on the spot make our vital interest manifest, and thus deterrent threats become credible. This is a strategy. It leaves numerous practical questions unanswered. What should be the design of the Force for carrying the strategy out? How can the required speed be achieved? How big should the Force be? How heavily equipped? What is the best way to defend a perimeter against indigenous attacks? These are matters for discussion and decision. This essay is about the strategy of the RDF, and not about its design. Its design, though not its details, follows from the strategy. The strategy, if accepted, tells us what we need to do, but not just how to do it.

Horizontal Escalation:
Sour Notes of a Recurrent Theme

JOSHUA M. EPSTEIN

INTRODUCTION

The deterrence of Soviet military aggression has been the basis of American national security policy since the Truman Administration. The means proffered to secure containment, however, have changed with each Administration since. But they have all partaken of two archetypal approaches: the symmetrical and the asymmetrical. The historian John Lewis Gaddis has characterized them succintly:

"Symmetrical response simply means reacting to threats to the balance of power at the same location, time, and level of the original provocation."

"Asymmetrical response involves shifting the location or nature of one's reaction onto terrain better suited to the application of one's strength against adversary weakness."[1]

Following the invasion of Afghanistan, former President Carter committed the United States to the deterrence of further Soviet aggression in the Persian Gulf region. While that deterrent commitment was affirmed intact by the Reagan Administration, the symmetrical thrust of the Carter Doctrine[2] was not; whether one dubs it "horizon-

Dr. Epstein is a Council on Foreign Relations International Affairs Fellow. This article was written while he was a Post-Doctoral Fellow at Harvard University's Center for International Affairs. While the author bears sole responsibility for all views herein expressed, he wishes to acknowledge the contributions of Barry R. Posen, Steven E. Miller, John Mearsheimer, Robert Art, Kenneth Waltz, and Melissa Healy.

[1] John Lewis Gaddis, "Containment: Its Past and Future," *International Security*, Spring 1981, Vol. 5, No. 4, p. 80. For a thorough analysis of American oscillations between the two approaches, see Gaddis' *Strategies of Containment* (New York: Oxford University Press, 1982).

[2] ". . . an attempt by any outside force to gain control of the Persian Gulf region— will be *repelled* by any means necessary, including military force" (emphasis mine). See 1980 State of the Union Address, U.S. Congress, Senate, Committee on Foreign Relations, "U.S. Security Interests and Policies in Southwest Asia," Hearings before the Subcommittee on Near Eastern and South Asian Affairs, Ninety-Sixth Congress, second session, February–March 1980, p. 350.

tal escalation'' or something else[3], the Reagan Administration's attraction to an asymmetrical conventional strategy for the Persian Gulf was quickly evident.

Shortly after taking office, Reagan Administration strategists reportedly issued guidelines to the military "to hit the Soviets at their remote and vulnerable outposts in retaliation for any cutoff of Persian Gulf oil." In Secretary Weinberger's view, "our deterrent capability in the Persian Gulf is linked with our ability and willingness to shift or widen the war to other areas."[4]

One possibility cited at the time was "to threaten the Soviet brigade in Cuba if Moscow or its surrogates move into the Persian Gulf." Direct conventional defense would certainly be attempted "whatever the odds," but the prospects for symmetrical response were accounted as grim "given the Soviets' inherent geographical advantages and their superior number of available ground forces."[5]

The same language was carried into the Administration's first Defense Posture Statement a year later.[6] But, in the interim, the strategy seemed to have assumed larger proportions. "If Soviet forces were to invade the Persian Gulf region, the United States should have the capability to hit back there or in Cuba, Libya, Vietnam, or the Asian land mass of the Soviet Union itself."[7] The list of remote "Soviet" vulnerabilities was longer and the Soviet homeland itself had emerged as a potential target for horizontal escalation. Similarly, the procurement of two additional large-deck nuclear aircraft carrier battlegroups was advocated not merely for their capacity to lash back at Soviet weak points, but, on the contrary, for the alleged "capability of a 15 carrier 600 ship Navy to fight and win in areas of *highest* Soviet capability"[8] (emphasis mine). But, as ever more challenging horizontal options emerged, the Administration's commitment to direct (symmetrical) defense was reaffirmed: "whatever the circumstances, we should be prepared to introduce American forces into the region

[3] "geographical escalation" and "war-widening strategy" are other names sometimes used.

[4] George C. Wilson, "U.S. May Hit Soviet Outposts in Event of Oil Cutoff," *The Washington Post*, July 17, 1981, p. 1.

[5] *Ibid.*

[6] For example, ". . . even if the enemy attacked at only one place, *we* might choose not to restrict ourselves to meeting aggression on its own immediate front. . . . A wartime strategy that confronts the enemy, were he to attack, with the risk of our counteroffensive against his vulnerable points strengthens deterrence and serves the defensive peacetime strategy." Caspar W. Weinberger, Secretary of Defense, *Annual Report to the Congress for Fiscal Year 1983* (hereafter referred to as FY 83 Posture Statement), pp. 116, 117.

[7] Leslie H. Gelb, "Reagan's Military Budget puts Emphasis on a Buildup of U.S. Global Power," *The New York Times*, Feb. 7, 1982, pp. Z6, Z7.

[8] John Lehman, Secretary of the Navy, "America's Growing Need for Seaborne Air Bases," *The Wall Street Journal*, March 30, 1982.

should it appear that the security of access to Persian Gulf oil is threatened."[9]

Both direct defense *and* asymmetrical response were apparently embraced; under the latter, not just points of Soviet weakness, but points of extreme Soviet strength as well were contemplated as horizontal targets. This "do everything" quality of the articulated strategy was compounded by the Administration's pointed rejection of planning around any specific set of prototypical (or real) contingencies (e.g., the $1 + 1/2$ or $2 + 1/2$ war sizing devices)[10] and its exhortations to prepare for "prolonged conventional wars simultaneously in several parts of the globe."[11]

Predictably, when the military was called upon to attach a price tag to the strategy, it was whopping: hundreds of billions—by some estimates $750 billion[12]—more than the $1.6 trillion Reagan Five Year Defense Plan. The strategy's requirements were reportedly "so grandiose that the Joint Chiefs of Staff says carrying them out would require 50 percent more troops, fighter planes, and aircraft carriers than are now deployed, along with another Marine amphibious force."[13]

It was against that sobering budgetary backdrop that William Clark, in the National Security Advisor's first major speech, announced, "there is not enough money available to eliminate all the risks overnight."[14] And having thus resurfaced, the budget constraint has since imposed a slackening in the planned pace of American military growth, in turn stimulating a more animated debate on the ranking of defense priorities.

Basic questions remain unresolved, however, concerning the advisability of a "war-widening strategy" *in principle*, particularly about its horizontal counter-offense component. And those underlying questions are not addressed merely by admitting a cutback in the pace of funding; the more basic issue is whether this course, this entire strategic direction, is advisable at all. Moreover, until that issue is settled, the debate on program priorities can only founder.

---

[9] George C. Wilson, "U.S. Defense Paper Cites Gap Between Rhetoric, Intentions," *The Washington Post*, May 27, 1982, p. 1.

[10] *FY 83 Posture Statement*, pp. 115-116. On the $1 + 1/2$ and $2 + 1/2$ war concepts, as peacetime planning devices, see William W. Kaufmann, "The Defense Budget" in Joseph A. Pechman (ed.) *Setting National Priorities, the 1983 Budget* (Washington, D.C.: The Brookings Institution, 1982), p. 81.

[11] "Flood and Leak at the Pentagon," *The New York Times*, Feb. 1, 1982, p. A-14. Richard Halloran, "Needed: A Leader for the Joint Chiefs," *The New York Times*, Feb. 1, 1982.

[12] Robert W. Komer, "Maritime Strategy vs. Coalition Defense," *Foreign Affairs*, Summer 1982, pp. 1128-1129. See also, "Flood and Leak."

[13] George C. Wilson, "U.S. Defense Paper."

[14] *Ibid*.

Recognizing that some—by no means all—within the Administration have "stepped back" to reexamine the strategy's appeal, it may therefore be constructive to raise some of the unanswered questions about "horizontal escalation". Five seem especially basic:

First, what is horizontal escalation supposed to do; what is the goal in an operational sense? Second, given some relatively concrete goal, how is the "proper" horizontal target selected? Related to that, in what ways might horizontal escalation affect the probability of vertical escalation by the U.S. or Soviet Union? Fourth, what are the risks of "counter-horizontal escalation" *by* the Soviets? Finally, are there otherwise avoidable diplomatic costs associated with the strategy?

Not only do these questions deserve thought, but the Administration's attraction to the strategy seems to rest on military premises that are questionable in their own right.

Having discussed these issues, the most important question of all—that of credibility—will be addressed. But, let us begin at the beginning.

THE QUESTION OF WARTIME OPERATIONAL GOALS

Without some sense of the operational goal of a military action, it is not possible to select its targets. Neither, *a fortiori,* is it possible to derive the forces required or to assess the adequacy of those already in being. While "carrying the war to other arenas" and "hitting the Soviets at their vulnerable outposts" may sound clear enough at first blush, such phrases in fact provide little guidance to the military planner, charged with designing a force, or to the public, charged with paying for it. What, exactly, is the goal of "horizontal escalation"?

Is it *to destroy something* in order *to punish* the Soviets, perhaps holding out the prospect of further punishment unless they comply with American terms, whatever those might be? Is it *to take something hostage,* hoping thereby to bargain a return to the pre-war status quo or some other political arrangement? Obviously, not both goals can be achieved: one cannot hold hostage what one has already destroyed.

Although it is hard to imagine many Soviet assets whose military acquisition would *compensate* the West for the loss of access to Persian Gulf oil, in principle, compensatory acquisition is another possible goal, one distinct from punishment or hostage-taking for bargaining purposes.

Perhaps the most intuitively appealing goals for horizontal escalation would be to *inhibit or to induce redeployments of Soviet forces,* thereby improving Western prospects for conventional defense in the original contingency. The appeal is natural enough: attacked at point A, one counters at point B in order (i) to "fix" Soviet forces at point B, preventing their use as reinforcements at point A, or (ii) to force the

Soviets to shift forces from A to B.

In the context of European war, the former has long been among the Navy's arguments for "opening up a second theater" by offensive fleet operations against Soviet Naval bases in the Western Pacific.[15] And, it is true that in a protracted conventional war between NATO and the Warsaw Pact, Soviet ground forces arrayed opposite China might be redeployed to the West as a third (or fourth) echelon of the Soviet European offensive. "Opening up a second theater" in the Pacific would allegedly tie down those Soviet forces, improving NATO's chances for conventional defense.

In fact, however, the Soviets' freedom to redeploy to Europe—or the Persian Gulf for that matter—their divisions on the Sino-Soviet border would depend primarily on the posture of the Chinese Army, not the US Navy. Admittedly, the Soviets might reinforce their Pacific Fleet's air forces with airpower normally deployed inland opposite China. But what real role could the corresponding Soviet ground forces play in either the Pacific sea battle or in defending Soviet naval shore facilities? A role significant enough to "fix" over forty ground divisions? That seems implausible.

Rather than inhibiting Soviet redeployments by "fixing" Soviet forces, geographical escalation could, in principle, *induce* Soviet redeployments. The object in that case would be to draw Soviet forces out of the original contingency, improving Western chances for success there. One open question in this regard is simply: when?

The Reagan five-year defense plan will, by definition, take half a decade to realize. At the end of that period, horizontal escalation might succeed in *forcing* Soviet wartime reallocations, but only if, in the interim, some ceiling on Soviet military growth had been reached. Otherwise, what's to prevent the Soviets from anticipating the strategy by simply *adding forces* in each theater over that interim period? After all, when the Sino-Soviet split presented them with "a new theater" (i.e., their Chinese frontier), the Soviets didn't shift many forces. True to Russian form, they essentially built. And, unless there's some "limit to growth," it may be hard to *force* Soviet reallocations, at least between theaters in the USSR.

To be sure, there may be military constraints in the Soviet offing. But if there are, the Administration has certainly not suggested them by its review of the Soviet military buildup and its projections of continuing growth as Soviet military *investment*[16] comes to fruition. In short, a reallocative goal for horizontal escalation seems to entail a

Soviet military growth ceiling, while the Administration's Soviet projections seem to deny the existence of any such limits.[17]

TARGETS: SOVIET VALUE, U.S. DIVERSION, AND VERTICAL ESCALATION

Punishment (destructive retaliation), hostage-taking, compensatory acquisition, fixing Soviet forces, or inducing their redeployment; these may not be the only possible rationales for horizontal escalation.

But, whatever its operational goal (punishment, hostage-taking, etc.), the compellent effectiveness of the horizontal action will surely depend upon the value placed *by the Soviets* upon its target. After all, the mere fact that a Soviet outpost is vulnerable doesn't make it valuable, as Secretary of Defense Weinberger recognizes: "If it (the counteroffensive) is to offset the enemy's attack, it should be launched against territory or assets that are of an importance to him comparable to the ones he is attacking."[18]

In practice, however, it may be difficult to identify a "horizontal target" which is at once of sufficient Soviet value to compel the behavior sought, but at the same time is not of such great value as to stimulate rash and grossly disproportionate (e.g., nuclear) Soviet responses.

It is an open question whether offensive sea control (attacking Soviet Fleets in their home waters) would be the most efficient way to secure Western sea lines of communication.[19] But, even if it otherwise were, such offensive naval operations could well run the nuclear risk, and not simply because they would involve hitting the Soviet homeland. Beyond that, in conducting offensive operations against either the Soviet Northern or Pacific Fleets, it might be difficult for the U.S. Navy to avoid sinking Soviet strategic ballistic missile submarines (SSBNs). And if American operations were to degrade, even inadvertently and by conventional means, the Soviets' strategic nuclear retaliatory capabilities, the Soviets might not *interpret* those operations as "conventional sea control," but as conventional precur-

---

[17] Some might argue that this criticism isn't fair because it presents horizontal escalation as a strategy toward which the US is building for the future when, in fact, they will claim, horizontal escalation is only an interim strategy until the U.S. can build up greater conventional defenses in the Gulf. But, if horizontal escalation is an interim measure with direct conventional defense the ultimate goal, then why is the Administration spending so much on carrier battle groups for "outyear" counteroffensives and so much less on programs directly related to Gulf defense (e.g., airlift and sealift) today?

[18] *FY 83 Posture Statement*, p. I-16.

[19] See *Navy Budget Issues* and Congressional Budget Office, *The U.S. Sea Control Mission: Forces, Capabilities, and Requirements*, June 1977. Still among the most concise essays on the factors involved in evaluating offense, defense, and requirements in each case is Arnold M. Kuzmack, *Where Does the Navy Go From Here?* (Washington, D.C.: The Brookings Institution, 1972).

sors to nuclear attack—conventionally executed nuclear damage-limiting first strikes, if you will.[20]

As for targets of too little value, were the Soviets to end up with control of oil fields in the Persian Gulf, they could certainly afford to buy a new merchant fleet,[21] had theirs been "swept from the seas" in bristling riposte to Gulf aggression. And regarding counteroffensives against Cuba, suppose, just for the sake of argument, that the Soviets were offered a straight trade: They "give up" Cuba and, in return, they get Iran's (or Saudi Arabia's) oil. Would Moscow turn it down? What assurance is there that, behind the compulsory fulminations, the Kremlin wouldn't be willing to let Cuba take a "horizontal beating" if it meant control of Gulf oil? And, if the Soviets would accept that trade, how "offsetting" would horizontal escalation against Cuba, in fact, be?

Not only may Administration strategists have exaggerated Cuba's value to Moscow, but horizontal escalation against Cuba was reportedly envisioned "if Moscow *or its surrogates* move into the Persia Gulf"[22] (emphasis mine). Are the Iraqis Soviet "surrogates?" Does that mean they have no goals of their own? Would the threat of American retaliation against Cuba (or anyone else for that matter) deter them? Would it deter Communist elements in Iran? The Syrians? The PDRY (South Yemen)?

Even if Moscow wished to bridle any of its surrogates lest we respond against "Cuba, Libya, Vietnam, or the Soviet Union itself," could they do it?

The main point, however, is that even with clear goals for horizontal escalation in mind, the selection of an appropriate target seems to require knowledge of the *Kremlin's* valuations. An uncertain affair even in peacetime, the problem would be compounded in war when, among other things, values change.[23] In addition to the problem of Soviet valuation, there is the problem of U.S. diversion.

Although contingency-counting has been rejected under the Administration's intellectual reforms, horizontal escalation nonetheless ensures that the U.S. confronts two contingencies (main plus horizontal) where it might have faced only one (main). And, even assuming that a horizontal target of the "proper" *Soviet* value were selected, the appropriate action against that target could require a significant

---

[20] By far the most comprehensive study of this important problem is Barry R. Posen, "Inadvertent Nuclear War? Escalation and NATO's Northern Flank," *International Security*, Fall 1982, Vol. VII, No. 2.

[21] Robert W. Komer, "Maritime Strategy vs. Coalition Defense," p. 1131.

[22] George C. Wilson, "U.S. May Hit Soviet Outposts," p. 1.

[23] This, and many other problems of conflict termination, are discussed in Fred Charles Ikle, *Every War Must End* (New York: Columbia University Press, 1971).

commitment of American forces, over and above those allocated to direct defense in the initial contingency.

The obvious question, therefore, is whether the U.S. would have to divert to horizontal offensives, forces that might otherwise have been applied (initially or as reinforcements) to the main defense, reducing the latter's prospects for success. If so, would not the strategy make it more likely that the U.S. find itself under pressure either (a) to concede defeat in the main contingency or (b) to use nuclear weapons there?

On the horizontal front, it should be noted that unless these counteroffensives are to be initiated preemptively; i.e., *before* the "provoking" Soviet attack—an option Mr. Weinberger has explicitly rejected[24]—then they will probably not achieve tactical surprise. Obviously, they might, but it would be imprudent to design forces on that assumption. And, on the prudent assumption that surprise would not be achieved, the horizontal target might enjoy a number of classical warning advantages (e.g., prepared defenses, cover, dispersal, etc.). These could well exacerbate the diversion problem and with it, the unpleasant problems of choice between humiliation and vertical (i.e., nuclear) escalation.[25]

Doubtless such considerations played a role in the Services' costing of the strategy: to avoid problems of diversion, one buys *much larger forces*.[26] But now that the Administration has essentially admitted that the forces necessary to hedge against the diversion problem are too expensive, retention of the strategy may be too risky.

Some, of course, argue just the reverse, that "because the development and acquisition of new weapons might be delayed, *more* emphasis would be placed on such flexible tactics as 'geographical escalation.' "[27] (Emphasis mine).

Admittedly, geographical escalation conjures up attractive images of "regaining the initiative", "turning the tables", and "making the Russians play by our rules." But this ought to suggest a further problem; namely, what if the Russians *do* decide to "play by our rules," and proceed to "counter-horizontal escalate" themselves?

---

[24] *FY 83 Posture Statement*, pp. 110–111.

[25] Indeed, in the worst of both worlds, the U.S. would divert so much force from the Gulf as to come under enormous pressure to use nuclear weapons there, while applying the large resultant counteroffensive force in such a way as to put the Soviets under equal pressure to use nuclear weapons on the horizontal front. Professor Huntington's proposal for a prompt conventional counteroffensive into Eastern Europe seems to invite this dangerous situation. See Samuel P. Huntington, "The Renewal of Strategy" in Samuel P. Huntington (Ed.), *The Strategic Imperative: New Policies for American Security* (Cambridge: Ballinger 1982).

[26] This is just the "flip side" of the Soviet solution discussed above. To avoid dangerous diversions (in the Soviet case, forced; in the U.S. case, self-imposed), build.

[27] Richard Halloran, "Reagan Aides see Pressure to Cut 1984 Military Budget," *The New York Times*, July 13, 1982, p. 1.

THE PROBLEM OF COUNTER-HORIZONTAL ESCALATION

Although the possibility was recognized by some Westerners at the time,[28] Khrushchev did not play "the Berlin card" in the Cuban missile crisis of 1962. Faced with an American "war-widening" move against Cuba, his successors might behave rather differently. One might imagine the following scenario: the Soviets invade Iran; we "hit" Cuba (or the Soviet brigade there); they "hit" West Berlin (or our brigade there). Then what? You got him to "play by your rules"; are you better off?

Is Cuba more valuable to the Soviets than West Berlin is to the Federal Republic? Would European leaderships dutifully "fall in" behind further American "initiatives" at that point?

Even assuming that the Soviets could attack the Berlin brigade "surgically," without killing West German citizens (the legal status of all West Berliners), would the U.S. allow it to be decimated without further response? If West Berlin had been sealed off, then at some point the brigade's survival might require airlift. Would the Soviets allow another Berlin airlift, or would they shoot down Western transports this time? Perhaps the airlift would "fight its way in," suppressing East German air defenses at a time of great tension and high military alert.

Whether or not one finds this particular scenario to be plausible, the point is that forcing the Soviets to "play by these rules" may not be in our interest; move and counter-move might quickly bring both sides to unforeseen and very unstable situations. And reversing the spiral might be exceedingly difficult.

DIPLOMACY FOR MILITARY PREMISES

Not only crisis management, but peacetime diplomacy as well may be compromised by a policy of "horizontal escalation."

The Soviets, Secretary Weinberger states, "can coerce by threatening—implicitly or explicitly—to apply military force".[29] But, mightn't a strategy of horizontal escalation, *predicated on the assumption that direct defense is infeasible,* facilitate that coercion?

In the Persian Gulf, one can only render Soviet threats the *more* credible, their local audiences the *more* compliant, by suggesting that direct conventional defense is unmanageable, "given the Soviets' inherent geographical advantages in the Persian Gulf region and their superior number of available ground forces."[30]

This, moreover, is a simplistic and misleading characterization of the Soviet-American conventional balance in the region. Geographical

---

[28] Herman Kahn, *On Escalation: Metaphors and Scenarios* (New York: Praeger, 1965), pp. 86–87.
[29] *FY 83 Posture Statement*, p. I-10.
[30] George C. Wilson, "U.S. May Hit Soviet Outposts," p. 1.

proximity does not *per se* constitute Soviet military access, and static pre-war "bean-counting" cannot reflect dynamic wartime effectiveness. The latter always depends on operational factors such as terrain, available avenues of advance (and their vulnerability), logistics, coordination, reconnaissance, flexibility, leadership, morale, combat technology, and troop skill. That fact is consistently bemoaned on the U.S. side, but is virtually neglected when assessing the Soviet threat. When such factors are accounted on *both* sides, in a balanced and systematic way, the prevalent assessment is seen to be overly pessimistic.[31]

Furthermore, while there are compelling reasons for the U.S. to avoid reliance on nuclear employment, the Soviets surely cannot ignore that possibility. And this, too, contributes to deterrence.

But does the attraction to "horizontal escalation" derive only from the unwarranted assumptions (a) that conventional defense is utterly infeasible and (b) that Soviet nuclear developments have stripped the U.S. strategic triad of deterrent value? Perhaps. But it often seems as though the true motivations run deeper—as though the advocates, at bottom, have turned away from the entire concept of limited war.[32]

WINNING

MacArthur said that "in war, there is no substitute for victory." Neither, of course, is there any substitute for national survival. While at various points, the Reagan Administration seems to have unqualifiedly adopted MacArthur's heroic dictum, at other points its strategists seem to be aware of the unheroic fact of nuclear life—"the difficulty that war invites the belligerents to regard the contest as mortal and to continue it until they are reduced to ruins."[33]

Over a decade ago, in an essay called "Peace Through Escalation?", Dr. Fred Ikle, now Under Secretary of Defense for Policy, put the enduring dilemma this way:

"If a nation can overwhelm all of the enemy's forces by escalating a war, the fighting will of course be brought to an end. . . . Short of inflicting such total defeat, successful escalation would have to induce the enemy

[31] Joshua M. Epstein, "Soviet Vulnerabilities in Iran and the RDF Deterrent," *International Security*, Fall 1981, Vol. VI, No. 2. See also Dennis Ross, "Considering Soviet Threats to the Persian Gulf," *International Security*, Fall 1981, Vol. VI, No. 2, and Keith A. Dunn, "Constraints on the USSR in Southwest Asia," *Orbis*, Fall 1981.

[32] In Secretary of the Navy John Lehman's view, the rapid growth of Soviet naval power has "eliminated the option of planning for a regionally limited naval war with the Soviet Union. It will be instantaneously a global naval conflict." Richard Halloran, "Reagan Selling Navy Budget as Heart of Military Mission," *The New York Times*, April 11, 1982.

[33] William W. Kaufmann, "Limited Warfare," in William W. Kaufmann (ed.) *Military Policy and National Security* (Princeton, New Jersey: Princeton University Press, 1956), p. 112.

government to accept the proffered peace terms. The trouble is, the greater the enemy's effort and cost in fighting a war, the more will he become committed to his own conditions for peace. Indeed, inflicting more damage on the enemy might cause him to stiffen his peace terms. . . . It is these opposed effects of escalation that make it so hard to plan for limited wars and to terminate them."[34]

In order, as Secretary Weinberger desires, "to prevent the uncontrolled spread of hostilities,"[35] it is obviously critical that the Soviets never see an advantage in opening new theaters or geographically widening a local war themselves. In that sense, a strategy of limited war, in fact does, and always has, required "horizontal" capabilities: 'you will not succeed at the initial point of attack and we will not be drawn off by attacks elsewhere; you must fight here and you cannot win here, so stop; indeed, don't start.'[36]

While multi-theater capabilities sufficient to *deny* the Soviets a war-widening strategy are thus essential to channel and limit conventional conflict should deterrence fail, it is far from clear that an American policy of *initiating* such expansions would foster military control or wartime diplomacy. It might, but having reviewed the risks, Dr. Ikle's observation is worth recalling:

"It is hard to say whether treason or adventurism has brought more nations to the graveyard of history. The record is muddied, because when adventurists have destroyed a nation they usually blamed "traitors" for the calamity.[37]

CREDIBILITY

If a strategy is to deter aggression, that strategy must be *credible.* We and our potential adversaries must believe at least two things about it. First, both sides must believe that, were deterrence to fail, the United States would actually operate its forces in accord with the strategy. Second, both must believe that such operations would be likely to achieve American wartime goals.

Failure on the second count often results in failure on the first. For example, Massive Retaliation, America's first great experiment in asymmetrical response, failed on the second requirement. The American goal was to contain Soviet expansion at military costs acceptable to the United States. But the strategy suggested that the U.S. would run a high risk of unacceptable damage in response to

---

[34] Fred Charles Ikle, *Op. Cit.,* pp. 41–42.

[35] *FY 83 Posture Statement,* p. III-101.

[36] For a fuller discussion, see Kaufmann, "Limited Warfare," in Kaufmann (ed.) *op. cit.*

[37] Fred Charles Ikle, *Op. Cit.,* p. 62.

even the most limited of Soviet encroachments. In the final analysis, not even the U.S. believed that we would operate our forces in such a way. And so, massive retaliation failed on the first count as well.[38]

Horizontal escalation—our most recent asymmetrical experiment—also fails to meet the basic requirements of credibility. It fails on the first count because it is not even clear what it would *mean* to operate American forces in accordance with the strategy: it is not clear what its targets would be or, more fundamentally, how one would go about determining them in wartime. Neither is it clear what military actions would be taken against the selected targets.

Horizontal escalation fails to meet the second requirement as well. It clearly runs daunting risks—of nuclear escalation or Soviet counter-horizontal—but the goals of horizontal escalation remain cloudy, in both the broader strategic sense (ultimate victory vs. limitation) and in the narrow operational sense (punishment, hostage-taking, etc.).

"The threat that leaves something to chance" may be credible. But threats that leave everything to chance most assuredly are not.

Now, as suggested at the outset, the Reagan Administration's early enthusiasm for the strategy seems to have cooled somewhat; it is certainly less vocal than it was. Logically, however, there are only two possibilities. Either horizontal escalation is the Administration's strategy or it isn't.

If it is, then the strategy is not credible. And if horizontal escalation is not the Administration's strategy, then *what is* the strategy? Given the economic costs allegedly required to support it, the American people surely deserve an answer.

---

[38] The seminal critique is Kaufmann's "The Requirements of Deterrence" in Kaufmann (ed), *Op. Cit.*

Suggestions for Further Reading

The literature on the uses of force in international relations is extensive. This list of books is by no means comprehensive, but it should be useful to those who wish to pursue in more depth the subjects covered in this book.

Raymond Aron, *The Great Debate*. New York: Doubleday, 1965.

Desmond Ball, *Politics and Force Levels: The Strategic Missile Program of the Kennedy Administration*. Berkeley: University of California Press, 1980.

Leonard Beaton and John Maddox, *The Spread of Nuclear Weapons*. New York: Praeger, 1962.

André Beaufre, *Deterrence and Strategy*. New York: Praeger, 1966.

Richard K. Betts, *Surprise Attack*. Washington, D. C.: The Brookings Institution, 1982.

Geoffrey Blainey, *The Causes of War*. New York: The Free Press, 1973.

Donald G. Brennan, editor. *Arms Control, Disarmament, and National Security*. New York: George Braziller, 1961.

Bernard Brodie, *Sea Power in the Machine Age*. Princeton: Princeton University Press, 1944.

———, *Strategy in the Missile Age*. Princeton: Princeton University Press, 1959.

Abram Chayes and Jerome B. Wiesner, editors. *ABMs An Evaluation of the Decision to Deploy an Antiballistic Missile System*. New York: New American Library, 1969.

Edward Meade Earle, editor. *Makers of Modern Strategy*. New York: Atheneum, 1966 (first published in 1941).

Lawrence Freedman, *The Evolution of Nuclear Strategy*. New York: St. Martin's Press, 1982.

J. F. C. Fuller, *Armaments and History*. New York: Scribner's, 1945.

B. H. Liddell Hart, *Deterrent or Defense*. London: Stevens and Sons, 1960.

———, *Strategy*. New York: Praeger, 1962.

Michael Howard, *The Franco-Prussian War*. London: Rupert Hart-Davis, 1968.

Jerome H. Kahan, *Security in the Nuclear Age.* Washington, D.C. The Brookings Institution, 1975.

Herman Kahn, *On Thermonuclear War.* Princeton: Princeton University Press, 1961.

William W. Kaufmann, *The McNamara Strategy.* New York: Harper and Row, 1964.

Klaus Knorr and Thorton Read, editors, *Limited Strategic War.* New York: Frederick A. Praeger, 1962.

Robert A. Levine, *The Arms Debate.* Cambridge: Harvard University Press, 1963.

Guenter Lewy, *America in Vietnam.* Oxford: Oxford University Press, 1978.

Edward N. Luttwak, *The Grand Strategy of the Roman Empire.* Baltimore; The Johns Hopkins University Press, 1976.

Salvador de Madariaga, *Disarmament.* New York: Coward-McCann, 1929.

Arthur J. Marder, *The Anatomy of British Sea Power.* New York: Alfred A. Knopf, 1940.

Etling E. Morison, *Men, Machines and Modern Times.* Cambridge: Massachusetts Institute of Technology Press, 1968.

Lewis Mumford, *Technics and Civilization.* New York: Harcourt, Brace and World, 1963 (first published in 1934).

John U. Nef, *War and Human Progress.* New York: W. W. Norton, 1968 (first published in 1950).

John Newhouse, *Cold Dawn—The Story of SALT.* New York: Holt, Rinehart and Winston, 1973.

Robert E. Osgood, *Limited War.* Chicago: The University of Chicago Press, 1957.

Anatol Rapoport, *Fights, Games, and Debates.* Ann Arbor: The University of Michigan Press, 1961.

Gerhard Ritter, *The Schlieffen Plan.* London: Oswald Wolff, 1958.

Theodore Ropp, *War in the Modern World.* New York: Collier Books, 1962.

Thomas C. Schelling, *The Strategy of Conflict.* Cambridge: Harvard University Press, 1960.

Jonathan Steinberg, *Yesterday's Deterrent.* New York: Macmillan, 1965.

Strobe Talbott, *Endgame—The Inside Story of SALT II.* New York: Harper and Row, 1979.

J. W. Wheeler-Bennett, *The Pipe Dream of Peace.* New York: W. Morrow, 1935.

E. L. Woodward, *Great Britain ai i the German Navy.* London: Frank Cass and Company, 1964 (first published in 1935).

Quincy Wright, *A Study of War.* 2 vols. Chicago: University of Chicago Press, 1942.

Contributors

Robert J. Art is Herter Professor of International Relations at Brandeis University.

Desmond Ball is Senior Resident Associate, Australian National University.

Bernard Brodie was affiliated with the RAND Corp. and is Professor of Political Science at the University of California at Los Angeles.

Frederic J. Brown served in the United States Army.

McGeorge Bundy is Professor of History at New York University.

Lewis A. Dunn is Special Assistant for Nuclear Affairs, Office of the Ambassador at Large, Department of State.

Joshua M. Epstein is International Affairs Fellow, Department of State, Council of Foreign Relations, 1980–83.

Charles Fairbanks is Professor of Political Science at Yale University.

John Lewis Gaddis is Professor of History at Ohio University.

Colin S. Gray is President of the National Institute for Public Policy.

Morton H. Halperin is Director, Center for National Security Studies.

Samuel P. Huntington is Professor of Government at Harvard University.

Robert Jervis is Professor of Political Science at Columbia University.

Karl Kaiser is Director of Research Institute of the German Society for Foreign Affairs, Bonn.

Edward L. Katzenbach, Jr. is Vice President of the University of Oklahoma.

George F. Kennan is Professor Emeritus at the Institute for Advanced Study, Princeton.

Georg Leber is Social Democratic member and Vice President of West German Bundestag.

Robert S. McNamara was Secretary of Defense and President of the World Bank.

Alois Mertes is Christian Democratic member of the Bundestag, member of its Foreign Affairs Committee, and foreign policy spokesman of the CDU/CSU Parliamentary Party.

Louis Morton is Professor of History at Dartmouth College.

Paul H. Nitze has for over thirty years served in high posts within the American Government in the national security field.

Stephen E. Ockenden is Legislative Assistant for Defense for Senator David Durenberger.

Robert E. Osgood is Director of the Washington Center of Foreign Policy Research and Professor of Political Science at the School of Advanced International Studies, Johns Hopkins University.

George H. Quester is Professor of Political Science at the University of Maryland.

Sir George Sansom was a writer and a British diplomat with extensive experience in the Far East.

Thomas C. Schelling is Professor of Economics at Harvard University.

Warner R. Schilling is Professor of Political Science at Columbia University.

Franz-Joseph Schulze was Commander in Chief of Allied Forces Central Europe and Deputy Chief of Staff, Allied Command Europe.

Gerard Smith has served in high posts within the American Government in the national security field.

Glenn H. Snyder is Professor of Political Science at the State University of New York at Buffalo.

Kenneth N. Waltz is Ford Professor of Political Science at the University of California at Berkeley.

Albert Wohlstetter was formerly with the RAND Corporation and was Professor of Political Science at the University of Chicago.

Roberta Wohlstetter is the author of *Pearl Harbor: Warning and Decision*.